Less managing. More teaching. Greater learning.

INSTRUCTORS...

Would you like your **students** to show up for class more **prepared**? *(Let's face it, class is much more fun if everyone is engaged and prepared...)*

Want ready-made application-level **interactive assignments,** student progress reporting, and auto-assignment grading? *(Less time grading means more time teaching...)*

Want an **instant view of student or class performance** relative to learning objectives? *(No more wondering if students understand...)*

Need to **collect data and generate reports** required for administration or accreditation? *(Say goodbye to manually tracking student learning outcomes...)*

Want to **record and post your lectures** for students to view online?

With **McGraw-Hill's** *Connect*® *International Business,*

INSTRUCTORS GET:

- Interactive Applications – **book-specific interactive assignments** that require students to APPLY what they've learned.

- Simple **assignment management,** allowing you to spend more time teaching.

- **Auto-graded** assignments, quizzes, and tests.

- **Detailed Visual Reporting** where student and section results can be viewed and analyzed.

- Sophisticated **online testing** capability.

- A **filtering and reporting** function that allows you to easily assign and report on materials that are correlated to accreditation standards, learning outcomes, and Bloom's taxonomy.

- An easy-to-use **lecture capture** tool.

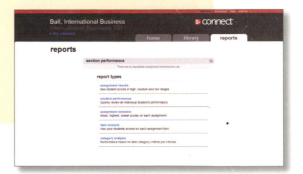

STUDENTS...

Want an online, **searchable version** of your textbook?

Wish your textbook could be **available online** while you're doing your assignments?

Connect® Plus International Business eBook

If you choose to use *Connect® Plus International Business*, you have an affordable and searchable online version of your book integrated with your other online tools.

Connect® Plus International Business eBook offers features like:

- Topic search
- Direct links from assignments
- Adjustable text size
- Jump to page number
- Print by section

STUDENTS...

Want to get more **value** from your textbook purchase?

Think learning management should be a bit more **interesting**?

Check out the STUDENT RESOURCES section under the *Connect®* Library tab.

Here you'll find a wealth of resources designed to help you achieve your goals in the course. You'll find things like **quizzes, PowerPoints, and Internet activities** to help you study. Every student has different needs, so explore the STUDENT RESOURCES to find the materials best suited to you.

Do Not Throw Away!

Welcome to the **CESIM** Global Challenge Simulation!

Experience the real world of truly interactive business simulation experience. During the simulation you will manage a global telecommunications company through fast-paced technological evolution and compete with your classmates on the simulated markets.

Your personal license code is:

FJ96GBh33UNL

To access the CESIM Global Challenge:

- Use a Web browser to go to **http://globalchallenge.cesim.com** or follow the link on the text Web site **http://www.mhhe.com/ball13e**

- Choose "Play the Game as a Student" and the registration starts.

- Enter the course code given to you by your instructor.

- Enter your personal license code exactly as it appears on this card.

- Fill in the other required information and choose your personal password and login.
  NOTE: You need to give a valid e-mail address as your login. This e-mail address will be used during the game to inform you about important deadlines and other necessary information.

Later you can access the system and play the game by just entering your login and password on the main page. You can also view the CESIM Global Challenge demo by choosing Demo on the main page (recommended 56-kbps or faster connection).

After you have registered and filled in all of the required information, you are guided through the rest of the set-up procedure. During the set-up procedure you are asked to choose your team, view schedule notes and read the game intro. Just follow the instructions on the screen.

Fine tune your teamwork skills and get ready to use everything you know about international business management!

Good luck!
CESIM Team and McGraw-Hill/Irwin

ISBN-13: 978-0-07-732460-5
MHID: 0-07-732460-9

INTERNATIONAL BUSINESS

THE CHALLENGE OF GLOBAL COMPETITION

BALL
GERINGER
MCNETT
MINOR

13th edition

McGraw-Hill Irwin

INTERNATIONAL BUSINESS: THE CHALLENGE OF GLOBAL COMPETITION

Published by McGraw-Hill/Irwin, a business unit of The McGraw-Hill Companies, Inc., 1221 Avenue of the Americas, New York, NY, 10020. Copyright © 2013, 2010, 2008, 2006, 2004, 2002, 1999, 1996, 1993, 1990, 1988, 1985, 1982 by The McGraw-Hill Companies, Inc. All rights reserved. Printed in the United States of America. No part of this publication may be reproduced or distributed in any form or by any means, or stored in a database or retrieval system, without the prior written consent of The McGraw-Hill Companies, Inc., including, but not limited to, in any network or other electronic storage or transmission, or broadcast for distance learning.

Some ancillaries, including electronic and print components, may not be available to customers outside the United States.

This book is printed on acid-free paper.

1 2 3 4 5 6 7 8 9 0 DOW/DOW 1 0 9 8 7 6 5 4 3 2

ISBN 978-0-07-811263-8
MHID 0-07-811263-X

Vice president and editor-in-chief: *Brent Gordon*
Editorial director: *Paul Ducham*
Executive editor: *John Weimeister*
Executive director of development: *Ann Torbert*
Development editor: *Jane Beck*
Editorial coordinator: *Heather Darr*
Vice president and director of marketing: *Robin J. Zwettler*
Marketing director: *Amee Mosley*
Marketing manager: *Donielle Xu*
Vice president of editing, design, and production: *Sesha Bolisetty*
Lead project manager: *Harvey Yep*
Senior buyer: *Carol A. Bielski*
Cover and interior designer: *Pam Verros*
Senior photo research coordinator: *Keri Johnson*
Photo researcher: *Ira C. Roberts*
Senior media project manager : *Susan Lombardi*
Typeface: *10.5/12 Times Roman*
Compositor: *Laserwords Private Limited*
Printer: *R. R. Donnelley*

Library of Congress Cataloging-in-Publication Data

International business : the challenge of global competition / Donald A. Ball . . . [et al.].—13th ed.
   p. cm.
   Includes index.
   ISBN-13: 978-0-07-811263-8 (alk. paper)
   ISBN-10: 0-07-811263-X (alk. paper)
   1. International business enterprises—Management. 2. International business enterprises.
3. International economic relations. I. Ball, Donald A.
   HD62.4.B34 2013
   658'.049—dc23
                                                         2011045058

Mike dedicates this edition to his parents, Ray and JoAnn, and his partner, Barbara, who have provided continued support and encouragement for his writing and other life activities.

Jeanne dedicates this edition to her finance professor, N. D. Quy; to her best friends, Nick Athanassiou and Raven McCrory; and to her research friends, ION, all of whom have helped her recognize and develop her strengths.

Michael dedicates this edition to his daughter, Amy, who has done an outstanding job of growing up since her mother passed away.

Don A. Ball

Don A. Ball, a consultant to multinational corporations, was a professor of marketing and international business for several years after leaving industry. He has a degree in mechanical engineering from Ohio State and a doctorate in business administration from the University of Florida. Ball has published articles in the *Journal of International Business Studies* and other publications. Before obtaining his doctorate, he spent 15 years in various marketing and production management positions in Mexico, South America, and Europe.

J. Michael Geringer

J. Michael Geringer is a professor of strategy and international business management at California Polytechnic State University in San Luis Obispo. He earned a BS in business at Indiana University and MBA and PhD degrees at the University of Washington. He has authored or edited more than 25 books and monographs, more than 130 published papers, and more than 40 case studies; he serves on the editorial boards of several leading international academic journals including Editor-in-Chief or Associate Editor for four journals; he served as the Saastamoinen Foundation Chair at the Helsinki School of Economics in Finland; he was the founding chair of the Strategic Alliances Committee of the Licensing Executives Society; he served as the chair of both the International Business and the Strategy and Policy divisions of the Administrative Sciences Association of Canada; and he is past chair of the Academy of Management's International Management division. His research has appeared in the *Strategic Management Journal, Academy of Management Journal, Journal of International Management, Columbia Journal of World Business, Management International Review, Journal of Management Studies, Human Resource Management Journal, Long Range Planning, Organisation Studies, Thunderbird International Business Review, and Journal of Applied Psychology,* among others. He has received 11 "best paper" awards for his research, including the Decade Award for most influential article from the *Journal of International Business Studies, and he received the Cal Poly's Distinguished Scholar Award in 2011.* His teaching performance has earned numerous awards in the United States, Canada, Asia, Africa, Australia, and Europe, including the University Distinguished Teacher Award. He was the first recipient of the International Educator Award from Cal Poly, and he endowed a scholarship for students to work and study internationally. He has been active in a range of charitable and service activities, including spearheading the adoption of a school in Soweto, South Africa, and fund-raising for public radio. In addition to working with universities around the world, Geringer is active in consulting and executive development for multinational corporations and executives from six continents. His clients have included Nokia; Lucent; Eastman Kodak; Sonera; Northern Telecom; Rautaruukki; Eastman Chemical; UPM Kymmene; Industry, Science & Technology Canada; Jiangsu Telecom Industrial; Hewlett-Packard; California Highway Patrol; Economic Council of Canada; Perlos; YIT; California Department of Transportation; Yahoo!; and Okobank, among others.

Jeanne M. McNett

Jeanne M. McNett is a researcher at Northeastern University in the College of Business Administration and formerly served as professor of management at Assumption College, in Worcester, Massachusetts, and the University of Maryland, Asian and European Divisions. She earned a PhD at the University of Massachusetts, Amherst, and an MBA at the Cass School of Business, City University, London. She has had expatriate assignments in Germany, the United Kingdom, Saudi Arabia, Japan, and Korea. Her interests include the role of culture in international business and the pedagogy of international management. Her publications include the *Blackwell Encyclopedia of Management, Vol. VI: International Management,* second edition (Oxford, UK: Blackwell Publishing, 2005), and the *Blackwell Handbook of Global Management* (Oxford, UK: Blackwell Publishing, 2004). Her teaching, research, and presentations have received many awards, including the Roethlisberger Best Paper of the Year Award from the *Journal of Management Education* and the Alpha Phi Alpha Teacher of the Year Award. Her articles have been included in journals and collections focused on teaching in the area of international business. In her "down time," she gardens, hangs out at the gym, and volunteers in the area of women's health care and health care policy.

Michael S. Minor

Michael S. Minor is professor of marketing and international business at the University of Texas, Pan American. He was educated at the University of North Carolina and Cornell and holds a PhD from Vanderbilt University. His research focuses on comparative consumer behavior, social network behavior, political risk, and the consumption of high-technology experiential products. He has published in the Journal of Retailing, Journal of Advertising, *Journal of International Business Studies, International Studies of Management and Organization, Journal of Services Marketing, International Business Review, Journal of Psychology and Marketing, Cyberpsychology and Behavior, Journal of Advertising Research,* and elsewhere. He is the coauthor with John C. Mowen and Todd Donovan of Understanding *Consumer Behavior: From Managerial Problems to Their Solutions.* He has written for business and popular media from *PCWeek* to *Tennessee Business Magazine.* He is past chair of the Consumer Behavior Special Interest Group, past vice chair of the Technology and Marketing Special Interest Group of the American Marketing Association, and a former member of the Global Marketing Special Interest Group's board of directors. He serves on multiple editorial advisory boards. He has won multiple teaching awards and was recently selected as the doctoral program professor of the year. His consulting experience includes work for UNCTAD's Division on Investment, Technology and Enterprise Development and for several U.S. and state government agencies. He has reviewed grant proposals for the Research Council of Norway as well as multiple U.S. agencies. He performs on guitar, dulcimer, and harmonica with the New Hallilujah Band and also plays mandolin and bass. A member of BMI, he has written more than two dozen country and inspirational songs.

Preface

Παγκόσμιο Business Los negocios internacionales Παγκόσμιο
Internationales Geschäft 國際商務 Gli Affari Internazionali
Negócios Internacionais Internationales Geschäft 國際商務

We are pleased to present the thirteenth edition of *International Business: The Challenge of Global Competition.*

Purpose and Scope of This Text

Whether students are advanced undergraduates or are in MBA programs, an international business course is an ideal venue for a varied number of questions. Our hope is that this book will answer these questions about business in different cultures, the impact of geography, why products are the same (or different) across cultures, why people have different practices, the effect of the Internet on international business, and many, many more. There are always new questions, and sometimes there are new answers to old questions.

International Business, thirteenth edition, is organized into three sections in order to maximize its utility to instructors and students alike. The opening section defines the nature of international business and the three environments in which it is conducted, as well as the nature and continuing importance of international institutions and how they affect business. Section Two focuses on the uncontrollable forces at work in all business environments and discusses their inevitable impact on business practice. We devote the final section of the book to a discussion of how managers deal with all the forces affecting international business. In the thirteenth edition, we have continued section-opening dialogues to help students better understand what they have learned and are about to learn.

Changes for the Thirteenth Edition

With each new edition we have been blessed by an expanding network of those making helpful suggestions. Professors, reviewers, and business professionals who bought the book or received it at a conference, and our own graduate and undergraduate students have made useful and constructive comments. We believe that *International Business,* thirteenth edition, continues to offer you a solid and superior text infused with current topics relevant to current challenges. In this edition, we have extensively revised and updated the material in each chapter to reflect recent world events and new international business issues. In response to instructor and student feedback, we have also attempted to improve the succinctness with which the material is presented, in order to reduce the overall length of this text.

As with every new edition, tables, figures, and graphs have been updated to include the most current data available as of the publication of this text. Keeping an international business text topical and current is a challenge, and we have worked hard to provide you with the most recent information possible. We have also updated examples where relevant and replaced dated examples where appropriate. We have reorganized Chapter 1 to increase its emphasis on motivations for internationalizing a company's business activities. We have consolidated our previous two chapters on international trade and foreign direct investment into a single, more focused Chapter 2. We have reorganized our new Chapter 3 to increase its focus on international institutions that influence international business. Our discussion of sociocultural forces in Chapter 4 has been substantially revised to incorporate enhanced discussion of frameworks for understanding different cultures, including those of Hall, Hofstede, and Trompenaars. Based on reviewer and user comments, we have deleted our prior Chapter 7, "Economic and Socioeconomic Forces," and have moved that content into other chapters. Discussion of trade forces has been combined with our discussion of political forces, creating our new Chapter 6, "Political and Trade Forces." Based on comments from our reviewers and users, our prior Chapter 11, "Labor Forces," has been consolidated with the chapter on human resource management, creating our new Chapter 17, "Managing Human Resources in an International Context." Reflecting increased interest from instructors and students, we have added a new chapter, Chapter 11, which addresses "Global Leadership Issues and Practices." As a result of these changes, we have reduced the overall number of chapters to 18 and the numbering of Chapters 2 through 18 has been modified. Learning objectives are clearly stated at the beginning of each chapter, with icons placed appropriately within the chapter text to highlight when each learning objective is addressed. We have retained our Worldview discussions to highlight key issues facing international managers and added discussion questions to each. We have added Global Debate boxes to provide the foundation for examining different perspectives on contemporary challenges that managers face in our global environment and have included discussion questions for each. To enhance the relevance of the content in the text, we have added a unique and innovative feature, The Global Path Ahead, that provides a concise vignette of a current student or recent graduate who has begun to pursue international business activities early in his or her career. The Global Path Ahead also includes a selection of global resources that students and graduates may use to pursue career opportunities related to the content of each chapter.

CHAPTER 1   THE CHALLENGING WORLD OF INTERNATIONAL BUSINESS

The opening case on the importance of international business experience has been updated, as has the popular Worldview box on buying American. New and updated examples have been added throughout the chapter to enhance understanding of key issues. The tables have been updated and refocused to improve understanding of key concepts, and the emphasis on growth of international firms and international business has been enhanced. Discussion of the debate on globalization of trade and investment has been placed into a new Global Debate box within the chapter. A discussion of the motives for entering foreign markets has been added. The minicase exercise at the end of the chapter, which deals with the ownership and nationality associated with many well-known companies and brands, has been updated in terms of products and companies.

CHAPTER 2   INTERNATIONAL TRADE AND FOREIGN DIRECT INVESTMENT

We have combined into a single chapter what had previously been two separate chapters addressing the empirical data and theory associated with international trade and foreign direct investment. This new Chapter 2 is now more focused, with an updated introduction and discussion of trade in goods and services. The data on international trade and investment have been updated throughout the chapter to reflect the most current figures available at the time of publication, and the presentation of these data has been improved to enhance the reader's ability to analyze and understand trends and traits of international trade. We have revised, reorganized, and clarified the discussion of theories of international trade and investment, and we added new examples in order to facilitate student comprehension of these topics. We have added a Global Debate box dealing with the issue of offshoring service jobs from the United States to India. There is increased coverage of emerging economies, particularly the BRIC (Brazil, Russia, India, China) nations, including an updated minicase at the end of the chapter that addresses Brazil's potential to become a global competitor in the information technology outsourcing business.

CHAPTER 3   INTERNATIONAL INSTITUTIONS FROM AN INTERNATIONAL BUSINESS PERSPECTIVE

Chapter 3's coverage of institutions includes monetary institutions, increasing its comprehensive coverage. Institutional theory is introduced to provide a framework for discussion of institutions. The general discussion has been refocused to address the actions of institutions as they affect international business rather than a descriptive summary. The World Trade

Organization (WTO) coverage summarizes the General Agreement on Tariffs and Trade (GATT), placing the WTO at the center and subordinating the historical discussion. The United Nations and EU coverage has been refocused to emphasize the impact of these institutions on the international business manager. Examples are updated, and new applications are included.

CHAPTER 4 SOCIOCULTURAL FORCES

In this first chapter of our second section, on international environmental forces, we expand our discussion of frameworks for cultural analysis. In addition, an increased emphasis is placed on how cultural dimensions affect the various functions of international business, from marketing to accounting. New examples and applications are added, and all data and examples are updated as well.

CHAPTER 5 NATURAL RESOURCES AND ENVIRONMENTAL SUSTAINABILITY

This chapter has been updated to reflect a direct focus on two critical challenges, global warming and depletion of energy sources. The section on geographical issues has been condensed some, while the areas included in sustainability have been expanded. The use of Porter's diamond is extended as a basis for discussion of the geographic factor conditions. New examples of sustainable practice are included. One example is a petroleum-based products business, so students gain a broader appreciation of the potentials of sustainable approaches.

CHAPTER 6 POLITICAL AND TRADE FORCES

This chapter has been focused to provide a more succinct coverage of political and trade forces. Discussion of ideological forces has been removed. Discussion of government ownership of business and privatization has been updated. The terrorism discussion has been expanded and updated, with the popular Worldview on terrorism in the Second Life virtual world revised and updated. Discussion and examples of country risk assessment has been revised and updated. The material on trade restrictions has been enhanced, and the Global Debate on sugar subsidies contains updated developments. The Global Path Ahead content and supporting resources provide valuable insights for the reader.

CHAPTER 7 INTELLECTUAL PROPERTY AND OTHER LEGAL FORCES

The increasing importance of intellectual property rights across the globe is further emphasized in this edition. The opening vignette provides a thought-provoking analysis of the implications of counterfeiting of pharmaceuticals. New examples and updated references are found throughout the chapter. The Worldview captures interesting new developments on the extension of intellectual property rights from within a virtual world and into the real world. Discussion of laws regarding taxation has been removed, because taxation is addressed in a more holistic manner in Chapter 18's discussion of accounting and financial management. There is new discussion of the potential threat to national sovereignty as a result of World Trade Organization decisions, as highlighted in a new Global Debate box on the 2011 decision on the American "dolphin-safe" labeling program. The discussion of the Foreign Corrupt Practices Act has been updated, along with increased discussion of anti-bribery and anti-corruption statutes elsewhere in the world.

CHAPTER 8 THE INTERNATIONAL MONETARY SYSTEM AND FINANCIAL FORCES

Chapter 8 is expanded to include coverage of the international monetary system as it affects the practice of international business. A short review of the development of monetary arrangements moves from the gold standard through the Bretton Woods system, including brief coverage of the Triffin paradox and the establishment of special drawing rights. The chapter then moves to a consideration of the floating system and contemporary currency arrangements. A new chart summarizes the evolution of the monetary system. The foreign exchange review is simplified. Taxes, inflation, and interest rates are reviewed with updated examples. Balance of payments accounts are presented in terms of their usefulness to the international manager.

CHAPTER 9 INTERNATIONAL COMPETITIVE STRATEGY

Chapter 9 introduces Section Three, on the organizational environment. We have revised the opening case on the use of scenario planning to help manage the strategic uncertainties associated with international business activities, and we have condensed the overall chapter to improve comprehension. The discussion has been expanded on why firms need to engage in strategic planning if they want to compete successfully in international markets. Throughout the chapter, we have included new and updated examples to promote the reader's comprehension of international strategy concepts and tools. There is an updated discussion, with examples, of mission, vision, and values statements and their roles in international strategy. There is a new Global Debate box addressing Google's values and strategy versus the opportunities within the Chinese marketplace. The Worldview on using regional strategies to compete globally has been updated. The popular minicase on Walmart's internationalization efforts at the end of the chapter has been updated to include the company's failures in Korea and Germany, its efforts to dramatically expand operations in China through acquisitions and internal growth, and its strategic plans to enter India and other emerging markets.

CHAPTER 10 ORGANIZATIONAL DESIGN AND CONTROL

The opening case on Kraft Foods has been updated to highlight the company's global reorganization of its structure in an effort to enhance Kraft's international competitiveness in a changing marketplace. The popular Worldview on Accenture's "virtual" global structure has been updated. There is a new Global Debate box on the issue of international transfer pricing and some of its implications. We have revised the minicase at the end, on SemiConnected Inc., and its potential for reorganization.

CHAPTER 11 GLOBAL LEADERSHIP ISSUES AND PRACTICES

This newly introduced chapter addresses an increasingly important issue facing international companies: the recruitment, development, and management of global leaders and global teams. The opening case focuses on the challenge of finding global leaders with the "right stuff" for addressing these new opportunities. We discuss the issue and importance of developing a global mindset and then address what global leadership is, how it differs from domestic leadership, and why it is important. In addition, we include a Worldview providing the consulting company Aperian's view on key global leadership activities. There is a discussion of the competencies required for effective global leadership, including Brake's Global Leadership Triad model and the Pyramid Model of Global Leadership. The Global Debate box addresses the appropriateness of women for global leadership positions. Issues and models associated with assessing, selecting, and developing global leaders are discussed. The importance of global teams and the challenges of leading such teams is addressed, including how traditional teams differ from global teams. Challenges of virtual and geographically dispersed teams are identified, as well as the topic of performance management in global teams. The chapter concludes with a discussion of leading global change, including change models. The Global Path Ahead vignette highlights a young global leader who developed his skills through a decade of different experiences abroad, and a minicase at the end of the chapter provides a cautionary tale of how a potential global leader can have his career derailed.

CHAPTER 12 ASSESSING INTERNATIONAL MARKETS

One of the points of this chapter's approach to market analysis is that it's not always obvious where potential markets are located. An example is that there is a growing market for motivational speakers—even in Iran! We update examples and include our advice on dealing with marketing research issues frequently encountered in developing economies.

CHAPTER 13   ENTRY MODES

This chapter has been reorganized in this edition. We begin with an examination of market entry through international social media, with an emphasis on social networks that are not tailored for U.S. audiences. We expand our discussion of exporting by discussing the benefits of exporting and the wide array of methods by which indirect and direct exporting can occur. The discussion of equity-based modes of entry is updated, and the discussion of joint ventures has an expanded section on benefits of joint ventures and on options for exercising control, even as a minority partner. There is an interesting new Worldview that examines challenges of forming and managing successful international joint ventures, using the Danone and Wahaha ventures in China as the focus. The Global Path Ahead has a vignette of a young international business professional who is managing market entry through a range of direct and indirect exporting options.

CHAPTER 14   EXPORT AND IMPORT PRACTICES

We discuss import and export processes, with a focus on the role of the small company new to exporting. The government resources section reflects major changes in the organization of export/import-related government support. The International Chamber of Commerce Incoterms are also updated, reflecting the consolidation of terms. A comparison chart outlining seller and buyer responsibilities described by Incoterms is also added to clarify what can be a confusing area for students. All information is updated, and the Worldview focuses on the U.S. Ex-Im Bank and its new president's commitment to the support of U.S. exporters.

CHAPTER 15   MARKETING INTERNATIONALLY

Current examples have an increasing focus on India and China. A new Worldview feature explores the impact of increased product development integration, involving R&D and marketing, on future locations for manufacturing. Such integration may lead to very different business models. In addition, a new minicase on Kraft's Athenos line of hummus and cheese products links to on-ine advertising. Examples and data are updated.

CHAPTER 16   GLOBAL OPERATIONS AND SUPPLY CHAIN MANAGEMENT

This chapter has been revised to make it more focused and succinct. The popular Zara case at the beginning of the chapter has been updated. The Worldview examines the continued success of Cognizant Technologies in using its innovative onshore/offshore approach to providing information technology services to customers around the world. The discussion of manufacturing systems has been made much more concise. In light of increasing petroleum prices and market uncertainties, we address the possibility that producing products "closer to home" is a more viable option than before. There is a much more concise discussion of the local manufacturing system. The Global Path Ahead vignette provides an overview of an effort by students to help develop intermediate technologies that may be more appropriate to emerging market contexts, such as Guatemala.

CHAPTER 17   MANAGING HUMAN RESOURCES IN AN INTERNATIONAL CONTEXT

Chapter 17's discussion of human resource management issues in international business has been reorganized to incorporate a portion of our prior discussion of international labor forces from Section Two. A new opening case addresses issues associated with expatriate positions. A new Worldview box examines the role of cultural backgrounds and nationality in selecting candidates for international positions. There is also a new Worldview box on the challenges associated with finding executives with the "right stuff" for positions internationally. We have added a Global Debate box on the appropriateness of women for international assignments, and the section on expatriates has been revised. The discussion of families of expatriates, including issues faced by trailing spouses and children, has been substantially revised. We have revised the discussion of challenges associated with repatriation, expatriate support services, and compensation and benefits for expatriates and other international personnel. A revised minicase at the end of the chapter deals with considerations facing an employee who is deciding whether to accept an international position that has been offered to her.

CHAPTER 18 INTERNATIONAL ACCOUNTING AND FINANCIAL MANAGEMENT

Chapter 18 places accounting at the beginning of the chapter, then moves on to financial management. The opening vignette is on sovereign wealth funds and their influence on private equity markets. Progress toward convergence of accounting standards is summarized and the basic assumption-level differences described, using institutional theory (covered in Chapter 3) to explain the differences at the theoretical level. The Global Reporting Initiative for triple-bottom-line accounting is included as an example of the general movement toward accountability. An ethics focus is on the development of for-profit microlending, a relatively new twist in an area that had been strictly not-for-profit. The pros and cons of this shift are presented. In the area of financial management, fronting loans have been included as a way to shift funds. An effort has been extended to make the chapter reader-friendly so that the nonspecialist student will be able to appreciate the creativity of contributions in the finance area. Examples and applications are updated.

GLOSSARY

The Glossary is a very extensive collection of definitions of documents, institutions, concepts, and terms used in international business. The Glossary is an extremely valuable resource for students and instructors.

New Features

With the thirteenth edition, we introduce an innovative and unique set of The Global Path Ahead boxes that appear at the end of each chapter. Each of these boxes provides a vignette of international business-related activities that current students or recent graduates have pursued, providing an opportunity for readers to envision their own, unique international paths that might be followed. These boxes also present valuable tools and insights to help students build a foundation for entering and excelling in international business activities and careers, providing links to resources that cover such topics as finding international job opportunities, building international skills and experience, gaining relevant knowledge and tools to increase success in finding and performing international business jobs, and learning from the practical experience and recommendations of peers who have successfully pursued opportunities involving international business activity.

The thirteenth edition also continues to use the innovative globalEDGE™ Research Tasks, created by Tunga Kiyak and Tomas Hult of the CIBER Center at Michigan State University. These end-of-chapter exercises challenge students to solve problems similar to those faced by practicing international business managers, and they acquaint students with the tools and data real managers use. The globalEDGE™ Research Tasks are ideal for Web-based courses. For example, in working on a product launch, students may be asked to compile a list of the top 10 countries in terms of their attractiveness for potential return of FDI. Students can access all the Internet resources needed to solve the problems at www.globaledge.msu.edu.

A new video collection features original business documentaries as well as network news footage. Videos correspond to the video cases (with discussion questions) available on the text's website at www.mhhe.com/ball13e.

Another source of new videos now available with the book is iGlobe, a ground-breaking online video website (www.mhhe.com/iglobe), where you can download two "on-demand" PBS videos per month about breaking stories on international business issues. The website is updated with new video selections each month, and the videos are archived monthly for easy accessibility. These streaming videos are complete with teaching notes and discussion questions. Key concepts for each video are identified to save you time! This is ideal for online courses or for homework assignments outside class.

Other Useful Elements

- Each chapter includes a Global Debate box that addresses international business issues that involve important dimensions associated with ethical or socially responsible activity.
- Each chapter includes current, relevant examples of business activities and developments in the increasingly critical emerging markets of the world.
- Worldview boxes highlight real-world applications of key concepts to help students relate the material they are learning to their own business careers.
- Learning Objectives are clearly identified at the beginning of each chapter, with special icons placed within the text to identify when each learning objective is being addressed.
- An extensive set of maps throughout the text gives students important geographic perspectives.
- End-of-chapter tools include Summaries, Key Words, Questions, globalEDGE™ Research Tasks, and Minicases to further help students in their comprehension.

CESIM: Global Challenge Simulation

This online simulation involving international markets for mobile handsets is packaged with new copies of the text. There are three market areas (North America, Europe, and Asia). The simulation presents a range of features that could be offered (affecting product differentiation), a choice of production sites (in Asia or North America), price options, and exposure to exchange rate fluctuations, among other issues and decisions. It can be used with 3 to 12 teams (6 to 50 students per simulation) and can involve teams from more than one class or university, if desired. There is an enhanced online support facility with the thirteenth edition, as well as an improved user interface to enhance the performance and appearance of the simulation. The simulation can be used at no additional expense for either instructors or students who use new copies of the text.

McGraw-Hill *Connect International Business*

 **Less Managing. More Teaching. Greater Learning.** McGraw-Hill *Connect International Business* is an online assignment and assessment solution that connects students with the tools and resources they'll need to achieve success.

McGraw-Hill *Connect International Business* helps prepare students for their future by enabling faster learning, more efficient studying, and higher retention of knowledge.

McGraw-Hill *Connect International Business* Features. *Connect International Business* offers a number of powerful tools and features to make managing assignments easier, so faculty can spend more time teaching. With *Connect International Business,* students can engage with their coursework anytime and anywhere, making the learning process more accessible and efficient. *Connect International Business* offers you the features described below.

Simple Assignment Management

With *Connect International Business,* creating assignments is easier than ever, so you can spend more time teaching and less time managing. The assignment management function enables you to:

- Create and deliver assignments easily with selectable end-of-chapter questions and test bank items.
- Streamline lesson planning, student progress reporting, and assignment grading to make classroom management more efficient than ever.
- Go paperless with the eBook and online submission and grading of student assignments.

Smart Grading

When it comes to studying, time is precious. *Connect International Business* helps students learn more efficiently by providing feedback and practice material when they need it, where they need it. When it comes to teaching, your time also is precious. The grading function enables you to:

- Have assignments scored automatically, giving students immediate feedback on their work and side-by-side comparisons with correct answers.
- Access and review each response; manually change grades or leave comments for students to review.
- Reinforce classroom concepts with practice tests and instant quizzes.

Instructor Library

The *Connect International Business* Instructor Library is your repository for additional resources to improve student engagement in and out of class. You can select and use any asset that enhances your lecture. The *Connect International Business* Instructor Library includes:

- E-book
- Instructor's Manual
- PowerPoint Slides
- Answers to the end-of-chapter globalEDGE Research Tasks
- Videos and Instructional Notes
- International Business Newsletter archives
- Access to interactive study tools like Business Around the World, Drag-and-drop maps, the Global Business Plan, and iGlobe

Student Study Center

The *Connect International Business* Student Study Center is the place for students to access additional resources. The Student Study Center:

- Offers students quick access to lectures, practice materials, eBooks, and more.
- Provides instant practice material and study questions, easily accessible on the go.
- Gives students access to the Personalized Learning Plan described below.

Student Progress Tracking

Connect International Business keeps instructors informed about how each student, section, and class is performing, allowing for more productive use of lecture and office hours. The progress-tracking function enables you to:

- View scored work immediately and track individual or group performance with assignment and grade reports.

- Access an instant view of student or class performance relative to learning objectives.
- Collect data and generate reports required by many accreditation organizations, such as AACSB.

Lecture Capture

Increase the attention paid to lecture discussion by decreasing the attention paid to note taking. For an additional charge Lecture Capture offers new ways for students to focus on the in-class discussion, knowing they can revisit important topics later. Lecture Capture enables you to:

- Record and distribute your lecture with a click of button.
- Record and index PowerPoint presentations and anything shown on your computer so it is easily searchable, frame by frame.
- Offer access to lectures anytime and anywhere by computer, iPod, or mobile device.
- Increase intent listening and class participation by easing students' concerns about note-taking. Lecture Capture will make it more likely you will see students' faces, not the tops of their heads.

McGraw-Hill *Connect Plus International Business*

McGraw-Hill reinvents the textbook learning experience for the modern student with *Connect Plus International Business*. A seamless integration of an e-Book and *Connect International Business*, *Connect Plus International Business* provides all of the *Connect International Business* features plus the following:

- An integrated e-Book, allowing for anytime, anywhere access to the textbook.
- Dynamic links between the problems or questions you assign to your students and the location in the e-Book where that problem or question is covered.
- A powerful search function to pinpoint and connect key concepts in a snap.

In short, *Connect International Business* offers you and your students powerful tools and features that optimize your time and energies, enabling you to focus on course content, teaching, and student learning. *Connect International Business* also offers a wealth of content resources for both instructors and students. This state-of-the-art, thoroughly tested system supports you in preparing students for the world that awaits.

For more information about Connect, go to www.mcgrawhillconnect.com, or contact your local McGraw-Hill sales representative.

Tegrity Campus: Lectures 24/7

Tegrity Campus is a service that makes class time available 24/7 by automatically capturing every lecture in a searchable format for students to review when they study and complete assignments. With a simple one-click start-and-stop process, you capture all computer screens and corresponding audio. Students can replay any part of any class with easy-to-use browser-based viewing on a PC or Mac.

Educators know that the more students can see, hear, and experience class resources, the better they learn. In fact, studies prove it. With Tegrity Campus, students quickly recall key moments by using Tegrity Campus's unique search feature. This search helps students efficiently find what they need, when they need it, across an entire semester of class recordings. Help turn all your students' study time into learning moments immediately supported by your lecture.

To learn more about Tegrity watch a 2-minute Flash demo at http://tegritycampus .mhhe.com.

Assurance of Learning Ready

Many educational institutions today are focused on the notion of *assurance of learning,* an important element of some accreditation standards. *International Business: The Challenge of Global Competition, 13e* is designed specifically to support your assurance of learning initiatives with a simple, yet powerful solution.

Each test bank question for *International Business: The Challenge of Global Competition, 13e* maps to a specific chapter learning outcome/objective listed in the text. You can use our test bank software, EZ Test and EZ Test Online, or in *Connect International Business* to easily query for learning outcomes/objectives that directly relate to the learning objectives for your course. You can then use the reporting features of EZ Test to aggregate student results in similar fashion, making the collection and presentation of assurance of learning data simple and easy.

AACSB Statement

The McGraw-Hill Companies is a proud corporate member of AACSB International. Understanding the importance and value of AACSB accreditation, *International Business: The Challenge of Global Competition, 13e* recognizes the curricula guidelines detailed in the AACSB standards for business accreditation by connecting selected questions in the text and/ or the test bank to the six general knowledge and skill guidelines in the AACSB standards.

The statements contained in *International Business: The Challenge of Global Competition, 13e* are provided only as a guide for the users of this textbook. The AACSB leaves content coverage and assessment within the purview of individual schools, the mission of the school, and the faculty. While *International Business: The Challenge of Global Competition, 13e* and the teaching package make no claim of any specific AACSB qualification or evaluation, we have within *International Business: The Challenge of Global Competition, 13e* labeled selected questions according to the six general knowledge and skills areas.

McGraw-Hill Customer Care Contact Information

At McGraw-Hill, we understand that getting the most from new technology can be challenging. That's why our services don't stop after you purchase our products. You can e-mail our Product Specialists 24 hours a day to get product-training online. Or you can search our knowledge bank of Frequently Asked Questions on our support website. For Customer Support, call 800-331-5094, e-mail hmsupport@mcgraw-hill.com, or visit www.mhhe.com/support. One of our Technical Support Analysts will be able to assist you in a timely fashion.

McGraw-Hill and Blackboard

McGraw-Hill Higher Education and Blackboard have teamed up. What does this mean for you?

1. **Your life, simplified.** Now you and your students can access McGraw-Hill's Connect™ and Create™ right from within your Blackboard course—all with one single sign-on. Say goodbye to the days of logging in to multiple applications.
2. **Deep integration of content and tools.** Not only do you get single sign-on with Connect™ and Create™, you also get deep integration of McGraw-Hill content and content engines right in

   Blackboard. Whether you're choosing a book for your course or building Connect™ assignments, all the tools you need are right where you want them—inside of Blackboard.
3. **Seamless Gradebooks.** Are you tired of keeping multiple gradebooks and manually synchronizing grades into Blackboard? We thought so. When a student completes an integrated Connect™ assignment, the grade for that assignment automatically (and instantly) feeds your Blackboard grade center.

4. **A solution for everyone.** Whether your institution is already using Blackboard or you just want to try Blackboard on your own, we have a solution for you. McGraw-Hill and Blackboard can now offer you easy access to industry leading technology and content, whether your campus hosts it, or we do. Be sure to ask your local McGraw-Hill representative for details.

To the long list of people to whom we are indebted, we want to add Professors Gary Anders, Arizona State University West; Gary Anderson, Bowling Green State University; John Anderson, University of Tennessee, Knoxville; Nicholas Athanassiou, Northeastern University; Robert T. Aubey, University of Wisconsin, Madison; Winston Awadzi, Delaware State University; Mark C. Baetz, Wilfred Laurier University; Bahman Bahrami, North Dakota State University; Rufus Barton, Murray State University; Lawrence Beer, Arizona State University; Joseph R. Biggs, California Polytechnic State University; S. A. Billon, University of Delaware; James R. Bradshaw, Brigham Young University; Sharon Browning, Northwest Missouri State University; Dennis Carter, University of North Carolina, Wilmington; Mark Chadwin, Old Dominion University; Aruna Chandras, Ashland University; John Cleek, University of Missouri, Kansas City; Gerald Crawford, University of North Alabama; Refik Culpan, Pennsylvania State University; Peter DeWill, University of Central Florida; Galpira Eshigi, Illinois State University; Christof Falli, Portland State University; Colette Frayne, California Polytechnic State University, San Luis Obispo; Prem Gandhi, State University of New York, Plattsburgh; Ellen Kaye Gerke, Alliant International University; Kenneth Gray, Florida Agricultural and Mechanical University; Robert Guffey, Elon College; Stanley D. Guzell, Youngstown State University; Gary Hankem, Mankato State University; Baban Hasnat, State University of New York, Brockport; Tom Hinthorne, Montana State University; Veronica Horton, University of Akron; Paul Jenner, Southwest Missouri State University; Bruce H. Johnson, Gustavus Adolphus College; Ahmad Karim, Indiana University–Purdue University, Ft. Wayne; Michael Kublin, University of New Haven; Eddie Lewis, University of Southern Mississippi; Carol Lopilato, California State University, Dominguez Hills; Mingfang Li, California State University, Northridge; Lois Ann McElroy Lindell, Wartburg College; Dorinda Lynn, Pensacola Junior College; Lynette Mathur, Southern Illinois University, Carbondale; Hugh J. McCabe, Westchester Community College; Fraser McLeay, University of Montana; Les Mueller, Central Washington University; Gary Oddon, San Jose State University; Darrell Neron, Peirce College; Ebele Oriaku, Elizabeth City State University; Jaimie Ortiz, Florida Atlantic University; Bill Pendergast, California Polytechnic State University–San Luis Obispo; Mike Peng, University of Texas–Dallas; Susan A. Peterson, Maricopa College; Jere Ramsey, California Polytechnic State University, San Luis Obispo; Tagi Sagafi-Nejad, Loyola College, Maryland; Rakesh Sambharya, Rutgers University; Eugene Seeley, Utah Valley State College; John Setnicky, Mobile College; V. N. Subramanyam, Lancaster University; Angelo Tarallo, Ramapo College; Jesse S. Tarleton, William and Mary College; John Thanopoulos, University of Akron; Kenneth Tillery, Middle Tennessee State University; Hsin-Min Tong, Redford University; Dennis Vanden Bloomen, University of Wisconsin, Stout; Heidi Vernon, Northeastern University; George Westacott, State University of New York, Binghamton; Terry Witkowski, California State University; Habte Woldu, University of Texas, Dallas; G. Bernard Yevin, Forsythe Technical Community College; Gregg Lattier, Lee College; Mr. Haryanto, Monmouth College; John C. Ruhnka, University of Colorado at Denver and Health Sciences Center; Juan F. Ramirez, Nova Southeastern University; Linda C. Ueltschy, Bowling Green State University; Macgorine Cassell, Fairmont State University; Scott C. Hammond, Utah Valley State College; Donald L Sparks, The Citadel; Donald Vest, Clark Atlanta University; Eugene Seeley, Utah Valley State College; Fifi Anastasiadis, Farmingdale State College; Hoon Park, University of Central Florida; Jeff W. Bruns, Bacone College; Jeffrey Kulick, George Mason University; John Ruhnka, University of Colorado at Denver; Kau C Pang, University of Alabama–Birmingham; Lilach Nachum, Baruch College; Phil Seder, Portland Community College; and Samit Chakravorti, Western Illinois University; and Yeqing Bao, University of Alabama, Huntsville. Attorney Mary C. Tolton, Esq., of the law firm Parker, Poe, Adams & Bernstein of Raleigh, North Carolina, provided valuable supplementary readings for the legal forces chapter; and we acknowledge the help of Denalee Eaton and Kimberly Gainey, students at California State University, Long Beach; Handan Vicdan and Ebru Ulusoy, PhD students at the University of Texas–Pan American; Sandra de los Santos and Elizabeth Reyes, members of the PhD program staff at the University of Texas–Pan American; and Pam Dineva and Ryan Smith, students at California Polytechnic University, San Luis Obispo.

We are also indebted to the following reviewers for helping us fine-tune the thirteenth edition to better meet market needs: Stuart Arends, Madonna University; Michael Banutu-Gomez, Rowan University; John Michael Cavendish, Salem International University; David Christensen, Boise State University; John Cipolla, Lynn University; Norb Elbert, Eastern Kentucky University; Mark Gabriel Fenton, Univeristy of Wisconsin–Stout; JoAnn Flett, Eastern University; David Geigle, Texas A&M University–Central Texas; Sara Jackson, University of the Incarnate Word; J. Leslie Jankovich, San Jose State University; Laura Lynn Kerner, Athens State University; Raihan Khan, SUNY–Oswego; Anthony Koh, University of Toledo; Jeffrey Kulick, George Mason University; Joseph Leonard, Miami University of Ohio–Oxford; Liliana Meneses, University of Maryland–University College; Hormoz Movassaghi, Ithaca College; Timothy Richard Muth, Florida Institute of Technology; Joseph Nowakowski, Muskingum University; Sam Okoroafo, University of Toledo; Eydis Olsen, Drexel University; Brian Satterlee, Liberty University; Eugene Seeley, Utah Valley University; Michael Smollar Volpe, University of Maryland-University College; Linda Carol Ueltschy, Bowling Green State University; James Wong, Shenandoah University; and Corinne Young, Saint Leo University.

Hundreds of professors have reviewed this text over its thirteen editions and have shaped it into the solid textbook it is. Their suggestions and feedback have been invaluable to us, and we very much appreciate their efforts and time.

We would like to offer our special thanks to the outstanding editorial and production staff from McGraw-Hill/Irwin who have worked so hard and so well to make this project succeed and stay on schedule, particularly John Weimeister, Jane Beck, Heather Darr, Donielle Xu, Elizabeth Steiner, Harvey Yep, Keri Johnson, and Ira Roberts. We feel honored to work with such a talented and professional team.

A World of Resources . . .

International Business: The Challenge of Global Competition continues to be the most objective and thorough treatment of international business available for students. Enriched with maps, photos, and the most up-to-date world data, this text boasts the collective expertise of one former and three current authors with firsthand international business experience, specializing in international management, finance, law, global strategy, and marketing—a claim no other text can make. Only Ball, Geringer, McNett, and Minor can offer a complete view of international business as diverse as the backgrounds of your business students.

Worldview Examples

Worldview features in every chapter offer compelling examples of how international business is affected by legal, political, economic, and social issues, helping students understand how interrelated these business strategy and policy issues are.

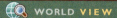 WORLD VIEW

Are Economic and Social Development Affected by Trade and Investment?

All economies are increasingly open in today's economic environment of globalization. Trade plays a vital role in shaping economic and social performance and prospects of countries around the world, especially those of developing countries. No country has grown without trade. However, the contribution of trade to development depends a great deal on the context in which it works and the objectives it serves.a

This quote is the way the United Nations Conference on Trade and Development (UNCTAD) began its groundbreaking report examining international trade and developing countries. International trade clearly has an important role in influencing nations' economic and social performance in a world of globalization. This role is even more fundamental in the case of developing countries. Yet the mere expansion of trade does not guarantee improvement for a country and its people. Rather, it is essential that trade performance be viewed in the context of its effects on employment levels, economic growth, development, and an improvement in the overall human condition.

To assist in efforts to ensure that trade plays a full and constructive role in enhancing growth and development, UNCTAD launched an ambitious initiative that included the Trade and Development Index (TDI). By capturing the interactions among a range of institutional, structural, financial, trade, and development factors underlying trade and development, the TDI attempts to provide a quantitative indication of a nation's trade and development performance and facilitate national and international strategies and policies that will enable trade to serve as an important tool for promoting development. Although UNCTAD created the TDI primarily for assessing performance in developing nations, to facilitate comparisons and insight, it also constructed the TDI for developed countries and for newly industrializing countries. Overall, 123 countries were evaluated and the 20 top- and bottom-ranked countries are listed in the accompanying table.

The average score for developed countries was 640, versus 467 for developing countries and 395 for the least developed countries. Seven major emerging economies (Brazil, Russia, India, China, Mexico, South Korea, and South Africa), which account for 45 percent of the world's population and more than 26 percent of global exports of goods and services, had an average TDI score of 509, and they have all evidenced increasing TDI scores. This indicates that the gap in development can be shrunk—and has been in the case of several nations. Overall,

compared with developed countries, developing countries evidence a continuing lag in such areas as physical infrastructure, human capital, financial intermediation, institutional quality, economic and social well-being, and trade performance.

The initial TDI evaluation revealed that the 30 highest-ranked nations were all developed countries, except for Singapore (#5), South Korea (#21), China (#25), Malaysia (#27), and Thailand (#29). This result is interpreted as evidence that few developing nations have been able to come close to the developed countries in terms of their trade and development performance. Nine of the bottom 10 nations are sub-Saharan African countries, accentuating the severity of the trade and development problems confronting sub-Saharan Africa and least developed nations in general. The best regional performance among developing nations was that of the countries of the East Asia and Pacific region, followed by the Middle East and North Africa region and the Latin America and Caribbean region. The regions of South Asia and of sub-Saharan Africa significantly lagged behind the other three regional groups in terms of their TDI scores.

A critical factor contributing to high TDI scores is trade liberalization. The importance of this factor is highest for countries with lower TDI scores, and vice versa. This suggests that the extent of trade liberalization has much greater importance for developing countries, and especially the least developed countries, than for developed nations. In general, over the longer term and in the absence of externalities or market failures, trade liberalization is an effective policy promoting development. However, efforts to liberalize too rapidly can also result in short-term adjustment problems.

Both external and internal factors were found to influence a nation's export performance. External factors include market access conditions (e.g., transportation costs, geography, physical infrastructure, trade barriers, competition) and other factors that influence demand for imports. Internal factors

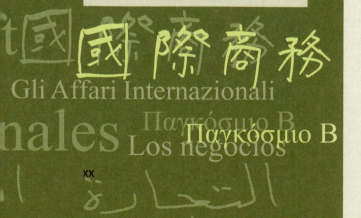

xx

Global debate

These boxed features in every chapter illustrate challenges that have faced companies and managers involved in international business, including issues relevant to ethical and socially responsible behavior. Students find these examples interesting and valuable, and considering these issues can better prepare them for making appropriate decisions when they engage in international business activities as part of their own careers.

The Global Path Ahead

Each box presents valuable tools and insights to help students build a foundation for entering and excelling in international business activities and careers. These boxes cover such topics as finding international job opportunities, building international skills and experience, gaining relevant knowledge and tools to increase success in finding and performing international business jobs, and learning from practical experience and recommendations from current students or recent graduates who have successfully pursued opportunities involving international business activity.

FIGURE 5.7

Map of Colombia

Instructive Maps

Numerous maps display valuable data and help students grasp geographic implications.

globalEDGE™ Research Tasks

Using the text and the globalEDGE™ website (www.globaledge.msu.edu), students solve realistic international business problems related to the types of tools and data sources international managers use to make informed decisions.

globalEDGE globalEDGE.msu.edu

Research Task

Use the globalEDGE site (http://globalEDGE.msu.edu/) to complete the following exercises:

1. You are working for a company that is deciding whether or not to enter South Asia. Top executives have requested a report on the natural environment in this region. Specifically, they are interested in gaining a better understanding of the main trends with respect to the land, air, and water. Using the South Asia Environment Outlook in the *South Asian Association for Regional Cooperation* website as reference, prepare a short report summarizing the key environmental trends in South Asia.

2. Your company wants to become more environmentally sustainable. Utilize resources available on the globalEDGE website regarding sustainable development and business to prepare a brief report that explains the concept of *sustainable* development and discusses why it is important for companies to engage in environmentally sustainable practices. In addition, compile a short list of steps that companies should take to become more environmentally sustainable.

Minicases

Minicases also appear at the end of each chapter. These brief scenarios challenge students to apply concepts discussed in the chapter to a real-world situation.

Minicase: The BlueGreen Alliance: A New Way of Thinking for Sustainability

In 2006, the United Steel Workers and the Sierra Club launched a collaboration to focus on environmental policy and expand the number of jobs and the quality of the jobs in the green economy. The collaboration surprised many because environmentalists and unions have been opposed on many issues in the past. For example, the environmentalists have opposed drilling for oil in the Alaska Arctic National Wildlife Refuge, which the unions supported. The unions have often opposed environmentalism because their belief was that it cost jobs. Yet, the collaboration found common ground and has been wildly successful, taking on many additional partners, including the Communications Workers of America, the Natural Resources Defense Council, the Service Employees International Union, the National Wildlife Federation, and the United Auto Workers. The BlueGreen Alliance unites more than 14 million members.

There are four main issues the BlueGreen Alliance is presently working on. The first has to do with increased investments in *clean energy* sources. This is a strategy to create green jobs, reduce global warming, and move the

United States toward energy independence. The second concern is *climate change*, and BlueGreen is urging passage of comprehensive climate change legislation. Such legislation would create jobs and reduce emissions. The *right trade policies* can lead, BlueGreen argues in its third concern, to a renewal of the American middle class if we increase trade and the jobs are located in the United States. The final concern is *green chemistry*. The BlueGreen Alliance is pushing for greater control of toxic chemicals and the development of safe alternatives through what it calls "green chemistry."[44]

Questions

1. Is the BlueGreen Alliance a partnership of convenience, or do you think it has the potential to move into a new way of approaching sustainability, with limits, interdependence, and equity?

2. The right trade policies, in a union view, may mean protectionist measures to build jobs. Do you think such a policy could fit into a sustainable approach?

Supplements for Instructors

Online Learning Center, www.mhhe.com/ball13e

The Online Learning Center (OLC) is a website that follows *International Business* chapter by chapter with digital supplementary content germane to the book. As students read the book, they can go online to take self-grading quizzes, review material, and work through interactive exercises. OLCs can be delivered multiple ways—through the textbook website, through PageOut, or within a course management system such as WebCT or Blackboard.

The following supplements are available for instructors who adopt this text:

Instructor's Manual

Written by coauthors J. Michael Geringer and Jeanne McNett, the Instructor's Manual will help save you valuable time preparing for the course by providing suggestions for heightening your students' interest in the material. Each chapter-by-chapter section presents concept previews, an overview of the chapter, a detailed chapter outline, suggestions and comments, student involvement exercises, and solutions to end-of-chapter material. The manual also includes video case teaching notes.

Test Bank

Written by the authors, the Test Bank contains approximately 100 questions per chapter in multiple-choice, true/false, and short-answer format. Each question is ranked for difficulty level and includes page references to the text.

PowerPoint Slides

Created by coauthors J. Michael Geringer and Jeanne McNett, this PowerPoint presentation includes key points from each chapter, sample figures from the text, and supplemental exhibits that help illustrate the main points in a chapter.

Videos

A new video collection features original business documentaries as well as news footage. Videos correspond to video teaching notes accessible on the instructor's side of the OLC.

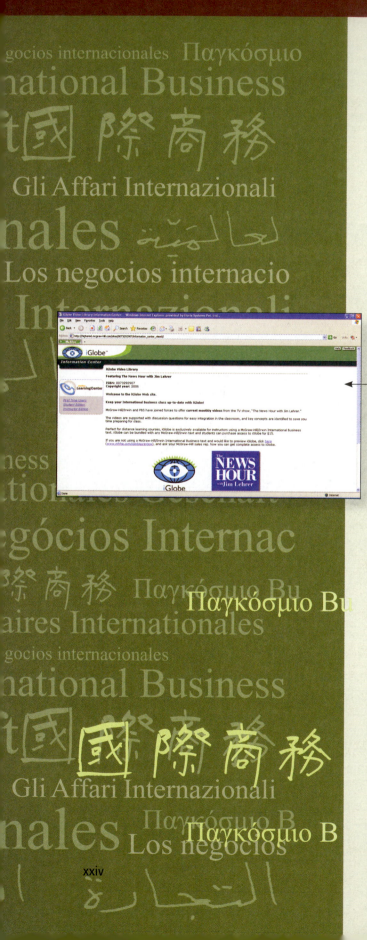

iGlobe

iGlobe is a ground-breaking online video website (www.mhhe.com/iglobe), where you can download two "on-demand" PBS videos per month on breaking stories on international business issues. The website is updated with new video selections each month, and the videos are archived monthly for easy accessibility. These streaming videos are complete with teaching notes and discussion questions. Key concepts for each video are identified to save you time! This is ideal for online courses or for homework assignments outside class.

International Business DVD Vol. 6 (ISBN 0077324676)

A revised and expanded *International Business* DVD of company mini-documentaries and newsreels sparks classroom discussions. Classic footage joins new stories to help you engage your students in international business topics.

Supplements for Students

CESIM: Global Challenge Simulation

This online simulation involving international markets for mobile handsets is packaged with new copies of the text. There are three market areas (North America, Europe, and Asia). The simulation presents a range of features that could be offered (affecting product differentiation), a choice of production sites (in Asia or North America), price options, and exposure to exchange rate fluctuations, among other issues and decisions. It can be used with 3 to 12 teams (6 to 50 students per simulation and larger classes can readily be accommodated by using multiple simulations simultaneously) and can involve teams from more than one class or university, if desired. The simulation is also well-suited for many online courses. There is an enhanced online support facility with the thirteenth edition, as well as an improved user interface to enhance the performance and appearance of the simulation. Use of this online simulation is free with new copies of this text.

Online Learning Center, www.mhhe.com/ball13e

The Online Learning Center (OLC) is a website that follows *International Business* chapter by chapter with digital supplementary content germane to the book. As students read the book, they can go online to take self-grading quizzes, review material, and work through interactive exercises.

Brief Contents

Contents

Contents   xxxi

CHAPTER 17

Managing Human Resources in an International Context 424

CHAPTER 18

International Accounting and Financial Management 454

List of Maps

INTERNATIONAL BUSINESS

Affaires Internationales

Los negocios internacionales

Gli Affari Internazionali

International Business

Παγκόσμιο Business

international Business 國際商務 Gli Affari Internazionali Los negoc
Affaires Internationales أحدا ذ
cios Internacionais Παγκόσμιο Business Los negocios internacionales
أحدا ذ Gli Affari Inter
egócios Internacionais Affaires Internationales
onales Geschäft Los negocios internacionales Παγκόσμι
ócios Internacionais Gli Affari Internazionali International Business
Παγκόσμιο Business 國際商務

section one

The Nature of International Business

The world we share is becoming increasingly interconnected in complex and interesting ways. Section One describes the nature and scope of international business and introduces the three environments in which international business managers must operate. How well they perform in their undertakings depends in great measure on their understanding of domestic, international, and foreign environments.

Chapter I discusses what international business is and also presents the concepts of the three environments and their forces. From the history of international business, we learn that international firms have been in existence for centuries, but that present-day global companies—characterized by explosive growth and closer central control of foreign operations—are markedly different from their predecessors. We discuss what is driving globalization of business and why firms go abroad, and examine the debate about pros and cons of globalization of business. We also examine the seven dimensions along which managers can globalize if they take their companies international.

In Chapter 2, information is presented to help you comprehend the dynamic growth and the magnitude of both international trade and foreign investment. We also provide an overview of the major theories of international trade and investment. A basic understanding of this material will help explain the actions already taken by managers and by government officials, and provide insight into what they plan to do in the future.

Chapter 3 discusses institutions that operate in the international environment and that may affect international businesses in fundamental ways. International institutions can be both a help and a hindrance to businesses, and the international institutions and agreements discussed in this chapter are organizations of governments, along with some private organizations, whose main purpose is political, economic, or a combination of the two. Some of these organizations have large amounts of power (such as the European Union), and others have less power, but all are important to business.

The Challenging World of International Business

In the past, complex international transactions were the domain of diplomats and international policy and business experts. Today a converging set of powerful economic, technological, demographic and geopolitical trends will demand that all citizens, not just the elite, have that kind of global fluency. Knowledge of the world is no longer a luxury, it is a necessity.

—*Nicholas Platt, President Emeritus of the Asia Society*

Why You Need International Business Experience and How to Get It

Gary Ellis, a young assistant controller for Medtronic, a *Fortune* 500 manufacturer of pacemakers and other medical equipment, was considered to be on the fast track for a top management position. However, company executives felt he first needed broader experience, so they sent him to head their European headquarters in Belgium. In his new job, Gary was responsible for many top-level duties and worked with an array of officials (labor, government, production, and marketing, as well as financial). Two years later, when the corporate controller's job in the company's home office in Minneapolis became vacant, Ellis was given the job due to the belief of Medtronic's chief executive officer (CEO) that successful executives of the future will be those who have lived for several years in another nation.

Medtronic is not the only firm with this belief. At FMC Corp., a heavy machinery and chemicals producer, the vice president for human resources suggested that by the end of the decade, anyone in a general management position in his company will have had direct international exposure and experience. Evidently, the boards of directors of many other American corporations have the same policy. Companies such as McDonald's, Coke, Kellogg, Alcoa, Altria, and Schering-Plough have all appointed leaders who had extensive experience as the heads of international operations, and approximately 30 percent of the top 700 CEOs in the United States have had international experience. William Sullivan, the CEO of Agilent Technologies, commented on his three years in Singapore as an operations manager by saying, "It was a real career changer. In today's environment, having that overseas experience is a big deal."[a] Pfizer's CEO, Henry McKinnell, commented on the impact of his 14 years overseas by saying, "I've had hundreds of experiences I'll never forget. They were invaluable in shaping me into the manager of a global company."[b] As Carlos Gutierrez, who was the CEO of Kellogg before becoming the U.S. secretary of commerce (2005–2009), said, "Having a foreign perspective gives you an advantage not only for doing business outside the U.S. but domestically, where we have the most diverse society in the world. There's a built-in understanding that differences exist and are good."[c]

Although many American managers want their top executives at company headquarters to have years of foreign experience, do CEOs of the major firms recognize

learning objectives

After reading this chapter, you should be able to:

LO1-1 **Understand** what international business is and why it is important.

LO1-2 **Comprehend** why and how international business differs from domestic business.

LO1-3 **Appreciate** that international business has a long and important history in the world's development.

LO1-4 **Appreciate** the dramatic internationalization of markets.

LO1-5 **Understand** the five kinds of drivers, all based on change, that are leading firms to internationalize their operations.

LO1-6 **Recognize** the key arguments for and against the globalization of business.

LO1-7 **Explain** the reasons for entering foreign markets.

LO1-8 **Recognize** that globalization of an international firm occurs over at least seven dimensions and that a company can be partially global in some dimensions and completely global in others.

the value of internationalized business education for all employees in management? Surveying the CEOs of the 162 largest firms on the *Fortune's* list of the 500 largest American corporations, we found that the CEOs strongly believed that: (1) an international orientation should be an important part of college business education; (2) international business skills and knowledge were important not merely for promotion to senior executive positions, but also for appointment to entry-level positions, and across a broad array of functional as well as cross-functional areas; and (3) the importance indicated in the preceding points was magnified for those companies that were anticipating increasing importance of international activities in the next five years.[d] For developing international skills, respondents believed that a number of courses in the international business curriculum are relevant to their companies. In addition to an introduction to international business, the internationally oriented courses that were viewed as being the most important for early career positions included topics related to (1) international strategy and competitiveness, (2) international legal and political issues, (3) international negotiation, and (4) foreign language. It appears from our study, then, that the CEOs of major American firms doing business overseas are convinced that the business graduates they hire should have some education in the international aspects of business. Clearly, the top executives from some of the largest corporations in the world are saying that they prefer business graduates who know something about markets, customs, and cultures in other countries. Companies that do business overseas have always needed some people who could work and live successfully outside their own countries, but now it seems that managers wanting to advance in their firms must have some foreign experience as well. As Roselinde Torres, president of U.S. operations of Mercer Delta Consulting said, "The hallmark of a great CEO is the ability to see an issue through a variety of lenses. International experience is one of the surest ways to add some new lenses."[e]

Did you note the reason for this emphasis on foreign experience for managers? It is increased involvement of the firm in international business. The top executives of many corporations want their employees to have a global business perspective. What about companies that have no foreign operations of any kind? Do their managers need this global perspective? They do indeed, because it will help them not only to be alert for both sales and sourcing opportunities in foreign markets, but also to be watchful for new foreign competitors preparing to invade their domestic market. In addition, according to recruiters, foreign experience reflects independence, re-sourcefulness, and entrepreneurship. People who work and support themselves overseas tend to be inquisitive, adaptive, and flexible—qualities that are valuable in today's work environment. Given this need by companies for internationally experienced personnel, what can you do to improve your chances to obtain an overseas post?

It can be valuable to take classes in the area of international business, perhaps leading to a degree in an international business–related field. In addition, even while you are in school or shortly after graduation, consider going abroad to study, to work (whether as a business intern, as a teacher, or even in such positions as bartender or child care provider), or to volunteer in community development activities. The experience of living and working in another culture can be important in personal development, as well as being a career booster. As Lauren DiCioccio said of her international experience as a cook and farm worker, "When I went, I was hesitant because people looked at me and were surprised that I would graduate with a degree from Colgate and take time off to work and backpack around Australia. So when I came back and had it on my résumé, I couldn't believe all of the interviews were about my time in Australia." Brandon Steiner, a 24-year-old teaching in Japan, said, "Having international experience under your belt—employers are enthusiastic. It looks good and is not a bad step out of college. It shows you already are open-minded."[f] Upon your return, this experience may help you to land a job that involves international business activities. Although most positions are based in a person's home country, they may involve some international travel to see clients or perform other job-related activities, thus, providing an opportunity for you to further broaden your international skills and experience.

If you already have a job, you can enhance your opportunities for international experience by making your boss and the human resource management department personnel aware of your interest and the fact that you have studied international business. Look for opportunities to remind them that you continue to be interested (performance review is a good time). Try to meet people in the home office who work with the company's foreign subsidiaries as well as visitors from overseas. As evidence of your strong interest in foreign employment, take additional international business courses and study foreign languages. Make sure that people in your company know what you are doing.

Throughout this book you will find examples of ways to develop, apply, and promote your international skills and experience, through features such as "The Global Path Ahead" vignettes of the international experiences of current students and recent graduates, and the "Resources for Your Global Career" suggestions that follow the vignette in each chapter. Hopefully, through effective application of these suggestions, you will build a successful foundation for your own international experiences!

[a]Erin White, "Future CEOs May Need to Have Broad Liberal-Arts Foundation," *The Wall Street Journal,* April 12, 2005, p. B4, www.uta.edu/pols/files/CEOsAndLiberalArts.pdf (May 28, 2011).

[b]Justin Martin, "The Global CEO: Overseas Experience Is Becoming a Must on Top Executives' Resumes, According to This Year's Route to the Top," *The Chief Executive,* January–February 2004, www.cristassociates.com/press/CEO_theglobalceo_020104.pdf (May 28, 2011).

[c]Carol Hymowitz, "Foreign-Born CEOs Are Increasing in U.S., Rarer Overseas," *The Wall Street Journal,* May 25, 2004, http://online.wsj.com/article/0,,SB108543349255419931,00.html (May 28, 2011).

[d]J. Michael Geringer and William R. Pendergast, "CEO Views on the Value of International Business Skills and Education," *The International Journal of Management and Business,* Vol. 1, September 2010, pp. 12–35.

[e]Martin, "The Global CEO."

[f]Hillary Chura, "A Year Abroad (or 3) as a Career Move," *The New York Times,* February 25, 2006, www.nytimes.com/2006/02/25/business/worldbusiness/25abroad.html (May 28, 2011).

What about you? Are you involved in the global economy yet? Please read the nearby Worldview box, "Are You Really Buying American?" and then think back to how you began your own day. After you awoke, you may have looked at your Casio watch for the time, checked your Samsung cell phone for messages, and turned on your Toshiba TV for the news and weather while you showered. After drying your hair with a Conair dryer, maybe you slipped into some Diesel jeans, quickly swallowed some Dannon yogurt and a glass of Mott's apple juice, brushed your teeth with Close-Up toothpaste, and drove off to class in your Honda with its Firestone tires and a tank full of Shell gasoline. Meanwhile, on the other side of the world, a group of Nike-clad Japanese students may be turning off their Apple computers after watching videos on YouTube.com and debating whether they should stop for hamburgers and Cokes at McDonald's or coffee at Starbucks. As they leave, they place their books and other materials into their JanSport backpacks, put on their North Face jackets and Oakley sunglasses, and turn on their iPods.

What do you and the Japanese students have in common? You are all consuming products made by *foreign-owned companies.* This is international business.

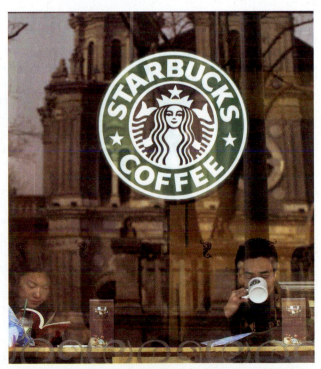

A Starbucks coffee store in Beijing China. Chairman Howard Schultz said China is the coffee chain's No.1 growth market.

Are You Really Buying American?

Consider the following scenario of a "typical" American family:

The Boltons, Mike and Barbara, live in the suburbs of Chicago. Mike is a manager with the Trader Joe's specialty grocery store chain. Barbara is an advertising executive for Leo Burnett Worldwide.

Barbara listens to the new Britney Spears CD on her Clarion car stereo in her 2011 Chrysler 200S convertible while driving home from work, stopping for gas at the Shell station. At the grocery store, she fills her cart with a variety of items, including Ragu spaghetti sauce, Hellmann's mayonnaise, Carnation Instant Breakfast drink, Wishbone salad dressing, CoffeeMate nondairy coffee creamer, Chicken-of-the-Sea canned tuna, Lipton tea, a half-dozen cans of Slim-Fast, Dannon yogurt, and several packages of Stouffer's Lean Cuisine frozen dinners. For a treat, she picks up some Ben & Jerry's ice cream, Toll House cookies, and a Butterfinger candy bar. She also grabs several cans of Alpo for their dog, Sassy, a box of Friskies, and a bag of Tidy Cat cat litter for their cat, Millie. She goes down the toiletries aisle for some Dove soap, Vaseline hand cream, Jergen's moisturizing lotion, and some Axe deodorant for Mike. Before finishing, she calls Mike on her Samsung cellular phone from Verizon Wireless to see if there is anything else he needs. He asks her to pick up some PowerBars for him to take to the gym during his lunchtime workouts next week. She also stops at the bookstore and picks up the new John Grisham book published by Random House, signing the credit card slip with her Bic pen.

After leaving his office, Mike stops at the BP gas station to fill his gas tank and checks the air pressure in his Firestone tires. He makes a quick stop at the video store to pick up *Spiderman* and a collection of *The King of Queens* episodes on DVD, before heading to the liquor store for a case of Miller Genuine Draft beer. He walks next door to the sporting goods store to pick up some Wilson racquetballs for his workouts next week.

Barbara's favorite TV show, *Jeopardy!*, is just starting as Mike comes in the door, so she pours herself a glass of Beringer wine from Napa Valley and turns on their Philips high-definition television while Mike prepares dinner.

All that you have read so far points to one salient fact: *all managers need to have a basic knowledge of international business to be able to meet the challenge of global competition.* Acquiring this knowledge consists, in part, of learning the special terminology of international business, an important function, as you already know, of every introductory course. To assist you in learning the international business "language," we've included a glossary at the end of the book and listed the most important terms at the end of each chapter. They also appear in bold print where they are first used in the text, with their definitions in the margin.

LO1-1 Understand what international business is and why it is important.

What Is International Business?

international business
A business whose activities are carried out across national borders

foreign business
The operations of a company outside its home or domestic market

Because international business is a relatively new discipline and is extremely dynamic, you will find that the definitions of a number of terms vary among users. To avoid confusion due to the range of different definitions of terms in international business, in this text we will employ the definitions listed here, which are generally accepted by managers:

1. **International business** is business whose activities are carried out across national borders. This definition includes not only international trade and foreign manufacturing, but also the growing service industry in areas such as transportation, tourism, advertising, construction, retailing, wholesaling, and mass communications.

2. **Foreign business** denotes the operations of a company outside its home or domestic market; many refer to this as business conducted within a foreign country. This term

While this may sound like a very typical evening for many Americans, foreign-owned firms produced nearly every item that the Boltons purchased or consumed:

- Trader Joe's is owned by a family trust set up by German businessman Theo Albrecht.
- Leo Burnett Worldwide is owned by Publicis of France.
- Sony Music of Japan produces and distributes Britney Spears' CDs.
- Japan's Clarion Co., Ltd. Produces Clarion car stereos.
- Italy's Fiat is the majority owner of Chrysler.
- The British-Dutch company, Royal Dutch Shell, owns Shell.
- Nestlé of Switzerland produces Alpo, Butterfinger, Carnation Instant Breakfast, CoffeeMate, Friskies, PowerBar, Stouffer's Lean Cuisine, Toll House, and Tidy Cat.
- Unilever, a British-Dutch multinational, makes Slim-Fast, Dove soap, Hellmann's, Ragu, Wishbone, Lipton, Vaseline, Axe, and Ben & Jerry's.
- Groupe Danone of France produces Dannon yogurt.
- Chicken-of-the-Sea is made by Thai Union International of Thailand.
- Japan's Kao owns Jergen's.
- Samsung cell phones are made by Korea's Samsung.
- Vodaphone Group plc of the United Kingdom owns 45 percent of Verizon Wireless.
- Bertelsmann AG of Germany owns Random House.
- Societe Bic of France produces Bic pens.
- Japan's Bridgestone owns Firestone.
- BP of the United Kingdom owns BP gas stations.
- Columbia Pictures, owned by Sony of Japan, released the *Spiderman* movies, Sony Pictures Television distributes *Jeopardy!* Sony Pictures Television distributes *The King of Queens.*
- SABMiller plc of the United Kingdom produces Miller beer.
- Amer Group of Finland owns Wilson Sporting Goods.
- Beringer Winery of Napa, California, is owned by Australia's Treasury Wine Estates.
- Philips televisions are produced and sold by Philips of the Netherlands.

This simple example reflects the impact of extensive foreign investments in the United States, especially in recent years. Even some of the best-known "American" products and brands are now produced by foreign firms.

Investments have also flowed outward from the United States. American companies such as Coca-Cola, Starbucks, McDonald's, the Gap, Microsoft, and Levi's are found in Japan, South Korea, China, Australia, Singapore, and nearly every European nation. American companies have also purchased a range of foreign companies and brands.

Question:

Why has there been almost no negative backlash among Americans to the flood of foreign investment into their country?

Sources: From T. R. Reid, "Buying American? Maybe Not; Many U.S. Brands European-Owned," *Washington Post*, May 18, 2002, p. E1; Nicholas Platt, "Make Global Skills a Top Priority," *Financial Times*, July 2, 2004, p. 13, http://proquest.umi.com/pqdweb?index=0&did=658025341&SrchMode=2&sid=1&Fmt=3&VInst=PROD&VType=PQD&RQT=309&VName=PQD&TS=1306613480&clientId=17870 (accessed May 28, 2011); and company websites (accessed May 28, 2011).

sometimes is used interchangeably with *international business,* although that will not be the practice in this book.

3. A **multidomestic company (MDC)** is an organization with multicountry affiliates, each of which formulates its own business strategy based on perceived market differences.

4. A **global company (GC)** is an organization that attempts to standardize and integrate operations worldwide in most or all functional areas.

5. An **international company (IC)** is a global or multidomestic company.

Although we primarily use the terms *global, multidomestic,* and *international* firms or companies, at times we may use *multinational enterprise (MNE)* or *multinational company (MNC)* interchangeably with *international company (IC),* inasmuch as both terms are employed in the literature and in practice.

Although you may find those who consider *multinational corporation* to be synonymous with *multinational enterprise* and *transnational corporation,*[1] the United Nations and the governments of many developing nations use *transnational* instead of *multinational* to describe any firm doing business in more than one country. The specialized agency, the United Nations Conference on Trade and Development (UNCTAD), for example, employs the following definition: "A transnational corporation is generally regarded as an enterprise comprising entities in more than one country that operate under a system of decision-making that permits coherent policies and a common strategy. The entities are so linked, by ownership or otherwise, that one or more of them may be able to exercise a significant

multidomestic company (MDC)
An organization with multicountry affiliates, each of which formulates its own business strategy based on perceived market differences

global company (GC)
An organization that attempts to standardize and integrate operations worldwide in all functional areas

international company (IC)
Either a global or a multidomestic company

influence over the others and, in particular, to share knowledge, resources and responsibilities with the others."[2] More recently, some academic writers have employed the term *trans-national* for a company that combines the characteristics of global and multinational firms: (1) trying to achieve economies of scale through global integration of its functional areas and at the same time (2) being highly responsive to different local environments (a newer name is *multicultural multinational*).[3]

What Is Different about International Business?

LO1-2 Comprehend why and how international business differs from domestic business.

International business differs from domestic business in that a firm operating across borders must deal with the forces of three kinds of environments—domestic, foreign, and international. In contrast, a firm whose business activities are carried out within the borders of one country needs to be concerned essentially with only the domestic environment. However, no domestic firm is entirely free from foreign or international environmental forces, because the possibility of having to face competition from foreign imports or from foreign competitors that set up operations in its own market is always present. Let us first examine these forces and then see how they operate in the three environments.

INFLUENCE OF EXTERNAL AND INTERNAL ENVIRONMENTAL FORCES

environment
All the forces surrounding and influencing the life and development of the firm

The term **environment** as used here means all the forces influencing the life and development of the firm. The forces themselves can be classified as *external* or *internal*. The external forces are commonly called **uncontrollable forces.** Management has no direct control over them, although it can exert influence–such as lobbying for a change in a law and heavily promoting a new product that requires a change in a cultural attitude. External forces consist of the following:

uncontrollable forces
External forces over which management has no direct control, although it can exert an influence

1. *Competitive:* kinds and numbers of competitors, their locations, and their activities.
2. *Distributive:* national and international agencies available for distributing goods and services.
3. *Economic:* variables (such as gross national product [GNP], unit labor cost, and personal consumption expenditure) that influence a firm's ability to do business.
4. *Socioeconomic:* characteristics and distribution of the human population.
5. *Financial:* variables such as interest rates, inflation rates, and taxation.
6. *Legal:* the many foreign and domestic laws governing how international firms must operate.
7. *Physical:* elements of nature such as topography, climate, and natural resources.
8. *Political:* elements of nations' political climates such as nationalism, forms of government, and international organizations.
9. *Sociocultural:* elements of culture (such as attitudes, beliefs, and opinions) important to international managers.
10. *Labor:* composition, skills, and attitudes of labor.
11. *Technological:* the technical skills and equipment that affect how resources are converted to products.

controllable forces
Internal forces that management administers to adapt to changes in the uncontrollable forces

The elements over which management does have some control are the internal forces, such as the factors of production (capital, raw materials, and people) and the activities of the organization (personnel, finance, production, and marketing). These are the **controllable forces** management must administer in order to adapt to changes in the uncontrollable environmental variables. Look at how one change in the political forces—the expansion of the European Union (EU) in 2007—affected all the controllable forces of firms worldwide that do business in or with the 27 EU member-nations. Suddenly these firms had to examine their business practices and change those affected by this new expansion. For example, some

European concerns and foreign subsidiaries in the EU relocated parts of their operations to other nations in the Union to exploit the lower wages there. Some American and Asian companies set up production in one of the member-countries to supply this giant free trade area. By doing this, they avoid paying import duties on products coming from their home countries.

THE DOMESTIC ENVIRONMENT

The **domestic environment** is all the uncontrollable forces originating in the home country that influence the life and development of the firm. Obviously, these are the forces with which managers are most familiar. Being domestic forces, however, does not preclude their affecting foreign operations. For example, if the home country is suffering from a shortage of foreign currency, the government may place restrictions on overseas investment to reduce its outflow. As a result, managers of multinationals find that they cannot expand overseas facilities as they would like to do. In another instance from real life, a labor union striking the home-based plants learned that management was supplying parts from its foreign subsidiaries. The strikers contacted the foreign unions, which pledged not to work overtime to supply what the struck plants could not. The impact of this domestic environmental force was felt overseas as well as at home.

THE FOREIGN ENVIRONMENT

The forces in the **foreign environment** are the same as those in the domestic environment except that they occur outside the firm's home country. However, they operate differently for several reasons, including those provided here.

Forces Have Different Values   Even though the kinds of forces in the two environments are identical, their values often differ widely, and at times they are completely opposed to each other. A classic example of diametrically opposed political-force values and the bewilderment they create for multinational managers involves the American export embargo on shipments of most goods to Cuba. This embargo meant that Cuba could not buy buses from a U.S. manufacturer. To circumvent the embargo, the Cuban government ordered the buses from the American firm's Argentine subsidiary. When word came from the firm's American headquarters that the order should not be filled because of the American embargo, the Argentine government ordered the Argentine subsidiary to fill the order. The Argentine government said that Argentine companies, of which the subsidiary was one, did not answer to the demands of a foreign government. The Argentine management of the subsidiary was in a quandary. Finally, headquarters relented and permitted its Argentine subsidiary to fill the order.

Forces Can Be Difficult to Assess   Another problem with foreign forces is that they are frequently difficult to assess. This is especially true of legal and political forces. A highly nationalistic law may be passed to appease a section of the local population. To all outward appearances, the government may appear to be against foreign investment; yet pragmatic leaders may actually encourage it. A good example is Mexico, which until 1988 had a law prohibiting foreigners from owning a majority interest in a Mexican company. However, a clause permitted exceptions "if the investment contributes to the welfare of the nation." IBM, Eaton, and others were successful in obtaining permission to establish a wholly owned subsidiary under this clause.

The Forces Are Interrelated   In the chapters that follow, it will be evident that the forces are often interrelated. This in itself is not a novelty because the same situation confronts a domestic manager. On the foreign scene, however, the kinds of interaction that occur and the outcomes may differ. For instance, the combination of high-cost capital and an abundance of unskilled labor in many developing countries may lead to the use of a lower level of technology than would be employed in the more industrialized nations. In other words, given a choice between installing costly, specialized machinery needing few workers and installing less expensive, general-purpose machinery requiring a larger labor force, management will frequently choose the latter when faced with high interest rates and a large pool of available workers. Another example is the interaction between physical and sociocultural forces. Barriers to the free movement of a nation's people, such as mountain ranges and deserts, help maintain pockets of distinct cultures within a country, and this has an effect on decision making.

THE INTERNATIONAL ENVIRONMENT

The **international environment** consists of the interactions (1) between the domestic environmental forces and the foreign environmental forces and (2) between the foreign environmental forces of two countries when an affiliate in one country does business with customers in another. This agrees with the definition of international business: business that involves the crossing of national borders.

For example, personnel at the headquarters of a multidomestic or global company work in the international environment if they are involved in any way with another nation, whereas those in a foreign subsidiary do not unless they too are engaged in international business through exporting or the management of other affiliates. In other words, a sales manager of Nokia's China operations does not work in the international environment if he or she sells cellular phones only in China. If Nokia's China operations export cell phones to Thailand, then the sales manager is affected by forces of both the domestic environment of China and the foreign environment of Thailand and, therefore, is working in the international environment. International organizations whose actions affect the international environment are also properly part of it. These organizations include (1) worldwide bodies (e.g., World Bank), (2) regional economic groupings of nations (e.g., North American Free Trade Agreement, European Union), and (3) organizations bound by industry agreements (e.g., Organization of Petroleum Exporting Countries).

Decision Making Is More Complex

Those who work in the international environment find that decision making is more complex than it is in a purely domestic environment. Consider managers in a home office who must make decisions affecting subsidiaries in just 10 different countries (many ICs are in 20 or more countries). They not only must take into account the domestic forces, but also must evaluate the influence of 10 foreign national environments. Instead of having to consider the effects of a single set of 10 forces, as do their domestic counterparts, they have to contend with 10 sets of 10 forces, *both individually and collectively,* because there may be some interaction.

For example, if management agrees to labor's demands at one foreign subsidiary, chances are it will have to offer a similar settlement at another subsidiary because of the tendency of unions to exchange information across borders. Furthermore, as we shall observe throughout this text, not only are there many sets of forces, but there are also extreme differences among them.

Self-Reference Criterion

Another common cause of the added complexity of foreign environments is managers' unfamiliarity with other cultures. To make matters worse, some managers will ascribe to others their own preferences and reactions. Thus, a foreign production manager, facing a backlog of orders, may offer her workers extra pay for overtime. When they fail to show up, the manager is perplexed: "Back home they always want to earn more money." This manager has failed to understand that the workers prefer time off to more money. This unconscious reference to the manager's own cultural values, called the **self-reference criterion,** is probably the biggest cause of international business blunders. Successful managers are careful to examine a problem in terms of the local cultural traits as well as their own.

A Brief History of International Business

While international business as a discipline is relatively new, as a business practice it is not, so let's briefly explore the history of international business.

Well before the time of Christ, Phoenician and Greek merchants were sending representatives abroad to sell their goods. Subsequently, a vast expansion of agricultural and industrial production in China stimulated the emergence of an internationally integrated trading system. The saying that "all roads lead to China" had relevance within the international trade system, because China was the world's leading manufacturing country for about 1,800 years, until it was replaced by Britain in about 1840.

The impact of the emerging international trading system was extensive. Politics, the arts, agriculture, industry, and other sectors of human life were profoundly influenced by the goods and ideas that came with trade. Public health was also affected. An interesting precursor to contemporary concerns about global health epidemics, such as severe acute respiratory syndrome (SARS) and the so-called swine flu, was international trade's association with the spread of the plague, one of the worst natural disasters in history. Believed to have originated in Asia, the plague moved west with traders and soldiers, carried by oriental rat fleas that lived on rodents that stowed away on ships and caravans. Called the Black Death in Europe and repeated in waves from the mid-1300s through the 1500s, the plague ravaged cities, caused widespread hysteria, and killed one-quarter of China's people and one-third of the population of Europe.[4]

The rise of the Ottoman Empire before 1300, ultimately spanning Europe, North Africa, and the Middle East, profoundly influenced the emerging trade routes for people, goods, money, animals, and microorganisms that spanned from England to China, across the Mediterranean and Northern Africa, and through Central Asia and the Indian Ocean region. The powerful central location of the Ottomans within this trading web had the effect of raising the cost of Asian trade for the Europeans. This spawned a search for sea routes to Asia, including expeditions that discovered the Americas.

In 1600, Great Britain's British East India Company, a newly formed trading firm, began to establish foreign branches throughout Asia, an action soon followed by many of the other European nations intent on exploiting trade opportunities for national advantage, including Portugal, the Netherlands, and France. In 1602, the Dutch East India Company was formed to carry out colonial activities in Asia and to open ocean trade routes to the East. The first company to issue stock, it is also frequently identified as the world's first multinational corporation.[5] By the end of the 1600s, ships commissioned by European trading companies regularly traveled to Asia via an interconnected Atlantic, Indian, and Pacific Ocean system of government-protected trade routes. Their goal was to acquire goods for sale or resale within various Asian markets and ultimately to return to Europe with valuable cargoes of cloth, spices, and other goods that would yield significant profits for investors. The 17th and 18th centuries have frequently been termed the "age of mercantilism" because the power of nations depended directly on the sponsorship and control of merchant capital, which expanded under the direct subsidization and protection of national governments. The concept of mercantilism is discussed in Chapter 2.

A number of multinational companies existed in the late 1800s. One of the first American companies to own foreign production facilities, have worldwide distribution networks, and market its products under global brands was Singer Sewing Machine. In 1868, it built a factory in Scotland and, by 1880, the company had become a global organization with an outstanding international sales organization and several overseas manufacturing plants. Other firms, such as J&P Coats (United Kingdom) and Ford Motor Company, soon followed, and by 1914, at least 37 American companies had production facilities in two or more overseas locations.[6] Interestingly, and quite a contrast to today's situation, in the 1920s *all* cars sold in Japan were made in the United States by Ford and General Motors and sent to Japan in knocked-down kits to be assembled locally. European companies were also moving overseas. For example, Friedrich Bayer purchased an interest in a New York plant in 1865, two years after setting up his plant in Germany. Then, because of high import duties in his overseas markets, he proceeded to establish plants in Russia (1876), France (1882), and Belgium (1908).[7]

As you have just read, multinational firms existed well before World War I, and the level of intracompany trade of multinationals in 1930, as a percentage of overall world trade, may have exceeded the proportion at the end of the 20th century.[8] Yet only in recent years have multinationals become the object of much discussion and investigation, especially concerning the increasing globalization of their operations.

Growth of International Firms and International Business

The size and the number of U.S. and foreign international concerns have been increasing rapidly in recent years, as have the levels of foreign direct investment (FDI) and exporting.

EXPANDING NUMBER OF INTERNATIONAL COMPANIES

UNCTAD, the United Nations agency in charge of all matters relating to FDI and international corporations, estimates that there are 82,000 transnational corporations with international production activities. These transnationals have approximately 810,000 foreign affiliates that collectively employ more than 78 million people. These transnationals account for approximately 25 percent of total global output and two-thirds of world trade. Foreign affiliates' sales have grown about 700 percent in the past 20 years.[9]

As a result of this expansion, the subsidiaries of foreign companies have become increasingly important in the industrial and economic life of many nations, developed and developing. This situation is in sharp contrast to the one that existed when the dominant economic interests were in the hands of local citizens. The expanding importance of foreign-owned firms in local economies came to be viewed by a number of governments as a threat to their autonomy. However, there has been a marked liberalization of government policies and attitudes toward foreign investment in both developed and developing nations since the early 1980s. Many government leaders know that local firms must obtain modern commercial technology in the form of direct investment, purchase of capital goods, and the right to use the international company's expertise if they are to be competitive in world markets.

Despite this change in attitude, there are still critics of large global firms who cite such statistics as the following to "prove" that host governments are powerless before them: In 2010, only 23 nations had gross national incomes (GNIs) greater than the total annual sales of Wal-Mart Stores, Inc., the company with the greatest level of sales in the world.[10] Further, when nations and corporations are ranked by GNI and total sales, respectively, 46 of the first 100 on the list are corporations. However, a nation's GNI and a company's sales are not directly comparable because GNI is a measure of value added, not sales. If a nation's total sales were computed, the result would be far greater than its GNI because there would be triple and quadruple counting. For example, suppose a steel manufacturer sells steel wire to a tire company, which uses it to build tires. Then the tire company sells the tires to automakers, which mount them on their automobiles, which they in turn sell to the public. Sales of the wire would be counted three times. However, in calculating GNI, governments merely sum the values added in each transaction, which is the difference between the sales of the company and the costs of materials bought outside the company. If company sales were measured by value added, Walmart's revenues of $405 billion would have been $22 billion on a value-added basis.[11] While Walmart's sales are about the same as Norway's GNI, when both the economy and the company are measured by the value added, Norway's economy is more than 18 times the size of Walmart.

A firm's size may at times give it bargaining power, as in the case of a government that wants a firm to set up a subsidiary because of the employment it will offer and the purchases it will make from other firms in that country. Yet, regardless of the parent firm's size, each subsidiary is a local company that must comply with the laws in the country in which it is located. If it does not, it can be subject to legal action or even government seizure.

FOREIGN DIRECT INVESTMENT AND EXPORTING ARE GROWING RAPIDLY

One variable commonly used to measure where and how fast internationalization is taking place is the increase in total foreign direct investment. **Foreign direct investment (FDI)** refers to direct investments in equipment, structures, and organizations in a foreign country at a level that is sufficient to obtain significant management control. It does not include mere foreign investment in stock markets. The world stock of outward FDI was $19.0 *trillion* at the beginning of 2010, which was more than nine times larger than what it was 20 years earlier, in 1990.[12]

foreign direct investment (FDI) Direct investments in equipment, structures, and organizations in a foreign country at a level that is sufficient to obtain significant management control; does not include mere foreign investment in stock markets

Of course, a substantial amount of international business involves exporting rather than FDI. **Exporting** is the transportation of any domestic good or service to a destination outside a country or region. It is the opposite of **importing,** which is the transportation of any good or service into a country or region, from a foreign origination point. Merchandise exports have grown faster than world output in nearly each of the past 60 years. World merchandise exports grew from $2.0 trillion in 1980 to $3.45 trillion in 1990, $6.46 trillion in 2000, and $15.24 trillion in 2010. This represents a nearly eightfold increase from 1980 to 2010, and with 2010 exports being 235 percent of the figure for 2000.[13] The level of service exports worldwide grew even more during this time, from $365 billion in 1980 to $781 billion in 1990, $1.5 trillion in 2000, and $3.7 trillion in 2010. This represented more than a tenfold increase between 1980 and 2010.[14] Trends regarding FDI and exporting, along with theories that help explain the level and location of exports and FDI, are discussed in Chapter 2. Figure 1.1 shows the growth in outward FDI and in services and merchandise exports from 1980 to 2010.

WHAT IS DRIVING THE GLOBALIZATION OF BUSINESS?

Although globalization is discussed everywhere—television shows, Internet chat rooms, political demonstrations, parliaments, management boardrooms, and labor union meetings— so far, it has no widely accepted definition. In fact, its definition continues to broaden. Now, for example, social scientists discuss the political, social, environmental, historical, geographic, and even cultural implications of globalization.[15] Some also speak of technological globalization, political globalization, and the like.

What Is Globalization?

The most common definition and the one used in international business is that of **economic globalization**—the tendency toward an international integration of goods, technology, information, labor, and capital, or the process of making this integration happen. The term *globalization* was first coined by Theodore Levitt in a *Harvard Business Review* article in which he maintained that new technologies had "proletarianized" communication, transport, and travel, creating worldwide markets for standardized consumer products at lower prices. He maintained that the future belonged to global corporations that did not cater to local differences in taste but, instead, adopted strategies that operated "as if the entire world (or major regions of it) were a single entity; [such an organization] sells the same things in the same way everywhere."[16]

The Drivers of Globalization

Five major kinds of drivers, all based on change, are leading international firms to globalize their operations: (1) political, (2) technological, (3) market, (4) cost, and (5) competitive.

Political There is a trend toward the unification and socialization of the global community. Preferential trading arrangements, such as the North American Free Trade Agreement and the European Union, that group several nations into a single market have presented firms with significant marketing opportunities. Many firms have moved swiftly to gain access to the combined markets of these trading partners, either through exporting or by producing in the area.

Two other aspects of this trend are contributing to the globalization of business operations: (1) the progressive reduction of barriers to trade and foreign investment by most governments, which is hastening the opening of new markets by international firms that are both exporting to them and building production facilities in them, and (2) the privatization of much of the industry in formerly communist nations and the opening of their economies to global competition.

Technological Advances in computers and communications technology are permitting an increased flow of ideas and information across borders, enabling customers to learn

FIGURE I.I

World
Merchandise
Exports,
Commercial
Services Exports,
and Outward
Foreign Direct
Investment,
1980–2010 (US$
trillions)

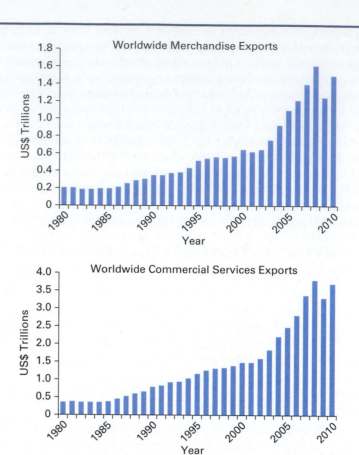

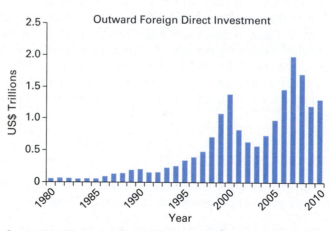

Sources: United Nations Conference on Trade and Development (UNCTAD), "FDI stock, by region and economy, 1990, 2000, 2008," *World Investment Report 2009* (New York: United Nations, 2009), p. 251; "Total Merchandise Trade," World Trade Organization, http://stat.wto.org/StatisticalProgram/WsdbExport.aspx?Language=E (May 28, 2011); and "Trade in Commercial Services," World Trade Organization, http://stat.wto.org/StatisticalProgram/WSDBStatProgramSeries.aspx?Language=E (May 28, 2011).

about foreign goods. Cable and satellite TV systems in Europe and Asia, for example, allow an advertiser to reach numerous countries simultaneously, thus creating regional and sometimes global demand. Global communications networks enable manufacturing personnel to coordinate production and design functions worldwide so that plants in many parts of the world may be working on the same product.

The Internet and network computing enable small companies to compete globally, because they make possible the rapid flow of information regardless of the physical location of the buyer and seller. Internet videoconferencing allows sellers to demonstrate their products to prospective buyers all over the world without the need to travel. It also permits international companies to hold corporate meetings between managers from headquarters and overseas subsidiaries without expensive, time-consuming travel. In addition, communicating by e-mail on the Internet is faster and more reliable than using postal mail and much less expensive than using a fax machine. Both Internet uses have given home office managers greater confidence in their ability to direct overseas operations.

Market   As companies globalize, they also become global customers. When Nokia announced its intention to set up a cell phone assembly plant in Chennai, India, suppliers of key components quickly confirmed that they would also establish plants adjacent to Nokia's facilities in order to avoid having a competitor capture the business. Likewise, for years, advertising agencies established offices in foreign markets when their major clients entered those markets to avoid having a competitor steal the accounts.

Finding the home market saturated also sends companies into foreign markets. According to a recent Dow Jones survey of the world's largest companies, 84 percent of the respondents expect that international markets will generate most of their growth in the next five years.[17] Indeed, the United States has only about 5 percent of the world's population, so the vast proportion of most companies' potential customers are located elsewhere.

Cost   Economies of scale to reduce unit costs are a common management goal. One means of achieving them is to globalize product lines to reduce development, production, and inventory costs. Management can also move production or other parts of the company's value chain to countries where costs are lower. Dramatic reductions in the cost of generating and transmitting information due to innovations in computing and telecommunications, as well as the decline in transportation costs, have facilitated this trend toward relocating activities worldwide.

Competitive   Competition continues to increase in intensity. New firms, many from newly industrialized and developing countries, have entered world markets in automobiles, computers, and electronics, for example. Another competitive driving force for globalization is the fact that companies are defending their home markets from competitors by entering the competitors' home markets to distract them. Many firms that would not have entered a single country because it lacked sufficient market size have established plants in

LO1-6 Recognize the key arguments for and against the globalization of business.

The Globalization Debate and You

Demonstrators at a World Trade Organization meeting

The merits of globalization have been the subject of many heated debates in recent years.[a] There have been extensive public protests about globalization and the liberalization of international trade at World Trade Organization meetings and at other gatherings of international organizations and leaders. The debate is, in many respects, waged by diametrically opposed groups with extremely different views regarding the consequences of globalization. Sifting through the propaganda and hyperbole spouted by both sides is a challenge. However, it is important to recognize the various perspectives on globalization, because their arguments can generate appeal (or rejection) both intellectually and emotionally. The contributions of free trade and globalization to dramatic reductions in worldwide poverty are contrasted with anecdotal stories of people losing their livelihoods under the growing power

(continued)

of multinationals. Likewise, increases in service sector employment are contrasted against losses in high-paying manufacturing jobs.

ARGUMENTS SUPPORTING GLOBALIZATION[a]

Free Trade Enhances Socioeconomic Development

That free trade is the best strategy for advancing the world's economic development is one of the few propositions on which almost all economists agree, not only because it is theoretically compelling but also because it has been demonstrated in practice. Data have shown a clear and definitive link between liberalization of trade and economic growth.[b] On a wide range of measures—poverty, education, health, and life expectancy—more people have become better off at a faster pace in the past 60 years than at any other time in history. Evidence is strong regarding the dramatic decline in both the proportion and the absolute number of destitute people. The World Development Indicators from the World Bank show that the number of people in extreme poverty fell from 1.5 billion in 1981 to 1.1 billion in 2001. Measured as a proportion of the population in developing countries, the decline was from 39.5 percent in 1981 to 21.3 percent in 2001. Between 1981 and 1999, the proportion of people in the East Asia and Pacific region living on less than $1 a day fell from 56 to 16 percent. In China, it plummeted from 61 to 17 percent. The proportion of people living in nations with daily food supplies under 2,200 calories per capita has declined from 56 percent in the mid1960s to less than 10 percent. Life expectancy in the developing world has nearly doubled since World War II, and infant mortality has decreased in all of the developing regions of the world. The proportion of children in the labor force fell from 24 percent in 1960 to 10 percent in 2000. Global literacy grew from 52 percent in 1950 to 81 percent in 1999, and on average the more globally integrated countries spend more on public education, especially in developing countries. Citizens from more globally integrated countries have greater levels of civil liberties and political rights. Within a generation's time, there has been an enormous improvement in the human condition, and every one of the development success stories was based on export-led growth facilitated by the liberalization of trade.

Of course, countries can reject globalization, and some have, including Myanmar, the Democratic Republic of Congo, Sierra Leone, Rwanda, Madagascar, Guinea-Bissau, Algeria, the Republic of Congo, Burundi, Albania, Syria, and Ukraine. They are among the most impoverished countries in the world. As an article in the *Financial Times* puts it, "They are victims of their refusal to globalize."[c]

Free Trade Promotes More and Better Jobs

Expanded trade is also linked with the creation of more and better jobs. Over the past two decades—a period of immense technological change and growth in trade—around 40 million more jobs were created than were destroyed in the United States. It is true that when a country opens to trade, just as when new technologies are developed, some of its sectors may not be competitive. Companies may go out of business, and some jobs will be lost. But trade creates new jobs, and these tend to be better than the old ones. The key is not to block change but, instead, to manage the costs of trade adjustment and to support the transition of workers to more competitive employment.

CONCERNS WITH GLOBALIZATION[d]

Those expressing concern with globalization have come from a range of sectors of society, and they express a correspondingly diverse set of concerns. Some fundamentally oppose the very process and outcomes of globalization on ideological grounds, while others may merely be concerned about finding ways to better manage globalization processes and the resulting outcomes. Some of the opponents' concerns may be viewed as naïve or clearly inconsistent with the preponderance of evidence. Other challenges to globalization may have theoretic merit or other supporting evidence and certainly may be worthy of discussion and the fostering of substantive change.

Although perspectives on the globalization debate may in many respects depend on one's values and ideology, thus further compounding efforts to reach a mutually agreed-on resolution, let us first ask this question: what are some of the primary concerns of the opponents of globalization? While many of the antiglobalizers concede that globalization "increases the size of the pie," they also claim that it has been accompanied by a broad array of injurious social implications. Among their concerns, let us briefly examine three primary ones here: (1) that globalization has produced uneven results across nations and people, (2) that globalization has had deleterious effects on labor and labor standards, and (3) that globalization has contributed to a decline in environmental and health conditions.

Globalization Has Produced Uneven Results across Nations and People

In stark contrast to the positive picture presented by supporters of globalization, opponents describe the painful impact of foreign investment and trade liberalization on the people of the world. Far from everyone has been a winner, they say. The promise of export-led growth has failed to materialize in several places. For example, most of Latin America has failed to replicate Asia's success despite efforts to liberalize, privatize, and deregulate its economies, with results ranging from disappointment in Mexico to catastrophe in Argentina. Similarly, efforts in sub-Saharan Africa have produced only limited benefits, and the share of the population living in extreme poverty there rose from 42 to 47 percent between 1981 and 2001. Open world markets, it seems, may offer the possibility of economic development—but the recipe is neither easy in its implementation nor universal in its outcomes.

Many opponents of globalization have claimed that there is a huge gap between the world's rich and poor

(continued)

and that globalization has caused that gap to increase. That there is a gap between rich and poor is unquestionable, but the evidence is perhaps not so clear regarding the charge that globalization has increased this inequality. Although Martin Wolf's analysis shows that income inequality has not risen in most developing countries that have integrated with the world economy, it does show that inequality has increased in some places, most notably in China. Inequality has risen in some high-income countries as well, but he attributes that more to the nature of technological change than to globalization. When income data are adjusted to reflect relative purchasing power, the inequality in income between poor and rich nations diminishes. Wolf also notes that while globalization of trade and investment is an enabler to improved income and living standards, the results may vary if obstacles exist such as poor governance or excessive borrowing.[e]

Globalization Has Had Deleterious Effects on Labor and Labor Standards

The issue of the impact of globalization on labor standards has become an oft-mentioned concern of workers in the United States and other nations. With trade liberalization through the World Trade Organization and increased mobility of capital, measures to keep a country's industries within its borders have been reduced, and companies have an easier time divesting their interests in one country and moving to another. Workers in developed countries frequently voice concerns that their jobs will migrate to developing nations where there are lower standards, and thus, lower costs, leading to the infamous "race to the bottom," where developed nations with more rigorous labor standards become disadvantaged. Indeed, the Labor Secretariat for the North American Free Trade Agreement (NAFTA) commissioned a report that found more than half of firms surveyed used threats to close U.S. operations as a tool to fight union-organizing efforts. Since NAFTA's inception and the subsequent reduction in trade and investment barriers, these threats have become more plausible. As reported by Alan Tonelson, "In fact, more than 10 percent of employers studied . . . 'directly threatened to move to Mexico,' and 15 percent of firms, when forced to bargain with a union, actually closed part or all of a factory—triple the rate found in the late 1980s, before NAFTA."[f]

The concern can run both ways, however. Although labor standards in developing countries are usually lower than in industrialized countries, they are rising—and evidence shows that multinationals investing in host nations pay higher wages, create new jobs at a faster rate, and spend more on R&D than do local firms. Developing countries may also view the imposition of more demanding labor standards within their borders as a barrier to free trade. They may feel that lower-cost labor constitutes their competitive advantage and that if they are forced to implement more stringent labor standards, then companies may no longer have an incentive to set up operations in their countries, damaging their prospects for improved economic development. As

the authors of *Globaphobia* ask, "Is it humane for the United States to refuse to trade with these countries because their labor standards are not as high as we would prefer? The consequence of taking this position is that many third-world workers will have no jobs at all, or must take jobs that pay even lower wages and have even worse working conditions than those currently available in the export-oriented sector."[g] A study by the Carnegie Endowment for International Peace found that Mexico's agricultural sector, which provides most of the country's employment, had lost 1.3 million jobs in the first decade since NAFTA was implemented. In addition, far from diminishing under NAFTA, the flow of impoverished Mexicans into the United States has risen dramatically, the study says.[h]

Globalization Has Contributed to a Decline in Environmental and Health Conditions

Regarding concerns of antiglobalization forces that globalization contributes to declining environmental standards, former president Zedillo of Mexico stated, "Economic integration tends to favor, not worsen the environment. Since trade favors economic growth, it brings about at least part of the necessary means to preserve the environment. The better off people are, the more they demand a clean environment. Furthermore, it is not uncommon that employment opportunities in export activities encourage people to give up highly polluting marginal occupations." Yet a difficulty caused by the North American Free Trade Agreement and the maquiladora program that began before NAFTA has been the substantial increases in ground, water, and air pollution along the Mexico–U.S. border. Damage to the environment has been caused by the many new production facilities and the movement of thousands of Mexicans to that area to work in them. In addition, some health and environmental issues extend beyond the scope of trade agreements. Some of NAFTA's rules on trade in services may cause governments to weaken environmental standards for sometimes hazardous industries like logging, trucking, water supply, and real estate development. For example, to comply with NAFTA's rules on trade in services, the Bush administration waived U.S. clean air standards in order to allow trucks based in Mexico to haul freight on U.S. highways. Globalization opponents argue that this could increase air pollution and associated health concerns in border states, as the aging Mexican truck fleet pollutes more than similar U.S. trucks and these vehicles do not use the cleaner fuels required in the United States. Protesters have also claimed that, under liberalized rules regarding the globalization of trade and investment, businesses have an incentive to move their highly polluting activities to nations that have the least rigorous environmental regulations or a lower risk of liability associated with operations that can create environmental or health-related problems. On the other hand, the economic growth fostered by globalization can help generate and distribute additional resources for protecting the environment, and improved trade and

(continued)

investment can enhance the exchange of more environmentally friendly technologies and best practices, particularly within developing nations.

Questions:

As you read the preceding synopsis of the complex issues and arguments of supporters and opponents of globalization, are you convinced one way or the other? Is there a way the debate can move beyond a simplistic argument for or against globalization and toward how best to strengthen the working of the global economy in order to enhance the welfare of the world and its inhabitants?

[a]"ICC Brief on Globalization," www.iccwbo.org/home/commercial_practice/case_for_the_global_economy/globalization%20brief/globalization_brief.asp (July 5, 2006); Paul Krugman, "The Good News," *The New York Times,* November 28, 2003, p. A31, www.nytimes.com/2003/11/28/opinion/the-good-news.html (May 28, 2011); Horst Kohler and James Wolfensohn, "We Can Trade Up to a Better World," *Financial Times,* December 12, 2003, p. 19, www.imf.org/external/np/vc/2003/121003.htm (May 28, 2011); and Martin Wolf, *Why Globalization Works* (New Haven, CT: Yale University Press, 2004).

[b]World Trade Organization, "The Case for Open Trade," www.wto.org/english/thewto_e/whatis_e/tif_e/fact3_e.htm (May 28, 2011).

[c]Kohler and Wolfensohn, "We Can Trade Up to a Better World."

[d]Gary Burtless, Robert Z. Lawrence, Robert E. Litan, and Robert J. Shapiro, *Globaphobia: Confronting Fears about Open Trade* (Washington, DC: Brookings Institution Press, 1998); Alan Tonelson, *The Race to the Bottom: Why a Worldwide Worker Surplus and Uncontrolled Free Trade Are Sinking American Living Standards* (Boulder, CO: Westview Press, 2002); Daniel Seligman, "On NAFTA's Tenth Anniversary, Americans Demand Safe, Clean and Fair Trade," Sierra Club, San Francisco, www.sierraclub.org/pressroom/releases/pr2003-12-23a.asp (May 2, 2010); John-Thor Dahlburg, "Protesters Tell a Different Tale of Free Trade," *Los Angeles Times,* November 20, 2003, p. A3, www.commondreams.org/headlines03/1120-05.htm (May 28, 2011); *Human Development Report 2003,* United Nations Development Program, New York, http://hdr.undp.org/en/reports/global/hdr2003/ (May 28, 2011); *World Development Indicators 2004,* World Bank, www.worldbank.org/data/countrydata/countrydata.html (May 28, 2011); and John Audley, Sandra Polaski, Demetrios G. Papademetriou, and Scott Vaughan, *NAFTA's Promise and Reality: Lessons from Mexico for the Hemisphere* (Washington, DC: Carnegie Endowment for International Peace, 2003).

[e]Martin Wolf, *Why Globalization Works* (New Haven, CT: Yale University Press, 2004).

[f]Tonelson, *The Race to the Bottom.*

[g]Burtless et al., *Globaphobia.*

[h]John Audley, Sandra Polaski, Demetrios G. Papademetriou, and Scott Vaughan, *NAFTA's Promise and Reality: Lessons from Mexico for the Hemisphere* (Washington, DC: Carnegie Endowment for International Peace, 2003).

the comparatively larger trading groups (European Union, Association of Southeast Asian Nations [ASEAN], Mercosur). It is one thing to be shut out of Belgium, but it is another to be excluded from all Europe.

The result of this rush to globalization has been an explosive growth in international business. Many of the issues associated with globalization are highly complex, and there is no single measure of globalization or of integration within the world economy. Each element of global integration can have different effects. Following are some of the arguments for and against the globalization process and its outcomes.

Motives for Entering Foreign Markets

LO1-7 Explain the reasons for entering foreign markets.

Now let us briefly examine the reasons international firms enter foreign markets, which are all linked to either (1) the desire to increase profits and sales or (2) the desire to protect these profits and sales from being eroded by competitors.

INCREASE PROFITS AND SALES

Enter New Markets   Managers are always under pressure to increase the sales and profits of their firms, and when they face a mature, saturated market at home, they begin to search for new markets outside the home country. They find that (1) markets with a rising gross domestic product (GDP) per capita and population growth appear to be viable candidates for their operations and (2) the economies of some nations where they are not doing business are growing at a considerably faster rate than is the economy of their own market.

New Market Creation   As we will discuss in Chapter 12, there are many ways in which potential new markets can be identified and assessed. Sources of potential market size and overall market growth rate can be found in publications such as the annual *Human*

Development Report of the United Nations Development Program (http://hdr.undp.org/en/). Reviewing data in such reports will reveal great variety in growth rates among countries when ranked by variables such as GDP (gross domestic product) per capita.

Data from sources such as the *Human Development Report* indicate that from a macro perspective, markets around the world are growing. However, this does not mean that equally good opportunities exist for all kinds of business. Perhaps surprisingly, economic growth in a nation causes markets for some products to be lost forever while, simultaneously, markets for other products are being created. Take the case of a country in the initial stage of development. With little local manufacturing, it is a good market for exporters of consumer goods. As economic development continues, however, managers see profit-making opportunities in (1) producing locally the kinds of consumer goods that require simple technology or (2) assembling from imported parts the products that demand a more advanced technology. Given the tendency of governments to protect local industry, the importation of goods being produced in that country will normally be prohibited or discouraged through taxes, tariffs, or other means once local production of those goods has been established. Thus, exporters of easy-to-manufacture consumer goods, such as paint, adhesives, toiletries, clothing, and almost anything made of plastic, will begin to lose this market, which now becomes a new market for producers of the inputs to these "infant industries."

Faster-Growing Markets   Not only are new foreign markets appearing, but many of them are growing at a faster rate than is the home market. A firm looking for a market large enough to support the local production of appliances or machinery, for example, might be attracted by the wealth, growth, and population size of Japan and Spain. When you examine the low GDP per capita and negative growth rates of many of the African nations, you realize why foreign direct investment in that entire continent is so low. Clearly, market analysts will investigate other factors, such as the political and legal situations (discussed in Chapters 6 and 7), but an examination of variables such as those contained in the *Human Development Report* mentioned earlier is a good place to start. Interestingly, 83 of the 182 countries in the 2009 *Human Development Report* for which data were available (46 percent) had average annual GDP per capita growth rates that were higher than the U.S. growth rate for the period 1990–2007.[18]

Improved Communications   This might be considered a supportive reason for opening up new markets overseas, because certainly the ability to communicate rapidly and less expensively with customers and subordinates by electronic mail, wireless and wired telephones, and videoconferencing has given managers confidence in their ability to control foreign operations. Advances in computer-based communications are allowing virtual integration, which permits firms to become more physically fragmented as they search the world for lower-cost inputs. For example, good, relatively inexpensive international communication enables large insurance, banking, software, and other firms to "body shop," that is, transmit computer-oriented tasks worldwide to a cheap but skilled labor force. The clients of numerous Indian software companies are in the United States. A few years ago, software teams were required to fly back and forth between the two countries. Now, at the end of the day, customers in the United States e-mail their problems to India. The Indians then work on the solutions and have them back in the United States before the Americans have had breakfast the next day. For their work, Indian software engineers often receive only 15 to 20 percent as much pay, as do their American counterparts.

Obtain Greater Profits   As you know, greater profits may be obtained by either increasing total revenue or decreasing the cost of goods sold, and often conditions are such that a firm can do both.

Greater Revenue   Rarely will all of a firm's domestic competitors be in every foreign market in which it is located. Where there is less competition, the firm may be able to obtain a better price for its goods or services. Increasingly, firms are also obtaining greater revenue by simultaneously introducing products in foreign markets and in their domestic markets as they move toward greater globalization of their operations. This can result in greater sales volume while lowering the cost of the goods sold.

Lower Cost of Goods Sold

Going abroad, whether by exporting or by producing overseas, can frequently lower the cost of goods sold. Increasing total sales by exporting not only will reduce research and development (R&D) costs per unit, but also will make other economies of scale possible. Another factor that can positively affect the cost of goods sold is the inducements—such as reduced taxes or subsidies for R&D—that some governments offer to attract new investment.

Higher Overseas Profits as an Investment Motive

There is no question that greater profits on overseas investments has been a strong motive for going abroad. *Business International,* for example, reported that 90 percent of 140 *Fortune 500* companies surveyed had achieved higher profitability on foreign than on domestic assets. One study of the 100 largest multinationals showed that only 18 of them earned more than 50 percent of their revenue overseas, but 33 earned more than 50 percent of their profits from foreign operations.

Let's now look at some reasons for going abroad that are more related to the protection of present markets, profits, and sales.

PROTECT MARKETS, PROFITS, AND SALES

Protect Domestic Market by Following Customers Overseas

Frequently, a firm will go abroad to protect its home market. Service companies (e.g., accounting, advertising, marketing research, banking, law) will establish foreign operations in markets where their principal accounts are located to prevent competitors from gaining access to those accounts. They know that once a competitor has been able to demonstrate to top management what it can do by servicing a foreign subsidiary, it may be able to take over the entire account. Similarly, suppliers to original equipment manufacturers (e.g., battery manufacturers supplying automobile producers) often follow their large customers. These suppliers have an added advantage in that they are moving into new markets with a guaranteed customer base.

Attack in Competitor's Home Market

Occasionally, a firm will set up an operation in the home country of a major competitor with the idea of keeping the competitor so occupied defending that market that it will have less energy to compete in the firm's home country.

Using Foreign Production to Lower Costs

A company may go abroad to protect its domestic market when it faces competition from lower-priced foreign imports. By moving part or all of its production facilities to the countries from which its competition is coming, it can enjoy such advantages as less costly labor, raw materials, and energy. Managers may decide to produce certain components abroad and assemble them in the home country, or, if the final product requires considerable labor in the final assembly, it may send the components overseas for this activity. Many nations, especially developing countries, offer export processing zones in which firms, mostly foreign manufacturers, enjoy almost complete absence of taxation and regulation of materials brought into the zones for processing and subsequent re-export.

Protect Foreign Markets

Changing the method of going abroad from exporting to overseas production is often necessary to protect foreign markets. Managers of a firm supplying a profitable overseas market via exports may begin to note some ominous signs that this market is being threatened.

Lack of Foreign Exchange

One of the first signs is a delay in payment by the importers. The importers may have sufficient local currency but may be facing delays in buying foreign exchange (currency) from the government's central bank. The credit manager in the exporting firm, by checking with his or her bank and other exporters, learns that this condition is becoming endemic—a reliable sign that the country is facing a lack of foreign exchange. In examining the country's balance of payments, the financial manager may find that the company's export revenue has declined while the import volume remains high. Experienced exporters know that import and foreign exchange controls are in the offing and that there is a good chance of losing the market, especially if they sell consumer products. In times of foreign exchange scarcity, governments will invariably give priority to the importation of raw materials and capital goods.

If the advantages of making the investment outweigh the disadvantages, the company may decide to protect this market by producing locally. Managers know that once the company has a plant in the country, the government will do its utmost to provide foreign exchange for raw materials to keep the plant, a source of employment, in operation. Because imports of competing products are prohibited, the only competition, if any, will have to come from other local manufacturers.

Local Production by Competitors

Lack of foreign exchange is not the only reason a company might change from exporting to manufacturing in a market. For instance, while a firm may enjoy a growing export business and prompt payments, it still may be forced to set up a plant in the market if competitors have also noticed their export volumes will support local production. If a competing firm moves to put up a factory in the market, management must decide rapidly whether to follow suit or risk losing the market forever. Managers know that many governments, especially those in developing nations, not only will prohibit further imports once the product is produced in the country but also will permit only two or three companies to enter so as to maintain a sufficient market for these local firms.

Downstream Markets

A number of Organization of Petroleum Exporting Countries (OPEC) nations have invested in refining and marketing outlets, such as filling stations and heating-oil distributors, to guarantee a market for their crude oil at more favorable prices. Petróleos de Venezuela, owner of CITGO, is one of the largest foreign investors in the United States.

Protectionism

When a government sees that local industry is threatened by imports, it may erect import barriers to stop or reduce these imports. Even threats to do this can be sufficient to induce the exporter to invest in production facilities in the importing country.

Guarantee Supply of Raw Materials

Few developed nations possess sufficient domestic supplies of raw materials. Japan and Europe are almost totally dependent on foreign sources for many important materials, and even the United States depends on imports for more than half of its consumption of aluminum, chromium, manganese, nickel, tin, and zinc. To ensure a continuous supply, manufacturers in the industrialized countries are being forced to invest, primarily in the developing nations where most new deposits are being discovered.

Acquire Technology and Management Know-How

A reason often cited by foreign firms for investing in the United States is the acquisition of technology and management know-how. Nippon Mining, for example, a Japanese copper mining company, came to Illinois and paid $1 billion for Gould, Inc. to acquire technology leadership and market share in producing the copper foil used in printed circuit boards for electronics products.

Geographic Diversification

Many companies have chosen geographic diversification as a means of maintaining stable sales and earnings when the domestic economy or their industry goes into a slump, since the industry or the other economies may still be at their peak in other parts of the world.

Satisfy Management's Desire for Expansion

The faster growth mentioned previously helps fulfill management's desire for expansion. Stockholders and financial analysts also expect firms to continue to grow, and those companies operating only in the domestic market have found it increasingly difficult to meet that expectation. As a result, many firms have expanded into foreign markets. This, of course, is what companies based in small countries, such as Nestlé (Switzerland) and Nokia (Finland), discovered decades ago.

The Seven Dimensions for Globalizing a Business

LO1-8 Recognize that globalization of an international firm occurs over at least seven dimensions and that a company can be partially global in some dimensions and completely global in others.

In organizing their international activities, there are at least seven dimensions along which management can globalize (standardize): (1) product, (2) markets, (3) promotion, (4) where value is added to the product, (5) competitive strategy, (6) use of non-home-country personnel, and (7) extent of global ownership in the firm. The possibilities range from zero standardization (multidomestic) to standardization along all seven dimensions (completely global). The challenge for company managers is to determine how far the firm should go with each one. Usually the amount of globalization will vary among the dimensions. For example, promotional activities for washing machines might be standardized to a great extent: people use them to get their clothes clean. However, for economic reasons, in poorer countries the machines must be simpler and less costly and, therefore, the product is not standardized worldwide. We return to this topic in various parts of the text, particularly in Chapter 15.

Organization of This Book

After describing the nature of international business and the institutions associated with it in Section One, we analyze several of the key uncontrollable forces that make up the foreign and domestic environments and illustrate their effect on management functions in Section Two. In Section Three, we reverse the procedure and deal with the management functions, demonstrating how they are influenced by the uncontrollable forces.

A solid understanding of the business concepts and techniques employed in the United States and other advanced industrial nations is a requisite for success in international

THE GLOBAL PATH AHEAD

Ryan Hultzman in Dalin, China: The Key Is to Get Beyond Your Comfort Zone

I was born and raised in San Jose, California. Sports have always played a big role in my life and I can't really think of a time growing up when I wasn't involved with either a baseball, swimming, or basketball team. Ever since I graduated from high school, most of my involvement in sports has been watching my favorite teams on TV, and I am hoping to find a job in San Jose upon graduation so I can get season tickets for the Sharks. I am hoping that I will get to travel a lot more after I graduate. Other than my time in China, I have only spent a week in Mexico on a cruise and five days visiting a friend in Germany. I would love to visit every continent by the time I am 30, so I hope to land a career that will allow me to do so.

I am a business major with a concentration in international management and a minor in psychology. At this point, my major career goal is to spend an extended period of time (over a year) working in another country. I know that this probably won't happen right away, but it is something that I will surely work toward. I have always been interested in traveling and learning about different cultures, and international business seemed like a great starting point to able to eventually work with people from different parts of the world.

I worked in Dalian, China for five months during the summer and fall of my senior year. I worked with AIESEC (an acronym for the Association Internationale des Étudiants en Sciences Économiques et Commerciales and the world's largest student-led organization) to get an international internship, because I

couldn't afford to study abroad. I chose to go to China because I wanted to challenge myself. The culture is extremely different

(continued)

from what I grew up with in the United States, and I wanted to live somewhere that would seriously challenge how I viewed the world. China has also been developing very rapidly, so I thought it would be interesting to experience that kind of growth first-hand.

In China, I worked as an English teacher. I mostly taught children 2 to 10 years old, but I also taught one adult class for a month. I had only been accepted for this opportunity about a month before I was supposed to start, so my preparation was fairly rushed. I had no background in Mandarin, so I did what I could to learn some basic phrases before I left. I asked around and found a couple of people who had previously spent time working in China and I asked them about their experiences and if they had any advice for me. I did a lot of research on the city I was going to be living in and tried to learn all I could about everyday life in China. Since I found this opportunity through AIESEC, my living arrangements and transportation from the airport were already established before I left, which was a huge benefit.

The most important thing I did to help myself adjust to the Chinese culture when I was abroad was make a few friends that I could really trust. I ended up living in a couple of different places with some great American and Canadian friends that I made, but it was invaluable having a couple of Chinese friends who I could rely on to help me out when I needed it. If I ever needed any help—anything from finding transportation to learning how to ask for a haircut—my friends were willing to provide their assistance.

I didn't really run into any reverse culture shock upon my return to the United States. I think a large part of that was due to the fact that I only spent five months in the country. My experience abroad definitely changed the way I view certain parts of my life, but I didn't have any trouble assimilating back into the U.S. culture.

I had to leave my first job in China after two months due to a contractual problem, so one of my biggest challenges was finding another place to work so I wouldn't have to cut my time abroad short. Chinese culture is strongly based on relationships, or *guanxi*, so I knew that my best shot for finding another job was to ask everyone I knew if they were aware of any jobs that were available for me. After a month of searching, I was offered a job at a kindergarten because my friend's boss knew the owner of the school and they were in need of a foreign English teacher.

Another big challenge for me was getting around in China without really knowing the language. Hand gestures can get you pretty far in most cases, but other things like being able to order food in a restaurant with menus that are written only in Chinese characters take some time. I had a Chinese tutor for the first two months, but once I left my first job I couldn't afford it any more, so I had to become very proactive in learning the necessities. I asked my bilingual friends a lot of questions and made flash cards so I could successfully navigate around the city on my own.

My greatest enjoyment from my time abroad was probably when one of my youngest classes started calling me "gēge lǎoshī" (in Mandarin, lǎoshī means teacher and gēge means older brother). Initially, the students referred to me as the "foreign teacher," but once they started calling me brother, I couldn't help but feel like my assimilation was complete.

I think my greatest learning points from my international experience have to be the things that I learned about myself. I felt like I grew more as a person in the five months I spent in China than any other time in my life. I have always seen myself as a very independent person, but my time abroad allowed me to prove it. I learned how to put my views and beliefs on hold in order to truly understand where people from different backgrounds are coming from.

As far as recommendations for success abroad, the most important thing is to keep an open mind. People view and value things very differently around the world and unless you can understand and appreciate their perspective, you won't be successful working with people from other cultures. Also, don't be afraid to step out of your comfort zone when you're abroad. Most of the best stories that I have from my time in China have to do with situations that I wouldn't normally put myself in back home and that is what made my time abroad so great.

Resources for Your Global Career

Exploring International Job Opportunities

More than likely, your first job in international business will *not* come with a business class airline ticket to Shanghai, Paris, or Rio de Janeiro and a "sky's the limit" expense account. More realistically, it will come with a desk, computer, fax machine, e-mail, and smartphone (e.g., BlackBerry, iPhone). Many entry-level jobs in international business involve managing import/export documentation to move shipments across international borders; tracking shipments by boat, plane, train, and truck; and following sales to make sure orders and payments are received—as well as dealing with foreign customers by phone, fax, and e-mail. Is this the glamour of international business? Probably not. But it is business, and it is international, and it does put your career track in the international arena, which is where you need to be to start your international business career. However, entry-level jobs in some small and medium-sized enterprises will involve short international visits to client meetings, conferences, trade shows, or corporate meetings in international locations. In addition to your willingness to take that all important entry-level international job and work to be successful at it, here are several other suggestions to build your international career:

- Inform your boss and your company's human resources department about your interest in a career in international business.

- Join several international business trade associations in your city and regularly attend their meetings:

  - *International Chamber of Commerce*—www.iccwbo.org/

  - *International Association of Business Communicators* (IABC)—www.iabc.com/

  - *International Trade Administration of the U.S. Department of Commerce* seminars and workshops—http://trade.gov/

  - *Federation of International Trade Associations* (FITA) offers a directory of international trade associations by specialty with locations—www.fita.org

(continued)

- Your state's Department of Commerce or Economic Development may offer workshops and seminars on international trade.

By attending these meetings, you will network and get to know their members so they get to know you and learn about your interest in a career in international business.

- Read international business publications and listen to international news and business broadcasts so you are current with issues, trends, and practices in international trade. Here are several:
  - *World Trade* (this is free)—www.worldtrademag.com/
  - *International Herald Tribune*—www.iht.com/
  - *Financial Times*—www.ft.com
  - *The Economist*—www.economist.com
  - *Reuters*—www.reuters.com
  - *BBC*—www.bbc.co.uk
  - Find a mentor to teach, guide, and assist you in building your international business career.
  - Be ready to travel internationally at a moment's notice—hold a valid passport.

If you are considering an international career but not sure where to look to find one, there are numerous websites with Internet listings for private industry and government jobs. The website for this book includes a broad range of sites, such as the following:

- The *Riley Guide* has hundreds of worldwide listings for companies and governments. The Targeting and Research section has information on Business and Employer Research and Living and Working Overseas: www.rileyguide.com

- *GoingGlobal.com* offers a wide range of information on international careers, international job search resources, job opportunities worldwide, and information to help build your international career: www.goinglobal.com/HotTopics.asp

- *Expertise in Labour Mobility* (ELM) is a knowledge provider on international work issues for companies and individuals entering the global workplace. ELM's "Looking for work in . . ." guides cover 40 countries and are "must have" tools for everybody involved in securing a job abroad: www.labourmobility.com

- *Escape Artist* provides a broad range of international job postings as well as related reference materials: www.escapeartist.com/jobs/overseas1.htm

- *International Jobs Center* provides extensive international business and international development job postings: www.internationaljobs.org/

- *Jobs Abroad* supplies listings for jobs in many nations of the world, along with other resources: www.jobsabroad.com/

- *International Careers and Jobs by Profession* provides resources for work abroad, study abroad, volunteering abroad, and international travel: www.transitionsabroad.com/listings/work/careers/keywebsitesprofessionspecific.shtml

- *Partnerjob.com* facilitates the geographic mobility of members' employees by helping find jobs for those employees' spouses and partners at their new location: www.partnerjob.com/

Alternatives for Working Globally—Consider International Jobs and Careers Other Than in Business

The first thought that typically comes to mind when you hear "International Careers" is a job in the corporate world working for a *Fortune 500* firm that services international markets and has a global reputation. This is not the only track into an international career. There are many outstanding international career opportunities for people with desirable interpersonal and language skills that are not in mainstream business but may require basic business expertise. Explore these options to become a part of the global workforce:

- Travel, Tourism and Hospitality—a major international industry found in virtually every country of the world.

- Engineering, Information Technology and Computer Science—experiencing major worldwide growth

- Health Professions and Health Care Management

- Translation and Language Teaching Abroad

- The Fine and Performing Arts

- Architecture

- Environmental and Natural Resource Management

- International Chambers of Commerce

- Foreign Trade Divisions of State Offices of Economic Development

- The U.S. Government

- U.S. Counselor Service

- Foreign Service—U.S. State Department

- The Central Intelligence Agency and the National Security Agency

- The Agency for International Development (AID)

- The Export-Import Bank

- The International Trade Commission

- U.S. Information Agency

- The Peace Corps

- International Education Exchange—teach abroad

- Volunteer and Social Service Agencies

The skills and experiences offered by any of these career options are highly sought after and readily transferable between the public and the private sector.

Look for International Internship Opportunities While You Are Still in School

- *Internships Abroad* is an internship program offered through Ohio University for internships in the United Nations, in the

(continued)

business. However, because transactions take place across national borders, three environments—domestic, foreign, and international—may be involved, instead of just one. Thus, in international business, the international manager has three choices in deciding what to do with a concept or a technique employed in domestic operations: (1) transfer it intact, (2) adapt it to local conditions, or (3) not use it overseas. International managers who have discovered that there are differences in the environmental forces are better prepared to decide which option to follow. To be sure, no one can be an expert on all these forces for all nations, but just knowing that differences may exist will cause people to "work with their antennas extended." In other words, when they enter international business, they will know they must look out for important variations in many of the forces that they take as given in the domestic environment. It is to the study of these three environments that this text is directed.

Summary

LO1-1 Understand what international business is and why it is important.

International business is business whose activities are carried out across national borders. International business is important because of the increasing scale and scope of activities that occur across national borders

LO1-2 Comprehend why and how international business differs from domestic business.

International business differs from its domestic counterpart in that it involves three environments—domestic, foreign, and international—instead of one. Although the kinds of forces are the same in the domestic and foreign environments, their values often differ, and changes in the values of foreign forces are at times more difficult to assess. The international environment is defined as the interactions (1) between the domestic environmental forces and the foreign environmental forces and (2) between the foreign environmental forces of two countries when an affiliate in one country does business with customers in another

LO1-3 Appreciate that international business has a long and important history in the world's development.

International business has a long and important history, extending thousands of years into the past. Politics, the arts,

agriculture, industry, public health, and other sectors of human life have been profoundly influenced by the goods and ideas that have come with international trade.

LO1-4 Appreciate the dramatic internationalization of markets.

Global competition is mounting as the number of international companies expands rapidly. The huge increase in import penetration, plus the massive amounts of overseas investment, means that firms of all sizes face competitors from everywhere in the world. This increasing internationalization of business is requiring managers to have a global business perspective gained through experience, education, or both

LO1-5 Understand the five kinds of drivers, all based on change, that are leading firms to internationalize their operations.

The five major kinds of drivers, all based on change, that are leading international firms to globalize their operations are as follows, with an example for each kind: (1) *political*—preferential trading agreements, (2) *technological*—advances in communications technology, (3) *market*—global firms become global customers, (4) *cost*—globalization of product lines and production helps reduce costs by achieving economies of scale, and (5) *competitive*—firms are defending their home markets from foreign competitors by entering the foreign competitors' markets.

LO1-6 Recognize the key arguments for and against the globalization of business.

Key arguments in support of the globalization include: (1) free trade enhances socioeconomic development, and (2) free trade promotes more and better jobs. Key concerns with the globalization of business include: (1) globalization has produced uneven results across nations and people, (2) globalization has had deleterious effects on labor and labor standards, and (3) globalization has contributed to a decline in environmental and health conditions.

LO1-7 Explain the reasons for entering foreign markets.

Companies enter foreign markets (exporting to and manufacturing in) to increase sales and profits and to protect markets, sales, and profits from being eroded by competitors.

LO1-8 Recognize that globalization of an international firm occurs over at least seven dimensions and that a company can be partially global in some dimensions and completely global in others.

The seven dimensions along which management can globalize (standardize) when organizing their international activities are: (1) product, (2) markets, (3) promotion, (4) where value is added to the product, (5) competitive strategy, (6) use of non-home-country personnel, and (7) extent of global ownership in the firm. The possibilities range from zero standardization (multidomestic) to standardization along all seven dimensions (completely global). A firm can have, and usually does have, an international strategy that is partially multidomestic in some dimensions and partially global in others.

Key Words

international business (p. 8)

foreign business (p. 8)

multidomestic company (MDC) (p. 9)

global company (GC) (p. 9)

international company (p. 10)

environment (p. 10)

uncontrollable forces (p. 10)

controllable forces (p. 10)

domestic environment (p. 11)

foreign environment (p. 11)

international environment (p. 12)

self-reference criterion (p. 12)

foreign direct investment (FDI) (p. 14)

exporting (p. 15)

importing (p. 15)

economic globalization (p. 15)

Questions

1. What are the differences among multidomestic, global, and international companies?

2. Business is business, and every firm has to find ways to produce and market its goods. Why, then, might managers be unable to successfully apply the techniques and concepts they have learned in their own country to other areas of the world?

3. Give examples to show how an international business manager might manipulate one of the controllable forces in answer to a change in the uncontrollable forces.

4. Although forces in the foreign environment are the same as those in the domestic environment, they operate differently. Why is this so?

5. What is the difference between the foreign environment and the international environment?

6. Why, in your opinion, do the authors regard the use of the self-reference criterion as "probably the biggest cause of international business blunders?" Can you think of an example?

7. Discuss some possible conflicts between host governments and foreign-owned companies.

8. "A nation whose GNI is smaller than the sales volume of a global firm is in no position to enforce its wishes on the local subsidiary of that firm." Is this statement true or false? Please explain your rationale.

9. Discuss the forces that are leading international firms to the globalization of their sourcing, production, and marketing.

10. What examples of globalization can you identify within your community? How would you classify each of these examples (e.g., international investment, international trade)?

11. Why is there opposition to globalization of trade and integration of the world's economy? Please assess the major arguments for and against such globalization efforts.

12. What are the reasons that explain why international firms would enter foreign markets?

13. You have decided to take a job in your hometown after graduation. Why should you study international business?

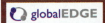
Use the globalEDGE site (http://globalEDGE.msu.edu/) to complete the following exercises:

1. The Emerging Market Global Players (EMGP) Project produces annual reports ranking the top *multinational enterprises* (MNEs) in emerging markets by their foreign assets. Locate the most recent annual report of Hungary, and identify the 10 largest nonfinancial Hungarian MNEs. In what industries are they classified? In how many countries do they have operations? In which regions of the world? Do you notice any similarities or differences in terms of the industries represented in the ranking and the regions where these MNEs operate? Prepare a short report summarizing your findings.

2. The *KOF Index of Globalization,* provided by the KOF Swiss Economic Institute, measures globalization on economic, social, and political dimensions. Provide a brief description of this index and its ranking. Specifically, what factors are considered in calculating the index? Find the most recent ranking, and identify the 10 countries with the lowest and highest Globalization Index. Do you notice any trends or similarities among the countries listed?

Minicase: Ownership of Companies and Brands

Which of the following companies or brands are owned by companies headquartered outside of the United States? Who are the owners and which country(ies) are the owners based in?

1. 7-Eleven Stores
2. Chesebrough-Pond (Vaseline)
3. Maybelline cosmetics
4. Diesel clothing
5. Aquafresh toothpaste
6. Baby Ruth candy bar
7. Holiday Inn
8. Arrowhead water
9. Columbia Pictures motion picture studios
10. Arco (gasoline)
11. Nerds candy
12. Popsicle frozen treats
13. Random House book publisher
14. Ralston Purina pet foods
15. Motel 6
16. Pinkerton National Detective Agency (Pinkertons)
17. Ban deodorant
18. RCA Records
19. Thinkpad laptop computers
20. Norelco electric shavers

International Trade and Foreign Direct Investment

If you care about global poverty and, for that matter, about equality, your aim should be to raise the growth rates of poor countries. Successful countries have all exploited global market opportunities, predominantly international trade and, to a more variable extent, foreign direct investment, to accelerate their growth. Successful globalization has, in short, reduced both poverty and inequality.

—*Martin Wolf, global business analyst*

Firms Invest Overseas, But They Also Export

The need for responding to such factors as (1) global competition, (2) liberalization by host governments in regard to foreign investment, and (3) advances in technology, were a major reason that American outward foreign direct investment (FDI) reached a record $1.20 trillion from 2006–2009. These figures represent more than 1.3 times the U.S. average a decade before (1996–1999). Inasmuch as foreign direct investment generally is used to set up or acquire assets to produce goods and services abroad, we might expect U.S. exports to have dropped as a result of the more than $2 trillion in U.S. FDI in the period 2000–2009. Have they?

Apparently not. Although some flows of exported goods and services from the United States to foreign markets have been replaced by production from these investments abroad, the overall level of American exports of goods and services increased from $1.1 trillion in 2000 to $1.8 trillion in 2010, an increase of 64 percent in a decade. The U.S. Department of Commerce states that approximately two-thirds of U.S. exports of goods are by U.S.-owned multinational corporations, with more than one-third of those exports being shipped by the U.S. parent to foreign affiliates.

To examine how important international business activities are for large American multinationals, we examined firms at the top of the *Fortune* Global 500 list of the largest multinationals. Among the companies examined, the ratio of foreign sales to total sales averaged nearly 60 percent. Many of these companies sell to 100 countries or more. Without sales and profits generated from foreign operations, the competitiveness of many of these companies would be seriously damaged, and some of them might be unable to remain in business. Yet, despite the fact that large international companies such as these typically have numerous production facilities overseas, it is usually not feasible for them to have a factory in every market. The foreign investment would be too great for them to attempt to set up production facilities in each market. Also, many markets are too small to support local manufacturing; they must be served by exports.

Although supplying overseas markets is essential to most major U.S. corporations, smaller firms also have activities overseas. According to the Exporter Data Base (a joint project of the International Trade Administration and the Census Bureau), small and medium-sized enterprises (SMEs) accounted for nearly 98 percent of all

2

U.S. exporters and nearly one-third of the total value of American exports. Categorizing SMEs as companies with fewer than 500 employees, an analysis of the Exporter Data Base reveals the following:

- The total number of American companies exporting goods in 2009 was 275,843. Of these exporters, 269,269 were SMEs. These numbers exclude companies that exported only services.

- SMEs accounted for 32.8 percent of the total value of U.S. exports.

- The total export revenues of SMEs was $308 billion in 2009. Canada was the most frequent export market, with 92,573 SMEs exporting to that country. Mexico was the second most popular, with 46,748 SME exporters, followed by the United Kingdom, Germany, China, Australia, and Japan.

- Overall, NAFTA countries represented more than 25 percent of U.S. merchandise exports by SMEs, valued at $90.5 billion. Canada purchased $49.6 billion in SME merchandise exports, followed by Mexico ($40.9 billion),

China ($23.5 billion), Japan ($19.6 billion), the United Kingdom ($17.1 billion), and Germany ($12.9 billion).

- In comparison to large companies, SMEs are highly dependent on initiatives undertaken by the U.S. government to open foreign markets to trade. Unlike large exporting companies, most SMEs lack offshore subsidiaries that can circumvent trade barriers and improve market access. More than half of all SME exporters operate from a single location in the United States.

Sources: United Nations Conference on Trade and Development, *World Investment Report,* "Annex Table 2: FDI Outflows, By Region and Economy, 1990–2009," www.unctad.org/templates/Page.asp?intItemID=5545&lang=1 (May 10, 2011); U.S. Census Bureau, "U.S. International Trade in Goods and Services," www.census.gov/foreign-trade/statistics/historical/ (May 10, 2011); U.S. Department of Commerce, Exporter Database, http://ita.doc.gov/td/industry/otea/edb/index.html (May 14, 2011); U.S. Census Bureau, "Profile of U.S. Exporting Companies, 2008–2009," April 12, 2011, www.census.gov/foreign-trade/Press-Release/edb/2009/ (May 10, 2011); and U.S. Department of Commerce, International Trade Administration, *Small and Medium Sized Exporting Companies: Statistical Overview, 2009,* www.trade.gov/mas/ian/smeoutlook/tg_ian_001925.asp (May 10, 2011).

International trade and investment have become fundamental to most people's lives. For example, much of the food we eat, the clothes we wear, the vehicles we drive, and the electronic goods that we use for work and pleasure are produced in other nations. Many of our jobs are dependent on exports, imports, or foreign investment. In this chapter, we examine (1) *international trade,* which includes exports and imports, and (2) *foreign direct investment*, which international companies must make to establish and expand their overseas operations. We will briefly examine key trends and traits of international trade and investment across the globe, and we will also present an overview of some of the most prominent theories that have been developed to explain the incidence and level of international trade and investment.

The following discussion of international trade first examines the volume of trade, including which nations account for the largest volume of the world's exports and imports. We then discuss the direction of trade and the trend toward increased regionalization of international trade. We examine the issue of major trading partners and their relevance for managers, and then we finish this section of the chapter by discussing several leading theories that help to explain international trade. The final section of the chapter will address foreign direct investment.

LO2-1 Appreciate the magnitude of international trade and how it has grown.

International Trade

VOLUME OF INTERNATIONAL TRADE

In 1990, a milestone was reached when the volume of international trade in goods and services measured in current dollars surpassed $4 trillion. By 2010, exports of goods and services had nearly quintupled, exceeding $18.9 trillion.[1] The dollar value of total world exports is greater than the gross national product of every nation in the world except the United States. One-fourth of everything grown or made in the world is now exported—another measure of the significance of international trade. Figure 2.1 illustrates the combined level of goods and services exports and imports as a percentage of gross domestic

FIGURE 2.1

Merchandise and
Services Trade as
a Percentage of
Gross Domestic
Product

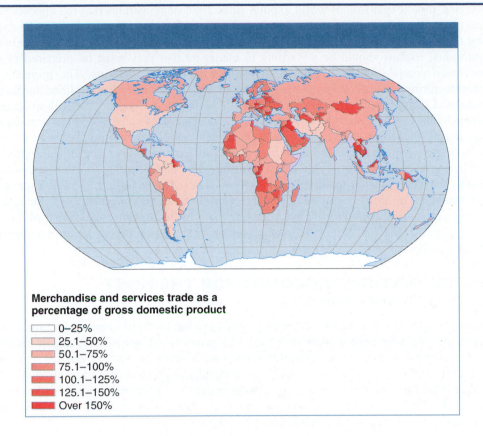

**Merchandise and services trade as a
percentage of gross domestic product**

☐ 0–25%
☐ 25.1–50%
☐ 50.1–75%
☐ 75.1–100%
☐ 100.1–125%
☐ 125.1–150%
☐ Over 150%

product for various nations. As can be seen, international trade has become a critical factor in the economic activity of many, if not most, of the countries of the world.

Of the $18.9 trillion in international trade in goods and services in 2010, exports of merchandise were $15.2 trillion, nearly five times what they had been 20 years earlier. While smaller in absolute terms, worldwide trade in services, at $3.7 trillion, has been growing faster than has trade in merchandise. The volume of world trade in services had reached a level that was more than 10 times what it had been in 1980.[2]

HOW EVEN HAS THE GROWTH IN TRADE BEEN?

As trade has grown globally, how even has this growth been? Have some nations fared better than others? Although the absolute value of their merchandise exports increased, the proportion of exports coming from the regions of North America, Latin America, Africa, and the Middle East decreased between 1980 and 2010. For example, the level of exports from Africa grew by more than 250 percent from 1980 to 2010, yet the region's proportion of overall world merchandise exports declined by half. In contrast, the proportion of merchandise exports from Asia increased by more than 90 percent between 1980 and 2010, with China accounting for nearly two-thirds of that increase. Although the European Union increased its proportion of world trade, the increase is attributable to the expansion of the EU to 27 member-countries.

The results for services exports share some similarity with merchandise exports. The extensive growth in the level of overall worldwide trade in services means that all of the regions and essentially all of the primary nations have experienced an absolute increase in the dollar volume of services exports. The proportion of world exports of commercial services accounted for by Latin America, the European Union, Africa, and the Middle East has evidenced an overall decline since 1980. However, the United States's proportion of services exports has risen by approximately one-third from 1980 to 2010. Asia has also been increasing its proportion of services exports at an even greater rate.

The rapid expansion of world exports since 1980 demonstrates that the opportunity to increase sales by exporting is a viable growth strategy and one that can benefit the exporting nations through the creation of jobs. At the same time, however, the export growth of individual nations should be a warning to managers that they must be prepared to meet increased competition from exports to their own domestic markets. The proportion of manufacturing value added that is located in developed countries has declined across most industrial sectors between 1995 and 2010, with the largest portion of that decline occurring since 2000.[3] Correspondingly, developing countries' share of value added has been increasing during this time, although the location of value-adding activities has been changing substantially. For example, while Africa and Latin America have not added appreciably to their proportion of worldwide manufacturing value added, the proportion generated by South and East Asia has quadrupled since 1980. These trends have important implications for managers in terms of not merely where there may be new markets (e.g., for machine tools or other capital goods used by expanding manufacturing sectors), but also where competition in manufacturing may be intensifying or where new sources of export competition might emerge.

WHICH NATIONS ACCOUNT FOR THE MOST EXPORTS AND IMPORTS?

Which nations are responsible for the large and growing levels of merchandise and services trade that we have seen worldwide? Table 2.1 presents the world's 10 largest nations in terms of exports and imports of merchandise and of services. As you can see, the largest exporters and importers of merchandise are generally developed countries, although China ranks in the top 5 on each list and India ranks in the top 10 for both imports and exports of services. These 10 largest exporters and importers collectively account for over half of all exports and imports for both merchandise and services.

| **TABLE 2.1** | **10 Leading Exporters and Importers in World Merchandise and Commercial Services, 2010 ($ billions)** |

Merchandise Exporters			Merchandise Importers			Service Exporters			Service Importers		
Rank	Nation	Value	Rank	Nation	Value	Rank	Nation	Value	Rank	Nation	Value
1	China	$1,578	1	United States	$1,968	1	United States	$515	1	United States	$358
2	United States	1,278	2	China	1,395	2	Germany	230	2	Germany	256
3	Germany	1,269	3	Germany	1,067	3	United Kingdom	227	3	China	192
4	Japan	770	4	Japan	693	4	China	170	4	United Kingdom	156
5	Netherlands	572	5	France	606	5	France	140	5	Japan	155
6	France	521	6	United Kingdom	558	6	Japan	138	6	France	126
7	South Korea	466	7	Netherlands	517	7	Spain	121	7	India	117
8	Italy	448	8	Italy	484	8	Singapore	112	8	Netherlands	109
9	Belgium	411	9	Hong Kong	442	9	Netherlands	111	9	Italy	108
10	United Kingdom	405	10	South Korea	425	10	India	110	10	Ireland	106

Sources: Central Intelligence Agency, *The World Factbook* (Washington, DC: CIA, 2011), www.cia.gov/library/publications/the-world-factbook/geos/xx.html (May 10, 2011); and World Trade Organization, "Trade Growth to Ease in 2011 but Despite 2010 Record Surge, Crisis Hangover Persists,"www.wto.org/english/news_e/pres11_e/pr628_e.htm#atable3 (May 10, 2011).

Direction of Trade

LO2-2 **Identify** the direction of trade, or who trades with whom, and trends in such trade.

What are the destinations of these merchandise exports? If you have never examined trade flows, you may think that international trade consists mainly of manufactured goods exported by the industrialized nations to the developing nations in return for raw materials. However, this is only partially correct. While more than half the exports from developing nations do go to developed countries, this proportion has been declining over the past 40 years, from 72 percent in 1970 to about 50 percent by 2010.[4] Also, approximately 70 percent of exports from developed economies go to other industrialized nations, not to developing countries.

The Increasing Regionalization of Trade   Although the direction of trade frequently changes over time among nations or regions of the world, the overall level of world trade continues to be dominated by trade that occurs with—not between—nations. For example, in 2009, 48 percent of the exports from North American nations went to other nations in North America, 52 percent of Asian nations' exports were to other Asian nations, and 72 percent of exports from European nations went to other European countries.[5] This regionalization of trade is reinforced by the development of expanded regional trade agreements (discussed in Chapter 3), such as the Association of Southeast Asian Nations (ASEAN), Mercosur in South America, and the European Union, which can can substantially alter the level and proportion of trade flows within and across regions. For example, most of Canada's exports go to the United States and more than 20 percent of American exports go to Canada, mainly as a result of the North American Free Trade Agreement and prior bilateral free trade treaties between these two nations.[6] The $163 billion value of U.S. exports to Mexico in 2010 was approximately five times the level in 1991.[7] Similarly, the proportion of overall exports accounted for by members of the regional trade agreement totaled 67 percent for the European Union, 25 percent for ASEAN, and 15 percent for Mercosur. Overall, there are more than 200 regional trade agreements in operation worldwide, and the share of world trade accounted for by members of these agreements increased from 37 percent in 1980 to more than 70 percent by 2011.

It appears that American exporters have made major inroads in developing country markets, which in turn are selling more to the United States. This is due in part to their increasing ability to export manufactured goods and the growing intracompany trade among international companies' affiliates. The fact that members of trade groups are increasingly selling more to each other is a development that will influence international companies' choices of locations for their plants and other operations.

Major Trading Partners: Their Relevance for Managers

An analysis of the major trading partners of a firm's home country and those of the nations where it has affiliates that export can provide valuable insights to management. Among the advantages to focusing attention on a nation that is already a sizable purchaser of goods coming from the would-be exporter's country are:

1. The business climate in the importing nation is relatively favorable.

2. Export and import regulations are not insurmountable.

3. There should be no strong cultural objections to buying that nation's goods.

4. Satisfactory transportation facilities have already been established.

5. Import channel members (merchants, banks, and customs brokers) are experienced in handling import shipments from the exporter's area.

6. Foreign exchange to pay for the exports is available.

7. The government of a trading partner may be applying pressure on importers to buy from countries that are good customers for that nation's exports. We have seen the efforts of the Japanese, Korean, and Taiwanese governments to persuade their citizens to buy more American goods. They have also sent buying missions to the United States.

MAJOR TRADING PARTNERS OF THE UNITED STATES

Table 2.2 shows the major trading partners of the United States. The top 15 trade partners accounted for 73 percent of the total exports from the United States and 75 percent of the total imports in 2010. The data indicate that the United States, an industrialized nation, generally follows the tendency we found earlier; that is, developed nations trade with one another. Mexico and Canada are major trading partners in great part because they share a common border with the United States. Freight charges are lower, delivery times are shorter, and contacts between buyers and sellers are easier and less expensive. Being joined with the United States in the North American Free Trade Agreement helps ensure that the three nations' mutual importance as trading partners will remain strong.

Of the top 15 nations that the United States imports from, 9 of these nations have remained on the list over the past 45 years, including Canada, Mexico, Japan, Germany, the United Kingdom, Italy, France, Venezuela, and Brazil. However, each nation's ranking has changed over time, and some new nations have been added to replace other nations that have become relatively less important as trade partners. Nations from Asia, besides long-term trade partner Japan, have become increasingly important trade partners in recent years. China, Singapore, South Korea, Taiwan, and India are supplying the United States with huge quantities of electronic products and components as well as a variety of largely labor-intensive manufactured goods, many of which are produced by affiliates of American international companies. Between 1991 and 2010, China rose from sixth to first place in exports to the United States and it also moved up to third place as an importer of U.S. goods (although the $92 billion level of Chinese imports was only 25 percent of the level of exports it sent to the United States).

Many of the same Asian countries appear as importers of American goods as well because (1) their rising standards of living enable their people to afford more imported products, and the countries' export earnings provide the foreign exchange to pay for them; (2) they are purchasing large amounts of capital goods to further their industrial expansion; (3) they are importing

TABLE 2.2	Major Trading Partners of the United States, Goods Only, 2010 ($ billions)					
	Exports			**Imports**		
Rank	**Country**	**Value**		**Rank**	**Country**	**Value**
1	Canada	$249		1	China	$365
2	Mexico	163		2	Canada	277
3	China	92		3	Mexico	230
4	Japan	61		4	Japan	120
5	United Kingdom	49		5	Germany	83
6	Germany	48		6	United Kingdom	50
7	South Korea	39		7	South Korea	49
8	Brazil	35		8	France	39
9	Netherlands	35		9	Taiwan	36
10	Singapore	29		10	Ireland	34
11	France	27		11	Venezuela	33
12	Hong Kong	27		12	Saudi Arabia	31
13	Taiwan	26		13	Nigeria	31
14	Belgium	26		14	India	30
15	Australia	22		15	Italy	29
Total		$1,278				$1,912

Source: U.S. Census Bureau, "Top Trading Partners," www.census.gov/foreign-trade/statistics/highlights/top/top1012yr.html (May 10, 2011).

raw materials and components that will be assembled into subassemblies or finished goods that will subsequently be exported, often to the United States; and (4) their governments, pressured by the American government to lower their trade surpluses with the United States, have sent buying missions to this country to look for products to import.

The analysis of foreign trade that we have described would be helpful to anyone just starting to search outside the home market for new business opportunities. The preliminary steps of (1) studying the general growth and direction of trade and (2) analyzing major trading partners would provide an idea of where the trading activity is. What kinds of products do these countries import from the United States? The U.S. Census Bureau maintains a site on the Internet with downloadable files of trade statistics. One entry, "About Foreign Trade" (www.census.gov/foreign-trade/about/index.html), contains extensive links to statistics on exports and imports, as well as information abourt the Exporter Database of all U.S. exporters. Another entry, "Foreign Trade" (www.foreign-trade.com/highlights.htm), has links to data on top trading partners by year, country, industry, product, and state. There are also tables on the Commerce Department's Export.gov website that list imports and exports from a range of different industries. These tables present multiyear data on levels of imports and exports between the United States and the other countries of the world, providing an idea of the size and potential attractiveness of various sectors. This site also has numerous guides for "Doing Business In" various countries, to help companies in successfully exploiting trade opportunities.

We have seen that the volume of international trade is large, growing, and critical to the economic performance of most nations. But why does this trade occur, both overall and between particular nations? To answer this question, we will briefly examine several of the leading theories of international trade. Understanding these theories is essential for international managers, because they frequently will be dealing with government officials trained in economics and must therefore be prepared to speak their language. When presenting plans requiring governmental approval, managers must take care that the plans are economically sound, because they are almost certain to be studied by economists and will often need to be approved by them. Marketers proposing large projects to government planners must be aware that the key determinant now is economic efficiency rather than mere financial soundness.[8] Moreover, knowledge of economic concepts in the areas of international trade and investment frequently provides insight into future government action.

Explaining Trade: International Trade Theories

LO2-3 **Outline** the theories that attempt to explain why certain goods are traded internationally.

Why do nations trade? This question and the equally important proposition of predicting the direction, composition, and volume of goods traded are what international trade theory attempts to address. Interestingly, as is the case with numerous economic writings, the first formulation of international trade theory was politically motivated. Adam Smith, incensed by government intervention and control over both domestic and foreign trade, published *An Inquiry into the Nature and Causes of the Wealth of Nations* (1776), in which he tried to destroy the mercantilist philosophy.

MERCANTILISM

Mercantilism, the economic philosophy Smith attacked, evolved in Europe between the 16th and 18th centuries. A complex political and economic arrangement, mercantilism traditionally has been interpreted as viewing the accumulation of precious metals as an activity essential to a nation's welfare. These metals were, in the mercantilists' view, the only source of wealth. Because England had no mines, the mercantilists looked to international trade to supply gold and silver. The government established economic policies that promoted exports and stifled imports. Import restrictions such as import duties reduced imports, while government subsidies to exporters increased exports. Those acts created a trade surplus which would be paid for in gold and silver, in addition to protecting jobs within the mercantilist nation. Of course, another outcome of mercantilism was the generation of benefits for certain economic groups, such as domestic merchants, artisans, and shippers, albeit at a cost to other groups such as consumers and emerging industrialists.

mercantilism
An economic philosophy based on the belief that (1) a nation's wealth depends on accumulated treasure, usually precious metals such as gold and silver, and (2) to increase wealth, government policies should promote exports and discourage imports

Although the mercantilist era ended in the late 1700s, its arguments live on. Many people still argue that exports are "good" for a country because they create jobs, while imports are "bad" because they transfer jobs from the importing country to other nations. This view essentially sees trade as a zero-sum activity, where one party must lose in order for another to gain. Similarly, a "favorable" trade balance still means that a nation exports more goods and services than it imports. In balance-of-payments accounting, an export that brings dollars to the country is called *positive,* but imports that cause dollar outflow are labeled *negative.*

In the United States and Europe, as well as a number of emerging markets in Asia, many managers believe that China remains a present-day "fortress of mercantilism" that raises barriers to imported goods while giving Chinese exporters an unfair advantage. Despite impressive economic growth and burgeoning trade surpluses, Chinese authorities have resisted efforts to revalue their currency, the yuan or renminbi. Instead, they have continued to hold the yuan within a tight trading range relative to the U.S. dollar. By limiting the extent to which the yuan can appreciate in value, the Chinese authorities have been accused of engaging in mercantilist behavior because they help the international cost-competitiveness of Chinese companies relative to that of companies from the United States and other nations. One study argues that 40 percent of the price advantage of companies from China is due to mercantilist policies of China's central government, including an undervalued currency, export subsidies, and lax regulatory oversight.[9]

THEORY OF ABSOLUTE ADVANTAGE

absolute advantage
Theory that a nation has absolute advantage when it can produce a larger amount of a good or service for the same amount of inputs as can another country or when it can produce the same amount of a good or service using fewer inputs than could another country

Adam Smith argued against mercantilism by claiming that market forces, not government controls, should determine the direction, volume, and composition of international trade. He argued that under free, unregulated trade, each nation should specialize in producing those goods it could produce most efficiently (for which it had an **absolute advantage,** either natural or acquired). Some of these goods would be exported to pay for imports of goods that could be produced more efficiently elsewhere. Smith showed by his example of absolute advantage that both nations would gain from trade.

An Example   Assume that a world of two countries and two products has perfect competition and no transportation costs. Suppose that in the United States and China (a) one unit of input (combination of land, labor, and capital) can produce the quantities of soybeans and cloth listed in the following table, (b) each nation has two input units that it can use to produce either soybeans or cloth, and (c) each country currently uses one unit of input to produce each of soybeans and cloth. If neither country imports or exports, the quantities shown in the table are also those that are available for local consumption. The total output of both nations is 4 tons of soybeans and 6 bolts of cloth

Commodity	United States	China	Total Output
Tons of soybeans	3	1	4
Bolts of cloth	2	4	6

In the United States, 3 tons of soybeans or 2 bolts of cloth can be produced with one unit of output. Therefore, 3 tons of soybeans should have the same price as 2 bolts of cloth. In China, however, because only 1 ton of soybeans can be produced with the input unit that can produce 4 bolts of cloth, 1 ton of soybeans should cost as much as 4 bolts of cloth.

The United States has an absolute advantage in soybean production (3 to 1). China's absolute advantage is in cloth making (4 to 2). Will anyone anywhere give the Chinese cloth maker more than 1 ton of soybeans for 4 bolts of cloth? According to the example, all American soybean producers should because they can get only 2 bolts of cloth for 3 tons of soybeans at home. Similarly, Chinese cloth makers, once they learn that they can obtain more than 1 ton of soybeans for every 4 bolts of cloth in the United States, will be eager to trade Chinese cloth for American soybeans.

Each Country Specializes   Suppose each nation decides to use its resources to produce only the product at which it is more efficient. The following table shows each nation's output. Note that with the same quantity of input units, the total output is now greater (a total output of 6 rather than 4 tons of soybeans, and 8 rather than 6 bolts of cloth).

Commodity	United States	China	Total Output
Tons of soybeans	6	0	6
Bolts of cloth	0	8	8

Terms of Trade (Ratio of International Prices)   With specialization, now the total production of both goods is greater, but to consume both products, the two countries must trade some of their surplus. What are the limits within which both countries are willing to trade? Clearly, the Chinese cloth makers will trade some of their cloth for soybeans if they can get more than the 1 ton of soybeans that they get for 4 bolts of cloth in China. Likewise, the American soybean growers will trade their soybeans for Chinese cloth if they get a bolt of cloth for less than the 1.5 tons of soybeans it costs them in the United States.

If the two nations take the midpoint of the two trading limits so that each shares equally in the benefits of trade, they will agree to swap 1.33 bolts of cloth for 1 ton of soybeans. Both will gain from specialization because each now has the following quantities:

Commodity	United States	China	Total Output
Tons of soybeans	3	3	6
Bolts of cloth	4	4	8

Gains from Specialization and Trade   Because each nation specialized in producing the product at which it was more efficient and then traded its surplus for goods that it could not produce as efficiently, both nations benefited. China gained 2 more tons of soybeans and the United States gained 2 more bolts of cloth.

Although Adam Smith's logic helped to convince many governments to dismantle trade barriers and encourage increased international trade, it failed to calm concerns of those whose countries lacked any absolute advantage. What if one country has an absolute advantage in the production of both soybeans and cloth? Will there still be a basis for trade?

THEORY OF COMPARATIVE ADVANTAGE

David Ricardo demonstrated in 1817 that even though one nation held an absolute advantage over another in the production of each of two different goods, international trade could still create benefit for each country (thus representing a positive-sum game, or one in which both countries "win" from engaging in trade). The only limitation to such benefit-creating trade is that the less efficient nation cannot be *equally* less efficient in the production of both goods.[10]

An Example   To illustrate how this can occur, let us slightly change our first example so that now China has an absolute advantage in producing *both* soybeans and cloth. Note that compared with China, the United States is less inefficient in producing soybeans (4 versus 5 tons produced from a single unit of input, or 80 percent as efficient as China)

Theory that a nation
having absolute
disadvantages in
the prodution of two
goods with respect
to another nation
has a comparative
or relative advan-
tage in the produc-
tion of the good in
which its absolute
disadvantage is less

than in manufacturing cloth (2 versus 5 bolts of cloth from a single unit of input, or 40 percent as efficient). Therefore, the United States has a **comparative advantage** in producing
soybeans.

Commodity	United States	China	Total Output
Tons of soybeans	4	5	9
Bolts of cloth	2	5	7

Each Country Specializes   If each country specializes in what it does best, its output
will be as follows:

Commodity	United States	China	Total Output
Tons of soybeans	8	0	8
Bolts of cloth	0	10	10

Terms of Trade   In this case, the terms of trade will be somewhere between the pre-
trade price ratios of 1 ton of soybeans for 1 bolt of cloth that Chinese soybean growers must
pay in China and the 1/2 bolt of cloth that American cloth makers must pay for 1 ton of
American soybeans.

Let us assume that the traders agree on an exchange rate of 3/4 bolt of cloth for 1 ton of
soybeans. Both will gain from this exchange and specialization, as the following table shows:

Commodity	United States	China
Tons of soybeans	4	4
Bolts of cloth	3	7

Note that this trade left China with 2 surplus bolts of cloth and 1 less ton of soybeans
than it had before specializing. However, the Chinese cloth manufacturers should be able
to trade 1 bolt of surplus cloth for at least 1 ton of soybeans elsewhere. Then the final result
will be as follows:

Commodity	United States	China
Tons of soybeans	4	5+
Bolts of cloth	3	6

Gains from Specialization and Trade   Gains from specialization and trade in this
case are 1 additional bolt of cloth for each of the United States and China, and about 1 more
ton of soybeans for China.

This simple concept of comparative advantage serves as a basis for international
trade, even when one nation has an advantage over another in the production of each of
the goods being traded. We have presented the theory of comparative advantage without
mentioning money; however, a nation's comparative advantage can be affected by differences between the costs of production factors in that country's currency and their costs
in other currencies. As we shall see in the next section, money can change the direction
of trade.

offshoring
Locating activities in
another nation

Comparative Advantage and Offshoring of Service Jobs from the United States to India

India, a nation with approximately 1 billion people, has relatively few other resources compared with developed nations. Therefore, it should have a comparative advantage in production of goods or services that require large amounts of labor and relatively little capital. However, India has an additional comparative advantage because many of its citizens speak English (which is taught in many Indian schools and universities rather than using one of the other 18 major languages and 844 dialects spoken in the country). Thus, labor has a relatively low price due to the large Indian workforce (about 450 million, with nearly 10 million additional people entering the workforce each year), high levels of unemployment or underemployment (officially an unemployment rate of 8 percent, but a poverty rate that exceeds 20 percent), and a large proportion of rural and unskilled workers. As Internet and cellular telephone communications continue to become less expensive, India increasingly is using its English-speaking pool of labor to export services—such as software engineering, telemarketing, reviews of credit or mortgage applications, preparation or review of legal documents, analysis of blood tests and other medical services, and claims processing—to foreign companies and their customers, a process known as **offshoring.**

At $76 billion in annual revenues in 2010-2011, the Indian information technology (IT) industry generated more than 5 percent of India's GDP, and the overall size of this sector is projected to grow to $225 billion in revenues by 2020 as a result of factors such as declining computer prices, new tax incentives, and the Indian government's efforts to connect the country's extensive and isolated rural areas with the outside world. *Fortune* 500 companies such as Amazon.com, IBM, and American Express, as well as a range of more moderate-sized firms, have already offshored millions of jobs. By 2015, it has been estimated that 3.4 million U.S. jobs, representing $136 billion in wages, will have been offshored, and India is well positioned to capture much of this business. According to Noshir Kaka of the consulting firm McKinsey, "This industry can do for India what automobiles did for Japan and oil for Saudi Arabia."

For example, 1.6 million U.S. individual and corporate tax returns were estimated to have been prepared in India in 2011. Documents obtained from taxpayers are scanned and shipped electronically to India, where forms are completed and sent back to the United States to be examined, approved, and signed by an American accountant. While a U.S. tax preparer might cost more than $3,000 per month during the peak tax season, a comparable Indian worker might cost less than $300. There is no requirement that the taxpayer be informed that the tax work is done abroad, and most accounting firms charge the same fees as those charged if the job is done by accountants in the United States, thus helping to boost profitability.

Companies in financial services and insurance have also been actively pursuing offshoring. More than 80 percent of global financial services companies have an offshore facility, and the range of services being offshored is rapidly being broadened. "Offshoring has released a new competitive dynamic. Larger firms are driving change across the financial services industry and using offshoring to open up a competitive advantage over their smaller rivals," said Chris Gentle of the professional services firm Deloitte. "Offshoring is fundamentally changing the way financial institutions do business, creating a global division of labor that demands new operating models, new structures and new management skills."

"This is a global industry in the throes of flux. It is a sector where [Indian companies] are rewriting the rules of the game. That is the difference that has become apparent and increasingly accepted," says Nandan Nilekani, CEO of the rapidly expanding Indian company Infosys Technologies. The basis for this change, he says, is the "global delivery model" being pioneered in India and replicated in other low-cost nations. In the IT sector, for example, a plentiful supply of Indian software engineers can work on projects "offshore," delivering the finished product to clients "on site" in the United States. "Our business innovation is forcing rivals to redesign the way they do things."

This disruptive change is threatening to transform the business models in operation across a broad range of industries. Although many people think of low-skill jobs like telemarketing and call centers when they think of offshoring to India, the sophistication and skill levels associated with processes being outsourced are rising rapidly. A big driver for this trend is the abundance of qualified personnel in India. A NASSCOM-McKinsey study found that India has 28 percent of the overall supply of skilled services personnel in low-cost nations, and these potential employees remain amazingly inexpensive. An Indian IT engineer earns a typical annual salary of less than $6,000 and one with a master's degree in business earns $8,500—about one-tenth the level of their American counterparts, although salary inflation is starting to reduce that gap.

Services represent 60 percent of the U.S. economy and employ up to 80 percent of American workers, so it is not surprising that the offshoring of service jobs has generated concerns across a broad spectrum of society. John Steadman, president of the Institute of Electrical and Electronics Engineers, cautioned, "If we continue to offshore high-skilled professional jobs, the U.S. risks surrendering its leading role in innovation." Andrew Grove, former Chairman of Intel Corp., warned that "it's a very valid question" whether the United States could lose its dominance in information technology as a result of this trend, as it did in electronics manufacturing.

(continued)

Responding to the offshoring to an Indian firm of calls from New Jersey welfare recipients about their benefits, state senator Shirley Turner said, "I was outraged. Here we are in New Jersey, as we are in every state, requiring welfare recipients to go to work. And yet, we were sending these jobs overseas . . . so that corporations can make more money." She noted that unemployed people do not pay taxes, and the loss of these tax revenues exacerbates budget deficits. Ironically, widespread publicity regarding concerns about offshoring may have hastened the trend by making more companies aware of the possible cost savings from such undertakings.

On the other hand, some have argued that offshoring will help to strengthen American industry and the economy as a whole. Offshoring is not necessarily a zero-sum game, where one Indian worker substitutes for one American worker. When American firms hire lower-cost labor abroad, they often must hire other workers to complement the increased level of foreign labor. Overseas expansion can also cause companies to modify the scope of activities undertaken in the United States, placing increasing emphasis on higher-value-added activities rather than the lower-skill positions that have been offshored. Shifting work to lower-cost locations abroad has the potential to lower prices in the United States, thus raising the purchasing power of American consumers, enhancing consumer spending and economic activity, and thereby creating more jobs. As *The Wall Street Journal* editorialized, "The world economy is a dynamic enterprise. Jobs created overseas generate jobs at home. Not just more jobs for Americans, but higher-skilled and better paying ones. At the same time, trade offers consumers a greater quantity and variety of goods and services for lower prices. David Ricardo lives."

Questions:

1. What advantages other than profit can be gained by offshoring?

2. What are the ethical considerations, if any, that a company faces in making a decision to offshore activities?

3. What might be the long-term implications of offshoring, from the perspective of the home country? The host country?

Sources: Business Monitor International, *The India Information Technology Report 2008* (London: Business Monitor International, 2008), www.businessmonitor.com/it/india.html (May 10, 2011); Meg Fletcher, "Moving Services Offshore," *Business Insurance*, June 2006, pp. 16–17; Joanna Slater, "In India, a Job Paradox," *The Wall Street Journal*, May 5, 2004, p. A12; Julie Gallagher, "Redefining the Business Case for Offshore Outsourcing," *Insurance & Technology*, April 2002, pp. A5, A8–A9; Khozem Merchant, "The Future on India's Shores," *Financial Times*, April 21, 2004, p. 8; "Outsourcing 101," *The Wall Street Journal*, May 27, 2004, p. A20; Rebecca Paley, "Fighting for the Down and Out(sourced)," *Mother Jones*, May/June 2004, pp. 20–21; Manjeet Kripalani and Pete Engardio, "The Rise of India," *BusinessWeek*, December 8, 2003, pp. 66–76; Robert Orr, "Offshoring Opens Gap in Financial Services Race," *Financial Times*, June 29, 2004, p. 9; SourcingNotes, "Offshoring Tax Returns Preparation to India," www.sourcingnotes.com/content/view/197/54/ (May 10, 2011); Heather Timmons, "India Feels Less Vulnerable as Outsourcing Presses On," *New York Times*, June 2, 2009, www.nytimes.com/2009/06/03/business/global/03outsource.html (May 10, 2011); and "China Steadily Closing Gap with India as Top BPO Destination," *The Economic Times*, November 12, 2010, http://articles.economictimes.indiatimes.com/2010-11-12/news/27606950_1_offshore-countries-outsourcing-industry-global-outsourcing (May 10, 2011).

HOW MONEY CAN CHANGE THE DIRECTION OF TRADE

Suppose the total cost of land, labor, and capital to produce the daily output of soybeans or cloth in the example on absolute advantage is $10,000 in the United States and 80,000 yuan in China. The cost per unit is as follows:

Commodity	Price per Unit	
	United States	**China**
Ton of soybeans	$10,000/3 = $3,333/ton	80,000 yuan/1 = 80,000 yuan/ton
Bolt of cloth	$10,000/2 = $5,000/bolt	80,000 yuan/4 = 20,000 yuan/bolt

To determine whether it is more advantageous to buy locally or to import, the traders need to know the prices in their own currencies. To convert from foreign to domestic currency, they use the *exchange rate*.

exchange rate
The price of one currency stated in terms of another currency

Exchange Rate   The **exchange rate** is the price of one currency stated in terms of the other. If the prevailing rate is $1=8 yuan, then 1 yuan must be worth 0.125 dollar.* Using

*If $1=8 yuan, to find the value of 1 yuan in dollars, divide both sides of the equation by 8. Then 1 yuan = 1/8 = $0.125.

the exchange rate of $1=8$ yuan, the prices in the preceding example appear to the U.S. trader as follows:

Commodity	Price per Unit (dollars)	
	United States	China
Ton of soybeans	$3,333	$10,000
Bolt of cloth	$5,000	$ 2,500

The American soybean producers can earn $6,667 more per ton by exporting soybeans to China than they can by selling locally,[†] but can the Chinese cloth makers gain by exporting to the United States? To find out, they must convert the American prices to Chinese yuan.

Commodity	Price per Unit (yuan)	
	United States	China
Ton of soybeans	26,664 yuan	80,000 yuan
Bolt of cloth	40,000 yuan	20,000 yuan

currency devaluation
The lowering of a currency's price in terms of other currencies

It is apparent that the Chinese cloth makers will export cloth to the United States because they can sell at the higher price of 40,000 yuan per bolt. The American cloth makers, however, will need some very strong sales arguments to sell in the United States if they are to overcome the $2,500 price differential.

Influence of Exchange Rate Soybeans to China and cloth to the United States will be the direction of trade as long as the exchange rate remains around $1=8$ yuan. But if the dollar strengthens to $1=24$ yuan, American soybeans will cost as much in yuan as do Chinese soybeans, and importation of American soybeans into China will cease. On the other hand, should the dollar weaken to $1=4$ yuan, then 1 bolt of Chinese cloth will cost $5,000 to American traders, and they will have little reason to import Chinese cloth into the United States. This example suggests that a nation can attempt to regain competitiveness in world markets through **currency devaluation** (lowering its price in terms of other currencies). Note that in many but by no means all cases, this action can leave domestic prices largely unchanged. This issue will be discussed further in Chapter 8.

SOME NEWER EXPLANATIONS FOR THE DIRECTION OF TRADE

The international trade theory we have been discussing was essentially the only theoretical explanation of trade available to us until the second half of the 20th century. Since that time, however, several other possible explanations for international trade have been developed. We will discuss several of them.

[†]For example, to calculate this figure, you would multiply the American price of $3,333 per ton of soybeans times 8 yuan per dollar, yielding a price of 26,664 yuan per ton.

resource endowment

Theory that countries export products requiring large amounts of their abundant production factors and import products requiring large amounts of their scarce production factors

Differences in Resource Endowments

Some countries have an abundance of resources, when compared to the endowments of other nations. For example, the United States has a large supply of fertile farmland, Chile has abundant supplies of copper, and Saudi Arabia has extensive amounts of crude oil. These differences in **resource endowments** can result in differences across countries in the opportunity cost of producing these resources. As a result, countries are likely to export those products that are less expensive for them to produce and to import products that are either unavailable domestically or that can be produced more cheaply in other nations. Theory based on differences in resource endowments would suggest that developed countries would be more likely to trade with developing countries, which have very different factor endowments, rather than with other developed countries that would have similar factor endowments. This theory can adequately explain international trade in primary products.

Overlapping Demand

In contrast to resource endowment–based theory, Swedish economist Stefan Linder theorized that customers' tastes are strongly affected by income levels, and therefore a nation's level of income per capita determines the kinds of goods its people will demand. Because an entrepreneur will produce goods to meet this demand, the kinds of products manufactured reflect the country's level of income per capita. Goods produced for domestic consumption will eventually be exported, due to similarity of income levels and therefore demand in other countries.

overlapping demand

Theory that trade in manufactured goods will be greater between nations with similar levels of per capita income, and that the goods traded will be those for which consumers in both countries demand the same good

The theory of **overlapping demand** thus deduces that international trade in manufactured goods will be greater between nations with similar levels of per capita income than between those with dissimilar levels of per capita income—the very situation observed in our review of trade data earlier in this chapter. Even though two developed countries may have similar factor endowments, which under the resource endowment theory would result in limited trade between them, these nations still can have a large volume of trade with each other. The goods that will be traded are those for which there is an *overlapping demand* (consumers in both countries are demanding the same good).[11] For example, if an American company such as Apple invents a sophisticated cell phone with advanced features for its home market, the best export opportunities for this phone will be in other advanced nations such as Japan and western European countries, even if these countries have their own domestic producers of cell phones. Note that the theory of overlapping demand differs from the theory of comparative advantage in that it does not specify in which direction a given good will go. In fact, this intraindustry trade occurs because of **product differentiation;** for example, Apple exports its cell phones to Europe and Japan and Sony-Ericsson exports cell phones to the United States, because consumers in these different markets perceive a difference in the brands.

product differentiation

The development of products that have unique differences, with the intent of positively influencing demand

International Product Life Cycle

The hypothesis of an **international product life cycle (IPLC)** was formulated by Raymond Vernon.[12] This concept, which concerns the role of innovation in trade patterns, views a product as going through a full life cycle from the internationalization stage to standardization. The initial innovation stage of the cycle borrows from Linder's theory of overlapping demand in terms of the motivations and response of entrepreneurs to perceived market opportunities. The subsequent three stages through which a product is said to pass are illustrated in Figure 2.2 and described next. This concept can be applied to new product introduction by firms in any of the industrialized nations, but because more new products have been successfully introduced on a commercial scale in the United States, let us examine the **IPLC** as it applies to this country.

international product life cycle (IPLC)

A theory explaining why a product that begins as a nation's export eventually becomes its import

1. *U.S. exports:* Because the United States possesses the largest population of high-income consumers of any country in the world, competition for their patronage is intense. Manufacturers are therefore forced to search constantly for better ways to satisfy their customers' needs. To provide new products, companies maintain large research and development laboratories, which must be in constant contact with suppliers of the materials they need for product development. The fact that their suppliers are also in this country facilitates

FIGURE 2.2

International
Product Life Cycle

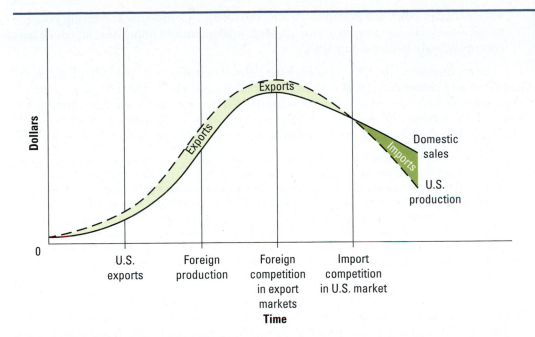

the contact.[13] In the early stages of the product life cycle, the design and the production methods are changing. By being close to the market, management can react quickly to customer feedback and more easily provide local repair services. These factors combine to make the United States a leader in new-product introduction. For a while, American firms will be the only manufacturers of the product; overseas customers, as they learn of the product, will therefore have to buy from American firms. The export market develops as the manufacturer ships products to these overseas customers.

2. *Foreign production begins:* Overseas consumers, especially those in developed nations, have similar needs and the ability to purchase the product. Export volume grows and may become large enough to support local production, especially in larger markets. The technology for producing the good has become fairly stable, and if the innovator is a multinational firm, it will often be sending its subsidiaries new-product information with complete details on how to produce it. Where there are no affiliates, foreign managers, as they learn of the product, will obtain licenses from the innovating company for producing the product (or else they may initiate efforts to imitate or invent around the innovator's technology in order to capture the market opportunity). Foreign production will begin, which also provides advantages of reduced costs for transportation and local communication. The American firm will still be exporting to those markets where there is no production, but its export growth will diminish as licensing and foreign direct investment substitute for exports as sources of supply to various international markets.

3. *Foreign competition in export markets:* Later, as early foreign manufacturers gain experience in marketing and production, their costs will fall. Saturation of their local markets will cause them to look for buyers elsewhere. They may even be able to undersell the American producers if they enjoy an advantage such as lower labor or raw material costs. In this stage, foreign firms are competing in export markets, and as a result, American export sales will continue to decline. By this stage, the innovating American firms may have developed newer versions of the product and begun scaling back production of the original product in order to begin focusing instead on the newer innovations.

4. *Import competition in the United States:* If domestic and export sales enable foreign producers to attain the economies of scale enjoyed by the American firm, they may reach a point where they can compete in quality and underprice American firms in the American market. From that point on, the U.S. market will be served exclusively (or nearly so) by imports. Televisions, footwear, and DRAM (dynamic random access memory)

semiconductor chips are examples of such products. This provides increasing pressure on the innovating company to achieve product innovation and improvement, which may correspondingly initiate a new IPLC.

Authors discussing the IPLC concept have claimed that this cycle may be repeated as the less developed countries (LDCs) with still lower labor costs obtain the technology and thus acquire a cost advantage over the more industrialized nations. Although little research has been done to substantiate the IPLC concept, a World Bank study seems to provide a plausible reason for these changes in production locations, as suggested in the following excerpt:

> *With countries progressing on the comparative advantage scale, their exports can supplement the exports of countries that graduate to a higher level. . . . A case in point is Japan, whose comparative advantage has shifted towards highly capital-intensive exports. In turn, developing countries with a relatively high human capital endowment . . . can take Japan's place in exporting relatively human capital–intensive products, and countries with a relatively high physical capital endowment, such as Brazil and Mexico, can take Japan's place in exporting relatively physical capital–intensive products. Finally, countries at lower levels of development can supplant the middle-level countries in exporting unskilled labor–intensive commodities.*[14]

Recently, attention has been given to the emergence of companies that have been termed "born globals," wherein companies become international in their operations almost from the beginning. Although some have argued that these firms may not internationalize their operations and products in the classic manner of the IPLC, they often increase commitment to international markets in a gradual way that may not be inconsistent with the IPLC concept.[15]

Economies of Scale and the Experience Curve

In the 1920s, economists began to consider the fact that most industries benefit from **economies of scale;** that is, as a plant gets larger and output increases, the average cost of producing each unit of output decreases. This occurs because larger and more efficient equipment can be employed, companies can obtain volume discounts on their larger-volume purchases, and fixed costs such as those of research and design and administrative overheads can be allocated over a larger quantity of output. Most manufacturing is subject to economies of scale, and mining and transportation industries also tend to benefit from increasing returns to scale. Production costs also drop because of the **experience curve.** As firms produce more products, they learn ways to improve production efficiency, causing production costs to decline by a predictable amount.[16]

Economies of scale and the experience curve affect international trade because they can permit a nation's industries to become low-cost producers without requiring that the nation have an abundance of a certain class of production factors. Then, just as in the case of comparative advantage, nations specialize in the production of a few products and trade with others to supply the rest of their needs. International trade is promoted because a nation's companies may not be able to fully achieve the potential scale economies through serving only the domestic market, even within countries as large as the United States. Examples include semiconductors, computers, and commercial aircraft. American consumers can benefit from higher quality and lower prices for these products because companies like Intel, Hewlett-Packard, and Boeing can spread very high fixed costs over sales within foreign as well as home markets.

National Competitive Advantage from Regional Clusters

National competitiveness involves a nation's ability to design, produce, distribute, or service products within an international trading context while earning increasing returns on its resources. A nation's ability to achieve sustained international success within a particular industry may be explained by variables other than the factors of production on which the theories of comparative advantage and resource endowment are based. For example, Alfred Marshall's seminal work on economic theory helped to explain why, in many industries, firms tend to cluster together on a geographic basis.[17] He suggested that geographic clusters appeared for three reasons: (1) advantages associated with pooling of a common labor force so that staffing requirements can be met quickly, even with unexpected fluctuations in demand; (2) gains from the development of specialized local suppliers whose operations and skills can be coordinated with the needs of the buyers; and (3) benefits that result within the geographic region from the sharing of technological information and corresponding enhancement of the rate of innovation.

Michael Porter, an economics professor at Harvard, extended the work of Marshall.[18] His Diamond Model of national advantage claims that four kinds of variables will have an impact on the ability of the local firms in one country to utilize the country's resources to gain a competitive advantage:

1. *Demand conditions:* the nature, rather than merely the size, of the domestic demand. If a firm's customers are sophisticated and demanding, it will strive to produce high-quality and innovative products and, in doing so, will obtain a global competitive advantage over companies located where domestic pressure is less. This might have been the case in the past, when international firms introduced their new products in home markets first (a condition of the international product life-cycle theory), but as more firms introduce new products globally, this variable will lose importance.

2. *Factor conditions:* level and composition of factors of production. Porter distinguishes between the basic factor endowments and the advanced factors (a nation's infrastructure, such as telecommunications and transportation systems, or university research institutes). He also distinguishes between created factors (e.g., from investments made by individuals, companies, or governments) and inherited factors (e.g., natural resources, location). Lack of natural endowments has caused nations to invest in the creation of the advanced factors, such as education of a nation's workforce, free ports, and advanced communications systems, to enable their industries to be competitive globally. Various Caribbean nations have upgraded their communications systems to attract banking and other service companies that have little dependence on the basic factors of production.

3. *Related and supporting industries:* suppliers and industry support services. For decades, firms in an industry, with their suppliers, the suppliers' suppliers, and so forth, have tended to form a cluster in a given location, often without any apparent initial reason. Yet these related and supporting industries serve as an important foundation for competitive success by providing a network of suppliers, subcontractors, and a commercial infrastructure. For example, the San Francisco Bay Area in California has a range of related and supporting industries for the personal computer industry. These include research, design, production, or service operations of such suppliers as semiconductor designers, semiconductor manufacturers, technologically savvy venture capitalists, and intellectual property rights lawyers, as well as related industries such as scientific equipment, electronics (e.g., MP3 players, "smartphones" such as the iPhone), telecommunications equipment, software developers, and a wide range of Internet-related companies.[19]

4. *Firm strategy, structure, and rivalry:* the extent of domestic competition, the existence of barriers to entry, and the firms' management style and organization. Porter states that companies subject to heavy competition in their domestic markets are constantly striving to improve their efficiency and innovativeness, which makes them more competitive internationally. For decades, firms in oligopolistic industries have carefully watched their competitors' every move and have even entered foreign markets because their competitors had gone there. For example, Japanese automakers such as Toyota, Honda, Nissan, and Mitsubishi have competed vigorously with each other for decades in their domestic marketplace, constantly pressuring each other to improve the quality and performance of their products or else risk the loss of market share. This vigorous competition has enabled these firms to develop world-leading capabilities in auto design and manufacturing. As soon as one of these companies ventures forth into a new international market such as the United States, Europe, or Southeast Asia for the sale or manufacturing of autos, the competitors tend to be close behind in order to avoid a decline in their relative international competitiveness.

In addition to these four variables, Porter claimed that competitiveness could be affected by government and chance. For example, competitiveness may be influenced through government policies such as incentives, subsidies, temporary protection from foreign competitors, or infrastructure development, or through random events such as the location and timing of research breakthroughs or luck.

Porter argues that these factors are fundamentally interrelated, creating a "virtuous circle" of resource generation and application, as well as responsiveness in meeting the demands of customers, as depicted in Figure 2.3.

SUMMARY OF INTERNATIONAL TRADE THEORY

LO2-4 **Explain** the size, growth, and direction of foreign direct investment.

International trade occurs primarily because of relative price differences among nations. These differences stem from differences in production costs, which result from:

1. Differences in the endowments of the factors of production.
2. Differences in the levels of technology that determine the factor intensities used.
3. Differences in the efficiencies with which these factor intensities are utilized.
4. Foreign exchange rates.

However, taste differences, a demand variable, can reverse the direction of trade predicted by the theory.

International trade theory shows that nations will attain a higher level of living by specializing in goods for which they possess a comparative advantage and importing those for which they have a comparative disadvantage. Generally, trade restrictions that stop this free flow of goods will harm a nation's welfare. Chapter 6's discussion of political forces examines a broad range of arguments that have been presented in support of restrictions on international trade of goods and services.

The topic we have been examining—international trade—exists because firms export. As you know, however, exporting is only one aspect of international business. Another—overseas production—requires foreign investment, the topic of the next section.

portfolio investment
The purchase of stocks and bonds to obtain a return on the funds invested

direct investment
The purchase of sufficient stock in a firm to obtain significant management control

Foreign Investment

Foreign investment can be divided into two components: **portfolio investment,** which is the purchase of stocks and bonds solely for the purpose of obtaining a return on the funds invested, and **direct investment,** by which the investors participate in the management of the firm in addition to receiving a return on their money. The distinction between these two components has begun to blur, particularly with the growing size and number of international mergers, acquisitions, and alliances in recent years. For example, investments

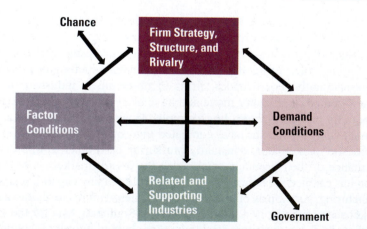

by a foreign investor in the stock of a domestic company generally are treated as direct investment when the investor's equity participation ratio is 10 percent or more. In contrast, deals that do not result in the foreign investor's obtaining at least 10 percent of the shareholdings are classified as portfolio investments. With the increasing pace of business globalization, it is not uncommon for companies to form strategic relationships with firms from other nations in order to pool resources (such as manufacturing, marketing, and technology and other know-how) while still keeping their equity participation below 10 percent. Financing from foreign venture capitalists also tends to be treated as a portfolio investment, although these investors frequently become actively involved in the target company's business operations, with the goal of ultimately realizing substantial capital gains when the target company goes public.

PORTFOLIO INVESTMENT

Although portfolio investors are not directly concerned with the control of a firm, they invest immense amounts in stocks and bonds from other countries. For example, data from the Department of Commerce show that persons residing outside the United States owned American stocks and bonds other than U.S. Treasury securities with a value of $5.3 billion at the beginning of 2010 (including $2.4 billion in corporate stocks), nearly 11 times the level achieved 20 years earlier, at the beginning of 1990.[20] The very substantial proportion of the increase in the valuation of American stock held by persons residing outside this country is associated with the large number and scale of acquisitions of U.S. companies by foreign companies.

Americans, by contrast, owned $5.5 billion in foreign securities at the beginning of 2010, which was more than 17 times the the corresponding level 20 years earlier, at the beginning of 1990.[21] Of the foreign securities held by Americans, $4.0 billion was in corporate stocks. This increase reflects net U.S. purchases of foreign stocks, acquisitions of foreign companies by U.S. companies, and price appreciation in many foreign stocks. As you can see, foreign portfolio investment is sizable and will continue to grow as more international firms list their bonds and equities on foreign exchanges.

FOREIGN DIRECT INVESTMENT

The following discussion examines the volume, level, and direction of foreign direct investment and the influence of international trade on foreign direct investment. This section discusses the overall level of foreign direct investment, as well as annual outflows and inflows of FDI.

The Outstanding Stock of FDI The *book value*—or the value of the total outstanding stock—of all foreign direct investment (FDI) worldwide was $19.0 trillion at the beginning of 2010.[22] Individuals and corporations from the United States had $4.3 trillion invested abroad, which was more than double the FDI of either of the next-largest investors, France and the United Kingdom. The proportion of FDI accounted for by the United States declined by 36 percent between 1980 and 2010, however, from 36 to 23 percent. During the same time period, the proportion of FDI accounted for by the European Union increased by nearly 31 percent, from 36 to 47 percent, although a portion of that increase was due to the inclusion of additional member-countries in the EU calculations. Japan's proportion of FDI declined from 12 percent in 1990 to 4 percent in 2010. Reflecting their continued economic development, developing countries have dramatically increased their share of FDI stock, from 1 percent in 1980 to 14 percent in 2010. Figure 2.4 highlights the rate of growth of FDI stock for selected nations and regions, particularly the M-BRIC emerging market economies, that is, Mexico, Brazil, Russia, India, and China.

An important development in the level of worldwide FDI is the emergence of what has been called the "bamboo network" of ethnic Chinese family businesses based outside of China. The 500 largest public companies in Asia that are controlled by overseas Chinese investors have more than $1 trillion in total assets, and this figure excludes these families' privately owned companies.[23] Ethnic Chinese are reported to be the largest cross-border investors in Malaysia, Thailand, Indonesia, Vietnam, the Philippines, and Hong Kong, and they are a major source of investment capital flowing into the Chinese mainland.

FIGURE 2.4

Stocks of Outward
Foreign Direct
Investment,
Selected Countries
and Categories,
1980, 1990, 2000,
and 2009 ($ billions)

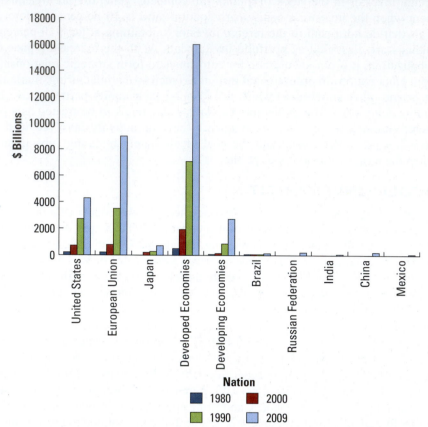

Sources: Various "Country Fact Sheets," *World Investment Report 2001*, United Nations Conference on Trade and Development, Geneva, October 2001; and *World Investment Report 2010,* United Nations Conference on Trade and Development, Geneva, www.unctad.org/Templates/webflyer.asp?docid=13423&intItemID=5539&lang=1&mode=downloads (May 10, 2011).

Another important development is the emergence of sovereign wealth funds, which are state-owned investment funds primarily from countries with either extensive commodity exports (e.g., petroleum) or trade surpluses. These funds were estimated to control approximately $4.3 trillion in assets in 2011.[24] Some observers are concerned not merely with the level of assets controlled by these funds, but also the potential for sometimes secretive state-owned investment funds to make decisions based at least partly on political or other noncommercial criteria.

Annual Outflows of FDI
Annual FDI outflows (the amount invested each year into other nations) hit a historical high in 2000—$1.2 trillion, more than 250 percent of the level in 1997.[25] However, the slowdown that began to hit most of the world's economies in late 2000 resulted in a subsequent decline in the overall level of annual FDI flows. By 2002, the total was only $537 billion, only about 44 percent of the 2000 figure. Outflows subsequently increased, reaching $2.3 trillion in 2007 before declining again, decreasing more than 50 percent to $1.1 trillion during the economic downturn of 2009.

The overall volume of outward FDI from developing nations in 2009 was 19 times the level in 1990, and the proportion of worldwide outward FDI that comes from developing nations increased from under 5 percent in 1990 to nearly 21 percent in 2009. Despite this increase, the vast proportion of outward FDI, nearly 80 percent, still originates from the developed countries. The United States and the EU have been accounting for the largest share of worldwide FDI—58 percent in 2009. The United States had been the leading source of FDI outflows through most of the 1990s and 2000s, although the proportion of worldwide outward FDI accounted for by the United States declined from an average of 21 percent in

1985–1996 to 18 percent for 2007–2009. American FDI outflows of $248 billion in 2009 exceeded the outflows of the second-largest source of FDI, France, by 69 percent. The European Union's proportion of outward FDI grew from an average of around 47 percent in 1985–1997 to a peak of 69 percent by 2005, before subsequently declining to 49 percent of global outward FDI from 2007–2009.

Much of this outward FDI has been associated with mergers and acquisitions. For example, historically, approximately two-thirds of the value of corporate investments made in the United States from abroad have been spent to acquire going companies rather than to establish new ones (similarly, the majority of American investments into foreign markets have gone to the acquisition of going companies). A number of reasons are responsible for this fact: (1) corporate restructuring in the United States caused management to put on the market businesses or other assets that either did not meet management's profit standards or were considered to be unrelated to the company's main business; (2) foreign companies wanted to gain rapid access in the United States to advanced technology, especially in computers and communications; (3) management of foreign firms felt that entrance into the large and prosperous American market could be more successful if they acquired known brand names rather than spending the time and money to promote new, unknown ones; and (4) increased international competitive pressures, including the pursuit of improved economies of scale, has led to restructuring and consolidation in many industries, and the acquisition of companies in major markets such as the United States has been a by-product of these industrial trends.

Annual Inflows of FDI   In which countries are investments being made, and where do the investments come from? The industrialized nations invest primarily in one another, just as they trade more with one another. An average of nearly 70 percent of annual FDI investments have been going into developed countries in recent years, although the proportion has fallen from 81 percent in 2000 to 51 percent by 2009.[26] The United States and the EU accounted for an average of more than 60 percent of all inward FDI from 1985 to 2004, exceeding 80 percent in 1999 and 2000, before declining to 49 percent by 2008. As noted earlier, much of this inward investment has gone to mergers and acquisitions made by companies whose businesses are confronting competition and consolidation globally. Japan has not been a significant recipient of inward FDI, averaging less than 1 percent of worldwide FDI from 1985 to 2009.

Worldwide, level of FDI flowing into the developing countries as a whole was 7.3 times larger in 2000 versus 1990, and it nearly doubled again between 2000 and 2009. Although the overall dollar value of FDI going to developing countries has been increasing substantially in recent years, the proportion of FDI funds going to these nations has fluctuated widely. The average from 1985 to 1995 was 28 percent, rising to 38 percent in 1996, declining to 18 percent in 2000, rising again to 40 percent in 2004, declining to 27 percent in 2007, and then rising to 43 percent in 2009. African nations have participated relatively little in the growing flow of inward FDI, accounting for an average of less than 3 percent of all inflows from 1985 to 2009. The small nation of Singapore (population 3 million) received almost as much foreign investment as the entire African continent did during this time. An encouraging trend is that the percentage of all inflows going to Africa increased from 0.7 percent in 2000 to an average of 3.7 percent for the 2007 to 2009 time period.

In Latin America, annual FDI inflows have fluctuated substantially during the past two decades. The proportion of worldwide inward FDI flows that have gone to Latin America increased from 3.8 percent in 1990 to 8.5 percent in 1995, then declined to 5.6 percent in 2000, before rising to 7.1 percent in 2005 and an average of 5.7 percent for 2007–2009. For Asia as a whole, total inflows to the region rose to a record $373 billion in 2008, nearly 1,300 percent of the average inward investments during 1985–1995. Asia accounted for 44 percent of all investments not directed to the United States and the European Union for the years 2008 and 2009. A particularly important trend is the proportion of Asian FDI that has been directed to China and its territories. Their combined proportion of Asian FDI was greater than 45 percent from 2007–2009, and it appears that some of the FDI previously directed toward other Asian nations might have been redirected toward these Chinese investments.

Are Economic and Social Development Affected by Trade and Investment?

All economies are increasingly open in today's economic environment of globalization. Trade plays a vital role in shaping economic and social performance and prospects of countries around the world, especially those of developing countries. No country has grown without trade. However, the contribution of trade to development depends a great deal on the context in which it works and the objectives it serves.a

This quote is the way the United Nations Conference on Trade and Development (UNCTAD) began its groundbreaking report examining international trade and developing countries. International trade clearly has an important role in influencing nations' economic and social performance in a world of globalization. This role is even more fundamental in the case of developing countries. Yet the mere expansion of trade does not guarantee improvement for a country and its people. Rather, it is essential that trade performance be viewed in the context of its effects on employment levels, economic growth, development, and an improvement in the overall human condition.

To assist in efforts to ensure that trade plays a full and constructive role in enhancing growth and development, UNCTAD launched an ambitious initiative that included the Trade and Development Index (TDI). By capturing the interactions among a range of institutional, structural, financial, trade, and development factors underlying trade and development, the TDI attempts to provide a quantitative indication of a nation's trade and development performance and facilitate national and international strategies and policies that will enable trade to serve as an important tool for promoting development. Although UNCTAD created the TDI primarily for assessing performance in developing nations, to facilitate comparisons and insight, it also constructed the TDI for developed countries and for newly industrializing countries. Overall, 123 countries were evaluated and the 20 top- and bottom-ranked countries are listed in the accompanying table.

The average score for developed countries was 640, versus 467 for developing countries and 395 for the least developed countries. Seven major emerging economies (Brazil, Russia, India, China, Mexico, South Korea, and South Africa), which account for 45 percent of the world's population and more than 26 percent of global exports of goods and services, had an average TDI score of 509, and they have all evidenced increasing TDI scores. This indicates that the gap in development can be shrunk—and has been in the case of several nations. Overall,

compared with developed countries, developing countries evidence a continuing lag in such areas as physical infrastructure, human capital, financial intermediation, institutional quality, economic and social well-being, and trade performance.

The initial TDI evaluation revealed that the 30 highest-ranked nations were all developed countries, except for Singapore (#5), South Korea (#21), China (#25), Malaysia (#27), and Thailand (#29). This result is interpreted as evidence that few developing nations have been able to come close to the developed countries in terms of their trade and development performance. Nine of the bottom 10 nations are sub-Saharan African countries, accentuating the severity of the trade and development problems confronting sub-Saharan Africa and least developed nations in general. The best regional performance among developing nations was that of the countries of the East Asia and Pacific region, followed by the Middle East and North Africa region and the Latin America and Caribbean region. The regions of South Asia and of sub-Saharan Africa significantly lagged behind the other three regional groups in terms of their TDI scores.

A critical factor contributing to high TDI scores is trade liberalization. The importance of this factor is highest for countries with lower TDI scores, and vice versa. This suggests that the extent of trade liberalization has much greater importance for developing countries, and especially the least developed countries, than for developed nations. In general, over the longer term and in the absence of externalities or market failures, trade liberalization is an effective policy promoting development. However, efforts to liberalize too rapidly can also result in short-term adjustment problems.

Both external and internal factors were found to influence a nation's export performance. External factors include market access conditions (e.g., transportation costs, geography, physical infrastructure, trade barriers, competition) and other factors that influence demand for imports. Internal factors

Level and Direction of FDI Even though it is impossible to make an accurate determination of the present value of foreign investments, we can get an idea of the rate and amounts of such investments and of the places in which they are being made. This is the kind of information that interests managers and government leaders. It is analogous to what is sought in the analysis of international trade. If a nation is continuing to receive

Top and Bottom Ranked Countries on the Trade and Development Index

Top-Ranked Countries			Bottom-Ranked Countries		
Rank	Country	TDI Score	Rank	Country	TDI Score
1	United States	743	103	Zimbabwe	395
				Pakistan	395
2	Germany	696	105	Syrian Arab Republic	392
3	Denmark	691		Chad	392
4	United Kingdom	682	107	Côte d'Ivoire	387
5	Singapore	675		Mauritania	387
6	Japan	668	109	Burkina Faso	386
	Sweden	668	110	Benin	384
8	France	664	111	Burundi	382
	Norway	664	112	Central African Republic	381
10	Canada	650		Zambia	381
	Switzerland	650	114	Ethiopia	379
12	Belgium	642	115	Cameroon	373
	Iceland	642	116	Guinea	372
14	Finland	636	117	Yemen	370
15	Ireland	630	118	Angola	364
16	Australia	628		Democratic Republic of Congo	364
17	Austria	627	120	Niger	362
18	New Zealand	623	121	Nigeria	350
19	Spain	619	122	Guinea-Bissau	339
20	Israel	610	123	Sudan	326

include supply-side conditions within a nation (e.g., raw materials, labor and capital costs, access to technology, economic policy, institutional environment). A country's extent of market access is particularly important, because limitations on access for foreign markets are a major cause of poor export performance.

Foreign direct investment (FDI) was found to have a significant and positive impact on export performance across all of the nations studied and for every time period studied. FDI has a key role in influencing the composition of exports, including the technological content and the development of export supply capacity, and especially in knowledge-based industries. The impact of FDI is strongest for the two poorest performing groups of exporters and at their early stages of export development.

UNCTAD emphasized that merely improving trade factors, such as liberalizing the trade environment, will yield only marginal benefits for a nation unless these efforts are done in conjunction with a focus on other factors associated with development and poverty reduction. There is a strong need for integration and consistency between trade policy and other social, political, and economic undertakings. For example,

nations must act simultaneously both on domestic capacity to supply goods and services and on access to foreign markets in order to produce strong performance. At early stages of development, important factors influencing domestic supply capacity include transportation infrastructure and macroeconomic stability.

Questions:

1. Why might trade and investment impact the social and economic development of a country?

2. What actions should a developing country take in order to enhance the potential benefits from international trade and development?

Sources: UNCTAD, Developing Countries in International Trade 2005: Trade and Development Index (New York: United Nations, 2005), www.unctad.org/templates/webflyer.asp?docid=6443&intItemID=1397&lang=1&mode=downloads (May 10, 2011); and UNCTAD, Developing Countries in International Trade 2007: Trade and Development Index (New York: United Nations, 2007), www.unctad.org/Templates/Page .asp?intItemID54388&lang51 (May 15, 2010).

appreciable amounts of foreign investment, its investment climate must be favorable. This means that the political forces of the foreign environment are relatively attractive and that the opportunity to earn a profit is greater there than elsewhere. Other reasons for investing exist, to be sure; however, if the preceding factors are absent, foreign investment is not likely to occur.

DOES TRADE LEAD TO FDI?

Historically, foreign direct investment has followed foreign trade. One reason is that engaging in foreign trade is typically less costly and less risky than making a direct investment into foreign markets. Also, management can expand the business in small increments rather than through the considerably greater amounts of investment and market size that a foreign production facility requires. Typically, a firm would use domestic or foreign agents to export. As the export business increased, the firm would set up an export department and perhaps hire sales representatives to live in overseas markets. The firm might even establish its own sales company to import in its own name.

Meanwhile, managers would watch the total market size closely because they would know that their competitors were making similar studies. Generally, because the local market would not be large enough to support local production by all the firms exporting to it, the situation would become one of seeing who could begin manufacturing there first. Experienced managers know that governments often limit the number of local firms making a given product so that those that do set up local operations will be assured of having a profitable and continuing business. This is especially important to developing countries that are dependent on foreign investment to provide jobs and tax revenue.

This sort of linear path to market expansion that we have just discussed is one that many international firms have taken and still take today. However, the new business environment of fewer government barriers to trade, increased competition from globalizing firms, and new production and communications technology is causing many international firms to disperse the activities of their production systems to locations close to available resources. They then integrate the entire production process either regionally or globally. As a result, the decision about where to locate may be either an FDI or a trade decision, illustrating just how closely FDI and trade are interlinked.

LO2-5 **Explain** several the theories of foreign direct investment.

Explaining FDI: Theories of International Investment

This section examines several of the leading theories of foreign direct investment, which comprises both ownership and control of international investments involving real or physical assets such as plants and other facilities, rather than theories regarding other types of international investment such as portfolios of stocks, bonds, or other forms of debt. Foreign direct investment involves the establishment of production or other facilities abroad, either through greenfield investment (the establishment of new facilities from the ground up) or cross-border acquisition (the purchase of an existing business in another nation). It is usually assumed that strategic motives will be the driving force for decisions to invest abroad, driven by desire to find new markets, access raw materials, achieve production efficiencies, gain access to new technologies or managerial expertise, enhance political safety of the firm's operations, or respond to competitive or other pressures in the external environment.[27]

MONOPOLISTIC ADVANTAGE THEORY

monopolistic advantage theory
Theory that foreign direct investment is made by firms in oligopolistic industries possessing technical and other advantages over indigenous firms

The modern **monopolistic advantage theory** stems from research showing that foreign direct investment occurs largely in oligopolistic industries rather than in industries operating under near-perfect competition. This means that the firms in these industries must possess advantages not available to local firms in order to overcome liabilities associated with being a foreigner—such as lack of knowledge about local market conditions, increased costs of operating at a distance, or differences in culture, language, laws and regulations, or institutions—that cause a foreign company to be at a disadvantage against local firms. Under this perspective, the advantages must be economies of scale, superior technology, or superior knowledge in marketing, management, or finance. Foreign direct investment takes place because of these product and factor market imperfections, which enable the multinational enterprise to operate more profitably in foreign markets than can local competitors.[28]

INTERNALIZATION THEORY

The **internalization theory** suggests that a firm may have superior knowledge, but due to inefficiency in external markets (i.e., transaction costs), the firm may obtain a higher price for that knowledge by using the knowledge itself, rather than by selling it in the open market. By investing in foreign subsidiaries for activities such as supply, production, or distribution, rather than licensing, the company is able to send the knowledge across borders while maintaining it within the firm. The expected result is the firm's ability to realize a superior return on the investment made to produce this knowledge, particularly as the knowledge is embodied in various products or services that are sold to customers.[29]

DYNAMIC CAPABILITIES

The **dynamic capability** perspective argues that ownership of specific knowledge or resources is necessary, but not sufficient, for achieving success in international FDI. The firm must also be able to effectively create and exploit dynamic capabilities for quality and/or quantity-based deployment, and these capabilities must be transferable to international environments in order to produce competitive advantage. Companies typically develop centers of excellence in order to develop distinctive competencies that will be subsequently applied to their investments within the host countries.

ECLECTIC THEORY OF INTERNATIONAL PRODUCTION

The eclectic theory, which combines elements of some of those we have discussed, is the most widely cited and accepted theory of FDI currently. Developed by Dunning, the **eclectic theory of international production** attempts to provide an overall framework for explaining why firms choose to engage in FDI rather than serve foreign markets through alternatives such as exporting, licensing, management contracts, joint ventures, or strategic alliances. This theory maintains that if a firm is going to invest in production facilities overseas, it must have three kinds of advantages:

1. *Ownership specific.* This is the extent to which a firm has or can develop a firm-specific advantage through ownership of tangible and intangible assets that are not available to other firms and can be transferred abroad. The three basic types of tangible or intangible ownership-specific advantages include knowledge or technology, economies of scale or scope, and monopolistic advantages associated with unique access to critical inputs or outputs. The advantage generates lower costs and/or higher revenues that will offset the added costs of operating at a distance within a foreign location.

2. *Location specific.* A foreign market must have specific characteristics, of an economic, social, or political nature (e.g., market size, tariff or nontariff barriers, or transport costs), that will permit the firm to profitably exploit its firm-specific advantages by locating to that market rather than from serving the market through exports.

3. *Internalization.* Firms have various alternatives for entering foreign markets, ranging from arm's-length market transactions to the use of hierarchy via a wholly owned

internalization theory
The concept that to obtain a higher return on its investment, a firm will transfer its superior knowledge to a foreign subsidiary, rather than sell it in the open market

dynamic capability
Theory that for a firm to successfully invest overseas, it must have not only ownership of unique knowledge or resources, but the ability to dynamically create and exploit these capabilities over time

eclectic theory of international production
Theory that for a firm to invest overseas, it must have three kinds of advantages: ownership specific, internalization, and location specific

subsidiary, as we will discuss in Chapter 13. It is in the firm's best interests to exploit its ownership-specific advantages through internalization in those situations where either the market does not exist or it functions inefficiently, causing the transaction costs of using market-based (arm's-length) options to be too high.

Because of the names of these three types of advantages that a firm must have, the eclectic theory of international production is sometimes referred to as the *OLI model*. This theory provides an explanation for an international firm's choice of its overseas production facilities. The firm must have both location and ownership advantages to invest in a foreign plant. It will invest where it is most profitable to internalize its monopolistic advantage.[30] These investments can be proactive, being strategically anticipated and controlled in advance by the firm's management team, or reactive, in response to the discovery of market imperfections.

There is one commonality to nearly all of these theories that is supported by empirical tests—the major part of direct foreign investment is made by large, research-intensive firms in oligopolistic industries. Also, all these theories offer reasons companies find it *profitable* to invest overseas. However, as we stated in Chapter 1, all motives can be linked in some way to the desire to increase or protect not only profits but also *sales* and *markets*.

THE GLOBAL PATH AHEAD

Kerry Thwing on Developing a Foundation in the International Area

The daughter of a travel agent, I was exposed to the "travel bug" as a baby. Ever since I can remember, my mother would plan yearly family vacations. Travel became a part of my life, and I would look forward to the adventures and experiences that would come with each trip. I was 16 when I decided to set out on

my first international solo excursion. I participated in a student exchange program to France, staying with a family in Cognac for a month and exploring Paris for a week. My life would not be the same had I chosen to stay home instead of taking a chance and leaving my comfort zone for this solo adventure. During that month abroad, I learned so much about myself and about others. I came home a wiser, more confident person. Now the travel bug had bitten me officially.

In college, I participated in three study abroad programs. My first year, I traveled to South America via a training ship as part of the Cal Poly at Sea study abroad program. We made port in Mexico, Chile, Peru, and Costa Rica. Then the summer of my second year, I studied in London, England. Finally, my fourth and final year at university, I studied in Adelaide, Australia. Though the ultimate purpose of these excursions was to complete the courses needed for my bachelor's degree in business administration, I learned so much more and such different things than I ever could have from a textbook or lecture. Travel can provide the ultimate education. Nothing can compare to the experience of leaving your comfort zone and observing your actions and the actions of others in a different environment.

Through international travel, not only will you learn about different cultures and values around the world, you will also learn many things about yourself. You can discover what you are truly capable of and you may be quite surprised by what you find. During my travels, there were many instances when things did not go as planned, but it is those times that are the most memorable for me. I was always pleasantly surprised by my ability to adapt and problem solve when put in a difficult situation. This is a skill that I learned through travel, and it has proven useful in many aspects of my life.

However, my favorite aspect of travel is the people that I have met, the connections to others that I have made. Throughout my time abroad, I have gained many great friends on a global scale. In fact, the majority of the relationships I have cultivated are related to my study abroad programs. It is important, especially when going with your friends to study abroad, to branch out and meet the locals. Not only will they be able to tell you about the city you are visiting, they will also teach you about the culture and may even become your new friends.

If I could give any piece of advice, I would say to take any chance you can to travel and experience new things. The only regrets I have are the opportunities that I did not take advantage of. In addition, take every chance you can *now* because you never know what will happen in the future. Personally, I decided to take the opportunity to return to Adelaide to complete my post-graduate education. I am currently residing in Adelaide and planning my next excursion abroad. I would encourage you to do the same as I do: explore every chance you can to spend time abroad.

Resources for Your Global Career

The successful international business professional looks beyond his or her home-country borders and continually explores and learns more about the world in which he or she lives and works. It is necessary to know and understand world facts and data, and to keep current with world events that will affect his or her ability to sucessfully engage in global business transactions.

Culture Cue. In dealing with your foreign counterparts, listen as much as you talk. Feel free to talk about your home country, but also ask the people you are meeting to tell you about their country, their customs, and their way of life. This type of conversation helps you to learn more about their part of the world, and it builds rapport. In many parts of the world, rapport and friendship must first be established before business will ever be discussed. This is a critical first step to doing business in many places in the world, including much of Latin America, the Middle East, and Asia.

Resources for Trade and FDI Statistics Worldwide:

CIA—The World Factbook: www.cia.gov/library/publications/the-world-factbook/

UNCTAD—United Nations Conference on Trade and Development Trade Statistics: www.unctad.org/Templates/Page.asp?intItemID=1584&lang=1

OECD—Organisation for Economic Cooperation and Development Statistics Portal: www.oecd.org/statsportal/0,2639,en_2825_293564_1_1_1_1_1,00.html

ISTIA—International Services Trade Information Agency: istia-services.org/

***Financial Times* FDI Portal:** www.locoonline.com/

JETRO—Japan External Trade Organization: http://www.jetro.org/

Multilateral Investment Agency of the World Bank Group FDI in Emerging Markets Portal: www.fdi.net/

FDI Intlligence: www.fdiintelligence.com/

Links to English language newspapers from around the world, listed by country: www.thebigproject.co.uk/news/

LO2-1 Appreciate the magnitude of international trade and how it has grown.

The volume of international trade in goods and services measured in current dollars exceeded $18.9 trillion in 2010. Merchandise exports, at $15.2 trillion, were nearly five times what they were in 1990. Services exports were only $3.7 trillion in 2008, but their rate of growth has been faster than that of merchandise exports.

LO2-2 Identify the direction of trade, or who trades with whom, and trends in such trade.

Developed countries tend to trade with developed countries and they account for a majority of the exports worldwide. More than half of the exports from developing countries also go to developed countries, although this proportion has been declining. The rise of regional trade agreements, as well as other factors, is transforming the volume and direction of world trade in merchandise and services. More than 70 percent of world trade now occurs between members of regional trade agreements.

LO2-3 Outline the theories that attempt to explain why certain goods are traded internationally.

Why do nations trade? Mercantilists did so to build up storehouses of precious metals. Later, Adam Smith's theory of absolute advantage showed that a nation will export goods that it can produce with less labor than can other nations. Ricardo then proved that even though a country is less efficient than other nations, that country can still profit by exporting goods if it holds a comparative advantage in the production of those goods.

Newer explanations for the direction of trade include the idea that a nation tends to export products requiring a large amount of a resource that is relatively abundant in that nation. In contrast to resource endowments, Linder theorized that because customers' tastes are strongly affected by income levels, a nation's income level per capita determines the kinds of goods they will demand. The kinds of goods produced to meet this demand reflect the country's income per capita. International trade in manufactured goods will be greater between nations with similar levels of per capita income. The international product life-cycle theory states that many products first produced in the United States or other developed countries are eventually produced in less developed nations and become imports to the very countries in which their production began. Porter helped to explain how nations can achieve competitive advantage through the emergence of regional clusters, claiming that four classes of variables are critical in this regard: demand conditions; factor conditions; related and supporting industries; and firm strategy, structure, and rivalry. Competitiveness can also be affected by government and by chance.

LO2-4 Explain the size, growth, and direction of foreign direct investment.

The book value of FDI was $19.0 trillion at the beginning of 2010. Although the largest source of this FDI, the proportion of global foreign direct investment accounted for by the United States has been declining, while the proportion accounted for by the European Union has risen. The proportion of FDI originating from the developing nations has also been increasing. On an annual basis, more than 85 percent of the outstanding stock of FDI at the beginning of 2010 came from developed countries.

The annual outflows of FDI often vary substantially, especially in conjunction with global economic cycles. Overall, nearly 8 percent of outward FDI originates from the developed countries, with nearly three-quarters of that money coming from the United States and the EU. In terms of desination for outward FDI, an average of nearly 70 percent of annual FDI investments have been going into developed countries in recent years, although the proportion is declining, with a majority of this investment occurring in the form of acquisitions of existing companies. The level of FDI flowing into developing countries was 7.3 times larger in 2000 versus 1990, and it nearly doubled again by 2009. The direction of FDI follows the direction of foreign trade; that is, developed nations invest in each other just as they trade with each other.

LO2-5 Explain several theories of foreign direct investment.

International investment theory attempts to explain why FDI takes place. Product and factor market imperfections provide firms, primarily in oligopolistic industries, with advantages not open to indigenous companies. The internalization theory states that firms will seek to invest in foreign subsidiaries, rather than license their superior knowledge, to receive a better return on the investment used to develop that knowledge. The dynamic capabilities perspective suggests that firms must have not only ownership of specific knowledge or resources, but also the ability to dynamically create and exploit capabilities in order to achieve success in FDI. The eclectic theory explains an IC's choice of its overseas production facilities. The firm must have location and ownership advantages to invest in a foreign plant. It will invest where it is most profitable to internalize its monopolistic advantage.

Key Words

mercantilism (p. 37)

absolute advantage (p. 38)

comparative advantage (p. 40)

offshoring (p. 40)

exchange rate (p. 42)

currency devaluation (p. 43)

resource endowment (p. 44)

overlapping demand (p. 44)

product differentiation (p. 44)

international product life cycle (IPLC) (p. 44)

economies of scale (p. 46)

experience curve (p. 46)

national competitiveness (p. 46)

portfolio investment (p. 48)

direct investment (p. 48)

monopolistic advantage theory (p. 54)

internalization theory (p. 55)

dynamic capability (p. 55)

eclectic theory of international production (p. 56)

Questions

1. How has trade in merchandise and services changed over the past two decades? What have been the major trends? How might this information be of value to a manager?

2. Knowing that a nation is a major trading partner of another signifies what to a marketing analyst?

3. Describe mercantilism, and explain why mercantilism has been argued to be a poor approach to use in order to promote economic development and prosperity.

4. a. Explain Adam Smith's theory of absolute advantage.

   b. How does Ricardo's theory of comparative advantage differ from the theory of absolute advantage?

5. "The greater part of international trade consists of an exchange of raw materials from developing nations for manufactured goods from developed nations." True or false? Explain.

6. Name some products that you believe have passed through the four stages of the international product life cycle.

7. Use Porter's Diamond Model of national advantage to explain why an emerging market such as Indonesia would be expected to experience great difficulty in achieving global competitiveness in a new industry sector such as "smart" cell phones or hybrid electric-gasoline automobile engines.

8. What are the different components of foreign investment? Why has the distinction between them begun to blur in recent years?

9. How has the level and direction of FDI changed over the past two to three decades, both overall and in terms of annual outflows and inflows? Why would this information be of relevance to managers?

10. According to theories presented in this chapter, why do companies engage in foreign direct investment?

---

globalEDGE globalEDGE.msu.edu

Research Task

Use the globalEDGE site (http://globalEDGE.msu.edu/) to complete the following exercises:

1. A.T. Kearney's annual *Global Services Location Index* (GSLI) evaluates the attractiveness of countries as an offshore destination. Locate the most recent study, and prepare a short report addressing the following questions: How is the Global Services Location Index calculated? According to the ranking, which 10 countries are the best destinations for providing outsourcing activities? Why do you think these countries are attractive as potential location for offshore services?

2. You are working at an automotive company that is currently searching for new opportunities for investment in emerging countries. Visit the *FDI.net* web portal, and find potential investment opportunities in the automotive sector. In which countries are the opportunities being offered? Select one of these opportunities and prepare a brief report summarizing what it entails.

Minicase: Can Brazil Become a Global Competitor in the Information Technology Outsourcing Business?

As the world becomes increasingly dependent on information technology (IT) products and services, the global IT outsourcing industry has expanded rapidly. Driven by global competitive pressures to reduce costs and focus on core competencies, corporations of all sizes have chosen to outsource and offshore many of their IT services. As a result, offshoring of IT services has been growing at a 40 to 50 percent compounded annual rate. Worldwide, India has established a strong leadership position in the IT outsourcing market, accounting for the largest share among countries. However, challenges have begun to emerge for India's IT sector, including increasing labor costs, inadequate physical infrastructure, and a daunting government bureaucracy, among other factors. Many nations, particularly emerging markets in Asia, Latin America, and eastern Europe, have been attempting to capture a share of the IT offshoring business because it is seen as a source of skilled jobs and a basis for improving overall economic development.

Although many people would associate the country with soccer or samba, Brazil has emerged as a global competitor in a range of sophisticated technology sectors. Now, Brazil has launched an active campaign to build a strong international competitive position in the IT offshoring business, trying to attract business that might otherwise be going to these other nations or regions.

Brazil's IT outsourcing sector is small relative to India's, but strong growth is projected based on the country's strengths along several dimensions. As the 5th largest country and 11th most powerful economy in the world, Brazil has a sophisticated telecommunications and network services infrastructure, one that has been rated higher than India or China on such key measures as network availability. Brazil has a tradition of strong engineering schools, capable of producing high-quality technical graduates. With nearly 300,000 people employed in IT services, the size of Brazil's domestic market for IT services is comparable to that of world-leading India, although a much smaller level of IT services are exported. The country has one of the world's most automated and sophisticated banking sectors and a dynamic domestic marketplace for IT software and support services. Brazil also offers a large base of affordable real estate for establishing corporate operations. Brazilian wage rates are about 40 percent of those for comparable hourly positions in the United States.. Employee turnover is only about 20 percent, versus the 40 percent rate that has been plaguing Indian IT companies. Total operating costs, which include labor, infrastructure costs, corporate taxes and incentives, are lower than competitors from most competing low-wage and moderate to-high wage nations. Brazil also boasts only a single time zone difference to the East Coast of the United States and four time zones for the U.S. West Coast and parts of

Europe. This minimal time zone difference provides Brazil with an advantage compared to competitors in China or India in terms of ease of access and coordination with clients and the offshore project support teams. Brazilian business practices, culture, and values are more Westernized than is common for nations such as India and China, which can facilitate shared understanding and effectiveness of working relationships with companies in the United States and western Europe. "The countries share many cultural references—music, movies, television shows, etc. You wouldn't have to explain who Mickey Mouse is to a Brazilian, but that may not necessarily be the case when it comes to somebody from India," explained Carlos Diaz, a vice president for Meta4. "Outsourcing is not just about completing a project; it is also about having a relationship with a vendor that you know and trust. This becomes much trickier when your outsourcing partner has different cultural sensibilities and is on the other side of the world," says Antonio Gil, Chairman of the Brazilian Association of Software and Services Export Companies. As Peter Bendor-Samuel, CEO of Everest, says, "'Yes' in Brazil typically means 'yes.' In India, it may mean 'no.'" Encouraged by strengths such as these, companies such as Accenture, Hewlett-Packard, Electronic Data Systems, Whirlpool, Gap Inc., and IBM have been expanding their offshoring activities in Brazil. In late 2010, IT consultancy CapGemini announced an investment of $298 million into CPM Braxis, a Brazilian IT service provider, in an effort to wrest leadership away from its other global competitors. Even competitors from India, such as Tata Consultancy Services, Infosys, and Wipro, have begun to aggressively expand into Brazil.

Despite the country's many strengths, Brazil also has some limitations. For example, underinvestment in electrical generation could make the country prone to the brownout and blackout problems that have plagued other emerging markets, including India. The Portuguese-speaking Brazilian population has also been characterized as being weak in terms of English-language skills, and there is a shortage of international experience among Brazilian technical and managerial ranks, which could be problematic for multinationals hoping to set up operations there. Only 7 percent of the population of nearly 190 million people has a university degree, and Brazil also suffers from a somewhat cumbersome regulatory climate, including inflexible labor laws, as well as a currency that has been prone to fluctuations over the past several decades. Even with wage inflation in India and China, Brazil's labor costs remain 30 to 40 percent higher. Brazil also has problems in terms of crime and social inequality, especially in big urban centers such as Rio de Janeiro and Sao Paulo.

Questions:

1. Use the theories of international trade and investment that have been presented in this chapter to help explain Brazil's intentions and actions regarding the international information technology sector.

2. What recommendations would you give to the Brazilian government and its outsourcing industry in order to improve their prospects for success in building a strong international competitive position in the information technology outsourcing business?

Sources: Diana Farrell, Martha Laboissiere, and Bruno Pietracci, "Assessing Brazil's Offshoring Prospects," *The McKinsey Quarterly*, 2007 (special edition: Shaping a New Agenda for Latin America), pp. 7–9; Todd Benson, "Brazil Aims to be Outsourcing Giant," *International Herald Tribune*, May 18, 2005, www.iht.com/articles/2005/05/17/business/outsource.php (May 10, 2011); Marco Silva, "Brazil as an Outsourcing Destination," www.sourcingmag.com/content/c060201a.asp (May 10, 2011); Gina Ruiz, "Brazil Seeks Outsourcing Dominance," www.workforce.com/section/hr-management/archive/feature/brazil-seeks-outsourcing-dominance/252397.html (May 10, 2011); Stephanie Overby, "Outsourcing: Brazil Blossoms as IT Services Hub," *CIO*, September 8, 2010, www.cio.com/article/610635/Outsourcing_Brazil_Blossoms_as_IT_Services_Hub (May 10, 2011); and Antonio Regalado, "Soccer, Samba and Outsourcing?" *The Wall Street Journal*, January 25, 2007, www.brazil-it.com/archives/2007/01/soccer_samba_an.php (May 10, 2011).

International Institutions from an International Business Perspective

Every institution not only carries within it the seeds of its own dissolution, but prepares the way for its most hated rival.

—*Dean William R. Inge, 1860–1954, Dean of St Paul's, London*

The United Nations Going Forward: The Paradox of its Evolution

At the closing of World War II, the victorious Allied powers gathered to create an institution to reduce the likelihood of future wars. In their optimism, they formed the United Nations, a supranational institution. According to historian Mark Mazower, the institution had two main objectives: first, to promote peace, since nations themselves and the League of Nations formed after WWI had failed miserably at this; and second, to extend the power of the Allies.* It is this last objective that is of special interest, because it can be understood as an attempt to institutionalize the influence of the Allied powers and to continue their control and dominance long after the war.

This last objective, Mazower argues in *No Enchanted Palace: The End of Empire and the Ideological Origins of the United Nations,* is an attempt to institutionalize their colonial approach and explains the Security Council membership (the United Kingdom, the United States, Russia, France, and China [originally the ROC, and since 1972, the PRC]) and their UN veto power.

The UN is not the empire's enforcer today, though. The major issue that has changed the UN into an organization that protects humanitarian and minority rights developed incrementally, beginning with the UN's endorsement of the creation of the sovereign state of Israel. Mazower points out that in the 1950s and 1960s, the UN supported self-determination; over time, this issue has moved the UN from a major supporter of empire to a forum for anti-colonialism. Today, political decisions are largely made by the G-20, the United States, the EU, NATO, and China—not the UN. The beauty of paradox.

The UN is still dominated by the major powers, yet rather than operate as an enforcer, its purpose centers around its members' shared appreciation of its function as a forum for discussion among all members and a place to share acceptance of legal and diplomatic norms. As a result of its role as a forum, the UN does some important things. It provides international standardization where needed, as with flight patterns and law of the sea, peacekeeping missions, disaster relief, care for refugees, and food security.

Mazower suggests that if we understand the origins and 65-year history of the UN, we will appreciate its evolution and judge it based on what it does. It is not a supranational moral force; it has not lost its moral purpose. It is not an enchanted palace. Rather, it has evolved to become an

learning objectives

In this chapter, you will learn about areas that will enable you to:

LO3-1 **Explain** the importance of international institutions to business decision makers and their firms.

LO3-2 **Describe** the various types of institutions, drawing on institutional theory.

LO3-3 **Outline** the United Nations as an institution and its relevance to international business.

LO3-4 **Describe** the purposes of the two global monetary institutions, the IMF and the World Bank.

LO3-5 **Discuss** the purpose of the World Trade Organization and its impact on international business.

LO3-6 **Discuss** the resources of the Organisation for Economic Cooperation and Development.

LO3-7 **Identify** the levels of economic integration and the effectiveness of the major trading blocs.

LO3-8 **Discuss** the EU, its impact, and its challenges going forward.

important forum, one that nations need in order to discuss and agree on issues that matter and one whose many technical agencies provide the background support needed for peaceful co-existence.

* Mark Mazower, *No Enchanted Palace: The End of Empire and the Ideological Origins of the United Nations,* Princeton, NJ: Princeton University Press, 2009.

We begin this chapter by examining the institutions that are most important to the international manager, moving from those that focus on global cooperation (such as the United Nations, the World Trade Organization, and the International Monetary Fund) to those whose concerns are mainly regional (such as regional trade alliances). Once we comment on why institutions are important to the international manager, we begin with a focus on basics: what institutions are and how they influence the firm.

Strong institutions are important for international decision makers. To illustrate their importance, think about the roles of China and the United States on the global stage: one a superpower, the other a rapidly developing nation preparing for a major global role. Martin Wolfe, chief economist at the *Financial Times,* notes that both nations are fated to cooperate.[1] Yet look at their differences: as Wolfe points out, one is a democracy, the other an autocracy; one is "a child of the enlightenment," the other an agrarian empire. Although working together will not be easy for either, international institutions encourage such efforts and make them more likely to succeed by developing multilateral solutions, in which all nations cooperate.

So at a basic level, institutions are important to business decision makers because they provide ways to settle conflict and resolve disagreements and they provide support and infrastructure for decision makers. For example, the World Trade Organization outlines trade practices among member nations and makes judgments when a member claims the rules have been violated.

The institutions we review in this chapter also provide opportunities for interesting careers. The United Nations and the Organisation for Economic Cooperation and Development routinely have career positions to fill in such fields as economics, languages, law, project management, and information technology. All of the institutions we cover have internship opportunities, as well. For more information, contact the specific organization through its website.

In this chapter, we examine the institutions that are most important to the international manager. The scope of these international institutions, all of which focus on various types of cooperation, is from global to regional; some are inclusive, with memberships composed of many countries, while others are exclusive and have relatively few member-nations. Most are groupings of governments, but there are private institutions that may be critically important to the international manager. Before we examine these institutions, we explore what institutions are and how we might understand their direct influence on the firm.

LO3-1 Explain the importance of international institutions to business decision makers and their firms.

new institutional theory
Understanding of institutions as social constructs, a collection of norms that structure the relations of individuals to one another

Institutions

WHAT ARE INSTITUTIONS AND WHY ARE THEY USEFUL?

Institutions are organizations constructed by a group, society, or culture to achieve a common goal that functions to "provide stability and meaning to social life."[2] A contemporary understanding of institutions suggests that they are a collection of norms that "regulate the relations of individuals to each other."[3] That is, institutions are socially constructed— a group, society, or culture constructs them—and they limit behavior. This approach to understanding institutions, called **new institutional theory,** suggests that decision makers in business might understand institutions as organized collections of basic rules and unwritten codes of conduct that limit and direct the decisions firms can make. Managers might well use a rules-of-the-game image to capture this view of institutions striving to reduce uncertainty in the firm's external environment.[4]

TYPES OF INSTITUTIONS

Institutions influence behavior in several ways. **Formal institutions** operate through laws and regulations, while **informal institutions** use norms, values, customs and ideologies.[5] Formal institutions, such as national governments, are major rule-setters, especially in the geographical area they control, but in some cases, far beyond their borders. Think of the power and the explicit rules of the European Union or of the United States tax authorities. The European Union's Directorate General for Competition is a body that influences the international firm's behavior when it wants to execute a merger or acquisition, even if the companies involved in the proposed transaction are not European. Why? Because if the merged business wants to sell into the EU, its merger or acquisition requires EU approval. The EU can also mandate product composition and computer code openness, as Microsoft has learned in regard to bundling software and sharing code. Formal institutions, then, function to constrain and regulate the firm's behavior through rules, laws, and sanctions—all mechanisms that enforce or coerce compliance. Firms comply with the rules of formal institutions because to do so makes sense; expedience is the basis of firm compliance.

While formal institutions use laws and regulations to gain compliance, informal institutions rely on norms, values, customs, and ideologies to mold behavior. We find two types of informal institutions, normative and cognitive. *Normative* informal institutions establish standards, "propagate principles, and broadly represent 'humanity'."[6] Examples of normative institutions are professional organizations and nongovernmental organizations (NGOs) that influence behavior through shared norms and values. The United Nations is also an informal normative institution. Behavior in this class of institution is influenced through shared norms; compliance is built on social obligation. For example, in the United Nations, members agree to abide by the UN's resolutions because they have so committed publicly to do so, they have accepted social obligations.

The other type of informal institution, the cognitive, is of tremendous importance to the international manager. *Cognitive* institutions use shared ideas to define reality by means of conceptual frameworks or schema. These concept-based informal institutions are often less explicit or tangible and less obvious to the non-native than are the formal institutions or informal normative institutions, because ideas are invisible. Different cognitive institutions contribute greatly to the challenges of international business. We can find examples of cognitive institutions in the contrast between the Japanese and American supplier relationship and in the Chinese concept of *guanxi*.

Supplier relationships contrast greatly between Japan and the United States. Remember our earlier image for institutions as setting the rules of the game? The "supplier game" in Japan calls for the supplier to build a relationship with the potential buyer. Such a relationship allows the firm to build knowledge about the reliability of the supplier, which is most important. Price, then, is likely to not be an early determinant of the buy decision in Japan. In contrast, in supplier relationships in the United States, the game is thought of differently. Price plays a more prominent initial role. Note, too, that the cultural custom in the United States is to share drinks after the deal is sealed, because drinks are a reward. But in Japan, drinks happen before the deal is structured, as a way to build the relationship, and continue during and after. None of these culture-based frameworks (role of price, role of shared drinks, and many other roles) that constitute the supplier process is formalized, yet these assumptions about the right way to negotiate with suppliers are institutionalized and operate to limit behavior choices and reduce uncertainty for the supplier and buyer in both Japan and the United States. Of course, they create uncertainty and confusion for those unaware that these cognitive institutions exist.

Guanxi, a Chinese institution that describes a type of relationship similar to a combination of social capital and mentoring, is another example of an informal cognitive institution. Difficult for non-Chinese to understand at times, *guanxi* relationships carry obligations that may be stronger than civic responsibilities and rational understandings of business situations. So delivering on a *guanxi* obligation may not make business sense to the Westerner,

LO3-2 Describe the various types of institutions, drawing on institutional theory.

formal institutions
Institutions that influence behavior through laws and regulations

informal institutions
Institutions that influence behavior through norms, values, customs and ideologies

but doing so makes perfect psychological and moral sense to the Chinese in such a mentoring relationship.

These examples illustrate that informal institutions, which consist of voluntary agreements or a set of shared assumptions, a bit like the mind's software,[7] exert a powerful influence on how decision makers in the firm understand their environment, and thus, the choices open to the firm in international activities. An international business scholar, Mike Peng, noted that in developing economies, informal institutions tend to play a greater role than in developed economies. One way to think of this relationship is that the informal institutions emerge to bring added order to the chaotic, unstructured environment in the developing economy, which lacks well-developed formal institutions.[8]

Richard Scott developed the framework we are using to describe the types of institutions international managers encounter. Figure 3.1 describes these types of institutions in more detail, including the basis of compliance to their rules or norms, how they institutionalize, the inherent logic at work in them, the basis of their legitimacy, and their indicators or evidence.[9]

To illustrate the importance of strong international institutions, let's think again about the roles of China and the United States on the global stage, one a rapidly developing nation preparing for a major global role, the other a superpower. As Martin Wolfe points out, one is a democracy, the other an autocracy; one "a child of the enlightenment," the other an agrarian empire. Although working together will not be easy for either, international institutions encourage such efforts and make them more likely to succeed by developing multilateral solutions, in which all member nations cooperate. For individual nations, agreeing to abide by a mutually negotiated UN resolution or a World Trade Organization rule is much more acceptable than agreeing to a bilateral negotiation, which tends to be zero sum, with a winner and a loser, and in which power and prestige are at stake. There is no humiliation at stake with a negotiated UN resolution that applies to all nations' behavior. Figure 3.2 shows the influence of institutions on firms, their managers and their behavior.

LO3-3 Outline the United Nations as an institution and its relevance to international business.

United Nations (UN) 192-member organization dedicated to the promotion of peace and stability of the world

The United Nations

The **United Nations (UN)** is probably the best-known worldwide organization. Its 192 member-nations are dedicated to the promotion of peace and global stability. Many of its activities relate directly to business and to the infrastructure on which business operations depend. For example, the UN is responsible for international agreements that directly affect commercial relationships, including much of the body of international law. In addition, as a stabilizing force in the world economy, the UN contributes to the conditions under which international business is conducted. Because the UN operates with voluntary agreements,

FIGURE 3.1

Institutions: Characteristics

Institution type:	Formal	Informal	
Social agreement is:	Regulative	Normative	Cognitive
Compliance based on	Expedience	Social obligation	Predisposition (taken for granted)
Institutionalization based on	Coercion	Norms	Imitation
Logic based on	Means to an end	Appropriateness	Conformance, orthodoxy
Legitimacy based on	Legal enforcement	Moral governance	Cultural support, concept correctness
Indicators/ Evidence	Rules, laws, sanctions,	Certification, accreditation	Prevalence, similarity

Source: J. McNett after W. R. Scott (1995) p. 10.

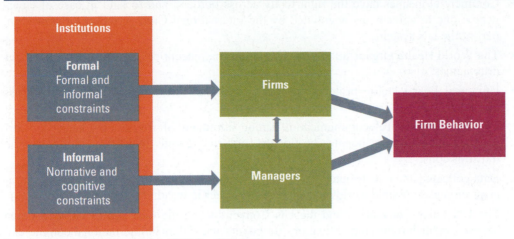

Source: Influenced by W. R. Scott (2008) and W. M. Peng (2002, 2008).

it is largely an informal institution. Here are some general areas in which the UN plays a significant role for international business:

- UN agreements set technical standards and norms. These standards and norms function as the "soft infrastructure" for the global economy. The United Nations Center for Trade Facilitation and Electronic Business (UN/CEFACT) has standardized trade documents and developed standards for electronic data exchange.

- UN efforts prepare the ground for investment in emerging economies and the development of their workforce through a focus on areas such as health, education, governance, and political stability. The United Nations Educational, Scientific, and Cultural Organization (UNESCO) actively promotes literacy for the world's approximately 1.25 billion adults and children (18 percent of the world's total population) who cannot read and write.

- Various UN agencies address the downsides of globalization, such as terrorism, crime, drugs, and arms traffic. Treaties that focus on areas of terrorism such as the taking of hostages have been developed so that agreed-upon responses among UN members exist.

- UN efforts to seek solutions to global environmental problems include the work of the UN Environment Programme (UNEP), the agency that laid the groundwork for the Climate Change Convention, leading to the Kyoto Protocol to reduce greenhouse gases. The UNEP has developed many initiatives that support sustainable business practices.

- The UN addresses education and health issues that require global-level solutions arrived at in partnership with businesses, through the Global Compact, an effort to partner private industry with groups in developing nations.

- The UN promotes social justice and human and labor rights. Central to these concerns is the UN Economic and Social Council.

- Efforts of the UN build the cornerstones of an interdependent world: trust and shared values. The Global Compact provides a framework for businesses that are committed to aligning their operations and strategies with 10 universally accepted principles in the areas of human rights, labor, the environment and anticorruption. This is one example of UN efforts to build trust and shared values.[10]

In addition to the general areas of impact on business just described, the UN has direct impact on the conduct of business in quite specific ways, because UN committees negotiate the global "rules of the game" for the international exchanges of goods, services, money, and information.

- When ships sail freely across the seas and through international straits, they are protected by rules legitimized in UN conferences.

- Commercial airlines have the right to fly across borders, and to land in case of emergency, due to agreements negotiated by the International Civil Aviation Organization, part of the UN system.

- The World Health Organization sets criteria for pharmaceutical quality and standardizes drug names.

- Universal Postal Union protocols prevent losses and allow the mail to move across borders.

- The International Telecommunication Union allotment of frequencies keeps the airwaves from becoming hopelessly clogged, and thus avoids interference among radio transmissions.

- Data collected and redistributed from member-states by the World Meteorological Organization make possible worldwide and country-specific weather forecasts.

- The UN Sales Convention and the UN Convention on the Carriage of Goods by Sea help to establish rights and obligations for buyers and sellers in international commercial transactions.[11]

In terms of direct business engagement with the UN, the site http://business.un.org/ lists collaborations with business, so you can see how many firms, including the National Basketball Association (NBA), Nike, Nestlé, Microsoft, and Starbucks partner with the UN.

UN ORGANIZATION

General Assembly
Deliberative body of the UN made up of all member-nations, each with one vote regardless of size, wealth, or power

Security Council
Main peacekeeping body of the UN, composed of 15 members including 5 permanent members

Economic and Social Council (ECOSOC)
UN body concerned with economic and social issues such as trade, development, education, and human rights

International Court of Justice (ICJ)
UN body that makes legal decisions involving disputes between national governments

The work of the United Nations is carried out through five active bodies, called *organs* in UN terminology. All UN member-nations are members of the **General Assembly,** the main deliberative body in which each nation has one vote regardless of its size, wealth, or power. The General Assembly acts by adopting resolutions that express the will of the member-nations. General Assembly decisions are normative and carry the heavy weight of world opinion, yet they have no legally binding force for governments or citizens in the member-nations. We are presently in the 65th session of the General Assembly, and its open meetings are available via webcast. The daily business of the General Assembly is contained in the *Journal of the United Nations,* available at www.un.org/en/documents/journal.asp in the six UN languages, Arabic, Chinese, English, French, Russian, and Spanish.

The UN **Security Council** has responsibility for maintaining international peace and security. Membership is five permanent members—China, France, the Russian Federation, the United Kingdom, and the United States—each having veto power, and 10 nonpermanent members elected by the General Assembly and representing specific regions to ensure every area is represented. This is the organ that historian Mark Mazower argues was intended to ensure that the Allies continued their political and economic domination after WWII, an effort which, he concludes, has achieved its opposite, the support of minorities and human rights. Presently, the Security Council's peacekeeping operations are active in 14 locations in Africa, the Americas, Europe, Asia and the Pacific, and the Middle East. The UN also sends political missions, such as the one now active in Afghanistan.[12] Current Security Council peacekeeping is illustrated in Figure 3.3 and includes more than 84,000 troops donated by 15 UN members.

The **Economic and Social Council (ECOSOC)** is concerned with economic and social issues, including trade, transport, industrialization, economic development, population growth, children, housing, women's rights, racial discrimination, illegal drugs, crime, social welfare, youth, the human environment, and food. ECOSOC makes recommendations on how to improve education and health conditions and promotes respect for and observation of the human rights and freedom of people everywhere. These are all actions that contribute to a high-quality workforce.

The **International Court of Justice (ICJ),** also known as the World Court, makes legal decisions involving disputes between national governments and gives advisory opinions. Because only nations litigate before the court, governments often intervene on behalf of corporations and individuals in their countries. Even though the court has worldwide

MISSIONS ADMINISTERED BY THE DEPARTMENT OF PEACEKEEPING OPERATIONS

MINURSO — Western Sahara
UNMIK — Kosovo
UNFICYP — Cyprus
UNIFIL — Lebanon
UNAMA* — Afghanistan
UNDOF — Syria
UNMOGIP — India and Pakistan

MINUSTAH — Haiti
UNOCI — Côte d'Ivoire
UNMIL — Liberia
MONUSCO — Dem. Rep. of the Congo
UNAMID — Darfur
UNMIS — Sudan
UNTSO — Middle East
UNMIT — Timor-Leste

Map No. 4259 Rev. 12(E) UNITED NATIONS
January 2011

* political mission

Department of Field Support
Cartographic Section

United Nations, *On the Front Line,* p. 13, http://www.unaids.org/en/media/unaids/contentassets/documents/document/2011/20110519_OnTheFrontLine.pdf. (accessed May 10, 2011).

jurisdiction to hear disputes between governments, it hears relatively few cases. There are presently three cases being heard and 16 cases pending.[13] The ICJ has 15 judges, who come from 15 different countries and serve nine-year terms, appointed by majorities of the General Assembly and the Security Council.

The **Secretariat,** headed by the secretary-general of the United Nations, is the UN's staff. The secretary-general is appointed by the General Assembly on the recommendation of the Security Council for a five-year renewable term. The eighth secretary-general, Ban Ki-Moon of Korea, began his first term in 2007. About 44,000 people from around the world make up the UN Secretariat staff.

Secretariat
The staff of the UN, headed by the secretary-general

UN MILLENNIUM DEVELOPMENT CAMPAIGN

The UN's Millennium Development Campaign was launched at the millennium, 2000. Its goal is to end poverty by 2015. The eight goals include ending hunger, gender equity, universal education, child health, maternal health, combat HIV/AIDS, environmental sustainability, and global partnership. One hundred eighty-nine government leaders have signed on to the Millennium Declaration and endorsed the urgency "to free our fellow men, women and children from the abject and dehumanizing conditions of extreme poverty, to which more than a billion of them are currently subjected."[14] The Millennium goals have fostered

Bretton Woods
1944 conference at which allied nations' treasury and central bank representatives met to establish the International Monetary Fund and the World Bank

International Monetary Fund (IMF)
Institution that fosters global monetary cooperation, financial stability, international trade, high employment and sustainable economic growth, and reduction of poverty

much institutional collaboration, both at the process and technical levels (e.g., the IMF) and the program levels (World Bank loans, UN development work, nongovernmental groups). These collaborations often involve businesses, both as contributors and suppliers to aid programs.

International Monetary Institutions

There are two global monetary institutions, the International Monetary Fund and the World Bank, both established at the Bretton Woods conference, called by the UN in 1944, near the end World War II and held at the Mount Washington Hotel in Bretton Woods, New Hampshire. **Bretton Woods** is significant because it resulted in the world's first negotiated agreement among independent nations to support trade through monetary institutions. These meetings, attended by representatives of the 44 allied nations, set up the **International Monetary Fund (IMF)** to establish rules for international monetary policies and their enforcement and the **World Bank** to lend money for development projects. Since then, the IMF purpose has gained depth and breadth, and now, in addition to fostering global monetary cooperation, it helps nations secure financial stability, facilitate international trade, promote high employment and sustainable economic growth, and reduce poverty.

INTERNATIONAL MONETARY FUND

The premise of the International Monetary Fund, which operates as a collaboration of nations, is that the common interest of all nations in a workable international monetary system far transcends their conflicting national interests.[15] The IMF promotes international monetary cooperation, including orderly exchange arrangements and payments systems, and makes funds available for balance-of-payments corrections. Each of the 187 members contributes funds, known as *quotas,* determined by the nation's relative size in the world economy. The number of votes a nation has is also determined by its quota. Currently, the quota formula is a weighted average of GDP (50 percent), openness (30 percent), economic variability (15 percent), and international reserves (5 percent).[16] Quota changes in 2011 included increases for 54 countries, including China, Korea, Turkey, Brazil, and Mexico, and was approved by IMF members in order to give these dynamic, developing economies a greater role in institutional decision making. Under the new quota system, China has become the third largest vote-holding nation with 6.07 percent of the total votes, while the United States has 16.479 percent, Germany has 5.308, and Japan 6.138.[17]

Quotas are denominated in **Special Drawing Rights (SDRs),** the IMF's unit of account that also serves as an international reserve asset. SDRs are like a paperless currency. The largest member of the IMF is the United States, with a current quota of SDR 37.1 billion (about $58 billion), and the smallest member is Tuvalu, with a current quota of SDR 1.8 million (about $2.7 million). The SDR's value is linked to a basket of currencies: the euro, Japanese yen, pound sterling, and U.S. dollar. The U.S. dollar equivalent of the SDR is posted daily on the IMF's website; the SDR value on July 5, 2011, was $1.60042.

The aggregate quotas form a pool of money from which the IMF can lend. Although the IMF officially deals solely with governments, it also collaborates with many other international institutions because IMF policies and actions have a profound impact on business worldwide. They set the monetary framework for trade. In this chapter, we discuss the major institutions the IMF works along side of in collaborative relationships, including the World Bank, the World Trade Organization and the UN. With the UN, collaboration is especially significant in relation to the UN's Millennium Goals. The IMF also collaborates with various civil society organizations that have complementary interests such as trade unions, nongovernmental organizations, governments, religious organizations, and other civic groups, in order to support their efforts to build financial stability and thereby create the conditions necessary to reduce poverty.

IMF AND EXCHANGE RATES

The IMF Articles of Agreement, which took effect in 1945, set up fixed exchange rates among member-nations' currencies, with **par value** based on gold and the U.S. dollar, which was valued at $35 per ounce of gold. Previously, the gold standard, which had used gold as the common denominator among currencies, had undergone severe pressure, such as during the Great Depression (1929–1933). To illustrate the Bretton Woods system, the British pound's par value was set at US$2.40, the French franc's at US$0.18, and the German mark's at US$0.2732. There was an understanding that the U.S. government would redeem dollars for gold and that the dollar was the only currency to be redeemable for gold. This new system, which lasted from 1944 to 1971, was a dollar-based gold exchange standard. Through it, the U.S. dollar became both a means of international payment and a reserve currency. Later, we will discuss the effects of this arrangement on the U.S. economy and how the currency exchange rate system has evolved. In 1971, President Nixon took the United States off the gold standard by literally closing the gold window at the U.S. Treasury, where people would queue to exchange currency for gold. As the IMF struggles today with core issues related to its purpose in a changing world, some economists think that exchange rates may be an area for renewed IMF focus.

CURRENT IMF ISSUES

The recent global financial crisis has broadened the criticism of the IMF's role in globalization. The IMF works to help economies manage the risks inherent in globalization such as globalized capital markets whose unpredictable and rapid changes challenge economies. IMF economists focus on providing technical assistance with exchange rate issues, macroeconomic policy and financial sector stability. And therein lies the issue.

World Bank
Institution that lends money for development projects

Special Drawing Rights (SDRs)
An international reserve asset established by the IMF

par value
Stated value

IMF aid is often tied to a country's following IMF advice for achieving increased financial stability, which often includes a reduction of both budget deficits and inflation. These measures, monetarist in their approach, actually tend to increase local poverty short term. They also inhibit the governments of developing nations that are implementing these monetarist measures from making significant progress in areas that are important to social development such as public health, poverty reduction, and education.

Important to note is the position the IMF is in. Its purpose is to help governments manage their economic adjustment to globalization, yet it has influence only on the nations to which it lends. The IMF does not presently lend to either China or the United States. Yet the U.S. deficit and the Chinese surplus (along with an overvalued currency) are the result, many argue, of major currency imbalances that have contributed to the global financial and economic crisis. In addition, when IMF advice to devalue currency was taken by borrowers in the past, it created domestic problems, and, China argues, was the leading cause of Japan's decline as a global power.[18] IMF intervention, although at times successful, has also led to significant social unrest, as it did in Argentina and Kenya.

Rebalancing the global economy is a critical IMF goal, and so far, the recovery has been uneven, with increased growth in developing economies and slower recovery in developed economies.[19] Going forward, the IMF realizes it needs to develop better tools and measures. In a post–financial crisis rethink, it has committed to questioning all of its traditional approaches and indicators.

Other criticisms of the IMF include that it has helped to strengthen the economies of dictatorial regimes, thereby contributing to the growth of markets attractive to American and European multinational firms. This critique is accurate. The IMF does not apply a political litmus test, but rather, an economic one. Presently, the IMF is changing its quota allocation to give developing nations a louder voice in decision making and undertaking a serious rethink of all that it does. These and other actions suggest that the IMF appears to have recognized at least the partial validity of these criticisms and is addressing them.

THE WORLD BANK

The World Bank was established along with the IMF at the Bretton Woods meeting in order to address development issues. Organized into two major and three smaller institutions, it functions as a nonprofit cooperative for its member-nations, able to pass on its ability to borrow funds at low rates to developing nations. Membership in the World Bank Group varies by institution, and the two major institutions, the International Bank for Reconstruction and Development (IBRD), also known simply as the World Bank, and the International Development Association (IDA) have 187 and 170 members, respectively. Both institutions loan to countries to support their development. The IBRD's focus is on middle-income nations with GDPs from $1,000 to $10,000 per capita, where 70 percent of the world's poor are located, and creditworthy poor nations. IDA focuses on the 79 poorest nations, 39 of which are in Africa. IDA provides interest-free loans, called *credits,* and grants for development projects, with the largest number of projects in the water, sanitation and flood protection, transportation, health, education, agriculture, and law and justice sectors. Begun in 1960, it has conducted projects totaling $221.9 billion,[20] saving lives and improving standards of living for hundreds of thousands of people. In recent years, IDA credits and grants have averaged $13 billion per year, and more than 50 percent have gone to Africa.[21] The healthy growth of these nations is important to business because billions of people are joining the world economy as their living standard rises. Developing nations account for more than half the increase in import demand since 2000; their share of global gross domestic product has risen to 43.4 percent in 2010, according to the World Bank.[22] The World Bank interactive map at http://geo.worldbank.org/ has map, satellite, and hybrid views of current World Bank projects.

There are three more institutions that participate in the World Bank Group. The International Finance Corporation (IFC) invests in companies and financial institutions in developing countries to build domestic capital markets so that local entrepreneurs have access to funding. The Multilateral Investment Guarantee Agency (MIGA) encourages FDI in developing economies and guarantees private-sector investment through political risk insurance, technical assistance, and dispute mediation. Finally, the International Centre for the Settlement of Investment Disputes (ICSID) helps to resolve disputes between governments and foreign investors, and, in that way, helps build foreign direct investment. Presently there are 121 cases being heard, and their procedural details are available for review. Among the cases is one filed by former Zimbabwean farmers against the Republic of Zimbabwe for the taking of their property, and another involves several tobacco companies, including Philip Morris, against the Republic of Uruguay.[23]

World Trade Organization

The **World Trade Organization (WTO)** is the only global international organization designed to establish and help implement rules of trade between nations. Since its beginning in 1995, the WTO's goal has been to reduce or eliminate trade barriers and restrictions worldwide to help producers of goods and services, exporters, and importers conduct their business by reducing costs. The WTO is a rules-based, member-driven organization with decisions negotiated by all the member governments. It negotiates member agreements to establish rules for equitable trade—rules that limit the possible actions governments may take in their trade relationships, thereby increasing trade flows. The WTO currently has 153 members, which represents 97 percent of world trade. All of these members sign on to every WTO agreement.

LO3-5 Discuss the purpose of the World Trade Organization and its impact on international business.

World Trade Organization (WTO)
An international organization that deals with rules of trade between nations

WTO PRINCIPLES

In WTO negotiations, members have established five basic principles, norms on which the global trade system rests:[24]

1. *Trade without discrimination.* This is the most-favored nation (MFN) principle, and it requires that nations treat all WTO members equally. If one nation grants another nation a special trade deal, that deal has to be extended to all WTO members. Another aspect of nondiscrimination is that foreigners and locals should be treated equally. In practice, this means that imported goods, once they are in the market, should not face discrimination.

2. *Freer trade, gradually, through negotiation.* Lower trade barriers encourage trade growth. WTO agreements establish "progressive liberalization" through gradual changes. Developing economies are given longer to make adjustments.

3. *Predictability, through binding and transparency.* Predictability helps businesses know what their real costs will be. The WTO operates with tariff "bindings," or agreements to not raise a specific tariff over a given time period. Such promises are as good as lowering a tariff because they give businesspeople realistic data. Transparency, making trade rules as clear and accessible as possible, also helps businesspeople anticipate a stable future.

4. *Promotion of fair competition.* Although many describe the WTO as a "free trade" organization, and it certainly does work toward trade liberalization, the WTO also realizes that trade relationships among nations can be exceedingly complex. Many WTO agreements support fair competition in agriculture, services, and intellectual property, discouraging subsidies and the dumping of products at prices below the cost of their manufacture.

5. *Encouragement of development and economic reform.* Three-quarters of WTO members are developing economies and those transitioning to market economies. These nations are active in the WTO's current **Doha Development Agenda** or extended conference. One of Doha's goals is that developed countries provide market access to goods from the very least developed countries and increase technical assistance for them. Developed countries have started to allow duty-free and quota-free imports for many products from the least developed countries, but agriculture remains a difficult area in which to build agreement.

Doha Development Agenda
WTO extended conference on trade

At 2001, WTO talks begun in Doha, Qatar, member governments agreed to launch a new agenda and to work on trade-related issues between developed and developing economies. The WTO membership has recognized that developing nations face constraints that limit their ability to benefit from the WTO trading system, especially on issues around trade in textiles, clothing, agriculture, and fish. The WTO initiated an aid program, the Aid for Trade initiative, in 2007 to provide assistance to WTO members for infrastructure, technical support, and productive capacity—three areas that affect a developing nation's ability to gain from trade agreements. In 2008, Aid for Trade received approval from all WTO members and its implementation over the last three years appears to have been effective. Yet the Doha Development Agenda has seen discord on many other issues connected to the trading needs of developing nations. Doha talks held in 2003 in Cancun, Mexico, collapsed when delegates from developing nations in Africa, the Caribbean, and Asia left the meeting over disagreement with the developed nations over agricultural issues. Twenty-one nations banded together to make the case that the agricultural subsidies wealthy nations pay to their own farmers undermine poor farmers around the world. In June 2004, the WTO delegates agreed to debate a proposal from the developing nations calling for the reduction and elimination of agricultural tariffs. Then in 2005, Brazil successfully sued the United States in the WTO over cotton subsidies. The United States and the EU have each agreed in principle to reduce agricultural subsidies. Ongoing Doha discussions were held in 2010 and are scheduled for 2011.

In addition to agriculture, property rights remain a difficult negotiation area for WTO members. We discuss intellectual property rights in Chapter 7, but we mention them here because, although they are a sticking point in the Doha discussions, some progress has been made in this area. Discussion of **trade-related intellectual property rights (TRIPS)** has so far led to agreement on 20-year patents and 50-year copyrights. Intellectual property rights violations are endemic in several industries, such as music, software, and pharmaceuticals, and tend to occur in a small group of developing countries, with music and software piracy rampant in China and pharmaceutical patent violations legendary in India, China, and Brazil. The WTO has negotiated a basic agreement that property rights should not take precedence over public health. Any country that adopts TRIPS will have the right to copy drugs patented before 1995. The WTO has also established a system of compulsory licensing that mandates that copyright holders license producers in developing countries. From 1972 to 2005, India did not have property rights protection for pharmaceuticals, which led to a huge generic drugs export market. India's joining the WTO agreement has provided patent protection for pharmaceuticals there while, at the same time, ensuring that its citizens have access to health care.

The Doha Round's discussions continue to be contentious. The recent global financial crisis, which the bloc of developing nations understands to have been caused by problems in developed nations yet solved largely by their own developing economies, has added some animosity and distrust to the discussions. Yet the major players are still in the discussions and have committed to moving Doha forward.[25] There are many issues of concern for WTO members, including farmers, women, and entrepreneurs all trying to build success in developing economies. China and India offer a sense of the WTO's possibilities. Together, they account for one-third of the global population, and in both countries, as a result of increased trade, absolute poverty has declined. All WTO members realize that for global trade to work, the rising tide must lift all boats. The future growth of world trade and the economic health of developed nations depend on getting globalization right so that all participants benefit from trade. New markets, an educated workforce, economic growth, and political stability in emerging nations are all important for international business.[26]

We must mention, though, the more cynical view of these international institutions that is touched on in this chapter's opening. It may be the case that the current problematic issues in many international institutions—including the IMF's lack of effectiveness in the global crisis, the World Bank's seeming loss of purpose, and the WTO's inability to resolve the problems in the Doha Round—are signs of the final efforts of the major post–World War II powers to maintain control of the global economy. If that is the case, true multilateralism lies ahead of us, with the fuller participation of India and China.

trade-related intellectual property rights (TRIPS)
Refers to the WTO agreement that protects copyrights, trademarks, trade secrets, and other intellectual property matters

IMF Sees a Growing Africa and So Does China

The IMF has increased its growth predictions for Africa in both 2010 and recently in 2011. Presently the IMF has forecast 5.5 percent growth for sub-Saharan Africa for 2011 and as much as 5.8 percent for 2012. Although African economies suffered in the recent financial crisis, with their growth cut at around 50 percent, they had resilient comebacks, largely based on increased trade with China and with other countries in Asia and Latin America. Most sub-Saharan African economies were able to avoid slipping into recession. African growth comes at a time when the United States and Europe are still dealing with recovering from the global recession.[a]

Africa's major trading partner is the EU, based on relationships from former colonial ties in many cases, but China has become one of Africa's major trading partners in the past few years, especially in the oil, minerals, and banking sectors. China is also active in FDI for infrastructure projects such as dams and highways. China is interested in Africa for energy-related natural resources, of course, but China also recognizes that Africa is online to emerge as a powerful, large market following India and China. China is good at taking a long-term view!

Questions:

1. What could China's activity in Africa mean for the U.S.?
2. What are some of the cultural issues a Chinese expat might face in Beijing?

[a]IMF, blog-imfdirect.imf.org/category/economic-outlook/ (accessed March 14, 2011).

Recently, in part, because WTO progress on trade liberalization and addressing the inequities of globalization has been slow, regional trade agreements have grown, to fill the gap. The WTO reports that in mid-2010, more than 474 regional trade agreements were in existence.[27] Agreements such as the European Union and the North American Free Trade Agreement may weaken the WTO, because they disrupt or limit the trade of excluded nations. Because most of these trade agreements are among developed nations, the impact on developing nations could be substantial. After a short focus on the Organisation for Economic Development, we will look at these trade agreements and the process they represent, economic integration.

Organisation for Economic Cooperation and Development

The **Organisation for Economic Cooperation and Development (OECD)** is often called the "rich man's club" because today it is composed of 34 of the wealthiest nations in the world (see Table 3.1).[†] Discussions leading to membership, though, are open to all nations committed to a market economy and a pluralistic democracy. The OECD supports governments in their efforts to increase economic growth, fight poverty, maintain financial stability, and help non-member-nations' economic development.[28]

Developed from an earlier World War II collaboration that administered distribution of the U.S. Marshall Plan aid in Europe, the OECD provides information on economic and other activities within its member-nations and is a forum through which to discuss shared economic and social policy issues. OECD publishes extensive research on a wide variety of international business and economic subjects. These publications and resource materials are valuable to researchers and businesspeople.

LO3-6 Discuss the resources of the Organisation for Economic Cooperation and Development.

Organisation for Economic Cooperation and Development (OECD) Group of developed countries dedicated to promoting economic expansion in its member-nations

[†]Note that OECD uses the British spelling of *organisation* in its name.

TABLE 3.1	OECD Member Countries		
Australia	France	Korea	Slovenia
Austria	Germany	Luxembourg	Spain
Belgium	Greece	Mexico	Sweden
Canada	Hungary	Netherlands	Switzerland
Chile	Iceland	New Zealand	Turkey
Czech Republic	Ireland	Norway	United Kingdom
Denmark	Israel	Poland	United States
Estonia	Italy	Portugal	
Finland	Japan	Slovak Republic	

The OECD has been instrumental in many areas, including encouraging member-nations to eliminate bribery, to establish a code of conduct for multinational companies, and to propose the adoption of specific legislation. The Business and Industry Advisory Committee (BIAC) of OECD, created in 1962 to represent business and industry, works in various areas that concern business, such as trade liberalization, sustainable development, e-commerce, taxation, and biotechnology. Information about the BIAC can be found at www.biac.org. OECD's highly regarded individual country surveys are found at www.oecd.org. They are a good complement to the Central Intelligence Agency's *World Factbook,* found at www.cia.gov/library/publications/the-world-factbook/, for reliable demographic and economic information. These sites are a good place to begin country-level research.

LO3-7 Identify the levels of economic integration and the effectiveness of the major trading alliances.

free trade area (FTA)
Area in which tariffs among members have been eliminated, but members keep their external tariffs

customs union
Collaboration that adds common external tariffs to an FTA

common market
Customs union that includes mobility of services, people, and capital within the union

complete economic integration
Integration on economic and political levels

Economic Integration Agreements

Often, economic cooperation begins with an agreement to have a free trade area, such as the North American Free Trade Agreement (NAFTA) among Canada, Mexico, and the United States. In a **free trade area (FTA),** tariffs are abolished among the members, but each member-nation maintains its own external tariffs on goods from countries in the rest of the world. So members have free trade among themselves but have their own individual trade restrictions with nonmember nations. Within the FTA, restrictions generally remain on the movement of services (such as accounting, insurance, and legal services), people (labor), and capital. An example of an FTA in addition to NAFTA is the Central American Integration System (Belize, Costa Rica, El Salvador, Guatemala, Honduras, Nicaragua, and Panama). There are also many FTAs (e.g., with South Korea) being negotiated but not yet in effect.

An FTA often develops into a **customs union,** an agreement that adds common external tariffs to the FTA. Examples are the Southern African Customs Union (SACU), with membership of South Africa, Lesotho, Namibia, Swaziland, and Botswana; the Common Market of the South (Mercosur or Mercosul), with membership of Argentina, Brazil, Paraguay, and Uruguay, plus the anticipated joining of Venezuela in 2011; and the Andean Community (Peru, Ecuador, Bolivia, and Colombia). FTAs are illustrated in Figure 3.4.

Progressing from the FTA and the customs union, the next level of economic integration is a **common market,** created when a customs union lifts restrictions on the mobility of services, people, and capital among the member-nations. Mercosur plans to develop in this direction. A common market is essentially a single market, so all of the barriers to trade, such as standards, borders, and taxes, become common. To achieve this level of economic integration, common market members establish common economic policies, an achievement that requires a great deal of political will.

Eventually the common market agreement may move toward an agreement for **complete economic integration,** as has happened with the EU. Such integration involves a high degree of political integration, which requires member-nations to surrender important elements of their sovereignty. For example, in the EU a central bureaucracy is responsible for coordinating and harmonizing tax rates, labor systems, education systems, and other social and legal

FIGURE 3.4   Free Trade Areas and Customs Unions

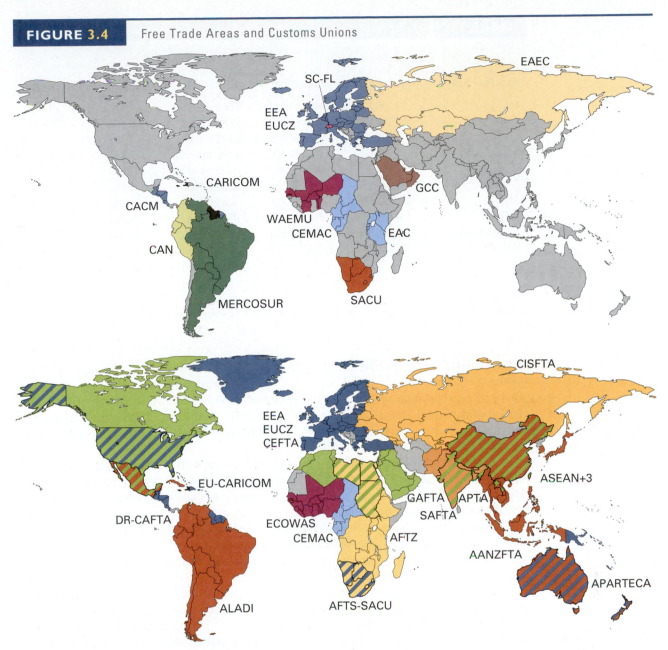

Source: http://en.wikipedia.org/wiki/File_Customs_unions.png.

systems for all EU members, while the European Central Bank develops monetary policy. A single currency, the euro, has been established to replace member-nations' currencies and is used in 17 of the member-states. It is also used by at least six non-EU countries or entities (such as the Vatican) as official currency.

Trading blocs such as FTAs and common markets impact the international firm due both to the cost reductions they bring to those inside the integrated area, through reductions in tariffs, quotas, and other trade barriers, and to the cost increases they bring to those firms outside the trading bloc. Table 3.2 compares the relative sizes of the major trading blocs and trading nations.

EXAMPLES OF ECONOMIC INTEGRATION AGREEMENTS

The **North American Free Trade Agreement (NAFTA)** created a free trade area among Canada, Mexico, and the United States that came into existence on January 1, 1994. Since its establishment, NAFTA has paved the way for strong economic growth

North American Free Trade Agreement (NAFTA)
Agreement creating a free trade area among Canada, Mexico, and the United States

TABLE 3.2   Major Regional Trading Blocs and Trading Nations

Regional Bloc	Area (sq km)	Population	GDP (US$)	GDP per Capita	Members
EU	3,976,372	492,387,344	$14.9 trillion	32,900	27
NAFTA	21,783,895	460,986,859	17.62 trillion	38,222	3
China	9,596,960	1,336,718,015	9.872 trillion	7,400	—
India	3,287,590	1,189,172,906	4.046 trillion	3,400	—
Russia	17,075,200	138,739,892	2.229 trillion	15,900	—
Canada	9,984,670	34,030,589	1.335 trillion	39,600	—
Mexico	1,972,550	113,724,226	1.56 trillion	13,800	—
ASEAN	4,435,830	591,841,000	1.496 trillion*	4,873	10
United States	9,826,675	313,232,044	14.72 trillion	47,400	—
World	6,928,198,253	6,790,062,216	74.43 trillion (2010 est.)	11,110 (2010 est.)	

*nominal, not PPP

Sources: CIA, *World Factbook,* 2011, www.cia.gov/cia/publications/factbook/, figures are estimates; ASEAN Trade Database, February 2011, www.asean.org.

and prosperity based on liberalized trade among the three members. Through NAFTA, the three countries have created one of the world's largest free trade zones—one of the most powerful productive forces in the global economy. Trade in North America is now virtually tariff free. The last trade area to have tariffs dropped was U.S. corn exports into Mexico, where the many small farmers have had transitional protection from U.S. corn imports.[29]

African countries have formed regional trade groups to promote economic growth throughout the continent. Most African countries, though, have their main trade relationships with developed countries, in many cases with former colonial powers. One exception to that observation must be made. China's increasing involvement in African trade and FDI is an interesting development that may lead to economic growth for Africa.[30] When China began its current reforms targeted toward development in the 1970s, it was poorer than Africa and faced more challenging institutional issues. Its education system was worse and its agricultural issues more daunting.

Except for South Africa and Nigeria, African economies are small and underdeveloped and, therefore, marginalized. Their governments face daunting challenges: infrastructure development; public health needs connected to HIV/AIDS, tuberculosis, and malaria; corruption; and insurgencies and civil wars. Their unstable environment is not conducive to economic growth, yet the economic collaborations persevere. Five of these groups are the Economic Community of West African States (ECOWAS), the Common Market for Eastern and Southern Africa (COMESA), the Southern African Development Community (SADC), the African Free Trade Zone (AFTZ), and the African Union (AU).

Mercosur or Mercosul, the Common Market of the South

A South American customs union of Argentina, Paraguay, Brazil, and Uruguay

Mercosur (Spanish) or **Mercosul** (Portuguese) is an acronym for the Common Market of the South, whose members are Argentina, Brazil, Paraguay, and Uruguay. Their goal is a common market and their alliance has made progress. Most trade within Mercosur is tariff free, and members have adopted a common external tariff on most products. Venezuela has been approved for membership and may join Mercosur soon. Regional trade agreements in Central and South America are mapped in Figure 3.5.

The Central American Free Trade Agreement (DR-CAFTA) includes the United States, Guatemala, Honduras, Nicaragua, El Salvador, Costa Rica, and the Dominican Republic. Although there is criticism of DR-CAFTA because it is asymmetrical (the aggregate GDP of the Central American members is equal to around 0.5 percent of the U.S. GDP), trade figures report substantial growth in the DR-CAFTA economies, a solid portion of which is attributable to the influence of this free trade area. Other Central and South American trade agreements include the Andean Community (CAN), whose members are Colombia, Peru,

FIGURE 3.5

Regional Trade
Agreements in
Central and South
America

Andean Community Central American Free Trade Zone Mercosur None
+ Dominican Republic, United States

Ecuador, and Bolivia. Venezuela decided in 2006 to withdraw from the Andean Community and is now on the threshold of membership in Mercosur.

In Asia, the **Association of Southeast Asian Nations (ASEAN)** was formed to foster peaceful relations among members and offer mutual protection against the growth of communism in their region. So it began as a cooperative military and security arrangement, something like the North American Treaty Organization (NATO). Military alliances have an impact on trade, so it is not surprising that ASEAN's security cooperation has led to economic cooperation. Because Southeast Asia is one of the fastest-developing and most dynamic economic regions in the world, ASEAN (Brunei, Cambodia, Indonesia, Laos, Malaysia, Myanmar [formerly Burma], the Philippines, Singapore, Thailand, and Vietnam) has increasing significance. ASEAN's initial agreement to noninterference in each other's internal affairs has allowed them to overcome conflict among themselves and to build the cohesion and mutual values needed for a common market. A subsidiary group, ASEAN+3 adds China, Japan, and South Korea to foster Asian cooperation and financial stability. ASEAN is mapped in Figure 3.6.

The European Union, which we look at next, has developed from a customs union to a common market and then beyond, with added political integration. Our review looks at the EU's development, then its basic organization, and finally, its impact and prospects.

Association of Southeast Asian Nations (ASEAN) Agreement among Southeast Asian nations that began as a security agreement and has developed toward a common market

The European Union

EU DEVELOPMENT

Left in a shambles by World War II, Europeans faced rebuilding their society aware that previous economic and political systems had failed them. Out of this awareness slowly developed a willingness to relinquish some aspects of national sovereignty for the greater

LO3-8 **Discuss** the EU, its impact, and its challenges going forward.

FIGURE 3.6

ASEAN Members

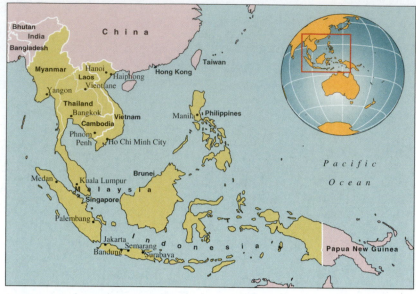

● Members of Association of Southeast Asian Nations (ASEAN).

Source: Association of Southeast Asian Nations

European Union (EU)
A body of 27 European countries committed to economic and political integration

economic and political good. In 1950, French foreign minister Robert Schuman began the process with the integration of the coal and steel industries into a common market, the European Coal and Steel Community (ECSC). The initial six members—Belgium, West Germany, France, Italy, Luxembourg, and the Netherlands—signed the Treaty of Rome in 1957, which established a common market among the six members. By 1967, this core group had established the European Community (EC), with a European Parliament, a European Commission, and a Council of Ministers. Then, in 1993, the EC members signed the Maastricht Treaty, which established the **European Union (EU),** with three areas of integration: the economic community, foreign policy, and domestic affairs. Denmark, Ireland, and the United Kingdom joined the EU's six founding members in 1973, followed by Greece in 1981; Spain and Portugal in 1986; and Austria, Finland, and Sweden in 1995. The European Union welcomed 10 new countries in 2004: Cyprus, the Czech Republic, Estonia, Hungary, Latvia, Lithuania, Malta, Poland, Slovakia, and Slovenia. In 2007, Bulgaria and Romania joined. Presently there are four candidate countries: Croatia, the former Yugoslav Republic of Macedonia, Iceland, and Turkey—all of which have been approved for accession with entry dates still to be set, and Serbia, Albania, Bosnia and Herzegovina, Montenegro, and Kosovo (under UN Security Council Resolution 1244) are in talks to join the candidates. Today, the European Union's 27 member-countries constitute most of the economic, industrial, and population strengths of Europe.[31] The population of the EU is about 500 million people, just under 60 percent larger than that of the United States. The EU has 7.3 percent of the world's population, and it is the largest trader in the world, with 17.1 percent of merchandise trade. In comparison, the United States is the second-largest trader, with 16 percent.[32] Notable are the western European countries that have rejected membership in the EU—Switzerland and Norway—both of which made the decision not to join based on national elections. Figure 3.7 shows a map of the present EU.

European Monetary Union (EMU) or Economic and Monetary Union
EU group that established use of the euro in the 17-country euro zone

The EU is a supranational body that has become a regional government. With passage of the Lisbon Treaty, which came into effect in 2009, the EU has modernized its institutions, made them more democratic, and moved forward with integration in the areas of foreign affairs, security, and justice. The **European Monetary Union (EMU),** or **Economic and Monetary Union,** as it is known in Europe, already has established a common currency used in 17 of the EU member-countries. The euro (€) is also used widely as a reserve currency, as an alternative to the dollar. The EU represents its members at the WTO and has

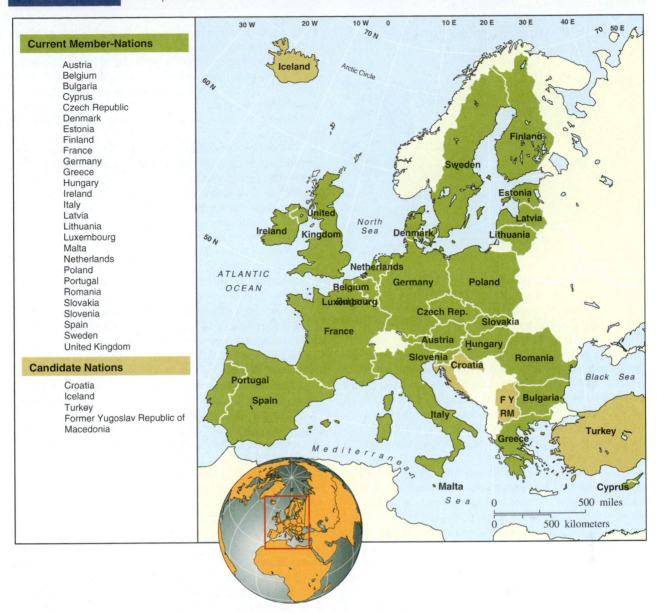

Current Member-Nations

Austria
Belgium
Bulgaria
Cyprus
Czech Republic
Denmark
Estonia
Finland
France
Germany
Greece
Hungary
Ireland
Italy
Latvia
Lithuania
Luxembourg
Malta
Netherlands
Poland
Portugal
Romania
Slovakia
Slovenia
Spain
Sweden
United Kingdom

Candidate Nations

Croatia
Iceland
Turkey
Former Yugoslav Republic of Macedonia

Source: European Union, http://europa.eu/abc/maps/index_en.htm, 12 March, 2011 © European Commission.

both the European Commission and the European Council presidents representing it at the G20 (Group of 20 nations' finance and central bank officials who meet to discuss key economic issues), in addition to the individual national representatives from France, Germany, Italy, and the United Kingdom. Recently, the European commissioner for economic and monetary affairs called for EU representation at the IMF as well.[33] EU members use EU passports and can move and work freely among EU countries, for the most part; the EU can tax member-nations directly and implement legislation directly in each of the member-nations; and the European Court of Justice has power to impose fines and other sanctions on individuals, companies, and member-nations that are found to violate EU agreements. A regional government is well under way.

The EU is organized into nine main institutions with functions similar to those performed by a national government. The **European Parliament** represents the people of Europe and is elected from member-states. Its sessions are available live at www.europarl.europa.eu. The **Council of the European Union** represents the member-states and is the

European Parliament
EU legislative body whose members are popularly elected from member-nations

Council of the European Union
The EU's primary policy-setting institution

THE GLOBAL PATH AHEAD

Katie Emick: International experience can target both inside and outside

I was born and raised in Morgan Hill, CA, until leaving for college in 2008. I spent much of my childhood travelling to our ranch in Oregon and going on annual camping trips, which instilled in me a deep love for the outdoors. I was very active in sports my whole life and went on to be MVP of the league for my varsity basketball team. I also participated in many triathlons, half-marathons, and other outdoor sporting events, trying to keep up with a family of professional athletes. My strong passion for the mountains has led me to become an active backpacker and snowboarder, and I hope to summit some of the world's tallest peaks during my lifetime.

While studying international business at Cal Poly in San Luis Obispo, I developed a more comprehensive understanding of the frameworks that govern international business and the many forces that drive the global arena. My most immediate goal following graduation is to work abroad as an intern or employee of an international company and gain tangible experience in dealing with the complexities of foreign environments. Given my partial fluency in Spanish and my strong interest in Latin America, I am pursuing opportunities in Spanish-speaking countries. I believe that to develop my full potential, I must immerse myself in an unfamiliar setting and harness the abundant learning opportunities that arise from living and working abroad.

Regarding long-term goals, my ideal profession would be in international management, coordinating strategic activities across a broad range of functions and countries. I hope to establish myself as a valuable asset in a multinational corporation by leveraging my ability to organize tasks, build cohesive networks, and respond to cultural diversity. I am also an active supporter of sustainable development and business practices, and will pursue a career that allows me to incorporate these values and foster sustainable solutions. At this stage in my life, my desire to pursue an international internship is inspired by a compelling drive to continue exploring, learning, and integrating myself into the global network. The opportunity to gain hands-on experience will enhance my business skills and cultural responsiveness, making me more qualified and better prepared for a career in international business.

I was exposed to the world of international business at an early age. My mother, a VP of Global Services for IBM, was constantly on international assignment, travelling to more than 30 countries a year. I became accustomed to the idea of a truly global career and was introduced to the inner workings of one of the world's largest and most global corporations. My mom has been very active in promoting the role of women in international business and implementing sustainable solutions around the world. With this upbringing, I developed a keen passion for travel, international networking, and sustainable development, and thus set my course towards a dynamic and geographically dispersed career.

In 2010, my mom, sister and I founded Rooted In Hope, a nonprofit organization dedicated to environmental awareness and sustainable growth. Although the organization is still in its early stages, we have successfully completed our first two international projects and are currently raising funds for future endeavors. The projects were based in Kenya, where Rooted In Hope volunteers and members of the local community planted over 3,000 trees. As Vice President and CFO of this organization, I have played an active role in global networking, project management, and financing operations, all of which have allowed me to apply and further develop my skills as an international business student.

Along with a lifetime of exposure to international business, my desire to pursue a career in the field has also been stimulated by my countless experiences travelling abroad. Prior to deciding on a college or a field of study, I travelled to Brazil and several countries in Europe and the Caribbean. These trips further heightened my interest in travel, and by the time I was admitted to Cal Poly, I was fully committed to studying international business. In my last year as an undergraduate, I travelled on Semester-at-Sea, where I had the opportunity to simultaneously study international business (on board the ship) and witness the context and concepts of what I was studying first-hand (in 13 countries).

During the Semester-at-Sea voyage, I visited 13 countries and over 30 major cities, many of which face the challenges of rampant poverty and overpopulation. To prepare for the voyage, and also out of interest and curiosity, I researched the locations where I would be travelling and made a "guide book" for myself. In addition, I spoke with many personal contacts who had experience in these foreign countries and who gave me important travel advice for each of the locations. I approached the voyage with adequate preparation and set off confidently with an open mind. The voyage confirmed my belief that, in order to make the most out of an international experience, one should enter foreign cultures filled with anticipation rather than expectation.

One of the many profound experiences I had during my trip was a visit to Varanasi, the oldest living civilization on Earth and the heart of the Hindu religion. At the banks of the river Ganges, Hindus engage in religious rituals and perform ceremonial cremations. While we were rowing down the river in a small boat, two corpses floated by (one baby and one adult male). Just yards away, Hindus were bathing and drinking the same sacred water. I allowed myself to take in the moment and absorb the images through a new set of eyes, trying to see life as these people see it. Shortly after, we weaved our way through the narrow crowded alleys, making way for cows and batting off overzealous vendors. I was lucky enough to be standing directly under a local Indian using his second story window as a lavatory. Talk about a tangible experience! (don't worry-no parasites transmitted . . .) The atmosphere painted a vivid contrast between the

(continued)

rapid development of Western society and the unchanged perpetuity of ancient traditions. My experiences in Varanasi penetrated and transformed my entire perspective of the world and existence, directly exposing me to the vast disparities that exist among cultures. This allowed me to expand my whole realm of consciousness and taught me more in the blink of an eye than I have learned in all my years as a student.

One of the biggest challenges I faced abroad was transportation within the countries, particularly the densely populated cities with weak infrastructure. The language barriers present obvious complications and the chaotic flow of traffic can be overwhelming to foreigners accustomed to the advanced transportation systems of developed countries. Even in advanced countries such as Japan, language barriers presented significant challenges. In many places, Americans are vulnerable targets for exorbitant pricing by locals, and it is difficult to dispute prices while avoiding confrontation. In some cases, I quickly learned the public transit systems and used them effectively to get around the large cities. However, I spent many times trying to cope with being utterly lost, completely ripped off, or trying to communicate using only gestures and drawings. Like learning foreign transit systems, most of the challenges I confronted abroad are ones that can only be understood and appreciated by experiencing them first-hand.

Another challenge I encountered while travelling with 600 other American students was witnessing the cultural insensitivity of some of the students I travelled with. Although this rarely resulted in immediate problems (unfortunately there are some exceptions), it left a lasting impression, which made me more conscious of my respect and behavior in foreign countries. The following is an excerpt from my travel journal, describing an experience on a bus from Casablanca to Marrakech:

I watched out the window as we passed primitive Berber villages, with huts made of mud and sand, donkeys pulling carts for miles, and children making games out of sticks and stones . . . I found it very upsetting that I was sitting by people talking about TV shows and trivial gossip, and complaining incessantly about the heat and the dust and everything in between. Meanwhile, our kind bus leader was giving detailed and fascinating information about the country and the landscape outside our windows. His accent was thick and it made each passing scene more meaningful. Unfortunately, it was difficult to hear him over the nonsense gibberish that filled the bus. The indifference, ignorance, and unwillingness to learn about the people and culture surrounded me, and made me even more appreciative of my journey. I was so grateful that I was one of the students on the bus struggling to hear what Abdul had to say, and I could sense the chasm between myself and those around me. I was here to learn, to grow, to rip myself from my comfort zone and plunge headfirst into an unforeseen world.

—September 15, 2010

It is difficult to sum up the enjoyment and gratification that has come from my international experiences. Each country offers a unique mix of cultures, religions, languages, laws, norms, landscapes, infrastructures and countless other defining characteristics. However, I found universal enjoyment in immersing myself in unfamiliarity, and the thrill of independently setting out on a dynamic and spontaneous adventure. The most indelible gratification came from my interactions with the people, who left lasting impressions throughout my entire journey.

Looking back, my greatest enjoyment was not bungee jumping off the tallest bridge in the world, shark diving with 18-foot great whites, sky-diving over the townships of South Africa, tobogganing down the Great Wall of China, or riding camels and ATVs through the Sahara desert. Although these were unforgettable and exhilarating experiences, they do not compare to the profound and irreplaceable interactions that I shared with people around the world, which impacted me in a way that is indescribable on paper. Two occasions worth mentioning are among my most meaningful and rewarding experiences abroad. I made it a point to visit the townships of South Africa and the slums of India during my travels. I did not want to spend my time solely as a tourist, and believed that experiencing first-hand the extreme poverty in these neighborhoods was an essential part of my learning experience.

In both countries, I decided to embark on a solo visit to these areas, despite the danger and risk of not being accompanied by an organized group. I went with another student, and in both cases, we were taken to the homes of our cab drivers. It was sketchy, to say the least, as we got further from the relative safety of the city and deeper into the maze of shantytowns. However, with increased risk came increased rewards. In South Africa, we were treated as celebrities throughout the neighborhood, and spent the afternoon simply living with the locals, sharing beers at the tavern, playing jump rope with the kids, and visiting the one-room shacks that serve as homes. This particular township is one of the most crime-ridden in the area, and therefore, its residents are not accustomed to visits by foreigners. I handed out stickers to the children, and was astonished by the excitement and appreciation that such a small gesture can evoke.

In Chennai, we visited the home of our cab driver who lived deep in the slums up a flight of stairs in a densely crowded neighborhood. The tuk-tuk made its way in the dark through a maze of narrow corridors lined with people, and I entered the unfamiliar world filled with a sense of subdued apprehension and overwhelming curiosity. We shared hours in the company of the residents, who humbly invited us into their one-room homes. My experience interacting with the children of these neighborhoods was one of compassion and mutual understanding. The following is an excerpt about my experience in the slums of Chennai:

I held a one month old baby who had her face painted, danced with the toddlers, played with a baby goat, and left the neighborhood singing the ABCs with a trail of kids following us. It was an absolutely surreal and amazing experience that left an indelible mark on me.

—November 1, 2010

During my travels abroad, I learned as much about myself as I did about the people and places I visited. One of my greatest learning points from my experience is just that . . . LEARN! Although I experienced and learned more during my travels than many people may in a lifetime, there is still an infinite amount of knowledge out there to discover and endless opportunities to explore. To make the most of my experiences abroad, I removed

(continued)

all self-imposed limitations and went into every experience with an open mind and a willingness to learn. I was reminded that the world can be very dangerous, and to be an international traveller, I must always be astute and remain constantly aware of my surroundings. I also learned that the world is kind, and that even as a foreigner, I can rely on the good human nature of people around the world to assist me in whatever way I may need. I learned to be more appreciative and grateful for the hand I was dealt, and to contribute to improving the livelihoods of the billions around the world who are not as fortunate. Most importantly, I embarked on a path of self-discovery that reminds me of my infinitesimal existence on this planet. However, I was also reminded that each and every person has the potential to create a positive impact and change the world for the better. Here are my recommendations for your international career development:

- Remove all self-imposed limitations and be whole-heartedly open to self-discovery.

- Embark on your journey with anticipation, not expectation!

- Be respectful and considerate of your surroundings. Understand fully where you are and be fully engaged in the setting. Don't be distracted by the trivial, irrelevant, or inconvenient . . . let your imagination take hold of the international experience and live in the moment.

- Keep a journal. Try to interpret events and record thoughts about intangible experiences. Photos can tell the story of what you did; use the journal to tell what you learned.

RESOURCES FOR YOUR GLOBAL CAREER

In addition to the major international institutions, the IMF (http://www.imf.org/), the World Bank (http://www.worldbank.org/), the WTO (http://www.wto.org/), others are playing increasingly

important roles in world development. For a detailed list of recognized international organizations written in English, French, German and Spanish, refer to: http://intosai.connexcc-hosting.net/blueline/upload/3listintinstite.pdf.

Paul Volcker stresses the need for international currency coordination and predicts the need for one global currency: http://www.deu.edu.tr/userweb/muge.tunaer/dosyalar/Volcker_Intl_Instit.pdf.

The International Financial Institutions Research Site at Wellesley College: http://www.wellesley.edu/Economics/IFI/

University of Wisconsin Directory of International Institutions: http://info.gradsch.wisc.edu/admin/gradcoordinators/iadmiss/index.html

From The World Bank—blogs, broadcasts and multimedia presentations on global issues and institutional initiatives worldwide: http://youthink.worldbank.org/

Broadcast speeches on globalization, international institutions, and the international economy from the "Conversations with History" series from the Institute of International Studies, University of California, Berkeley: http://globetrotter.berkeley.edu/PubEd/research/globalization.html

Podcast: American Higher Education Is Going Global: Implications for CIOs, National Networks, and Federal Policymakers: http://www.educause.edu/blog/gbayne/PodcastAmericanHigherEducation/167670

IBM's Global CEO Study: The Enterprise of the Future: http://www.ibm.com/ibm/ideasfromibm/us/ceo/20080505/

Organizations addressing issues of business ethics, institutional governance, corporate responsibility, ethical treatment of employees, and anticorruption worldwide:

International Business Ethics Institute: http://www.business-ethics.org/

Ethics World: http://www.ethicsworld.org/

European Commission
Body responsible for the EU's day-to-day operations

European Central Bank
The central bank for Europe's single currency, the euro

European Court of Justice
The highest court of the EU, it interprets EU law

primary policy-setting institution of the EU. When the Council meets, the nation's minister who represents the specific area being discussed serves as the representative of the member-nation. For example, when financial matters are discussed, the 27 finance ministers of all member-nations participate. Council decisions are supranational and are set forth in regulations and directives. Recent directives deal with foreign policy issues (terrorism, weapons of mass destruction control, Burma/Myanmar) and issues of health and safety (flu tracking and precautions, disaster planning, workplace safety equipment, computer use rules, and environmental safety for workers). The **European Commission** administers the daily operations of the EU. It consists of 27 commissioners, one from each member-nation. Commission members are nominated by their countries, appointed by the Commission president-elect, and then approved by a vote of the European Parliament. The remaining six EU institutions focus on financial and social issues and include the **European Central Bank (ECB)** and the **European Court of Justice (ECJ).**

THE EU'S IMPACT ON INTERNATIONAL BUSINESS

The EU is a major world political and economic force. Its directives have superseded 27 sets of national rules and harmonized hundreds of thousands of national standards, labeling laws, testing procedures, and consumer protection measures covering everything from toys to food, stock brokering to teaching. The 27 nations have scrapped more than 60 million customs and tax formalities at their shared borders and are on the verge of implementing a harmonized patent system. The EU is the world's largest trading economy, a large source of FDI outflows, and the source of approximately 20 percent of the world's total output. The introduction of the euro is one of the most significant achievements of the EU.

These EU successes significantly impact how managers conduct business in several ways. The use of a common currency and common import and export processes have reduced the cost of doing business within the EU. A number of EU regulations have major impacts in the United States, Japan, China, and elsewhere because of the EU's size and importance as a trading partner. EU standards are advanced, especially in environmental and sustainability requirements. For example, in an effort to prevent electronic equipment waste, the EU requires recycling of all equipment, including cell phones, computers, household appliances, and televisions. It requires 80 percent recovery by weight for larger appliances, 75 percent for IT and telecommunications equipment, and 70 percent for small appliances. In addition, the manufacturers are required to provide collection for the waste that is not from private households. We may expect even more progress with continued European integration.

Microsoft is an example of a company whose business practices have been substantially influenced by the EU. In 2004, the European Commission ordered the company to pay €497 million, share its software code with competitors, and offer an unbundled version of the Windows operating system. Microsoft complied. Then, in 2005, the EU ruled that Microsoft would be fined $2.37 million per day if the software code it provided competitors didn't have better documentation. In 2008, the EU imposed a $1.35 billion fine, because Microsoft had not complied fully with its 2004 order to share code. In 2009, the EU announced that it would investigate Microsoft's Internet Explorer bundling with Window's operating systems, an investigation that was settled when Microsoft agreed to allow consumers to choose from among 12 competing browsers, including Explorer, all accessible on a choice screen. The point is clear: if foreign companies want access to the EU market, they must conduct business by the European Union's rules, often at the global level as well as within the EU.

THE EU GOING FORWARD

The EU has evolved beyond a free trade agreement, such as NAFTA and Mercosur, and made substantial progress in economic and political integration. It has, as the CIA *World Factbook* points out, "its own flag, currency (for some members), and law-making abilities, as well as diplomatic representation and a common foreign and security policy in its dealings with external partners."[34] The global financial crisis hit some European countries hard, though, and created challenges for the financial health and stability of the EU, especially within the Eurozone.

As the financial crisis began to recede, largely due to infusions from the European Central Bank (ECB) into banks, the concern focused on a sovereign debt crisis in some of the eurozone countries, including Greece, Spain, Ireland, Portugal, and Italy. This development points out the EU's lack of a federal treasury and budget. The fiscal policies of the EU are contained in the Stability and Growth Pact, an agreement that sets limits on member-nations' debt and deficits, with fines for violation. Yet the fines are voted in the European Council and have not been enforced on the larger economies, France and Germany, when they ran deficits. Clearly, this is an area for EU development. The EU did vote to support Greece and other endangered economies with a plan administered by the ECB and loans.

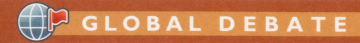
Do International Institutions Weaken the Nation-State?

One of the major forces of opposition to global institutions such as we have reviewed in this chapter are groups concerned with their nation's *sovereignty,* briefly understood as the authority of their nation to govern itself. Many groups hold that supranational agreements are an assault on the nation's independence. Their concern is that, for example, UN treaties and conventions would weaken the power of their nation to make its own decisions. A specific example of this is found in the U.S. refusal to ratify the UN Convention on the Rights of the Child, which would, the claim is, hold international law over state and federal laws protecting the rights of parents to make decisions related to their children's upbringing and education. The Kyoto Protocol on Climate Change is another example. The argument here is that such an international agreement on emissions would modify the power of the state and federal government to regulate in this area. Ratification of foreign treaties and agreements requires a two-thirds vote in the Senate.

One of the counterarguments to the sovereignty position is that the benefits gained from joining in such supranational agreements far outweigh their trade-offs. This is especially the case with issues whose limits do not fall on international borders, such as climate change and pollution.

Questions:

1. Do international institutions such as the UN weaken the power of nation-states?

2. What might be the consequences of a world without international institutions?

This chapter has reviewed major global institutions and focused on their importance to managers engaged in international business. Institutions matter to the conduct of international business because they operate to limit the available choices, thereby simplifying the environment. An international manager can benefit greatly by being aware of their strengths and contributions. Next, we move from institutions to address the environmental forces to which the international manager has to adjust, beginning with sociocultural forces.

Summary

LO3-1 Explain the importance of international institutions to business decision makers and their firms.

Institutions exist to limit and direct choices decision makers can make, so they limit the choices open to the firm. Institutions accomplish this constraint by simplifying the external environment. Whether the institution is formal or informal, it establishes rules, ways of acting, and ways of thinking (formal, informal normative, and informal cognitive) that achieve compliance through force, social norms, and shared assumptions that have the effect of reducing the number of options open to the firm or establishing the rules of the game. Their importance to business is that they simplify the external environment in ways that can help business understand and operate in their external environment.

LO3-2 Describe the various types of institutions, drawing on institutional theory.

Institutions are divided into formal and informal, based on how they influence behavior. Formal institutions use laws and regulations, while informal institutions use customs and ideologies. Informal institutions may be either normative or cognitive. Normative institutions work through values and norms, while the cognitive institutions work through schema or shared sets of assumptions that shape our meaning-giving.

We have reviewed the United Nations, the World Trade Organization, and the two monetary institutions—the World Bank and the International Monetary Fund—as examples of global institutions. We have also looked at OECD. Many other global institutions exist, of course, at all levels, including firms and nongovernmental organizations. Among these are the economic integration agreements. There are many other bases for regional institutions. Our focus has been on those of broadest significance to the international firm.

LO3-3 Outline the United Nations as an institution and its relevance to international business.

The United Nations is an informal, normative institution. Governments comply with their UN agreements based on moral principles and social obligation. At the same time, looking at the parts of the UN, the Peacekeeping Force could be seen as a formal institution that uses the regulatory power of coercion to extract compliance. The UN's work is carried out through five main bodies or organs: the General Assembly, the Security Council, the Economic and Social Council, the International Court of Justice, and the Secretariat. The General Assembly is a forum in which every nation has one vote; the Security Council focuses on peace and security and has permanent members and elected members; the Economic and Social Council addresses issues related to trade, education, health, and other economic and social issues; the International Court of Justice hears cases between nations; and the Secretariat, headed by the secretary-general, is the administrative arm of the UN. The UN has a variety of agencies throughout the world that work to promote peace and stability and to facilitate trade and economic activity. International organizations such as the United Nations can have profound influence on international businesses. By providing a forum for governments to talk to each other, the United Nations contributes toward peace and stability, conditions that stimulate international business. Such dialogue also results in collaborative efforts that support multilateral cooperation in areas of immediate concern to business, such as maritime agreements, communication accords, and other rules and standards. In addition, many of these institutions support development projects, which stimulate business directly, through their contracts and also through their support of the development of markets.

LO3-4 Describe the purposes of the two global monetary institutions, the IMF and the World Bank.

The basic idea of the IMF is that a workable monetary system is in the interests of all nations. Its Articles of Agreement outline the purpose of the fund in six points: to promote international monetary cooperation, to facilitate the expansion and balanced growth of international trade, to promote exchange stability and orderly exchange arrangements among members, to assist in the establishment of a multilateral system of payments, to make the fund's resources available for balance-of-payments corrections, and to shorten the duration and lessen the disequilibrium of members' balance of payments. The World Bank, including the IBRD and the IDA, lends money for development projects in middle-income and creditworthy poor countries. In the poorest countries, it provides low-interest loans and grants for projects designed to help them develop infrastructure, health and education, and other areas connected to development.

LO3-5 Discuss the purpose of the World Trade Organization and its impact on international business.

The WTO attempts to reduce trade barriers worldwide in order to facilitate trade. Its membership is composed of the world's major trading countries, so it has the potential to significantly influence world trade. The WTO routinely issues decisions on trade disputes between countries. The Doha Development Agenda of the WTO has been stalled and faces difficult negotiations in the areas of agricultural subsidies of developed nations, enforcement of rules and rulings, and intellectual property rights.

LO3-6 Discuss the resources of the Organisation for Economic Cooperation and Development.

The OECD conducts extensive research on a wide variety of international business and economic subjects, and it produces highly regarded individual country surveys. These resource materials are valuable to researchers and businesspeople as they develop an understanding of markets.

LO3-7 Identify the levels of economic integration and the effectiveness of the major trading blocs.

The four major forms of economic integration are the free trade area (tariffs abolished among members), the customs union (a free trade agreement plus a common external tariff), the common market (a customs union plus mobility of services, people, and capital), and complete integration (a common market plus a common currency and additional economic and political integration). NAFTA has been quite effective, while Mercosur, whose goal is a common market, has faced difficulties recently. African economic integration efforts have faced difficulties, as well, and they endure. The EU has been markedly successful and able to weather the instability of the recent financial crisis and the ensuing fallout in its weaker economies.

LO3-8 Discuss the EU, its impact, and its challenges going forward.

The EU is a supranational entity with 27 European member-nations, 17 of which share a common currency. Its purpose is to integrate the economies of its member-nations, creating a trading region where goods, services, people, and capital move freely. In recent years, the EU has made major steps toward political union as well. The EU is a regional government and has regulatory power over social and environmental matters, including mergers and business operations, in Europe. The depth and breadth of its market gives the EU de facto influence on businesses worldwide. The EU's success at monetary integration reduces the risk for businesses within the EMU. The EU can be seen as one large market with fewer restrictions than existed among the 27 nations before integration. The recent financial crisis severely challenged the EU, especially when several of its weaker economies approached default on sovereign debt. So far, the EU appears to have weathered these challenges.

Key Words

new institutional theory (p. 64)

formal institutions (p. 65)

informal institutions (p. 65)

United Nations (UN) (p. 66)

General Assembly (p. 68)

Security Council (p. 68)

Economic and Social Council (ECOSOC) (p. 68)

International Court of Justice (ICJ) (p. 68)

Secretariat (p. 69)

Bretton Woods (p. 70)

International Monetary Fund (IMF) (p. 70)

World Bank (p. 71)

Special Drawing Rights (SDRs) (p. 71)

Questions

1. What are the characteristics of informal cognitive institutions, and why are they of special significance to international business managers?

2. The UN may be best known for its peacekeeping missions, but it also has many agencies involved in activities that directly impact business. Comment on the UN's influence on a single trade transaction.

3. Sovereign wealth funds and high reserves are held by many developing nations today, and they were the major market for IMF loans in the past. How might the IMF adjust to a world in which fewer countries need their loans?

4. In your judgment, do bilateral trade agreements such as NAFTA and Mercosur undercut the WTO?

5. The U.S. Congress approved NAFTA, despite strong trade union and labor opposition. Do you agree with labor's opposition? Explain.

6. Mercosur's main trading partner is with the EU rather than the United States. Why might this be the case?

7. Why is OECD known as "the rich man's club"? Does it impact only rich countries?

8. Using concepts from new institutional theory, describe three bodies or organs of the EU.

9. What impact can the EU have on businesses external to the EU?

10. Criticism of international institutions such as the UN or the EU often goes to sovereignty, the authority of the state to govern itself. The argument is that the institution violates the sovereignty of the nations. One of the counterarguments to this assertion is that the benefits gained from joining the international institution can be positive and outweigh the sacrifice in sovereignty. Give several examples of this counterargument, drawing on institutions we have reviewed.

Research Task

 globalEDGE.msu.edu

Use the globalEDGE site (http://globalEDGE.msu.edu/) to complete the following exercises:

1. You work at a company that manufactures low-cost computers and is currently considering entering India. Use the *World Development Indicators* (WDI)—the World Bank's premier data compilation of data on development—to gather information on this country. Prepare a short report focusing on the economic policy and external debt, education, and infrastructure of India as it applies to your company's product.

2. The *Organisation for Economic Cooperation and Development* (OECD) publishes an Economic Survey, approximately every two years, for each OECD country. Each survey provides OECD's assessment and recommendations on the main economic challenges faced by the individual country. Find the Economic Surveys of France, Italy, and the United Kingdom for the most recent year. Summarize the key challenges facing each economy. Do you notice any similarities among the countries in terms of the challenges they are facing?

Minicase: Use of International Institutions— Setting Up a 100 Percent Owned Subsidiary

You are researching direct foreign investment possibilities in African countries in the energy sector, either 100 percent owned or with a local partner. Which organizations discussed in this chapter would you look to for help in developing a list of criteria for your decision?

International Environmental Forces

In Chapter 1, we stated that many practices followed at home can be transferred intact to other countries. However, we also mentioned that because of the differences in environmental forces, some ways of doing business must be adapted to local conditions or changed completely.

In Section Two, we examine these forces to see how they differ from those we encounter at home. We begin Section Two with Chapter 4, which discusses cultural forces and points out that the variety of attitudes and values among cultures affects managers of all the business functions in ways that can require them to behave differently than they would have done at home. Next we look at the physical forces—location, topography, and climate, along with natural resources and environmental sustainability (Chapter 5).

In Chapter 6, we investigate the political forces that affect the success or failure of a foreign venture, including their influence on international trade. Some of these are nationalism, terrorism, unstable governments, trade restrictions and government-owned businesses.

Intellectual property and other legal forces, the subject of Chapter 7, represent an additional set of constraints within which firms must operate.

Finally, our discussion moves to the international monetary system and financial forces in Chapter 8. Topics here include currency exchange risks, currency exchange controls, taxation and inflation, and the balance of payments accounts.

91

Sociocultural Forces

Speaking about cultural differences among Europeans . . . it is no good focusing on similarities and common interests and hoping things will work out. We have to recognize the differences and work with them."

—Dr. Allan Hjorth, Copenhagen Business School, trainer in cross-cultural behavior

Six Quick Rules of Thumb for Doing Business across Cultures

Knowing your customer is just as important anywhere in the world as it is at home, whether you are aiming to sell computers in Abidjan or soft drinks in Kuala Lumpur. Each culture has its logic, and within that logic are real, sensible reasons for the way they do things. The businessperson who can figure out the basic pattern of the culture will be increasingly effective interacting with foreign clients and colleagues. The following six rules of thumb are helpful:

1. *Be prepared.* Whether traveling abroad or selling from home, approach a foreign market having done your homework. A mentor is most desirable, complemented by lots of reading on social and business etiquette, history and folklore, current affairs (including relations between your two countries), the culture's values, geography, sources of pride (artists, musicians, sports), religion, political structure, and practical matters such as currency and hours of business. Read local newspapers. The Internet can be a helpful source of information, and a good site for international newspaper links is www.refdesk.com/paper.html/.

2. *Slow down.* Americans are clock-watchers. In many countries, Americans are seen to be in a rush—in other words, unfriendly, arrogant, and untrustworthy. In other countries, the Japanese and Germans are considered to be somewhat time-obsessed.

3. *Establish trust.* Often, American-style crisp business relationships will get you nowhere. Product quality, pricing, and clear contracts compete with the personal *relationship and trust* that are developed carefully and sincerely over time. The marketer must be established as *simpatico,* worthy of the business and dependable in the long run.

4. *Understand the importance of language.* Obviously, translations must be done by a professional who speaks both languages fluently, who has a vocabulary sensitive to nuance and connotation, and who has talent with the idioms and imagery of each culture. Having an interpreter is often critical and may be helpful even when one of the parties speaks the other's language.

5. *Respect the culture.* Manners are important. The traveling representative is a guest in the country and must respect the host's rules. As a Saudi Arabian official states in one of the *Going International* films, "Americans in foreign countries have a tendency to treat the natives as foreigners, and they forget that actually it is *they* who are the foreigners themselves!"

learning objectives

After reading this chapter, you should be able to:

LO4-1 **Describe** what culture is.

LO4-2 **Explain** the significance of national-level culture differences for international business.

LO4-3 **Describe** Hall's concept of high and low context.

LO4-4 **Describe** Hofstede's framework.

LO4-5 **Outline** Trompenaars' dimensions.

LO4-6 **Discuss** the sociocultural aspects of culture as a phenomenon.

6. *Understand components of culture.* Any region is a sort of cultural iceberg with two components: surface culture (fads, styles, food, etc.) and deep culture (attitudes, beliefs, values). Less than 15 percent of a region's culture is visible, and strangers to the culture must look below the surface. Consider the British habit of automatically lining up on the sidewalk when waiting for a bus. This surface cultural trait seems to reflect a deep cultural desire to lead neat and controlled lives. Or think of the Japanese victim's response to the March 2011 earthquake and tsunami. Knowledge about other cultures and how they affect the way people do business may show businesspeople working in a culture different from their own that their solutions are not always the appropriate ones.

Understanding that our way is not the only way or the best way is the first step in learning to use cultural differences to gain a strategic advantage. Mishandling or ignoring cultural differences can cause numerous problems, such as lost sales, the departure of competent employees, and low morale that contributes to low productivity. When cultural differences are blended successfully, however, they can result in innovative business practices superior to those that either culture could produce by itself.

Source: Lisa Hoecklin, "Managing Cultural Differences," www.latinsynergy.org/strategicjointventure.htm#CHILE (December 27, 2000; inactive March 16, 2011); "How to Negotiate European Style," *Journal of European Business,* July–August 1993, p. 46; and "Japanese Punctuality," http://joi.ito.com/achives/2005/04/28/japanese_punctuality.html (August 4, 2006; inactive March 16, 2011).

What Is Culture?

 LO4-1 Describe what culture is.

There are many useful definitions of culture. Most anthropologists, whose focus is on culture, view it as the *sum total of the beliefs, rules, techniques, institutions, and artifacts that characterize human populations.*[1] In other words, culture consists of the "individual worldviews, social rules, and interpersonal dynamics characterizing a group of people set in a particular time and place."[2] Most anthropologists also agree that:

1. Culture is *learned;* we are not born with a culture.
2. The various aspects of culture are *interrelated.*
3. Culture is *shared, patterned, and mutually constructed through social interaction.*
4. Culture *defines the boundaries* of different groups.[3]

> *"Culture is a little like dropping an Alka-Seltzer into a glass—you don't see it, but somehow it does something."*
>
> —*Hans Magnus Enzensberger*

sociocultural
Description of the social world through which we observe the effects of culture

Society is composed of people living within their cultural frameworks, so, to understand a specific group (either an organization or a society), how it works, and what its norms and values are, we need to understand its culture. Yet culture cannot be directly observed; we have to learn about it by observing the social world in which it exists. Because of their close linkage, the concepts *social* and *cultural* are often combined into the term **sociocultural,**[4] and we follow this practice. Culture occurs at all levels, within all groups, so it is evident in organizations, social groups, ethnic groups, and regional groups. Here, we are interested in culture at the national level; you will also want to pay attention to understanding the organization's culture and the various local subcultures.

When people work in societies and cultures different from their own, they have to communicate across cultural borders, with cultures they may not understand. A failure to communicate across one cultural border is problematic; such problems are magnified with the multiple cultures of a firm's foreign markets. In addition, most societies consider their culture superior to all others (**ethnocentricity**). Given that, every culture's members tend to think that its ways are best, most attempts by outsiders to introduce their home culture approach in a business environment (the "German way" or the "British way") will be met with stubborn resistance.

ethnocentricity
Assuming one's own culture to be superior to other cultures

How do international businesspeople learn to live with, work in, and meet business goals in other cultures? The first step is to realize that the other cultures are different from their own.

Then they need to learn the characteristics of those cultures so that they may adapt to them. The anthropologist E. T. Hall claims this can be accomplished in only two ways: (1) spend a lifetime in a culture or (2) undergo an extensive training program that covers the main characteristics of a culture, including the language. Such a program is much more than a briefing on a country's customs. It is a study of what culture is and what it does, building an understanding of the various ways in which human behavior has been institutionalized in the country.[5]

Hall suggests that to be successful in their relationships with people in other countries, international businesspeople need to be students of culture. They need factual knowledge about the different culture, which is relatively easy to obtain, but they must also become sensitive to the nuances of cultural differences, a type of knowledge more difficult to obtain. Most newcomers to international business do not have the opportunities Hall recommends. They need to hit the ground running, so to speak, and can rarely afford the time necessary for in-depth study of new cultures. They can, however, take the important first step of realizing that there *are* other cultures. In this chapter, we point out some of the important areas of sociocultural difference that concern businesspeople. We hope that you will remember that there are cultural differences for which you must look, and that you will seek out opportunities to build your knowledge of other cultures.

The concept of culture is broad; it includes everything. Ethnologists break their study of culture into focused areas such as aesthetics, attitudes and beliefs, religion, material culture, language, societal organization, education, legal characteristics, and political structures. We will look at several of these specific areas once we review the significance of culture for business and explore several conceptual frameworks international managers find useful as they build their understanding of other cultures.

As we explore culture, we need to be reminded that the national characteristics of culture we discuss are generalizations. They are broadly true, but they follow a normal distribution curve, and there are always exceptions. Furthermore, characteristics or characterizations may change over time. The Scandinavians were considered by a 10th-century writer to be "the filthiest race God ever created," and a noted 18th-century writer was amazed at the lack of German military spirit and how easygoing Germans were compared to the French.[6]

Culture Affects All Business Functions

Everything we do is influenced by culture, and most of us realize that about other cultures, but not always about our own. To think about how national cultural differences can affect the functional areas of a business with an international presence is a good place to begin our focus on culture.

LO4-2 **Explain** the significance of national-level culture differences for international business.

MARKETING

In marketing, the wide variation across cultures in attitudes and values requires that many firms use different marketing mixes in different markets. To develop effective marketing campaigns, the marketer has to understand the foreign market the firm is selling into, and the understanding has to be beyond a surface awareness of differences. The closer the marketer can come to understanding how potential purchasers in the target market give meaning to what occurs in their worlds and how they think their worlds should be, the better. Many businesses have made costly mistakes with product introductions into foreign markets, in physical property design, inappropriate copy for advertisements, and pricing. Through these errors, they learn the importance of understanding their markets, even though acquiring knowledge about a new culture is both time consuming and expensive. Major misunderstandings in marketing due to cultural misunderstandings abound. One international marketing consultant tracks and reports on them in a blog and on a website: www.deborahswallow .com/2009/08/20/cross-cultural-marketing-blunders.

HUMAN RESOURCES

Sociocultural values play key roles in motivation and evaluation of employees. In some cultures, individual effort is rewarded, while in others, group effort is more highly valued. Other values that come into play in human resources (HR) often connect to attitudes toward status. Is social status something we earn, through achievements (what we do), or is it a result of our

Disneyland: Successes and Failures, One after Another

Why is it that Disneyland Paris had problems with falling attendance and losses while Tokyo's Disneyland and Disney Sea have steadily increasing attendance and are the most profitable Disney parks? Why is it, too, that, while Tokyo Disneyland is so successful, Hong Kong Disneyland is struggling? The experts who predicted that Tokyo Disneyland attendance would peak in the first year and then taper off were wrong; it has increased steadily. The park owes some of its success to its location in a metropolitan area of 35 million people, but a cultural change that may be the result of its close local partnership is believed to be a major reason for its success. Some say that Walt Disney Productions has written a new chapter in Japanese social history by popularizing the idea that family outings can be fun. Families now account for half of the park's visitors. An executive of Disney states, "Leisure was not always a part of the Japanese lifestyle. Fathers used to see family outings as a duty."

In Paris, the early staggering losses at Disneyland stemmed from the high interest costs and high overheads, many of which were caused by cultural errors. Disneyland Paris is a solo project for Disney; there is no local operating-level partner. To cover the project's $4 billion cost, Disney put up just $170 million for 49 percent of the operation, and public shareholders paid $1 billion for the 51 percent they own. The $2.9 billion balance was borrowed at interest rates of up to 11 percent. Disney management expected to reduce the debt by selling the six big hotels it had built, but the $340-per-night price it charged had kept them about half full. Moreover, the guests weren't staying as long or spending as much as Disney had expected.

Disney executives believed, incorrectly, that they could change the French attitude of not wanting to take their children from school during the school year, as Americans do, and of not wanting to take more short breaks during the year, instead of one long vacation during the month of August. If these changes had happened, and the French used their shorter vacations to visit Disneyland Paris, this would have given Euro Disney steady, high attendance all year rather than for just one month.

One reason the European visitors didn't spend as much per visit as Disney had predicted was the extremely high prices. Almost two years passed before Disney lowered them. Another reason the guests didn't spend more, even though in this case they wanted to, was also due to a cultural problem: the breakfast debacle. Apparently, a decision involving millions of dollars in revenue was based not on research but only on what someone told Disney. One executive said, "We were told that Europeans don't take breakfast, so we downsized the restaurants." However, when the park opened, everyone wanted breakfast and wouldn't settle for just croissants and coffee; they wanted bacon and eggs. Disney tried to serve 2,500 breakfasts in hotel restaurants seating 350 people. The Disney solution for the French public, known worldwide as connoisseurs of good eating: prepackaged breakfasts delivered to hotel rooms. Disney also decided initially not to serve alcohol, as is their policy in the United States. They misjudged the local transport scene, as well, expecting Europeans to take golf cart transportation from their hotels to the park, while the Europeans wanted to walk. So ample sidewalks were built.

family's social position (who we are)? For example, Americans, who expect to be promoted based on their accomplishments, often are surprised to learn of the significant role schooling in the "right" institutions and family background play in this process in Great Britain. Differences in attitudes toward authority, another sociocultural variable, may also lead to personnel problems. Is the expected role of the manager to be the *patron,* an authoritarian figure responsible for their employees' welfare? Or is the manager one among equals? Is the control process of an annual review widely seen as a way to credit the employee's work and help the employee grow or as a way to exact higher labor output from the worker? The answers to these questions, which are important to HR practices, frequently lie in deeply embedded cultural values.

PRODUCTION

Production managers have found that cultural values and attitudes toward change can seriously influence the acceptance of new production methods. Plant layout is also influenced by culture. The assembly line is the product of minds socialized in a linear culture in which the task receives primary focus, not the social relationship. Contrast the linear system with the Uddevalla approach found in some Volvo plants in Sweden in the 1980s, where small, autonomous teams assembled the total car in several hours.[7] In procurement, sociocultural norms and rules structure the way the firm acquires resources. In much of Asia, procurement often exists in a web of social relationships and friendships, whereas in the United States, transparency and price frequently drive the process.

After 1995, Disneyland Paris worked to correct the cultural and financial errors that kept attendance down and losses up. The park cut admission prices by 22 percent and hotel rates by one-third. In addition to the original expensive, sit-down restaurants that Disney mistakenly believed all Europeans would demand, cheaper fast food is now available in self-service restaurants. Instead of marketing the park to Europe as if it were a single country, Disneyland Paris has offices in all the main European capitals, and each office tailors tour packages to fit its own market. Today, Disneyland Paris is one of France's top tourist attractions and a major attraction for Europe, as well.

Tokyo Disneyland was next on Disney's development list. Disney had learned from its Parisian mistakes. In Japan, Disney partnered with a local company, so they had ready access to local knowledge. Disneyland Tokyo has been successful beyond forecast. Then came Hong Kong Disney, a 48–52 joint-venture partnership with the Hong Kong government. Yet, to the surprise of Disney, Hong Kong has been struggling since its opening in 2005. Just as in Paris, Hong Kong Disney stumbled early, with low attendance and confusion among guests as to what to expect. Disney responded with a new marketing campaign and dozens of changes inside the park, including more seats because Chinese guests take an average of 10 minutes longer to eat than Americans. Management has also taken steps to see that Mandarin speakers don't accidentally get in the lines to hear English-speaking guides.

The issues in Hong Kong, though, seem to be more related to the product concept rather than to execution issues. People in Hong Kong don't get the Disney magic. They don't have the Disney fairytale stories lodged deeply in their collective unconscious, the way Westerners do (and as the Japanese acquired after WWII). Local visitors in Hong Kong are only 41 percent of all visitors, while in Tokyo they are 96.8 percent. So, Disney will add non-Disney characters and themes. Another issue is that Hong Kong taxpayers, whose government owns the majority share in Disney, want more transparency about Disneyland results: the Hong Kong government has not been transparent in its release of Disney's results, and the local community wants more details about financial results. So, citizens are angry about their government's investment, an emotion that further challenges the growth of Disney's magic. Perhaps, when they understand their investment more fully, they'll visit and help Hong Kong Disney build its magic.

Meanwhile, Disney is moving ahead with plans for China, in Shanghai, which will be many times larger than the Hong Kong theme park. Here, there are also local partners with a majority stake. The planned opening is 2014. We'll be able to see if Disney applies what it has learned in Paris, Tokyo, and Hong Kong, as China comes online.

Questions:

1. Why did Disney go solo and avoid joint ventures or other collaborations in its foreign market entries?

2. Do you think Disney, a peculiarly American fantasy concept, can appeal to Asians who don't have much knowledge of American culture?

Sources: "Euro Disney's Fortunes Turn as Number of Visitors Rises," *Financial Times*, November 14, 1997, p. 13; "The Kingdom inside a Republic," *The Economist*, April 13, 1996, pp. 66–67; "Tokyo Disney Shifts Japanese Ideas on Leisure," *The Columbian*, May 1, 1994, p. F7; "Mickey n'est pas fini," *Forbes*, February 14, 1994, p. 42; "Euro Disney's Wish Comes True," *The Economist*, March 19, 1994, p. 83; Merissa Marr and Geoffrey A. Fowler, "Chinese Lessons for Disney," *The Wall Street Journal*, June 12, 2006, pp. A1, A5; "Disneyland Resort Paris," Wikipedia, http://en.wikipedia.org/wiki/Disneyland_Resort_Paris (accessed March 20, 2011); "Mojo Eludes Disney in Hong Kong," *Japan Times*, February 4, 2010, http://search.japantimes.co.jp/cgi-bin/nn20100204f1.html (accessed March 20, 2011).

ACCOUNTING AND FINANCE

A culture's accounting controls directly relate to the culture's assumptions about the basic nature of people. Are the controls tight throughout the organization, perhaps suggesting low levels of trust at cultural levels, or loose, suggesting that the culture assumes people will act honestly, even when they are not closely monitored? Are the controls administered by formal institutions, gaining compliance through rules and sanctions, or by informal institutions, gaining compliance through social norms (described in Chapter 3)? Treasurers realize the strength of sociocultural forces when, armed with excellent balance sheets, they approach local banks, only to find that the banks in some cultures attach far more importance to who they are than to how strong their companies are or how strong they appear to be on paper. Also, in some cultures financial statements are notoriously unreliable, because the local culture allows creative accounting to keep the tax man away.

PREFERRED LEADERSHIP STYLES

Leadership traits vary by culture, as well. Is the usual relationship between leader and followers hierarchical or more lateral? Is the leadership model paternalistic? Heroic? Does the ideal leader come up through the ranks, or is the ideal leader someone placed in the leadership position due to family or status? The function of leadership also may be understood differently, depending on culture. Does leadership integrate a group of people or does it provide direction for a collection of individuals?

Frameworks to Understand Cultures

We have seen that sociocultural forces are important to international business. Increasingly, one useful way managers quickly build a general sense of what to expect in a culture is to use an analytical framework. These frameworks help managers build ways to understand behavior patterns across cultural borders. As we review these frameworks, remember that their use is comparative: our own culture functions as an implicit reference point.

The studies of national-level differences in values on which the frameworks are based include work by Kluckhohn and Strodtbeck,[8] Hall,[9] House,[10] Hofstede,[11] Trompenaars,[12] and Schwartz.[13] Here, we briefly look at three of these frameworks, those developed by Hall, Hofstede, and Trompenaars. This material is an introduction to a rich area of research in several disciplines, including international business, marketing, psychology, anthropology, and sociology. Vas Taras has a "Catalogue of Instruments for Measuring Culture" that lists 143 separate instruments. (www.vtaras.com/Culture_Survey_Catalogue). Hall's theoretical framework is simple and yet powerful; Hofstede's dimensions are empirically derived and have received significant attention from both managers (because they apply easily) and scholars (because they raise significant methodological issues); Trompenaars' work integrates concepts that are derived from the social sciences. If you find yourself interested in further study in this area, Schwartz's work merits your attention. His focus is on values, and his analysis clusters them into openness to change, self-transcendence, self-enhancement, and conservation. House's Globe Study, an ambitious and interesting project that examines leadership patterns around the globe, uses value and practice dimensions to measure culture and may also be useful.

LO4-3 Describe
Hall's concept of high and low context.

HALL'S HIGH AND LOW CONTEXT

context
The relevant environment

Hall offers a classification of cultures based upon communication styles and, specifically, on the role that **context** plays in the communication patterns. The context of the communication act is the relevant environment beyond the explicit communication. For example, part of context may be the speaker's and participants' body language, place in the room, and who speaks before and after the speaker. In a high-context culture, the participants have social ties that are long-standing and close, so people know what the communication will be from long experience with the other and from communication signals. In a low-context culture, the relationships are of shorter duration and so more of the communication has to be explicit. In our families, we probably find a higher context, even though we may be members of low-context cultures.

Hall suggests that in high context (HC), the communication tends to be implicit and indirect. Context plays an exceedingly strong role, actually carrying much of the meaning. In these cultures, such as Japan, China, Latin America, and the Middle East, communication is more subtle and inferred. (See Figure 4.1.)

In contrast, Hall notes that people in low-context cultures have explicit communication patterns. They do not rely so greatly on the context of the communication. The explicit communicator is direct and unambiguous: what you say is what you mean. In North America, communication tends to be low context (LC), direct, and to-the-point. In LC cultures, to "tell it like it is" is understood to be a positive trait. Figure 4.2 shows examples of HC and LC cultures, along with examples of the concept applied to occupations.

Now we look at the social dimensions of Hall's framework. In LC cultures, people tend to have many connections that endure for short time periods. Because the stored mutual history is minimal, explicit communication ensures that the intended meaning is communicated. In HC culture societies, people have close connections over a long period of time, so much of the meaning is already known because it resides in the context. Figure 4.1 shows these communication relationships and further describes behaviors connected with these two communication patterns.

monochronic
Having to do with linear time, sequential activities

Hall's work also suggests that LC cultures tend to be **monochronic,** with time characterized as linear, tangible, and divisible into blocks, consistent with the economic approach to time.[14] Monochronic time emphasizes planning and the establishment of schedules, with

FIGURE 4.1   High and Low Context Attributes

High Context

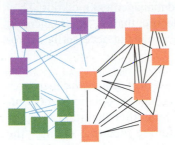

- Less verbally explicit communication, less written/formal information
- More internalized understandings of what is communicated
- Multiple cross-cutting ties and intersections with others
- Long term relationships
- Strong boundaries—insider/outsider
- Knowledge is situational, relational
- Decisions and activities focus around personal face-to-face relationships, often around a central authority person

Low Context

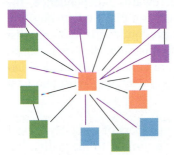

- Rule oriented, people play by external rules
- More knowledge is codified, public, external, and accessible.
- Sequencing, separation—of time, of space, of activities, of relationships
- More interpersonal connections of shorter duration
- Knowledge is more often transferable
- Task-centered. Decisions and activities focus around what needs to be done, division of responsibilities.

Source: Modified from www.culture-at-work.com/highiow.html (accessed june 5, 2010).

significant energy put into the maintenance of established schedules. In contrast, HC cultures tend to be **polychronic.** That is, two or more activities are carried out within the same clock block; switching among activities can be both desirable and productive. We think of this as multi-tasking.[15]

polychronic
Having to do with simultaneous activities, multi-tasking

HOFSTEDE'S FIVE DIMENSIONS

Hofstede, a Dutch business researcher and consultant trained in anthropology, developed his framework from surveys he administered to global IBM employees in the late 1960s, and later augmented them. His framework is concerned primarily with work values.[16] He developed four dimensions with which to classify the survey data that underlie and differentiate cultures: individualism-collectivism, power distance, uncertainty avoidance, and masculinity-femininity. In collaboration with researchers in Asia, he later added a fifth dimension, long-term orientation, having recognized that his earlier work represented a Western

LO4-4 **Review**
Hofstede's framework.

FIGURE 4.2

Examples of High- and Low-Context Cultures and Occupations

High Context	High Context
Japanese	
Chinese	Human resources
Arab	Marketing/Sales
Greek	Management
Mexican	
Spanish	Manufacturing
Italian	Products
French	R&D
French Canadian	
English	Technical
English Canadian	Information Systems
American (US)	
Scandanavian	Engineers
German	Finance
German-Swiss	
Low Context	Low Context

Confucian dynamism
Another term for long-term orientation

perspective. This fifth dimension is sometimes referred to as **Confucian dynamism.** His initial database had not included Asian cultures because IBM had little exposure in Asia when Hofstede did the studies. These five dimensions provide managers with a way to understand how national-level cultural differences affect organizations and management methods. They also assist in showing that management skills are culturally specific; that is, "a management technique or philosophy that is appropriate in one national culture is not necessarily appropriate in another."[17] Now to the dimensions.

Individualism-Collectivism[18]

The individualism-collectivism dimension measures the degree to which people in the culture are integrated into groups. People in highly *collectivistic* cultures belong to strong, cohesive in-groups that look after them in exchange for loyalty. The force of this dimension can be illustrated with the Japanese saying: "the nail that sticks up gets hammered down." In contrast, people in highly *individualistic* cultures are more loosely connected and look after themselves and their immediate family. The United States is highly individualistic; the culture rewards independence; the education system rewards outstanding individuals. This dimension plays out strongly in employee motivation and decision making. Countries with predominantly individualist cultures are the United States, Canada, the United Kingdom, Australia, the Netherlands, New Zealand, Sweden, France, and Germany. Cultures that are collectivist include Guatemala, Ecuador, Panama, Indonesia, Pakistan, Taiwan, China, Japan, and West and East African countries.

Power Distance

Power distance is the extent to which members of a society expect and accept power to be distributed unequally. Power distance is similar to inequality, but defined from below, not from above. The dimension suggests that a society's level of inequality is endorsed by followers as well as by leaders. In large power distance societies, seniority, age, rank, and title are important. People will want directions, and formality is emphasized. In a small power distance environment, a consultative style of leadership predominates, informality tends to be the norm, and there is equal distance among people. For example, from season ticket holders of box seats at major sporting events to fast-food workers, just about everyone in the United States self-identifies as middle class. Examples of large power distance cultures are Malaysia, Guatemala, Panama, Philippines, Arab countries, India, West African countries, and Singapore. Examples of small power distance countries include Austria, Israel, Denmark, New Zealand, the Republic of Ireland, Sweden, Norway, Canada, the United States, and Germany.

Uncertainty Avoidance

Uncertainty avoidance describes a society's comfort with uncertainty. Hofstede points out that this dimension "ultimately refers to man's search for Truth" because it describes the extent a culture programs its members to feel either uncomfortable or comfortable in unstructured situations. Cultures that avoid uncertainty try to minimize the possibility of such situations by "strict laws and rules, safety and security measures." Strong uncertainty avoidance cultures resist change, including career change and organizational change, expect clear procedures, and preserve the status quo. Weak uncertainty avoidance cultures see conflict as having positive aspects, expect innovation, encourage risk taking, and reward career change. Examples of strong uncertainty avoidance cultures are Greece, Portugal, Guatemala, Uruguay, Japan, France, Spain, and South Korea. Examples of weak uncertainty avoidance cultures include Singapore, Jamaica, Denmark, Sweden, Hong Kong, the United States, Canada, Norway, and Australia.

Masculinity-Femininity

The *masculinity-femininity* dimension describes the distribution of roles between the genders. Hofstede's data indicate that "women's roles across cultures differ less than do men's, and that men's values among countries vary considerably, from very assertive and competitive and maximally different from women's values on the one side, to modest and caring and similar to women's values on the other." The assertive pole is masculine, and the caring one feminine. "The women in feminine countries have the same modest, caring values as the men; in the masculine countries they are somewhat assertive and competitive, but not as much as the men, so that these countries show a gap between men's values and women's values." Note that this dimension is about *the gap between* men and women's roles in the culture. In a feminine culture, there is relatively less variation between male and female roles, which suggests that leadership and decision-making roles would be equally open to men and women. In a feminine culture, quality of work life is important, people work in order to live, and environmental issues matter from a business perspective. In a masculine culture, male roles are more likely to be task focused and female roles relationship focused, achievements are emphasized, economic growth is central, people live in order to work, and business performance is the primary goal. Examples of masculine cultures include Japan, Austria, Venezuela, Italy, Mexico, and the Philippines. Examples of feminine cultures include Sweden, Norway, the Netherlands, Denmark, Costa Rica, and Finland. A word of caution: to think that feminine cultures are not concerned with production and business success is an error. Just think of the globally successful Scandinavian firms in order to correct your misapprehension: IKEA, Nokia, Lego, Volvo, Ericsson, H&M, Bang & Olufson, and Carlsberg begin the list.

Long-Term Orientation/Confucian Dynamism[19]

This is the added dimension, as a result of a study among students in 23 countries around the world, using a questionnaire designed by Chinese scholars. Hofstede describes it as dealing with Virtue regardless of Truth, that is, the level to which people in the culture will persevere to overcome obstacles they cannot overcome with will or strength. In long-term-oriented societies, people value actions and attitudes that affect the future: persistence/perseverance, thrift, saving face at the group level, and shame. In short-term-oriented societies, values connected to the present and past are stronger: respect for tradition, fulfilling social obligations, high consumption patterns, and protecting face at the individual level. Because this dimension is often misinterpreted, a brief chart is shown in Table 4.1. Table 4.2 presents the scores for Hofstede's five dimensions for about one-third of the countries in his sample.

Figure 4.3 plots the scores for selected nations on the power distance and uncertainty avoidance dimensions. The Latin American countries in the second quadrant had high power

---

TABLE 4.1 Characteristics of Long-Term and Short-Term Orientation

Long-Term Orientation Characteristics	Short-Term Orientation Characteristics
Social order	Personal survival/security
Hierarchical relationships	Personal respect/dignity
Collective face-saving	Individual face-saving
Long-term planning	Short- to medium-term planning
Thrift-centered	Spending-centered
Long-term outcomes	Short- to medium-term outcomes
Examples	**Examples**
China	Pakistan
Hong Kong	Nigeria
Taiwan	Philippines
Japan	Canada
South Korea	Zimbabwe
India	United Kingdom
Brazil	United States
Singapore	Germany

Source: Modified from Ting-Toomey, Table 3.5.

TABLE 4.2

TABLE 4.2 — Selected Scores for Hofstede's Cultural Dimensions

Country	Power Distance	Uncertainty Avoidance	Individualism	Masculinity	Long-Term Orientation*
Mexico	81	82	30	69	
Venezuela	81	76	12	73	
Colombia	64	80	13	64	
Peru	90	87	16	42	
Chile	63	86	23	28	
Portugal	63	104	27	31	
China	80	30	20	66	118
Japan	52	92	46	95	80
United States	50	46	91	62	29
Australia	49	51	90	61	31
South Africa (SAF)	49	49	65	63	
New Zealand	45	49	79	58	30
Canada	39	48	80	52	23
United Kingdom	35	35	89	66	25
Ireland	28	35	70	68	

*Data for long-term orientation have not been collected for many countries yet, so these are blank.

Source: Geert Hofstede, "Cultural Dimensions in Management and Planning," *Asia Pacific Journal of Management*, January 1984, p. 83.

distance and strong uncertainty avoidance. These scores suggest that lines of communication in organizations in these countries will be vertical, employees will prefer directive management styles, and risk taking will be avoided. By clearly defining roles and procedures, the organizations are very predictable. The Anglo nations in the fourth quadrant had small power distance and weak uncertainty avoidance. Organizations in these countries are characterized by less formal controls and fewer layers of management, along with more participative leadership styles. Relationships tend to be informal. Note, too, that Japan and China have quite different scores.

FIGURE 4.3

Plot of Selected Nations on Power Distance and Uncertainty Avoidance

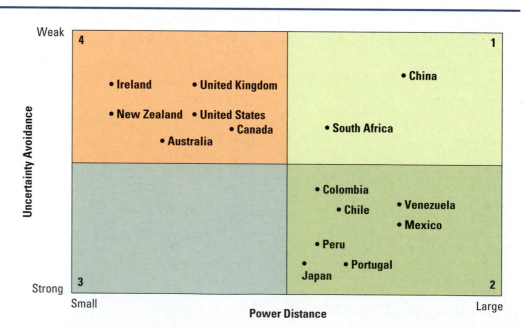

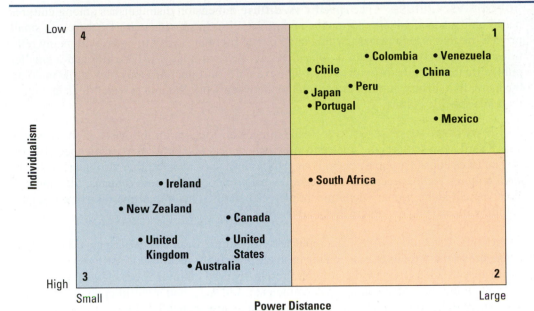

FIGURE 4.4

Plot of Selected
Nations on
Individualism and
Power Distance

The scores for individualism and power distance are plotted in Figure 4.4. The Latin and Asian countries (first quadrant) scored relatively high on power distance and weak on individualism. Employees tend to expect their organizations to look after them and defend their interests. They expect close supervision and managers who act paternally. On the other hand, people in the Anglo countries (third quadrant) have small power distance and high individualism, suggesting that they would prefer to do things for themselves and would not expect organizations to look after them.

TROMPENAARS' SEVEN DIMENSIONS

Fons Trompenaars, trained as an economist, is also Dutch. His seven-dimension framework for understanding culture is derived from the social sciences, and his initial data are from 47 countries, later greatly expanded in collaboration with Hampden-Turner. The first five dimensions address the culture's patterns for relationships among people, and the final two have to do with time and nature.[20] Trompenaars' dimensions are interesting because, unlike Hofstede's dimensions, which describe values, many of Trompenaars' dimensions describe the behavior that is the result of the underlying cultural value. For example, the specific-diffuse dimension describes the behavior to which values about privacy lead. In a specific culture, the idea that privacy is close and the entry barriers high leads to social patterns that are specific.

Universalism vs. Particularism (rules vs. relationships) This dimension addresses whether rules or relationships regulate behaviors. A culture's values that are **universalist** apply to all people. The rules are for everyone in all situations. **Particularist** values consider the context. Universalist cultures tend to be rules-based, while particularist cultures tend to be relationship-based. The United States tends to be moderately rules-based (in ethics, for example, we think that everyone should follow the guidelines or rules), whereas in other cultures, the judgment is situational—it all depends.

Individualism vs. Communitarianism This dimension has to do with whether people plan their actions with reference to individual benefits or group benefits. You will note its similarity to Hofstede's individual-collectivism dimension.

Neutral vs. Affective (unemotional vs. emotional) This dimension describes the culture's rules for display of emotions. People in neutral cultures tend to withhold emotional expression, while people in affective cultures are much more expressive.

LO4-5 Outline Trompenaars' dimensions.

universalism
Condition in which concepts apply to all

particularism
Condition in which context determines what concepts apply

communitarianism
Belief that the group is the beneficiary of actions

neutral vs. affective
Withholding emotion vs. expressing emotion

specific vs. diffuse
Life divided into public and private vs. life undifferentiated

Specific vs. Diffuse   The **specific vs. diffuse** dimension distinguishes among cultures based on the social patterns for public and private life. In *specific* cultures, there is a small private life that is kept private, with a large public life that is easy to enter, with many relationships that may be brief. In a *diffuse* culture, there is a large private life and a smaller public life that is more difficult to enter. For example, introductions may play a role in doing business. In a diffuse culture, the distinction between work life and private life is less clear than in a specific culture.

achievement vs. ascription
What a person does vs. who a person is

Achievement vs. Ascription   This dimension focuses on the basis of social status and reward, with status being related to either who a person is or what a person does. *Ascription* cultures consider who a person is by family lineage or age, or other attributes. *Achievement* cultures are meritocracies that reward what you do. In the United States, for example, achievement is the primary determinant of social status. This dimension may be especially helpful with staffing and interpersonal dynamics.

Attitudes toward Time   Trompenaars' time dimension has two aspects. The first is where the primary focus exists—on the past, the present, or the future. Past-focused cultures use history as a lens to view the present. Present-focused cultures focus on what is happening now. Future-oriented cultures plan, anticipate, and see a better world evolving. The second aspect to the time dimension is whether actions are sequential (linear) or synchronous (polychronic).

Attitudes toward the Environment   The relationship with nature is the basis of this dimension. Is the culture in harmony with nature, or does our understanding of the natural order of things (i.e., culture) suggest that we control nature? North American Anglo cultures tend to assume that they are meant to dominate nature. This can-do attitude does not allow natural obstacles such as oceans and mountains get in the way of progress. Other cultures may be more inclined to seek harmony with nature rather than to dominate it. The impact of this dimension influences areas such as infrastructure development and also ways people think about obstacles in the external world. Do they adjust or reconfigure?

Figure 4.5 illustrates an application of Trompenaars' dimensions to China, Mexico, and the United States.

SUGGESTIONS FOR USING THE FRAMEWORKS

As we conclude this review of culture frameworks, a caveat about how to use them is in order: both Hofstede's and Trompenaars' data represent a normal distribution within a national culture of the specific dimension. The score of each dimension represents its mean for each country, the central tendency. Thus, you will find people in the culture at all points on the distribution curve. The dimensions suggest that people from a specific culture tend to think and behave in a certain way. Do remember that such generalizations are at best sophisticated stereotypes of the complex culture we are trying to understand.[21] They are best used to establish likelihood and to predict; they can be misleading because they ignore complexity and subtlety. This is an important caution.

Remember, too, that these data have been analyzed on a national level and do not recognize the existence of subcultures. Cultural frameworks are useful tools, especially when we recognize their limitations. The frameworks help us to set expectations so that we can begin to build an understanding, but we are not wedded to these expectations. As humans, we are infinitely variable. As Shakespeare has Hamlet observe, "What a piece of work is a man! how noble in reason! how infinite in faculties! in form and moving how express and admirable!"[22]

LO4-6 Discuss the sociocultural aspects of culture as a phenomenon.

Sociocultural Aspects of Culture

Now that we have discussed what culture is, its importance to international business managers, and the frameworks available to help build our understanding of specific cultures, we focus on some of the sociocultural aspects of cultural variation—that is, how a society's

FIGURE 4.5

Examples of
Country Rankings
on Trompenaars'
Dimensions

China	
Dimension	
Universal --- X ----	Particularist
Individualist ----------------------------------- X --------	Collectivist
Neutral----------------------------------- X -----------	Affective
Specific--X---	Diffuse
Achievement------------------------------------- X --	Ascription

Mexico	
Dimension	
Universal ----------------------------X----------------	Particularist
Individualist -------------X-------------------------	Collectivist
Neutral-------------------------------------- X -	Affective
Specific----------------------------X-------------	Diffuse
Achievement------ X ---------------------------------	Ascription

United States	
Dimension	
Universal -- X -----------------------------------	Particularist
Individualist - X ---------------------------------	Collectivist
Neutral-------------------------------- X ---------------	Affective
Specific------------ X ---------------------------	Diffuse
Achievement- X -----------------------------------	Ascription

culture manifests or shows itself. Culture manifests in everything, and we look briefly at some of the major areas, aesthetics, religion, material culture, language, and social organization. We close with brief observations about an area in which there is often confusion, and where many cross-culturally confusing signals are sent: gift giving.

AESTHETICS

Aesthetics describe a culture's sense of beauty and taste and is expressed in many areas, most directly in art, drama, music, folklore, and dance.

aesthetics
A culture's sense of beauty and good taste

Art   Art including color and form, is of particular interest to international businesspeople because of its symbolic meanings. Colors carry different meanings in different cultures. For example, the color of mourning is black in the United States and Mexico, black and white in the Far East, red in South Africa, and purple in Brazil and Thailand. Green is a propitious color in the Islamic world, and any ad or package featuring green is looked at favorably there.

Aesthetics apply to our ideas about our bodies and their physical beauty, as well. The view of an ideal weight differs markedly across cultures. Often, in richer countries, the better-off are thinner, while in poorer countries, the poorer are thinner. In Japan, sumo athletes are obese, and in some areas of Nigeria, girls enter "fattening rooms" to bulk up. Tattoos are another aspect of body aesthetic value differences across cultures. In some cultures, they are seen as beauty-enhancing, while in others, a desecration. The oldest preserved human, the Iceman found between Austria and Italy, is tattooed. In an interesting reversal, at one time in

Japan, criminals were tattooed by authorities as a way to identify them, a negative meaning. Today, the Yakuza tattoo themselves to establish their in-group identity.

Music and Folklore

Musical tastes vary across cultures, and, although commercials with music are generally popular worldwide, the marketer must know what kind of music each market prefers. Thus, a commercial that used a ballad in the United States might be better received if accompanied by the tune of a bolero in Mexico or a samba in Brazil.

A culture's folklore can disclose much about a society's way of life. The incorrect use of folklore can sometimes cost the firm a share of the market. For example, associating a product with the cowboy would not obtain the same results in Chile or Argentina as in the United States, because in those countries, the cowboy is a far less romantic figure—it is just a job. On the other hand, Smirnoff's use of an image of late revolutionary leader Ernesto "Che" Guevara in an advertisement for spicy vodka sparked controversy in Cuba, where Guevara is a national hero.[23] In many areas, especially where nationalistic feeling is strong, local firms have been able to compete successfully with foreign affiliates by making use of indigenous folklore in the form of slogans and proverbs. An example of this is the use of Colonel Sanders' statues outside KFC stores in Japan. This marketing draws on the Japanese respect for elders and the perceived Japanese-ness of the Colonel. Loy Weston, who established KFC in Japan, claims that luck was in play here, but that luck was based on tremendous cultural sensitivity.

RELIGION

Religion, an important component of culture, is responsible for many of the attitudes and beliefs affecting human behavior. A knowledge of the basic tenets of the religions of your markets will be useful as you build your understanding of those cultures. Each religion has various forms and traditions within it and expresses its beliefs through particular kinds of worship and prayer, rituals, dietary rules, and modes of dress.[24] Knowledge of the local religion will also help you to communicate your respect for the culture. The following paragraphs describe briefly the main beliefs or principles that define five major religions.

Christianity has many denominations, but all of them share a belief that there is one God who is revealed through human history. Christians believe that Jesus was God's Son who came to earth as a man and lived in Israel, then called Palestine; he was killed about 30 C.E. by authorities of the Roman Empire, but came back to life and ascended to heaven. Christians claim that all who profess their belief in the Resurrection of Jesus will be received into heaven after death.

Islam began in the 7th century C.E. and, like Christianity and Judaism, originated in the Middle East. From an Arabic word meaning, "submitting," Islam also professes belief in one God, Allah. Muslims (those who practice Islam) focus on living their lives according to God's will, which is revealed through the "Qur'an" (the Scripture) and a long line of messengers. Mohammed is revered as the last and most important prophet of the religion and is said to have received the words of the Qur'an directly from God in a series of visions.

Buddhism was founded between the 6th and 4th centuries B.C.E. in northeastern India. Based on the teachings of Siddhartha Gautama, a royal prince who became known as the Buddha (Enlightened One), it encompasses several schools of thought, established over the centuries by different teachers. In general, Buddhists believe that earthly life is a continuous cycle of birth and death (reincarnation) that is the cause of human suffering. When we finally escape this cycle to achieve a state of being called "nirvana": we become, like the Buddha, enlightened.

Hinduism is the oldest of the major world religions and began in India around 2500 B.C.E. Hindus believe in one Supreme Reality, called Brahman, which takes many forms and names. Hindus seek to be in harmony with Brahman by living an ethically good life through self-discipline, the sharing of wealth, and following the teachings of the

TABLE 4.3	Followers of Five Major World Religions	
Religion	**Number of followers (in millions)**	**Cultural Tradition**
Christianity	2,200	Abrahamic religions
Islam	1,650	Abrahamic religions
Buddhism	1,500	Indian religions
Hinduism	1,000	Indian religions
Judaism	18	Abrahamic religions

Sources: World Christian Database Gordon–Conwell Theological Seminary Centre for the Study of Global Christianity, http://world christiandatabase.org; Pew Forum, http://pewforum.org/Mapping-the-Global-Muslim-Population.aspx; *CIA World Factbook,* 2011, www. cia.org; "Philosophy of Religion". *Encyclopædia Britannica.* 2010, www.britannica.com/EBchecked/topic/497132/philosophy-of-religion (all accessed March 19, 2011).

Scriptures (Vedas). Like Buddhists, they believe in reincarnation (the cycle of rebirth) and seek to escape it to achieve union with God.

Judaism began about 1900 B.C.E. in Israel, then known as Canaan, and shares the belief that God acts in human history, especially in times of struggle and oppression. The "Tanak," Judaism's Scripture, tells the story of how the Jews were repeatedly conquered and enslaved by foreign powers, but were freed by God's power acting through figures such as Abraham, Moses, and David. Jews believe that God made a "covenant" or promise to protect them as long as they continue to believe in and worship the one God.[25]

Table 4.3 shows the world's five major religions, while Figure 4.6 maps the major religions.

MATERIAL CULTURE

material culture or artifacts

All human-made objects; concerned with *how* people make things (technology) and *who* makes *what* and *why* (economics)

Material culture or artifacts are all the human-made objects of a culture; people who study material culture are concerned with *how* people make things (technology) and *who* makes *what* and *why* (economics). Every culture has certain parts of its material culture of which it is especially proud. Some awareness of these objects and the meaning they have for people in the culture can communicate interest in the culture.

LANGUAGE

Probably the most apparent cultural distinction that the newcomer to international business perceives is in language. Differences in the spoken language are readily discernible, and after a short period in the new culture, variations in the unspoken language become apparent, as well. Language is an important key to a culture, and without it, people find themselves locked out of all but a culture's perimeter. As illustrated in Chapter 5, spoken languages demarcate cultures just as physical barriers do. In fact, nothing equals the spoken language for distinguishing one culture from another.

Even though many global businesspeople speak English, when they buy, they often want to do business in their own language. The foreign seller who speaks the local language has a competitive edge. Figure 4.7 shows a map of the major languages of the world.

Nonverbal communication, or the unspoken language, can often tell businesspeople something that the spoken language does not—if they can understand it. High-context cultures tend to use unspoken language more intensively than do low-context cultures and thus, people in HC cultures often have developed advanced "reading ability" of unspoken language. Because context plays such an important role in their home culture, they are aware of this medium. Eye contact, posture, and subtle facial expressions are all cues on which HC cultures rely.

Gestures are a common form of cross-cultural communication, yet they vary from one region to another. For instance, Americans and most Europeans understand the thumbs-up

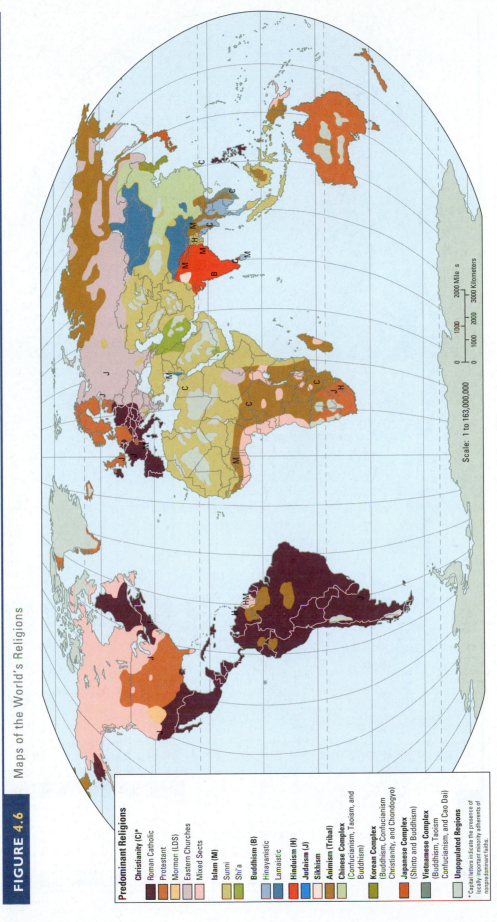

FIGURE 4.6 Maps of the World's Religions

Predominant Religions

Christianity (C)*
- Roman Catholic
- Protestant
- Mormon (LDS)
- Eastern Churches
- Mixed Sects

Islam (M)
- Sunni
- Shi'a

Buddhism (B)
- Hinayanistic
- Lamaistic

Hinduism (H)
Judaism (J)
Sikhism
Animism (Tribal)

Chinese Complex
(Confucianism, Taoism, and Buddhism)

Korean Complex
(Buddhism, Confucianism Christianity, and Chondogyo)

Japanese Complex
(Shinto and Buddhism)

Vietnamese Complex
(Buddhism, Taoism Confucianism, and Cao Dai)

Unpopulated Regions

* Capital letters indicate the presence of locally important minority adherents of nonpredominant faiths.

Scale: 1 to 163,000,000

0 1000 2000 3000 Kilometers
0 1000 2000 Mile s

Source: Map 18, "World Religions," *Student Atlas of World Geography*, 3rd ed., by John L. Allen. Copyright 2003: The McGraw-Hill Companies, Inc.

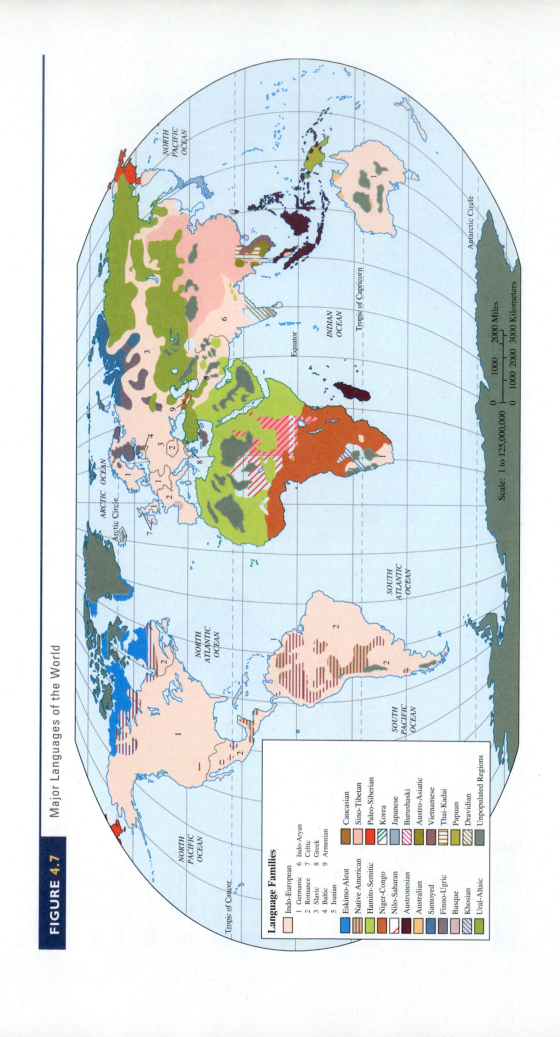

FIGURE 4.7   Major Languages of the World

Language Families

Indo-European

1 Germanic   6 Indo-Aryan
2 Romance   7 Celtic
3 Slavic   8 Greek
4 Baltic   9 Armenian
5 Iranian

Eskimo-Aleut
Native American
Hamito-Semitic
Niger-Congo
Nilo-Saharan
Austronesian
Australian
Samoyed
Finno-Ugric
Basque
Khosian
Ural-Altaic

Caucasian
Sino-Tibetan
Paleo-Siberian
Korea
Japanese
Burushaski
Austro-Asiatic
Vietnamese
Thai-Kadai
Papuan
Dravidian
Unpopulated Regions

Scale: 1 to 125,000,000

0   1000   2000 Miles
0   1000   2000   3000 Kilometers

gesture to mean "all right," but in southern Italy and Greece, it transmits a vulgar message. Similarly, making a circle as the "OK" sign, with the thumb and the forefinger, is friendly in the United States, but it means, "you're worth nothing" in France and Belgium and is vulgar in Greece and Turkey.

The unspoken language also includes spatial relationships, including aspects of workspaces. In the United States, an office door that is closed suggests a request for privacy; the normal position of the door is open. Germans regularly keep their doors closed. Hall suggests that the closed door does not mean that the person behind it wants no visitors, but only that he or she considers open doors to be sloppy and disorderly.[26] Office size and location can mean different things in different cultures. In the United States, the higher the status of the executive, the larger and more secluded the office, but in the Arab world, the company president may be in a small, crowded office. In Japan, the senior person is likely to be closest to the center of the room, and the least valuable places on an office floor are by the windows. The French also locate important department heads in the center of activities, with their assistants located outward on radii from this center.

Conversational distances, the space between people in a conversation, tend to vary across cultural borders, as well. For example, they tend to be much smaller in the Middle East than in Anglo cultures. Seeing two people with differing expectations for conversational distance, such as an American and a Saudi, move across a floor as one tries to close the space and the other expand it is not uncommon at social gatherings, if you watch for it. Conversational distances vary by gender as well, and comfortable distance may also vary by the degree of familiarity of the parties involved.

SPECIAL FOCUS: GIFT GIVING

Gift giving is an important aspect of every international manager's life, and a confusing aspect for many. In all cultures, some sort of entertainment outside of office hours and the exchange of gifts are part of the process of getting better acquainted. In high-context cultures and cultures with large power distance, the etiquette for gift giving is markedly different than in low-context cultures and cultures with small power distance.

Marcel Mauss, an anthropologist who looked at gifts in early societies, theorized that gift giving operated within the society as a way to acknowledge interrelationships and obligations. Mauss argued that in "archaic" societies, individual, family, and communal interests combined to make a social system that needed to acknowledge interrelationships and obligations.[27] He suggests that gift giving creates reciprocal relationships involving three obligations: the obligation to give, to receive, and to reciprocate. A gift has a magiclike quality, he points out, because it carries with it more than the item itself; it carries some of the giver—and that quality results in an obligation of the receiver to reciprocate. Thus, the ritual of gift giving in international business is important because it creates a social bond to be a giver, a receiver, and one obligated to the other. This series of roles and reciprocal obligations creates solidarity.

The first point about gifts from a practical viewpoint is to figure out how the ritual plays out. What constitutes an acceptable gift in the culture, and what is the role of gift giving? In Japan, for example, one never gives an unwrapped gift or visits a Japanese home empty-handed. A gift is presented with the comment that it is only a trifle, which implies that the humble social position of the giver does not permit giving a gift in keeping with the high status of the recipient. The recipient, in turn, will not open the gift in front of the giver, in order to spare him or her any embarrassment. The intention of gift giving in Japan is to convey thoughtfulness and consideration for the receiver, who, over time, builds up trust and confidence in the giver.

Every country will have an etiquette and set of implicit rules around the giving of gifts: their timing, their value, how they are presented. Know what these are.[28] Many organizations have policies related to gift giving designed to separate this cultural pattern from bribery or extortion, so managers will want to keep their organization's guidelines in mind.

When in Rome, Should You "Do as the Romans Do" . . . and Feel Comfortable about It?

Overseas travel, whether for work or vacation, may place us in the position of needing to decide whether to follow local practices. With some local practices, there is no choice. When in Britain, you drive on the left side of the road. Some local practices, though, may not seem to make sense, while others may seem liberating. The Japanese protect delicate tatami mats by removing their shoes. Do you conform? If you are a non-Muslim woman, do you wear a headscarf and long cloak when in a conservative Islamic country such as Saudi Arabia?

At a more complex level, other customs may conflict with our home culture's moral or perhaps legal standards. If you are from a country where cannabis is illegal or reserved for medicinal use, do you visit the Grasshopper, a cannabis coffee shop, when you are in Amsterdam? If you are American and you observe the drinking age of 21, do you drink in environments where there is no drinking age?

At the business level, do you follow the corporate tax law as you would in your home country, or do you underreport and then negotiate, along with the locals, in Italy? Do you pay fixers or agents, invisible hands, in cultures where this is a process widely followed? Agreed, such practices will contradict most company ethical codes, but what if your competitors follow such practices? If you are American, do you follow the Foreign Corrupt Practices Act in cultures where your competition greases palms? Do you outsource your legal or moral issue to an agent? The issue here is, to what extent should we follow local practices and conform to local customs? What do you think?

Questions:

1. Are all actions that conform to local customs morally defensible?

2. Recommend an approach to resolving ethical issues in the international arena.

SOCIETAL ORGANIZATION

Every society structures its social relationships, and these patterned arrangements of relationships define an important aspect of culture. There are two main classes of social institutions, based on the conditions of their formation: *kinship* and *free association.*

The family is the basic unit of institutions based on kinship. Unlike the American family, which is generally composed of parents and their children, families in many nations are extended to include all relatives by blood and by marriage. Many of these cultures will be high context. For the foreign firm, this extended family is a source of employees and business connections. The trust that people place in their relatives may motivate them to buy from a supplier owned by their cousin's cousin, even though the price is higher. Local personnel managers may fill the best jobs with family members, regardless of qualifications. Although the extended family is large, each member's feeling of responsibility to it is strong. This practice goes against the common Western idea that nepotism is to be avoided, except in family businesses.

Associations not based on kinship may be formed by age, gender, or common interest.[29] These groups are important for international managers to understand, because they influence behavior at a fundamental level and their rules and organization are likely to differ across cultural borders. Consumer organizations, for example, have forced firms to change their products, promotion, and prices. A new kind of association has emerged with Facebook and other social networks, with their own unwritten cultural rules. In the spring of 2011, we are seeing that they have a significant influence on international political organizations in the Middle East. We can expect to see much more e-influence on firms.

In Chapter 4, we have looked at what culture is and its significance for international business, reviewed three of the most useful cultural dimension frameworks, and addressed some of the more significant sociocultural aspects of societies, including aesthetics, religion, material culture, and language. Moving forward to other external forces that managers must address and over which they have limited control, please remember that all of these forces are influenced by culture. You might think of culture as a collection of rules, many of them unwritten, that social groups use to solve their problems and differentiate themselves from one another. Understanding culture at a significant level provides international managers with a rich way to build understanding, and possibly value, across cultural borders.

Mallory Wedeking: Attitude Is Everything!

Mallory Wedeking has studied and worked in Uganda and Rwanda. When asked to give advice to students studying international business and wondering if it is for them, she has some very interesting observations. Here are her comments:

My concentration in school is entrepreneurship and my career goals are to pursue a career in business in the context of International Development. I became interested in International Business when I first traveled after I graduated high school. Interacting with different cultures and different lifestyles inspired in me creativity and a desire to learn. I craved the excitement and added texture to doing business in an international context.

The most influential time abroad I have experienced would be the four months I studied in Uganda and Rwanda, two countries located in East Africa. While I was there, in addition to studying, I was also able to do an internship through the non-profit Food for the Hungry. My duties in the internship involved working with a rural village in Eastern Africa to help foster economic development and financial responsibility within the community.

I chose this location because I desired to expand my knowledge and cultural awareness beyond that of the Western, developed world. Obviously, I knew I was going to experience a much broader cultural gap than I had in Europe and was nervous about the transition. I briefly familiarized myself with the culture (which would definitely be necessary in more formal cross-cultural interactions), but most of the cultural awareness, including "Dos" and "Don'ts," I learned along the way. I learned early on that mistakes were unavoidable and that the attitude in which you deal with them is what matters.

Learning another culture is truly a humbling experience. Along those lines, if I had to give anyone advice in working abroad, I would have to say that attitude is everything. Cultural miscommunications will happen no matter how much you prepare ahead of time. I do not think I would have been able to learn in the capacity that I did if I wasn't able to get back up on my feet (literally, in some cases) and keep moving forward. Also, I would recommend understanding the phases of culture shock and being able to properly identify where you are in order to deal with your current feelings and emotions. There is a tendency at certain points of culture shock to retreat from the culture and surround yourself with only things familiar and comfortable. I experienced this feeling two months into my stay abroad, often retreating with my fellow American students and watching movies like Ferris Bueller's Day Off or Star Wars. I had to force myself to continue interacting with the Ugandan people, against all my other desires.

Surprisingly, I found that returning to the United States was a much more difficult cultural adjustment than arriving in East Africa. One reason was because I had not expected that my home for twenty years of my life could feel overwhelming and unfamiliar. It took about six months to completely feel comfortable here again. I learned that the process cannot be rushed, and it is important to give yourself time to really absorb everything you learned while abroad. You shouldn't expect or want yourself to be the same exact person you were before you left.

My greatest enjoyment while I was working abroad was finding different ways to connect with people. I realized that though we were worlds apart culturally, not to mention mileage, there were so many ways we could relate to each other, especially through song and dance. Emphasizing the things you have in common, rather than the differences (which easily outnumber the commonalities), is so important in learning to relate with one another. After all, we are all human, and that's a huge thing in common!

I would highly recommend working internationally. The daily surprises keep things interesting and teach you invaluable qualities and skills. Even traveling for pleasure purposes or studying abroad teaches you skills such as being adaptable, thinking and making decisions quickly, learning on the go and developing advanced communication skills, all of which are extremely desirable to employers.

Resources for Your Global Career

Test your Cultural IQ and knowledge of business etiquette by taking the international cultural quizzes on these links:

- http://www.getcustoms.com/2004GTC/quiz.html
- http://www.mannersinternational.com/etiquette_tips_business.asp
- *The Economist:* Country Briefings and "Doing Business In . . ." Series: http://audiovideo.economist.com/?fr_chl=a841d118e68f7ad627812b42ce2cb5a134fc691e&rf=bm

Here are your etiquette and protocol guides for doing business in major cities and countries in the world—you can never learn enough!

- http://www.economist.com/blogs/gulliver/etiquette/
- http://www.executiveplanet.com/index.php?title=Main_Page

(continued)

Summary

LO4-1 Describe what culture is.

Anthropologists, who study culture, describe it as the *sum total of the beliefs, rules, techniques, institutions, and artifacts that characterize human populations.* In other words, culture consists of the "individual worldviews, social rules, and interpersonal dynamics characterizing a group of people set in a particular time and place." Most anthropologists also agree that:

1. Culture is *learned;* we are not born with a culture.
2. The various aspects of culture are *interrelated.*
3. Culture is *shared, patterned, and mutually constructed through social interaction.*
4. Culture *defines the boundaries* of different groups.

LO4-2 Explain the significance of national-level culture differences for international business.

Everything we do is influenced by culture, and most of us realize that about other cultures, but not always about our own. National cultural differences affect the functional areas of international business. For example, assumptions about the need for controls in accounting systems rest of cultural values having to do with trust. Leadership is greatly influenced by culture. What is leadership thought to be? Is it patriarchal and hierarchical? It the leader one among equals? HR practices are greatly influenced by cultural values as well. What is the role of social class in employee relationships? Is employee evaluation a development aid or an adversarial process? Every business action is influenced by national-level cultural values. Organizational and local-level values also play a role.

LO4-3 Describe Hall's concept of high and low context.

In a high-context culture, the participants have social ties that are long-standing and close, so people know what the communication will be from long experience with the other and from communication signals. In a low-context culture, the relationships are of shorter duration, and so more of the communication has to be explicit. In our families, we probably find a higher context, even though we may be members of low-context cultures. In high context (HC), the communication tends to be implicit and indirect. Context plays an exceedingly strong role, actually carrying much of the meaning. In these cultures, such as Japan, China, Latin America, and the Middle East, communication is more subtle and inferred. In contrast, Hall notes that people in low-context cultures have explicit communication patterns. They do not rely so greatly on the context of the communication. The explicit communicator is direct and unambiguous: what you say is what you mean.

LO4-4 Describe Hofstede's framework.

Hofstede's framework is concerned primarily with work values. It originally had four dimensions that were used to classify the survey data that underlie and differentiate cultures: individualism-collectivism, power distance, uncertainty avoidance, and masculinity-femininity. In collaboration with researchers in Asia, he later added a fifth dimension, long-term orientation. This fifth dimension is sometimes referred to as Confucian dynamism.

LO4-5 Outline Trompenaars' dimensions.

Trompenaars' seven-dimension framework for understanding culture is derived from the social sciences, and his initial data are from 47 countries, later greatly expanded in collaboration with Hampden-Turner. The first five dimensions address the culture's patterns for relationships among people, and the final two have to do with time and nature. Trompenaars' dimensions are interesting because, unlike Hofstede's dimensions, which describe values, many of Trompenaars' dimensions describe the behavior that is the result of the underlying cultural value. His dimensions are universalism vs. particularism (rules vs. relationships), individualism vs. communitarianism, neutral vs. affective (unemotional vs. emotional), specific vs. diffuse, achievement vs. ascription, attitudes toward time, and attitudes toward the environment.

LO4-6 Discuss the sociocultural aspects of culture as a phenomenon.

Culture is not directly observable. The sociocultural aspects of cultural are how a society's culture manifests or shows itself. Culture manifests in everything. The major areas include aesthetics, religion, material culture, language, and social organization.

sociocultural (p. 94)

ethnocentricity (p. 94)

context (p. 98)

monochronic (p. 98)

polychronic (p. 99)

Confucian dynamism (p. 100)

universalism (p. 103)

particularism (p. 103)

communitarianism (p. 103)

neutral vs. affective (p. 103)

specific vs. diffuse (p. 104)

achievement vs. ascription (p. 104)

aesthetics (p. 105)

material culture or artifacts (p. 108)

Questions

1. Drawing on Hall's high and low context, describe some of the communication issues that might well arise when an Arab company officer who has spent his career in the Middle East is sent on temporary assignment to Germany for a year to integrate a process developed in one of the Middle East production facilities.

2. If you are a Mexican who has just accepted a short-term assignment in Ireland, what are some of the expectations you may have about Irish behavior, drawing on Hofstede's cultural dimensions?

3. Thinking about the definitions and descriptions of culture offered in this chapter, would you expect the objective discipline of accounting to be influenced by culture?

4. If you had the choice of sending either an American or a Mexican, both equally qualified and at about the same level and in the same functional areas, to Japan for a three-year assignment, why might sending the Mexican offer less risk?

5. How could Trompenaars' universalism-particularism dimension be helpful in sorting out confusion in the international division over ethical behavior?

6. Give a short description of an example of Trompenaars' achievement-ascription dimension.

7. If you were advising a French colleague on her first work assignment to your home culture, and she asked you what aspects of the material culture she should pay attention to, what advice would you give her?

8. What is the significance of the extended family for international managers?

9. Some societies view change differently than do Americans. What impact does this have on the way Americans operate in those areas?

10. Discuss the role of gift giving in high-context societies.

Research Task

globalEDGE   globalEDGE.msu.edu

Use the globalEDGE site (http://globalEDGE.msu.edu/) to complete the following exercises:

1. Assume you own an exporting company that specializes in consumer products. You have been selling your products in several different countries but have yet to enter the Asian market. You have chosen Singapore as the first Asian country to enter. Because you have not previously sold your products in any Asian market, you think it would be a good idea to form a strategic alliance with a local firm. You strongly believe that first impression is important. Therefore, you have decided to collect some information regarding the business culture and local habits of Singapore from the *Kwintessential* website. Prepare a short report on the most shocking characteristics that may influence business interactions in this country.

2. The cultural distance of countries in which your firm operates is one of the many explanations of significant differences that your U.S.-based employees face when traveling to different affiliates worldwide. Typically, an index of cultural distance can be determined by summing the differences of country-level scores such as those introduced by Hofstede's cultural dimensions. At the present time, your firm has operations in Turkey,

Poland, Costa Rica, South Africa, and Indonesia. Using the *Hofstede Cultural Dimensions Resource Center* based on studies involving cultural dimensions to assess all five countries, determine which affiliates are located in a culture that is least and most similar to the United States. As there are four main components of each overall cultural distance score, which component(s) can be considered most influential for each country?

Minicase: Who Gets the Assignment?

Your international company headquartered in New Jersey is sending an expatriate to China for a three-year assignment to staff up and run a new branch of its industrial products business. The main Chinese customers are using the products in their Middle Eastern and North African petroleum operations. You are chair of the selection committee, have extensive overseas experience, and presently serve as VP, Human Resources. There were 12 internal people interested in the position, and your committee has narrowed this to three final candidates who want this assignment. Here are the candidates:

Tom is a mid-level finance manager with stellar performance reviews. He has no foreign experience and would like to develop his career in this direction. He is single, has an MBA, and has been out of school for 20 years. His background is in finance at the undergrad level, which he studied at Ohio State, only 50 miles from his hometown. He is involved in the local Council on Foreign Relations and is an accomplished athlete.

Firdaus is a deputy VP of HR at corporate. Her family emigrated from Yemen to Chicago when she was in grade school, and she speaks reads and writes Arabic, both classical and the Yemen dialect. She is married, with two children. Her husband George is a professor of history and does not speak Arabic. She has a Ph.D. in engineering, joined the company on the operations side, and has made the mid-career transition to HR successfully. She finished her PhD at the University of London before she began with the company and is now early mid-career. Her performance reviews are stellar. She encountered an incident at the company's headquarters several years ago when there was a discussion about her wearing a headscarf, but this was resolved without her changing her practice. She is well known and well liked throughout HQ. Her husband is ready to take a leave of absence for three years to accompany her.

Gunther is VP of the German-based EU company. His functional background is accounting, and he is credited with the success of the company in the EU. He built the business from a small operation in Frankfurt to the EU sector leader in only seven years. He speaks German and English and is known for being well-organized and "button-upped." His work is timely, accurate, and detailed. Gunther's boss, the president of the international side, was a bit surprised that Gunter expressed interest in this position, because it is perceived as junior to the position he has now, although it would have an equivalent title on paper. Gunter has an undergraduate degree in anthropology and took graduate-level accounting courses earlier in his career.

The company would like someone who could get the operation up and running, stay for three years, and then transfer the position to a local hire they would develop for the responsibility. Drawing on the culture dimensions that we have reviewed, along with your business knowledge, whom would you recommend for the position?

Natural Resources and Environmental Sustainability

Climate change may prove to be the most important business issue of the 21st century. Managers who wish to be responsible to shareholders and the broader community must be prepared to face the challenges and opportunities presented by our shifting climate. Trillions of dollars, millions of lives, thousands of species—infinite solutions.

—*Stanford University's Graduate School of Business,*
The MBA's Climate Change Primer

Switzerland, Where Geography Drives Competitive Advantage: Geography, Watches, Chocolate, and Cheese

Watches, lace, carvings, chocolate, cheese, precision machinery, pharmaceuticals—what do they have in common? All are produced in Switzerland; all have a high value per kilo; the Swiss versions are known for their quality; and Switzerland's natural resources, or lack of them, are partially responsible for their being produced in Switzerland. To appreciate why this is so, consider the following: (1) Switzerland is mostly mountainous, with little level land; (2) it is close to the heavily populated lowlands of western Europe; (3) transportation across the mountains to these markets is relatively expensive; and (4) Switzerland has practically no mineral resources.

One way to overcome these endowment disadvantages—lack of local sources of raw materials and high transportation costs—is to import small amounts of raw materials, add high value to them, and export a lightweight finished product. The Swiss have done precisely this with the manufacture of watches. They import small volumes of high-quality Swedish steel costing in the range of 40¢ per ounce that they then convert to watch movements selling for $60 per ounce. Because of their light weight, the cost of transporting these movements to market is minimal. Precision machinery and pharmaceuticals are other products that minimize the need for importing bulky raw materials. For all of these products, emphasis is placed on the value added by manufacturing, a process that is based on skill, care, and tradition.

Now let's look at the highly protected Swiss agricultural sector. Although the mountain slopes do not support much agriculture, they are adequate for raising cattle and goats. Production of milk is no problem, but getting it to its major markets outside Switzerland is. Fluid milk is bulky in relation to its value and expensive to transport. The dairymen do to the milk what the watchmakers do to the steel—convert it to a concentrated, high-value product: cheese. Because Swiss cheesemakers have no advantage over their counterparts in the lowland dairying areas nearer to the important markets, they have to compete on the basis of high quality and reputation, which they have carefully promoted.

The plentiful supply of milk is responsible for another product: milk chocolate. The Swiss import the raw chocolate and convert the milk into another high-value-per-kilo product. Certainly, the Swiss manufacturer pays higher transportation costs to bring sugar and chocolate in and ship

learning objectives

After reading this chapter, you should be able to:

LO5-1 **Describe** how geographical features of a country or region create contextual differences that contribute to economic, cultural, political, and social conditions important to international business.

LO5-2 **Apply** Porter's diamond model to a discussion of geographical features.

LO5-3 **Summarize** the importance to business of inland waterways and outlets to the sea.

LO5-4 **Outline** the nonrenewable and renewable energy options available and their broad business implications.

LO5-5 **Describe** the issues related to nonfuel minerals that concern international business.

LO5-6 **Describe** the concept of environmental sustainability and its potential influence on business.

LO5-7 **Explain** the major characteristics of sustainable business.

LO5-8 **Discuss** the utility of the stakeholder model for sustainable business.

the finished product out than does Hershey in Pennsylvania. Again, the Swiss product must be perceived to be superior so that it will bring a higher price to offset the greater costs.

Source: Adapted from Rhoads Murphey, *The Scope of Geography*, 2nd ed. (Skokie, IL: Rand McNally, 1973), pp. 65–67.

The scope of *natural resources* is quite broad. We begin with a consideration of the geographic basics—location, topography, and climate—and how they influence business. Then we continue with a focus on the major natural resources for energy and nonfuel minerals. Our consideration of natural resources leads directly to concerns about their stewardship. The final section addresses those issues through a focus on environmental sustainability.

Geography

LO5-1 Describe how geographical features of a country or region create contextual differences that contribute to economic, cultural, political, and social conditions important to international business.

Switzerland is a good example to illustrate how geography—location, topography, climate, and natural resources—can have a profound impact on the way people organize their activities. Here, we explore how the physical environment provides the basic context for our economic lives. Think about the Swiss and their watches, chocolates, cheese, precision machinery, and pharmaceuticals. These high value per kilo, high quality products provide a creative way to overcome Switzerland's lack of local raw materials and its high transportation costs, both of which are endowment disadvantages. For watches, the Swiss import high-quality Swedish steel costing 40¢ per ounce and convert it to watch movements selling for $60 per ounce. Because of their low weight, the cost of transporting these movements to market is minimal. Swiss dairies do to milk what the watchmakers do to the steel—convert it via processing to concentrated, high-value products: cheese and chocolates that compete on the basis of reputation and quality.[1]

We consider the physical elements of a location as largely uncontrollable forces because, much like the foreign environmental forces we discussed earlier, they are the givens around which managers must adjust their strategies as they make efforts to compensate for and adjust to differences in these forces among markets. An additional way to explain the importance of the environment and natural resources is to examine Michael Porter's diamond (see Figure 5.1), a model developed to explain differing levels of success among the many national players in world markets.[2]

Competitive Advantage: Porter's Diamond

LO5-2 Apply Porter's diamond model to a discussion of geographical features.

Porter's diamond model considers four aspects of a country's economic environment that affect its competitive position: factor conditions; related and supporting industries; demand conditions; and firm strategy, structure, and rivalry. Porter suggests that competitively successful countries are the ones that have the most favorable diamonds. The geographic attributes of a country are a core part of its *basic factor* conditions, its inherited assets over which the country has either no or quite limited control, such as topography, climate, and natural resources. Porter distinguishes between basic factors, those that a country inherits, such as the mountains and lack of natural resources for the Swiss, and *advanced factors*, those a country can readily mold, such as the labor force and infrastructure. He makes the interesting point that local *disadvantages* in factor conditions can actually function as *advantages* and become a force for innovation. His thinking is that adverse conditions such as local terrain and climate or scarce raw materials at the basic-factor level, or labor shortages at the advanced-factor level, force firms to develop new methods, and this innovation may lead to a national competitive advantage. Awareness of a nation's factor conditions is important for the international firm.

Going back to the Swiss example of high-value-added, concentrated goods, the Swiss have developed expertise areas that take into account their geography, in this case, mostly constraints (basic factors), by developing advanced factor conditions that recognize and incorporate their basic, inherited conditions. The Swiss have built an educated, skilled, and specialized workforce; they protect agriculture against foreign competition; they pursue neutrality, thus keeping trade relationships open; they have established a reliable transportation system that overcomes their topographical challenges; and they have encouraged high levels of savings, so they can draw on both domestic and foreign savings in Switzerland. Switzerland has taken a

FIGURE 5.1

Firm Strategy, Structure, and Rivalry

Factor Conditions

Demand Conditions

Related and Supporting Industries

Source: Reprinted by permission of the *Harvard Business Review.* "The Competitive Advantage of Nations" by Michael E. Porter, March–April 1990, p. 77. Copyright © 1990 by The President and Fellows of Harvard College; all rights reserved.

strategic approach to developing its resources by recognizing its basic endowments and building its advanced endowments. This approach has led to the Swiss competitive advantage in the areas of watches, precision machinery, chocolate, pharmaceuticals, and cheese, among others.

Location: Political and Trade Relationships

Where a country is located, who its neighbors are, and how its capital and major cities are situated are also basic factor conditions. How these factors contribute to the way a country builds its competitive advantage should be part of the general knowledge of international businesspeople. If the firm has an understanding of these aspects of its foreign markets, it, too, can share in the benefits they confer. Location helps explain many of a country's political and trade relationships, as the following focus on Austria will illustrate. While our focus here is on one country to illustrate the relationships among location, politics, and trade, remember that every country will have its own set of such relationships.

At the height of the Cold War, Austria's location enabled that country to be a political bridge between the noncommunist nations of the West and the communist nations of the East (see Figure 5.2). In addition, Austria's political neutrality made it a popular location

FIGURE 5.2

Austria and Her
Neighbors: A Cold
War Map

for the offices of international firms servicing eastern European operations. Furthermore, because Austria had led the Austro-Hungarian Empire until 1918, the Austrians were completely familiar with the cultures and practices of those neighboring countries to which they had once been joined. Finally, Vienna, Austria's capital, was close to both Czechoslovakia (today the Czech Republic and Slovakia) and Hungary. Austria took advantage of its location to (1) increase trade with the East, (2) become the principal financial intermediary between the two regions, and (3) strengthen its role as the regional headquarters for international businesses operating in eastern Europe.

In 1991, when the collapse of the Soviet bloc (COMECON, consisting of Bulgaria, Czechoslovakia, East Germany, Hungary, Romania, Poland, the Soviet Union, Cuba, Mongolia, and Vietnam) forced eastern European enterprises to reorient their trade toward the West, Austria's location and relationships allowed Austrian entrepreneurs to capture an important share of the West's exports to the East.

Geographical proximity is often a major reason for trade between nations and plays a role in the formation of trading groups, as well. With proximity, knowledge of the country is likely, delivery faster, freight costs lower, and service costs lower, too. The major trading partners of the United States—Canada and Mexico—lie on its borders. Geographical proximity is evident in the formation of trading groups such as the EU, Mercosur, ASEAN and NAFTA. Proximity also helps to explain why Japan has been one of China's largest sources of imports and a major trading partner, at least until the Tohoku earthquake in March 2011.

Topography

Surface features such as mountains, plains, deserts, and bodies of water contribute to differences in economies, cultures, politics, and social structures wherever they occur, both in nations and in regions of a single country. These topographic features, the features on the land's surface, can both hinder and aid physical distribution. They also may require that products be altered. For example, the effects of altitude on food products require a change in baking instructions at heights above 3,000 feet. Internal combustion engines begin to lose power at 5,000 feet, which may require the manufacturer of gasoline-powered machinery to use larger engines. Because **topography** contributes so powerfully to the factor conditions of a given location, we examine its major components: mountains, plains, deserts, and bodies of water.

topography
The surface features of a region

Mountains are barriers that tend to separate and impede exchange and interaction, whereas level areas (plains and plateaus) facilitate exchange and interaction, unless climate makes exchange unlikely, as in the Sahara and Gobi Deserts. The extent to which mountains serve as barriers depends on their massiveness, ruggedness, and transecting valleys. One example of such a barrier is the Himalaya Mountains. Travel across them is so difficult that transportation between India and China is by air or sea rather than overland. The contrast between the cultures of the Indo-Malayan people living to the south of the mountains and those of the Chinese living to the north is evidence of the Himalayas' effectiveness as a barrier. Another example of the influence of mountain barriers is found in Afghanistan, where mountains dominate the landscape, running northeast to southwest through the center of the country, including the Hindukush ("Hindu Killer") area. More than 40 percent of Afghanistan lies above 6,000 feet.[3] For comparison, In the United States, there are only two peaks east of the Mississippi River that hit 6,000 feet: Mt. Mitchell in North Carolina and Mt. Washington in New Hampshire. In Afghanistan, high passes transect the mountains, creating a network for caravans. There are at least 10 major ethnic groups and 33 languages spoken in Afghanistan,[4] evidence of the ability of mountain ranges to separate populations. Figure 5.3 illustrates Afghanistan's topography. In similar fashion, the Alps, Carpathians, Balkans, and Pyrenees have long separated the Mediterranean cultures from those of northern Europe.

Nations whose mountain ranges divide them into smaller regional areas, such as Afghanistan and Switzerland, pose a challenge to businesspeople in the form of regional markets, each with its own distinctive industries, climate, culture, dialect, and sometimes even language. In addition to Afghanistan and Switzerland, Spain, China, and Colombia present the challenge of mountain ranges. In Spain, Catalonia and the Basque country (see

The Central Asian Hindu Kush runs from north central Pakistan through eastern and central Afghanistan.

Figure 5.4) have separate languages, Catalan and Euskara, along with sizable minorities that wish to secede from Spain to form a separate nation. Although the Basques and the Catalans can speak Spanish, when they are among themselves they use their own languages, which are unintelligible to other Spaniards. This creates the wide range of problems that are found wherever there are language differences. In Catalonia and the Basque country, Spanish-speaking managers do not attain the empathy with their local employees that they do in other parts of Spain, and sales representatives who speak the local language are more

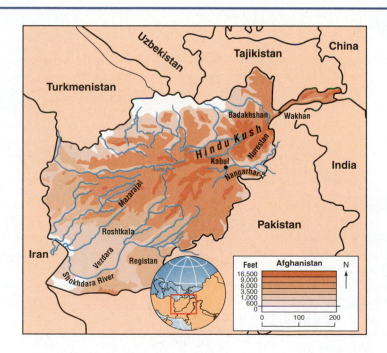

FIGURE 5.3

Map of Afghanistan Mountains

The green wall of China, here in Taipusi, Inner Mongolia, has been planted to fend off the encroaching Gobi Desert.

FIGURE 5.4

Map of Spain

0   100   200 Millas

0   100   200 Kilómetros

effective. These language differences increase promotional costs if, to be more effective, companies choose to prepare their material in Euskara, Catalan, and Spanish.[5] A similar situation holds for Switzerland, whose language borders are illustrated in Figure 5.5.

In China, dozens of languages, each having many dialects, developed in villages separated by mountains. This language diversity caused communication problems that hindered economic development until the government decreed Mandarin, known in China as *Putonghua*, to be the official language in 1956. Today, though, many dialects persist. The written language is shared among the many language groups, but spoken language is virtually incomprehensible across language borders. You can compare the Chinese language map in Figure 5.6 to the topographical map to see that language areas and topography correspond.

In Colombia, three ranges of the Andes run like spines from north to south to divide Colombia into four separate areas, each with its own culture and dialects (see Figure 5.7). Depending on the product, marketers may need to create four distinct promotional mixes. In addition, Colombia has a range of climates due to the great differences in altitude throughout habitable parts of the country. The variation from hot and humid at sea level in Barranquilla to cold and dry in Bogotá creates production and inventory challenges for a manufacturer that must produce a distinct product and package for each climate zone.

Deserts and tropical forests also separate markets, increase the cost of transportation, and create concentrations of population. More than one-third of the earth's surface consists of arid and semiarid regions located either on the coasts, where the winds blow away from the land, or in the interior, where mountains or long distances cause the winds to lose their moisture before reaching these regions. Every continent has deserts and tropical forests, and every western coast between 20 and 30 degrees north or south of the equator is dry. Only in latitudes where there is a major source of water, as in Egypt, is

FIGURE 5.5   Map of the Cantons and Major Language Areas of Switzerland

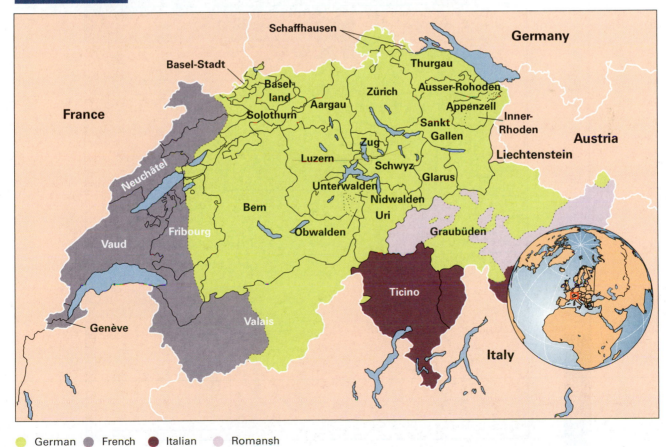

- German   French   Italian   Romansh

FIGURE 5.6 Topographical and Language Maps of China

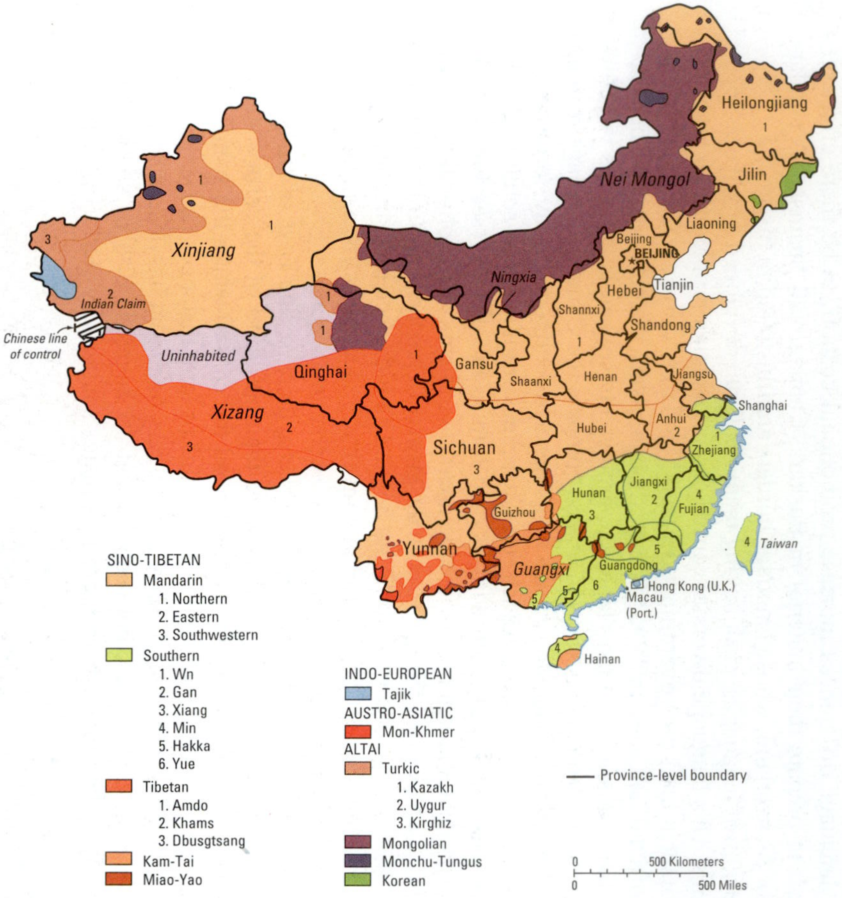

Language Map (top)

Heilongjiang
Jilin
Liaoning
Nei Mongol
Ningxia
Gansu
Qinghai
Xizang
Xinjiang
Uninhabited
Sichuan
Yunnan
Guangxi
Guizhou
Hunan
Hubei
Shaanxi
Shanxi
Henan
Hebei
BEIJING
Tianjin
Shandong
Jiangsu
Shanghai
Anhui
Zhejiang
Jiangxi
Fujian
Guangdong
Hainan
Taiwan
Hong Kong (U.K.)
Macau (Port.)

Indian Claim
Chinese line of control

Province-level boundary

500 Kilometers
500 Miles

SINO-TIBETAN

Mandarin
1. Northern
2. Eastern
3. Southwestern

Southern
1. Wu
2. Gan
3. Xiang
4. Min
5. Hakka
6. Yue

Tibetan
1. Amdo
2. Khams
3. Dbusgtsang

Kam-Tai
Miao-Yao

INDO-EUROPEAN
Tajik

AUSTRO-ASIATIC
Mon-Khmer

ALTAI
Turkic
1. Kazakh
2. Uygur
3. Kirghiz

Mongolian
Monchu-Tungus
Korean

Topographical Map (bottom)

China
International boundary
Province-level boundary
National capital
Province-level capital
Railroad
Road

Autonomous regions and municipalities in italics

500 Kilometers
500 Miles

RUSSIA
KAZAKHSTAN
KYRGYZSTAN
TAJ.
AFG.
PAK.
INDIA
NEPAL
BHUTAN
BANGLADESH
BURMA
LAOS
THAILAND
CAMBODIA
VIETNAM
MONGOLIA
NORTH KOREA
SOUTH KOREA
PHILIPPINES

Astana
Bishkek
Almaty
Semey (Semipalatinsk)
Barnaul
Novosibirsk
Omsk
Bratsk
Chita
Irkutsk
Ulan-ude
Ulaanbaatar
Khabarovsk
Harbin
Changchun
Shenyang
Dalian
Beijing
Tianjin
Hohhot
Baotou
Yinchuan
Lanzhou
Xining
Golmud
Urumqi
Korla
Kashi
Burqin
Lhasa
Thimphu
Kathmandu
New Delhi
Agra
Leh
Mandalay
Myitkyina
Rangoon
Chiang Mai
Bangkok
Vientiane
Hanoi
Hue
Nanning
Haikou
Kunming
Guiyang
Chengdu
Chongqing
Wuhan
Zhengzhou
Xian
Taiyuan
Shijiazhuang
Jinan
Qingdao
Nanjing
Shanghai
Hefei
Nanchang
Changsha
Guangzhou
Hong Kong
Macau
Fuzhou
Xiamen
Kao-hsiung
Taipei
Seoul
Pyongyang

HEILONGJIANG
JILIN
LIAONING
NEI MONGOL
NINGXIA
GANSU
QINGHAI
XIZANG (TIBET)
XINJIANG
SICHUAN
YUNNAN
GUIZHOU
GUANGXI
GUANGDONG
HUNAN
HUBEI
HENAN
SHAANXI
SHANXI
SHANDONG
HEBEI
JIANGSU
ANHUI
ZHEJIANG
JIANGXI
FUJIAN
HAINAN
CHONGQING

Special Administrative Regions

Lake Baikal
Lake Balkhash
Yellow Sea
East China Sea
South China Sea
Hainan Dao
Taiwan
Luzon
Manila

Amur
Ob
Irtysh
Amu
Indus
Ganges
Brahmaputra
Irrawaddy
Salween
Mekong
Yangtze
Huang He
Xi
Hai
Songhua
Tumen
Demarcation Line

Indian claim
Chinese line of control
Line of Control

30
15
45
75
90
105
120
135

FIGURE 5.7

Map of Colombia

Colombia
— Department, Intendencia and Comisar'a Boundaries   ● Elevations above 14,000 meters

there a concentration of population. Nowhere is the relationship between water supply and population concentration better illustrated than in Australia, a continent the size of the continental United States but with only 22.6 million inhabitants, in contrast to the U.S. population of 311 million. Australia's coastline is humid and fertile, whereas the huge center of the country is mainly a desert closely resembling the Sahara. Figure 5.8 illustrates this by a focus on land use. Because of its topography, Australia's population concentrates along the coastal areas in and around the state capitals, which are also major seaports, and in the southeastern fifth of the nation, where more than one-half of the population lives. Her topography gives Australia one of the highest percentages of urban population in the world, at about 93 percent.

At the other extreme from deserts, tropical rain forests also are a barrier to economic development and human settlement, especially when they are combined with a harsh climate and poor soil. This occurs in the tropical rain forests located in the Amazon basin, Southeast Asia, and the Congo. Except in parts of West Africa and Java, rain forests are thinly populated and little developed economically. For example, the greatest rain forest of them all—in the Brazilian Amazon basin—covers more than 1 million square miles (equivalent to one-fourth of the U.S. land area) and occupies one-half of Brazil; it is inhabited by just 4 percent of the country's population. Only true deserts have a population density lower than the Amazon's one person per square mile. There is one other topographical feature that is neither a desert nor a tropical forest, yet it has the features of

FIGURE 5.8

Land Use Map of
Australia

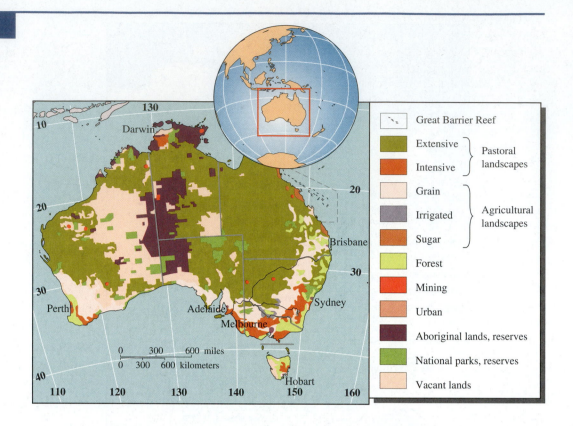

these formations: the Canadian Shield. This is a massive area of bedrock covering one-half of Canada's landmass that is swept by polar air that permits a growing season of only four months. Its population density is low, with only 10 percent of Canada's population in this region.

International managers know that in more densely populated nations, marketing and distributing their products costs less because population centers are closer, communication systems are better, and more people are available for employment. Therefore, when they compare population densities such as Canada's 3 inhabitants per square kilometer, Australia's 3, Brazil's 23, and the United States' 33 with the Netherlands' 401 or Japan's 336, they know not to draw the wrong conclusions.[6] They are aware that the populations in Canada, Australia, and Brazil are highly concentrated in a relatively small area, because of deserts, tropical rain forests, and, in Canada's case, the shield.

LO5-3 **Summarize** the importance to business of inland waterways and outlets to the sea.

Bodies of Water

Bodies of water, unlike mountains, deserts, and tropical forests, attract people and facilitate transportation. A world population map clearly shows that bodies of water have attracted more people than have areas remote from water (see Figure 5.9). Densely populated regions coincide with rivers, lakes, and seacoasts.

Water is necessary for life and critical for industry, yet invisible to most consumers when used in agriculture and manufacturing. For example, as much as 2,400 liters are used to produce one hamburger, while 11,000 liters can be used in the production of a pair of jeans.[7] Although water is an abundant natural resource, its abundance is not reflected in patterns of water distribution. In general, the world's poor lack access to clean water. As an example, in the slums of Dar es Salaam, Tanzania's largest city, 1,000 liters of water could cost $8. The same amount in the wealthy areas of the same city would cost $0.34, and $0.68 in the United States, according to the not-for-profit organization WaterAid.[8]

One significant feature associated with bodies of water is the **inland waterway,** significant because it provides inexpensive access to interior markets. Before the construction of railways, water transport was the only economically practical carrier for bulk goods moving over long distances. Water transport increased even after the building of railroads; today, in every continent except Australia, which has no inland waterways, extensive use is still made of water transportation. The importance of waterways relative to railroads, however, has diminished everywhere with one exception—Europe's **Rhine waterway,** the world's most important inland waterway system.

Cargo ships passing through Germany on Europe's main transportation artery, the Rhine waterway.

To illustrate the Rhine's significance, consider this: one-half of Switzerland's exports and nearly three-fourths of its imports pass through the city of Basel, the Swiss inland port (see Figure 5.10). From ancient times, shipments have moved among the Netherlands, Belgium, Germany, France, Austria, Liechtenstein, and Switzerland by means of the Rhine and its connecting waterways. The Rhine–Main–Danube Canal, completed in 1992, creates access from the Netherlands and the North Sea through 15 countries to the Black Sea. From there, shipments can continue to Moscow over the interconnected system of the Volga and Don Rivers. Not many ships undertake the entire 30-day voyage from Rotterdam to the Black Sea, which is 3,500 kilometers, but this waterway has stimulated shipping over shorter east–west routes, such as Nuremburg to Budapest and Vienna to Rotterdam. Increasingly, firms have been turning

Rhine waterway
A system of rivers and canals that is the main transportation artery of Europe

inland waterway
Waterway that provides access to interior regions

FIGURE 5.9   World Population Map

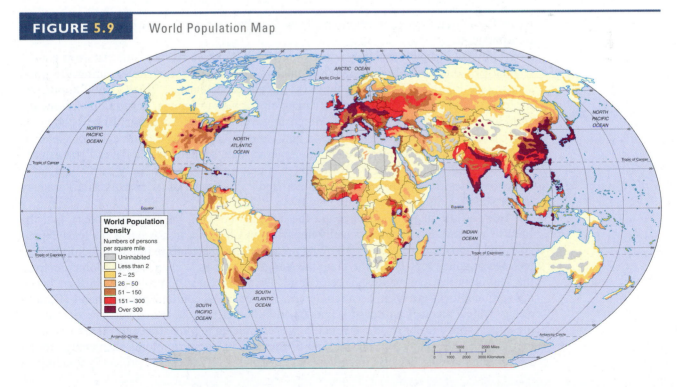

World Population Density

Numbers of persons per square mile

- Uninhabited
- Less than 2
- 2 – 25
- 26 – 50
- 51 – 150
- 151 – 300
- Over 300

FIGURE 5.10   Map of Rhine–Main–Danube Canal

Source: Center for International Earth Science Information Network (CIESIN), Columbia University, and Centro Internacional de Agricultura Tropical (CIAT). Used by permission, http://ciesin.columbia/edu/gpw.

to the Rhine waterway as an environmentally friendly and more economic alternative to road transportation.

A review of major inland waterways in South America includes the Amazon and its tributaries, which offer some 57,000 kilometers of navigable waterways during the flood season (see Figure 5.11). Oceangoing vessels can reach Manaus, Brazil (1,600 kilometers upstream), and smaller river steamers can go all the way to Iquitos, Peru (3,600 kilometers from the Atlantic). Farther south, the Mercosur governments of Argentina, Brazil, Paraguay, and Uruguay are developing the Paraná and Paraguay Rivers as a trade corridor connecting the vast landlocked interior of South America with seaports at the River Plate estuary near Montevideo (see Figure 5.12). Although at present the rivers are only partly navigable, Argentina uses river ports on the Paraná to handle 25 percent of its exports, and Paraguay imports most of its fuel on the Paraguay River.

In Asia, the major waterways are the Yangtze (China), the Ganges (India), and the Indus (Pakistan). Rivers are especially important in China because water is the least expensive, and often the only, means of moving industrial raw materials to the manufacturing centers. Oceangoing vessels can travel up the Yangtze as far as Wuhan, 1,000 kilometers from the sea. Now that the massive Three Gorges Dam hydroelectric project is finished, when navigational locks are open, oceangoing vessels are able to continue past Wuhan to Chongquing, which becomes an inland seaport 2,400 kilometers from the ocean. The dam itself, the largest concrete dam ever constructed, was completed in May 2006 and filled to capacity in October 2008. The reservoir the dam creates is 650 kilometers long, displacing around 1.9 million persons. Because of anticipated environmental issues (the project is flooding an

FIGURE 5.11

Source: https://www.cia.gov/library/publications/the-world-factbook/maps/maptemplate_br.html

FIGURE 5.12

Natural Resources and Environmental Sustainability   **Chapter 5**   131

area comparable to the Grand Canyon in the United States, but with three gorges), as well as human rights and archeological issues, the World Bank refused to fund the dam. At the International Rivers Network site, a group critical of the ecological impact of the dam, you can view video of the dam and its construction and join a virtual river cruise. See www. internationalrivers.org/node/6193/.

The United States depends heavily on two waterways, which provide 40,000 km of inland navigation. The Great Lakes–St. Lawrence waterway enables ocean freighters to travel 3,700 kilometers inland, thus transforming lake ports into ocean ports. The other waterway, the Mississippi River, connects the Great Lakes to the Gulf of Mexico and is especially important for carrying bulky commodities such as cotton, wheat, coal, timber, and iron ore. Most of the navigable rivers in the United States are in the eastern half because in the West, steep grades, hydroelectric dams, and variable flow make navigation impossible. The West's navigable rivers include the Columbia, Sacramento, and San Joaquin. The Columbia–Snake River system allows navigation inland 750 km to Lewiston, Idaho.

Historically, navigable waterways with connections to the ocean have been important because they have permitted the low-cost transportation of goods and people from a country's coast to its interior, and today they are the only means of access from the coasts of many developing nations. In Africa, where 14 of the world's 20 landlocked developing countries are located, access to the coast can be a major issue. With landlocked nations, governments must construct costly, long truck routes and extensive feeder networks for relatively low volumes of traffic. Furthermore, the governments that control the coastlines near landlocked countries are in positions to exert considerable political influence. An example of this situation is found with the Mercosur governments of Argentina, Brazil, Paraguay, and Uruguay and the Paraná and Paraguay Rivers Trade Corridor, which connects the landlocked interior of South America, Bolivia, and Paraguay, with seaports, as illustrated in Figure 5.12. Outlets to the sea for landlocked nations and regions are an important political and economic issue.

Climate

climate
Meteorological conditions, including temperature, precipitation, and wind, that prevail in a region

Climate (temperature, precipitation, and wind) is important because it sets the limits on what people can do, physically and economically. Where the climate is harsh, there are few human settlements, and where it is permissive, there tends to be population density. However, climate is not deterministic—it allows certain developments to occur, but it does not cause them. In terms of Porter's diamond, although climate is an inherited asset as a factor condition, technology can be applied to modify its impact. Similar climates occur in similar latitudes and continental positions, and the more water-dominated an area, the more moderate its climate.

We should mention in our discussion of climate that for centuries, some writers have used climatic differences to explain differences in human and economic development. This explanation, known as the North–South divide, suggests that the greatest economic and intellectual development has occurred in the temperate climates of northern Europe and the United States because the less temperate climates limit human energy and mental powers.[9] However, businesspeople must not be taken in by such ethnocentric reasoning that fails to explain the difference in the level of technology employed in the 1600s by the inhabitants of northeastern North America and northern Europe. Clearly, other factors—such as the Industrial Revolution, population size, and location—have contributed to the North–South development differences. Jared Diamond's Pulitzer Prize–winning *Guns, Germs, and Steel: The Fates of Human Societies* explores the basis of these factors that contribute to differing levels of development.[10] Diamond argues that the gaps in technology among human societies are caused by environmental differences amplified by feedback loops and that these differences do not lead to intellectual or moral superiority. World Bank studies have shown that many of the factors responsible for underdevelopment in tropical nations are present because of the tropical climate: continuous heat and the lack of winter temperatures offer no constraints for reproduction and growth of weeds, insects, viruses, birds, and parasites, and this results in destroyed crops, dead cattle, and people infected with debilitating diseases.[11] Techniques are becoming available to control pests and parasites, and once this is accomplished, the very characteristics that are now detrimental to tropical Africa will give it advantages over the temperate zones in agriculture. The resulting income is anticipated to create a market in tropical Africa that could easily surpass that of the Middle East. As a parallel example in North America, we might recall the huge development shift from the northern to the southern U.S. states, supported as it was by two technological innovations, DDT for malaria and air conditioning.

Location, topography, and climate form the basic, inherited context for business ventures. Try as the Swiss might to alter things, Switzerland is likely to continue to be a mountainous country with long, snowy winters on a heavily populated plain at the foot of the Alps. Of course, people may undertake massive modifications: Holland, situated below the North Sea level, has protected itself through a system of dykes. Singapore has greatly increased its landmass by reclaiming land from the surrounding sea, as have the Japanese in their landfill expansion into Tokyo Harbor. Such modification of an inherited factor illustrates Porter's idea of changing a disadvantage to an advantage. Yet, for the most part, location and topography tend to be permanent facts, while climate, although not deterministic, may set limits difficult to modify. In fact, often such attempts may backfire. In contrast, natural resources, our next focus, present businesspeople with sources of raw materials that, unlike location, topography, and climate, are extractable and malleable.

Natural Resources

What are **natural resources?** For our purposes, they are anything supplied by nature on which people depend. The principal natural resources important to business productive capacity are those from which we can source energy and nonfuel minerals. The final section of this chapter addresses the sustainability of natural resources.

ENERGY

Natural resources that are sources for energy are either nonrenewable or renewable. The nonrenewable sources are fossil fuels, including petroleum, coal, and natural gas; once we use them, their supplies are depleted. Nuclear energy is also nonrenewable, but on a quite different scale than are the fossil fuels. Among renewable energy sources are hydroelectric, wind, solar, geothermal, waves, tides, biomass, and ocean thermal energy conversion. Figure 5.13 illustrates the evolution of the world's marketed energy supply by fuel from 1980 to 2030. You can see that nonrenewables have dominated the market. We look first at these major **nonrenewable energy** sources and then at the renewable sources.

NONRENEWABLE ENERGY SOURCES

Petroleum   Petroleum, or crude oil, has been a cheap source of energy and a raw material for plastics, fertilizers, and other industrial applications. The world is running out of oil, but exactly when is uncertain. Fifty years at current consumption rates seems an optimistic estimate.[12] Analysts widely agree that we will reach the peak in oil production within the next 10 years, if we haven't already reached it, and supplies available for extraction will go into decline.[13] Once we know that peak oil has been reached, our economies will enter a transition period in which there will be an increasing gap between what the market needs in petroleum products and what can be supplied at a reasonable price. OECD economies are based on fossil fuels, as are the economies of developing nations that are moving forward in their industrial evolutions, such as China and India. In addition to depleted oil supplies, there are also above-ground issues that will drive up the cost of petroleum.[14] Among them are the political unrest in the Middle East, home of major petroleum deposits; the financial crisis; and the Japanese earthquake, tsunami, and nuclear emergency in March 2011. Another factor that influences petroleum availability is that the easy sources have

natural resources
Anything supplied by nature on which people depend

nonrenewable energy sources
The principal nonrenewable energy sources are the fossil fuels—petroleum, coal, and natural gas—and nuclear power

FIGURE 5.13

World Marketed
Energy Use by Fuel
Type, 1980–2030

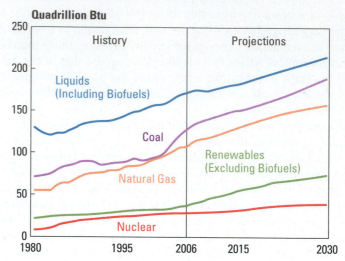

Quadrillion Btu

Sources: **History:** Energy Information Administration (EIA), *International Energy Annual 2006* (June–December 2008), web site www.eia.doe.gov/iea. **Projections:** EIA, World Energy Projections Plus (2009).

already been tapped, and now the reserves that are more difficult to harvest will need to be used. Estimates of oil reserves are uncertain for a number of reasons:

- New discoveries continue to be made in proven fields with the aid of improved prospecting equipment.

- Political issues affect territories available for exploration and production. Political unrest limits access to potential sites, and governments control access to their natural resources. More than one-third of the world's oil and gas comes from the Middle East and North Africa.

- Improved techniques such as steam and hot-water injection enable producers to obtain greater output from wells already in operation and put new areas into operation.

- Automated, less expensive equipment may lower drilling costs; for instance, wellheads located on the ocean floor can replace expensive offshore platforms, once the technology is developed to avoid leakage and spills. This innovation allows a company to profitably work smaller-sized discoveries that otherwise it would not touch.

Nevertheless, no one doubts that we face serious dependency and supply issues with oil. A group of oil industry professionals, the Association for the Study of Peak Oil and Gas, agrees that we are probably in the peak production time period right now,[15] and their critical question is: How long do we have to make adjustments before the price of oil becomes prohibitive? The U.S. Energy Information Administration projects that world energy consumption will continue to increase through 2035; with dramatic increases in developing countries such as China and India as they industrialize.[16] Figure 5.14 illustrates marketed or sold energy use by region. Oil is projected to remain the world's dominant energy source in this period, with reductions seen after 2020. The U.S. Energy Information Administration's projections also suggest a slow decline going forward. Table 5.1 shows what we probably have to draw on to meet these increasing energy needs, the greatest oil reserves by country, along with their reserve to production ratios at current production levels. The reserve-to-production ratio tells us how long the reserve supply is forecast to last, at current consumption levels. Then Figures 5.15 and 5.16 show these reserves categorized by investment risk and political risk, two other variables that affect their availability. Note that, increasingly, oil reserves are controlled by governments that face domestic political unrest or that limit the access of the major western oil companies. Note, too, the revolutions and unrest in Libya, Tunisia, Saudi Arabia, Bahrain, Yemen, and Egypt in the spring of 2011.

There are unconventional sources of petroleum whose attractiveness increases as conventional sources are depleted. These include oil sands, oil-bearing shale, coal, and natural

gas. In addition to being a source for petroleum, the last two are also used to generate energy on their own. The world's major oil sands are located in Canada (Athabasca, in Alberta), Venezuela, and the Republic of Congo. The sands contain bitumin, a tarlike crude oil, and place Canada first in heavy oil reserves and second only to Saudi Arabia in overall proven reserves. Oil-bearing **shale** is fine-grained sedimentary rock that yields 25 liters or more of liquid hydrocarbons per ton of rock when heated to 500°C, whose largest known source is the three-state area of Utah, Colorado, and Wyoming, in the United States. Oil shale has remained underdeveloped because of the availability of less expensive conventional oil, the environmental problems of waste rock disposal, and the great quantities of water needed for processing. Recent technological advances, along with oil price increases, make oil recovered with minimal environmental impact from shale economically feasible, although Greenpeace and other environmental groups have campaigned against oil shale projects, claiming that extracting the oil from shale creates four times the greenhouse impact as does

shale
A fissile rock (capable of being split) composed of laminated layers of claylike, fine-grained sediment

FIGURE 5.14

Marketed Energy Use by Region

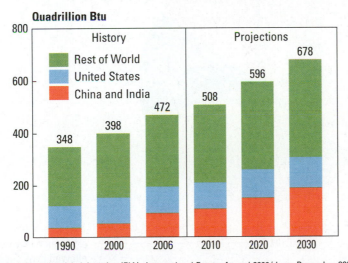

Sources: **History:** Energy Information Administration (EIA), *International Energy Annual 2006* (June–December 2008), web site www.eia.doe.gov/iea. **Projections:** EIA, World Energy Projections Plus (2009).

TABLE 5.1	World Oil Reserves by Country as of January 2010, Top 14

Rank	Country	Proved Reserves (billions of barrels)	Reserve to Production Ratio	Share of World Production*
1	Saudi Arabia	267	72 years	10.2%
2	Canada	179	149	3.3
3	Iran	138	95	4.0
4	Iraq	115	150	2.1
5	Kuwait	104	110	2.6
6	United Arab Emirates	98	88	2.9
7	Venezuela	87	107	2.7
8	Russia	60	17	9.9
9	Libya	41	66	1.7
10	Nigeria	36	41	2.4
11	Kazakhstan	30	59	1.4
12	United States	21	8	7.5
13	China	16	11	3.9
14	Qatar	15	46	0.9

*Energy Information Administration, www.eia.doe.gov/emeu/international/oilproduction.html (accessed March 24, 2011); www.nationmaster.com/graph/ene_oil_res-energy-oil-reserves (accessed March 24, 2011).

extracting conventionally drilled oil, and that investing in the development of more non-renewable energy sources, when we know that eventually we have to switch to renewable energy sources, doesn't make sense. Yet, as conventional sources of oil become depleted,

FIGURE 5.15

Worldwide Proven Oil Reserves by Investment Risk

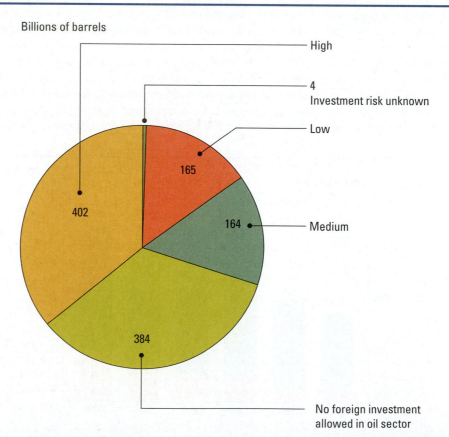

Billions of barrels

High

4
Investment risk unknown

Low

165

Medium

164

402

384

No foreign investment allowed in oil sector

Source: www.gao.gov/new.items/d07283.pdf.

FIGURE 5.16

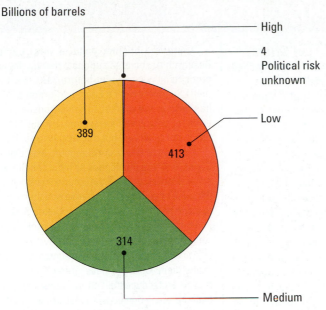

Billions of barrels

High

4
Political risk
unknown

Low

389

413

314

Medium

Source: www.gao.gov/new.items/d07283.pdf.

these synthetic petroleum sources such as oil sands and oil-bearing shale have become more useful. Presently oil-bearing shale is commercially processed in China, Estonia, Brazil, Germany, Israel, and Russia. These unconventional sources are often grouped together as **heavy oil** and are seen as the future by oil companies.

Coal and natural gas can also be converted to oil through a complex chemical process. During the South Africa apartheid boycotts in the 1980s, when oil exporters refused to sell South Africa oil, the South African government commercialized the German-developed Fischer-Tropsch process to obtain oil from coal through a catalyzed chemical reaction. Coal is put under pressure at high temperature and is converted to crude gas. After cooling and purification, the gas passes through a conversion process that produces high-value chemical components and synthetic oil.[17] A similar process can be used with natural gas.

Oil companies have long had a problem disposing of large, isolated gas reserves that are too far from markets to be profitable. However, converting the gas to a liquid allows for it to be produced profitably and moved to world markets less expensively than is possible with the gaseous form. Using this process, oil companies can use gas that, in the past, has been burned off, and they are being refined with a greener process than other refining methods use. Thus, what began as an import substitution project has developed into a new energy source for South Africa. Chevron has a joint venture with Sasol, the innovative South African petrochemical company, for worldwide use of its gas-to-liquid (GTL) technology. Sasol has projects in Qatar, Gabon, Mozambique, Nigeria, Germany, China, India, and the United States. The U.S. military, the country's largest consumer of oil, is using alternatives such as synthetic oil and encouraging their development. The Air Force plans to buy 25 percent of its jet fuel from synthetic sources by 2016, and the Pentagon is actively exploring the use of synthetic fuels throughout the Defense Department.[18]

Nuclear Power   Nuclear power was predicted to be on its way out because waste material storage is problematic and accidents at the plants can be dangerous over large distances, as we learned from Chernobyl, the 1986 Ukrainian nuclear disaster and as we are relearning with the Japanese nuclear crisis at Fukushima in the spring of 2011. Currently, the nuclear industry is in crisis as governments review the safety of their reactors and, at least temporarily, their commitments to nuclear power. With the cost increases of oil and the pressure for reduced carbon-burning fuels to meet climate-change targets, nuclear power had been predicted to grow from 6 percent in 2008 to 8 percent in 2035. The International

heavy oil
Oil that does not flow easily and cannot be drawn from wells

How Immediate Is the Fossil Fuel Crisis?

How do we know when our oil reserves have reached their midpoint and are starting to decline? The answer to that important question is a critical point of contention, a bit like figuring out when we've fished the next-to-the-last fish from the ocean. You don't know for sure until it has happened. Specialists are divided and of many, even contradictory, judgments and predictions. Goldman Sachs analysts and OPEC officials themselves have said that the price of oil could hit $200 a barrel within two years. One school of analysts argues that oil production has already reached its peak and is on the decline. The peak oil theory, developed by Marion Hubbert, a geologist for Shell, holds that oil's decline will follow a bell curve. This terminal decline, fringe analysts warn, would bring us out of our cars and our economy to a standstill. Chaos would ensue. The time has come to stash in survival guides and freeze-dried food, to get ready for the economic collapse.

Increasingly this evidence is reaching people beyond the eccentric fringe so that regular citizens are becoming concerned about their carbon footprint. The largest proven oil reserves are in Saudi Arabia, and we know little of what is actually happening there. Satellite reconnaissance might suggest that the Saudis are having to push harder to get more out of the world's largest field, Ghawar. After all, Ghawar has been a major source of energy for our fossil-fuel economy for 75 years. Matthew Simmons, author of *Desert: The Coming Saudi Oil Shock and the World Economy*, has reviewed outputs of the world's oilfields, noting that 20 percent of the world's oil consumption is sourced from old fields, and no new fields in their league have been discovered in almost 30 years. In addition, many of the producers face political unrest and nationalism in countries with sizable reserves: Nigeria, Russia, Iran, Iraq, and Venezuela among them.

There is a brighter point of view. Cambridge Energy Research Associates suggests that no decline in ability to produce oil would occur before 2030. Guy Caruso, head of the U.S. government's Energy Information Administration, has faith in the market to drive consumer behavior, government policy, and innovation. He thinks that the primary risk is not reserves, but above-the-ground political issues.

Developed world consumption, especially in the United States, will face challenges as India and China draw from the same supplies to build their economies. People realize that the price of oil is destined to rise and that they have to adjust to these realities. To many in the United States, conservation and the development of renewable resources look like a reasonable path, much more so than five years ago. Conservation and a call for renewable energy sources is becoming mainstream. Colleges have green dorms, where residents recycle and reduce their energy consumption. Recycling has become commonplace in most areas. Towns are erecting wind power and solar farms to meet their municipal needs. And SUV gas guzzlers, one of the valued American indulgences, are becoming burdensome beyond their value.

Increased gas efficiency in our vehicles; improved domestic oil supply, including untapped reserves; deep sea drilling; the application of new technologies to coal; and the increase of ethanol production are ways to address the oil scarcity/unavailability issue in the United States. True, increased production of ethanol reduces food production at a time when there are worldwide food shortages and food prices are rising dramatically.[19]

Questions:

1. Does a developed country have a moral duty to produce food over fuel crops when hunger is a global issue?

2. What's your best thinking on how immediate the fossil fuel crisis may be? Is it immediate, or do we have another good 50 to 100 years to figure out our transition to new energy sources?

Energy Agency is now suggesting that nuclear power may actually decline over the next few years.[20] Yet, nuclear power plants generate little pollution in their normal operation, so as the price of oil rises and new designs are available, nuclear power use increased.

Until the Fukushima incident, caused by the tsunami that followed the Sendai earthquake, fewer nuclear plants were being retired, and those in service were being used at higher capacity. Higher nuclear growth was expected in developing countries, where most of the reactors under construction are located. China, India, Korea, and Russia have ambitious nuclear plants coming online or under construction. The International Atomic Energy Agency (IAEA) lists 65 nuclear plants under construction, the majority in China (27), Russia (11), Korea (5), and India (5)[21] China has 13 plants in operation, and was committed to a sixfold increase by 2020.[22] The U.S. Nuclear Energy Institute reports that more than 20 nuclear power plant licenses are being actively pursued in the United States, although there is significant concern about safety issues.[23] In addition, France has turned heavily to nuclear generation while making a concerted effort to curb fossil fuel consumption and develop a strategic energy security policy. France produces 75 percent of its electricity by nuclear power and has one of the lowest rates of greenhouse gas emissions in the industrialized world. Strong commitment to nuclear power has enabled France to go from a net importer of electricity to the world's largest exporter. If the price of oil stays high and the safety issues that Fukushima may bring to the fore can be resolved, nuclear power is likely to continue to grow from its present 15 percent share of the world's electricity grid, 24 percent share in OECD countries, and 34 percent in the EU.[24] Despite the dangers of earthquakes, tsunamis, spent fuel storage, and radiation, nuclear energy has very low carbon emissions, and its use also contributes to energy self-sufficiency, as is the case with France.

Coal   Coal, much like nuclear power, was predicted to be on its decline as an energy source, largely because it pollutes heavily, but just the opposite is the case: coal's consumption is projected to increase 56 percent through 2035, largely due to increases in China and India. However, because other fuel sources are developing at a faster pace than is coal, its share of world primary energy consumption is projected to increase only slightly, from 27 percent in 2007 to a projected 28 percent in 2030.[25] Non-OECD member countries in Asia, the largest of which are China and India, are projected to account for 95 percent of the expected global increase in the use of coal through 2030. China's coal consumption has increased so dramatically that in 2007, its global market price nearly doubled.

The United States is now an exporter of coal to China, and this has led to increased pay for miners and increased demand for mine, port, and rail workers. The United States has coal reserves to last 146 years at projected consumption rates, which puts the United States at the top of countries with substantial recoverable coal reserves.[26] See Table 5.2 for a comparative listing of the top six countries with coal resources, contrasting to those with oil and gas. The United States has the world's major coal deposits, with Russia, China, Australia–New Zealand, and India following. In terms of coal consumption, China's projected increase is massive, largely because China uses coal for much more than electricity generation. Coal is a major industrial fuel (see Figure 5.17).

Unfortunately, burning coal frequently creates emissions that are directly responsible for global warming, although there are clean coal technologies being developed. They promise to reduce emissions from coal-fired plants by venting the emissions deep into the ground, by pulverizing the coal before it is burned, and by using the South African conversion process to change the coal to a gas before it is burned. Through their use of coal, China, India, and the United States contribute greatly to greenhouse gases. In the United States, the Environmental Protection Agency ruled in December 2009 that greenhouse gases threaten public health, so now the federal government can enact regulation of tailpipe and smokestack emissions. The **Kyoto Protocol,** the United Nations Framework Convention on Climate Change, calls for nations to work together to reduce global warming by reducing their emissions of the gasses that contribute to it, carbon dioxide first among them. To date, the United States is the only industrialized country that has signed and not ratified the Kyoto Protocol. The concern in the United States was that the burden to reduce greenhouse gas emissions would

Kyoto Protocol
United Nations Framework Convention on Climate Change, which calls for nations to reduce global warming by reducing their emissions of the gases that contribute to it

TABLE 5.2	Top Six Countries' Coal's Distribution by Country, in Contrast to Oil and Gas

Coal		Oil		Gas	
United States	28.3%	Saudi Arabia	19.9%	Russia	26.9%
Russia	18.6	Canada	13.3	Iran	15.9
China	13.6	Iran	10.1	Qatar	14.3
Non-OECD Europe and Eurasia	10.3	Iraq	8.6	Saudi Arabia	4.1
Australia and New Zealand	9.2	Kuwait	7.7	United States	3.8
India	6.7	Venezuela	7.4	United Arab Emirates	3.4

Source: U.S. Energy Information Administration, *International Energy Outlook*, May 2009, Tables 4, 6, and 9.

FIGURE 5.17

Coal Consumption
in Selected World
Regions, 1980–2030

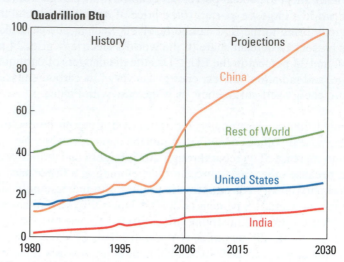

Quadrillion Btu

History / Projections

China

Rest of World

United States

India

Sources: **2006:** Energy Information Administration (EIA), *International Energy Annual 2006* (June–December 2008), web site www.eia.doe.gov/iea. **2015 and 2030:** EIA, World Energy Projections Plus (2009).

be born by the industrialized economies and be harmful to the United States' economy. Others wanted binding targets and timetables for both industrialized and developing economies.

Natural Gas   Natural gas is the cleanest burning among the fossil fuels, its greenhouse gas emissions significantly less than with oil or coal. This increased burning efficiency means gas has much lower contributions to acid rain, solid waste and water pollution than do other fossil fuels. As oil prices increase, natural gas consumption is expected to increase as a substitute fuel, with a 47 percent projected increase through 2030. That estimate may actually increase, given the possible impact of the Fukushima nuclear disaster on the use of nuclear power. Gas is a reasonable substitute for nuclear in that it has a small carbon footprint.

International Energy Agency Report, 2010   The International Energy Agency (IEA) is an energy policy advisor to its 28 member-nations, founded during the oil price shocks of 1973–1974 and with a focus today on energy-related security, environmental protection, and economic development. IEA's 2010 report on the future of energy technologies[27] suggests that an energy revolution is under way, based on low-carbon technologies. Gas and nuclear power are at the center of this revolution, along with new extraction methods and low-carbon burning technologies. Increased fuel efficiency in transportation, the use of biofuels, and some alternative approaches to fueling transportation such as the use of hydrogen and electricity could drop oil demand by 27 percent.

Yet the report points out that carbon dioxide emission trends run counter to the repeated warnings of the United Nations Intergovernmental panel on Climate Change, which calls for reductions of at least 50 percent of the 2000 emission levels in order to limit the long-term global average temperature rise. Climate change is occurring at a faster rate than originally predicted, and the reduction in emissions is immediately necessary to prevent climate change at dangerous levels. The next decade is critical.

The IEA director, Nobuo Tanaka, concludes that the energy revolution is necessary and achievable. It doesn't ask us to do more with less, but rather, to continue growth, fueling it with reasonable and more costly alternatives. Let's hope we have the courage to move forward.

RENEWABLE ENERGY SOURCES

Everyone accepts that some day in the future renewable energy sources will replace fossil fuels, either because the price of nonrenewable energy sources will become too high relative to the cost of developing sustainable renewable sources or because the sources themselves will be unavailable, due to either depletion or political and risk issues. In addition, there is growing concern about the impact of carbon dioxide emissions produced by coal and oil on climate change. There are seven alternative energy sources whose commercial development is widely tracked: wind power, biomass fuels, solar photovoltaic power, concentrating solar thermal power, geothermal power, ocean energy, and hydropower. There are other forms of alternative energy under development and used in small applications, but at this point, these are the seven sources that have commercial viability (see Figure 5.18).

None of these alternative sources of energy is available everywhere, but all appear to have applications under appropriate conditions. In 2009, growth in the renewable sector outpaced growth in the nonrenewable sector in both the European Union and the United States, and growth in the renewable energy markets developing countries has been rapid, especially in Argentina, Costa Rica, Egypt, Indonesia, Kenya, Tanzania, Thailand, Tunisia, and Uruguay. *Renewables 2011 Global Status Report*,[28] the most frequently referenced report on renewable energy business and policy, confirms that more than half of the existing renewable power capacity is now in developing countries. In fact, renewable energy appears to have reached a tipping point. No longer confined to industrialized countries, in *2011* renewables comprised fully half of the new global power generating capacity from all sources and constituted 16 percent of global power consumption. In four markets, renewables have replaced the traditional energy sources of fossil fuels and nuclear. These markets are power generation, transport fuels, heating and cooling, and rural/off-grid energy services. Many categories of renewable energy technologies grew from 15 to 50 percent in the period 2005 through 2010. The top five countries for non-hydro renewable power were the United States, China, Germany, Spain and India. Including hydropower, China, the United States, Canada, Brazil, and India tied with Germany were the top countries for total installed renewable capacity. Clearly, there is national-level support for the inevitable transition from fossil fuels to renewables, and countries are beginning to make policy commitments to the transition. Presently over 118 countries have put in place renewable energy targets or promotions. This figure is up from 55 countries in 2005.

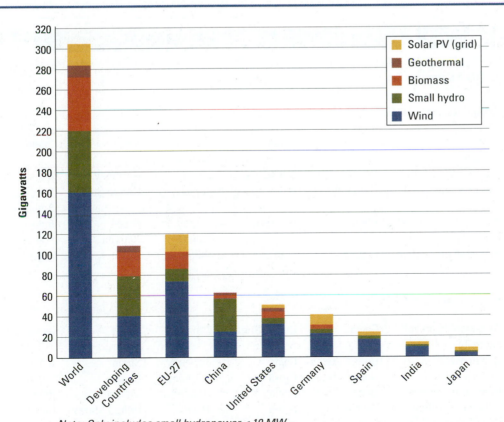

FIGURE 5.18

Renewable Power Capacities, Developing World, EU, and Top Six Countries

Note: Only includes small hydropower < 10 MW

Source: Renewable Energy Policy Network for the 21st Century, *Renewable 2010 Global Status Report*, www.ren21.net.

FIGURE 5.19

Share of Global
Electricity from
Renewable Energy

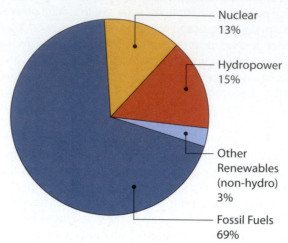

Source: *Renewables 2010 Global Status Report.*

During the five years from 2005–2011 there was consistent high growth in the sector year after year. Global wind power capacity grew the most in developing countries, including China, which now accounts for over half the global market. Solar photovoltaics more than doubled in 2010, while more than half the total capacity of concentrating solar thermal power was added during 2010. Ethanol production increased by 17 percent. Biomass and geothermal, with applications both for power and heat, also grew strongly. As Figure 5.19 suggests, although the transition has begun, renewable energy is still a small portion of the world's energy supply, yet it is a growing part. Table 5.3 shows the leading nations in renewable energy sources by their investment, their added sources, and their existing capacity as of 2010. Now we focus briefly on each of the seven major renewable energy sources.

TABLE 5.3	Top Five Countries in Renewables				
Top 5 Countries	**1**	**2**	**3**	**4**	**5**
Annual Amounts for 2009					
New capacity investment	Germany	China	United States	Italy	Spain
Wind power added	China	United States	Spain	Germany	India
Solar PV added	Germany	Italy	Japan	United States	Czech Republic
Solar hot water/heat	China	Germany	Turkey	Brazil	India
Ethanol production	U.S.	Brazil	China	Canada	France
Biodiesel production	France–Germany	France–Germany	United States	Brazil	Argentina
Existing Capacity 1/1/2010					
Renewables power capacity	China	United States	Canada	Brazil	Japan
Wind power	United States	China	Germany	Spain	India
Biomass power	United States	Brazil	Germany	China	Sweden
Geothermal power	United States	Philippines	Indonesia	Mexico	Italy
Solar photovoltaic	Germany	Spain	Japan	United States	Italy
Solar hot water/heat	China	Turkey	Germany	Japan	Greece

Source: Compiled from data in Renewables 2010 Global Status Report

Wind power, both on land and offshore, increased 41 percent in 2009, despite the economic crisis, and maintained that level in 2010. From 2005 to 2010, the average annual growth rate of wind power capacity has been 27 percent. Wind power's global capacity has doubled in less than three years. China represents one-third of the world's capacity and continued as the top installer in 2010, while it had only 2 percent of the world's wind power in 2004. Trends are toward offshore development and small scale community projects. 11 countries have off-shore wind farms. Denmark meets 20 percent of its electricity demand with wind power. The majority of offshore capacity is in Europe, with the UK and Denmark leading. China has installed the first major offshore wind project outside of Europe, and the United States has approved a major wind farm in Massachusetts, off the coast of Cape Cod. Small-scale wind systems, either connected to the grid or off-grid, are found in China, the United States, and the UK. The projections for wind power are strong, with new interest in Africa and extended projects under way in China.

Biomass is a category of renewable energy fuels based on photosynthesis, the process through which plants transform the sun's energy into chemical energy. It is derived from agricultural, forestry, and municipal waste and also from some crops grown expressly for fuel. Biomass can be solid (straw, wood chips), liquid (vegetable oils and animal slurries) or gas (biogas) and is usually used to generate power through combustion. A growing development within this sector is the co-firing of biomass fuels with coal, a process that reduces harmful emissions and can use existing coal power generating facilities. Ethanol is a type of biomass fuel and, coincidentally, the source of alcohol in alcoholic beverages. Its use has risen dramatically as the cost of oil has increased beyond ethanol's production cost. Like other biofuels, ethanol burns cleaner than does gasoline, so its use reduces carbon emissions. Corn, wheat, and sugarcane are among the most popular sources of ethanol. Brazil led the world in developing biomass fuel, meeting more than 40 percent of its gasoline demand with ethanol produced from sugarcane, and also pioneered the concept of flexible-fuel vehicles (FFVs). Biomass heating has expanded as well, and in Sweden, biomass is now the primary energy source for heat. In Sweden, biomass energy for heating exceeded that of oil, 32 to 31 percent. As of 2011, China leads the world in biomass applications for household heating.

Solar photovoltaic power (PV) is power based on the voltage created when certain materials are exposed to light. The photovoltaic effect was first observed by the French physicist Alexandre-Edmond Becquerel in 1839, so it has taken some time to commercialize, but now it is well on its way. Solar cells are being used to generate power in well over 100 countries, and it is the fastest growing power technology, including the fossil fuels. Grid-connected capacity (not including private home installations that do not generate power to a larger grid) increased between 2005 and 2010 at an annual average rate of 60 percent and doubled in 2010. Global PV installations are six times what they were in 2004. Germany has been a major force in the development of PV. There has also been growing interest in small-scale off-grid systems, accounting for 5 percent of the global market. PV has also been growing as a source for heating and cooling, especially in Turkey, Cyprus, and the EU.

Concentrating solar thermal power (CSP) uses mirrors or lenses to collect sunlight that heats water running in tubes behind the collector surface. This heat then drives an engine, often a steam turbine, connected to an electrical power generator. CSP is categorized as a different type of power than solar PV, based on the difference in technology. CSP plants have been growing in the United States and Spain, and there are new installations in Algeria, Egypt, and Morocco.

Geothermal power derives from the heat stored in the earth and may involve many technologies. Heat can be drawn from hot water or steam reservoirs deep in the earth that are accessed by drilling, from geothermal reservoirs that create hot springs, and directly from the earth's close-to-the-surface temperature of 50°F to 60°F. The heat can be used directly or to generate electricity. Both Turkey and Iceland have had more than 200 percent growth in this area between 2005 and 2010. The United States brought six new plants online in 2009. Iceland generates 25 percent of its electricity with geothermal power, and the Philippines generates 18 percent. Seventy nations have projects under way in this rapidly expanding geothermal market. Direct use of geothermal for heating, bathing, and industrial applications grew faster in the 2005–2010 period than did its use for power generation.

wind power
Power derived from the wind, as with a windmill

biomass
A category of fuels whose energy source is photosynthesis, through which plants transform the sun's energy into chemical energy; sources include corn, sugarcane, and wheat

solar photovoltaic power (PV)
Type of power based on the voltage created when certain materials are exposed to light

concentrating solar thermal power (CSP)
Uses mirrors or lenses to collect sunlight heats water running in tubes behind the collectors.

geothermal power
Power derived from heat stored in the earth.

ocean energy
Power derived from the ocean, either as a result of the sun's heat on the ocean or the mechanical energy of the tides and waves.

Ocean energy results from two sources: the sun's heat on the water and the mechanical energy of the tides and waves. It is the least mature of the renewable energy sources, but interest is building in wave, tidal, and ocean thermal energy conversion systems. There is a barrage (dam) successfully generating power at La Rance, off the coast of France, that began in 1966. Portugal also has a commercial wave plant and plans to expand it, while the UK operates the only commercial-scale tidal turbine to generate electricity. There are at least 25 countries involved in some sort of ocean energy development activity. China, India, the U.S. and the UK have ocean energy projects underway.

hydropower
Power derived from the force of moving water.

Hydropower draws on the energy of moving water to generate power and supplied 16 percent of global electricity in 2010. China doubled its hydropower capacity during the 2004–2010 period, when the Three Gorges Dam project came fully online. In Africa, the Tekeze Dam came online in Ethiopia. In rural areas of Africa that are un-electrified, small hydro plants are often used to replace diesel generators. The forecasts are for large-capacity increases in hydropower, with major plants being finished in Brazil, China, India, Malaysia, Russia, Turkey, and Vietnam. Small-scale hydro applications are also expected to increase.

NONFUEL MINERALS

LO5-5 Describe the issues related to nonfuel minerals that concern international business

Although much of the world's attention to natural resources has centered on the discovery and development of new and cleaner energy sources, there are some mineral natural resources about which governments and industry need to think strategically. Nonfuel minerals are used in all areas of modern living, from house construction to the manufacture of computers and motor vehicles. Chrome and manganese are indispensable for hardening steel; platinum is a vital catalytic agent in the oil-refining process and is used in automotive catalytic converters; and vanadium is used in forming aerospace titanium alloys and in producing sulfuric acid.

rare earths
A group of 17 elements used in technological applications.

Rare earths are a group of 17 elements used in technological applications such as in high-end magnets in U.S. weapons, petroleum refining, and lasers. China controls 95 percent of the export market and announced in early 2011 that it expects to need to import these materials soon. It had previously imposed export quotas. Those quotas, which have been loosened recently, last year drove the price up threefold in Japan, the largest importer of rare earths. Prices of some rare earths jumped more than 1,000 percent.[29] In the United States, there is discussion in Congress to limit Chinese participation in the U.S. mining sector and lobby against World Bank loans to China if they abandon their exports in this sector. Rare earths are not actually rare; most of them are widely dispersed. The problem is that they do not occur often in concentrations that make their mining commercially viable, hence the *rare*. Table 5.4 illustrates the main sources of totally import-dependent mineral imports into the United States.

With rare earths, we have concluded our review of the major natural resources, the factor conditions on which all business rests. These resources are what the firm has to work with as it explores ways to add value. Now we move to the challenging issue of how we work with what we have—how we use these resources. Currently, we face a two-part energy crisis: the eventual depletion of nonrenewable fossil fuels and climate change due to global warming. This crisis is being driven by climate change, which has hit us ahead of the depletion reality, and its resolution requires global cooperation. The triggers for climate change lie in emissions from the same carbon-based fuels whose limited supply contributes to the first part of the crisis. One response to this entire crisis would be to speed up the development of clean energy sources, to make our transition before necessity dictates it. Such an environmentally sustainable approach is exactly what we consider next.

LO5-6 Describe the concept of environmental sustainability and its potential influence on business.

Environmental Sustainability

The concept of sustainability has broad scope. *Sustainability* is about maintaining something, and that something might be the environment, society, the economy, people within the economy, or the organization. Increasingly, when we use the term *sustainability* in a business context, we mean a wide array of these applications.[30] By its very nature, sustainability is a systems concept. The thing we are trying to sustain (a business, a way of life, the natural world) exists within a larger system, and if that larger system is not sustained, the subsystem is unlikely to survive. For example, are the Everglades likely to be sustained if

TABLE 5.4 U.S. Minerals Ranked by Net Import Reliance—2010

Commodity	Percent Imported	Major Sources (2006–2009)
Arsenic (trioxide)	100	Morocco, China, Belgium
Asbestos	100	Canada
Bauxite and Alumina	100	Jamaica, Brazil, Guinea, Australia
Cesium	100	Canada
Fluorspar	100	Mexico, China, South Africa, Mongolia
Graphite (natural)	100	China, Mexico, Canada, Brazil
Indium	100	China, Canada, Japan, Belgium
Manganese	100	South Africa, Gabon, China, Australia
Mica, sheet (natural)	100	China, Brazil, Belgium, India
Niobium (columbium)	100	Brazil, Canada, Germany, Estonia
Quartz crystal (industrial)	100	China, Japan, Russia
Rare earths	100	China, France, Japan, Austria
Rubidium	100	Canada
Strontium	100	Mexico, Germany
Tantalum	100	Australia, China, Kazakhstan, Germany
Thallium	100	Russia, Germany, Netherlands
Thorium	100	United Kingdom, France, India, Canada
Yttrium	100	China, Japan, France

Note: Excludes mineral fuels.

Source: USGS, *Mineral Commodity Summaries, 2011.*

temperature and precipitation change significantly? As this example illustrates, the likelihood of a specific local geography or culture being sustained if the larger environment is not sustained is quite slim. In this way, sustainability is actually local and global at the same time; any specific location involves systems that are global. This simultaneity is what the phrase, "Act locally, think globally" tries to capture.

We might also consider sustainability from the consumption side. Sustainable consumption has been thought of frequently as a limitation on business. Yet Aron Cramer, CEO of BSR , the leading Corporate sustainability consultants, points out that "in a world where our consumption patterns outpace the planet's ability to regenerate resources by 30 percent, businesses that figure out how to deliver enhanced value by radically reducing material inputs and engaging consumers on product use will be well-positioned for success."[31]

Environmental sustainability rests on the commitment of business to operate without reducing the capacity of the environment to provide for future generations.[32] Thus, in addition to thinking locally and globally at the same time, the environmentally sustainable firm also has to think of its competitive present and the needs of future generations at the same time. Such approaches usually consider the ecological, social, and economic systems in which the business functions, that is, its natural, social, and economic worlds. In this section, we look at the characteristics of sustainable business practices and explore an application of the *stakeholder model* to sustainability.

CHARACTERISTICS OF ENVIRONMENTALLY SUSTAINABLE BUSINESS

There are three characteristics of the rapidly evolving sustainable business practices that are widely agreed upon: limits, interdependence, and equity.[33] *Limits* address the reality that environmental resources are exhaustible. Water, soil, and air can become toxic, and their use needs to be informed by awareness of that danger. The current focus on greenhouse gases and their contribution to global warming offers one example of limits. Recognizing the limits of the earth's atmosphere to absorb emissions and incorporating this recognition into how the business

environmental sustainability
Economic state in which the demands placed upon the environment by people and commerce can be met without reducing the capacity of the environment to provide for future generations

LO5-7 **Explain** the major characteristics of sustainable business.

operates is an ecologically responsible decision that supports sustainability. Extractive industries such as mining and oil offer ready examples of how limits can function. Freeport-McMoran has recognized limits in its mining operations in Papua, Indonesia, where it pays special attention to ecological issues. In contrast, Shell Oil is widely recognized as not recognizing limits in Nigeria. There are reported to be oil spills every year in southern Nigeria that dwarf the Deepwater Horizon disaster in the Gulf of Mexico in 2010. In addition to doing what is right, the business that learns how to reduce emissions before its competitors do and before emission levels are controlled by government regulation develops a valuable competitive advantage.

Interdependence describes the relationships among ecological, social, and economic systems. Action in one of these systems affects the other two. This interdependence can be seen often in stark dimensions in international examples. In its extractive operations in Papua (formerly Irian Jaya), Indonesia, Freeport-McMoran has built towns, settled wild areas, and developed rich copper and gold mines in remote places that required engineering feats to access. These areas had been the hunting grounds of indigenous hunter-gatherer tribes, among them the Kamoro and Amungme. The arrival of Freeport caused considerable local social stress. Freeport's operations involve some river and stream pollution from tailings, which are abated. Freeport-McMoran also provides health care and education for the indigenous peoples in the area, employs locals, and appears to have made extensive efforts to be a good citizen and a socially responsible neighbor. Yet, critics point out that the first-world technology and advancement the company brings to this area is threatening the continued existence of the indigenous people, through development and education. Imagine the strains on a social system in which parents, wearing loincloths and using poisoned blow arrows to kill game, are living as traditional hunter-gatherers, while their children are being educated to cruise the Internet and eat Western-style food. The interrelatedness of economic, social, and ecological systems in examples such as these is complex because the issues go beyond pollution and infringement of hunting grounds to complicated ethical and social issues related to development. Freeport-McMoran has recognized the interdependence of social, ecological, and economic systems in Papua and works hard at being a good corporate citizen. A similar challenge exists with Shell Oil in the Ogoni tribal lands in Nigeria, yet Shell's approach appears to value the economic sustainability of the business over the sustainability of ecological and social systems. In less stark dimensions, filmmaker Michael Moore's eulogy to Flint, Michigan, *Roger and Me*, explores the economic, social, and ecological implications of GM's decision to move production out of Flint. His argument is that GM ignored, and took no responsibility for, the interdependence of ecological, social, and economic systems.

Equity in distribution suggests that for the system interdependence to work, there cannot be vast differences in the distribution of gains. All stakeholders have to benefit to some degree from the value added by the business activities. In a globalizing world, where information is increasingly more open, vast inequities may lead to unrest and violence. An example of corporate challenges presented by lack of equity in distribution is found in Shell's southern Nigeria operations, which have been forced to shut down several times after raids by groups claiming to speak for the locals. The tribe claims they

An aerial view of a giant mine run by the U.S firm Freeport-Mcmoran Cooper & Gold Inc at the Grassberg mining operation. Indonasia will not hesitate to sue U.S. mining giant Freeport-McMoran if it fails to follow through on recommendations to stop pollution from its Papua operations, Environment Minister Rachmat Witoelar said.

have been "cheated of oil wealth pumped from their land by the central government and oil companies." Shell local employees have undertaken work stoppages as part of demands for equitable pay, and Shell has been forced to cut production by 25 percent, in a market of rising demand.[34] Political tensions related to equity in distribution have also informed Venezuelan and Bolivian oil businesses. Figure 5.20 illustrates the relationships among the ecological, social, and economic aspects of a business and how sustainability is achieved. The ecological context of the business—its environment—must be able to sustain itself and bear the impact of the business. The social context needs to be able to bear the impact of the business and have equity. The economic context has to be viable and equitable. Where these all intersect, the firm achieves sustainability.

Increasingly, companies will need to make decisions about setting limits on how their operations affect the environment, as a result of either consumer pressure or government regulation. They will also encounter increased signs of the interdependence that exists among the social, economic, and ecological systems that form the context for their business. When there is equity in distribution, such interdependence can work to the benefit of the firm and its stakeholders. Equity in distribution requires a business model that allocates gain from the business's value creation to a wide array of stakeholders, under the principle that a rising tide raises all boats. Sam Palmisano, CEO of IBM, refers to this new way of understanding business in his frequent observations about how IBM needs to end its colonial company model and move on to a truly globally integrated model where high levels of trust persist among all stakeholders.[35] Sustainable business models are complex, involving more stakeholders and more basic areas than do the more traditional business models. Areas that are most commonly involved are:

Alternative fuels	Office maintenance
Brownfield remediation	Pollution prevention
Corporate accountability	Social investing
Ecological development	Sustainable technology
Ecotourism	Transportation alternatives
Energy conservation	Waste reduction
Green building design	Water conservation

We'll now look more closely at the basic stakeholder model as a way for the firm to approach sustainability.

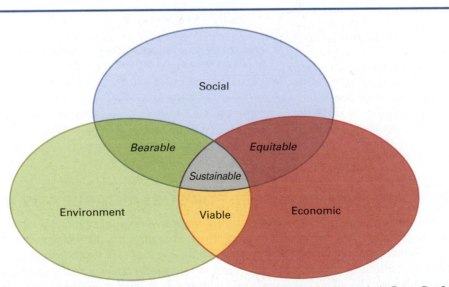

Source: *From W.M. Adams, 2006, "The Future of Sustainability: Re-Thinking Environment and Development in the Twenty-First Century, Report of the IUCN Renowned Thinkers, March 29, 2011, p. 16. Reprinted with permission.*

FIGURE 5.20

Context for Sustainability

Why Europe Leads the Way: The Environment and Business

While the United States has been lowering environmental standards and stepping away from cooperation on environmental treaties (Kyoto Protocol, International Seabed Authority), the European Union has pushed onward to raise environmental standards. Today, they have some of the highest standards in the world. Many of the European environmental regulations address the waste and toxic pollution that are by-products of manufacturing. Among EU initiatives are required vehicle recycling, elaborate tracing and checks on genetically modified crops, electronics recycling, bans on the most toxic chemicals used in electronics, required chemical testing, and required green design.[a]

The EU has come to accept an approach to environmentalism known as the *precautionary principle*. This approach suggests regulation at the first sign of a possible danger rather than waiting for research to establish the facts. The precautionary principle puts the onus on the industry to prove that its products are not dangerous. In marked contrast, the U.S. approach tends to focus on developing solutions for existing problems: "If it ain't broke, don't fix it."

In the late 1960s, soon after publication of environmentalist Rachel Carson's book *Silent Spring* (1962), the United States led the world in environmental awareness, legislation, and responsibility. Congress established the Environmental Protection Agency (EPA) and passed the National Environmental Policy Act, the Clean Air Act, the Endangered Species Act, and the Clean Water Act. Yet, recently, the EU has far outpaced the United States in this area. Why? There is no one simple explanation for such a shift, but demographic and cultural differences are part of the answer.

Most Europeans live in densely populated cities so that environmental problems such as air and water pollution have a stronger, more directly observed impact on them than they do on the more spread-out, rural, and suburban American population. Another reason for the shift may be attributable to culture. The United States was founded to protect individual citizens from a meddlesome, intrusive state. The United States is exceedingly individualistic, and business practices are thought of as acts of individual freedom. In Europe, communal values are stronger than in the United States. Business is thought to have quite a different purpose, one that includes obligations to society and higher levels of social responsibility than found in the United States.

One example of the contrast in approach to sustainability is the recent EU chemical industry regulation: Registration,

Evaluation, and Authorization of Chemicals (REACH). REACH requires chemical companies to manage the risks from chemical substances, gather information on them that will allow for their safe handling, and register the information in a central database. The regulation also calls for the progressive substitution of dangerous chemicals when alternatives have been identified. The purpose of the EU regulations, which require that chemical companies show that their materials are not harmful, is to close the knowledge gap that exists between the public's awareness of the risks of chemicals and what the industry itself knows.

In the United States, the Toxic Substances Control Act authorizes the Environmental Protection Agency to regulate chemicals that pose an unreasonable risk to humans and the environment. The EPA has required testing for fewer than 200 of the 62,000 chemicals that were being used when the EPA review began, in 1979. The EPA also requires a pre-manufacturing review of new chemicals. Of the 32,000 chemicals that have been submitted for review, the EPA has taken action to reduce the risk of around 3,500 substances.[b]

Unlike the U.S. approach, REACH reverses the burden of proof so that industry, both producers and importers of substances, rather than the government, assumes responsibility for providing the necessary information and taking effective risk management measures. In Europe, business has social responsibilities that in the U.S. are met by government regulation. Interestingly, the U.S. government and chemical producers lobbied against REACH, claiming it would be a technical barrier to trade, in violation of WTO rules.[c] The European approach recognizes that business needs to be sustainable, while in the United States, the government acts as a watchdog.

Questions:

1. Do you think a European approach to toxic substances could work in the United States? Explain your reasoning.

2. Recalling the culture dimensions we reviewed in Chapter 4, do they support the proposition that culture helps to explain the EU's approach to environmental issues

[a]The Environment: European Union, http://europa.eu/pol/env/index_en.htm (accessed April 3, 2011).

[b]"GAO Letter on Chemical Regulation," November 4, 2005, GAO-06-217R, www.gao.gov/new.items/d06217r.pdf (accessed April 3, 2011).

[c]"The New Rules Project, Environment Sector," www.newrules.org/environment/euchem.html (accessed April 3, 2011).

LO5-8 **Discuss** the utility of the stakeholder model for sustainable business.

THE STAKEHOLDER MODEL FOR SUSTAINABLE BUSINESS

The traditional model of doing business is an economic one, focusing on an input-process-output approach, where the goal is profitability above all. One difficulty in moving from this traditional model of doing business to a sustainable model is that our thinking has been molded by the traditional approach, and for good reason: it has worked well. We also tend to resist change. The adage "If it ain't broke, don't fix it" has remarkable sway. We don't see that the model is broken because we tend to focus on the economic and ignore the ecological and social parts of the context. In order for managers to keep both the big picture context and the details in their minds simultaneously, use of the stakeholder model is helpful. **Stakeholder theory**[36] was developed by R. Edward Freeman, and it differs from the traditional economic business model because it calls for managers to identify and consider the network of tensions caused by competing demands within which any business exists. The traditional economic model of business considers a far narrower scope of influences (employees, owners, and suppliers) that are driven by the single goal of creating profits. Stakeholder theory forces a business to address *underlying values and principles*. It "pushes managers to be clear about how they want to do business, specifically, what kind of relationships they want and need to create with their stakeholders to deliver on their purpose."[37] Stakeholder theory also suggests that the tensions among the varying stakeholders in a business environment can be balanced. Business then becomes about a network of relationships in the larger social context and the responsibilities that develop from them. In stakeholder theory, profits are a *result* of value creation rather than the primary driver in the process, as in the economic model. Freeman points out that there are many companies whose operations are consistent with stakeholder theory, including Johnson & Johnson, eBay, Google, and Lincoln Electric.

To achieve this balance among competing tensions that characterizes the stakeholder approach, the company needs to see itself in relation to its stakeholders and then view itself in a social context as Figure 5.21 illustrates. Consideration of this context, which leads to building relationships to discuss these issues both with the company itself and within its larger context, leads the company to clearly identify its purpose, principles, and responsibilities. Built on these discussions, the company is able to identify limits for its operations so that what it does is ecologically responsible and acceptable to its stakeholders; analyze and manage the various interdependencies among the ecological, social and economic systems that form the context of the business; and address ways to achieve equity of distribution. Thomas Merton, the Trappist Monk and philosopher, captured the reality of interdependence and the underlying value the stakeholder approach contains when he observed that "(T)he whole idea of compassion is based on a keen awareness of the interdependence of all these living beings, which are all part of one another, and all involved in one another."[38]

One way a company can measure its activities in this larger context and share the results is to use **triple-bottom-line (3BL) accounting.** Here, the company measures its social and environmental performance in addition to its traditional economic performance. We discuss this approach more in Chapter 18 when we consider international accounting. For an example of triple-bottom-line reporting, see Freeport-McMoRan's Sustainable Development Reports at www.fcx.com. The company's public materials suggest it is using a stakeholder

stakeholder theory
An understanding of how business operates that takes into account all identifiable interest holders

triple-bottom-line (3BL) accounting
An approach to accounting that measures the firm's social and environmental performance in addition to its economic performance

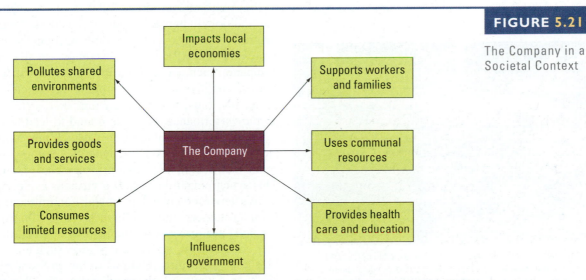

FIGURE 5.21

The Company in a Societal Context

Source: "Your Company in a Societal Context," Slide 7 from Pathways PowerPoint presentation *Sustainability and Business,* World Resources Institute, *Reprinted with permission.*

approach, increasing value, and contributing to the quality of life for its constituencies, including locals, while operating low-impact mining.

Interface Inc. offers an impressive example of the transfer to sustainability under the leadership of its founder, Ray Anderson. Influenced by the social and business writer Paul Hawken,[39] Anderson has made what he calls a mid-course correction. Interface manufactures the trendy modular carpeting Flor, and this change is especially notable because Interface products are spun from petroleum products. Anderson grasped that nature was a self-organizing systems that met its needs with abundance and no waste. In the last 13 years, Interface has come to realize that nature itself has some fundamental operating principles: it "runs on sunlight and other renewable energy sources, it fits form to function, it recycles everything and it is extremely efficient—never creating excess or wasting—and, finally, it rewards cooperation."[40] The challenge was to translate these principles into a new model for business. This process for Interface involved the need to address sustainability on seven fronts. The first front they focused on was the elimination of waste. This involved redesigning the products and processes so that there was no waste, that whatever was waste in one process would be nutrients for the next cycle of production, manufactured into new resources. The next challenge was to make emissions benign. All toxic substances need to be eliminated in its emissions, factories with no smokestacks, so to speak. Renewable energy sources need to be incorporated in all of Interface's activities—and will be 100 percent incorporated by 2020. Closing the loop, the fourth challenge, entails converting waste into raw materials and keeping organic materials uncontaminated so they can be returned to nature. Resource-efficient transportation is the fifth challenge, and it includes employee commutes. Sensitizing stakeholders involves creating a culture that uses sustainability principles to improve the livelihoods of all Interface stakeholders. The final challenge is to redesign commerce, to create a new business model based on sustainability that draws on delivering value through sustainability.[41] Thus began what has been so far a very successful 16-year effort to transform Interface into a sustainable business. Its "ecometrics" are impressive, as you can see on its Web site, where you can also view the company's 3BL report. As a petrochemical-dependent company, Interface has made remarkable progress toward sustainability: energy use is down 43% per unit, 30% of their energy is renewable, greenhouse gases have been reduced 44 %, waste sent to landfills is down 77%, water use per unit is down 80%, and recycled or bio-based materials are used in 36% of their manufacture.

Patagonia, the international outdoor gear company, is another business that has environmental sustainability at the core of its mission. In the 1970s, the climber Yvon Chouinard founded Patagonia with the goal of providing equipment for "clean climbing," that is, climbing that minimizes environmental impact: "Patagonia exists as a business to inspire and implement solutions to the environmental crisis." Patagonia recognizes that the traditional approach to doing business, focusing on quarterly earnings and generally accepted accounting principles (GAAP), is not sustainable in that it is not complete. Such accounting does not account for negative externalities such as environmental degradation and social ills; thus, it creates an unrealistic view of economic performance, and it is bound to lead to an environmental crisis. Patagonia's "ecosystem model" for sustainability relies on the synergies among the environmental, social, and economic elements of a business. This synchronization creates a virtuous cycle: the company's environmental and social commitment attracts loyal customers and employees, which improves the financial performance of the firm, which facilitates further commitment, and so on. Within such an approach, business can inspire solutions to the environmental crisis.[42] As Chouinard observed years ago, "No business can be done on a dead planet. A company that is taking

Interface's ReEntry® 2.0, a process that reclaims old carpet and converts it into recycled raw materials, diverted 28 million pounds of carpet from landfills in 2010. Since 1995, ReEntry has diverted a cumulative total of 228 million pounds of carpet and carpet scraps.

the long view must accept that it has an obligation to minimize its impact on the natural environment."[43] On the production side, Patagonia uses recycled materials, both in its building construction and in its products. Plastic soda cans are the source of much of the fleece, and organic cotton is used exclusively. Patagonia also has introduced the Footprint Chronicles program that traces the ecological impact of the manufacture of select products. This approach transparently addresses the trade-offs global sourcing creates and evaluates the ecological impact of various sourcing decisions, sharing all of this information with its stakeholders. Designed to educate stakeholders to the complexities of sourcing decisions, Footprint Chronicles avoids simplifying what is a complex set of issues and is a bit like listening in on an ethics class discussion. See "The Footprint Chronicles" at www.patagonia.com/web/us/contribution/patagonia.go?assetid=23429&ln=150/.

Chapter 5 has covered many topics of importance to the international manager. We began with a focus on how location, topography, and climate can influence business, drawing on Porter's diamond model. We then looked at natural resources and moved on to look at environmental sustainability.

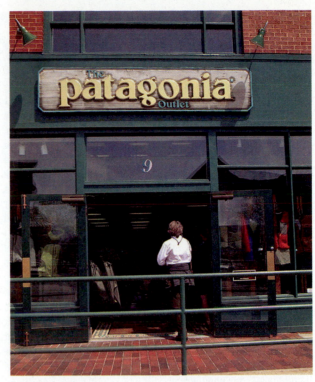

Patagonia retail site.

THE GLOBAL PATH AHEAD

Jeremy Capedevielle: Sustainability Work in Ecuador

I graduated from Cal Poly–San Luis Obispo with a concentration in International Business with an emphasis in Entrepreneurship. My curiosity involving the intricacies of culture and relationships

in the international context piqued my interest in IB, and a trip to New Zealand gave me a further glimpse into the world of limitless possibilities that further engaged my entrepreneurial spirit. Upon graduation, I had no idea as to the direction my life would lead, but one thing I was certain of was that I would embark on a trip to explore foreign lands for six months or longer.

Following graduation, I worked and saved money for four months, enjoyed many beautiful days upon the beaches of Southern California, read to my heart's desire, and reflected upon the topics of my choosing. It was the first time in a while when I took the time for myself to survey the wide and far stretching lands of my life and is probably one of the most important periods of my life. After methodically pulling pieces together, I discovered a direction that offered potential to fulfill my needs, both personally and professionally; that is, to work with and create organizations that are more conducive to people's happiness and personal well-being.

During that beautiful Southern California summer, I felt more strongly than ever that whatever the future had in store for me, traveling and experiencing foreign landscapes would be the best thing I could do for myself then. At the very least, I'd gain new insights, have my perspective and construction of the world challenged, and learn a new language. South America sparked my interest primarily due to its less-explored nature and my enthusiasm continued as I learned more about its highly diverse cultural and ecological landscapes. After making the necessary preparations and obtaining an insight into the cultural and political contexts in which I'd be traveling, I booked a flight to Panama and soon after travelled to South America.

(continued)

After sailing through the San Blas Islands and seemingly endless seas from Panama to Cartagena, Colombia, I lived with a family for two months in Cali, Colombia. They introduced me to their incredibly warm and vibrant culture. I gained a further glimpse into the Cali lifestyle and the weekend life on the "fincas" (farms), learned to salsa (Cali is the "salsa capital of the world"), and independently taught English language courses. Cali is where I really experienced "culture shock." Some of it came from the different pace of culture and angles at which the world is viewed, but I attribute the majority of my culture shock to my lack of Spanish speaking abilities. I'm grateful to those who worked with me to communicate and connect out of sheer interest for me as a person, but when groups gathered, alienated is a good way to describe the way I felt. My basic Spanish wasn't nearly enough to keep up, and the pace of conversation swept over me like a wave—leaving me with only tones, vibrations and a feeling as to where the current of conversation was pulling. Although lacking the local language provides a different type of learning experience in itself, it also leads to missed opportunities for connecting and understanding. For those wishing to explore lands where a different language is spoken, I recommend at least an intermediate understanding of the language beforehand, scheduling home stays with locals, and arranging private language lessons upon arrival.

After leaving Cali, I headed south to the most ecologically diverse country in the world, Ecuador. What I expected to be a short trip through Ecuador's beautiful landscapes en route to Peru has evolved into a longer-term expedition and tremendous opportunity. Within days of arriving in Quito, I came across the coordinator of a volunteer program and soon after found myself volunteering with the charity, Great Aves [www.greataves.org/], teaching English and assisting with community development projects in rural communities of Amazonian Ecuador.

Great Aves' approach strives to enhance education throughout the communities with which it works in order to help develop sustainable businesses and implement more efficient agricultural methods, all the while maintaining a conscious mindset of the impacts each action has on the environment. After working at every level within the Great Aves organization, I increasingly became impassioned by the project and found myself in the role of Coordinator of the Amazon Conservation and Community Development project. Successful sustainable community development is a challenging endeavor that requires a deep understanding of the communities with whom we work, a clear picture of local resources available to help meet its needs, and the tact to develop this information into a working model that serves to bridge the gap between theory and implementation. I've learned it is extremely important to work ideas of progress and education around the ways of the community with which we work, rather than develop plans and attempt to mold the community to those.

Volunteering has offered me an incredible learning experience that I simply never would have obtained had I traveled from place to place without taking time to get involved at the local level. I am constantly provided with new insights as I interact and work with the local communities. I have learned that, with respect to the communities Great Aves is involved with,

"deadlines" or "appointments" more often than not translate to "best case scenarios" and giving, especially within the community development sector, must be entered into with some caution as it tends to lead to expectations.

My goal in writing this piece is to inspire and urge my readers to venture outside the road more commonly traveled. The vast amount of pressure felt upon graduation can be, from my experience and observations, frightening and overwhelming. Yet, this pressure alleviates as a view of the world and its endless range of possibilities is revealed. We, as Americans, come from a place that provides the opportunity to decide, as individuals, where to step next. That is a reality I have become more grateful for as I learn more about restrictions elsewhere. It is not the only way, but openly exploring realms outside of our own borders is one of the best ways to learn more about ourselves and the world in which we live. It can be a difficult and sometimes overwhelming task, but try your best to be true to yourself. Challenge assumptions, observe the things that give you joy, and continually ask yourself—what do I love to do and how can I align this with a life that provides for what I need?

Resources For Your Global Career

Do you Know Your World's Geography? Test your knowledge of the locations of cities of the world by playing this interactive game: http://www.minijuegosgratis.com/juegos/hwdykyworld/hwdykyworld.html

For a comprehensive world geography and related data resource: http://geography.about.com/

Do you know how fast the world changes? This site shows you real-time data changes for global statistics: http://www.peterrussell.com/Odds/WorldClock.php

Are You Respectful of the Growing Worldwide Green Movement? "Going Green" is rapidly becoming an issue in virtually every public, private, for-profit and nonprofit organization worldwide. It is shifting from an environmental movement to that of a political ideology. As companies support "green" they also identify and even create opportunities to provide social value and enhanced business profitability at the same time. The businessperson who can do both for a company will be increasingly valuable. Here are two Web sites that offer a wide range of information on "green": http://www.globalgreens.org/index.php (specifically the streaming video conference speeches) and http://www.greens.org/

Advocacy on Green and Social Responsibility Issues Many global organizations support the Green Movement and social responsibility in general by advocating for environmentally and economically sound practices to protect not only the environment, ecosystems, public health, but also indigenous peoples of the world. Four such organizations are ELAW (Environmental Law Alliance Worldwide), http://www.elaw.org/news/ebulletin/text.asp; GRACE, http://www.gracelinks.org/; Net Impact (founded by students and focused on helping new generation leaders learn about and take action regarding social responsibility-related business issues), http://www.netimpact.org/; and UNEP (United Nations Environment Programme), http://na.unep.net/. Explore

(continued)

the links on these sites to learn more about advocacy programs on a global scale because they do affect world business.

Global Environmental and Sustainability Career Options To explore internships or career opportunities in environmental or sustainability-related areas, take a look at Web sites such as these:

Great Green Careers, http://www.greatgreencareers.com/?utm_content=GGC+05.15.11+MEN&utm_campaign=MEN_MISC&utm_source=iPost&utm_medium=email

CampusAccess.com, http://www.campusaccess.com/internships/environmental.html

Environmental Career Opportunities (ECO), http://www.eco-jobs.com/environmental-internships.htm

Conservation International, http://www.conservation.org/Pages/default.aspx

Earthworks, http://www.earthworks-jobs.com/

Environmental Career Center, http://environmentalcareer.com/

International Environmental and Development, http://www.iedonline.net/jobs_interns.htm

Green Energy Jobs, http://www.greenenergyjobs.com/

Summary

LO5-1 Describe how geographical features of a country or region create differences that contribute to economic, cultural, political, and social conditions that are important to international business.

Mountains separate people. They divide nations into smaller regional markets that often have distinct cultures, industries, and climates. Sometimes, even the languages are different. Deserts and tropical forests act as barriers to people, goods, and ideas.

LO5-2 Apply Porter's diamond model to a discussion of geographical features.

Location, topography, climate, and natural resources are inherited factors that underlie inputs that companies draw on. Local disadvantages in factor conditions can be recognized as advantages and become a force for innovation. Adverse conditions such as local terrain and climate or scarce raw materials, at the basic-factor level, force firms to develop new methods, and this innovation may lead to a national comparative advantage. Hence, understanding these factors is important.

LO5-3 Summarize the importance to business of inland waterways and outlets to the sea.

Waterways have an effect opposite to mountains and deserts; they bring people together. Water transportation has increased even after the building of railroads and highways. Various European firms are shipping goods in barges on the Rhine waterway instead of using highways.

LO5-4 Outline the nonrenewable and renewable energy options available and their broad business implications.

Nonrenewable energy sources include petroleum, both from conventional sources and nonconventional sources such as shale, oil sands, coal, and natural gas. Other nonrenewable sources are coal, nuclear power, and natural gas. Renewable energy sources include hydroelectric, wind, solar, geothermal, waves, tides, biomass, and ocean thermal energy conversion. Each of these energy sources has a cost that affects its use. As nonrenewable sources approach depletion, renewable sources will become more widely applied as their relative cost decreases.

LO5-5 Describe the issues related to nonfuel minerals that concern international business.

Nonfuel mineral natural resources have been taken for granted, but supplies indicate that they are an area about which governments and industry need to think strategically. Nonfuel minerals are used in all areas of modern living. Rare earths are a subset of these minerals—a group of 17 elements used in technological applications such as high-end magnets in U.S. weapons, petroleum refining, and lasers. China controls 95 percent of the export market and announced in early 2011 that it expects to need to import these materials soon. Prices of some rare earths recently have jumped up more than 1,000 percent.

LO5-6 Describe the concept of environmental sustainability and its potential influence on business.

Environmental sustainability rests on the commitment of business to operate without reducing the capacity of the environment to provide for future generations. Increasingly, companies will need to make decisions about setting limits on how their operations affect the environment, and they will also encounter increased signs of the interdependence that exists among the social, economic, and ecological systems that form the context for their business.

LO5-7 Explain the major characteristics of sustainable business.

There are three characteristics of evolving sustainable business practices that are widely agreed upon: limits, which apply to the ecological system; interdependence, which applies to the social system as well as to the other two; and equity in distribution, which applies to the economic system.

LO5-8 Discuss the utility of the stakeholder model for sustainable business.

Stakeholder theory forces a business to address its underlying values and principles. Stakeholder theory encourages managers to articulate clearly how they want to do business. What kind of relationships do they want and need to create with their stakeholders to deliver on their purpose? In this way, operating with stakeholder theory leads to a public discussion about responsibility of the business toward all stakeholders and among all stakeholders.

Key Words

topography (p. 122)
inland waterway (p. 129)
Rhine waterway (p. 129)
climate (p. 132)
natural resources (p. 133)
nonrenewable energy sources (p. 133)
shale (p. 135)
heavy oil (p. 137)

Kyoto Protocol (p. 139)
wind power (p. 143)
biomass (p. 143)
solar photovoltaic power (PV) (p. 143)
concentrating solar thermal power (CSP) (p. 143)
geothermal power (p. 143)
ocean energy (p. 144)

hydropower (p. 144)
rare earths (p. 144)
environmental sustainability (p. 145)
stakeholder theory (p. 149)
triple-bottom-line (3BL) accounting (p. 149)

Questions

1. Of the 38 nations listed by the UN as the least developed nations in the world, 16 are landlocked. How might being landlocked contribute to slower development? Remember that Switzerland is landlocked as you think through this question.

2. Comment on the potential of oil shale and oil sands as future energy sources.

3. a. Why do you suppose the blank areas on a population map generally coincide with the areas of higher elevation on a topographical map?

   b. Why are the tropics an exception to this rule?

4. "International businesspeople, unless they are in the business of refining minerals or petroleum, have no need to concern themselves with world developments in natural resources." Agree or disagree with this assertion, explaining your reasoning.

5. Mountains, deserts, and tropical rain forests are generally culture barriers. Explain.

6. In 2005, Switzerland, a landlocked country, won the America's Cup sailing competition. How might this be explained using Porter's factor conditions?

7. From an international businessperson's point of view, how would you apply what you have learned about factor conditions as you explore locations for manufacturing?

8. Explain how the stakeholder model applies to a specific example of sustainable business. This example can be from your community, the business press, or a class discussion.

9. How is the concept of sustainable business practice both local and global?

10. Can a petroleum-based business incorporate sustainable characteristics?

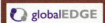
Use the globalEDGE site (http://globalEDGE.msu.edu/) to complete the following exercises:

1. You are working for a company that is deciding whether or not to enter South Asia. Top executives have requested a report on the natural environment in this region. Specifically, they are interested in gaining a better understanding of the main trends with respect to the land, air, and water. Using the South Asia Environment Outlook in the *South Asian Association for Regional Cooperation* website as reference, prepare a short report summarizing the key environmental trends in South Asia.

2. Your company wants to become more environmentally sustainable. Utilize resources available on the globalEDGE website regarding sustainable development and business to prepare a brief report that explains the concept of *sustainable* development and discusses why it is important for companies to engage in environmentally sustainable practices. In addition, compile a short list of steps that companies should take to become more environmentally sustainable.

Minicase: The BlueGreen Alliance: A New Way of Thinking for Sustainability

In 2006, the United Steel Workers and the Sierra Club launched a collaboration to focus on environmental policy and expand the number of jobs and the quality of the jobs in the green economy. The collaboration surprised many because environmentalists and unions have been opposed on many issues in the past. For example, the environmentalists have opposed drilling for oil in the Alaska Arctic National Wildlife Refuge, which the unions supported. The unions have often opposed environmentalism because their belief was that it cost jobs. Yet, the collaboration found common ground and has been wildly successful, taking on many additional partners, including the Communications Workers of America, the Natural Resources Defense Council, the Service Employees International Union, the National Wildlife Federation, and the United Auto Workers. The BlueGreen Alliance unites more than 14 million members.

There are four main issues the BlueGreen Alliance is presently working on. The first has to do with increased investments in *clean energy* sources. This is a strategy to create green jobs, reduce global warming, and move the United States toward energy independence. The second concern is *climate change*, and BlueGreen is urging passage of comprehensive climate change legislation. Such legislation would create jobs and reduce emissions. The *right trade policies* can lead, BlueGreen argues in its third concern, to a renewal of the American middle class if we increase trade and the jobs are located in the United States. The final concern is *green chemistry*. The BlueGreen Alliance is pushing for greater control of toxic chemicals and the development of safe alternatives through what it calls "green chemistry."[44]

Questions

1. Is the BlueGreen Alliance a partnership of convenience, or do you think it has the potential to move into a new way of approaching sustainability, with limits, interdependence, and equity?

2. The right trade policies, in a union view, may mean protectionist measures to build jobs. Do you think such a policy could fit into a sustainable approach?

Political and Trade Forces

In nearly every economic crisis, the root cause is political, not economic.
—*Former Prime Minister Lee Kuan Yew of Singapore*

Branding and Rebranding a Country

In February 2008, a new nation was born—Kosovo, a former province of Serbia. As one means of putting this new nation "on the map," the advertising agency Ogilvy developed a 10-foot-high, 79-foot-long, 3-foot-deep metal sculpture spelling the word "newborn." On the day the country was established, citizens signed the sculpture. It is now part of the landscape in the new capital, Pristina.

At about the same time, in a different part of the world, Israel also was engaged in a "rebranding" effort. Just over 60 years since the nation's founding, Israel is trying to attract more visitors by rebranding as a "lifestyles-oriented destination." Israel's public relations problem is serious. Except for Iran, it has the lowest public perception of any country in the world. The gap between an advanced level of economic and social development and a low image creates a burden that hinders its attraction as a destination for tourism or economic activity. So Israel, in addition to launching a campaign called "Women of the Israeli Defense Forces" which ran in *Maxim,* a men's magazine, has country websites on MySpace and Facebook and a blog, Israeli.org. These efforts are intended to shift perceptions of Israel from lenses of war, occupation, and religion to "a human lens." In Kosovo, the task is to develop any perception of the country at all. Further, the country will need to dissociate itself from the violence that has plagued that part of the world for a number of years. However, on a positive note, the $5.9 million "Kosovo—The Young Europeans" branding campaign that was developed by the advertising agency BBR Saatchi & Saatchi won the top award in the nation branding category at the 2010 M&M Awards ceremony in London. According to the organizers of the competition, "the judges were particularly impressed by the 'genuinely intriguing' nature of the campaign, by the very cost effective activation, and by the results."

Source: Ron Friedman, "Re-branding Israel? If only I Could," *Jerusalem Post,* February 11, 2010, www.jpost.com/Israel/Article.aspx?id=168506 (accessed June 23, 2011); "Kosovo 'Nation Branding' Campaign Wins M&M Award," http://nation-branding.info/2010/10/09/kosovo-nation-branding-campaign-wins-mm-award/ (June 23, 2011); and David Kaufman, "Best Face Forward: How Israel, Approaching Sixty, Is Rebranding Itself to Attract More Visitors," *AdWeek,* March 17, 2008, pp. 20–21, http://nyi-www.brandweek.com/aw/content_display/esearch/e3i47dc2082d6980ced5f03bf7b4b0e4072?pn=3 (June 23, 2011).

6

learning objectives

After reading this chapter, you should be able to:

LO6-1 **Discuss** nationalization and privatization of business.

LO6-2 **Explain** what terrorism is and the range of activities that terrorists can engage in, as well as countermeasures that companies and their employees might take.

LO6-3 **Evaluate** the importance to business of government stability and policy continuity.

LO6-4 **Explain** country risk assessment by international business.

LO6-5 **Discuss** types of trade restrictions and the arguments for imposing them.

157

In many ways, the political climate of a country in which a business operates is as important as the country's topography, its natural resources, and its climate. Hospitable, stable governments can encourage business investment and growth despite geographic or weather obstacles and a scarcity of natural resources. The opposite is equally true. Some areas of the world that are relatively blessed with natural resources and manageable topography and weather have been little developed because of government instability. Occasionally, a country's government is hostile to investment in its territory by foreign companies, even though they might provide capital, technology, and training for development of the country's resources and people.

Many of the political forces with which business must cope have ideological sources, but there are a large number of other sources. These sources include nationalism, government-owned business, terrorism, and unstable governments, among other factors. The international company itself can also be a political force. Some firms have budgets or sales larger than the gross national income (GNI) of some of the countries with which they negotiate. Although budgets and GNIs do not translate directly into power, it should be clear that companies with bigger budgets and countries with bigger GNIs possess more assets and facilities with which to negotiate.

This chapter provides an indication of the types of risks political forces pose to private business. As we shall see, some of the risks can stem from more than one political force. We also look at some of the ways international trade is heavily influenced by political forces.

Government Ownership of Business

LO6-1 Discuss nationalization and privatization of business.

One might assume that government ownership of the factors of production is found only in communist countries, but that assumption is not correct. From country to country, there are wide differences in the industries that are government-owned and in the extent of government ownership.

WHY FIRMS ARE NATIONALIZED

Governments put their hands on firms for a number of reasons. Some of these reasons are (1) to extract more money from the firms, if the government suspects that the firms are concealing profits; (2) profitability—the government believes it can run the firms more efficiently and make more money; (3) ideology; (4) job preservation—to save jobs by putting dying industries on life-support systems; (5) because the government has pumped money into a firm or an industry, and control usually follows money; and (6) happenstance, as with the nationalization after World War II of German-owned firms in Europe.

UNFAIR COMPETITION?

Where government-owned companies compete with privately owned companies, the private companies sometimes complain that the government companies have unfair advantages. Some of the complaints are that: (1) government-owned companies can cut prices unfairly because they do not have to make profits, (2) they get cheaper financing, (3) they get government contracts, (4) they get export assistance, and (5) they can hold down wages with government assistance.

Another advantage state-owned companies may enjoy over privately owned business comes in the form of direct subsidies: payments by the government to those companies. The EU Commission has been trying to discourage such subsidy payments. For years it has required annual financial reports from state-controlled companies as part of a crackdown on the subsidies that can distort competition.

privatization
The transfer of public sector assets to the private sector, the transfer of management of state activities through contracts and leases, and the contracting out of activities previously conducted by the state

Privatization

Britain's former prime minister, Margaret Thatcher, was a leader of the **privatization** movement. During her years in office, Thatcher decreased state-owned companies from a 10 percent share of Britain's GNP to 3.9 percent. She sold more than 30 companies, raising some $65 billion. Similarly, from 1975 to 1989, Chile's Pinochet sold government stakes in

FIGURE 6.1

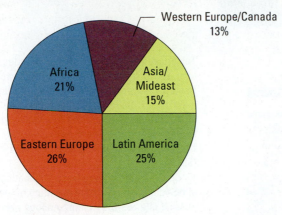

Source: "Privatization Worldwide Summary," prepared for the Transnational Corporations and Management Division of the United Nations. Used here by permission of the author, Michael S. Minor.

more than 160 corporations and 16 banks and more than 3,600 agro-industrial plants, mines and real estate, not including the return of property expropriated during the previous government of Salvador Allende.

PRIVATIZATION ANYWHERE

Privatization does not always involve ownership transfer from government to private entities. Activities previously conducted by the state may be contracted out: Mozambique has contracted a British firm to run its customs administration, and Thailand has private companies operating some of the passenger trains of its state-owned railroad. Germany's *Deutsche Post* was privatized and is often counted as a privatization success story. In general, the solvency and stability of the banking sector were found to be improved by the privatization of industrial and commercial companies. Privatized companies have improved their profitability more rapidly, which has led to notable improvements in the banks' loan portfolios.[1]

Figure 6.1 shows privatization by geographic region. The percentages in the figure total 100 without reference to the United States; neither the U.S. government nor the individual state governments are participating substantially in the privatization trend.

Government Protection

A historical function of government, whatever its ideology, has been the protection of the economic activities—farming, mining, manufacturing, and so forth—within its geographic area of control. These activities must be protected from attacks and destruction or robbery by bandits, revolutionaries, foreign invaders, or terrorists. In 1990, the Iraqi armed forces invaded Kuwait, quickly overwhelming the defenders of that smaller country.

The aftermath of this war demonstrates the influence of politics on business. In gratitude for American fighting in Desert Storm, Kuwait and other Gulf Cooperation Council countries—Saudi Arabia, Qatar, Bahrain, the United Arab Emirates, and Oman—bought some $36 billion of American arms. But in a 1997 competition to sell Kuwait 72 self-propelled howitzers, a Chinese company beat out an American company's widely considered superior versions. In private conversations, Kuwaiti officials said their reasons for buying Chinese had nothing to do with range, price, or accuracy and everything to do with politics. It seems China suggested it would withhold its support at the United Nations for extending trade sanctions against Iraq unless Kuwait gave the estimated $300 million order to the Chinese company. "Sometimes you get to a state when you feel you're being blackmailed," a senior Kuwaiti official said. "We lean toward the U.S. equipment, but we have to find a way to please the Chinese and not upset them in the Security Council."[2]

Terrorism in Second Life

Terrorism has been around for decades in the real world. However, terrorism attacks are no longer exclusive to the real world. Recently, several attacks occurred in the virtual world environment called "Second Life." A group of dissatisfied older residents of the virtual world started to protest against the "authoritarian leadership" of the Second Life founding company Linden Labs. The group named themselves the Second Life Liberation Army (SLLA).

SLLA members were frustrated because of the rapid increase of newcomers and by the entrance of real-world companies into Second Life. As they claim, nobody asked them anything about the change that occurred and were made solely by Linden Labs. They're arguing that by being residents of this world, they should have more voice in decision making. They also made an official statement of demands:

The establishment of basic "rights" for Second Life players. Having consulted widely we now believe the best vehicle for this is for Linden Labs to offer public shares in the company. We propose that each player is able to

---

LO6-2 Explain
what terrorism is and the range of activities that terrorists can engage in, as well as countermeasures that companies and their employees might take.

terrorism
Unlawful acts of violence committed for a wide variety of reasons, including for ransom, to overthrow a government, to gain release of imprisoned colleagues, to exact revenge for real or imagined wrongs, and to punish nonbelievers of the terrorists' religion

TERRORISM

Terrorism involves unlawful acts of violence committed for a wide variety of reasons, including for ransom, to overthrow a government, to gain release of imprisoned colleagues, to exact revenge for real or imagined wrongs, and to punish nonbelievers of the terrorists' religion. Since at least the 1970s, various groups have hijacked airplanes, shot and kidnapped individuals, and bombed people and objects. Al Qaeda is by no means the only terrorist organization in the world. Among the better-known groups involved in terrorism are the Irish Republican Army (IRA), Hamas, Hezballah, Abu Nidal and other Islamic fundamentalist groups, the Basque separatist movement (ETA), the Japanese Red Army, the German Red Army Faction, and various terrorist organizations in Latin America.

A number of organizations rank countries and territories for their level of terrorism risk. For example, the 2010 Terrorism Risk Index from the global risk advisory company Maplecroft listed the 10 highest risk nations (in order) as Somalia, Pakistan, Iraq, Afghanistan, Palestinian Occupied Territory, Columbia, Thailand, Philippines, Yemen, and Russia.[3]

Kidnapping for Ransom   Kidnapping is another weapon used by terrorists. The victims are held for ransom, frequently very large amounts, which provides an important source of funds for the terrorists. Estimates are that there are 8,000 to 10,000 ransom and kidnapping situations per year and that kidnappers take home up to $500 million. One firm engaged in corporate risk consulting notes that large ransoms can be physically daunting—$1 million in mixed $20 and $100 bills weighs about 66 pounds! Mexican kidnappings have increased by more than 300 percent since 2005, and pirates from Somalia are hijacking dozens of ships per year in the Indian Ocean, holding an estimated 700 hostages at a time.[4]

Paying Ransom Becomes Counterproductive   The hostage business is booming. A remarkable deal concluded in the Philippines explains why.

buy one share for a set-price. This would serve both the development of the world and provide the beginnings of representations for avatars [residents of the virtual world] in Second Life.

The SLLA organized several terrorist attacks on various companies operating in SL. The attacks, which began in late 2006 included bombs planted outside the Reebok store; a bomb that hit the ABC headquarters; a helicopter that flew into the Nissan building; and forced entry into the American Apparel store, attacking several customers. Although there are no real victims in these cases, the goal is to create confusion that will cause unpleasant experiences for other residents and companies.

How did companies react? Some companies took the attacks seriously. In Nissan's case they responded similarly as they would in a real-world attack situation. Nissan online officials cleaned up the crime scene, removed the bodies, and put them in virtual coffins. Although they treated the attack seriously, they still did not close their business.

On the other hand, the American Apparel store closed its business and moved out. ABC took precautions in order to protect its sites, especially its most popular site called Sandbox. On that site, visitors are allowed to build objects, and ABC officials found that several objects were inappropriate for ABC. To prevent that, it started to monitor the site and visit it on a regular basis.

Companies that expand their business into Second Life are harmed by those attacks. Fearing broader impacts, the U.S. Congress held a hearing about a potential link between virtual worlds like Second Life and terrorism, including the potential to launder funds for terrorist organizations. More chillingly, some security experts believe that in the wake of the closure of training camps in Pakistan and elsewhere, the virtual world is being used as a training ground for future missions in "First Life"—the real world.

Source: Sharon Weinberger, "Congress Freaks Out over Second Life Terrorism," *Wired*, April 4, 2008, www.wired.com/dangerroom/2008/04/second-life/ (June 23, 2011); Preeti Aroon and Dean Takahashi, "Terrorists in Second Life," *Foreign Policy*, March–April 2008, p. 93; Iain Thomson, "Cyber-Terrorists Storm Second Life," *What PC?* February 22, 2007; Natali O'Brien, "Virtual Terrorists," July 31, 2007, www.theaustralian.com.au/news/features/virtual-terrorists/story-e6frg6z6-1111114072291 (accessed June 23, 2011); and Wayne Porter, "Exclusive Interview with Second Life Liberation Army and Reflections on Snow," December, 4, 2006, www.revenews.com/wayneporter/exclusive-interview-with-second-life-liberation-army-leader-slla/ (June 23, 2011).

Libya's Colonel Muammar Qaddafi, trying to shake off that country's pariah status, bought the release of several Western hostages held by a band of Islamist bandits in the Philippines. The price was about $1 million each. The kidnappers evidently learned two lessons: holding a few hostages keeps the army away, and grabbing more keeps the money rolling in. Within weeks after receiving the ransom money, the Philippine kidnappers bought new weapons and a new speedboat with which to capture more people to sell.[5] As an illustration of the global reach of terrorism, the Philippine group, which calls itself Abu Sayyaf, is thought to have links with al Qaeda.

Countermeasures by Industry   Insurance to cover ransom payments, antiterrorist schools, and companies to handle negotiations with kidnappers have come into being. The insurance, which is called KRE (kidnap, ransom, and extortion) and generates $500 million in premiums each year, can pay for the ransom, the fees of specialist negotiators, the salary of the hostage, and counseling for the victim and the family. Fees for the security of CEOs have ranged up to $1.7 million per year for Larry Ellison, former chairman of Oracle Corp., down to $239 for a home-alarm monitoring service for the chair of Valero Energy Corp.[6]

As kidnapping and extortion directed against businesses and governments have become common fund-raising and political techniques for terrorists, insurance against such acts has grown into a multimillion-dollar business. The world's largest kidnapping and extortion underwriting firm is located in London. The firm, Cassidy and Davis, says that it covers some 9,000 companies. Cassidy and Davis runs antiterrorism training courses for executives, with subjects ranging from defensive driving techniques—escape tactics and battering through blockades—to crisis management. Country-by-country risk analyses are instantly available on international computer hookups.

Antiterrorist surveillance detection and evasive driving training are also available. International Training Inc. (ITI) teaches some 5,000 students each year how to frustrate would-be assassins and kidnappers. The students are company executives and high-wealth individuals. To enhance your chances of success with your driver's training, you can harden your automobile. For example, Carat Security Group offers multilayered ballistic glass, protected car floors, run-flat tires and protected fuel tanks for the automobiles of potential victims. It cites the recent violence in Mexico as a boon to the armored car industry.

Chemical and Biological Terrorism

In 1995, the Aum Shin Rikyo cult launched a nerve gas attack in the Tokyo subway that killed 12 people and injured 5,500, many of whom suffered severe nerve damage. A malfunction in the bomb delivery system is believed to have prevented thousands of additional casualties. Sarin was the nerve gas used in the Tokyo subway attack. Chemical information about sarin is available on the Internet, making threats possible from self-taught terrorists anywhere.

Government Stability

LO6-3 Evaluate the importance to business of government stability and policy continuity.

stability
Characteristic of a government that maintains itself in power and whose fiscal, monetary, and political policies are predictable and not subject to sudden, radical changes

instability
Characteristic of a government that cannot maintain itself in power or that makes sudden, unpredictable, or radical policy changes

Government **stability** can be defined in two ways. One can speak of either a government's ability to maintain itself in power, or the stability or permanence of a government's policies. It is safe to generalize that business prospers most when there is a stable government with permanent—or gradually changing—policies. **Instability** on the other hand is when a government cannot maintain itself in power or makes sudden, unpredictable, or radical policy changes. It is hard for business to flourish when government is unstable.

Stability and Instability

Example of Zimbabwe Zimbabwe was a relatively rich African country that was a net exporter of food. After a successful liberation movement against white-minority rule, the Zimbabweans elected resistance leader Robert Mugabe as prime minister in 1980. In the 1990s he decided to seize land and equipment from big farms and redistribute them to small landholders. People close to Mugabe were able to get the best of the land, but they have failed to work it and produce food.

There is now a severe food shortage, and the country depends on foreign aid. But the aid-donating countries have grown impatient with corruption and are cutting back their aid. It is also generally conceded that Mugabe stole the presidential election in 2008. The resulting instability caused a loss of confidence by potential foreign investors, so money, expertise, and technology are no longer coming in. Poverty and starvation are the lot of many Zimbabweans.

International Companies

International business is not merely a passive victim of political forces. It can be a powerful force in the world political arena. About half of the world's 100 biggest economic units are firms, not nations.

International companies (ICs) repeatedly make decisions about where to invest, where to conduct research and development, and where to manufacture products. The country or area in which an investment is made or where a laboratory, research facility, or manufacturing plant is located can benefit as jobs are created, new or improved technology becomes available, or products are produced that can be exported or substituted for imports.

Of course, the IC will seek the country and area in which it can operate most beneficially and profitably. It will negotiate with the national and local areas in which it is considering an investment or plant location in efforts to maximize benefits such as tax breaks, infrastructure improvements, and worker training programs.

The financial size of many ICs provides them with a strong negotiating position. And an IC's power need not rest solely on size. It can come from the possession of capital, technology, and management skills, plus the capability to deploy those resources around the world. An IC may have the processing, productive, distributive, and marketing abilities necessary for the successful utilization of raw materials or for the manufacture, distribution, and marketing of certain products. Those abilities are frequently not available in developing countries. Recognition of the desirability of IC investments is growing.[7] For example, China has operations in a wide variety of African states, such as oil exploration in Chad, the Congo, and Guinea, and building projects in Ivory Coast, Nigeria, and Angola.

TABLE 6.1   Country Risk Rankings

Economist.com Country Operational Risk, February 2009		Euromoney Country Risk Rankings, March 2011	
1 equals highest level of operational risk		Higher numbers represent higher levels of country risk; ranks of 100 reviewed nations	
1	Sudan	100	Mozambique
2	Kyrgyz Republic	99	Algeria
2	Kenya	98	Belarus
2	Nigeria	97	Seychelles
5	Chad	96	Paraguay
6	Ecuador	95	Nigeria
7	Eritrea	94	Mongolia
8	Tajikistan	93	Venezuela
9	Venezuela	92	Albania
10	Uzbekistan	91	Lebanon
11	Turkmenistan	90	Argentina
12	Zimbabwe	89	Ukraine
13	Myanmar	88	Egypt
14	Iraq	87	Macedonia
14	Guinea	86	Serbia

Source: Adapted from "Risky Business: Doing Business Is Getting Riskier in Many Countries around the World," *The Economist*, March 16, 2009, www.economist.com/node/13251992?story_id5E1_TPNVTJJN&CFID5172695079&CFTOKEN576845053 (June 23, 2011); and "Country Risk March 2011: Country Rankings and Acknowledgements," *Euromoney*, www.euromoney.com/Article/2773235/Country-risk-March-2011-Country-rankings-and-acknowledgements.html (June 23, 2011).

Country Risk Assessment

The political events of recent years have caused firms to concentrate much more on country risk assessment. **Country risk assessment (CRA)** is an evaluation, conducted by a bank or business, that assesses a country's economic situation and policies and its politics to determine how much risk exists of losing an investment. Because of recent turmoil, firms that had already done CRA updated and strengthened the function, and many other companies began to engage in the practice.

TYPES OF COUNTRY RISKS

Country risks are increasingly political in nature. Among them are wars, revolutions, and coups. Less dramatic, but nevertheless important for businesses, are government changes caused by election of a new government that may be hostile to private business and particularly to foreign-owned business.

The risks may be economic or financial. Countries may have persistent balance-of-payments deficits or high inflation rates. Repayment of loans may be questionable. Labor conditions may cause investors to pause. Labor productivity may be low, or labor unions may be militant. Laws may be changed in regard to such subjects as taxes, currency convertibility, tariffs, quotas, and labor permits. The chances for a fair trial in local courts must be assessed. And terrorism may be present. If it is, can the company protect its personnel and property?

INFORMATION CONTENT FOR CRA

The types of information a firm will need to judge country risks vary according to the nature of its business and the length of time required for the investment, loan, or other involvement to yield a satisfactory return.

LO6-4 Explain country risk assessment by international business.

country risk assessment (CRA)
An evaluation, conducted by a bank or business, that assesses a country's economic situation and policies and its politics to determine how much risk exists of losing an investment or not being paid

Nature of Business   Consider the needs of a hotel company compared with those of mining companies. Sometimes variations exist between firms in the same industry or on a project-to-project basis also. The home country of the company may be a factor: does the host country bear a friendly attitude toward the home country or not?

Length of Time Required   Export financing usually involves the shortest period of risk exposure. Typically, payments are made within 180 days—usually less—and exporters can get insurance or bank protection.

Bank loans can be short, medium, or long term. However, when the business includes host-country assembly, mixing, manufacture, or extraction of oil or minerals, long-term commitments are necessary. With long-term investment or loan commitments, risk analysis entails inherent problems that cannot be resolved. Most such investment opportunities require 5, 10, or more years to pay off. But the utility of risk analyses of social, political, and economic factors decreases rapidly over longer time spans.

WHO DOES COUNTRY RISK ASSESSING?

General or specific analyses; macro or micro analyses; and political, social, and economic analyses have been conducted for years. The Conference Board located bits and pieces of CRA being performed in various company departments—for example, the international division and the public affairs, finance, legal, economics, planning, and product-producing departments. Sometimes the people in one department were unaware that others in the company were similarly involved.

Outside consulting and publishing firms are another source of country risk analysis. As CRA has mushroomed in perceived importance, a number of such firms have been formed or have expanded. Some of the better-known outside consulting and publishing firms for CRA include:

- Business Environment Risk Intelligence (BERI) S.A.
- Business Monitor International.
- Coface.
- Control Risk Solutions.
- Economist Intelligence Unit (EIU).
- Euromoney.
- Eurasia Group.
- STRATFOR.
- *Harvard Business Review*'s Global Risk Navigator.
- The PRS Group.
- Standard and Poor's Rating Group.
- Moody's Investor Services.

Instead of or in addition to using outside consultants, a number of firms have hired such experts as international business or political science professors or retired State Department, CIA, or military people.

Trade Restrictions

LO6-5 **Discuss** types of trade restrictions and the arguments for imposing them.

Perhaps no foreign event (except fashion shows) is the subject of more writing by journalists than trade. For example, we are currently witnessing trade restrictions on rice, even as world food prices may increase as much as 40 percent. Infant industry arguments are being made in China; genetically modified and related food restrictions have appeared in Europe. Although we have strong theory in support of free trade's benefits, the WTO is experiencing difficulty getting the trade negotiations completed successfully due to political barriers, and this is likely to be exacerbated in coming years with more inflationary pressure, climate-related problems, and resource limitations.

The government officials who make decisions about import restrictions are particularly sensitive to the interest groups that will be hurt by the international competition. These groups consist of a small, easily identified body of people or organizations—as contrasted to the large, widespread number of consumers who typically benefit from free trade. In political debates over a proposed import restriction, the protectionist group will usually be united in exerting pressure on government officials, whereas pro-trade consumers rarely mount an organized effort.

ARGUMENTS FOR TRADE RESTRICTIONS

A number of arguments have traditionally been presented in support of efforts to restrict trade. We address several of the most common such arguments here, as well as associated rebuttal arguments.

National Defense

The national defense argument for trade restrictions suggests that certain industries need protection from imports because they are vital to security and must be kept operating even though they are not competitive with foreign suppliers. For example, the U.S. shoe industry requested that Congress impose restrictions because growing reliance on imported footwear was "jeopardizing the national security of the United States." Speaking to the Armed Services Committee of the U.S. Congress, the president of the Footwear Industry of America stated: "In the event of war or other national emergency, it is unlikely that the domestic footwear industry could provide sufficient footwear for the military and civilian population. . . . Improper footwear can lead to needless casualties and turn sure victory into possible defeat." A Defense Department spokesman said he knew of no plan to investigate the prospects of a wartime shoe crisis. Furthermore, federal law already requires the armed forces to buy U.S.-made footwear exclusively.[8]

Critics of the defense argument claim it would be far more efficient for the government to subsidize a number of firms to maintain sufficient capacity for wartime use only. Moreover, a subsidy would clearly indicate to taxpayers the cost of maintaining these companies in the name of national security—something that some interests may not want known. Currently, most American ocean shipping companies receive government subsidies without which they could not remain in business because of the competition from foreign firms with lower operating costs. In this way, we have a merchant marine ready in case of hostility, and we know what this state of readiness costs us.

Similar arguments have been offered in support of bans on the export of advanced technologies. Such bans, proponents argue, prevent valuable technologies from being used to strengthen competitors, especially militarily. However, these bans can reduce export revenues for the country's manufacturers by closing off potential markets. The bans can also impede efforts to sustain international market share and fund continued innovation, enabling competitors from other nations to improve their competitiveness.

Sanctions to Punish Offending Nations

A related argument for imposing trade restrictions is to inflict economic damage on other nations in order to punish them or otherwise encourage them to modify behavior. A common approach is to pass legislation that prohibits trade with the "offending" nation.

But sanctions not only seldom achieve their goal of forcing change in the targeted country; they also tend to produce collateral economic damage in the nations applying them.[9] Economic sanctions during the 1990s may have cost the United States some $15 billion to $23 billion annually in exports, in addition to losses resulting from restrictions on foreign direct investment, capital flows, tourism, and other sources of income or output.[10] During the time, that the United States was imposing sanctions on Iraq that prohibited American firms from doing business there, companies from France, Russia, and other nations were generating billions of dollars from business contracts from which American firms were excluded.

Protect Infant (or Dying) Industry

Advocates for the protection of an infant industry may claim that in the long run the industry will have a comparative advantage but that firms need protection from imports until the required investment capital is obtained, the labor force is trained, production techniques are mastered, and economies of scale are achieved. Without the protection, advocates argue, a firm will not be able to survive because lower-cost imports from more mature foreign competitors will underprice it in its local market.

Efforts to protect emerging industries are not limited to developing nations, of course. For example, former Representative Ken Salazar of Colorado argued for the maintenance of a protective 54-cents-a-gallon import duty on foreign-produced ethanol, including imports from low-cost producer Brazil, in order to give "our infant industries a greater chance to grow." The cost of subsidizing the American ethanol industry is estimated at $1 billion to $5 billion annually.[11]

A related argument concerns the protection of a "dying" industry, one threatened by an onslaught of imports that endangers the survival of domestic companies and the jobs they provide. Under this argument, it takes time to make the necessary adjustments to move labor and capital out of the industry and into other sectors. Protecting the industry from imports can therefore facilitate a smoother transition. This logic has been used in justifying protection for textiles and footwear in the United States and Europe. Other aid, such as subsidies for relocating to different geographic areas and for providing assistance to displaced workers, may also be part of the proposed solution.

Protect Domestic Jobs from Cheap Foreign Labor
Protectionists who use this argument usually compare lower foreign hourly wage rates to those paid in their home country. They conclude that foreign exporters can flood the home country's market with low-priced goods, and thus simultaneously eliminate jobs of home-country workers. The first fallacy of this argument is that wage costs are neither all of the production costs nor all of the labor costs, so a comparison merely based on relative hourly wages would be misleading.

Second, the productivity per worker may be much greater in richer countries because of more capital per worker, superior management, and advanced technology. As a result, the labor cost component of the goods being produced could be lower even though wages are higher.

Scientific Tariff or Fair Competition
Supporters of this argument say they believe in fair competition. They simply want an import duty that will bring the cost of the imported goods up to the cost of the domestically produced article. This will eliminate any "unfair" advantage that a foreign competitor might have because of superior technology, lower raw material costs, lower taxes, or lower labor costs. It is not their intent to ban exports; they wish only to equalize the process for "fair" competition. If this were law, no doubt the rate of duty would be set to protect the least efficient producer, thereby enabling the more efficient domestic manufacturers to earn large profits. The efficient foreign producers would be penalized, and, of course, their comparative advantage would be nullified. The impact on consumers might also be viewed as unfair, since the import duty would result in an increase in the prices that they pay.

Retaliation
Representatives of an industry whose exports have had import restrictions placed on them by another country may ask their government to retaliate with similar restrictions. An example of how retaliation begins is the ban by the European Union (EU) on imports of hormone-treated beef from the United States. Because the use of hormones in animal production is considered a health hazard in the EU, the European Union closed its market to American beef (12 percent of total U.S. meat exports) in 1988. American beef producers complained that no scientific evidence supported the claim, and the United States promptly retaliated by putting import duties on about $100 million worth of EU products, including boneless beef and pork, fruit juices, wine coolers, tomatoes, French cheese, and instant coffee. The EU then threatened to ban U.S. shipments of honey, canned soybeans, walnuts, and dried fruit worth $140 million. In reply, the United

States announced that it would follow the EU ban with a ban on all European meat. If that had happened, about $500 million in U.S.–EU trade would have been affected.

Generally, disputes like these go to the World Trade Organization (WTO). After having its beef banned by the EU for eight years, the United States launched a formal dispute settlement procedure with the WTO in May 1996, challenging the ban. When the WTO Appellate Body announced that the EU ban had been imposed without reason, the EU declared that it would implement the Appellate Body ruling, but it did not comply by the date set by the WTO. The WTO authorized the United States to retaliate, resulting in imposition of a 100 percent import duty on a list of EU products with an annual trade value of $116.8 million. In 2003, the EU announced a new directive that it asserted was in compliance with the WTO's ruling, although it still banned most American and Canadian beef. The United States claimed the new EU guidelines still violated WTO requirements and maintained sanctions. In 2009, the two sides agreed that the Americans would lift sanctions gradually, corresponding with a phased increase in allowed importation into the EU of hormone-free beef from the United States. In 2011, a year ahead of schedule, the United States ended retaliatory sanctions on EU goods. The EU still has until 2012 to honor its part of the deal, or else face a renewal of sanctions.[12]

Dumping   Retaliation also occurs for **dumping.** The WTO defines dumping as selling a product abroad for less than (1) the average cost of production in the exporting nation, (2) the market price in the exporting nation, or (3) the price to third countries. A manufacturer may dump products to sell excess production without disrupting prices in its domestic market, as a response to cyclical or seasonal factors (e.g., during an economic downturn or at the end of a fashion season), or as a way to raise market share. A manufacturer may also lower its export price to force the importing nation's domestic producers out of business, expecting to raise prices once that objective is accomplished. This latter behavior is called *predatory dumping*.

dumping
Selling a product abroad for less than the cost of production, the price in the home market, or the price to third countries

The United States became the first country to prohibit dumping of foreign goods into its own market in 1916 (there is no U.S. law prohibiting American firms from dumping their goods abroad, though). Dumping is now within the domain of the WTO, which is the recipient of many related complaints through appeals by countries opposing the imposition of antidumping protections against their companies. Most governments retaliate when dumping is perceived to be harming local industry

New Types of Dumping   There are at least five new kinds of dumping for which fair-trade lobbies consider sanctions to be justified in order to level the playing field for international trade. In reality, these special-interest groups calling for level playing fields are seeking to raise the production costs of their overseas competitors to protect local high-cost producers. The classes of dumping include:

1. *Social dumping*—unfair competition caused by firms, usually from developing nations with lower labor costs and poorer working conditions, which undermines social support systems, including worker benefits.

2. *Environmental dumping*—unfair competition caused by a country's lax environmental standards. It has been argued that globalization provides incentives to national governments to set weak environmental policies, particularly for industries whose plants can be relocated internationally.

3. *Financial services dumping*—unfair competition caused by a nation's low requirements for bank capital-asset ratios.

4. *Cultural dumping*—unfair competition caused by cultural barriers aiding local firms.

5. *Tax dumping*—unfair competition caused by differences in corporate tax rates or related special breaks. Slovakia was accused of tax dumping because its low corporate tax rate and generous incentive policies were perceived to give it an advantage over other European nations in attracting investment from multinationals.[13]

subsidies

Financial contributions, provided directly or indirectly by a government, which confer a benefit, including grants, preferential tax treatment, and government assumption of normal business expenses

countervailing duties

Additional import taxes levied on imports that have benefited from export subsidies

Subsidies   Another cause of retaliation may be **subsidies** that a government makes to a domestic firm either to encourage exports or to help protect it from imports. Some examples are cash payments, government participation in ownership, low-cost loans to foreign buyers and exporters, and preferential tax treatment. For example, as shown in Figure 6.2, the OECD nations provide billions of dollars per year in subsidies to their farmers. Perhaps the greatest damage caused by this assistance is its effect on the millions of farmers in the poorest nations. High customs duties restrict access to wealthy countries' markets, while subsidized overproduction in developed countries artificially depresses prices in world markets, harming the income of farmers in poorer nations. Most of the agricultural subsidies in developed countries go to a small percentage of recipients, usually large enterprises. The nearby Global Debate box provides a more detailed example of subsidies for sugar producers in the United States.

Competitors in importing nations frequently ask their governments to impose **countervailing duties** to offset the effects of a subsidy. In the United States, when the Department of Commerce receives a petition from an American firm claiming that imports from a particular country are subsidized, it first determines whether a subsidy actually was given. If so, Commerce imposes countervailing duties equal to the subsidy's amount.

FIGURE 6.2

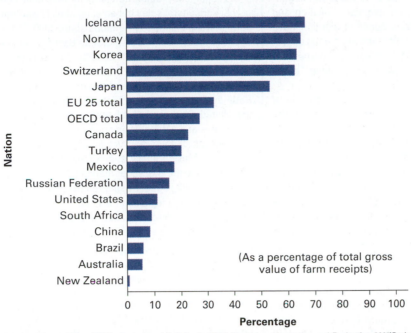

(As a percentage of total gross value of farm receipts)

Source: Adapted from OECD, *Agricultural Policies in OECD Countries: Monitoring and Evaluation 2007*(Paris: OECD, 2007), www.oecd.org/document/0/0,3343,en_2649_33727_39508672_1_1_1_1,00.html (June 23,2011).

GLOBAL DEBATE

Sugar Subsidies: Sweet for Producers, Not for Consumers

Although they lack comparative advantage in sugar production, the United States, Japan, and the EU, among others, have maintained strong protection for their domestic sugar industries. A World Bank report called sugar the "most policy-distorted of all commodities." Protectionism by developed countries harms foreign sugar producers, many of which are poor farmers in developing countries, by reducing demand and prices for their product. Oxfam estimated, for example, that EU sugar supports had caused Malawi to experience losses that exceeded its total budget for primary health care. Before being forced by the WTO into making changes in November 2005, the EU maintained domestic sugar prices that were triple world market prices.

In the United States, sugar tariffs have been in place since 1789. Imports are allocated through tariff-rate quotas among 40 nations and limited to about 15 percent of the U.S. market, except in years when there is a shortfall in the U.S. domestic supply, as in 2005 after Hurricane Katrina. High price supports result in overproduction of sugar domestically, yet at the same time the price of raw sugar in the United States has averaged more than double the world price during the past decade, costing American consumers and businesses an estimated $4 billion annually. The benefits are highly concentrated among a small number of companies. A mere 1 percent of sugar growers enjoys 42 percent of the benefits from protectionist U.S. sugar policies.

Nicaraguan Jackson Riveras carries a load of freshly cut sugarcane on a plantation near Turrucares of Alajuela, Costa Rica. Like many Nicaraguan immigrants, Ramirez came to Costa Rica to work the harvest season in order to earn higher wages and send money back to his family.

(continued)

Excess sugar production also contributes to environmental problems. In Florida, for example, pollution and disruption of water flows from sugar production have been cited as a major contributor to environmental degradation of the Everglades. Similar pollution concerns have been voiced in South Texas, where the annual "burn" sends burnt chaff into the sky.

Mechanization has eliminated the labor intensity of producing sugar from sugar beets or sugarcane in the United States. Sugar is produced in 18 states and supports 146,000 American jobs, although only about 60,000 people now work directly in the production or refining of sugar. Movement to free trade in sugar would result in an estimated loss of fewer than 2,500 workers in the sugar industry, meaning that the cost for each protected job is more than $1.5 million. In addition, protection of the U.S. sugar industry has cost thousands of jobs in other sectors, such as food and beverage manufacturing. For example, sugar accounts for 32.7 percent of the total cost of producing breakfast cereals, and high sugar prices led to the loss of an estimated 112,000 jobs at sugar-consuming companies between 1997 and 2009. High sugar prices were also a major factor in companies' decisions to relocate operations to non-U.S. sites, especially Canada and Mexico, contributing to an increase in imports of sugar-containing products. As one Commerce Department executive said, "We are seeing U.S. jobs move to countries that don't have the competitive disadvantage of high sugar prices that we face in the United States."

Efforts to reform protection of the sugar industry have made limited progress, at least partly due to the strength of the sugar lobby. Sugar accounts for less than 1 percent of U.S. agricultural sales but an estimated 17 percent of all agricultural political contributions since 1990. "It's a very effective lobby," commented Claude Barfield of the American Enterprise Institute. "They've traditionally given a lot of money to both parties." Sugar lobbying resulted in the complete exclusion of sugar from the U.S.–Australia free trade agreement, the first bilateral trade treaty in which the United States required that a product be entirely excluded—and a dangerous precedent.

However, change may yet occur. In 2008, the United States and Mexico finally ended their decade-long battle over access to the U.S. sugar market under NAFTA, with all barriers to trade in sugar being removed between the two countries. In 2011, legislation was introduced into the U.S. Congress to completely eliminate sugar subsidies, although the likelihood of its passage was questioned by many.

Source: Bill Straub, "Lugar Again Sets Sights on Sugar Subsidies," *Evansville Courier & Press*, www.courierpress.com/news/2011/apr/03/no-headline---04a0xsugar/ (June 23, 2011); Investors.com, "Close the Candy Store," April 12, 2011, www.investors.com/NewsAndAnalysis/Article/568924/201104121859/Close-The-Candy-Store.aspx (June 23, 2011); Mary Barley, "Big Sugar and the Everglades," *The Gainesville Sun*, April 8, 2011, www.gainesville.com/article/20110408/NEWS/110409559/-1/news?p=all&tc=pgall&tc=ar (June 23, 2011); Michael Schroeder, "Sugar Growers Hold Up Push for Free Trade," *The Wall Street Journal*, February 3, 2004, p. A13; and Oxfam International, "Dumping on the World: How EU Sugar Policies Hurt Poor Countries," March 2004.

Other Arguments   The arguments we have examined are probably the ones most frequently given in support of trade restrictions. Others include the use of protection from imports to (1) permit diversification of the domestic economy or (2) improve the balance of trade. You should have gathered from this discussion that protection from imports generally serves the narrow interests of a special-interest group at the expense of many. Although the application of trade restrictions can sometimes buy time for the protected industry to modernize and become more competitive in the world market, a real danger exists that a nation's trading partners will retaliate with restrictions of their own, causing injury to industries that have received no protection. Let's examine these restrictions, beginning with tariff barriers.

TARIFF BARRIERS

tariffs

Taxes on imported goods for the purpose of raising their price to reduce competition for local producers or stimulate local production

Tariffs, or import duties, are taxes levied on imported goods primarily for the purpose of raising their selling price in the importing nation's market to reduce competition for domestic producers. A few smaller nations also use them to raise revenue on both imports and exports. Exports of commodities such as coffee and copper are commonly taxed in developing nations. However, imposition of tariffs can result in retaliation that is harmful rather than helpful for a country and its well-being.

For example, in the late 1920s, declining economic fortunes caused American farmers to lobby Congress for tariff protection on agricultural products. Over time, more domestic producers joined with agricultural interests, seeking their own protection from foreign competitors. The resulting legislative proposal increased tariffs for more than 20,000 items across a range of industries. The broad support for the legislation caused the Democratic and Progressive parties to join the Republicans on October 28, 1929, in supporting the Smoot-Hawley Tariff Act to establish some of the highest levels of tariffs ever imposed.

That day the stock market crashed, falling 12 percent. In the following months, 34 foreign governments filed protests against Smoot-Hawley. Nevertheless, on June 17, 1930, President Herbert Hoover signed the bill. The result was a trade war that engulfed most of the world's economies. World trade plummeted from $5.7 billion in 1929 to $1.9 billion in 1932, unemployment skyrocketed, and the world entered a decade-long economic depression.

Ad Valorem, Specific, and Compound Duties

Import duties are (1) ad valorem, (2) specific, or (3) a combination of the two called compound. An **ad valorem duty** is stated as a percentage of the invoice value of the product. For example, the U.S. tariff schedule states that flavoring extracts and fruit flavors not containing alcohol are subject to a 6 percent ad valorem duty. Therefore, when a shipment of flavoring extract invoiced at $10,000 arrives in the United States, the importer is required to pay $600 to U.S. Customs before taking possession of the goods. A **specific duty** is a fixed sum of money charged for a specified physical unit of the product. A company importing dynamite in cartridges or sticks suitable for blasting would have to pay $0.37 per pound irrespective of the invoice value. When the flavoring extracts and fruit flavors just mentioned contain more than 50 percent alcohol by weight, they are subject to a specific duty of $0.12 per pound plus a 3 percent ad valorem. Thus, on a $10,000 shipment weighing 5,000 pounds, the importer would have to pay a **compound duty** of $900 [($.12 × 5,000 pounds) + (0.03 × $10,000) = $600 + $300]. Note that in an inflationary period, a specific duty soon loses its importance unless changed frequently, whereas the amount collected from an ad valorem duty increases as the invoice price rises. Sometimes, however, an exporter may charge prices so much lower than domestic prices that the ad valorem duty fails to close the gap. Some governments set *official prices* or use *variable levies* to correct this deficiency.

Official Prices

Official prices are included in the customs tariff of some nations. The official price guarantees that a certain minimum import duty will be paid irrespective of the actual invoice price. It thwarts a fairly common arrangement that numerous importers living in high-duty nations have with their foreign suppliers, whereby a false low invoice price is issued to reduce the amount of duty to be paid. The importer sends the difference between the false invoice price and the true price separately.

Variable Levy

One form of **variable levy,** which guarantees that the market price of the import will be the same as that of domestically produced goods, has been used by the EU for imported grains. Calculated daily, the duty level is set at the difference between world market prices and the support price for domestic producers.

Lower Duty for More Local Input

Import duties are set by many nations in such a way that they encourage local input. For example, the finished product ready for sale to the consumer may have a 70 percent duty. However, if the product is imported in bulk so that it must be packaged in the importing nation, the duty level may be 30 percent. To encourage some local production, the government may charge only a 10 percent duty on the semifinished inputs. These situations can provide opportunities for foreign manufacturers of low-technology products, such as toiletries, to get behind a high-tariff wall with very modest investments.

When tariffs are assessed at very low rates, they are sometimes referred to as *nuisance tariffs*. That is because importers are still required to go through the frequently lengthy process of paying these tariffs, even though their low levels may no longer serve their original intention, such as protecting domestic producers.

NONTARIFF BARRIERS

Nontariff barriers (NTBs) are all forms of discrimination against imports other than the import duties we have been examining. As nations reduced import duties, nontariff barriers assumed greater relative importance, and their use has been increasing. For example,

ad valorem duty
An import duty levied as a percentage of the invoice value of imported goods

specific duty
A fixed sum levied on a physical unit of an imported good

compound duty
A combination of specific and ad valorem duties

variable levy
An import duty set at the difference between world market prices and local government-supported prices

nontariff barriers (NTBs)
All forms of discrimination against imports other than import duties

government-required testing and certification requirements have increased exponentially since the mid-1990s. NTBs can take many forms, including the quantitative and nonquantitative ones discussed next, and the additional costs they impose on producers and exporters help to discourage trade.

Quantitative

One type of quantitative barrier is **quotas,** which set numerical limits for specific kinds of goods that a country will permit to be imported during a specified period. If the quota is *absolute,* once the specified amount has been imported, further importation for the rest of the period (usually a year) is prohibited. Quotas are generally *global;* that is, a total amount is fixed without regard to source. They may also be *allocated,* in which case the government of the importing nation assigns quantities to specific countries. The United States allocates quotas for specific tonnages of sugar to 40 nations. Some goods are subject to *tariff-rate quotas,* which permit a stipulated amount to enter duty-free or at a low rate, but when that amount is reached, a much higher duty is charged for subsequent importations.

Some producers have used transshipping to evade allocated quotas. In such cases, the finished goods are first shipped to a country with an unfilled quota, where the goods are labeled as products of that country, and then shipped to the quota-imposing nation. Prior to the ending of the Multi-Fiber Agreement in 2004 that limited textile imports from other nations, this deceptive labeling scheme was estimated to have brought $2 billion in illegal clothing imports from China into the United States annually. Gitano, for example, pled guilty to charges of fraud for importing Chinese blouses labeled "Made in the Maldives Islands."

For many years there has been an agreement among nations against imposing quotas unilaterally on goods (except agricultural products). Therefore, governments have negotiated **voluntary export restraints (VERs)** with other countries (e.g., the Japanese government established a VER to restrict the number of automobiles that its manufacturers could export to the United States annually, and the Canadian government agreed to a VER to limit the amount of Canadian lumber to be exported to the United States).

Orderly Marketing Arrangements

Orderly marketing arrangements are VERs consisting of formal agreements between the governments of exporting and importing countries to restrict international competition and preserve some of the national market for local producers. Usually, they stipulate the size of the export or import quotas that each nation will have for a particular good.

Nonquantitative Nontariff Barriers

Many international trade specialists claim that the most significant nontariff barriers are the nonquantitative type. Governments have tended to establish nontariff barriers to obtain the protection formerly afforded by import duties. A study of nonquantitative barriers revealed more than 800 distinct forms, which may be classified under three major headings: (1) direct government participation in trade, (2) customs and other administrative procedures, and (3) standards.

1. *Direct government participation in trade.* The most common form of direct government participation is the subsidy. Besides protecting industries through subsidies, as was mentioned earlier, nearly all governments subsidize agriculture. Agricultural support programs are often promoted as being targeted toward protecting smaller farms and traditional rural economies. However, in most OECD nations, the largest 25 percent of farms receive between 60 and 80 percent of the total level of agricultural support.[14]

   Government procurement policies are also trade barriers because they usually favor domestic producers and restrict purchases of imported goods by government agencies. Policies may also require that products purchased by government agencies have a stipulated minimum *local content.* Since the WTO Government Procurement Agreement went into effect, most nations have opened their government business to foreign bidders to comply with its requirements. However, as noted by the EU, the American government still has policies in place that may substantially interfere with international trade. For example, similar to practices in Canada and elsewhere in the world, the Buy America Act has a range of measures that either prohibit public sector organizations from purchasing from foreign suppliers of goods or services or hinder such purchases through mechanisms such as requirements for local content or the provision of advantageous pricing terms for American suppliers. The Department of Defense, which is the U.S. government's largest public procurement agency, excludes foreign suppliers from many contracts.[15]

2. *Customs and other administrative procedures.* These barriers cover a large variety of government policies and procedures that either discriminate against imports or favor exports. For example, in China, a product being imported may be subject to different rates of duty, depending on the port of entry and an arbitrary determination of the customs value. Because of this flexibility, customs charges often depend on negotiations between Chinese customs officials and managers. It is alleged that corruption is often involved.[16]

Governments have also found ways to discriminate against the exportation of services. When serving international markets, airlines face a number of situations in which the national airline receives preferential treatment, such as in the provision of airport services, airport counter locations, and number of landing slots. Other examples of discrimination are the Canadian government's giving tax deductions to local businesses that advertise on Canadian TV, but not doing so when they use American stations across the border, and Australia's requiring that television commercials be shot in Australia.

3. *Standards.* Both governmental and private standards to protect the health and safety of a nation's citizens certainly are desirable, but for years exporting firms have been plagued by many standards that are complex and discriminatory. For example, the European Parliament passed biotech food labeling requirements that impose mandatory traceability of genetically modified (GM) organisms and stringent labeling of foods that contain GM ingredients. The requirements include labels stating "This product is produced from GM organisms" and strict limits on mixing GM and non-GM ingredients in food exported to the EU. The United States is one of the world's leading producers and exporters of GM crops, with 75 percent of soybeans, 71 percent of cotton, and 34 percent of corn being GM. In the United States and Canada, 55–63 percent of customers see GM food as "bad," while this rises to 81 percent and 89 percent disapproving in Germany and France, respectively.[17]

Exporting companies need to be informed about the changing status of tariff and nontariff barriers in the countries where they are doing business or would like to do business. Those that have stayed away from markets with extremely high import duties or nontariff barriers, such as product standards or customs procedures designed to keep out foreign products, may find these barriers no longer exist.

COSTS OF BARRIERS TO TRADE

Trade restraints in the United States and other countries cost consumers tens of billions of dollars per year, while benefiting a relatively small number of companies in the protected sectors of the economy. The sugar industry provides an interesting example of this situation, as discussed in the earlier Global Debate, "Sugar Subsidies: Sweet for Producers, Not for Consumers."

Sugar is not an isolated example of the costs associated with trade barriers. A recent study of just 20 product groups in protected industries showed that the average consumer cost per job saved was $231,289 per year. This means that consumers paid more than seven times the average annual compensation of manufacturing workers to preserve jobs through import constraints. Many of these sectors have been shielded from imports for 45 years or more. Studies done in other countries show similar results.[18]

Fernando Villanueva: "There Is So Much Beauty in the World."

Fernando Villanueva has advice for others wanting to join him in international business. He is from Palo Alto, California, completed a bachelor's degree in International Business at the California Polytechnic State University San Luis Obispo, and financed most of his own college education. He has been dancing Mexican Folklore since the age of 15, and he is pasionate about traveling and meeting new people. Here's his advice about pursuing a career in international business:

My interest in obtaining a degree in International Business first arose after I traveled to France in 1998. I was 16 at the time. I had the opportunity to participate in a program called The Experiment in International Living. This program allowed me to experience the French culture by living with a French family and taking language courses with people from all over the world. Ever since then, I knew international business was the right place for me.

A year after graduating from Cal Poly, I was able to work and live in the Czech Republic thanks to an AIESEC traineeship with the Univerzita Pardubice. Some of my responsibilities were conducting research work for business-related articles, coordinating and conducting presentations for professors in the European Union, coordinating events for students in the Erasmus program, and editing and reviewing articles being considered for publication. While working for the Univezita Pardubice, I was credited as one of the official translators/editors in two published books. I was also able to travel for work or leisure to Austria, Belgium, Czech Republic, Denmark, Egypt, England, Finland, France, Germany, Greece, Hungary, Italy, Luxembourg, Netherlands, Poland, Scotland, Slovakia, Spain, Sweden, Turkey, and Wales.

When traveling to new destinations, I always try to research the country and city I will be visiting. This allows me to have some basic knowledge of where I am going. My experience with locals

has been that they appreciate my efforts to familiarize myself with their city beforehand. Knowing some basic words or phrases has always been helpful and equally appreciated. Another thing I try to do when in a new country is eat the traditional local dishes. I try to avoid spending a lot of time with other foreigners, interacting instead with the locals. I have found that this helps me adapt to the culture and people much more quickly.

The reason I chose to be an AIESEC trainee was to obtain experience working internationally, thus making me a valuable asset for any company I choose to work for in the future. Having successfully completed my traineeship will show future employers that I am able to adapt to new environments and successfully function in complex situations. Thanks to my experience with AIESEC, I have learned how to communicate and work with people from all over the world.

Two of my biggest challenges while working abroad, and with people from various parts of the world, were adjusting to the different modes by which business was conducted and to bureaucracy. Ever since my first international experience, I have had to remind myself that business is not always conducted in the same mode in each country and that I must be able to adjust to new forms of business practices. Working with other government entities can be challenging; I have accepted this fact and I try to not let this discourage me from working with them. I have discovered that achieving good cooperation with other government entities and learning to work with them can be beneficial for both me and the company I work for.

I have really enjoyed working abroad because it has allowed me to travel to various countries and it has also allowed me to acquire the ability to successfully function in nearly any business environment, both internationally and domestically. While in these countries, I have met many interesting and amazing people, and I have maintained a good relationship with many of the people I have met throughout this experience. I have learned a lot from the people I have met, both professionally and personally. Thanks to my international experience, I have learned that culturally we are all different, yet we also share a lot in common. I have found this to be true no matter where I have traveled.

When you are visiting a country that you do not reside in, always remember that you are a guest of that country—no matter what your purpose for visiting may be. A recommendation I have for anyone who is, or will be, working internationally is to not assume that the way things are done back home is always the way things are done everywhere else. Telling a person that he or she is doing a task wrong just because they are doing that task in a different way than it is done back home normally does not go well. Also, people do not like to hear what you believe is wrong about their country and what makes yours better. If you focus most of your energy on pointing out what is wrong, or what you hate, about the country you are visiting you will lose the opportunity to see what is great about it. There is so much beauty in the world; allowing yourself to have the opportunity to see a small part of it is truly amazing.

(continued)

Resources for Your Global Career

Your Understanding of the Impact of Political Risk and Geopolitics on International Business

Every international business transaction is affected by two governments, that of the home country and that of the host country. You must abide by the laws, rules, and regulations of each country. You must also understand the political orientation of each country and geographic region in which you do business because the government and its political structure will determine your ability to do business in that country. Geopolitics goes well beyond government and politics. It includes, but is not limited to, such issues as:

- Country and regional economics.
- Terrorism and its support or condemnation.
- Military alliances.
- Human rights.
- Religion and the degree of separation between "church and state."
- Public policy.
- Natural resources.
- Governmental stability.
- Attitudes toward dumping and counterfeiting products.
- Arms control.
- Chemical and biological warfare.
- Nuclear proliferation and threat.

Political risk assessment is a major component of doing a potential market entry analysis to determine the feasibility and risks of entering into a specific foreign market. Keeping current with the ever-changing global political scene and doing political risk assessment in market entry planning are two critical tools of the successful international business professional.

Your Primer on World Terrorism: To understand the incidence and scope of world terrorism, suspected or identified, look at the Global Incident Map, a real-time global display of terrorism and other suspicious events updated as they are reported: www.globalincidentmap.com/user.php.

Resources for Geopolitical Issues and Careers: To build your base of understanding of current geopolitical events and to help you locate internship and career opportunities in this area, the following resources may be useful:

- STRATFOR gives reports and analyses of geopolitical events as they relate to global economics and trade, energy, military, politics, terrorism and security: www.stratfor.com
- SIPRI (Stockholm International Peace Research Institute) provides in-depth information on Political Risk issues: www.sipri.org
- EURO Intelligence provides daily reports on macroeconomic, financial, and political issues focusing on Europe: www.eurointelligence.com/
- FP (Foreign Policy) PASSPORT, foreign policy blog: http://blog.foreignpolicy.com/node
- Foreign Policy Association: www.fpa.org/
- *World Politics Review*—a foreign policy and national security daily: www.worldpoliticsreview.com/
- Techniques for Assessing and Managing Risk in International Markets: http://findarticles.com/p/articles/mi_qa3615/is_200712/ai_n21279424?tag=rbxcra.2.a.1
- *Oxford Analytica* analyzes the implications of international developments and their impact on corporations, governments, financial, and international institutions: www.oxan.com

For internships or career opportunities in geopolitical-related organizations, see websites such as the following:

- U.S. Department of State: www.state.gov/p/io/empl/
- Foreign Policy Association: www.fpa.org
- Devex—International Development: www.devex.com/jobs

Summary

LO6-1 Discuss nationalization and privatization of business.

From time to time governments take firms or organizations out of private and into government hands. Some of the reasons for this are (1) to extract more money from the firms, (2) profitability, (3) ideology, (4) job preservation, (5) because the government has pumped money into a firm or an industry, and (6) happenstance. Where government-owned companies compete with privately owned companies, the private companies sometimes complain that the government companies have unfair advantages. Governments sometimes sell government assets to private parties or contract with private firms to perform functions usually performed by governments. That is called privatization.

LO6-2 Explain what terrorism is and the range of activities that terrorists can engage in, as well as countermeasures that companies and their employees might take.

Terrorism involves unlawful acts of violence committed for a wide variety of reasons, including for ransom, to overthrow a government, to gain release of imprisoned colleagues, to exact revenge for real or imagined wrongs, and to punish nonbelievers of the terrorists' religion.

Terrorism introduces instability into a country, making it difficult for businesses to know what the political environment will be in the future, and some terrorist groups have developed a global reach. In some cases, terrorism is also personally hazardous to firm employees and to their families. Some countermeasures that can be taken include insurance for covering kidnapping, ransom, and extortion; antiterrorist surveillance and evasive driving training; and using specialists for handling negotiations with kidnappers.

LO6-3 Evaluate the importance to business of government stability and policy continuity.

Businesses can operate under almost any set of rules as long as those rules don't change often, so that businesses can make plans. When policy (tax rates is an example) changes frequently, businesses have difficulty complying with the rules, as well as difficulty setting prices, employment policies, etc.

LO6-4 Explain country risk assessment by international business.

Country risk assessment is a form of assessment that includes political risks, but also others, such as difficulties in remitting profits, local content requirements, possible terrorist action, and the like. Businesses may choose to have CRA done inside the firm, the firm may hire outsiders, or even both.

LO6-5 Discuss types of trade restrictions and the arguments for imposing them.

In response to demands for protection, governments impose import duties (tariff barriers); nontariff barriers, such as quotas, voluntary export restraints, and orderly marketing arrangements; and nonquantitative nontariff barriers, such as direct government participation in trade, customs, and other administrative procedures and standards for health, safety, and product quality. Special-interest groups demand protection for defense industries so that their country will have these industries' output in wartime and will not depend on imports, which might not be available. New industries in developing nations frequently request barriers to imports of competing products from developed countries. The argument is that the infant industry must have time to gain experience before having to confront world competition. Protectionists argue for protection from cheap imports by claiming that other countries with lower hourly labor rates than those in the protectionist's nation can flood the protectionist's nation with low-priced goods and take away domestic jobs. Others want "fair" competition, that is, an import duty to raise the cost of the imported good to the price of the imported article to eliminate any "unfair" advantage that the foreign competitor may have. This, of course, nullifies the comparative advantage. Companies will also demand that their government retaliate against dumping and subsidies offered by their competitors in other countries.

Key Words

privatization (p. 158)

terrorism (p. 160)

stability (p. 162)

instability (p. 162)

country risk assessment (CRA) (p. 163)

dumping (p. 167)

subsidies (p. 168)

countervailing duties (p. 168)

tariffs (p. 170)

ad valorem duty (p. 171)

specific duty (p. 171)

compound duty (p. 171)

variable levy (p. 171)

nontariff barriers (NTBs) (p. 171)

quotas (p. 172)

voluntary export restraints (VERs) (p. 172)

orderly marketing arrangements (p. 172)

Questions

1. Why might governments nationalize firms, and why might a government-owned firm have an unfair advantage over privately owned companies?

2. What options does a company have for helping to prevent terrorism or to better manage terrorist actions if they occur?

3. Why might business fear sudden changes in government policies?

4. How can ICs use their strengths to influence government policies?

5. Is country risk assessment an exact science? Explain.

6. It seems that free, unrestricted international trade, in which each nation produces and exports products for which it has a comparative advantage, will enable everyone to have a higher level of living. Why, then, does every country have import duty restrictions?

7. "We certainly need defense industries, and we must protect them from import competition by placing restrictions on competitive imports." True or false? Is there an alternative to trade restrictions that might make more economic sense?

8. It seems entirely reasonable for a government to undertake efforts to protect a new or recently established—often called an "infant"—industry. Why, then, might international trade professionals argue against governmental efforts to protect a new or recently established industry?

9. According to the WTO, what is dumping? Why would a government be opposed to having their citizens or businesses be able to obtain products at lower costs?

10. "Workers are paid $20 an hour in the United States but only $4 in Taiwan. Of course, we can't compete. We need to protect our jobs from cheap foreign labor." What are some possible problems with this statement?

11. There are two general classifications of import duties: tariff and nontariff barriers.

   a. Describe the various types of tariff barriers.

   b. What are some of the nontariff barriers?

 globalEDGE.msu.edu

Research Task

Use the globalEDGE site (http://globalEDGE.msu.edu/) to complete the following exercises:

1. Your company is considering opening a new factory in Latin America. As such, the strategic management division is in the process of evaluating the specific locations for such an operation. The pool of candidate countries has been narrowed to Colombia, Panama, and Paraguay. By using Country Insights, a resource provided by globalEDGE, prepare a short report comparing the risks of conducting business in these countries. Based on this information, in which country would you open the new factory?

2. You work for a national chain of clothing stores that is considering importing textiles from India into the United States. You want to determine whether the goods are subject to import quotas. Using information provided by the *U.S. Customs and Border Protection*, prepare a report highlighting the elements that determine whether a shipment is subject to this type of trade restriction.

Minicase: Is Your Chocolate the Result of Unfair Exploitation of Child Labor?

When you last savored a bar of rich chocolate, a cup of hot cocoa, or a piece of chocolate cake or scoop of chocolate ice cream, did you know that you may have unwittingly been consuming a product made with child slaves?

Chocolate is one of the most-traded agricultural products in the world. The top 10 chocolate-consuming nations are all developed countries in Europe or the United States, yet about 70 percent of the world's cocoa is produced in West Africa. In practice, beans from different nations are usually mixed together during their exportation and transport to processing plants in the importing nations. So Hershey bars, Snickers, M&Ms, KitKats, Nestlé chocolates, fudge, hot chocolate—essentially all of these delicacies that are regularly enjoyed by hundreds of millions of consumers—will include cocoa from West Africa, especially the Côte d'Ivoire (Ivory Coast). With about 46 percent of the world's total cocoa production, Côte d'Ivoire produces nearly twice the level of the second-largest cocoa producer, Ghana.

Results of a survey on child labor in West Africa, released in 2002, found that 284,000 children were working in hazardous conditions on West African cocoa farms, with the majority (200,000) working in Côte d'Ivoire. Nearly two-thirds of the child laborers were under the age of 14. Working conditions were described as slave-like, with 29 percent of the surveyed child workers in the Côte d'Ivoire indicating that "they were not free to leave their place of employment should they so wish." Many of these children had been brought into the cocoa-growing areas from distant regions of the Côte d'Ivoire or from poverty-stricken countries such as Burkina Faso, Mali, and Togo, often after being kidnapped. Some of the child laborers had been sold by their parents in the expectation that the child's earnings would be sent home. Although paid less than 60 percent of the rate of adult workers, children frequently worked for more than 12 hours per day, 6 days a week, and were regularly beaten. More than half of the children applied pesticides without protective gear. Only 34 percent of the children working on cocoa farms went to school, which was about half the level for children who were not working on cocoa farms. The rate of school enrollment was even lower for girls.

These child laborers seemed to be trapped in a vicious cycle: they were forced into work due to kidnapping or economic circumstances faced by themselves and/or their families; they earned subsistence wages; and because most had not been to school and had minimal skills, their prospects for seeking other employment options were limited.

Efforts to raise awareness of the exploitation of child labor in the cocoa industry faced great challenges, and even today, a majority of consumers seem unaware of the circumstances behind the production of their favorite chocolate treats. Yet the atrocious nature of the child labor situation in the cocoa industry compelled the media, public interest groups, and others to continue their efforts. Hard-hitting news stories began to appear on television and radio and in magazines and newspapers across North America and Europe.

Fearing the implications of boycotts, trade sanctions, or certification and labeling requirements in key markets such as the United States and Europe, representatives from the chocolate industry attempted to develop a strategy for dealing with the problem. The Chocolate Manufacturers Association hired former senators George Mitchell and Bob Dole to lobby against legislation establishing certification and labeling requirements. Once that defeat was secured, the industry agreed to self-regulate and attempted to change the child labor practices. A protocol for the industry was developed that established a timetable for eliminating child labor and forced labor in the production of cocoa. A self-imposed deadline was set for establishing a viable monitoring and certification system: July 1, 2005.

Some important cocoa-producing nations have worked with the International Labor Organization and the International Programme on the Elimination of Child Labour (IPEC) to establish national programs to eliminate child labor in their countries. However, as of 2010, there was evidence suggesting that child labor continued to be a widespread problem in Côte d'Ivoire and Ghana. Industry representatives have complained that progress toward eliminating child labor in cocoa production has been hindered by traditional culture in the agriculturally based producing nations, compounded by civil war and other complications.

In the absence of prompt and effective action by the chocolate and cocoa industry, a number of companies have begun producing fair-trade-certified chocolate. Through observing a strict set of guidelines associated with fair-trade certification, these companies guarantee that a consumer of one of their chocolate products is "not an unwitting participant in this very inhumane situation." Fairtrade Labeling Organizations International, a consortium of fair-trade organizations from Canada, the United States, Japan, Australia, New Zealand, and 15 European nations, establishes certification standards.

Fair-trade practices essentially involve international subsidies to farmers in developing countries, ensuring that farmers who are certified as engaging in fair-trade practices will receive a price for their produce that will at least cover their costs of production. By providing a price floor, fair-trade practices protect Third World farmers from the ruinous fluctuations in commodity prices that result from free trade practices. At the same time, fair-trade certification requires that farmers engage in appropriate social, labor, and environmental practices, such as paying livable wages and not using child or slave labor. In addition to the cocoa program, fair-trade certification programs have been implemented for a range of other products, such as coffee, bananas, nuts, spices, tea, and crafts.

Although still a nascent movement, sales of fair-trade certified products are growing and are projected to reach $9 billion in 2012. Will there be a similar result for chocolate? Already, more than 50 companies make fair-trade chocolate products in the United States, including ClifBar, Cloud Nine, Newman's Own Organics, Scharffen Berger, and Sweet Earth Chocolates.

Questions

1. Should labor practices in another country be a relevant consideration in international trade? Why or why not?

2. With regard to trade in products such as cocoa, what options are available to governments, businesses, and consumers for dealing with practices such as child labor or slave labor in other countries? What are the implications associated with each of these options?

3. How would international trade theorists view the fair-trade movement?

Source: "Cocoa Production in Cote d'Ivoire," http://en.wikipedia.org/wiki/Cocoa_production_in_C%C3%B4te_d%27Ivoire (June 23, 2011); Jose D. Perezgonzalez, "Child Labor in Cocoa Production—2010," Journal of Knowledge Advancement and Integration, 2011, pp. 1–4, www.lulu.com/product/ebook/child-labour-in-cacao-production/15575910 (accessed June 23, 2011); "Fairtrade Certification," http://en.wikipedia.org/wiki/Fairtrade_certification (June 23, 2011); "Slave-Free Chocolate," http://vision.ucsd.edu/~kbranson/stopchocolateslavery/main.html (June 23, 2011); and "Fair-Trade Q&A," www.globalexchange.org/campaigns/fairtrade/fairtradeqa.html (accessed June 23, 2011).

Intellectual Property and Other Legal Forces

The role which the Court [International Court of Justice] plays, through the power of justice and international law . . . is widely recognized and evidenced by the number of cases on the Court's docket. . . . It is not uncommon that these cases deal with issues concerning international peace and security. In performing its dispute resolution function, the Court, which embodies the principle of equality of all before the law, acts as a guardian of international law, and assures the maintenance of a coherent international legal order.

—*Judge Shi Jiuyong, former president of the International Court of Justice, to the General Assembly of the United Nations*

Counterfeit Pharmaceuticals: A Health and Intellectual Property Challenge Worldwide

You are feeling under the weather while traveling abroad, so you visit a doctor, fill your prescription at a local pharmacy, and swallow a pill with your bottled water. Soon you will be feeling better. Or will you? Are the pharmaceuticals you just ingested genuine or fake?

A special kind of challenge confronting both developed and developing nations is the counterfeiting of pharmaceuticals. Counterfeiting is the use of a well-known manufacturer's brand name on illicit copies of the firm's merchandise. Besides the production of exact copies of branded pharmaceuticals, other kinds of pharmaceutical counterfeiting include: (1) making products that contain the correct active ingredients but in the wrong proportions, (2) making products that do not contain any active ingredients, and (3) making products that contain toxic ingredients or other impurities.

With an estimated $75 billion of worldwide sales in 2010, 90 percent higher than 2005 and increasing at nearly double the rate of legitimate pharmaceutical sales, counterfeit drugs represent an industry that is growing rapidly in size–and in its risk to public health–worldwide.[a] The globalization of manufacturing supply chains has meant more steps, and more geographic spread, between the production and consumption of drugs. About half of all drugs sold through "questionable" Internet pharmacies are estimated to be counterfeit, according to the World Health Organization (WHO). The proportion of counterfeit drugs ranges from under 1 percent in some developed countries to 10 to 50 percent in developing nations.[b] "Counterfeiters can make more money than hard-drug traffickers, and they have less of a chance to go to prison," according to Interpol policewoman Aline Plançon.[c] The profit margin from selling counterfeit Viagra, for example, is roughly 10 times that from selling heroin, and the legal consequences are lower. While traffickers of hard drugs may face prison or death, those trafficking in counterfeit pharmaceuticals usually face charges under trademark, fraud, or similar laws.

Counterfeit Products Can Be Dangerous

Besides causing legitimate manufacturers to lose sales, fake drugs sometimes bring tragedy to users when, as is common, they fail to perform as well as the original.

1. In Mexico, officials confiscated 15,000 counterfeit burn remedies because many contained sawdust or dirt and caused raging infections, while hundreds of infants and others

learning objectives

After reading this chapter, you should be able to:

LO7-1   **Discuss** the complexity of the legal forces that confront international business.

LO7-2   **Explain** the possibilities for international dispute settlement.

LO7-3   **Recognize** the need and methods to protect intellectual property.

LO7-4   **Explain** the risk of product liability legal actions.

LO7-5   **Discuss** some of the U.S. laws that affect international business operations.

were killed in recent years in Bangladesh, Panama, Nigeria, Haiti, and India after using cough syrup containing diethylene glycol, a toxic chemical used for making antifreeze.

2. The World Health Organization estimates that 25 percent of antimalarial medicines used in developing nations are counterfeit or substandard—more than 50 percent in parts of Africa and Asia—which contributes to malarial outbreaks and associated illness and death. Among the chemicals discovered in malaria pills are the antibiotic erythromycin, an ingredient for the street drug ecstasy, and an active incredient from the erectile dysfunction drug, Viagra.

3. In 2008, the European Union tracked and seized more than 34 million illegal pills during a two-month investigation, and the U.S. Food and Drug Administration has repeatedly warned consumers about "potentially significant risks" associated with counterfeit Lipitor, Viagra, and other popular prescription drugs that are sold by pharmacies in Mexican border towns or through online sources to U.S. consumers.[d]

The problem of counterfeiting is not limited to the pharmaceutical industry, of course. Troubling levels of counterfeit goods have been reported across a broad array of products, ranging from music, books, and clothing to aircraft parts, semiconductors, computer software, agricultural pesticides and fertilizers, and pet food. Indeed, the Federal Bureau of Investigation considers counterfeiting and other forms of theft of intellectual property to be "the crime of the 21st Century."[e]

Combating Imitations

A range of public and private sector organizations have organized efforts to fight the rapidly spreading global outbreak of counterfeit drugs.

This includes the Pharmaceutical Security Institute (which tracks pharmaceutical counterfeiting), the European Alliance for Access to Safe Medicines (which is working to exclude counterfeit and substandard medicines from supply chains), and the WHO-sponsored International Medical Products Anti-Counterfeiting Taskforce (IMPACT). Progress is being made in raising awareness of the nature and extent of the problem, developing appropriate legislation and enforcement efforts to locate and punish offenders, and identifying innovative ways of ensuring the safety of pharmaceutical supply chains from raw material to consumer. Despite these efforts, protecting the health of consumers and the intellectual property rights of pharmaceutical makers and other companies remains an ongoing challenge worldwide.

[a]Estimate by the U.S.-based Center for Medicines in the Public Interest, NanoGuardian, "NanoGuardian Extends NanoEncryption Technology to Pre-Filled Syringes and Vial Caps," www.nanoguardian.net/pressDisplay.php?pressNum=35 (accessed June 25, 2011).

[b]U.S. Food and Drug Administration, "Counterfeit Drugs Questions and Answers," December 2, 2010, www.fda.gov/Drugs/DrugSafety/ucm169898.htm (accessed June 25, 2011); and Sarah Everts, "Fake Pharmaceuticals," *Chemical & Engineering News* 88, no. 1 (January 4, 2010), pp. 27–29, http://pubs.acs.org/cen/science/88/8801sci1.html (accessed June 25, 2011).

[c]Ibid.

[d]World Health Organization, "WHO Calls for an Immediate Halt to Provision of Single-Drug Artemisinin Malaria Pills," www.who.int/mediacentre/news/releases/2006/pr02/en/ (accessed June 25, 2011); World Health Organization, "Counterfeit Medicines," www.who.int/medicines/services/counterfeit/impact/ImpactF_S/en/ (accessed June 25, 2011); and "Counterfeit Lipitor, Viagra, and Evista Sold in Mexican Border Towns," www.medicinenet.com/script/main/art.asp?articlekey=47114 (accessed June 25, 2011).

[e]Jon W. Dudas, "Statement of Jon W. Dudas, Acting Undersecretary of Commerce for Intellectual Property and Acting Director of the United States Patent and Trademark Office Before the Committee on Judiciary, United States Senate, March 23, 2004," www.ogc.doc.gov/ogc/legreg/testimon/108s/dudas0323.htm (accessed June 25, 2011).

Although seldom as severe as those associated with deadly counterfeit pharmaceuticals, myriad issues related to intellectual property and other legal forces confront international companies wherever they operate. Participants in international business should understand the enormous breadth and depth of laws and legal issues in various jurisdictions worldwide. Anyone studying legal forces affecting international business soon realizes that the variety of these forces complicates the task of understanding the laws.

While on the one hand, businesses must be aware of laws in order to comply, on the other hand, businesses also expect that laws will assist them when necessary. An issue of great concern to businesses that operate internationally is the stability of a host government and its legal system. When a business enters a country, the firm needs to know whether the country's host government will be able to protect the foreign business with an adequate legal system. The legal system must be able to enforce contracts and protect the basic rights of employees. In examining international legal forces, one must keep in mind that a stable government and an adequate court system are necessary to ensure a welcome environment for foreign businesses.

This chapter examines international law and international dispute settlement, including those dealing with intellectual property and other key company assets. It also looks at specific national laws that influence international business.

International Legal Forces

RULE OF LAW

International businesspeople need to determine whether a country is governed by the rule of law, instead of rule by a political dictatorship or rule by a powerful elite. If a country's legal system is based on the rule of law, this encourages foreign investment because foreign businesses know that their interests will be protected. Following the rule of law also makes ensuring protection of human rights of local people easier.

For example, Hong Kong has an advantage over Shanghai in attracting foreign investors because Hong Kong has a tradition of law adopted from British colonial days, while Shanghai courts tend to favor Chinese litigants. This disparity in legal systems between the two cities is seen to give Hong Kong an advantage as a location for foreign firms.[1]

WHAT IS INTERNATIONAL LAW?

Each sovereign nation is responsible for creating and enforcing laws within its jurisdiction. Once laws cross international borders, the matter of enforcement is complicated by the necessity of agreement between nations. The same concepts that apply to domestic laws do not always apply to international law.

What is called *international law* can be divided into public international law and private international law. **Public international law** includes legal relations between governments, including laws concerning diplomatic relations between nations and all matters involving the rights and obligations of sovereign nations. In contrast, **private international law** includes laws governing the transactions of individuals and companies crossing international borders. For example, private international law would cover matters involved in a contract between businesses in two different countries.

SOURCES OF INTERNATIONAL LAW

International law comes from several sources, the most important of which are bilateral and multilateral **treaties** between nations. Treaties are agreements between countries and may also be called *conventions, covenants, compacts, or protocols*. International organizations such as the United Nations have provided a forum for creation of many treaties. The UN has sponsored many conferences that have led to multinational agreements on a range of matters, including postal delivery and use of driver's licenses in other countries. Also, the International Court of Justice, an organ of the UN, creates international law when it decides disputes brought before it by member-nations.

Another source of international law is customary international law, which consists of international rules derived from customs and usage over centuries. An example of customary international law is the prohibition against genocide (there is also a specific international statute against genocide), or the immunity from prosecution of visiting foreign heads of state.

EXTRATERRITORIALITY

Many countries, including the United States and members of the European Union, often attempt to enforce their laws outside their borders. This is referred to as **extraterritorial application of laws.** This attempt to enforce laws abroad is done not by force but through traditional legal means. For example, the U.S. government imposes taxes on U.S. citizens and U.S. permanent residents regardless of either the source of income or the residence of the taxpayer. If a U.S.

LO7-1 Discuss the complexity of the legal forces that confront international business.

public international law
Legal relations between governments

private international law
Laws governing transactions of individuals and companies that cross international borders

treaties
Agreements between countries, which may be bilateral (between two countries) or multilateral (involving more than two countries); also called *conventions, covenants, compacts,* or *protocols*

extraterritorial application of laws
A country's attempt to apply its laws to foreigners or non-residents and to acts and activities that take place outside its borders

citizen is living in Madrid and receives all of her income from Spanish sources; the United States will still expect the taxpayer to comply with U.S. tax laws. Likewise, when U.S. companies operate in other countries with U.S.-based personnel, the U.S. companies must comply with U.S. laws, including employment laws. Of course, these companies must also comply with the laws of the host country. Extraterritorial application of laws has been extended in many other areas including antitrust, employment, and environmental laws. Also, the Alien Tort Statute allows non-U.S. nationals to file lawsuits in U.S. courts for alleged violations of international law. In 2010, Coca-Cola was sued (in New York) for alleged violence against workers in Guatemala.

International Dispute Settlement

LO7-2 Explain the possibilities for international dispute settlement.

litigation
A legal proceeding to determine and enforce a particular legal right.

LITIGATION

Litigation, which is a legal proceeding conducted in order to determine and enforce particular legal rights, can be extremely complicated and expensive. In addition to involving the trial itself, most lawsuits in the United States entail lengthy pretrial activities, including a process called *discovery*. Discovery is the means of finding facts relevant to the litigation that are known to the other side, including obtaining documents in the other side's possession. Some discovery methods can seem quite intrusive because courts grant parties great latitude in obtaining information in the possession of the opposing side. Discovery is one reason many people outside the United States dislike litigation in the United States.

Litigation involving disputes that cross international lines can arise in both state and federal courts. Special rules exist for obtaining discovery in other countries, and they vary from country to country. Some countries freely allow U.S. litigators to obtain discovery. Others have restrictions. For example, if discovery is to occur in Switzerland even in a case involving only U.S. parties, permission must be obtained from Swiss authorities. Failure to obtain permission may result in penalties, including possible criminal sanctions.

One of the major problems usually involved in cross-border litigation is the question of which jurisdiction's law should apply and where the litigation should occur. Each country (and each state in the United States) has elaborate laws for determining which law should apply and where litigation should occur. As with any other disputed matter, the final decision on these issues rests with the court. Occasionally, courts in two countries (or two states) will attempt to resolve the same dispute. Again, this is resolved by reference to the particular choice of law provisions and can be quite complicated. For this reason, it is prudent to include in contracts a choice-of-law clause and a choice-of-forum clause in the event of a dispute. A *choice-of-law clause* in a contract specifies which law will govern in the event of a dispute. For example, if there is a U.S. seller and an Australian buyer, the parties may agree that Australian law would govern any dispute. A *choice-of-forum clause* in a contract specifies where the dispute will be settled. For example, the parties in the preceding example may agree to have the dispute decided in California state courts in Los Angeles County, California.

PERFORMANCE OF CONTRACTS

Whenever businesses enter into agreements with other businesses, the possibility exists that there may be problems getting the other side to perform its obligations. No worldwide court has the power to enforce its decrees. The worldwide courts that do exist, such as the UN's International Court of Justice, rely on the voluntary compliance of the parties before it. Each nation in the world is a sovereign nation and has its own rules for recognizing decrees and judgments from other nations.

When contracting parties are residents of a single country, the laws of that country govern contract performance and any disputes that arise between the parties. That country's courts have jurisdiction over the parties, and the courts' judgments are enforced in accordance with the country's procedures. When residents of two or more countries contract, those relatively easy solutions to dispute resolution are not available. Enforcing contracts that cross international lines is often quite complicated.

United Nations Solutions   When contract disputes arise between parties from two or more countries, which country's law is applicable? Many countries, including the United States, have ratified the UN Convention on the International Sale of Goods (CISG) to solve such problems.

The CISG established uniform legal rules to govern the formation of international sales contracts and the rights and obligations of the buyer and seller. The CISG applies automatically to all contracts for the sale of goods between traders from different countries that have ratified the CISG. This automatic application will take place unless the parties to the contract expressly exclude—opt out of—the CISG.

Private Solutions—Arbitration   As mentioned before, many people outside the United States dislike the U.S. court system. Likewise, many U.S. businesspeople dislike or at least fear litigation in other countries. For these reasons, international businesspeople often agree that any disputes will be resolved by arbitration, rather than by going to court in any country. **Arbitration** is a dispute resolution mechanism that is an alternative to litigation. Arbitration is usually quicker, less expensive, and more private than litigation, and it is usually binding on all parties. At least 30 organizations now administer international arbitrations, the best known of which may be the International Court of Arbitration of the International Chamber of Commerce in Paris. In addition, London and New York are centers of arbitration. Some organizations specialize in the type of arbitration cases they will consider. For example, the World Intellectual Property Organization (WIPO) Arbitration and Mediation Center handles technological, entertainment, and intellectual property disputes. In 2009 the Center settled a dispute between Research in Motion Ltd. and a private party over domain names using variations of the word BLACKBERRY.[2] The International Centre for the Settlement of Investment Disputes specializes, logically, in investment disputes.

In summary, people and businesses may prefer arbitration for several reasons. They may be suspicious of foreign courts. Arbitration is generally faster than law courts, where cases are usually backlogged. Arbitration procedures are usually more informal than court procedures. Arbitration may be confidential, avoiding the perhaps unwelcome publicity accompanying an open court case. And generally it may be less expensive.

Other organizations are working toward a worldwide business law. For example, the 11 **Incoterms** of the International Chamber of Commerce and its Uniform Rules and Practice on Documentary Credits receive almost universal acceptance, and new definitions of some Incoterms went into effect in 2011. These terms are explained in Chapter 14. (See Table 7.1 for examples of commonly used Incoterms for water transport.) The UN Commission on International Trade Law and the International Institute for the Unification of Private Law are doing much useful work. The Hague-Vishy Rules on Bills of Lading sponsored by the International Law Association have been adopted by a number of countries.[3]

arbitration
A process, agreed to by parties to a dispute in lieu of going to court, by which a neutral person or body makes a binding decision

Incoterms
Universal trade terminology developed by the International Chamber of Commerce

DESPITE LEGAL UNCERTAINTIES, INTERNATIONAL BUSINESS GROWS

Despite legal uncertainties of doing business in other countries, international business activities will increase in the future. For this reason, international businesspeople must be aware of the legal environment in which they find themselves. Legal systems vary significantly from country to country, and it is important to understand the differences. The assumptions one makes on the basis of the U.S. legal system may not apply in other countries.

TABLE 7.1	Examples of Incoterms

1. *FAS (free alongside ship—port of call).* The seller pays all the transportation and delivery expense up to the ship's side and clears the goods for export.
2. *CIF (cost, insurance, freight—foreign port).* The price includes the cost of the goods, insurance, and all transportation and miscellaneous charges to the named port of final destination.
3. *CFR (cost and freight—foreign port).* CFR is similar to CIF except that the buyer purchases the insurance, either because it can be obtained at a lower cost or because the buyer's government, to save foreign exchange, insists on use of a local insurance company.

Intellectual Property

intellectual property
Patents, trademarks, trade names, copyrights, and trade secrets, all of which result from the exercise of someone's intellect

patent
A government grant giving the inventor of a product or process the exclusive right to manufacture, exploit, use, and sell that invention or process

A *patent* is a government grant giving the inventor of a product or process the exclusive right to manufacture, exploit, use, and sell that invention or process. *Trademarks* and *trade names* are designs and names, often officially registered, by which merchants or manufacturers designate and differentiate their products. *Copyrights* are exclusive legal rights of authors, composers, creators of software, playwrights, artists, and publishers to publish and dispose of their works. *Trade secrets* are any information that a business wishes to hold confidential. All are referred to as **intellectual property.**

Trade secrets can be of great value, but each country deals with and protects them in its own fashion. The duration of protection differs, as do the products that may or may not be protected. Some countries permit the production process to be protected but not the product. International companies must study and comply with the laws of each country where they may want to manufacture, create, or sell products.

PATENTS

In the field of **patents,** the International Convention for the Protection of Industrial Property, sometimes referred to as the Paris Union, provides some degree of standardization. This convention is adhered to by 173 countries.

A major step toward the harmonization of patent treatment is the European Patent Organization (EPO). Through EPO, an applicant for a patent need file only one application in English, French, or German to be granted patent protection in all 27 EU member-states. Before the EPO, an applicant had to file in each country in the language of that country. Often multiple companies are involved. For example, the U.S. Supreme Court ruled in 2008 on a U.S. patent for computer chipsets, which South Korea's LG Electronics Inc. licensed to Intel Corp. When a Taiwan manufacturer used the chips, LG sued.

As indicated in the introductory vignette for this chapter, the prescription drug industry relies heavily on patents and other intellectual property. Multinational pharmaceutical companies say they need years of patent protection to recoup expensive investments in research and development of new drug treatments. Pfizer Inc. has a blockbuster drug in Lipitor, an anti-cholesterol drug: Pfizer's revenue from Lipitor is about $13 billion per year. Pfizer's patent ran out in June 2011—so Pfizer negotiated an agreement with Indian generic-drug maker Ranbaxy Laboratories Ltd. to keep Ranbaxy's generic version off the U.S. market until November 2011. This extension for Pfizer is important, given that revenues average more than $1 billion per month.[4]

The World Intellectual Property Organization (WIPO) is a UN agency that administers 24 international intellectual property treaties. WIPO advises developing countries on such matters as running patent offices and drafting intellectual property legislation. Interest in intellectual property matters has been growing in developing countries. There is also another agreement called TRIPS (trade-related aspects of intellectual property) that operates under the aegis of the World Trade Organization, as mentioned in Chapter 3. In addition, in late 2010 the United States, European Union, Mexico, Japan, Morocco, New Zealand, Singapore, Switzerland, Australia, South Korea, and Canada reached an "agreement in principle" for ACTA, the Anti-Counterfeiting Trade Agreement.[5] Passage of the agreement may make it easier for border inspectors to search laptops for pirated contents, for example. Opponents allege that the ACTA would negatively affect the flow of information on the Internet.

At the UN, smaller nations have been mounting attacks on the exclusivity and length of patent protection. They want to shorten the protection periods from the current 15 to 20 years down to 5 years or even 30 months. But multinational companies are resisting the changes. They point out that the only

Many companies such as Coca-Cola market their products throughout the world and understand the importance of protecting trademarks worldwide

TABLE 7.2	The International Framework for IP Protection

Organization	Parent
World Intellectual Property Organization (WIPO)	UN
Trade Related Aspects of Intellectual Property (TRIPS)	WTO
Anti-Counterfeiting Trade Agreement (ACTA) (Proposed)	Free-standing

incentives they have to spend the huge amounts required to develop new technology are periods of patent protection long enough to recoup their costs and make profits.

An added dimension is the growth of so-called patent trolls, who can be likened to modern-day highway robbers cashing in on loopholes in IP protection. These are lawyers and investors who buy patents that were mistakenly granted, mostly to failed companies. In one case, a patent troll claimed that a patent bought for about $50,000 was infringed by Intel's microprocessors and threatened to sue Intel for $7 billion in damages. This is a fascinating subworld populated not just by trolls but also patent pirates, patent thickets, and the like.

TRADEMARKS

Trademarks can be a shape, a color or design (such as the Levi's small red tag on the left side of the rear pockets of its jeans), a catchy phrase, an abbreviation, or even a sound. Although blacksmiths who made swords in the Roman Empire may have been the first to use trademarks, Löwenbräu and Stella Artois claim use since the 14th century. Trademark protection varies from country to country, as does its duration, which may be from 10 to 20 years (with possible renewals). Such protection is covered by the Madrid Agreement of 1891 for most of the world, although there is also the General American Convention for Trademark and Commercial Protection for the Western Hemisphere. In addition, protection may be provided on a bilateral basis in friendship, commerce, and navigation treaties.

An important step in harmonizing the rules on trademarks was taken in 1988 when regulations for a European Union trademark law were drafted. A single European Trademark Office known as the Office of Harmonization in the Internal Market (OHIM) is responsible for the recognition and protection of proprietary marks in all EU countries, including trademarks belonging to companies based in non-EU member-countries.

TRADE NAMES

Trade names (name of a business) are protected in all countries that adhere to the International Convention for the Protection of Industrial Property, which was mentioned earlier in connection with patents. Goods bearing illegal trademarks or trade names or false statements about their origin are subject to seizure upon importation into these countries.

COPYRIGHTS

Copyrights are protected under the Berne Convention of 1886, which is adhered to by 164 countries, the WIPO Copyright Treaty, and the TRIPS Agreement, to which all WTO members agree to abide.

TRADE SECRETS

Trade secrets are any information that is not generally known to the public and that a business wishes to hold confidential. Trade secrets may include formulas, processes, patterns, designs, or other information or sets of information that could give a company an economic advantage over its competitors. The value of a trade secret is maintained by not allowing it to be publicly known, and companies must exercise reasonable efforts to ensure that trade secrets are not disclosed. While protection of trade secrets is not subject to expiration after a set period of time, as with patents, there is no guarantee of the protection of trade secrets if another party independently discovers the information.

trademark
A shape, a color, design, catchy phrase, abbreviation, or sound used by merchants or manufacturers to designate and differentiate their products

trade name
A name used by merchants or manufacturers to designate and differentiate their products

copyright
Exclusive legal rights of authors, composers, creators of software, playwrights, artists, and publishers to publish and dispose of their works

trade secret
Any information that a business wishes to hold confidential

Virtually Ripped Off? Intellectual Property Issues in Second Life's Virtual World

Second Life virtual world.

The Second Life virtual world, once considered a haven for geeks, has reached mainsteam success with more than 20 million users worldwide. It is a self-sufficient universe with everything the real (read "first") world has, including intellectual property rights. Introduced in the previous chapter as a potential new staging area for terror, here we consider it as a potential rat's nest for IP issues.

As the virtual world becomes more and more like the real world, the need for realism increases. Brand owners are finding that their trademarked products appear online without their authorization. Virtual lawyer, Benjamin Duranske, found 15 shops advertising Ferrari cars; 40 stores selling virtual Rolex and Chanel watches; and another 50 that carried sunglasses branded as Gucci, Prada, Rayban, and Oakley.

Creaters of virtual goods for sale in virtual worlds are also expressing concern with violation of their intellectual property rights. Linden Lab, which owns Second Life, was sued by an entrepreneur who created virtual erotic "SexGen" beds and other goods that he sold to residents in Second Life. The entrepreneur sued, claiming that Linden Lab permitted Second Life residents to counterfeit his creations and sell them for Linden dollars (known as L$). His lawsuit claimed, "The manner in which this has occurred is akin to the knockoff handbags and purses sold near Canal Street in New York City." Another entrepreneur, who sells virtual clothing in Second Life, joined the lawsuit, alleging that by allowing other marketers to copy and sell fake versions of her designs, Linden Labs was infringing on her copyright. These two litigants are seeking class-action status

Standardizing Laws around the World

Many attempts have been made to standardize laws among various countries. To international business, the advantage of standardization is that business flows much better when there is a uniform set of rules. Worldwide harmonization is progressing slowly, though, in most areas. For now, businesspeople must confront the reality of differing standards.

In the tax area, there are tax conventions, or treaties, among nations. Each country tries to make each such treaty as similar as possible to the others, and so patterns and common provisions may be found among them.

In antitrust, the EU member-nations operate under Articles 81 and 82 of the Treaty of Rome, which are similar to the antitrust laws in the United States. In an unusual bilateral move, Germany and the United States signed an executive agreement on antitrust cooperation. This was the first attempt by national governments to cooperate on antitrust matters concerning firms operating in both countries. There have been proposals to create worldwide agreements on antitrust.

Some agreement exists in the field of international commercial arbitration, including enforcement of arbitration awards. If the disputed contract involves investment from one country into another, it can be submitted for arbitration by the International Center for Settlement of Investment Disputes at the World Bank. Chapter 3 covered a number of other UN-related organizations and other worldwide associations. Each of them has some harmonizing or standardizing effect on laws in the member-countries.

The UN Convention on the International Sale of Goods (CISG) provides some uniformity in international sales agreements for those parties who elect to use it. It has been signed by 74 states. There have been attempts to make accounting and bankruptcy standards

in U.S. District Court in California. They claim, "Linden Lab has created in Second Life a system in which it directly engages in piracy, actively allows its users to engage in piracy by providing the tools for it, and by which it profits from its own piracy and the piracy of its users."

So, who cares? First, these virtual knockoffs are bought and sold, in Second Life, and although L$ are used, L$ can be exchanged for real currency. Admittedly the sums are still small, with the equivalent of only about $29 million in L$ in circulation during the first quarter of 2011.[a] Courts are still trying to determine how to handle the issues raised by lawsuits involving virtual worlds like Second Life. Regarding the lawsuit mentioned above, Eric Goldman of Santa Clara University's High Tech Law Institute said, "It's not an easy case. This particular area of law is unsettled."

A greater risk is that companies producing trademarked goods and services in the real world may lose their ability to exploit the virtual site for their own marketing purposes in the future. Further, they may meet with opposition when they try to renew their trademarks from rivals who say they have abandoned their rights by failing to police third-party use. Finally, there is simply the issue of loss of control. In a similar situation, the British telecom company BT was unhappy to find that the central character in a PlayStation 2 game, "The Getaway," pretends to be a BT engineer before carrying out a killing spree.

It's worth noting that Second Life is just the tip of the virtual world iceberg: there are many other virtual worlds such as China-based HiPiHi, Germany-based Twinity and Smeet, New Zealand–based SmallWorlds, U.S.-based IMVU and Kaneva, and Canada-based Utherverse. Reflecting this concern, there is a Second Life Patent and Trademark Office (SLPTO) runs by SL inhabitants. Linden Labs, creator of Second Life, has started a "Brand Center" office to protect its own "Second Life" name and logo.

Questions:

1. What should be the relationship beween rights—and their enforcement—associated with intellectual property in a virtual world game context and those in a "real"world?

2. With the proliferation of virtual worlds in cyberspace, how can a company effectively monitor the variety of different sites in order to effectively protect its intellectual property rights?

[a]George Trefgarne, "Brussels Clears Way for $220bn Merger," *The Telegraph*, www.telegraph.co.uk/finance/4468341/Brussels-clears-way-for-220bn-merger.html (June 25, 2011); and Stephen Castle, "EU Fine Sends Message to Microsoft and Others," www.nytimes.com/2008/02/27/technology/27iht-msft.4.10498942.html (accessed June 25, 2011).

Source: "The Brand Reality of the Virtual World," *Managing Intellectual Property*, December 1, 2007, www.managingip.com/Article/1788109/The-brand-reality-of-the-virtual-world.html (accessed June 25, 2011); "Second Life," http://en.wikipedia.org/wiki/Second_Life (accessed June 25, 2011); Wendy David, "Second Life Sued for Allowing Sale of Imposter Virtual Goods," www.mediapost.com/publications/?fa=Articles.showArticle&art_aid=113576 (accessed June 25, 2011); and http://virtuallyblind.com/2008/03/26/sl-brand-center/ (accessed June 25, 2011).

---

uniform worldwide. A Model Law on Cross-Border Insolvencies from UNCITRAL (UN Commission on International Trade Law) served as the basis for Chapter 15 of the U.S. Bankruptcy Code, for example.

Two standardizing organizations are the International Organization for Standardization (ISO) and the International Electrotechnical Commission (IEC). The IEC promotes standardization of measurement, materials, and equipment in almost every sphere of electrotechnology. The ISO recommends standards in other fields of technology. Most government and private purchasing around the world demands products that meet IEC or ISO specifications.

Some Specific National Legal Forces

COMPETITION LAWS

Competition laws (known in the United States as **antitrust laws**) are intended to prevent inappropriately large concentrations of economic power, such as monopolies. Actions brought to enforce competition laws or antitrust laws usually involve government actions brought against business, but also may involve business actions against other businesses.

U.S. Laws and Attitudes Are Different—But the Differences Are Narrowing
U.S. antitrust laws are strict, and they are vigorously enforced. They are laws to prevent price fixing, market sharing, and business monopolies. The U.S. Department of Justice is charged with enforcing U.S. antitrust laws. Other countries and the European Union are becoming more active in the antitrust field, and more than 80 countries

competition laws
The EU equivalent of antitrust laws

antitrust laws
Laws to prevent inappropriately large concentrations of power and the potential abuse of such power through price fixing, market sharing, and business monopolies

now have antitrust laws. The EU Commission is responsible for enforcing EU competition policy. In addition to enforcing competition policy against businesses, the EU Commission also has the power to force EU member-governments to dismantle state monopolies that block progress toward an open, communitywide market.[6]

A number of important differences in antitrust laws, regulations, and practices exist between the United States, other nations, and the EU. One difference is the *per se* concept of the U.S. law. Under the U.S. laws, certain activities, such as price fixing, are said to be illegal *"per se."* This means that they are illegal even though no injury or damage results from them. The EU Treaty of Rome articles dealing with restrictive trade practices do not contain the per se illegality concept of U.S. antitrust law. For example, a cartel that allows consumers a fair share of the benefits is legally acceptable in the EU. Also, the treaty is not violated by market dominance—only by misuse of that dominance to damage competitors or consumers.

The U.S. focus on antitrust legislation is concerned with the impact of the business deal on the consumer, while the EU is more concerned about the industry's competitive structure and thus pays attention to rivals' objections. In Japan, antitrust legislation was introduced by the United States during its occupation of Japan after World War II. This legislation, the Japanese Anti-Monopoly Law, was modeled on U.S. antitrust law and did not harmonize well with the existing cooperative *zaibatsu* (conglomerates) the Japanese government had established. In fact, the Japanese approach to a rational development of the economy regarded antitrust measures as an impediment. However, with increasing foreign presence, Japanese companies have incorporated antitrust thinking into their strategies. Because the Japanese culture so values cooperation, this is a challenge, especially when it comes to cartels.[7]

Japan's "Toothless Tiger"
Japan's Fair Trade Commission (FTC), whose responsibility is to enforce antitrust laws, has been nicknamed the "toothless tiger." It is viewed as one of the weakest bodies in Japanese government, easily bullied by other powerful ministries, such as finance and international trade and industry (MITI), which have vested interests in ensuring that Japan's traditional, collaborative ways of doing business prevail. Most of the FTC's targets are small, foreign, or weak; when it has investigated powerful industries such as domestic cars, car parts, and construction, it has punished them at worst with "recommendations." The recommendations are usually accepted by the targeted company. If not, hearings follow, and then directives. However, Japanese courts lack power to hold defendents in contempt for failure to comply with the FTC's cease and desist orders.

A major difference between American and Japanese trust busting is that around 90 percent of U.S. complaints are initiated by private parties, while in Japan a private antitrust action can be brought only if the FTC has investigated the case first. Because of Japan's limited discovery laws, the only way the FTC can obtain information on a firm is to raid it. As a result, the FTC won't make a move unless it is sure the laws are being broken. It is almost impossible to be sure of that without information. Given all this, it is easy to understand why the FTC is considered to be a toothless tiger, limited "to merely gumming violators hard."[8]

Worldwide Application of U.S. Antitrust Laws
The U.S. government often attempts to enforce its antitrust laws extraterritorially. For example, a grand jury in Washington, D.C., indicted three foreign-owned ocean shipping groups on charges of fixing prices without getting approval from the U.S. Federal Maritime Commission. The other governments, European and Japanese, protested bitterly, arguing (1) that shipping is international by definition, so the United States has no right to act unilaterally, and (2) that the alleged offenses were both legal and ethical practices outside the United States. The U.S. Supreme Court has repeatedly permitted overseas application of U.S. antitrust laws, although recent court decisions appear to have curtailed the potential of foreign plaintiffs to use U.S. courts in order to seek relief.[9]

EU Extraterritorial Application of Its Competition Policy
Like the U.S. Department of Justice, the EU Commission has increasingly sought enforcement of its competition policy abroad when there is an effect on commerce within the EU. For example, the EU Commission had to give its approval before merger talks between America Online and Time Warner could proceed. Before its approval was given to the merger, AOL–Time Warner had to agree to sever all ties with the German media group Bertelsmann. The EU has also viewed Microsoft as anticompetitive and in 2008 fined the firm €899 million ($1.3 billion).[10]

Criminal Cases
U.S. antitrust laws contain both civil and criminal penalties.* A decision by the U.S. federal court of appeals held that criminal antitrust laws apply to foreign companies even if the conspiracy took place outside the United States. While earlier decisions had permitted U.S. antitrust laws to be used against foreign companies in civil cases, this decision, which was against Nippon Paper Industries, set the precedent that antitrust laws could be used also to get criminal convictions.

Proposal for Global Antitrust Approval
It is often difficult for international businesses to comply with the variety of antitrust laws worldwide. A good example is Microsoft. In the 1990s, the U.S. government and several U.S. states brought antitrust actions against Microsoft. The actions continued well into the early 21st century. The EU also brought several actions against Microsoft, one of which we mentioned earlier. In 2008, China began examining whether Microsoft has a monopoly position. The Microsoft case is a good example of how one company with international operations can get bogged down with antitrust laws in multiple jurisdictions. In light of the numerous countries that impose antitrust rules worldwide, many argue that greater worldwide cooperation in antitrust enforcement is needed. Some think that the WTO is the proper avenue for such worldwide cooperation. Others believe an international antitrust authority would be appropriate. Reaching such an agreement would be difficult because of the differing interests involved.[11] The U.S. government has proposed a world organization for the clearance of antitrust issues. If approved, the organization would probably take the form of a clearinghouse for merger filings. Calls for such an entity are increasing because of the multinational nature of most large mergers.

Tariffs, Quotas, and Other Trade Obstacles
Trade obstacles are legal forces as well as political and financial forces. For that reason, we mention them again here. Every country has laws on these subjects. The stated purpose of a tariff is to raise revenue for the government, but it may serve the additional objective of keeping certain goods out of a country. Quotas limit the amount or source of imports.

There are many other forms of protection or obstacles to trade in national laws. Some are health or packaging requirements. Others deal with language, such as the mandatory use of French on labels and in advertising, manuals, warranties, and so forth, for goods sold in France, including websites located on servers physically in France. When Vietnam catfish imports into the United States flooded the market, lawyers for the U.S. catfish industry successfully argued that the Vietnamese product was not catfish but a different family of fish. After this failed to stop the imports, they reversed themselves and alleged that these catfish were being "dumped" on the U.S. market.[12] Table 7.3 provides a sampling of trade barriers.

In many countries, U.S. and EU exports may encounter weak patent or trademark protection, high tariffs, quarantine periods, and a variety of other obstacles.

The United States has many options in dealing with trade obstacles abroad. It can impose retaliatory barriers on products from countries imposing barriers against U.S. goods. It sometimes uses tariffs and quotas. It also uses a form of quota called by some "voluntary"

---

*Civil liability calls for payment of money damages. Criminal liability may result in fines or imprisonment.

TABLE 7.3   Worldwide Examples of Tariffs and Other Trade Barriers

Product	Destination	Barrier
U.S. rice	Japan	Government managed rice imports allocate U.S. rice almost exclusively to nonconsumer use (e.g., industrial food processing or re-export as food aid) and without identifying source as U.S. rice
European wines and spirits	India	Federal and state additional duties of 150 percent or more
Diammonium phosphate fertilizer	China	Value-added tax exemption for all phosphate fertilizers except diammonium phosphate, giving benefit to domestic fertilzer producers
Internet gambling from EU providers	United States	Discriminatory legislation
Commercial aircraft	EU	EU government subsidies to Airbus, reducing its risks versus those faced by Boeing of the United States and other aircraft manufacturers
Motion pictures	Canada	Prohibition on non-Canadian films shown on Canadian Broadcasting Corporation networks between 7 p.m. and 11 p.m. unless released at least 2 years previously and not in the top 100 grossing films for at least 10 years
U.S. poultry and pork	Russia	Import restrictions (quotas)

Source: Office of U.S. Trade Representative, *2010 National Trade Estimate Report on Foreign Trade Barriers,* www.ustr.gov/about-us/press-office/reports-and-publications/2010 (accessed June 25, 2011); and European Commission, "Report to the Trade Barriers Regulation Committee," http://trade.ec.europa.eu/doclib/docs/2009/june/tradoc_143405 .pdf (accessed June 25, 2011).

 GLOBAL DEBATE

A Threat to National Sovereignty? America's Dolphin-Safe Tuna Labeling versus the WTO

In May 2011, a World Trade Organization panel ruled that long-standing American "Dolphin Safe" labeling requirements for tuna violated international trade rules. As the first case examining the compatibility of voluntary product labeling with the WTO agreement, results of this finding against the United States could establish an important precedent—for governments, public interest organizations, consumers, and other stakeholders—of other informational labeling efforts worldwide.

First a bit of background on the case. In 1959, fishermen in the Pacific Ocean region stretching from southern California to South America began using purse seine fishing methods to harvest tuna. *Purse seining* deploys a wall of netting a mile or more in length that encircles entire schools of fish, the bottom is pulled closed like a drawstring purse, and everything inside the net is pulled into a boat to be processed. Dolphins in this part of the Pacific tend to swim in schools above large schools of tuna, so fishing fleets seek out dolphins and encircle them with nets in order to capture the tuna that swim below. While successful in netting tuna, consequences for dolphins can be catastrophic. Millions of dolphins were trapped in nets and drowned between 1959 and 1972, and dolphin populations plummeted. Congress passed the Marine Mammal Protection Act (MMPA) in 1972, which prohibited the use by American tuna fisherman of fishing methods that would cause dolphin deaths. In 1988, the MMPA was amended to ban tuna imports from nations whose fishing fleets caught

(*continued*)

tuna using purse seine nets. In 1990, the Dolphin Protection Consumer Information Act (DPCIA) was passed by Congress, and the "dolphin safe" label was created. Tuna caught with purse seine nets were prohibited from using this label in the United States. These actions dramatically reduced dolphin deaths, from 500,000 per year in the 1960s to 15,550 in 1992 and further declines since then, reducing the threat to endangered dolphin populations. The cost of implementing dolphin-safe labeling legislation, conducting negotiations with foreign governments, and preventing the sale of tuna caught with dolphin-unsafe methods was estimated by the Congressional Budget Office at $6 million per year.

The WTO ruling represents a victory for Mexico's three largest tuna producers: Grupo Herdez, Grupo Maritimo Industrial, and Pescados Industrializados, which collaborated with the Mexican ministries of Agriculture and Economy in the long-running battle to sell tuna in the United States. Beginning in 1980 under the WTO predecessor, the General Agreement on Tariffs and Trade (GATT), Mexico has repeatedly challenged American "dolphin safe" standards in what was dubbed "GATT-zilla versus Flipper." The most recent case was filed by Mexico in 2008. Although 315,000 tons of tuna were imported into the United States in 2010, Mexico asserted that "dolphin safe" standards resulted in unreasonably greater challenges to sell their tuna in the United States and violated trade rules.

"Dolphin safe" labeling is a voluntary measure, and tuna harvested with "dolphin unsafe" methods can legally be sold in the United States (but not with the "dolphin safe" label), which appears to comply with WTO guidelines. However, the WTO ruled that "dolphin safe" was a technical regulation rather than a standard. The WTO asserted that anything impeding nonlabeled tuna's "marketing opportunities in the United States" represents a barrier to trade and that "dolphin safe" labeling violates Article 2.2 of the WTO agreement, which prohibits technical regulations that are "more trade-restrictive than necessary to fulfill a legitimate objective." Therefore, the United States must discontinue the "dolphin safe" labeling program or face WTO sanctions. There is limited opportunity for the United States to appeal the ruling, and because the United States agreed to the WTO treaty, Article VI of the U.S. Constitution holds that the WTO agreement "shall be the Supreme Law of the Land; and the Judges in every State shall be bound thereby."

This WTO ruling on "dolphin safe" labeling has been viewed by some as evidence that trade agreements such as the WTO can erode national policies enacted on the basis of public interest and welfare. Several observers have expressed concern that the WTO has established a dangerous precedent that could be extended to a range of other public policy issues, such as environmental protection (e.g., habitat protection, clean air and water) or food chain safety (e.g., limitation on use of potentially damaging fertilizers or pesticides, existence of genetically modified organisms in food products).

Questions:

1. Do you think that the WTO should be able to prohibit voluntary labeling efforts that provide information of potential value to consumers in a particular nation? Why or why not?

2. Should the WTO be able to overrule nations when national laws are based on sound science? How could the WTO ensure that the science behind local laws and regulations is sound and not a cover for protectionism?

3. Some people have argued that member nations give up national sovereignty rights by joining the WTO and allowing that organization to make decisions that are not in the best interest of a particular nation, especially since many WTO meetings are not open to the public. Do you agree with this interpretation and, if so, what could be done to address the situation?

Source: World Trade Organization, "Difference between a Technical Regulation and a Standard," *Technical Information on Technical Barriers to Trade*, www.wto.org/english/tratop_e/tbt_e/tbt_info_e.htm (June 26, 2011); Food and Agriculture Organization of the United Nations, "Tuna Purse Seining," www.fao.org/fishery/fishtech/40/en (June 26, 2011); Sam Williford, "WTO Eliminates 'Dolphin Safe' Labeling," *Economy in Crisis*, May 23, 2011, www.economyincrisis.org/content/wto-eliminates-%E2%80%9Cdolphin-safe%E2%80%9D-labeling, June 26, 2011); "U.S. Constitution—Article 6," www.usconstitution.net/xconst_A6.html (June 26, 2011); Public Citizen, "U.S. Dolphin-Safe Tuna Labeling Rule Deemed a WTO Violation," May 20, 2011, http://citizen.typepad.com/eyesontrade/2011/05/us-dolphin-safe-tuna-labeling-rule-deemed-a-wto-violation.html (June 26, 2011); American Albacore Fishing Association, "WTO Court Rules Against US Dolphin Safe Label Requirement," May 24, 2011, www.americanalbacore.com/wto-court-rules-against-us-dolphin-safe-label-requirement (June 26, 2011); and Loraine Mitchell, "Dolphin-Safe Tuna Labeling," *Economics of Food Labeling*, pp. 22-25, http://agritrade.cta.int/en/layout/set/print/content/view/full/4738 (June 26, 2011).

restraint agreements (VRAs) and by others "voluntary" export restraints (VERs). *Voluntary* is in quote marks because these barriers are imposed by the U.S. government on the exporting countries. The inevitable result is higher costs to American consumers, because exporters send only the higher-priced top of their lines and importers charge more for scarcer products. The United States is not the only country that imposes VRAs and VERs on its trading partners—far from it. Japan, Canada, the EU countries, and many others require that countries exporting to them "voluntarily" limit the number or value of goods exported.

Torts are injuries inflicted on other people, either intentionally or negligently. Tort cases in the United States may result in awards of very large sums of money. Other countries have tort laws that restrict the amount of money that can be obtained in tort actions.

Product Liability

One important area of torts, especially in the international arena, is **product liability.** Product liability laws hold a company and its officers and directors liable and possibly subject to fines or imprisonment when its product causes death, injury, or damage. Such liability for faulty or dangerous products was a growth area for the U.S. legal profession beginning in the 1960s. Liability insurance premiums soared, and there were concerns that smaller, weaker manufacturing companies could not survive. In the 1980s that boom spread to Europe and elsewhere. As foreign firms buy or build U.S. plants, they are being hit by the same liability and insurance problems have long been faced by U.S. companies.[13]

Manufacturers of products are often held to a standard of **strict liability,** which holds the designer/manufacturer liable for damages caused by a product without the need for a plaintiff to prove negligence in the product's design or manufacture. There are several reasons to believe that the impact of strict liability on product designers and manufacturers in Europe and Japan will not be as heavy or severe as it is in the United States. The EU allows companies to use "state-of-the-art" or "developmental risks" defenses, which allow the designer/manufacturer to show that at the time of design or manufacture, the most modern, latest-known technology was used. They also are permitted to cap damages. By comparison, damages awarded by American juries have been in the hundreds of millions of dollars.

Other differences in legal procedures in the United States compared with those in Europe and Japan will limit or prevent product liability awards by European and Japanese courts. As mentioned, in the United States, but not elsewhere, lawyers take many cases on a contingency-fee basis, whereby the lawyer charges the plaintiff no fee to begin representation and action in a product liability case. The lawyer is paid only when the defendant settles or loses in a trial, but then the fee is relatively large, running between one-third and one-half of the settlement or award. In addition, outside the United States, when the defendant wins a lawsuit, the plaintiff is often called upon to pay all the defendant's legal fees and other costs caused by the plaintiff's action.

In the United States, product liability cases are heard by juries that can award plaintiffs actual damages plus punitive damages. As the name indicates, punitive damages have the purpose of punishing the defendant, and if the plaintiff has been seriously injured or the jury's sympathy can be otherwise aroused, it may award millions of dollars to "teach the defendant a lesson." Outside the United States, judges, not juries, hear product liability cases. Judges are less prone to emotional reactions than juries are, and even if the judge is sympathetic toward a plaintiff, punitive damages are not awarded by non-U.S. courts.

Punitive Damage Effects

Multimillion-dollar punitive damage awards by U.S. courts have caused foreign firms to keep their products out of the United States. For instance, Axminster Electronics, a British firm whose devices help prevent crib death by monitoring a baby's breathing, does not sell in the United States because it cannot secure product liability insurance. Within the United States, every drug company knows that if a person uses a drug and subsequently gets ill, there is a chance that a jury somewhere in the United States may impose liability on the manufacturer and order it to pay damages.

Buyer Beware in Japan

The Japanese law on product liability requires that the plaintiff prove design or manufacturing negligence, which is difficult with complex, high-tech devices. The plaintiffs' difficulties are exacerbated by the unique Japanese legal procedures to provide discovery, the process by which plaintiffs can seek defendants' documents relevant to their cases. Discovery is available to plaintiffs in U.S. courts but is limited in Japan.[14]

MISCELLANEOUS LAWS

Individuals working abroad must be alert to avoid falling afoul of local laws and police, army, or government officials. Some examples make the point.

- A Plessey employee, a British subject, was given a life sentence in Libya for "jeopardizing the revolution by giving information to a foreign company." Saudi Arabia may strictly enforce sanctions against importing or drinking alcohol and wearing revealing clothing. Foreigners in Japan who walk out of their homes without their alien registration cards *(gaikakujin toroku)* can be arrested, as happened to one man while he was carrying out the garbage. An Australian writer was sentenced in Thailand to three years in jail for writing a novel (seven copies sold) that insulted the crown prince. Brunei has caned nearly 500 foreigners since 2004 for settling illegally in the sultanate.

- A New York law firm, International Legal Defense Counsel (ILDC), has made a reputation by dealing with countries where American embassies and consulates are of little legal help. One of its cases involved a Virginia photographer named Conan Owen, who agreed to transport a package of cocaine from Colombia to Spain, where he was arrested and slapped with a stiff prison sentence. The U.S. Attorney General personally interceded with no success, and Owen languished in prison for nearly two years. Then, ILDC obtained his freedom through the use of a bilateral prisoner transfer treaty that permits American inmates in foreign jails to do their time in a facility back home. Once in the United States, Owen was quickly freed.

U.S. Laws That Affect the International Business of U.S. Firms

LO7-5 Discuss some of the U.S. laws that affect international business operations.

Although every law relating to business arguably has some effect on international activities, some laws warrant special notice. We will look briefly at several U.S. laws. Although many U.S. laws affect activities of international firms, there has not been a successful effort to coordinate them. Some are even at cross-purposes, and some diminish the ability of U.S. businesses to compete with foreign companies.

FOREIGN CORRUPT PRACTICES ACT

During the 1970s, revelations of **questionable or dubious payments** by American companies to foreign officials rocked governments in the Netherlands and Japan. Congress considered corporate bribery "bad business" and "unnecessary." As a result, the **Foreign Corrupt Practices Act (FCPA)** became law. Key provisions of the act involve bribery of foreign officials and requirements for transparency of accounting transactions.

There are a number of uncertainties about terms used in the FCPA. An interesting case in point involves "grease." According to the FCPA's drafters, the act does not outlaw *grease,* which refers to facilitating payments made solely to expedite nondiscretionary official actions. Such actions as customs clearance and telephone calls have been cited. However, there is no clear distinction between supposedly legal grease payments and illegal bribes. To confuse matters further, U.S. Justice Department officials have suggested that they may prosecute some grease payments anyway under earlier antibribery laws written to get at corruption in the United States. The act is very broad in what constitutes a foreign official, and the government's relevant criterion for a bribe is not the amount but rather the intent of the payment.

questionable or dubious payments
Bribes paid to government officials by companies seeking to purchase contracts from those governments

Foreign Corrupt Practices Act (FCPA)
U.S. law against making payments to foreign government officials for special treatment

Other doubts raised by the FCPA concern the accounting standards it requires for compliance. That matter is connected to questions about how far management must go to learn whether any employees, subsidiaries, or agents may have violated the act; even if management were unaware of an illegal payment, it could be in violation if it "had reason to know" that some portion of a payment abroad might be used as a bribe.*

The FCPA makes it unlawful to bribe foreign government officials to obtain or retain business. Facilitating payments for routine government actions such as visa issuance, import approvals, and the processing of government papers are permissible under the FCPA. In January 2010, nearly two dozen U.S. corporate executives were indicted in an undercover "sting" operation for bribing an African minister of defense. After a record-setting level of enforcements in 2010, there are indications that increased efforts at enforcement of the FCPA will produce a growing level of prosecutions and fines in subsequent years.[15]

Critics believed that the FCPA would harm American companies' competitiveness abroad because it would demand of American companies a higher standard of behavior than was common in the competitive environment. Congress decided that the potential economic damage to exports would be minimal and that the only companies that would be hurt would be those whose only means of competing was through the payment of bribes. The United States actively lobbied the international community to introduce similar legislation, which it did in 1997, with the OECD Convention on Bribery. In response, the FCPA was amended in 1998 to incorporate antibribery conventions developed by the OECD.

You may wonder if U.S. laws on bribery place U.S. businesses at a disadvantage in international competition. What seems to have happened on the bribery front is interesting. The FCPA, along with the OECD convention and the UN initiative, have brought a discussion of bribery and transparency out into the open. Such discussions were further stimulated by the Asian financial crisis of 1997, one of whose causes was widely attributed to lack of transparency in financial dealings. Having an international reputation for transparency and being perceived as "aboveboard" have become increasingly important for global companies. There appears to be a strong move for company values that support integrity in the belief that integrity is better for business than are corrupt activities.

Other Antibribery or Anticorruption Statutes

There are other laws regulating corruption and bribery. Among the most noteworthy is the UN Convention against Corruption (UNCAC), signed by more than 151 countries as well as the EU as of 2011.[16] The UNCAC goes beyond bribery to address a broader range of corruption, such as general abuse of power and trading in official influence, as well a the recovery of assets from officials accused or convicted of engaging in corruption.

In 2011, the United Kingdom Bribery Act came into force, which includes penalties for corporate failure to prevent bribery. The person engaging in a bribe does not need to be British and the act of bribery does not need to have occurred in the United Kingdom. A corporation can be charged under this law as long as it engages in "a business or part of a business" in the United Kingdom, suggesting that this law may be applied extraterritorially. As new legislation, this act is accompanied by a substantial amount of uncertainty regarding what would qualify as adequate procedures to prevent bribery and how broadly the association with potential bribe-payers is interpreted (e.g., are joint venturers liable for the actions of their partners?).[17]

Measuring Likelihood of Bribery Abroad: The Bribe Payers Index

The organization Transparency International publishes a bribe payers index (see Table 7.4). This index assesses the likelihood that firms from industrialized nations will engage in bribery abroad. Its data for 2008 (the latest survey) are based on a survey of 2,742 respondents from 26 countries.

*Other words with similar connotations are *dash, squeeze, mordida, piston, cumshaw,* and *baksheesh.*

TABLE 7.4 Bribe Payers Index

Country	Rank for Year of Study			
	1999	2002	2006	2008
Canada	2	5	5	1
Belgium	8	6	9	1
Switzerland	5	2	1	3
Netherlands	6	6	8	3
United Kingdom	7	8	6	5
Germany	9	9	7	5
Japan	14	13	11	5
Australia	2	1	3	8
Singapore	11	9	12	9
France	13	12	15	9
United States	9	13	9	9
Spain	12	11	13	12
Hong Kong	n.a.	15	18	13
South Korea	18	18	21	14
Taiwan	17	19	26	14
South Africa	n.a.	n.a.	24	14
Italy	16	17	20	17
Brazil	n.a.	n.a.	23	17
India	n.a.	n.a.	30	19
Mexico	n.a.	n.a.	17	20
China	19	20	29	21
Russia	n.a.	21	28	22

* n.a. = data not reported.

Source: Transparency International, *Bribe Payers Index 2008,* www.transparency.org/policy_research/surveys_indices/bpi (June 24, 2011); Transparency International, *Bribe Payers Index 2006,* www.transparency.org/policy_research/surveys_indices/bpi/bpi_2006 (June 24, 2011); Transparency International, *Bribe Payers Index 2002,* www.transparency.org/policy_research/surveys_indices/bpi/bpi_2002 (June 24, 2011); Transparency International, *Bribe Payers Index 1999,* www.transparency.org/policy_research/surveys_indices/bpi/bpi_1999 (June 24, 2011); and Transparency International, "TI Report: Emerging Economic Giants Show High Levels of Corporate Bribery Oversees," December 9, 2008, www.transparency.org/news_room/latest_news/press_releases/2008/bpi_2008_en (accessed June 24, 2011).

ACCOUNTING LAW

Investor confidence in the integrity of financial reporting and corporate governance has been shaken by financial scandals worldwide. This crisis of confidence has substantially damaged the economic prospects of numerous companies, employees, retirees, customers, suppliers, and other stakeholders.

U.S. accounting practice is guided by the Securities and Exchange Commission (SEC) and the Financial Accounting Standards Board (FASB) and follows standards known as generally accepted accounting principles (GAAP), while most other countries, including those in the EU, follow standards issued by the International Accounting Standards Board (IASB) known as the International Financial Reporting Standards (IFRS). These standards differ in many aspects, but a number of projects looking toward convergence are expected to be completed in 2015. This area is further explored in Chapter 18.

THE GLOBAL PATH AHEAD

Rory Burdick: Career Launch in International

Rory Burdick graduated from California Polytechnic State University with a business major and economics minor, both with an international concentration. Then he traveled, just for the adventure of it all. The following are comments he has made about this journey.

After completing my courses at Cal Poly, I joined a group of friends who were traveling to South Africa from East Asia. I went on to travel through London, Amsterdam, Berlin, and Prague. After emptying my bank accounts, I returned to San Francisco to work in various technology startups.

I joined a successful startup whose customer base eventually grew to a size that required 24/7 customer support, and the decision was made to implement "follow-the-sun" coverage across the United States, Europe, India, and China. This decision led to my first international work experience—managing the training of these offshore support groups. During this project, I learned how to overcome cultural, communication, and time zone issues. A college friend moved to Paris, which was a good excuse for a road trip originating in Amsterdam, then traveling through Paris, Marseille, Barcelona, back to Paris through the Pyrenees, and finally returning to Amsterdam.

Shortly after that road trip, I was approached with an opportunity to interview for a position at Google. Once a part of Google, I joined a small global team and traveled on assignment to Atlanta, New York, and Frankfurt. A director visiting my group in Mountain View mentioned he was looking for someone to take a position in Brazil. Knowing very little about the country or the opportunity, I expressed interest and arranged an interview with the hiring manager, which led to a six-month assignment in São Paulo that included a short assignment in Buenos Aires. Since

returning to the United States, I have spent time with my family in British Columbia and Nuevo Vallarta, and I am writing this profile from Sardinia, Italy.

I'd like to tell you my personal travels have been well-thought-out cultural excursions, but in reality I've chosen my destinations for surfing (South Africa, Mexico), snowboarding (Canada, Santiago), festivals (Europe, Jamaica), and the opportunity to travel with good friends in countries with favorable exchange rates! After joining Google, I worked hard to establish myself with local management as an ambitious self-starter who could be trusted with difficult projects where individual contributors would have minimal support from management. Once established as a strong individual contributor and leader, I was asked to travel to locations that were short-handed or needed project-specific burst labor. My travels enabled me to interface with employees from different locations around the world, which helped me make a name for myself. This strategy allowed me to make a case for taking the position in Brazil for a related group in a position I had never before performed.

Roughly four months passed between initially expressing my interest and being offered the position in Brazil, but I only had three weeks to prepare for departure! After the initial interview, I was given the names of several people who had worked or were currently working in South America. Some were Americans like me, and others were Brazilians who had grown up in or around São Paulo. I conducted a series of informational interviews with these staff members to hear what they had to say about their experiences. I asked about the culture of Brazil, personal safety, cost of living, and what the city of São Paulo had to offer. All of them had insightful comments, but nothing would fully prepare me for my assignment.

I can honestly say my time in Brazil was both the most challenging and most rewarding experience of my life. São Paulo has one of the most ethnically diverse populations in the world, and because of this I blended in with everyone else. I inherited a project that was behind schedule and suffered from various vendor and contractor issues, as well as internal customer issues. I had to quickly find solutions despite my language shortcomings, while maintaining a positive relationship with our Brazilian business partners. I managed this by closely watching the cultural norms of those around me and maintaining a positive attitude with a quiet confidence. By demonstrating my desire to perform well and my interest in establishing positive relationships, my Brazilian counterparts were extremely interested in working with me to find mutually beneficial solutions to the hurdles we faced.

There were many amazing aspects of my trip, but three stand out from the rest. Portuguese is a beautiful language with elements of Italian, Spanish, and French. Being thrown into full submersion without any previous experience was quite humbling, but it has provided me with a language foundation that allows me to communicate with most Latin populations. In addition to their beautiful language, it is hard not to fall in love with the Brazilian people and their culture. Warm and outgoing, they were eager to engage me in conversations ranging from my family back home to political issues we face as new American

(continued)

cultures. Most importantly for me, I was able to singlehandedly bring a project back onto schedule while building relationships in an international context.

Relocating to a foreign country for an employment opportunity is an exciting and overwhelming experience that is difficult for anyone to prepare for fully. While I would definitely recommend talking to people or reading about the culture and history of the country you will be visiting, even more important is language and a positive attitude. My experience has been that people are curious about and outgoing toward visitors who show interest in learning about them. The more able you are to communicate with people, the more they will tell you about their culture, their country and themselves. The knowledge I have gained from my studies pales in comparison to what I have learned from interacting with people on a personal level.

Resources for Your Global Career

International Law and Culture Cue

When traveling and conducting business globally, always keep in mind that the laws of many countries are steeped in the country's religious heritage. This means that breaking a law in these countries may also be seen as an act of huge disrespect for one's religious beliefs. World religions such as Muslim, Hindu, and Buddhism, also termed "code religions," clearly define accepted behavior and serve as a basis for the laws in countries where these religions are dominant. Become sensitive to and respectful of the religious influences in the countries with which you trade. It is wise to show respect and interest when others may tell you about their religious beliefs, but be astute to keep your religious preferences and beliefs to yourself. Never put yourself in a position where your religious beliefs may be interpreted as superior to those of the country you are in. You just might also be breaking a local law.

Your Worldwide Resources for Foreign and International Law:

- EISIL (Electronic Information System for International Law): www.eisil.org/
- American Bar Association Section on International Law: www.abanet.org/intlaw/home.html
- Careers in International Law: www.luc.edu/law/career/pdfs/International.pdf
- Career Resources in International Law, www.nyls.edu/centers/harlan_scholar_centers/center_for_international_law/career_resources
- International Law Review Association: http://studentorgs.law.smu.edu/ILRA
- Finding Foreign Law Online when Going Global: www2.lib.uchicago.edu/~llou/global.html
- Foreign and International Law Resources: www.washlaw.edu/forint/alpha/a.html
- Worldwide Legal Directories: www.hg.org/internat.html
- International Law Blog: http://blogs.law.harvard.edu/internationallaw/
- Worldwide Legal Resources and Legislation Affecting Marketing: www.theglobalmarketer.com/law/index.jsp
- Worldwide Legal Directories and Resource for International Law Articles: www.hg.org/guides.html
- International Intellectual Property Law Resources: www.asil.org/ip1.cfm and www.lib.uchicago.edu/e/law/intlip.html

LO7-1 Discuss the complexity of the legal forces that confront international business.

International business is affected by many thousands of laws and regulations issued by states, nations, and international organizations. Some are at cross-purposes, and some diminish the ability of firms to compete with foreign companies.

LO7-2 Explain the possibilities for international dispute settlement.

International dispute settlement possibilities include litigation and arbitration. Litigation across borders often raises the issue of which jurisdiction's law should apply and where the litigation should occur. Arbitration is often less expensive, faster, and more informal than litigation. Both litigation and arbitration face difficulties in enforcement.

LO7-3 Recognize the need and methods to protect your intellectual property.

Patents, trademarks, trade names, copyrights, and trade secrets are referred to as intellectual properties. Pirating of those properties is common and is costly for their owners. The UN's World Intellectual Property Organization (WIPO) was created to administer international property treaties, as was TRIPS, a WTO agency with a similar purpose.

LO7-4 Explain the risk of product liability legal actions.

Product liability refers to the civil or criminal liability of the designer or manufacturer of a product for injury or damages it causes. In several ways, product liability is treated differently in the U.S. legal system than it is in other countries. For example, only in the United States does one find lawyers' contingency fees, jury trials of these cases, and punitive damages. Although the principle of strict liability has been adopted in Europe, defendants are permitted to use state-of-the-art defenses and countries can put a cap on damages. Product liability is virtually unknown in Japan.

LO7-5 Discuss some of the U.S. laws that affect international business operations.

Many U.S. laws affect international business operations, both of U.S. and of foreign companies. The United States applies federal employment laws to any U.S. company operating anywhere. This extraterritoriality means that U.S. companies operating in foreign countries are required to follow U.S. employment law as it applies to U.S. nationals. The Foreign Corrupt Practices Act also applies to U.S. businesses in their foreign operations and to foreign businesses that conduct operations in the United States.

Key Words

public international law (p 183)

private international law (p 183)

treaties (p 183)

extraterritorial application of laws (p 183)

litigation (p 184)

arbitration (p 185)

Incoterms (p 185)

intellectual property (p 186)

patent (p 186)

trademark (p 187)

trade name (p 187)

copyright (p 187)

trade secret (p 187)

competition laws (p 189)

antitrust laws (p 189)

torts (p 194)

product liability (p 194)

strict liability (p 194)

questionable or dubious payments (p 195)

Foreign Corrupt Practices Act (FCPA) (p 195)

Questions

1. What is the significance of determining whether a country follows the rule of law?

2. How does international law differ from national law? What are the sources of international law?

3. What objections do other countries have to extraterritorial application by the United States of its laws?

4. Why do many people from outside the United States dislike engaging in litigation in the United States?

5. What are advantages of submitting contract disputes to arbitration instead of to litigation in courts?

6. What are the primary types of intellectual property, and why do companies concern themselves with intellectual property issues?

7. What are competition laws, and how do the laws and the approaches differ between the United States and other parts of the world?

8. Are tariffs the only type of obstacle to international trade? If not, name some others.

9. Can product liability be criminal? If so, in what sorts of situations would product liability become criminal behavior?

10. What is the Foreign Corrupt Practices Act? What arguments or evidence can you identify in support or opposition to laws such as the FCPA?

Research Task

globalEDGE.msu.edu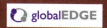

Use the globalEDGE site (http://globalEDGE.msu.edu/) to complete the following exercises:

1. Your company is considering expanding to Singapore. Because of this, top management is hoping to better understand the intellectual property (IP) laws of this country. Using the *Intellectual Property Office of Singapore* (IPOS) website, prepare a short report on trademark protection in Singapore. In your report, include a discussion addressing the following: (a) the benefits of trademark registration, (b) registrable and unregistrable marks, and (c) the steps in the application process.

2. Transparency International's *Corruption Perceptions Index* (CPI) is a comparative assessment of a country's integrity performance. Provide a description of this index and its ranking. Using the most recent data, identify the five countries with the lowest and the five with the highest CPI scores according to this index. Do you see any trends between CPI scores and the level of economic and social development of a country?

A California-based company is expanding very well and has just made its first large export sale. All of its sales and procurement contracts up to now have contained a clause providing that if any disputes arise under the contract, they will be settled under California law and that any litigation will be in California courts.

The new foreign customer, who is Italian, objects to these all-California solutions. She says she is buying and paying for a large volume of the products, so before finalizing the sales contract she says that the California company should compromise and allow Italian law and courts to govern and handle any disputes.

Questions:

1. You are the CEO of the California company, and you very much want this large export order. You are pleased with the service your law firm has given, but you know it has no international experience. What are the various forms of dispute resolution available to your California company? What are the advantages and disadvantages of each for your company?

2. In deciding whether to only use California law for settling litigation or to allow the foreign customer's home nation of Italy as the venue for litigation, would your analysis be any different if the customer was from China? From Russia? From the United Kingdom? Why or why not?

The International Monetary System and Financial Forces

The function of money is not to make money but to move goods. Money is only one part of our transportation system. It moves goods from man to man. A dollar bill is like a postage stamp: it is no good unless it will move commodities between persons. If a postage stamp will not carry a letter, or money will not move goods, it is just the same as an engine that will not run. Someone will have to get out and fix it.

—*attributed to Henry Ford in a speech at the Ford Motor Company*

International Monetary Arrangements and Terrorism

As we all realize, two critical requirements for international terrorism are funding and secrecy.

Terrorist operations are costly, and funding them involves an ability to launder money, to disguise its sources, and to move it unmonitored across international borders. So government focus on terrorists' international monetary arrangements is critical: if the money flow can be monitored, operations may be forecast. If the flow can be stopped, terrorism will stop. Today, traditional banking activity, with its records, electronic trails and reporting requirements, won't work for terrorists, although it did in 2001. The 9/11 terrorists were funded via bank wire transfers to a U.S. bank in Florida where several of the conspirators had accounts.[a] Let's look at some ways terrorist funding is thought to be transferred today and how governments have been responding to the financial institutions that serve terrorism.

The transfer method that attracts the most attention is hawala. This is an informal way to transfer value that leaves few or no traces and is very popular with foreign workers who want to transmit money home. They give the funds to their local hawala, with directions about who should receive it. The hawala then contacts his counterpart in the destination, and the designated recipient can draw the funds. Hawala arose in medieval times before the development of banks to support trade across geographic distance. Brokers at both ends of the transaction operate as agents for people wanting to transmit money. The brokers run balances that can be can be settled over time through either cash or non-cash transactions. Although the hawala keeps detailed records, these are private and there is no record of a money transfer. The sender receives no contract or receipt, no legal documentation; it all works on trust and honor. The deal may be communicated via phone, fax, or e-mail. Often the hawalas are part of the same extended family, although this is not always the case. If you think back to Chapter 4 and Hall's context, hawalas are culturally high context. Hawalas make a small commission on the transaction, plus they may make something on the exchange rate, although their rates often are better than those available at banks. You can see how hawalas meet the support needs for terrorists. The majority of hawala transactions are legal, and they serve an important function well.

Many other ways to transfer value without a trail exist. One way is to manipulate invoices so that excess value is transferred to the payee. An invoice for $200,000 inflated 30 percent transfers $60,000 without record. There are

8

also schemes to divert trade, to use charities, and to use Internet-based payments. Each of these approaches is complex and not easily traceable.[b]

Every industrialized nation's treasury is at work monitoring money laundering that may be supporting terrorism. There are also international coordination efforts. The Financial Action Task Force on Money Laundering (FATF), established by the G7 countries, develops and promotes policies that make money laundering more difficult and more risky. FATF works closely with the IMF, the World Bank, the United Nations, and national bodies such as the U.S. Department of the Treasury. FATF regularly reviews and reports on country anti-laundering standards in place in specific countries, publishing the results of their audits. If the FATF report is critical, all governments are notified to advise their banks and other financial institutions to give special attention to any transactions in the listed countries by exercising appropriate due diligence and caution. The financial world is watching the listed countries closely. These measures actually force the transfer of value to less obvious methods in less obvious institutions.

What suggestions does FATF offer to help safeguard against terrorism, from the finance side? Its recommendations include criminalizing the financing of terrorism; freezing and confiscating terrorist assets; reporting suspicious transactions related to terrorism; tracking parallel or alternative remittance systems, such as hawala; and monitoring wire transfers, nonprofit organizations, and cash couriers. In the United States, the Department of the Treasury lists countries, individuals (designated nationals), and networks that have been sanctioned by the U.S. government. Treasury refers to these sanctions as 311 actions, named after the section of the USA Patriot Act that provides the Secretary of the Treasury with options to target specific organizations. You can see the updated 311 list at www.treasury.gov/resource-center/terrorist-illicit-finance/311-Actions/Pages/311-Actions.aspx/.

[a]Nikos Passas, "Fighting Terror with Error: The Counter-Productive Regulation of Informal Value Transfers," *Crime, Law and Social Change* 45 (2007), pp. 315–66.

[b]Conversation with Nikos Passas, April 1, 2011.

The international monetary system consists of institutions, agreements, rules, and processes that allow for the payments, currency exchange, and movements of capital across international borders that are required by international transactions.[1] To gain a sense of how the international monetary system has evolved, it's useful to build an understanding of how the institutions and arrangements that facilitate payments across national borders have evolved. So, we begin this chapter with a review of the gold standard and the Bretton Woods system. We have already discussed the two monetary institutions that were developed at the Bretton Woods meetings in 1944: the International Monetary Fund (IMF) and the World Bank (see Chapter 3). Here, we examine one of them more closely, the IMF. The IMF plays a central institutional role in the international monetary system by providing the rules of the international monetary system "game." Then we consider the emergence of the current floating exchange rate system. We also look briefly at the Bank for International Settlements. Following our focus on the international monetary system, we look at the major financial forces that help to shape a firm's international context. These forces include fluctuating currency values, currency exchange controls, taxation, and inflation and interest rates. We conclude with a focus on how the monetary exchanges among nations are recorded. This happens through a system called the balance-of-payments accounts, and we also look at their relevance for the international manager.

LO8-1 Describe the international monetary system's evolution.

The International Monetary System

A BRIEF HISTORY: THE GOLD STANDARD

Based on its scarcity and easily assessed level of purity, gold has been trusted as a way for people to store value, exchange value, and measure value since ancient times. From about 1200 A.D. to the present, the price of gold has generally been going up.[2] From ancient times until the last part of the 19th century, international traders used both bullion and gold and silver coins. However, as trade grew, carrying large amounts of gold became impractical. Think about it: gold is heavy, it has transportation and storage costs, it does not earn interest, and it needs safekeeping. Its bulk makes it an obvious target for thieves. These drawbacks led to paper script that was backed by governments with a pledge to exchange the script for gold at a fixed rate.

In 1717, Sir Isaac Newton, the great mathematician and master of the English mint, established the price of gold in terms of British currency at 3 pounds, 17 shillings, 10.5 pence per ounce, putting England de facto on the **gold standard.** Prior, the silver standard had been used. Most trading or industrial countries followed England's move and adopted the gold standard. Each country set a certain number of units of its currency per ounce of gold, and the ratios of their gold equivalence established the exchange rate between any two currencies on the gold standard. For example, if 5 British pounds were pegged at 1 ounce of gold and 10 French francs were pegged at 1 ounce, then the exchange rate would have been 2 French francs per British pound, or 0.5 pound per franc.

gold standard
The use of gold at an established number of units per currency

Except during the Napoleonic Wars, England stood willing to convert gold to currency, or vice versa, until World War I, which began in 1914. During those two centuries, more than 90 percent of world trade was financed in London.[3] The cost of World War I forced Britain to sell a substantial portion of its gold and suspend gold exchange. Other warring countries, including Germany, France, and Russia, suspended the exchange of paper money for gold and stopped exports of gold. Between World War I and World War II, which began in 1939, there was a short flirtation with renewal of the gold standard, but it was not successfully reestablished.

The simplicity of the gold standard was a large part of its appeal. When there were trade imbalances, they would be corrected by a flow of gold in the direction of the surplus. The money supply would rise or fall in direct relation to the gold flows. Although the gold standard has not been the international monetary system for many years, it continues to have some ardent advocates—most economists not among them—who call for a return to the gold standard and fixed exchange rates. The heart of their argument is expressed in one word: *discipline.* Under the gold standard, a government cannot create money that is not backed by gold. Therefore, no matter how great the temptation to create more money

Iranian currency trader counts gold coins, "Iranians' political hedge fund."

for political advantage, a government cannot do so without the required amount of gold.[4] Unfortunately, this discipline sacrifices a government's monetary flexibility. For example, a government could not increase money supply to ward off a recession on the gold standard. Such flexibility is necessary in a globalized monetary system, where quick adjustments to wide swings in a currency's value may be necessary. Economist Paul Krugman points out that this flexibility is why the 1987 stock market crash did not cause a depression similar to that of 1929.[5]

LO8-2 **Explain** the Triffin paradox.

BRETTON WOODS SYSTEM

Bretton Woods system
The international monetary system in place from 1945 to 1971, with par value based on gold and the U.S. dollar

Allied government representatives met at Bretton Woods in New Hampshire in 1944 to plan for post–World War II monetary arrangements. Their consensus was that stable exchange rates were desirable, but experience might dictate adjustments. They also agreed that floating or fluctuating exchange rates had proved unsatisfactory, although the reasons for this opinion were little discussed. These meetings established the IMF, which we reviewed in our discussion of global institutions. The IMF Articles of Agreement contained the rules for a new international monetary system, the **Bretton Woods system,** also called the gold exchange standard and the fixed rate system, which served as the basis of the international monetary system from 1945 to 1971.

fixed exchange rate
Specific currency exchange equivalence upheld by government

The new system set up **fixed exchange rates** among member-nations' currencies, with **par value** based on gold and the U.S. dollar, which was valued at $35 per ounce of gold. For example, the British pound's par value was US$2.40, the French franc's was US$0.18, and the German mark's was US$0.2732. There was an understanding that the U.S. government would redeem dollars for gold and that the dollar was the only currency to be redeemable for gold. This dollar-based gold exchange standard established the U.S. dollar as both a means of international payment and a reserve currency for governments to hold in their treasuries.

par value
Stated value

reserves
Assets held by the central bank, used to back up government liabilities

The Bretton Woods system supported substantial international trade growth during the 1950s and 1960s. Other countries changed their currency's value against the dollar and gold, but the U.S. dollar remained fixed. This meant that the United States, in order to satisfy the growing demand for reserves (because countries would hold dollars as a proxy for gold), had to run a balance-of-payments deficit. That is, in the United States, the flow of dollars out was greater than the flow in; the demand on dollars for holding outside the country was greater than those that flowed in as a result of export sales and foreign investment. From 1958 through 1971, the United States ran up a cumulative deficit of $56 billion. The deficit was financed partly by use of the U.S. gold reserves and partly by incurring liabilities to foreign central banks. **Reserves** are held by the central bank or treasury and used to back its liabilities; reserves may include various hard currencies (Japanese yen, U.S. dollar, British pound sterling, EU euro) and gold. U.S. gold reserves shrank from $24.8 billion to $12.2 billion.[6] During this period, those liabilities increased from $13.6 billion to $62.2 billion.[7] By 1971, the U.S. Treasury held only 22 cents worth of gold for each U.S. dollar held by those banks.

Triffin paradox
A national currency that is also a reserve currency will eventually run a deficit, which leads to lack of confidence in the reserve currency and a financial crisis

There's an interesting paradox associated with reserve currencies that was first pointed out by economist Robert Triffin: such a deficit, which is unavoidable, would eventually inspire a lack of confidence in the reserve currency, which would lead to a financial crisis. That is, the more dollars foreigners held, the less confidence they had in the currency. Known as the **Triffin paradox,** that is exactly what happened when, after trade deficits in the late 1960s, President Charles De Gaulle pushed the Bank of France to redeem its dollar holdings for gold. Eventually, in 1971, President Nixon suspended the dollar's convertibility into gold.

special drawing rights (SDR)
An international reserve asset established by the IMF; the unit of account for the IMF and other international organizations

Bretton Woods had tried to make adjustments to avoid the impending crisis by creating an international reserve asset, **special drawing rights (SDR),** in 1969. The SDR's value is based on a basket of four currencies: the euro, the Japanese yen, pound sterling, and the U.S. dollar. The IMF, its 185 members, and 15 other official international institutions use the SDR as its unit of account, as does another financial institution, the Bank for International Settlements. Yet today, the SDR has limited use as a reserve asset, and its

Central Reserve/National Currency Conflict

Every member of the IMF keeps a *reserve account,* a bit like a savings account, with holdings the country can draw on when needed to finance trade or investments or to intervene in currency markets. Countries with the largest reserve accounts are China, Japan, Taiwan, Russia, Korea, India, and Hong Kong. The reserve assets are gold, foreign exchange, SDR, and reserve positions in the IMF. The U.S. dollar has been the most used central reserve asset in the world since the end of World War II; at the end of March 2011, roughly 34 percent of the world's reserve assets were held in dollars and 15 percent in euros. Since 2007, the trend has been downward for the dollar and the euro. The dollars, held in the form of U.S. Treasury bonds, earn interest, so the more dollars held in the central reserve account, the better. But the countries holding those U.S. dollars in their foreign reserve accounts don't want their central reserve asset to lose value, and therein lies a contradiction: at some point, holding large numbers of U.S. dollars (or any other product) in supply causes them to lose value.

At the same time, the U.S. dollar is the national currency of the United States, whose government must deal with inflation, recession, interest rates, unemployment, and other national, internal problems. The U.S. government uses fiscal and monetary policies to meet those problems—raise or lower taxes, decisions on how to spend available revenue, growth or contraction of the money supply, and rate of that growth or contraction.

It would be only accidental if the national interests of the United States in dealing with its internal problems were to coincide with the interests of the multitude of countries holding U.S. dollars in their central reserve asset accounts. For example, the United States may be slowing money supply growth and raising taxes to combat U.S. inflation, while the world needs more liquidity, in the form of U.S. dollars, to finance growth, trade, or investment. Or the United States may be stimulating its economy through faster money supply growth and lower taxes at a time when so many U.S. dollars are already outstanding that their value is dropping—not a happy state of affairs for countries holding U.S. dollars.

It was a quirk of history that thrust the currency of the United States into this conflicting role. The IMF hoped that a nonnational asset, the SDR, would rescue the U.S. dollar and the world from this conflict.

Questions:

1. What are the advantages of the SDR?

2. China holds considerable dollars in its foreign reserves. How do the U.S. and Chinese governments' interests in the dollar coincide? How might they conflict?

Source: Remarks by Chairman Alan Greenspan, November 14, 2005. See www.federalreserve.gov/boarddocs; IMF Currency Composition of Official Reserves, www.imf.org/external/np/sta/cofer/eng/index.htm (accessed April 13, 2011).

ability to serve as a safety net should the international monetary system run into serious difficulty has yet to be tested. The daily valuation of the SDR can be checked at www .imf.org/external/np/fin/data/rms_sdrv.aspx/.

FLOATING CURRENCY EXCHANGE RATE SYSTEM

After trade deficits in the late 1960s, when President Charles de Gaulle pushed the Bank of France to redeem its dollar holdings for gold, President Nixon announced in 1971 that the United States would no longer exchange gold for the paper dollars held by foreign central banks. This action took the U.S. dollar out of its role as a stabilizer for the international monetary system. The shock caused currency exchange markets to remain closed for several days, and when they reopened, they began to develop a new system for which few rules existed. Currencies were floating, based on market forces, and the stated US$ value of $35 per ounce of gold was now meaningless because the United States would no longer exchange any of its gold for dollars.

Two attempts were made to agree on durable, new sets of fixed currency exchange rates, one in December 1971 and the other in February 1973, resulting in the Smithsonian Agreements. Both times, however, banks, businesses, and individuals felt that the central banks had pegged the rates incorrectly, and the speculators were correct each time. By March 1973, the major currencies were floating in the foreign exchange markets, and this system of **floating currency exchange rates** still prevails. The agreement that established the rules for the floating system was accepted by IMF members after the fact, at a meeting in Jamaica in 1976. Known as the **Jamaica Agreement,** it allows for flexible exchange rates among IMF members, while condoning central bank operations in the money markets to smooth out volatile periods. The Jamaica Agreement also demonetized gold; it was abandoned as a reserve currency. Such is our trust for gold's value, though, that it is still used by many nations as a reserve currency.

LO8-3 Describe the floating currency exchange rate system, including the IMF currency arrangements.

floating currency exchange rates Rates that are allowed to float against other currencies and are determined by market forces

Jamaica Agreement The 1976 IMF agreement that allows flexible exchange rates among members

CURRENT CURRENCY ARRANGEMENTS

Initially, the IMF recognized three types of currency exchange arrangements, but it later extended the categories to eight. These eight categories of exchange rate arrangements that the IMF now uses to describe how countries position their currencies in relation to other currencies are explained here, ranging from not having any legal tender to having fixed and then freely floating exchange rate arrangements—that is, they are characterized by their degree of flexibility.

- *Exchange arrangement with no separate legal tender:* one country adopts the currency of another or a group of countries adopt a common currency. An example of the first is the U.S. dollar's use in El Salvador, Panama, and Ecuador. An example of the second is the European Union's euro being used as shared currency in 17 EU member-countries.

- *Currency board arrangement:* a legislated commitment to exchange domestic currency for a specific foreign currency at a fixed rate. The currency board arrangement commits the government to hold foreign reserves equal to its domestic currency supply. Hong Kong and Bulgaria, Estonia and Lithuania use currency boards.

- *Conventional fixed peg arrangement:* a "peg," or fixed-rate relationship where exchange rate fluctuations are allowed within a narrow band of less than 1 percent. The peg could be to one currency or to a basket of currencies. The Saudi riyal is, in effect, pegged in this way to the U.S. dollar.

- *Pegged exchange rate within a horizontal band:* a peg arrangement in which the exchange rate fluctuations are allowed to be greater than 1 percent around a central rate (e.g., Denmark's krone pegged to the euro).

- *Crawling peg:* a currency is readjusted periodically at a fixed, preannounced rate or in response to changes in indicators (e.g., at various times Mexico, Botswana, Costa Rica, and Iran).

- *Crawling band:* currency readjustment to maintain fluctuation margins around a central rate (Denmark's krone to the euro).

- *Managed floating with no preannounced path for the exchange rate:* a monetary authority actively intervenes on the exchange market without specifying or making public its goals and targets. Algeria, India, Malaysia, and Singapore are examples of this approach. China relaxed a 10-year yuan peg in 2005 and allowed it to be managed against a basket of trading currencies. In May 2010, the Chinese government signaled a possible further relaxation of its control of the yuan exchange rate float.

- *Independently floating exchange rates:* rely on the market. There may be interventions, yet they are conducted to moderate the rate of change rather than to establish the currency's level. Examples of countries following this approach are the United States, Mexico, Japan, South Africa, Switzerland, Canada, India, and the United Kingdom.

The floating exchange rate system, with its various approaches, seems to be meeting its recent challenges, several of which—including a central bank liquidity crisis in the spring of 2008 and an ensuing global financial crisis—have been severe. In addition to economic policy, coordination by the G7 countries (France, Germany, Italy, Japan, the United States, the United Kingdom, and Canada, sometimes with Russia making a G8) has emerged as a key factor in the foreign exchange (FX) markets. In a recent coordinated intervention to stop the rise of the Japanese yen after the 2011 earthquake, central banks in Japan, Europe, and North America stabilized the strengthening yen, thereby stabilizing financial markets and avoiding a global crisis. This intervention is discussed in the WORLDview feature.

As G7 central banks have become more adept at influencing currency movements, the explosive growth in the volume of currencies being traded in the world's foreign exchange markets challenges their efforts. From an annual volume of roughly $18 billion in 1979, foreign exchange transactions are in the rage of $4 trillion daily, up 71 percent since 2004 and 20 percent since 2007.[8] This amount exceeds the reserves of the richest

G7 Foreign Exchange Intervention

After the Japanese earthquake that struck on the east coast of Honshu on March 11, 2011, the yen strengthened considerably. In the first week after the earthquake, it hit an all-time high against the U.S. dollar of ¥76.25. This strengthening may seem illogical at first, because we would expect that a country facing a disaster would have a weakening currency. There was severe damage to Japan's economy and the Bank of Japan pumped in liquidity to provide market stability. All the more reason to expect that the yen would weaken. But instead, the yen strengthened, threatening the stability of global economic markets.

The yen strengthened on speculation by currency traders that Japanese global businesses would repatriate money to contribute to Japan's recovery. So the Bank of Japan, followed by European and North American central banks, intervened in the market. The *Financial Times* reports that within hours, the yen reversed course. The yen moved quickly to above ¥80 to the dollar, and has continued to weaken.

This G7 intervention was the first in 10 years and was prompted by the disorderly trading pattern in the yen against the dollar, threatening financial stability far beyond Japan, on a global level.

Questions:

1. With a natural disaster, why would we expect a country's currency to weaken?

2. Why were the G7 so quick to intervene?

Source: Peter Graham, "Action by G7 Marks Turning Point for Yen," *Financial Times*, Foreign Exchange Special Report, March 23, 2011, p. 2.

countries, such as China at $2.5 trillion in March 2010, so the market has increasing leverage to influence exchange rates. For example, if the foreign exchange market players believe the Japanese yen should be stronger in US$ terms, the yen will strengthen in spite of any government market intervention. The floating exchange system seems to be able to respond to market movements with flexibility and relative order. Table 8.1 summarizes currency arrangements.

Floating currencies can move against one another quickly and in large swings. Such changes have many causes, including political events, expectations, disasters, and government economic policies, such as allowing trade imbalances and deficits. These currency fluctuations create major uncertainties that managers protect against through a process called *hedging,* which is explained in Chapter 18, when we consider financial management in an international context.

TABLE 8.1	Summary of Currency Arrangements		
System	**Gold**	**Bretton Woods Fixed Gold Exchange**	**Floating**
Pros	Simplicity	Fixed rates	Flexibility (free/managed float, peg)
	Widely trusted	Supported trade growth	Reflects market forces
	Imposes monetary discipline		Handles huge volume
Cons	Impractical with large trade flows	Balance of payment deficit for U.S.	Wide swings in currency values
	Holding costs	U.S. government liabilities to foreign central banks	
		Shrinking U.S. gold reserves	
Controlling Mechanism	Gold flows: price-specie-flow mechanism (Hume)	Government adjusted rates against dollar Dollar constant against gold	Market forces with some government intervention

BANK FOR INTERNATIONAL SETTLEMENTS

One more institution that is an important part of the international monetary system is the **Bank for International Settlements (BIS).** BIS is an international organization of central banks that exists to build cooperation among them to foster monetary and financial stability. Central bankers of major industrial countries meet at least seven times a year at the BIS in Basel, Switzerland, to discuss the global financial system. BIS is the oldest international financial institution in the world, having been founded in 1930 to address war reparations imposed on Germany by the Treaty of Versailles. Today, the BIS has four main functions: a banker for central banks, a forum for international monetary cooperation, a center for research, and an agent or trustee for governments in various international financial arrangements. The BIS is known as the most discreet financial institution in the world, an explanation for its being often overlooked, both as an institution and as a physical site. If you've spent time in Basel, you know the round tower of the BIS just outside the main train station heading toward downtown. There is no sign identifying the building.

Having reviewed the basics of the international monetary system, we now are ready to focus on the financial forces external to the firm and largely uncontrollable that influence the context in which international managers make decisions. These forces include currency exchange rate fluctuation and exchange risk, as well as other financial forces that are external to the firm and have a great impact on the firm's management, such as currency exchange controls, taxation, inflation, and national-level balance-of-payments account balances. Although *uncontrollable* means that, these financial forces originate outside the business and are beyond its influence, financial managers of a company are not helpless in the face of these forces. Possible ways to manage around them are discussed in Chapter 18, when we consider financial management.

Financial Forces

We begin our review of financial forces with a focus on fluctuating currency values, examining foreign exchange (FX), FX quotation, causes of exchange rate movement, and exchange rate forecasting.

FLUCTUATING CURRENCY VALUES

In a post–Bretton Woods monetary system, freely floating currencies fluctuate against each other. At times, central banks intervene in the foreign exchange markets by buying and selling large amounts of a currency in order to affect the supply and demand of the particular currency. These interventions are not announced, but can be deduced, as in the example, we considered earlier of the G7 intervention to weaken the Japanese yen after the Japan earthquake. Yet, for the most part, the major currencies (the U.S. dollar, the British pound sterling, the Japanese yen, and the euro) are allowed by their central banks to fluctuate freely against each other. These fluctuations may be quite large. For example, in January 1999, the euro rate was established at US$1.1667. In May 2000, the euro had sunk to US$0.8895, a 23.75 percent drop. Then the trend reversed and by June 2006, the euro was trading at US$1.2644, an increase of 42.14 percent. Two years later, by early June 2008, the euro was trading at US$1.5768. Yet, by May 2010, one euro was back to US$1.28, as a result of the Greek economy's bailout problems encountered by the European Union that uncovered key flaws in the single European currency system. In March 2011, the euro was at $1.4434. Figure 8.1 presents these data, but in euro terms (i.e., how many euros one dollar would buy during this same time period). Clearly, there is significant movement in these currencies' values.

Such fluctuations have considerable impact on financial transactions. This impact of exchange rate changes on the direction of trade was discussed in Chapter 2 as one of the factors that determines whether importing or manufacturing locally is more advantageous. Another example, exaggerated for effect, will underscore the importance of currency exchange rate fluctuation to the firm. Imagine that you are operating with U.S. dollar earnings and that in May 2010 you signed a purchase agreement for the amount of $100,000,

vehicle currency
A currency used as a vehicle for international trade or investment

intervention currency
A currency used by a country to intervene in the foreign currency exchange markets, often to buy (strengthen) its own currency

Bank for International Settlements (BIS)
Institution for central bankers; operates as their bank

FIGURE 8.1

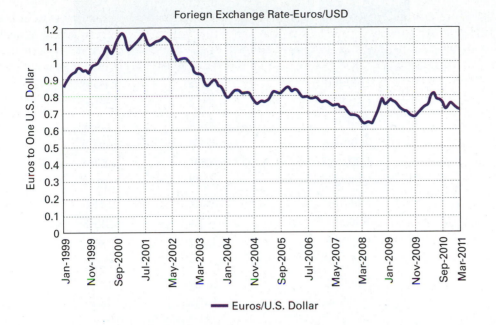

Foreign Exchange Rate-Euros/USD

Euros to One U.S. Dollar

— Euros/U.S. Dollar

reciprocal currency

In FX, using the dollar as the base currency, a currency that is quoted as dollars per unit of currency instead of in units of currency per dollar; also known as *direct quote*

payable in euros when you receive your purchase. At that time, the cost of each euro was US$0.8895. Now, years later (for the sake of our example), your purchase arrives, but the cost of each euro has risen to US$1.50, so every euro costs you US$0.6105 more than it did when you committed to the purchase. Your $100,000 purchase will cost you $161,050 or $61,050 more in U.S. dollars, a substantial difference.

We now look at why these currency fluctuations occur, that is, what forces determine exchange rates. We begin with a brief review of how exchange rates are determined and then move on to the more interesting area, what causes their fluctuation.

spot rate

The exchange rates between two currencies for delivery within two business days

Foreign Exchange

People often like to do business in their own currency because, generally, they don't like to assume the risk that can accompany currency exchange. Foreign exchange quotations—the price of one currency expressed in terms of another—are reported in the world's currency exchange markets in terms of the U.S. dollar, and increasingly, the euro, and the local currency. Historically, the US$ has had a central role as a main central reserve asset of many countries, a **vehicle currency,** and an **intervention currency.** This role continues, while the Japanese yen and the euro are increasingly joining the dollar in these functions.[9]

forward rate

The exchange rate between two currencies for delivery in the future, usually 30, 60, 90, or 180 days

EXCHANGE RATE QUOTATIONS

Table 8.2 is the listing of currency exchange rates on April 9, 2011. Prices are given for buying (bid) and selling (ask or offer). Assuming that you are operating in dollars, depending on the transaction, you might want to look at how much of the foreign currency you can purchase per U.S. dollar or its **reciprocal**, how many U.S. dollars a unit of the other currency would buy.

The exchange rate for a purchase or trade on April 9 for delivery within two days is known as the **spot rate.** The spot rate for the euro on April 9, 2011, in dollar terms, was $0.69106. There is also a **forward currency market** that allows managers to lock in purchases of currencies at known rates. The **forward rate** is the cost today for a commitment to buy or sell an agreed amount of a currency at a fixed, future date, usually on a 30-, 60-, 90-, or 180-day basis. The forward market rates can help you get a sense of where traders expect the currency to be headed. The *Financial Times* quotes forward rates for several currencies: the yen, the UK pound, the euro, and the U.S. dollar.

LO8-6 **Discuss** how foreign exchange is quoted.

forward currency market

Trading market for currency contracts deliverable 30, 60, 90, or 180 days in the future

TABLE 8.2	Average Exchange Rates on Saturday, April 9, 2011	
Saturday, April 9, 2011	**Bid**	**Ask**
EUR/USD	1.44705	1.44856
USD/EUR	0.69034	0.69106
USD/JPY	84.69	84.84
USD/CAD	0.95484	0.95610
USD/CHF	0.90593	0.90744
EUR/JPY	122.63	122.78
EUR/GBP	0.88334	0.88460
EUR/CHF	1.31201	1.31353
GBP/CHF	1.48404	1.48604
GBP/JPY	138.73	138.93
GBP/USD	1.63766	1.63916
GBP/EUR	1.13045	1.13207

Source: www.oanda.com/currency/converter/.

bid price
Highest priced buy order that is currently in the market

ask price
Lowest priced sell order that is currently in the market

Until now, we have not discussed the way the FX market operates. Most of the transactions are *over the counter (OTC),* meaning that there is no actual trading floor; trades are done electronically. The market is composed of banks and other large financial institutions such as pension funds and mutual funds. As mentioned earlier, prices consist of a **bid price** and an **ask price,** with the bid lower than the ask. The difference between the two prices, the *bid–ask spread,* provides a margin for the bank or agency. The rates listed in financial publications and sites are the interbank rates, for customers buying large quantities, usually US$1 million or more. The rates charged to small customers are much less favorable to the customer.

As you can imagine, the FX markets are large, liquid, and quite competitive, with 24-hour trading through international banks. The Bank for International Settlements reported daily turnover averages in the foreign exchange markets in the $4 trillion range for 2010. The FX markets are largely unregulated, as well. A *Wall Street Journal* article described them as "a Wild West of global capitalism . . . Unlike major stock and commodities markets, the foreign-exchange market, or FX, operates with virtually no government or regulatory oversight."[10]

LO8-7 Describe the factors that influence exchange rate movement.

Causes of Exchange Rate Movement

monetary policies
Government policies that control the amount of money in circulation and its growth rate

fiscal policies
Policies that address the collecting and spending of money by the government

Since 1973, the relative values of floating currencies and the ease of their convertibility have been set by market forces, influenced by many factors. These factors include such considerations as supply and demand forecasts for the two currencies; relative inflation in the two countries; relative productivity and unit labor cost changes; political developments, such as expected election results; expected government fiscal, monetary, and currency exchange market actions; balance-of-payments accounts; and a psychological aspect.[11] Monetary and fiscal policies of the government, such as decisions on taxation, interest rates, and trade policies, and other forces external to the business, such as world events, all may play significant roles in this process. **Monetary policies** control the amount of money in circulation, whether it is growing, and, if so, at what pace. **Fiscal policies** address the collecting and spending of money by the government.

As the earlier list of possible factors suggests, what determines exchange rates is wide and potentially complex, such that economists have not yet developed an accepted theory to explain them. Economists have been able to determine several *parity relationships*—that is, relationships of equivalence—among some of the various factors involved in exchange rate movements. It is those to which we now move our attention, because awareness of them supports an international manager's understanding of FX markets. Two of these relationships, interest rate parity and purchasing power parity, are fundamental to our further consideration of exchange rates. They both rest on and are applications of the **law of one price,** which states that in an efficient market, like products will have like prices. If price differences exist, the process of **arbitrage** (buying and selling to make a profit with no risk) will quickly close any gaps and the markets will be back at equilibrium.

When the law of one price is applied to interest rates, it suggests that interest rates vary to take account of differing anticipated levels of inflation. The economic explanation of this relationship, which results in interest rate parity, is known as the **Fisher effect.** It states that the real interest rate will be the nominal interest rate minus the expected rate of inflation. Where the real rate of interest (rr) is equal to the nominal interest rate (rn) minus the expected rate of inflation (I):

$$rr = (rn) - I$$

Thus, an increase in the expected inflation rate will lead to an increase in the interest rate. A decrease in the expected inflation rate will lead to a decrease in the interest rate. An investor would want to earn more in a high-inflation environment to compensate for the effect of inflation on the investment.

An interesting aspect of interest rate parity is known as the **international Fisher effect,** which simply says that the interest rate differentials for any two currencies reflect the expected change in their exchange rates.[12] For example, if the nominal interest rate in the United States is 5 percent per year and in the EU it is 3 percent, we would expect the dollar to decrease against the euro by 2 percent over the year or the euro to strengthen against the dollar by that same amount.

A second parity relationship is **purchasing power parity (PPP).** PPP shows the number of units of a currency required to buy the same basket of goods and services in the foreign market that one dollar would buy in the United State, or in another home market with that market's currency. It is the result of the law of one price applied to a basket of commodity goods. PPP suggests that for a dollar to buy as much in the United Kingdom as in the United States, the cost of the goods in the UK should equal their U.S. cost times the exchange rate between the dollar and pound. This relationship is expressed in the following equation, where P is the price of a basket of commodity goods,

$$£P(\$/£) = \$P$$

Another way to think about what PPP theory states is that currency exchange rates between two countries should equal the ratio of the price levels of their commodity baskets. This relationship is expressed in the following equation, where P is the price of a basket of commodity goods,

$$£P(\$/£) = \$P$$

For example, if a basket of goods costs $1,500 in the United States and £1,000 in the United Kingdom, the PPP exchange rate would be $1.50/£. If, in the trading market, the actual spot exchange rate was $2/£, the pound would be overvalued by 33 percent, or, equivalently, the dollar undervalued by 25 percent.

The Economist, a British weekly magazine, presents a playful application of PPP theory in its "Big Mac index," substituting a Big Mac for a basket of goods. This index suggests that in the long term, many of the developing countries' currencies are undervalued and the euro and many European currencies are overvalued. The Big Mac PPP is the exchange rate that would have a Big Mac in other countries costing as it does in the United States. You can check the latest Big Mac index and view a video explaining *The Economist*'s efforts to make economics as simple as it ought to be at www.economist.com/markets/bigmac. So, for example, in October 2010 in China, the Big Mac in U.S. dollars at the prevailing yuan–dollar exchange rate cost $2.18, whereas in the United States a four-city average price was $3.71. In effect, the yuan is 41 percent below the implied PPP exchange rate. That's a

---

law of one price
Concept that in an efficient market, like products will have like prices

arbitrage
The process of buying and selling instantaneously to make profit with no risk

Fisher effect
The relationship between real and nominal interest rates: The real interest rate will be the nominal interest rate minus the expected rate of inflation

international Fisher effect
Concept that the interest rate differentials for any two currencies will reflect the expected change in their exchange rates

purchasing power parity (PPP)
PPP shows the number of units of a currency required to buy the same basket of goods and services in the foreign market that one dollar would buy in the United States or other home market

pretty inexpensive burger. *The Economist* claims that in the long run, its Big Mac index performs pretty well, with many of the discounted and premium-fetching currencies correcting. Remember, too, that the price of a Big Mac represents more than a basket of tradable goods, the situation PPP theory describes. For example, the McDonald's service level we may receive with our Big Mac can't be traded, nor can McDonald's brand image. Nevertheless, the Big Mac index is a helpful and playful way to get a quick sense of relative currency values and where they may be heading. Looking at the latest version of the Big Mac index might help you choose your next bargain vacation spot.

Now that we have reviewed two parity relationships, interest rate parity, which includes the Fisher effect and the international Fisher effect, and purchasing power parity, we can look more closely at exchange rate prediction.

EXCHANGE RATE FORECASTING

LO8-8 Outline the approaches to exchange rate forecasting.

Because exchange rate movements are so important to all aspects of international business—production, sourcing, marketing, and finance—many business decisions take the risk of exchange rate movement into consideration. There are several approaches to forecasting, and three of the main ones are the efficient market approach, the fundamental approach, and the technical approach. We briefly examine each.

The **efficient market approach** assumes that current prices fully reflect all available relevant information in the environment. This also suggests that forward exchange rates are the best possible predictor of future spot rates because they will have taken into account all the available information. For example, if interest rates are different between two countries, the forward rate will reflect this (international Fisher effect). The efficient market approach does not suggest that the forward rate will be the future spot rate with perfect accuracy. Rather, the divergences will be random. An approach related to the efficient market approach is called the **random walk hypothesis,** and it holds because of the short-term unpredictability of factors, the best predictor of tomorrow's prices is today's prices.[13]

The **fundamental approach** to exchange rate prediction looks at the underlying forces that play a role in determining exchange rates and develops various econometric models that attempt to capture the variables and their correct relationships. Eun and Resnick, two noted international finance scholars, have surveyed the research on the various fundamental models and conclude that "the fundamental models failed to more accurately forecast exchange rates than either the forward rate model, which we have termed the efficient market model, or the random walk model."[14]

The third approach to exchange rate forecasting, **technical analysis,** looks at history and then projects it forward. It analyzes historic data for trends and then, assuming that what was past will be future, projects these trends forward. Technical analysts think in terms of waves and trends. There is no theoretical underpinning to the technical approach, and scholarly academic studies tend to dismiss it. Yet currency-trading marketing materials suggest that traders often use it.

As for the performance of these various approaches, research by Eun and Sabherwal on the exchange rate forecasts of major commercial banks indicates that the 10 banks in the study could not outperform the random walk model.[15] Their findings also suggest that the forward exchange rate and the spot rate were both about equal in value for predicting future exchange rates. The evidence available indicates that neither the technical nor the fundamental approach outperforms the efficient market approach. Additional research suggests that combining forecasts generated by these and additional models may be helpful.

We have examined a major financial force that international managers have to address— foreign exchange fluctuations, their causes, and their prediction. How managers actually deal with the risk that such currency fluctuation exposure creates is a topic we address in Chapter 18. There are many other financial forces that confront international managers than those we will discuss. For example, tariffs are a financial force because they represent increased costs and can change without notice. You can see the current U.S. tariff schedule at the U.S. International Trade Commission Web site (www.usitc.gov/tata/hts/bychapter/index.htm). One interesting aspect of the tariff schedule is how specific it is. For example, in Harmonized Tariff Schedule (HTS) category 0704.10.20, cauliflower, the tariff rate is 2.5 percent

efficient market approach
Assumption that current market prices fully reflect all available relevant information

random walk hypothesis
Assumption that the unpredictability of factors suggests that the best predictor of tomorrow's prices is today's prices

fundamental approach
Exchange rate prediction based on econometric models that attempt to capture the variables and their correct relationships

technical analysis
An approach that analyzes data for trends and then projects these trends forward

Debate: Fixed FX Rates, Perhaps Hooked to Gold, or Floating Rates, Hooked to Faith?

Most economists support the idea that floating exchange rates are beneficial for the world economy. A small minority of experts advocates a return to the gold standard and fixed exchange rates. Let's further consider this choice.

In the early 1970s, the U.S. government could not continue to guarantee that dollars floating around the world would be convertible to gold at the agreed rate. So, the U.S. decoupled the dollar from gold, with the immediate effect that the world's currency exchange rates were not fixed any more.[a]

The economists, Obstfeld and Rogoff, argue that the main reason exchange rates could not stay fixed was the rapid evolution of world capital markets since the 1950s. Because the volume of global transactions started exceeding most countries' foreign exchange reserves, governments could no longer intervene effectively to sustain the value of their currency. Until the volume of trade grew, governments would buy or sell significant amounts of their currencies in the global markets in an effort to sustain their currency's supply and demand equilibrium. At the same time, a speculative attack on a specific currency by the "market" could cause a run on a currency that a government could not counter. As we have already seen, with the advent of the Internet, in less than 15 years the amount of *daily* foreign exchange transactions has increased from $1 trillion in 1994 to more than $4 trillion in 2010. Thus, it is difficult to imagine the day when the main currency regimes around the world would be dominated by fixed rate relationships.

Even if a central bank could support its currency effectively, the impact on the rest of the economy could be considerable. In this chapter, we have discussed the relationship between exchange rates and interest rates. In an environment where currency A is becoming relatively stronger than currency B, the interest rates in country A are likely to be higher than those in country B. This increases the cost of doing business in country A versus country B. Moreover, interest rate movements, exchange rate values, and inflationary pressures tend to be interlinked. Finally, the role of speculators cannot be overlooked. The currency market impressions of a currency's reputation can be enough to scare buyers away from a perceived weak currency toward a strong one. As with any other buying–selling relationship, this will weaken further the currency that buyers are fleeing from and strengthen the one they are going to. Then, the strengthening currency has a negative impact on that country's ability to export.

The discussion up to here shows that we may not like "floating exchange rates" for whatever reasons, but is there an alternative in today's globalized economy and global capital markets? What are the key arguments for trying to "fix" exchange rates? Two are as follows:[b]

First, exchange rate changes increase the risk and cost of trade for industries that are based on producing goods. These industries have products that have to be shipped from one country to another. This process is associated with a time lag from when an order is placed, to when the producer ships, to when the buyer receives a product. These three points in time may be associated with very different exchange rates among the currencies of the two countries involved. Whether it is the manufacturer or the buyer or both who bear the risk, there are ways to minimize foreign exchange risk related to timing. All these ways introduce a new cost to the transaction. Had the exchange rate been fixed, this cost would not arise.

Second, exchange rate fluctuations may lead to protectionist measures that can impede trade and deprive a country's people from trade benefits. Yet, fixing the exchange rate means that the government is also depriving itself of the ability to manage its monetary policy. Finally, fixed-rate proponents say that fixed exchange rates impose monetary discipline on a government. A long, logical explanation shows, however, that this implies isolation from actions of other governments, an impossible option today.

Questions:

1. Given the preceding discussion, what is your own broad conclusion about the viability of fixed or floating exchange rates?

2. What are the key arguments for fixed exchange rates?

[a]M. Obstfeld and K. Rogoff, "The Mirage of Fixed Exchange Rates," *Journal of Economic Perspectives* 9, no. 4 (1995), pp. 73–96.

[b]P. B. Kenen, "Fixed versus Floating Exchange Rates," *Cato Journal* 20, no. 1 (2000), pp. 109–13.

---

between June 5 and October 25, when the U.S. crop is being harvested. If the cauliflower is cut or sliced, the rate is 14 percent at any time. We now look at some of the most significant additional financial forces, beginning with currency exchange controls, and then move on to taxation, inflation and interest rates, and balance-of-payments effects.

Currency Exchange Controls

A government can limit the amount of its currency that can be exchanged for another currency in a particular transaction. Controls differ greatly from country to country and even within a country, depending on the type of transaction. In general, the developed countries have

LO8-9 Discuss the influence of currency exchange controls on international business.

few or no currency exchange controls, but these nations are a minority of the world's countries. Many developing countries, though, such as Mexico, have reduced or eliminated such controls in order to encourage foreign investment. The international business manager must be aware of whether currency exchange controls exist both before and while doing business in any country, because the currency exchange control situation can change quickly.

Convertible currencies can be exchanged for other currencies without restrictions. Known as hard currencies, these include the Japanese yen, the U.S. dollar, the British pound, and the euro. When a currency is nonconvertible, its value is arbitrarily fixed, typically at a rate higher than its value in the free market. In such a case, the government imposes exchange controls to limit or prohibit the legal use of its currency in international transactions. The government also requires that all purchases or sales of other currencies be made through a government agency. Limitations might also restrict the amount of domestic currency transferred into foreign currency. Such restrictions may influence a firm's ability to repatriate profits, that is, return profits to the home country. A black market inevitably springs up alongside such currency restrictions, but it is of little use to the international manager, who wants to abide by the laws.

Countries put limitations on the convertibility of their currency when they are concerned that their foreign reserves could be depleted. Foreign reserves are a source of currency for foreign debt service, import purchases, and other demands for foreign currency that domestic banks might encounter. The Ukraine, South Africa, Pakistan, and China have exchange controls. The Chinese renminbi is convertible in current accounts (accounts for day-to-day banking) but not capital accounts (longer-term accounts), although recent hints in the international financial press suggest that China may be loosening controls so that the renminbi could become a hard currency, used for trade and as a part of foreign reserves.

When a government requires the firm to have permission to purchase foreign currency, the exchange rates often are above the free-market rate. If the government doesn't grant permission or if the cost of foreign currency is too high, the blocked currency can be used only within the country. Such repatriation limitations usually present international managers with the problem of finding suitable products and investments within the country or establishing other arrangements to move their stored value beyond the country's border, such as barter or swaps with other foreign firms needing local currency inside the country.

LO8-10 Summarize the influences of differences in taxation and inflation rates on international business.

Taxation

We mentioned the legal aspects of taxation in Chapter 7. Taxation is also a financial force whose impact is significant. If a corporation can achieve a lower tax burden than its competitors have, it can lower prices to its customers or generate higher revenue with which to pay higher wages and dividends. Governments around the world widely use three types of taxation to generate revenue: income tax, value-added tax (VAT), and withholding tax. The *income tax* is a direct tax on personal and corporate income. Table 8.3 compares corporate taxation rates in selected countries. The effective tax rate may be lower due to tax breaks that are a result of effective lobbying, tax planning strategies, and creative accounting. The *New York Times* recently reported that in 2010, General Electric paid no U.S. taxes and received a tax benefit of $3.2 billion.[16] This, despite the 35 percent U.S. corporate tax rate.

TABLE 8.3   Corporate Tax Rates, 2011

Country	Percent
Switzerland[a]	8.5–21.17
Ireland	12.50
Germany[b]	15.83
Canada	16.50
Turkey	20.00
China[c]	25.00
Netherlands	25.50
Finland	26.00
United Kingdom	28.00
Mexico	30.00
Australia	30.00
Japan	30.00
Brazil	34.40
India	33.99
France	34.43
United States (on worldwide income, plus any state taxes)	35.00

[a] incl canton rates and vary by location

[b] may vary by location

[c] lower rates for some industries

Source: The Tax Foundation, *National and State Income Tax Rates,* 2011, www.taxfoundation.org/taxdata/show/23034.html (accessed April 12, 2011). *Reprinted with permission.*

A *value-added tax (VAT)* is a tax charged on the value added to a good as it moves through production from raw materials to final purchaser. It is really a sales tax whose payment documentation from one stage to another from production through to the final buyer becomes important for tax credits, because the seller collects the tax for the goods sold and then receives credits for VAT already paid earlier in the production process. Countries that levy value-added taxes are permitted by World Trade Organization (WTO) rules to rebate the value-added taxes to exporters, an incentive that makes the exports less expensive and thus more competitive.

The third general tax category is the *withholding tax.* This is an indirect tax levied on passive income (income such as dividends, royalties, and interest) that the corporation would pay out to nonresidents, people, or companies in another tax jurisdiction. Countries establish bilateral tax treaties to categorize passive-income withholding rates. For example, on interest the United States withholds 30 percent from residents of non–tax treaty countries. From UK residents, it withholds nothing, while from residents of Pakistan it withholds 30 percent.

International companies need to understand tax laws in each country in which they operate and how those tax laws relate to tax laws in other countries. This additional tax burden can create financial risk, but it can also be an opportunity for savings, given good tax planning.

Inflation and Interest Rates

Inflation is a trend of rising prices. Some economists hold that it is caused by demand exceeding supply, while others view the cause as an increase in the money supply. All, however, agree that in an inflationary economy, prices increase. Table 8.4 shows inflation levels in selected countries. Japan, the EU, and the United States have had relatively good records in keeping inflation down in recent years. Historically, Latin American countries have had inflation troubles. However, these trends have been gradually reversed. Brazil experienced 3,118 percent inflation in 1990 and was able to decrease this to 5.9 percent in 2010. The overall highest inflation rate to date was found in Zimbabwe, where it reached 14.9 billion percent in July 2008. Most inflation is measured by a *consumer price index (CPI),* the price changes for a basket of consumer goods.

TABLE 8.4   Country Inflation Rates

Country	Percent Inflation Latest[a]	Percent Inflation 2010
Argentina	10	10.9
Australia	2.7	2.7
Brazil	6.3	5.9
Chile	3.4	3.0
China	4.9	4.6
Euro area	2.6	2.2
France	1.7	1.8
Germany	2.10	1.7
Greece	4.4	5.2
India	8.82	9.47
Ireland	2.2	1.3
Italy	2.5	1.9
Japan	0.0	0.0
Nigeria	11.1	11.8
Russia	9.5	8.8
Spain	3.6	3.0
Switzerland	1.0	0.5
Turkey	4.0	6.4
United Kingdom	4.4	3.7
United States	2.1	1.5
Venezuela	29.6	27.2

[a]Percent inflation latest is for the year ending on April 1, 2011.

Source: *From Trading Economics, http://www.tradingeconomics.com/World-Economy/Inflation-Rates.aspx (accessed April 12, 2011). Reprinted with permission.*

Inflation, a financial force external to companies, affects the firm in several major ways. First, the inflation rate determines the real cost of borrowing in capital markets. You'll recall the Fisher effect from our discussion of exchange rates. When the firm operates in multiple countries, it has multiple currency exposures, and the complexity of dealing with inflation increases because inflation rates vary among countries. Should management decide to raise capital, should this be done through equity or debt? In which capital markets? In what currency? These are the critical questions answers to which inflation rates play a role.

Further, increasing inflation rates encourage borrowing (debt) because the loan will be repaid with inflated, cheaper money. But high inflation rates bring high interest rates because banks have to offer more reward to draw in deposits. Then, inflation may discourage lending because lenders may fear that, even with high interest rates, the amount repaid plus interest would be worth less than the amount lent. Thus, there is a relationship between inflation and interest rates. And we have seen in our discussion of the international Fisher effect, there is a relationship between currency exchange rate trends and interest rates. So, there is a relationship between inflation and currency exchange rates. Inflated currencies tend to weaken. In inflated economies, instead of lending, the money holder may buy something that is expected to increase in value, thereby further fueling inflation. In Brazil during a recent inflationary period, farmers would hoard their crops, not bring them to the market, and then use them in barter for imported farming equipment and Mercedes cars. Lenders have begun to use variable interest rates, which rise or fall with inflation, to shift financial risk to the borrower. This shift requires that the borrower be much more careful about borrowing. The original rate and any future changes are based on a reference interest rate, such as the U.S. prime rate (rate of interest banks lend to their best customers) or the London Interbank Offer Rate (the bank-to-bank interest rate in London—LIBOR).

Andrew Crane: Develop Experience with Global Financial Forces by Traveling and Working Abroad!

I was raised in San Diego, CA, and developed a passion for surfing early in my life. As a result, I have been able to surf almost every day since I was 12 years old. While I was at university at Cal Poly in San Luis Obispo, I remained an avid surfer, even being named the MVP on the school's surf team. I ultimately earned a B.S. degree in Business Administration with a concentration in entrepreneurship.

Besides surfing, I also have a passion for travel and all things international. From an early age, I have been exposed to foreign cultures through family travels abroad, and I was able to develop fluency in Spanish as well as English. Then, during my years as a university student, I would save money during the school year in order to allow me to travel during the summers. I studied abroad in Spain for one quarter during my junior year, and also used that opportunity to travel a bit elsewhere in Europe. My career goals are to be involved in startup business projects and to own and operate my own business one day soon, preferably one that will either be located outside the U.S. or that will involve extensive international travel.

I have traveled throughout 32 countries so far in my life, mainly in Latin America, Europe, and Africa, as well as spending some time in Australia and Indonesia. For my work experiences in Africa and Latin America, I was involved with a non-governmental organization (NGO) that needed someone who was enthusiastic about working in foreign countries and was fluent in Spanish. My job in the Dominican Republic consisted of relationship management between a micro-finance institution and the donor partner from the United States. I also reviewed the financial operations of the Dominican partner as well as translated English/Spanish for business meetings and field visits. My work in Africa consisted of work in the area of microfinance for schools, helping to promote greater affordability in the educational sector.

My international work experience began after graduating from high school, when I received an opportunity to intern with a NGO in Peru, Nicaragua, and the Dominican Republic. Later, while at university, I had the good fortune to find a job in Nicaragua as a property management liaison at an upscale resort community by the ocean. I decided to push my university graduation back a term in order to work in this management position for six months. It turned out to be one of the best decisions of my life, resulting in the most fun experience abroad that I have had so far.

While working in Nicaragua, I really developed an appreciation for that country's people and also for working with the land. Maybe it's my Southern roots, but I really enjoyed planting trees and even overseeing a farming project. The people there were so wonderful, and I still keep in contact with some of the people who worked for me as well as people I lived with.

My experience in Nicaragua also taught me quite a bit about management, corporate politics, and communication. On the management end of things, I learned how to delegate tasks to anywhere from 6 to 24 men under my control and to manage the tasks they were doing at different places on the property at the same time. As for corporate politics, I learned a lot about the political factors that drive the decisions of upper management. And as for communication, due to the lack of receiving it from my superiors, I learned the importance of communicating effectively with one's subordinates. It's really difficult to please all parties when nobody knows what they are supposed to be doing.

Immediately after graduating from university, I worked for a couple of months in Africa. It was an excellent learning opportunity. At the same time, the language barrier that I encountered while working in Africa represented perhaps the biggest challenge that I have had to address in my work abroad. As I discovered during my work in Ghana and Rwanda, you will always find quite a few nationals who do not speak English – even when English is the country's official language. I dealt with this by hiring a sharp intern for US$100 a month. This fellow was not only able to translate proficiently, but also assist in my work, making it money well spent.

In terms of preparation for my travels, I suppose there are only so many things one can do to prepare oneself for living in another culture. I have personally found that the most important aspect of being prepared for working abroad is having an open mind. Once you are able to realize this, along with understanding that most of the rest of the world does not run on the Western orientation toward time, business is much easier to conduct in foreign countries!

My advice to those who are interested in exploring international business: go travel, step out of your comfort zone, and see what unexpected opportunities life will throw your way. Consider going to a country and simply hanging out for a month or so. You would be amazed at how many opportunities there are for Westerners in the developing world once you get involved in the local scene. However, most of the time you have to be in that specific country to hear about them. It's not as if job opportunities like these are posted on craigslist.org or jobs.com.

Resources for Your Global Career

Knowing How to Follow the International Money Trail

Money is what business—international or domestic—is all about. Understanding currencies, currency fluctuations, exchange rates, and the mechanics of buying and selling foreign currency are

(continued)

fundamental tools of the international business professional, and these tools are used daily in the practice of international trade. In fact, *arbitrage*, or foreign currency trading, is growing into an increasing profitable commodity market in banks and financial institutions worldwide. The information here will help you understand how to follow the international money trail.

How Currencies Are Designated

Virtually every country in the world has its own currency and the euro (€) is the now the single currency of most EU countries. Some countries like Japan with the yen (¥) and Great Britain with the pound sterling (£) use symbols to identify their currencies. Most world currencies use the first letter of the currency name such as "P" but globally this can be confusing. Does P20 mean 20 pesetas, pesos, pounds, pataca, pa'anga, or another currency? And, if it means 20 pesos, are they pesos from Mexican, Bolivia, Argentina, Chile, Colombia, or some other country? To address this confusion, the international banking community developed the ISO 4217 set of currency abbreviations to standardize how currencies are identified.

ISO 4217 uses three-letter abbreviations such as USD for the United States dollar. When currencies are defined by supranational entities, the ISO 4217 system assigns two-letter entity codes starting with "X" to be used in place of country codes as in the case of XCD for the Central Caribbean dollar.

Depending on whether you are using e-mail, news, or the Web, some currency symbols may be used but many others *should not* be used. In e-mail and news, the only currency symbol that may safely be used is $ (the dollar symbol). To express a value in any other currency you should use the ISO 4217 abbreviation. For £ 10, GBP 10 should be used. In HTML, the only currency symbols that may be used safely are: "$" for dollar, "¢" for cent, "£" for pound, "¥" for yen, and "¤" to show a generic currency. To show the value of any other currency, the ISO 4217 abbreviation should be used.

Source: http://www.jhall.demon.co.uk/currency/ (accessed June 3, 2011).

World Fact: According to the Sauder School of Business at the University of British Columbia, there are 245 countries and territories in the world, each with a currency. Some countries use a common currency such the GBP in UK countries and the USD in Puerto Rico.

Source: http://fx.sauder.ubc.ca/currency_table.html (accessed June 3, 2011).

Your Worldwide Resources:

- Currency converter for 164 currencies: http://www.oanda.com/convert/classic
- Track currency value fluctuations: http://www.x-rates.com/
- See what individual country currencies look like: http://www.banknotes.com/images.htm

- ISO 4217 abbreviations for all of the world's currencies: http://fx.sauder.ubc.ca/currency_table.html
- Expand or just brush up on your financial language at this comprehensive glossary of financial terms and phrases: http://www.investorwords.com/
- Links to the world's major stock exchanges: http://www.tdd.lt/slnews/Stock_Exchanges/Stock.Exchanges.htm
- Links to worldwide stock and commodities exchanges: http://www.libraries.rutgers.edu/rul/rr_gateway/research_guides/busi/stocks.shtml
- Overview of commodity exchanges: http://www.unctad.org/infocomm/exchanges/ex_overview.htm
- To read the *Financial Times:* http://www.ft.com/home/

Starting Your Career in International Finance—Where Do You Look for a Job?

The allure and the rewards of a career in international finance—being a power broker dealing in stocks and bonds, commodities, or currency on a 24/7 basis across the time zones of the globe—can be quite dramatic. So where are the jobs in international finance located? Where are the major financial markets of the world? The top 11 banking centers of the world are as follows:

1. New York
2. London
3. Hong Kong
4. Singapore
5. Tokyo
6. Chicago
7. Zurich
8. Geneva
9. Shenzhen
10. Sydney
11. Shanghai

Source: http://www.huffingtonpost.com/2010/03/15/worlds-top-financial-cent_n_498394.html#s73819&title=11_Shanghai (accessed June 3, 2011)

For job and career information within areas of international finance, the following Websites can be valuable:

- Fincareer.com, http://www.fincareer.com/
- GoAbroad.com, http://jobs.goabroad.com/search/finance/jobs-abroad-1
- International Finance Corporation, a World Bank Group, http://www.ifc.org/ifcext/careers.nsf/Content/CurrentOps
- Kiva, a global organization devoted to microfinance, http://www.kiva.org/

As Table 8.5 suggests, April 2011 interest rates in most countries vary across a small range. This trend may be explained by the integration of financial markets as they become more globalized. In the 13 countries in Table 8.5, the average interest rate was 3.58 percent. A similar figure in 1993 was 6.9 percent.

Finally, inflation rates cause the cost of the goods and services produced in a country to rise, and thus the goods and services become less competitive globally. Producers in the high-inflation country find export sales more difficult. Such conditions may lead

TABLE 8.5   Sample Interest Rates

Central Bank or Country	Percent Interest Rate for April 2011
Bank of England	0.50
Bank of Japan	0.10
European Central Bank	1.25
Federal Reserve	0.25
Swiss National Bank	0.25
The Reserve Bank of Australia	4.75
Bank of Canada	1.00
Brazil	11.75
China	6.06
India	6.75
South Korea	3.00
Mexico	4.50
Turkey	6.50

Source: www.worldinterestrates.info/ (accessed April 13, 2011).

to balance-of-payments deficits in the trade account, so under these conditions management must be alert to government policy changes that attempt to correct these deficits. Such changes could include more restrictive fiscal or monetary policies, currency controls, export incentives, and import obstacles. Because monitoring balance-of-payment accounts is important, we now take a look at them.

Balance of Payments

The **balance of payments (BOP)** is a record of a country's transactions with the rest of the world. BOP data are of interest to international businesspeople for several reasons. First, the balance of payments reveals demand for the country's currency. If a country is exporting more than it imports, there will be a high demand for the currency in other countries in order to pay for the exported goods. This demand may well create pressure on the exporter's currency, in which case, it might be expected to strengthen. Conversely, when a country imports more than it exports, the currency might be expected to weaken, or, if not a floating currency, to be devalued. Faced with a trade deficit, a government might lean toward restrictive monetary or fiscal policies. Currency or trade controls could be introduced. The BOP trend also helps managers predict what sort of changes in the economic environment might develop in the country. This prediction could impact their choice of strategic risks to take in a specific country.

balance of payments (BOP)
Record of a country's transactions with the rest of the world

BOP Accounts   The BOP accounts are recorded in double-entry bookkeeping form. Each international transaction is an exchange of assets with a debit and a credit side. Payments *to* other countries, funds flowing out, are tracked as debits (−), while transactions that are payments *from* other countries, funds flowing in, are tracked as credits (+). The statement of a country's BOP is divided into several accounts and many subaccounts, as outlined in Figure 8.2.

LO11 **Explain**
the significance of the balance of payments to international business decisions.

Deficits and Surpluses in BOP Accounts   The BOP current account and capital account add up to the total account. A deficit in the current account is always accompanied by an equal surplus in the capital account, and vice versa. Let's see how this works. If you purchase a case of French wine in the United States for $200, your payment, as it heads out of the United States and to the French winery, will be recorded as a debit in the U.S. current account. Once the winery receives your dollars, it has to do something with them. If the treasurer of the winery decides to deposit your payment in a dollar account at a U.S. bank,

FIGURE 8.2   Balance of Payments Major Accounts

I. Current Account

Net changes in exports and imports of goods and services—tangibles and intangibles.

    A. Goods or *merchandise account*—tangibles; net balance known as the *trade balance*.

    B. *Services account*—intangibles.

    C. *Unilateral transfers*—transfers with no reciprocity (gifts, aid, migrant worker earnings), to satisfy the needs of double-entry recording, entry made that treats the aid or gift as purchase of goodwill.

II. Capital Account

Net changes in a nation's international financial assets and liabilities; credit entry occurs when resident sells stock, bonds, or other financial assets to nonresident. Money flows to resident, while resident's long-term international liabilities (debit entry) increase.

    A. *Direct investment*—located in one country and controlled by residents of another country.

    B. *Portfolio investment*—long-term investments without control.

    C. *Short-term capital flows*—such as currency exchange rate and interest rate hedging in the forward, futures, option, and swap markets; volatility and transaction privacy make this entry the least reliable measure.

III. Official Reserves Account

    A. *Gold* imports and exports.

    B. *Foreign exchange* (foreign currencies) held by government.

    C. *Liabilities* to foreign central banks.

the amount will show up as a credit in the U.S. capital account. If the winery exchanges your dollar payment for euros, then the bank receiving the dollars will have to make a decision about how to spend or invest the dollars. Sooner or later, these dollars will show up as a credit on the U.S. account.

Contrary to the commonly held belief, a current account deficit is not always a sign of bad economic conditions. It means that the country is importing capital. This is no more unnatural or dangerous than importing wine or cheese. The deficit is a response to conditions in the country. Among these conditions could be excessive inflation, low productivity, or inadequate saving. In the case of the United States, a current account deficit could occur because investments in the United States are secure and profitable. If there is a problem, it is in the underlying conditions and not in the deficit per se.[17] Countries with relatively high price levels, gross national products, interest rates, and exchange rates, as well as relatively low barriers to imports and attractive investment opportunities, are more likely to have current account deficits than are other countries.[18]

In recent years, the United States has had a substantial deficit in its current account. Citizens of the United States are importing more goods than they are exporting, yet exporting more services than they are importing. There also is a surplus in the U.S. capital account. Those dollars that leave the United States to pay for imported goods come back into the United States in the form of foreign-owned investments (e.g., Treasury bills and investment property in New York City). So let's remember that a deficit or surplus in the current account cannot be explained or evaluated without simultaneously examining an equal surplus or deficit in the capital account.

In our review of the monetary system and financial forces, we have briefly examined three currency arrangements: gold, the Bretton Woods system (which was a modified fixed rate system), and a floating system. We've also looked at our current monetary system and the Bank for International Settlements. Then we reviewed the major financial forces with which the firm has to work: fluctuating currency values, currency exchange controls, taxation, inflation, and interest rates. Finally, we reviewed the balance of payments accounts and their significance to the international manager.

LO8-1 Describe the international monetary system's evolution

The gold standard operated to support trade until 1914. Currencies were pegged to gold and adjustments were made by the exchange of gold. Next followed a period of fixed rates known as the Bretton Woods system, with the U.S. dollar exchangeable for gold. This pushed the United States into a persistent deficit and reduced gold in the U.S. reserves. The United States stopped the exchange of dollars for gold, and the dollar was allowed to float freely against other currencies on the open market. This began the period of floating exchange rates, which is where we are now. The IMF's Smithsonian Agreement worked out the rules and exchange regimes for the floating system, ranging from free floats to dirty floats to pegged currencies.

LO8-2 Explain the Triffin paradox.

When the U.S. dollar was used as a reserve currency and backed by gold, the United States, in order to satisfy the growing demand for reserves (because countries would hold dollars as a proxy for gold), was forced to run a balance-of-payments deficit. That is, in the United States the flow of dollars out was greater than the flow in; the demand on dollars for holding outside the country was greater than those that flowed in as a result of export sales and foreign investment. There's an interesting paradox associated with reserve currencies that was first pointed out by economist Robert Triffin: such a deficit as the United States experienced because the U.S. dollar was the international reserve currency is unavoidable. It eventually inspires a lack of confidence in the reserve currency, which leads to a financial crisis. That is, the more dollars foreigners held the less confidence they had in the currency.

LO8-3 Describe the floating currency exchange rate system, including the IMF currency arrangements.

Floating currency exchange rates are rates that are allowed to float against other currencies and that are determined by market forces. There are eight categories of exchange rate arrangements that the IMF now uses to describe how countries position their currencies in relation to other currencies. They range from not having any legal tender to having fixed and then freely floating exchange rate arrangements—that is, they are characterized by their degree of flexibility. The eight categories are no separate legal tender, currency board arrangements, fixed peg, peg within a horizontal band, crawling peg, crawling band, managed float, and independent float.

LO8-4 Discuss the purpose of the Bank for International Settlements.

The purpose of the Bank for International Settlements is to operate as a central bankers' bank. In addition, it serves as a forum for central bankers' discussions, leading to international monetary cooperation; as a center for research; and as an agent or trustee for governments in various international financial arrangements.

LO8-5 Explain the impact of fluctuating currency values.

Fluctuating currency values affect costs and valuation, so they are a critical factor in decision making for the firm. Marked and sudden shifts in currency exchange rates have increased under the current free-floating system, which presents a risk for the firm. Factors that influence exchange rate movement include basic supply and demand of the currency, interest rates, inflation rates, expectations of the future, and the monetary and fiscal policies of the government.

LO8-6 Discuss how foreign exchange is quoted.

The exchange rate is either spot or forward. The spot rate is for a purchase or trade for delivery within two days. The forward rate is the cost today for a commitment to buy or sell an agreed amount of a currency at a fixed, future date. There is a bid and an ask, and the market itself it an over-the-counter market. Quotations for one currency are in terms of another currency.

LO8-7 Describe the factors that influence exchange rate movement.

Since 1973, the relative values of floating currencies have been set by market forces, influenced by many factors. These factors include such considerations as supply and demand forecasts for the two currencies; relative inflation in the two countries; relative productivity and unit labor cost changes; political developments, such as expected election results; expected government fiscal, monetary, and currency exchange market actions; balance-of-payments accounts; and a psychological aspect. What actually determines exchange rates is wide and potentially complex, such that economists have not yet developed an accepted theory to explain them. Economists have been able to determine several *parity relationships*—that is, relationships of equivalence—among some of the various factors involved in exchange rate movements. These include interest rate parity and purchasing power parity.

LO8-8 Outline the approaches to exchange rate forecasting.

There are three major approaches to exchange rate forecasting: the efficient market approach, the fundamental approach, and the technical approach. The efficient market approach assumes that current prices fully reflect all available relevant information in the environment, so forward exchange rates are the best predictor of future spot rates because they will have taken into account all the available information. The fundamental approach looks at the underlying forces that play a role in determining exchange rates and develops various econometric models that attempt to capture the variables and their correct relationships. Technical analysis analyzes historic data for trends and then, assuming that what was past will be future, projects these trends forward.

LO8-9 Discuss the influence of currency exchange controls on international business.

Governments can restrict the exchange of their currency for other currencies, which may greatly affect international business. These controls limit the amount of foreign currency purchases or exchanges made inside the country. These limits may differ for citizens and noncitizens and may limit the firm's ability to pay for imports and to repatriate profits. Governments set currency exchange controls to reduce depletion of their foreign currency reserves. The international business manager must be aware of whether currency exchange controls exist both before and while doing business in any country, because the currency exchange control situation can change quickly.

LO8-10 Summarize the influences of differences in taxation and inflation rates on international business.

Financial forces beyond the control of the firm, such as differences in taxation and inflation rates, can influence the firm greatly, so they must be monitored and predicted constantly. Taxes increase the firm's costs, whether they are value-added taxes or income taxes. Inflation is a trend toward higher prices and is measured by the consumer price index. Inflation is accompanied by higher interest rates. The firm will want to limit exposure in inflation-prone economies and make decisions about debt in a strategic way. Inflation also affects consumer decisions.

LO8-11 Explain the significance of the balance of payments to international business decisions.

The balance of payments, which reveals demand for the country's currency, is a significant sign of potential issues. By monitoring BOP data, the firm can build a sense of a possible future. If a country is exporting more than it imports, there will be a high demand for the currency in other countries in order to pay for the exported goods. This demand might be expected, via supply and demand, to cause the currency to strengthen. Conversely, when a country imports more than it exports, the currency might be expected to weaken, either in the market or through government action. Faced with a trade deficit, a government might lean toward restrictive monetary or fiscal policies. Currency or trade controls could be introduced. The BOP trend over time also helps managers predict what sort of changes in the economic environment might develop in the country. This prediction could affect their choice of strategic risks to take in a specific country.

Key Words

gold standard (p. 205)

Bretton Woods system (p.. 206)

fixed exchange rate (p. 206)

par value (p. 206)

reserves (p. 206)

Triffin paradox (p. 206)

special drawing rights (SDR) (p. 206)

floating currency exchange rates (p. 207)

Jamaica Agreement (p. 207)

Bank for International Settlements (p. 210)

vehicle currency (p. 210)

intervention currency (p. 210)

reciprocal currency/direct quote (p. 211)

spot rate (p. 211)

forward currency market (p. 211)

forward rate (p. 211)

bid price (p. 212)

ask price (p. 212)

monetary policies (p. 212)

fiscal policies (p. 212)

law of one price (p. 213)

arbitrage (p. 213)

Fisher effect (p. 213)

international Fisher effect (p. 213)

purchasing power parity (PPP) (p. 213)

efficient market approach (p. 214)

random walk hypothesis (p. 214)

fundamental approach (p. 214)

technical analysis (p. 214)

balance of payments (BOP) (p. 221)

Questions

1. Briefly outline the advantages and disadvantages of the gold system.

2. Was the Bretton Woods system bound to fail?

3. You are on a business trip from Portugal to the United States for 90 days, and you have a per diem expense account of euro 400 per day, no receipts required. This per diem is advanced to you before the trip (euro 36,000). You deposit it into your checking account and use your Portuguese (euro) credit card to cover your costs while in the United States. After the first two weeks of your trip, the dollar weakened against the euro by 15% percent. What ethical dilemma might this currency fluctuation present for you?

4. If all nations used the SDR, what might the impact be on business?

5. If your firm is generating considerable revenues in operations in a country that suddenly and without warning imposes exchange controls that prohibit the purchase of foreign currency within the country and the export of the currency, what are some of the issues you will want to discuss with your regional finance staff?

6. Your U.S. firm is about to sign a contract to supply services to a bank in Beijing, with a up-front payment agreement of 50 percent. Would you want this payment in U.S. dollars? Why or why not?

7. While the Federal Reserve has been slashing interest rates, the European Central Bank is holding interest rates steady. Could this policy difference have influenced the relative strength of the dollar against the euro? Why?

8. Your Boston-based company earned 54 percent of its profits from Germany and France. Given your answer in question 7, are you happy today? Why?

9. Your Munich-based company earns 64 percent of its revenues from high precision auto component exports to the United States. You need to expand manufacturing capacity, and the U.S. market has great growth potential for your product. Given your answer in question 7, where would you add capacity, in Germany or the United States? Why?

10. Why should managers regularly monitor the BOP of the countries in which their business operates?

 globalEDGE.msu.edu

Research Task

Use the globalEDGE site (http://globalEDGE.msu.edu/) to complete the following exercises:

1. Your company imports video equipment from Japan to sell in the United States. The exchange rate fluctuations over the past year have had a significant impact on your bottom line. In preparing an annual report for your company, you would like to include a one-year *currency chart* showing the movement of the U.S. dollar versus the Japanese yen. Describe the pattern you see. Over the past year, has the dollar gained or lost ground versus the yen?

2. As an entrepreneur, you are interested in expanding your business to either Germany or Australia. As part of your initial analysis, you would like to know how much minimum investment is needed to enter each of these markets. To have an appropriate estimate, you hire a consulting firm to perform an initial investment analysis. The consulting firm provides a short report concerning the level of minimum investment needed for each country. Taken from the report, the minimum investment amounts enclosed are: 24 million euros (EUR) or 30 million Australian dollars (AUD). To make a clear comparison by using current *exchange rates*, you must convert each currency to U.S. dollars and suggest which country provides the better investment.

Minicase: SDR Exchange Risk

The Asian Development Bank (ADB), a multilateral development bank owned by its 67 members whose primary goal is poverty reduction, makes its loans in SDR. As of September 2010, these loans totaled $44.3 billion, with the largest borrowers being China, Indonesia, India, Pakistan, and the Philippines. The ADB covers the exposure of its capital resources, $114.8 billion, by selling into the forward market the currencies that make up the SDR basket. Why would the ADB hold SDR instead of dollars or euro? What are the currency amounts that make up the SDR? To learn more about the SDR basket, visit http://imf.org/external/np/fin/data/rms_sdrv.aspx.

ernational Business 國際商務 Gli Affari Internazionali Los negoci
affaires Internationales ...
cios Internacionais Παγκόσμιο Business Los negocios internacionales
Gli Affari Intern
 négocios Internacionais Affaires Internationales
onales Geschäft Los negocios internacionales Παγκόσμ
cios Internacionais Gli Affari Internazionali 國際商務
Παγκόσμιο Business International Business

section three

The Organizational Environment

In the preceding two sections, the primary focus has been on the broad environmental context in which international businesses compete. Section One introduced you to issues regarding the nature of international business, including international business, trade, investment, and the institutional context in which international business functions. Section Two discussed forces that affect international business and with which management must cope.

In Section Three, our attention shifts away from the external environment and focuses instead on the business itself, including actions that managers can take to help their companies compete more effectively as international businesses. In identifying potential management responses and solutions to problems caused or magnified by the foreign and international environments, this book is intended to be only an introduction to international business. Deeper discussions into specific areas can be found in textbooks specializing in those areas.

Chapter 9 deals with the concept of international competitive strategy and how companies use strategic planning techniques to address international business opportunities and challenges. Moving from

a consideration of strategy to how the firm is organized, Chapter 10 looks at organizational design and the different ways in which international companies can be structured. Chapter 11 examines issues associated with global leadership. Our attention then focuses on markets in the international environment. Chapter 12 deals with assessing and analyzing international markets. Chapter 13 explores ways in which a company can enter international markets, including practices and procedures for exporting and importing. Chapter 14 examines practices associated with importing and exporting. Chapter 15 explores international marketing and ways that it differs from domestic marketing. The final three chapters address other important functional areas of the international company. Chapter 16 deals with operations management in international companies, including management of international supply chains. Chapter 17 presents material on managing human resources in international businesses, particularly nonexecutive, technical, or sales employees. Finally, Chapter 18 covers management issues of a financial or accounting nature that arise in conjunction with international business activities.

International Competitive Strategy

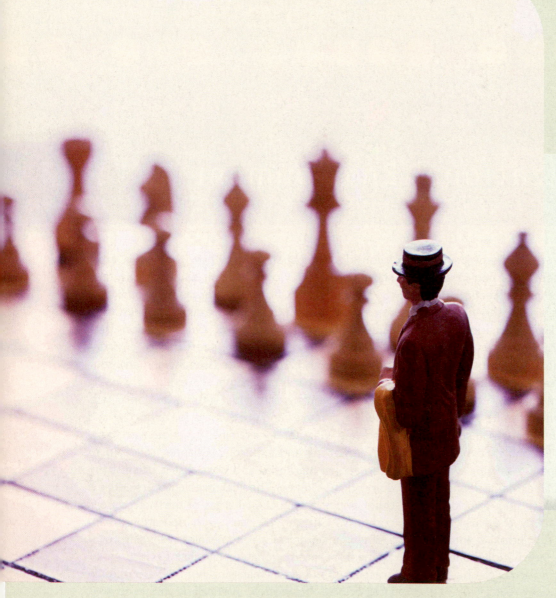

What business strategy is all about—what distinguishes it from all other kinds of business planning—is, in a word, competitive advantage. Without competitors there would be no need for strategy, for the sole purpose of strategic planning is to enable the company to gain, as effectively as possible, a sustainable edge over its competitors.

—*Kenichi Ohmae, McKinsey & Company consultant*

Thinking Strategically about the Future in an Uncertain World

What would happen if the prices of oil or food were to skyrocket (as they did during 2011) or suddenly crash? What are the chances of a host government nationalizing an industry, such as Bolivia did in its oil and natural gas sector in 2006? What would happen if world credit markets dried up, as happened after the subprime mortgage debacle in 2007? What are the implications of increasing urbanization and industrialization in emerging markets, such as India, China, or Brazil? Efforts to identify and assess changes in environmental forces, which were discussed in Section Two of this book, are a key aspect of scenarios—stories about possible futures—that the global energy company Royal Dutch Shell employs in its strategic planning process. The objective of this process is to force executives to question their assumptions about the environments in which the company operates and successfully incorporate the uncertainty and potential changes that might profoundly affect their strategic and operational performance around the world.

Recently, companies like Shell have begun modifying their approach to using scenarios in their strategic planning efforts. Formerly, the planners made the scenarios and presented them to the line managers—a kind of "show and tell." There was no involvement of the managers. Now there is an emphasis in the company on getting managers to bring scenarios into their decision processes because Shell's top management is convinced that scenario building is an important management tool.

The objective of scenario planning is to envision possible futures in a more realistic light, plan for uncertainties and discontinuous events, and develop strategies to help a company cope with these potential future states. Scenario planning helps emphasize that the business environment is uncertain and might evolve in totally different ways, thus helping to challenge traditional perspectives regarding the organization and its environment. This provides a useful context for developing long-term strategic plans, as well as shorter-term contingency plans, which are appropriate for risky and uncertain operating situations. Scenario planning gives close attention to external and internal factors that may normally not be considered relevant but that have influence on the future.

Scenarios are plausible and challenging stories, but they are not forecasts; that is, they do not extrapolate from past data to make predictions. In fact, they are a means to force managers to realize that their assumptions based on past experience no longer apply. Also, if managers have thought out the possible outcomes, they should be quicker to react when one of those outcomes occurs. As Shell's former planning head expresses it, "They can remember the future."[a]

Managers typically work in teams of six to eight people to build scenarios. They first agree about the decision that must be made and then gather information by reading, observing, and talking with knowledgeable people. Next, the team works to identify the driving (environmental) forces and the "critical uncertainties" (the unpredictables) and prioritizes them. Three or four scenarios are commonly prepared, based on issues critical to the success of the decision. Each should depict a credible future and not be written to show the best-case, worst-case, and most likely situations. The team then identifies the implications of the scenarios and the leading indicators management must follow.

A member of a consulting firm that trains managers to use scenarios writes:

Using scenarios is rehearsing the future, and by recognizing the warning signs and the drama unfolding, one can avoid surprises, adapt, and act effectively. Decisions which have been pretested against a range of what fate may offer are more likely to stand the test of time, produce robust and resilient strategies, and create distinct competitive advantage. Ultimately, the end result of scenario planning is not a more accurate picture of tomorrow, but better decisions today.[b]

The uncertainty of the world seems to have increased rather dramatically in recent years, especially in the aftermath of events such as the 9/11 tragedy in the United States; instability in global oil, food, and credit markets; or the earthquake and tsunami that struck Japan in 2011. As a result, it is likely that international companies and their managers will demonstrate an increased interest in scenario planning as an essential part of their strategic planning activities.

Source: A. J. Vogl, "Big Thinking," *Across the Board* 41, no. 1 (January–February 2004), pp. 27–33; Julie Verity, "Scenario Planning as a Strategy Technique," *European Business Journal* 15, no. 4 (January 2003), pp. 185–95; "20:20 Vision," *Global Scenarios,* www.shell.com/b/b2_03.html (March 15, 1998); and Hugh Courtney, "Decision-Driven Scenarios for Assessing Four Levels of Uncertainty," *Strategy and Leadership* 31, no. 1 (2003), pp. 14–22.

[a]"A Glimpse of Possible Futures," *Financial Times,* August 25, 1997, p. 8.

[b]"Using Scenarios," *GBN Scenario Planning,* www.gbn.org/usingScen.html (March 20, 1998).

In the preceding two sections of this book, the primary focus has been on the broad environmental context in which international businesses compete. This discussion has included the theoretical framework for international trade and investment; the international institutions that influence international business; and the sociocultural, political, legal, financial, economic, and physical forces that influence the international business environment. Our attention now shifts away from the external environment, and we focus instead on the business itself, including the actions managers can take to help their companies compete more effectively as international businesses. In this chapter, we discuss the concept of international strategy and how companies use strategic planning and the analysis of competitive forces to improve their global competitiveness.

The Competitive Challenge Facing Managers of International Businesses

In Chapter 1, we discussed some of the important reasons that motivate companies to pursue international business opportunities, including the potential to increase profits and sales through access to new markets; to protect existing markets, profits, and sales; and to help satisfy management's overall desire for growth. However, in order to succeed in today's global marketplace, a company must be able to quickly identify and exploit opportunities wherever they occur, domestically or internationally. To do this effectively, managers must fully understand why, how, and where they intend to do business, now and over time. This requires that managers have a clear understanding of the company's mission, a vision for how they intend to achieve that mission, and an understanding of how they plan to compete with other companies. To meet these challenges, managers must understand the company's strengths and weaknesses and be able to compare them accurately to those of their worldwide competitors. Strategic planning provides valuable tools that help managers address these global challenges.

What Is International Strategy, and Why Is It Important?

International strategy is concerned with the way firms make fundamental choices about developing and deploying scarce resources internationally.[1] International strategy involves decisions that deal with which products or services to offer, which markets to enter, and how to compete. It deals with all the various functions and activities of a company and the interactions among them, not merely a single area such as marketing or production. To be effective, a company's international strategy needs to be consistent among the various functions, products, and regional units of the company (internal consistency) as well as with the variety of demands associated with operating in the international competitive environment (external consistency).

The goal of international strategy is to achieve and maintain a unique and valuable competitive position both within a nation and globally, a position that has been termed **competitive advantage.** This suggests that the international company must either perform activities different from those of its competitors or perform the same activities in different ways. To create a competitive advantage that is sustainable over time, the international company should try to develop skills, or **competencies,** that (1) create value for customers and for which customers are willing to pay; (2) are rare, because competencies shared among many competitors cannot be a basis for competitive advantage; (3) are difficult to imitate or substitute for; and (4) are organized in a way that allows the company to fully exploit and capture the value from the competitive potential of these valuable, rare, and difficult-to-imitate competencies.[2]

Managers of international companies that are attempting to develop a competitive advantage face a formidable challenge because resources—time, talent, and money—are always scarce. There are many alternative ways to use these scarce resources (e.g., which nations to enter, which technologies to invest in, and which products or services to develop and offer to customers), and these alternatives are not equally attractive. A company's managers are forced to make choices regarding what to do and what *not* to do, now and over time. Different companies make different choices, and those choices have implications for each company's ability to meet the needs of customers and create a defensible competitive position internationally. Without adequate planning, managers are more likely to make decisions that do not make good sense competitively, and the company's international competitiveness may be harmed.

Global Strategic Planning

WHY PLAN GLOBALLY?

As was discussed in the various chapters of Section Two, companies are confronting a set of environmental forces that are increasingly complex, global, and subject to rapid change. In response, many international firms have found it necessary to institute formal global **strategic planning** to provide a means for top management to identify opportunities and threats from all over the world, formulate strategies to handle them, and stipulate how to finance and manage the strategies' implementation. Strategic plans help ensure that decision makers have a common understanding of the business, the strategy, the assumptions behind

LO9-1 Explain international strategy, competencies, and international competitive advantage.

international strategy
The way firms make choices about acquiring and using scarce resources in order to achieve their international objectives

competitive advantage
The ability of a company to have higher rates of profits than its competitors

competencies
Skills or abilities required in order to adequately complete a task

strategic planning
The process by which an organization determines where it is going in the future, how it will get there, and how it will assess whether and to what extent it has achieved its goals

the strategy, the external business environment pressures, and their own direction, as well as promote consistency of action among the firm's managers worldwide. Strategic plans also encourage participants to consider the ramifications of their actions in the firm's other geographic and functional areas. These plans provide a thorough, systematic foundation for raising key questions about what a business should become and for making decisions regarding what resources and competencies the company should develop, when and how to develop them, and how to use those competencies to achieve competitive advantage. This is intended to help the organization respond more effectively to challenges than its competitors. Strategic planning is also intended to increase the likelihood of strategic innovations, promoting the development, capture, and application of these new ideas in order to promote success in a challenging competitive environment. McKinsey's "Global Survey" revealed that 85 percent of respondents perceived their company's business environment to be "more competitive" or "much more competitive" than it was five years earlier, with the intensity of competition increasing for both small and large companies and across all industries.[3] Despite complaints about the challenges of effectively implementing planning efforts, especially within large and international companies, Bain & Company's "Management Tools and Trends" survey reported that strategic planning continues to be among the most commonly used management tool among global executives, and it is the tool with the highest reported level of satisfaction.[4]

GLOBAL STRATEGIC PLANNING PROCESS

LO9-2 Describe the steps in the global strategic planning process.

strategic planning
The process by which an organization determines where it is going in the future, how it will get there, and how it will assess whether and to what extent it has achieved its goals

Global **strategic planning** is a primary function of a company's managers, and the ultimate manager of strategic planning and strategy making is the firm's chief executive officer. The process of strategic planning provides a formal structure in which managers (1) analyze the company's external environments, (2) analyze the company's internal environment, (3) define the company's business and mission, (4) set corporate objectives, (5) quantify goals, (6) formulate strategies, and (7) make tactical plans. For ease of understanding, we present this as a linear process, but in actuality, there is considerable flexibility in the order in which firms take up these items. In company planning meetings that one of the authors attended, the procedure was iterative; that is, during the analysis of the environments, committee members could skip to a later step in the planning process to discuss the impact of a new development on a present corporate objective. They then often moved backward in the process to discuss the availability of the firm's assets to take advantage of the environmental change. If they concluded that the company had such a capability, the committee would try to formulate a new strategy. If a viable strategy was developed, the members would then establish the corporate objective that the strategy was designed to attain.

You will note that the global planning process, illustrated in Figure 9.1, has the same basic format as the planning process for a purely domestic firm. As you know by now, most activities of the two kinds of operations are similar. It is the variations in the values of the uncontrollable forces that make the activities in a worldwide corporation more complex than they are in a purely domestic firm.

Analyze Domestic, International, and Foreign Environments

Because a firm has little opportunity to control these forces, its managers must know not only what the present values of the forces are but also where the forces appear to be headed. An environmental scanning process similar to the market screening process described in Chapter 12 can be used for continuous gathering of information. Yet recognition of the nature and implications of the current and future domestic, international, and foreign environments is an essential input into the global strategic planning process.

While recognition of changes in key environmental forces is a necessary strategic task for managers of international companies, it is not sufficient. Management must also develop and implement appropriate responses to these changes. A study by the consulting company McKinsey & Company found that, worldwide, most executives agree that environmental, social, and business trends are more critical to company strategy than was

FIGURE 9.1   The Global Strategic Planning Process

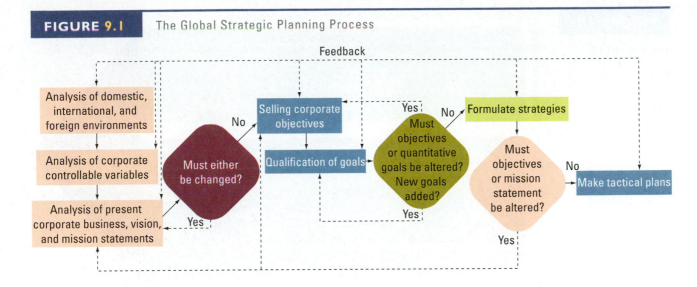

the case five years ago.[5] Despite this, relatively few companies appear to act on key international trends that they observe, often due to a lack of the necessary skills and resources for addressing whether, how, and when to act in order to deal effectively with these environmental forces.

Analyze Corporate Controllable Variables

An analysis of the forces controlled by the firm will also include a situational analysis and a forecast. The managers of the various functional areas will either personally submit reports on their units or provide input to a planning staff that will prepare a report for the strategy planning committee.

Often management will analyze the firm's activities from the time raw materials enter the plant until the end product reaches the final user, what is frequently called a **value chain analysis.** As part of this process, management must address three key questions about the business:

1. Who are the company's target customers?
2. What value does the company want to deliver to these customers?
3. How will this customer value be created?

The value chain analysis itself focuses primarily on the third question, and it refers to the set of value-creating activities that the company is involved with, from sources for basic raw materials or components to the ultimate delivery of the final product or service to the final customer. A simplified value chain is shown in Figure 9.2. The goal of this analysis is to enable management to determine the set of activities that will comprise the company's value chain, including which activities the company will do itself and which will be outsourced. Management must also consider where to locate various value chain activities (e.g., should assembly be done in the company's home nation, located in a lower-cost location abroad, or located close to a customer abroad?). It is also necessary for management to examine the linkages among the activities in the value chain (e.g., between sales and product development, in order to ensure that customer needs are effectively communicated and incorporated in new products). Linkages must be examined not merely across activities within the company but also in terms of managing relationships with external entities such as suppliers, alliance partners, distributors, or customers within and across nations. The desired outcome of this analysis is the identification and establishment of a superior set of well-integrated value chain activities and the linkages among these activities, a system that will permit the organization to more effectively and efficiently develop, produce, market, and sell the company's products and services to the target customers, thereby creating the basis for global competitive advantage.

value chain analysis
An assessment conducted on the chain of interlinked activities of an organization or set of interconnected organizations, intended to determine where and to what extent value is added to the final product or service

FIGURE 9.2

The Value Chain

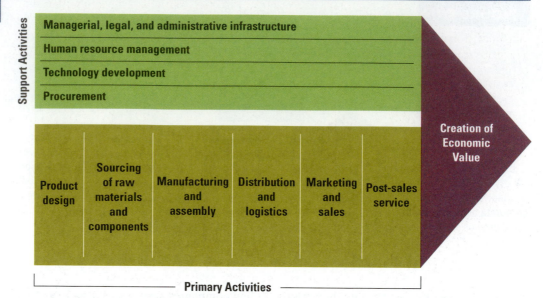

Source: Adapted from M. E. Porter, *Competitive Advantage* (New York: Free Press, 1985).

Knowledge as a Controllable Corporate Resource

In today's highly competitive, rapidly changing, and knowledge-intensive economy, companies have the potential to achieve competitive advantage through leveraging their organizational knowledge across national boundaries. This organizational knowledge base includes the capabilities of employees (individually and in teams) as well as the knowledge that gets built into the overall organization through its various structures, systems, and organizational routines. As a valuable, scarce, and often unique organizational resource, knowledge is increasingly recognized as the basis for competitive advantage. As a result, managers are undertaking efforts to identify and evaluate the pool of knowledge that is contained within their companies on a global basis, including assessments of which knowledge and associated competencies will be the foundation for the company's future success. This process is frequently referred to as **knowledge management.** To help accelerate the acquisition, development, and exploitation of competitively valuable knowledge, managers are developing sets of techniques and practices to facilitate the flow of knowledge into and within their companies, to build knowledge databases, to transfer best practices within and across their international network of operations, and otherwise to create the foundation for a knowledge-based competitive advantage.

To effectively manage knowledge, companies must encourage individuals to work together on projects or somehow share their ideas. Much valuable knowledge is **tacit,** which means that it is known well by the individual but is difficult to express verbally or to document in text or figures. As a result, systems are needed in order to convey this tacit knowledge to others, possibly by converting it into **explicit,** codified knowledge and then making this knowledge accessible quickly and effectively to other employees who need it. In addition, to effectively design and deliver products that meet customers' needs, it is often necessary to gain access to valuable knowledge of suppliers, customers, and other partner organizations as well. In some cases, it is even necessary to establish company facilities in other locations in order to gain access to this knowledge. For example, Nokia and Ericsson, which are international leaders in telecommunications technology, both established offices in the Silicon Valley. Their objective was to tap into the latest thinking of suppliers and customers located in that region and then transfer this knowledge back to their respective headquarters in Europe. Companies face an ongoing challenge of creating mechanisms that will systematically and routinely identify opportunities for developing and transferring knowledge and for ensuring that subsidiaries are willing and able both to share what they know and to absorb knowledge from other units of the company. They also must ensure that this proprietary knowledge is managed in a way that will protect it from diffusion to competitors, in order to help the company maintain its competitiveness over time.

knowledge management
The practices that organizations and their managers use for the identification, creation, acquisition, development, dispersion, and exploitation of competitively valuable knowledge

tacit knowledge
Knowledge that an individual has but that is difficult to express clearly in words, pictures, or formulae, and therefore difficult to transmit to others

explicit knowledge
Knowledge that is easy to communicate to others via words, pictures, formulae, or other means

After the analysis of corporate controllable variables, the planning committee must answer questions such as the following: What are our strengths and weaknesses? What are our human and financial resources? Where are we with respect to our present objectives? Have we uncovered any facts that require us to delete goals, alter them, or add new ones? After completing this internal audit, the committee is ready to examine the company's mission, vision, and values statements.

Define the Corporate Mission, Vision, and Values Statements

These broad statements communicate to the corporation's stakeholders (employees, stockholders, governments, partners, suppliers, and customers) what the company is, where it is going, and the values that will guide the behavior of the organization's members. Some firms combine two or all three of these into a single statement, whereas others have separate statements. The **mission statement** defines the purpose for a company's existence, including its business, objectives, and approach for reaching those objectives. A **vision statement** is a description of the company's desired future position, of what it hopes to accomplish if it can acquire the necessary competencies and successfully implement its strategy. In contrast, a **values statement** is intended to be a clear, concise description of the fundamental values, beliefs, and priorities of the organization's members, reflecting how they want to behave with each other and with the company's customers, suppliers, and other members of the global community. A Booz Allen Hamilton/Aspen Institute survey of corporations in 30 countries revealed that 89 percent of these organizations had explicit, written statements of corporate values and that greater success in linking a corporation's values to its operations was related to superior financial results.[6]

Some Examples

The South Korean multinational Samsung states the following about its mission and management philosophy:

> We will devote our human resources and technology to create superior products and services, thereby contributing to a better global society.[7]

Amazon.com states the following about the vision for that company:

> Our vision is to be earth's most customer-centric company; to build a place where people can come to find and discover anything they might want to buy online.[8]

Sumitomo Corporation of Japan states its nine basic values as being:

> (1) Integrity and Sound Management: To comply with laws and regulations, while maintaining the highest ethical standards, (2) Integrated Corporate Strength: To create no boundaries within the organization; always to act with a company-wide perspective, (3) Vision: To create a clear vision of the future, and to communicate to share it within the organization, (4) Change and Innovation: To accept and integrate diversity in values and behavior, and to embrace change as an opportunity for action, (5) Commitment: To initiate, own, and achieve organizational objectives, (6) Enthusiasm: To act with enthusiasm and confidence, and to motivate to others through such action, (7) Speed: To make quick decisions and act promptly, (8) Human Development: To fully support the development of others' potential, and (9) Professionalism: To achieve and maintain high levels of expertise and skills.[9]

After defining any or all of the three statements, management must then set corporate objectives.

Set Corporate Objectives

Objectives direct the firm's course of action, maintain it within the boundaries of the stated mission, and ensure its continuing existence. For example, Intel's mission is to "delight our customers, employees, and shareholders by relentlessly delivering the platform and technology advancements that become essential to the way we work and live." Its objectives are stated as (1) extend our silicon technology and manufacturing leadership, (2) deliver unrivaled microprocessors and platforms, (3) grow profitability worldwide, and (4) excel in customer orientation.[10] How does Intel know whether it achieves these objectives? How will the company assess whether it has successful in attempting to "deliver unrivaled microprocessors and platforms," for example?

LO9-3 Explain the purpose of mission statements, vision statements, values statements, objectives, quantified goals, and strategies.

mission statement
A broad statement that defines the organization's purpose and scope

vision statement
A description of the company's desired future position if it can acquire the necessary competencies and successfully implement its strategy

values statement
A clear and concise description of the fundamental values, beliefs, and priorities of the organization's members

Google's Values and Strategy versus the China Opportunity

Google, the world's leader in the global Internet search engine business, with more than two-thirds of global net searches, has actively promoted its ethical values—including its unofficial motto of "don't be evil"—as a foundation for its business activity. In 2006, Google entered the rapidly growing and potentially lucrative Internet search market in China. To obtain permission for entry, Google agreed to modify its operating approach to fit with Chinese requirements to censor Internet searches, particularly those involving certain socially or politically sensitive topics. Google's decision to engage in censorship, taken after much soul-searching, reflected a belief that the company's participation might contribute to a gradual loosening of Beijing's restrictions on free speech. The company included a disclosure on its site, stating that some search information had been removed, in an effort to raise awareness of censorship among Chinese Internet users. "I actually feel like things really improved" in the initial years after Google's entry, co-CEO Sergey Brin said. "We were actually able to censor less and less."[a]

By the end of 2009, Google had gained 36 percent of the Chinese market, second only to local company Baidu and far outdistancing rivals such as Microsoft and Yahoo. Google's Chinese revenues, estimated at $300 million in 2009 and projected at $600 million in 2010, had the potential to reach $5 billion to $6 billion by 2014.[b]

However, Google decided that its reputation for ethical behavior was more valuable than the potential returns from China's search engine market. In a highly publicized move on January 12, 2010, Google announced it would stop obeying censorship requirements on its Chinese site. This decision was triggered by increasingly strict government requirements to limit Internet freedom in that country, as well as a series of highly sophisticated cyberattacks on its servers in the United States, allegedly originating in China. Google's chief legal officer, David Drummond, asserted that these attacks were, "almost singularly focused on getting into Gmail accounts specifically of human-rights activities, inside China or outside." They were "all part of an overall system bent on suppressing expression, whether it was by controlling Internet search results or trying to surveil activists."[c] CEO Eric Schmidt stated, "We like what China is doing in terms of growth. . . we just don't like censorship."[d]

Despite a series of tense negotiations with the Chinese government, on March 22, 2010, Google shut down its Chinese search site. Google moved its Chinese-language search activities to Hong Kong, a special administrative region which has broader protection of free speech under the "one country, two systems" approach that was established in 1997, when the British handed over control of their former colony.

Brin, who was born in the Soviet Union and whose family experienced government repression prior to emigrating to the United States, explained Google's move by stating, "in some aspects of their (China's) policy, particularly with respect to censorship, with respect to surveillance of dissidents, I see the same earmarks of totalitarianism (as in the former Soviet Union), and I find that personally quite troubling."[e] This argument ultimately prevailed over CEO Schmidt and others who believed that Google should maintain its presence in China. "One of the reasons I am glad we are making this move in China is that the China situation was really emboldening other countries to try and implement their own firewalls," said Brin.[f] "Ultimately, I guess it is where your threshold of discomfort is. So we obviously as a company crossed that threshold of discomfort."

Google's high-profile exit was applauded by many, both inside and outside the company. By positioning Google as a champion of free speech, it reinforced Google's well-publicized "don't be evil" motto and reputation for ethical values and behavior, a reputation that had been questioned as a result of the company's Chinese censorship activities. Mitch Kapor, a well-known Silicon Valley venture capitalist, stated that, "More businesses ought to follow 'gut principles' and shareholders and customers ought to support and encourage them to do so."[g] Google's decision to exit China was also expected to enhance customers' perceived trust in the company and its commitment to protect customers' personal information. This is a particularly important consideration, because Google's business model increasingly emphasizes cloud computing—an approach by which data that individuals and businesses currently keep on their own computers will instead be stored online, making it accessible from virtually any computer or wireless device. Implementation of such a model requires a high level of trust that a company such as Google will protect these data. As one of Google's former Chinese employees stated, "If what Google does in China makes its data seem unsafe, then Google's global strategy is gone."[h]

However, Google's decision to exit the Chinese search engine market was not without its detractors. The Chinese government expressed displeasure with Google's highly visible actions, stating, "Google has violated its written promise it made when entering the Chinese market by stopping filtering its searching service and blaming China in insinuation for alleged hacker attacks. This is totally wrong. We're uncompromisingly opposed to the politicization of commercial issues, and express our discontent and indignation to Google for its unreasonable accusations and conducts."[i] Li Yizhong, Minister of Industry and Information Technology, said, "I hope Google can respect Chinese rules and regulations. If you insist on taking this action that violates Chinese laws, I repeat: You are unfriendly and irresponsible, and you yourself will have to bear the consequences."[j] The highly publicized actions threatened

(continued)

Google's ability to compete in the world's largest and fastest growing Internet market, leaving the company exposed to the risk that the Chinese government could block access for users from the Chinese mainland. Although a complete blockage of access did not occur initially, repeated interruptions of Google searches initiated in China raised concerns about the reliability and long-term commercial viability of Google's services for China-based customers. Chinese Foreign Ministry spokesperson Qin Gang said, "The one whose reputation has been harmed isn't China, rather it is Google."[k]

Google's actions also potentially aided local Chinese competitors. Baidu saw its market share increase by nearly 10 percent, to 64 percent, in the three months after Google's announcement, along with a 60 percent increase in its stock price. International rivals also stood to benefit. Microsoft's senior manager for regulatory policy, Cornelia Kutterer, stated, "We have done business in China for over 20 years, and we intend to continue our business in China," reaffirming Microsoft's intention to adhere to local laws, including Chinese censorship requirements.[l] A Microsoft spokesperson said, "If we do a great job with the product, then we will hopefully attract more share."[m] A number of Google's partners terminated or sharply scaled back their involvement with the company. For example, Tom Group Ltd. removed Google's search service from its Chinese Internet portal and Motorola announced plans to provide links to other search engines on its phones in China. China's second largest wireless carrier, China Unicom, announced that it would drop Google as the company's default search engine for its newest smartphones. "We are open to cooperating with any handset makers and companies. But they must obey China's regulations," said Unicom president Lu Yimin.[n]

Question: Did Google make a good decision to leave China? What do you think?

Google headquarters in China

[a]Ben Worthen, "Soviet-born Brin Has Shaped Google's Stand on Chinva," *Wall Street Journal Online*, March 13, 2010 (accessed August 25, 2011)

[b]Tim Bradshaw, David Gelles and Richard Waters, "Realism Lies behind Decision to Quit," *Financial Times*, March 24, 2010, p. 6 (accessed August 25, 2011)

[c]L. Gordon Crovitz, "Google Search Result: Hong Kong; The Company Had to Maintain the Trust of Its Users," *Wall Street Journal Online*, March 29, 2010 (accessed August 25, 2011)

[d]Rebecca Blumenstein and Stephen Fidler, "Google Takes Aim at Beijing Censorship; CEO Schmidt Hopes to 'Apply Some Pressure,' as Business Leaders Voice Concerns about Growing China-U.S. Tension," *Wall Street Journal Online*, January 30, 2010 (accessed August 25, 2011)

[e]Jessica E. Vascellaro, "Google's Brin Talks about China Gamble," *Wall Street Journal Online*, March 24, 2010 (accessed August 25, 2011)

[f]Jessica E. Vascellaro, "Brin Drove Google to Pull Back in China," *The Wall Street Journal*, March 25, 2010, p. A1 (accessed August 25, 2011)

[g]Ibid

[h]Matthew Forney and Arthur Kroeber, "Google's Business Reason for Leaving China: Of Reputation and Revenue," Wall Street Journal Online, April 6, 2010 (accessed August 25, 2011)

[i]Anonymous, "China Calls Google's Actions 'Wrong,'" *Informationweek Online*, March 23, 2010 (accessed August 25, 2011)

[j]Jason Dean, Geoffrey A. Fowler, and Aaron Back, "China Threatens Google; Beijing Raises Tension in Censorship Spat: 'You Are Unfriendly and Irresponsible,'" *Wall Street Journal Online*, March 13, 2010 (accessed August 25, 2011)

[k]Loretta Chao, "Google Braces for Fallout in China," *The Wall Street Journal*, March 24, 2010, p. B1 (accessed August 25, 2011)

[l]Sharon Gaudin, "Google, China Play Game of Cat and Mouse," *Computerworld*, April 5, 2010, p. 8 (accessed August 25, 2011)

[m]Geoffrey A. Fowler and Loretta Chao, "Google Exit Would Open a Door for Microsoft," *Wall Street Journal Online*, March 16, 2010 (accessed August 25, 2011)

[n]Aaron Back and Loretta Chao, "Google Weaves a Tangled Chinese Web," *Wall Street Journal Online*, March 25, 2010 (accessed August 25, 2011)

Quantify the Objectives   To enhance a company's ability to develop and implement an effective strategy, one that will enable the company's objectives to be attained, it is important that efforts be made to quantify these objectives. Of course, strategic planning for international operations typically involves a range of qualitative as well as quantitative factors, which complicates efforts to quantify objectives. When objectives can be quantified in a relevant manner, they should be. However, despite the strong preference of most top managers for verifiable objectives, they frequently do have nonquantifiable or directional goals. Incidentally, objectives do tend to be more quantified as they progress down the organization to the operational level, because, for the most part, strategies at one level become the objectives for the succeeding level.

Up to this point, only *what, how much,* and *when* have been stipulated. *How* these objectives are to be achieved will be determined in the formulation of strategies.

Formulate the Competitive Strategies

LO9-4 Explain home replication, multidomestic, regional, global, and transnational strategies and when to use them.

competitive strategies
Action plans to enable organizations to reach their objectives

Generally, participants in the strategic planning process will formulate alternative **competitive strategies** and corresponding plans of action that seem plausible considering the directions the external environmental forces are taking and the company's strengths, weaknesses, opportunities, and threats (something that endangers the business, such as a merger of two competitors, the bankruptcy of a major customer, or a new product that appears to make the company's product obsolete).

When developing and assessing strategic alternatives, it is important to remember that companies competing in international markets confront two opposing forces: reduction of costs and adaptation to local markets. To be competitive, firms must do what they can to lower costs per unit so that customers will not perceive their products or services as being too expensive. This often results in pressure for some of the company's facilities to be located in places where costs are low, as well as for developing products that are highly standardized across multiple nations.

However, in addition to responding to pressures to reduce costs, managers also must attempt to respond to local pressures to modify their products to meet the demands of the local markets in which they do business. This modification requires that the company differentiate its strategy and product offerings from nation to nation, reflecting differences in distribution channels, governmental regulations, cultural preferences, and similar factors. However, modifying products and services for the specific requirements of local markets can involve additional expenses, which can cause the company's costs to rise.

As a consequence of these two opposing pressures, companies basically have five different strategies that they can use for competing internationally: home replication, multidomestic, regional, global, and transnational. As suggested in Figure 9.3, the strategy that would be most appropriate for the company, overall and for various activities in the value chain, depends on the amount of pressure the company faces in terms of adapting to local markets and achieving cost reductions. Each of these strategies has its own set of advantages and disadvantages, as summarized here, which must be carefully considered when making decisions about the strategy an international company will choose to deploy.

FIGURE 9.3

Cost and Adaptation Pressures and Their Implications for International Strategies

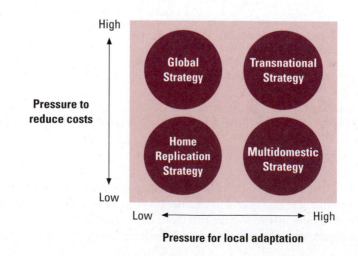

Home Replication Strategy

According to this typology, companies pursuing a home replication strategy typically centralize product development functions in their home country. After they develop differentiated products in the home market, these innovations are then transferred to foreign markets in order to capture additional value. To be successful, the company has to possess a valuable distinctive competency that local competitors lack in the foreign markets. The company's home-country headquarters usually maintains tight control over marketing and product strategy, and the primary responsibility of local subsidiaries is to leverage home-country capabilities. The extent of local customization of product offerings or marketing strategy tends to be limited. As a result, once local demand and circumstances justify such an investment, the company will tend to establish manufacturing and marketing functions in each major country in which it does business. This strategy can be appropriate if the company faces relatively weak pressures for local responsiveness and cost reductions. When there are strong pressures for local responsiveness, however, companies pursuing a home replication strategy will be at a disadvantage compared with competitors that emphasize customization of the product offering and market strategy for local conditions. Companies pursuing a home replication strategy may also face high operating costs, due to duplication of manufacturing facilities across the markets they serve.

Multidomestic Strategy

A multidomestic strategy tends to be used when there is strong pressure for the company to adapt its products or services for local markets. Under these circumstances, decision making tends to be more decentralized in order to allow the company to modify its products and to respond quickly to changes in local competition and demand. Subsidiaries are expected to develop and exploit local market opportunities, which means that knowledge and competencies should be developed at the subsidiary level. By tailoring its products for specific markets, the company may be able to charge higher prices. However, local adaptation of products usually will increase the company's cost structure. To effectively adapt products, the company will have to invest in additional capabilities and knowledge in terms of local culture, language, customer demographics, human resource practices, government regulations, distribution systems, and so forth. Adapting products too much to local tastes may also take away the distinctiveness of a company's products. For example, KFC's chicken outlets in China are highly popular because they are perceived to reflect American values and standards, something that might be lost if the company tried to adapt the stores and products to be more like other Chinese food outlets. The extent of local adaptation may also change over time, as when customer demands start to converge due to the emergence of global telecommunications, media, and travel, as well as reduced differences in income between nations. The cost and complexity of coordinating a range of different strategies and product offerings across national and regional markets can also be substantial.

Global Strategy

A global strategy tends to be used when a company faces strong pressures for reducing costs and limited pressure to adapt products for local markets. Strategy and decision making are typically centralized at headquarters, and the company tends to offer standardized products and services. Overseas offices are expected to adopt the most efficient strategies found within the entire corporation. Value chain activities are often located in only one or a few geographic locations to assist the company in achieving cost reductions due to economies of scale. International subsidiaries are expected to transmit information to headquarters and to submit to centralized controls imposed by headquarters. There tends to be strong emphasis on close coordination and integration of activities across products and markets, as well as the development of efficient logistics and distribution capabilities. These strategies are common in industries such as semiconductors (e.g., Intel) or large commercial aircraft (e.g., Boeing). However, global strategies may also confront challenges such as limited ability to adjust quickly and effectively to changes in customer needs across national or regional markets, increased transportation and tariff costs for exporting products from centralized production sites, and the risks of locating activities in a centralized location (which can, for example, cause the firm to confront risks from political changes or trade conflicts, exchange rate fluctuations, and similar factors).

Transnational Strategy

A transnational strategy tends to be used when a company confronts simultaneous pressures for cost effectiveness and local adaptation and when there is a potential for competitive advantage from responding to both of these two divergent forces. The location of a company's assets and capabilities will be based on where it would be most beneficial for each specific activity, neither highly centralized as with a global strategy nor widely dispersed as with a multidomestic strategy. International subsidiaries are expected to contribute actively to the development of the company's capabilities, as well as to develop and share knowledge with company operations worldwide. Typically, "upstream" value chain activities, such as product development, raw materials sourcing, and manufacturing, will be more centralized, while the "downstream" activities, such as marketing, sales, and service, will be more decentralized, located closer to the customer. Of course, achieving an optimal balance in locating activities is a challenge for management, as is maintaining this balance over time as the company faces changes in competition, customer needs, regulations, and other factors. Management must ensure that the comparative advantages of the locations of the company's various value chain activities are captured and internalized, rather than wasted due to limitations of the organization's people, structures, and coordination and control systems. The complexity associated with the strategic decisions, as well as the supporting structures and systems of the organization, will be much greater with a transnational strategy. Caterpillar, for example, has tried to manufacture many of the standardized components of its products in a few locations worldwide. At the same time, the company has set up assembly operations in each major market, sometimes accompanied by specialized local production capability, thereby promoting its ability to tailor products to local needs.

Standardization and Planning

While the preceding discussion addressed basic strategic alternatives at a business or corporate level, it should be remembered that not all activities of an organization confront the same mix of globalization and localization pressures. For example, historically, more aspects of research and development and manufacturing have been standardized and coordinated worldwide by companies than has been the case for other value chain activities such as marketing. Many top executives believe marketing strategies are best determined locally because of differences among the various foreign environments. Yet there remains a desire within many international companies to achieve benefits from standardizing various elements of marketing strategies as well as the total product itself, which leads to their inclusion in the global strategic planning process. In making such strategic plans, however, companies must look beyond what makes sense under current circumstances and also consider how the situation may change in the future and the implications of these changes. This need to focus on the future helps explain companies' increasing use of scenarios in the planning process.

scenarios

Multiple, plausible stories about the future

Scenarios

As the introductory vignette suggests, because of the rapidity of changes in the uncontrollable variables, many managers have become dissatisfied with planning for a single set of events. Instead, they have turned to **scenarios,** multiple, plausible stories for probable futures. Their significant contributions to strategy development merit additional focus. Scenario analysis allows management to assess the implications for the company of various economic conditions and operating strategies. Scenarios integrate a variety of ideas about the future, including key certainties and uncertainties, and present these ideas in a useful and comprehensible manner. Managers can brainstorm various "what-if" scenarios, raising and challenging their assumptions and projected outcomes before committing to a specific course of action. Often, the what-if questions reveal weaknesses in current strategies. Some of the common kinds of subjects for scenarios are large and sudden changes in sales (up or down), sudden increases in the prices of raw materials, sudden tax increases, and a change in the political party in power.

Regional Strategies for Competing Globally

Many researchers in the field of international business have argued that the emergence of broad economic liberalization, declining transportation costs, advances in telecommunications and computer technology, and other factors have produced a "borderless" world. In such a world, it has been argued that a global strategy is an appropriate or even necessary approach for multinational companies to adopt in order to achieve success.

Multinationals do represent a major force driving economic globalization, with the 500 largest multinational enterprises being responsible for about half of world trade and more than 90 percent of the global stock of foreign direct investment. Yet investigations of large multinationals in manufacturing and service sectors reveal that most of these companies generate the majority of their revenues within a single region rather than having broad and deep penetration of international markets as a whole. For the large majority of these firms, an average of about 80 percent of their worldwide revenues are generated within their home region of the three largest economic regions of North America, the European Union, and Asia. These data suggest that, at least for most companies and industries, the world marketplace is triad-based rather than global in nature.

Some researchers have suggested that this triad-based competitive situation, sometimes termed *semiglobalization,* may merely reflect a stage in the evolution of international companies. From this perspective, increased globalization of sales and other value chain activities may be expected to occur over time as companies accumulate sufficient international experience and are thus able to more fully and successfully extend their reach globally. Experimentation and innovation with business models may be necessary in order to accomplish this. There may also be a "threshold of internationalization" beyond which a multinational's performance may decline, at least until the competencies necessary for more globally dispersed operations are able to be developed and managed successfully. In fact, some research that has found that multinationals' revenues tend to be concentrated in a single nation also suggests that broader assessment of value chain activities than merely sales—including sourcing of labor, capital, production, and knowledge—might produce a less region-centric interpretation of multinationals' strategies.

Nevertheless, one result of this recent research on the region-based nature of multinational sales is the potential value to be derived from thinking of international strategy within the context of a region-by-region perspective, rather than merely a nation-by-nation versus a global basis. In part, this argument emphasizes the continued heterogeneity that companies may encounter in the world's marketplaces, such as differences in local cultures, discriminatory treatment from national or regional governments or other governing bodies, and complexities of dealing with multiple institutions in the host markets. To the extent that a multinational's market position varies substantially across regions, strategies may also need to vary by region in order to accommodate the differing competitive circumstances that confront an international company. Yet, even when considering the appropriate strategy to use within each region, it may be useful to consider the relative extent of pressure for local adaptation versus pressure to reduce costs, as discussed in this section, "Formulate the Competitive Strategies."

Source: Alan M. Rugman and Alain Verbeke, "A Perspective on Regional and Global Strategies of Multinational Enterprises," *Journal of International Business Studies* 35, no. 1 (2004), pp. 3–18; J. Michael Geringer, Paul W. Beamish, and Richard C. DaCosta, "Diversification Strategy and Internationalization: Implications for MNE Performance," *Strategic Management Review* 10, no. 2 (1989), pp. 109–19; Lei Li, "Is Regional Strategy More Effective Than Global Strategy in the U.S. Service Industries," *Management International Review* 45, special issue (2005), pp. 37–57; Pankaj Ghemawat, "Semiglobalization and International Business Strategy," *Journal of International Business Studies* 34, no. 2 (2003), pp. 138–52; Eden Yin and Chong Ju Choi, "The Globalization Myth: The Case of China," *Management International Review* 45, (2005), pp. 103–20; Allen J. Morrison, David A. Ricks, and Kendall Roth, "Globalization versus Regionalization: Which Way for the Multinational?" *Organizational Dynamics* 19, no. 3 (1991), pp. 17–29; and Pankaj Ghemawat, "Regional Strategies for Global Leadership," *Harvard Business Review*, December 2005, pp. 98–108.

Although the origins of scenario planning are unclear, the multinational company Royal Dutch Shell is widely recognized as a pioneer in popularizing the technique. Shell made scenario planning a staple of its strategic planning efforts more than 30 years ago, when it was confronted with a severe and unexpected global oil shortage. In dealing with such uncertainty and change, traditional strategic planning approaches based on extrapolation of historical conditions are of limited value. Managers find it difficult to break away from their existing view of the world, one that results from a lifetime of training and experience. Through presenting other ways of seeing the world, scenarios allow managers to envision alternatives that might lie outside their traditional frame of reference. Such an approach is particularly useful for international companies that face high levels of change and uncertainty regarding political, technological, competitive, and other forces because it allows management to anticipate and prepare for opportunities and threats that cannot be fully predicted or controlled.[11]

In his classic book, *The Art of the Long View,* Peter Schwartz identifies the following seven steps to successful scenario planning:

1. Determine the area, scope, and timing of the decisions with greatest relevance to or impact on your organization.

2. Research existing conditions and trends in a wide variety of areas (including those areas you might not typically consider).

3. Examine the drivers or key factors that will likely determine the outcome of the stories you are beginning to build.

4. Construct multiple stories of what could happen next.

5. Play out what the impact of each of these possible futures might be for your business or organization.

6. Examine your answers and look for those actions or decisions you'd make that were common to all two or three of the stories you built.

7. Monitor what does develop so as to trigger your early response system.[12]

The primary value of scenario planning efforts is not so much the strategic plans that are created but, instead, the transformation in strategic thinking that results from this activity. Scenarios should be developed in a manner that is consistent with and helps to clarify the priorities of the company, and these stories are then tied into strategic and operational decisions that a company must make today and over time. Scenarios are frequently used as a learning tool for preparing standby or contingency plans, enhancing the company's ability to perform within uncertain international markets.

contingency plans
Plans for the best- or worst-case scenarios or for critical events that could have a severe impact on the firm

Contingency Plans

Many companies prepare **contingency plans** for worst- and best-case scenarios and for critical events as well. Every operator of a nuclear power plant has contingency plans, as do most producers of petroleum and hazardous chemicals since such

ecological disasters as BP's 2010 oil spill in the Gulf of Mexico occurred. Because of the important impact on profits of changes in the prices of jet fuel, contingency planning is a common strategic activity for domestic and international airlines. The deadly terrorist attacks on the World Trade Center in New York and the Pentagon in Washington, DC, on September 11, 2001, reminded many organizations of the importance of developing contingency plans to ensure the effective continuation of their operations in the event that their headquarters or other key locations are attacked or otherwise incapacitated for a period of time.

Prepare Tactical Plans

Because strategic plans are fairly broad, tactical (also called *operational*) plans are a requisite for spelling out in detail how the objectives will be reached. In other words, very specific, short-term means for achieving the goals are the objective of tactical planning. For instance, if the British subsidiary of an American producer of prepared foods has as a quantitative goal a 20 percent increase in sales, its strategy might be to sell 30 percent more to institutional users. The tactical plan could include such points as hiring three new specialized sales representatives, attending four trade shows, and advertising in two industry periodicals every other month next year. This is the kind of specificity found in the tactical plan.

STRATEGIC PLAN FEATURES AND IMPLEMENTATION FACILITATORS

Sales Forecasts and Budgets

Two prominent features of the strategic plan are sales forecasts and budgets. The **sales forecast** not only provides management with an estimate of the revenue to be received and the units to be sold but also serves as the basis for planning in the other functional areas. Without this information, management cannot formulate the production, financial, and procurement plans. **Budgets,** like sales forecasts, are both a planning and a control technique. During planning, they coordinate all the functions within the firm and provide management with a detailed statement of future operating results and the resources required to achieve those outcomes.

sales forecast
A prediction of future sales performance

budget
An itemized projection of revenues and expenses for a future time period

Plan Implementation Facilitators

Once the plan has been prepared, it must be implemented. Two of the most important plan implementation facilitators that management employs are policies and procedures.

Policies   Policies are broad guidelines issued by upper management for the purpose of assisting lower-level managers in handling recurring problems. Because policies are broad, they permit discretionary action and interpretation. A policy is intended to economize managerial time and promote consistency among the various operating units. For example, if a company's distribution policy states that sales will be made through wholesalers, marketing managers throughout the world would know that they should normally use wholesalers and avoid selling directly to retailers. Similarly, publicity regarding the widespread occurrence of bribery in various international markets has prompted numerous companies to issue policy statements condemning this practice. Managers have thus been put on notice by these statements that they are not to offer bribes.

policies
Broad guidelines intended to assist lower-level personnel in handling recurring issues or problems

Procedures   Procedures prescribe how certain activities will be carried out, thereby ensuring uniform action on the part of all corporate members. For instance, most international corporate headquarters issue procedures for their subsidiaries to follow in preparing annual reports and budgets. This assures corporate management that whether the budgets originate in Thailand, Brazil, or the United States, they will be prepared using the same format, which facilitates comparison.

procedures
Specified ways of performing a particular task or activity

Performance Measures

A key part of strategic planning is measuring performance in order to assess whether the strategy and its implementation are proceeding successfully or whether modifications may need to be made. Companies need to consider at least three types of measures when assessing strategic performance: (1) measures of the company's success in obtaining and applying the required resources, such as financial, technological, and human resources; (2) measures of the effectiveness of the company's personnel, within and across the firm's international network of operations, in performing their assigned jobs; and (3) measures of the company's progress toward achieving its mission, vision, and objectives and doing so in a manner consistent with the company's stated values.[13] A range of concepts and tools, including the balanced scorecard and triple-bottom-line accounting, have been promoted as alternatives for helping to measure strategic performance. For example, the balanced scorecard approach is based on an integration of strategic planning with a company's budgeting processes, and short-term results from the balanced scorecard can serve as a means of monitoring progress in achieving strategic objectives across four dimensions: financial, customer, internal, and learning and growth.

KINDS OF STRATEGIC PLANS

Time Horizon
Although strategic plans may be classified as short, medium, or long term, there is little agreement about the length of these periods. For some businesses, long-range planning may be for a five-year period. For others, such as manufacturers of commercial aircraft, this would be the length of a medium-term plan; their long range might cover 15 years or more. Short-range plans are usually for one to three years; however, even long-term plans are subject to review annually or more frequently if a situation requires it. Furthermore, the time horizon will vary according to the age of the firm and the stability of its market. A new venture in a field such as social networking (e.g., Facebook) or Internet television (e.g., Brightcove) is extremely difficult to plan for more than three years in advance, but a five- or six-year horizon may be sufficient for a mature company in a steady market.

Level in the Organization
Each organizational level of the company will have its level of plan. For example, if there are four organizational levels, as shown in Figure 9.4, there will be four levels of plans, each of which will usually be more specific than the plan that is at the level above. In addition, the functional areas at each level will have their own plans and sometimes will be subject to the same hierarchy, depending mainly on how the company is organized.

METHODS OF PLANNING

top-down planning
Planning process that begins at the highest level in the organization and continues downward

Top-Down Planning
In **top-down planning,** corporate headquarters develops and provides guidelines that include the definition of the business, the mission statement, company objectives, financial assumptions, the content of the plan, and special issues. If there is an international division, its management may be told that this division is expected to contribute $350 million in profits, for example. The division, in turn, would break this total down among the affiliates under its control. The managing director in Germany would be informed that the German operation is expected to contribute $35 million; Brazil, $8 million; and so on. An advantage of top-down planning is that the home office, with its global perspective, should be able to formulate plans that ensure the optimal corporatewide use of the firm's scarce resources. This approach may also promote creativity, because a corporatewide perspective on market opportunities may yield insights that are not readily observable lower in the organization, such as by managers within individual national markets.

Disadvantages of top-down planning are that it restricts initiative at the lower levels and shows some insensitivity to local conditions, particularly within ethnocentric management teams. Furthermore, especially in an international company, there are so many interrelationships that consultation is necessary. Can top management, for example, decide on rationalization of manufacturing without obtaining the opinions of the local units as to its feasibility?

bottom-up planning
Planning process that begins at the lowest level in the organization and continues upward

Bottom-Up Planning
Bottom-up planning operates in the opposite manner. The lowest operating levels inform top management about what they expect to do, and the total becomes the firm's goals. The advantage of bottom-up planning is that the people responsible for attaining the goals are formulating them. Who knows better than the subsidiaries'

directors what and how much the subsidiaries can sell in their respective geographic regions? Because the subsidiaries' directors set the goals with no coercion from top management, they feel obligated to make their word good. Their hands-on perspective may allow them to recognize potentially innovative opportunities to create and leverage value within their local markets, thus serving as a basis for improved performance or even strategic experimentation. However, bottom-up planning has a disadvantage: because each affiliate is free to some extent to pursue the goals it wishes to pursue, there is no guarantee that the sum total of all the affiliates' goals will coincide with those of headquarters. When discrepancies occur, extra time must be taken at headquarters to eliminate them.

Iterative Planning   It appears that **iterative planning** is becoming more popular, especially in global companies that seek to have a single global plan while operating in many diverse foreign environments. Iterative planning combines aspects of both top-down and bottom-up planning. An example of iterative planning is the approach used in 3M. In 2010, 3M generated 65.5 percent of its $26.7 billion in sales from outside the United States, where it has operations in more than 60 nations and sales in more than 200. Strategic planning plays a key role in the company's resource allocation decisions and global expansion. Figure 9.4 illustrates how 3M's iterative planning process functions. Planning starts with the operating managers of the company's six operating business segments, who analyze strengths and weaknesses and external forces, such as new technology and government regulatory changes; perform a competitor analysis; and determine the company resources they will need to achieve their objectives. Their plans then go to the market group, in which from three to five business divisions are typically located. They are reviewed by the market group management and consolidated for presentation to the strategic planning committee, consisting of the 12 vice presidents at headquarters who represent the markets into which the market groups are divided. The plans are reviewed, and the results of this review are discussed with the market group management. Any differences between market and market group managements are reconciled.

iterative planning
Repetition of the bottom-up or top-down planning process until all differences are reconciled

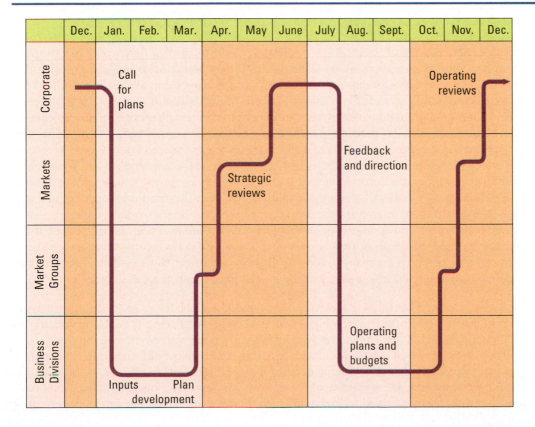

FIGURE 9.4

3M Strategic Planning Cycle

Two months later (July), the corporate headquarters' management committee, to which the strategic planning committee vice presidents belong, reviews the plans and votes on spending priorities. Feedback and direction are given to the business divisions, which then prepare operating plans and budgets by December and submit them to headquarters. They are finalized with corporate worldwide plans. Then, a few days before the December operating reviews, the management committee holds brainstorming sessions to discuss trends and developments over the coming 15 years. The general manager of each business division presents the best picture possible for that industry for the period. The outcome of this meeting is a broad guide for strategic planning. Although operating managers do the planning, the director and staff of a planning services and development unit provide an analysis of 3M's 20 principal competitors worldwide and any other information the divisions require. They also try to identify opportunities and new products.

NEW DIRECTIONS IN PLANNING

LO9-5 **Describe** the methods of and new directions in strategic planning.

Strategic planning, particularly in the more traditional, bureaucratic form that is still practiced in some corporations, has been described as a calendar-driven ritual, not an exploration of the company's potential. This traditional strategic planning approach commonly consists of a company's CEO and the head of planning getting together to devise a corporate plan, which would then be handed to the operating people for execution. Too frequently, companies' annual strategic planning processes have become ritualistic and devoid of discovery, with planners working "from today forward, not from the future back, implicitly assuming, whatever the evidence to the contrary, that the future will be more or less like the present."[14] Tending to generate projections based on historical conditions and performance, this traditional planning approach tends to fall victim to collective—and frequently outdated—mind-sets about the competitive environment. Not surprisingly, the resulting strategic planning documents often fail to be implemented successfully.

Increasingly, the old process is being replaced by a *strategic management* approach, which combines strategic thinking, strategic planning, and strategic implementation and which is increasingly recognized as a fundamental task of line management rather than merely specialized planners in staff positions. Although still susceptible to problems such as groupthink, this more contemporary approach attempts to incorporate changes in three areas: (1) who does the planning, (2) how it is done, and (3) the contents of the plan.

Who Does Strategic Planning?

Although CEOs report that they would like to spend about one-third of their workday on strategy, strategic planning is no longer something that only the company's most senior executives do.[15] Top management, at the urging of strategy consultants, is assigning strategic planning to teams of line and staff managers from different business, geographic, and functional areas, much as it has done with process-improvement task forces and quality circles. Frequently these teams include a range of ages—from junior staff members who have shown the ability to think creatively to experienced veterans near retirement age who will "tell it like it is." Another difference between the new and the old approaches: traditional planning is a company activity done in seclusion; now, the new approach often includes interaction with such parties as important customers, distributors, suppliers, and alliance partners, in order to gain firsthand experience with the firm's markets. Other important stakeholders such as governments or stakeholder activists are also relevant influences, if not necessarily direct participants, in this strategic planning process. Incorporating these diverse perspectives can help a company to identify creative and effective ways to address the challenge of increasingly uncertain and changing international competitive environments.

How Strategic Planning Is Done

The rapid rise in the levels of uncertainty in many areas of international business, combined with the challenge of quantifying factors relating to sociopolitical and other worldwide developments associated with environmental forces such as those discussed in Section Two, made it clear to top managers of many affected companies that there was no point in making detailed five-year forecasts when various international crises were exposing the nonsense of many previous forecasts. Instead, many firms have moved toward less structured formats and much shorter documents. The top management of companies generally accepts that, to be effective, strategic planning processes should permit ideas to surface from anywhere in the organization and at any time. As indicated earlier in Figure 9.1, objectives and strategies are intertwined, as are tactics and strategy. If the planning team is unable to come up with suitable tactics to implement a strategy, the strategy must be altered. In a similar fashion, if strategies cannot be formulated to enable the firm to reach the objective, the objective must be changed.[16]

Contents of the Plan   The contents of the plan are also different. Many top managers say they are much more concerned now with focusing on issues, strategies, and implementation and with incorporating creative, forward-looking ideas that are essential to competitive success within a changing and uncertain international environment. In the contemporary global competitive environment, where firms often must place bigger bets on new technologies and other competitive capabilities, companies cannot afford to devote large amounts of money in one direction only to discover years later that this was the wrong direction for investing. Instead, competition in today's global competitive environment requires an approach to strategic planning that effectively incorporates a long-term perspective to strategic decision making and resource allocation decisions.

SUMMARY OF THE INTERNATIONAL PLANNING PROCESS

A good way to summarize the new direction in planning is to quote Frederick W. Gluck, from the consulting firm McKinsey & Co. Gluck says that if major corporations are to develop the flexibility to compete, they must make the following major changes in the way they plan:

1. Top management must assume a more explicit strategic -decision-making role, dedicating a large amount of time to deciding how things ought to be instead of listening to analyses of how they are.

2. The nature of planning must undergo a fundamental change from an exercise in forecasting to an exercise in creativity.

3. Planning processes and tools that assume a future much like the past must be replaced by a mind-set that is obsessed with being first to recognize change and turn it into a competitive advantage.

4. The role of the planner must change from being a purveyor of incrementalism to being a crusader for action and an alter ego to line management.

5. Strategic planning must be restored to the core of line management responsibilities.[17]

THE GLOBAL PATH AHEAD

Eduardo Rangel: Growth in International through Experience

Eduardo Rangel was born in the United States and spent his pre-school years in Tijuana, Mexico, where his family lived while his father commuted to work in the United States. Here are some of his observations about how he got involved in international business:

Although I was born in San Diego, CA, my family continued living in Tijuana, Mexico. It made sense to my father to save money by living in Mexico and working in the United States. When I was five years old, we moved together to San Diego. Without any academic guidance, I nearly skipped college altogether and joined the military, but I caved in to peer pressure in high school and applied to colleges like most of my friends. At this point, my life, including school, was a personal path of trial and error, a lot more wrong choices than right ones.

Following a three-year stint in community college, I transferred to California State University–Northridge to try my chances there, concentrating in international business. Then they canceled their International Business concentration, so I decided to transfer again to Cal Poly in San Luis Obispo, CA. Although I was taking general courses to satisfy graduation requirements for a business degree at Cal Poly, I directed most of my attention to the international business classes.

(continued)

I was in search of an international position in business after graduation, rather than immediately finding a job in the United States, in order to move outside of my comfort zone. As a result, I joined a student club, AIESEC, which gave me the opportunity to apply for international internships. As a member of the Cal Poly chapter of AIESEC, a global youth organization that engages in international student exchange internships, I actively participated in club events and info sessions. I became aware of internship opportunities they offered in Asia, my first choice for working abroad. After much consideration, I selected Beijing, China, to participate in a nine-month internship during my senior year. China was among the most discussed themes in my business classes, and by working in Beijing I figured I could learn about a new culture, beyond the popularized images presented in various mass market sources (e.g., *Lonely Planet, National Geographic, New York Times*). My decision-making process to take the initiative to go to China can best be described by Nike's slogan, "Just Do It."

I decided to arrive in Beijing three months before the beginning of my internship in order to take an intense Mandarin course at a local university during the first month, and then to travel around China. The point was to let the process of culture shock and jet lag take its course. Having a simple structure, like going to class and walking around the city, enabled me to improve my assimilation into the local culture.

Many of my colleagues were greatly affected by culture shock, and as a result, they became reluctant to accept their new standard of living in Beijing. Culture shock is a feeling of anxiety, loneliness, and confusion that people sometimes experience when living in another country. My friends struggled with the concept of accepting another country's values. Ultimately, some of them decided to leave the country and head back home. Being open minded is crucial in this instance.

I vividly remember a dismal week in Beijing, when I disconnected myself from any interaction with friends and colleagues and stayed in my room waiting for some comforting advice. I called one of my professors from Cal Poly, asking for help to regain the lost enthusiasm that existed when I first arrived in China. I began explaining to her I had been taking my time in China for granted by working long hours and ignoring invitations from friends to travel. She suggested I have fun and enjoy myself and return to feeling like a visitor again. She reminded me that I needed to maintain the perspective that I was a visitor and I needed to enjoy my time in China and continually be learning about the local culture.

In China, I worked with United Education Culture Exchange (UECE). Part of my role was to uphold and reflect an American image to our clients. UECE offers a vast array of programs for Chinese students who want to participate in a cultural exchange by either working or studying in the United States. UECE sponsors their U.S. visa and assists them with accommodations and obtaining their social security cards. I specifically dedicated most of my time to the Work & Travel USA program. Every Wednesday and Friday, we had students come in at 14:00 for a presentation I developed in English, followed by an on-site interview to assess their English fluency. Although many clients failed to understand my presentation in English, the intention was to give UECE credibility by having an American presence, a branding effort of sorts.

Near the end of my internship, UECE organized a press conference to commemorate the success of the Work & Travel USA program. Leading up to the event, we toured universities in China to present our program on campuses on a large scale. We interviewed more than 5,000 students in 15 universities and accepted 700 students into the program, a 1,000 percent increase from the previous year. Government officials, distinguished guests, and the local media were present for this lavish event, and I was at the center of it. I made the keynote presentation, in English, thanking everyone for attending and outlining the goal of the Work & Travel USA program. The press conference was a celebration of our achievements, a very satisfying culminating experience for my Beijing internship.

After returning to the United States from Beijing, I spent a quarter at Cal Poly completing my bachelor's degree. Then I returned to work for another two years in Beijing, China, exploring the culture and learning the language. The global recession served as a convenient excuse to stay longer in Beijing, because I was earning a good income and lived well there. Ultimately, I returned to the States, and having traveled to more than 10 countries and living in three of them already has fueled my desire to continue learning about other people.

Here's what Eduardo mentioned as important things he learned from his work in China:

Patience Being productive in an international company does not necessarily equate to feeding or pushing ideas to your superiors immediately after beginning your new position in the company. Most companies in China are micromanaged and subordinates seldom approach their superiors about any dispute or concerns. Most foreigners mistakenly apply the same work habits from their home country to their host country. When they push their method onto their colleagues, the colleagues feel uncomfortable.

Theoretical vs. Experiential Learning Reading about the importance of a business card in China cannot replace the physical exchange during a meeting with a prospective Chinese client. The concept of *guanxi,* literally translating to "relationships," continues after the card exchange with dinners and involves

(continued)

constant communication. At times, the managers and I would have dinners with high-ranking school or government officials in order to maintain an already established relationship. This is perceived as a way to solidify friendships by proving a client's worth. *Guanxi* is a term that I learned about in my international business courses, but I did not realize its importance until I was partaking in such behavior in my internship.

Knowing Your Objective Make a plan or outline of what you want to achieve from your trip, while also recognizing that there is always room to be flexible. I saw many foreigners stuck in China without any idea as to what their next objective would be. They stayed in China for work just because it was easy, it was all they knew to do. Being focused on one's career goals is necessary in order to have an international career in business, rather than merely a business career in China.

Resources for Your Global Career

Companies operating globally must continually monitor competitors and analyze competitors' activities in foreign markets just as it is accepted business practice in domestic markets. A complication for international strategic planning efforts is that new competition can virtually arise from any corner of the world at any time—24/7—and they may compete in virtual markets as well as in "bricks-and-mortar" markets. Companies must realize that future competitors can

develop in second- and third-world markets just as effectively as they can be found in developed markets. This means that environmental scanning and an array of analytical tools become even more critical to effective strategic planning when doing business on a global scale.

International Strategic Planning Resources

International market research reports for strategic planning:
www.export.gov/mrktresearch/index.asp
www.eia.doe.gov/countries/
Webcasts on various issues of global strategy and global strategic planning:
http://jobfunctions.bnet.com/Management/Strategy/Global+Strategy/?tag=content;breadcrumb
Perspectives on international business strategy:
www.strategy-business.com/global_perspective
http://findarticles.com/p/articles/mi_m4256/is_n4_v18/ai_13928532/
http://jobfunctions.bnet.com/Management/Strategy/International+Strategy/?&tag=content;breadcrumb
Examples of international strategic plans and approaches:
Global strategic plan for eradication of malaria:
www.rollbackmalaria.org/forumV/docs/gsp_en.pdf
Heart Health Inc.:
http://findarticles.com/p/articles/mi_pwwi/is_200803/ai_n24932155/
Global strategic planning through company situational analysis:
http://findarticles.com/p/articles/mi_m1038/is_n5_v37/ai_15859250/

Summary

LO9-1 Explain international strategy, competencies, and international competitive advantage.

International strategy is concerned with the way in which firms make fundamental choices about developing and deploying scarce resources internationally. The goal of international strategy is to create a competitive advantage that is sustainable over time. To do this, the international company should try to develop skills, or competencies, that are valuable, rare, and difficult to imitate and that the organization is able to exploit fully.

LO9-2 Describe the steps in the global strategic planning process.

Global strategic planning provides a formal structure in which managers (1) analyze the company's external environment, (2) analyze the company's internal environment, (3) define the company's business and mission, (4) set corporate objectives, (5) quantify goals, (6) formulate strategies, and (7) make tactical plans.

LO9-3 Explain the purpose of mission statements, vision statements, values statements, objectives, quantified goals, and strategies.

Statements of the corporate mission, vision, and values communicate to the firm's stakeholders what the company is and where it is going, as well as the values to be upheld among the organization's members in their behaviors. A firm's objectives direct its course of action, and its strategies enable management to reach its objectives.

LO9-4 Explain home replication, multidomestic, regional, global, and transnational strategies and when to use them.

When developing and assessing strategic alternatives, companies competing in international markets confront two opposing forces: reduction of costs and adaptation to local markets. As a result, companies basically have five different strategies that they can use for competing internationally: home replication, multidomestic, global, transnational, and regional. (Regional strategies are included because, as some researchers have argued, considering them is of value as few firms are truly global in their scope and operations.) The most appropriate strategy, overall and for various activities in the value chain, depends on the amount of pressure the company faces in terms of adapting to local markets and achieving cost reductions. Each of these five strategies has its own set of advantages and disadvantages.

LO9-5 Describe the methods of and new directions in strategic planning.

Strategic planning is traditionally done in a top-down, bottom-up, or iterative process. Operating managers, rather than dedicated staff planners, now have assumed a primary role in planning. Firms use less structured formats and much shorter documents. Managers are more concerned with issues, strategies, and implementation.

Key Words

Questions

1. What is international strategy, and why is it important?

2. What is the difference between strategic planning conducted in domestic companies and that conducted in international companies?

3. Suppose that competitor analysis reveals that the American subsidiary of your firm's German competitor is about to broaden its product mix in the American market by introducing a new line against which your company has not previously had to compete in the home market. The environmental analysis shows that recent weakness in the dollar–euro exchange rate is expected to continue, making American exports relatively less expensive in Germany. Do you recommend a defensive strategy, or do you attack your competitor in its home market? How will you implement your strategy?

4. You are the CEO of the Mesozoic Petrochemical Company and have just finished studying next year's plans of your foreign subsidiaries. You are pleased that the African regional unit's plan is so optimistic because that subsidiary contributes heavily to your company's income. But OPEC is meeting next month. Should you ask your planning committee, which meets tomorrow, to construct some scenarios? If so, about what?

5. Your firm has used bottom-up planning for years, but the subsidiaries' plans differ with respect to approaches to goals and assumptions—even the time frames are different. How can you, the CEO, get them to agree on these points and still get their individual input?

6. What are the main strengths and weaknesses of each of the competitive strategies: home replication, multidomestic, regional, global, and transnational? Under what circumstances might each strategy be more or less appropriate?

7. What strategic issues arise as a firm considers an international transfer of skills and products resulting from its distinctive competencies in its home country?

8. What is scenario analysis? Why would scenario analysis be of value to an international company? What might limit the usefulness of such an approach?

Research Task

 globalEDGE.msu.edu

Use the globalEDGE site (http://globalEDGE.msu.edu/) to complete the following exercises:

1. You work in a multinational corporation whose vision is "to be the world's leading company in the electrical equipment industry." Management wants to know how well it is doing with respect to its vision. Use the *Forbes Global 2000* most recent ranking to compile a list of the world's top 10 biggest public companies in the electrical equipment industry. What countries are these top companies from? What criteria does *Forbes* use to rank the companies?

2. You are working for a company that is planning to invest in a foreign country. Management has requested a report regarding the attractiveness of alternative countries based on the potential return of foreign direct investment (FDI). A colleague mentioned a potentially useful tool called the *FDI Confidence Index,* which is updated periodically. Find this index, and provide information regarding how the index is constructed. Which countries are ranked in the top 20 based on the FDI Confidence Index?

Founded in Rogers, Arkansas, by Sam Walton in 1962, Walmart has developed into the largest retailer in the world, with 2010 sales of more than $405 billion. Embodying high levels of service, strong inventory management, and purchasing economies, Walmart overpowered competitors and became the dominant firm in the U.S. retail industry. After rapid expansion during the 1980s and 1990s, Walmart faced limits to growth in its home market and was forced to look internationally for opportunities.

When Walmart opened its first international location in 1991, many skeptics claimed that Walmart's business practices and culture could not be transferred internationally. Yet, the company's globalization efforts progressed at a rapid pace. Its more than 4,263 international retail units employ more than 660,000 associates in 15 international markets. Walmart's international sales exceeded $100 billion in 2010—24.7 percent of the company's total, and a level that is expected to increase substantially over the next decade.

Globalizing Walmart: Where and How to Begin?

When Walmart began to expand internationally, it had to decide which countries to target. Although the European retail market was large, to succeed there Walmart would have had to take market share from established competitors. Instead, Walmart deliberately selected emerging markets as its starting point for international expansion. In Latin America, it targeted nations with large, growing populations—Mexico, Argentina, and Brazil—and in Asia it aimed at China. Because the company lacked the organizational, managerial, and financial resources to simultaneously pursue all of these markets, Walmart pursued a very deliberate entry strategy for the emerging markets, focusing first on the Americas rather than the more culturally and geographically distant Asian marketplace.

For its first international store, opened in 1991 in Mexico City, the company used a 50–50 joint venture. This entry mode helped Walmart manage the substantial differences in culture and income between the United States and Mexico. Its Mexican partner, the retail conglomerate, Cifra, provided expertise in operating in the Mexican market and a base for learning about retailing in that country. Leveraging its learning from the Mexican experience when it entered Brazil in 1996, Walmart took a majority position in a 60–40 venture with a local retailer, Lojas Americana. When subsequently entering Argentina, Walmart did so on a wholly owned basis. After gaining experience with partners, in 1997 Walmart expanded further in Mexico by acquiring a controlling interest in Cifra, which it renamed in 2000 to Walmart de México S. A. de C. V. By 2011, Walmart operated more than 1,766 units in Mexico, accounting for more than half of all supermarket sales in Mexico.

Still, learning the dos and don'ts was a difficult process. "It wasn't such a good idea to stick so closely to the domestic Walmart blueprint in Argentina, or in some of the other international markets we've entered, for that matter," said the president of Walmart International. "In Mexico City we sold tennis balls that wouldn't bounce right in the high altitude. We built large parking lots at some of our Mexican stores, only to realize that many of our customers there rode the bus to the store, then trudged across those large parking lots with bags full of merchandise. We responded by creating bus shuttles to drop customers off at the door. These were all mistakes that were easy to address, but we're now working smarter internationally to avoid cultural and regional problems on the front end."[a] Walmart's initial entry into Brazil used greenfield store sites and emphasized aggressive pricing to build market share, but the French retailer Carrefour and other Brazilian competitors retaliated, launching a costly price war. Walmart's strength in international sourcing was initially of limited assistance in Brazil, since the leading sales category—food—was primarily sourced locally, where Carrefour and others already had strong relationships with local suppliers. Over time, Walmart changed its competitive emphasis to customer service and a broader merchandise mix than smaller local companies could match. The company also pursued acquisitions to supplement internal growth, buying 118 Bompreço stores in 2004 and 140 Sonae stores in 2005. By 2011, Walmart was the third-largest retailer in Brazil, operating 434 stores.

The Challenge of China

The lure of China, the world's most populous nation, proved too great to ignore. Walmart was one of the first international retailers in China when it set up operations in 1996. Before Walmart's arrival, state-owned retailers typically offered a limited range of products, often of low quality, and most stores were poorly lit, dirty, and disorganized.

Concerned about their potential impact on local firms, Beijing restricted the operations of foreign retailers. These restrictions included requirements for government-backed partners and limitations on the number and location of stores. Initially, Walmart's partner was Charoen Pokphand, a Thai conglomerate with massive investments in China and a strong track record with joint ventures. This venture was terminated after 18 months, due to differences regarding control. A new venture was subsequently formed with two politically connected partners, Shenzhen Economic Development Zone and Shenzhen International Trust and Investment Corporation, and Walmart was able to negotiate a controlling stake in the venture. The first Chinese Walmart store was in Shenzhen, a rapidly growing city bordering Hong Kong. The company concentrated its initial activities in Shenzhen while it learned about Chinese retailing.

Walmart had many well-publicized miscues while learning how to do business in China. For example, some household items found at American Walmarts are not found in the Chinese stores. "Their shopping list isn't as extensive as ours. If you ask the majority of people here what a paper towel is, they either don't know or they think it's some kind of luxury item," said the president of Walmart China.[b] The company eliminated matching kitchen towels and window curtains, because the wide variety of Chinese window sizes caused people to make their own curtains. Consumers purchased four times the number of small appliances projected, but Walmart no longer tries to sell extension ladders or a year's supply of soy sauce or shampoo to Chinese customers, who typically live in cramped apartments with limited storage space. Yet, although "people say the Chinese don't like sweets, we sure sell a lot of M&Ms," said Joe Hatfield, president of Walmart's Asian retailing operations.[c]

Operationally, the scarcity of highly modernized suppliers in China frustrated Walmart's initial attempts to achieve high levels of efficiency. Bar coding was not standardized in China, and retailers had to either recode goods themselves or distribute labels to suppliers, procedures that increased costs and hindered efficiency. Pressured to appease the government's desire for local sourcing of products, while maintaining the aura of being an American shopping experience, Walmart's solution was to source about 85 percent of the Chinese stores' purchases from local manufacturers but heavily weight purchasing toward locally produced American brands (such as products from Procter & Gamble's factories in China). Walmart also mass-markets Chinese products that were previously available only in isolated parts of the country, such as coconut juice from Guangdong province, hams and mushrooms from rural Yunnan, and oats from Fujian province.

Walmart also learned the importance of building relationships with agencies from the central and local governments and with local communities. Bureaucratic red tape, graft, and lengthy delays in the approval process proved to be aggravating. The company learned to curry favor through actions such as inviting Chinese officials to visit Walmart's American headquarters, assisting local charities, and even building a school for the local community. Walmart expected its small-town folksiness to be a strong asset in China. "Price has been an issue, but there's always somebody who can undersell you. A young person who's smiling and saying, 'Can I help you?' is a big part of the equation. Most places in this country you don't get that," said the president of Walmart International.[d] "Over the last two years, Walmart has learned a tremendous amount about serving our Chinese customers, and our excitement about expanding in the market and in Asia has never been stronger."[e]

In 2006, Walmart outbid competitors Carrefour, the United Kingdom's Tesco, and Lianhua of China to acquire Trust-Mart, a chain of more than 100 supercenters located in 20 cities across China. This acquisition immediately gave Walmart the largest network of food and department stores in China. By 2011, Walmart operated 279 retail units in China. Walmart estimated that its operations in China could be nearly as large as in the United States within 20 years, and the lessons Walmart has learned have positioned the company to exploit future market-opening initiatives in China.

A Different Approach for Entering Canada and Europe

After focusing initial international expansion efforts on large developing nations, Walmart began to pursue the Canadian and European markets. Strong, entrenched competitors in these mature, developed country markets hindered Walmart's prospects for obtaining critical mass solely through internal growth. Rather than first developing its retail operations from scratch, as in Latin America and Asia, Walmart entered via acquisitions.

The company entered Canada in 1994 by acquiring 122 Woolco stores. Walmart quickly restructured the money-losing Canadian operations, applying many of the practices that had been successful in the United States. Transition teams were brought in from the United States to help with the transformation, and within two years the Canadian operations were profitable. Its 317 stores account for more than 35 percent of the Canadian discount- and department-store retail market.

In Europe, Walmart entered Germany by acquiring the 21-unit Wertkauf hypermarket chain in 1998 and 74 Interspar stores in 1999. The company entered the United Kingdom in 1999 by acquiring the 229-store ASDA Group. Walmart was the second-largest supermarket chain in the United Kingdom by 2011, with 371 stores, but it has been losing ground to industry leader Tesco Plc. These acquisitions allowed Walmart to build market share quickly within the highly advanced and competitive European retail market.

Walmart's rapid European market share growth was accompanied by difficulties. The acquisition of two German companies based in different cities within a year proved too much for the company's limited European infrastructure. Top management positions were filled with U.S. expatriates, many of whom lacked German language skills. Efforts to centralize purchasing and leverage Walmart's famous competencies in information systems and inventory management were stymied by problems with suppliers that were not familiar with such practices. The introduction of Walmart's "always low prices" approach met resistance from competitors and regulators. Indeed, the company was ordered by Germany's Cartel Office to raise prices, charging that Walmart had helped to spark a price war by illegally selling some items below cost. Walmart also challenged existing retail practices regarding hours of operation. Laws required shops to close by 8 p.m. on weekdays and 4 p.m. on Saturdays and to remain closed on Sundays. In response, Walmart stores began to open by 7 a.m., two hours earlier than most competitors. These changes sparked vehement opposition from smaller competitors and employees' unions.

Walmart Germany struggled to build a strong competitive base, sustaining estimated losses of more than $1 billion. Lacking the scale of operations to create competitive advantage, and facing strong competition in a mature marketplace, in 2006 Walmart sold its German operations to a competitor, Metro. "We had a difficult time in Germany from the get-go," said Walmart's Amy Wyatt. "Looking at the international business around the world and where we would have the greatest impact on growth and investor return, it became increasingly clear that given the German business environment, we could never obtain the scale and results we desired."[f] That same year, Walmart announced that it was selling its Korean operations after failing to achieve successful scale and due to difficulties adjusting to the peculiarities of the Korean marketplace.

India: Anticipating the Opening Up of a Billion-Person Market

Although it is the world's eighth-largest retail market at more than $350 billion and has 400 million people with disposable income, the inefficiency of the Indian retail sector is well known. More than 95 percent of retail sales are made through nearly 15 million tea stands, newspaper stalls, and mom-and-pop stores. Strict government barriers have prevented foreign-owned retail businesses, although that situation is changing. "Many smart people—much smarter than I—believe that India could be the next China," said John Menzer, the former head of Walmart's international operations and current vice chair of the company's U.S. stores. "So, certainly, as a retailer it's a place where we'd like to be."[g]

However, exploiting the potential of India could be a major challenge, particularly given the country's notoriously frustrating bureaucracy and poor infrastructure. Walmart will have to learn to manage highly protectionist and anti-capitalist political parties, a bad road system, frequent power outages, difficulties acquiring appropriate plots of land, and lack of adequate distribution and cold-storage systems, among other concerns. One industry participant said, "Where will they run their Volvo trucks here? They will probably have to have bullock carts and handcarts in their supply chain."[h] The diversity of the country could also prove problematic, with 18 official languages, 6,000 castes and subcastes, and widely varying regional consumer cultures. Savvy new Indian chains, such as Provogue and Shoppers' Stop, are starting to emerge, and nationalistic sentiments may produce much consternation for expansion efforts of foreign companies such as Walmart.

In preparation for an eventual opening of the market, Walmart began building a foundation by establishing relationships with Indian suppliers, distributors, and consumers. "What we found in China as we get stores on the ground and get more mass, we get to know a lot more of the suppliers. And when we know the suppliers, it gives us the opportunity to learn the product of the suppliers and actually export them," said Mr. Menzer.[i] In 2007, Walmart established Bharti Walmart, a 50–50 joint venture with Bharti Enterprises, a leader in mobile telecommunications. The venture's first store opened in 2009. Due to the constraints on retailing, this venture is technically focused on the wholesale market, selling only to large institutional or wholesale buyers while the company builds up its infrastructure and skills for an eventual liberalization of the retail market. However, due to limited restrictions, more than 30,000 members joined this first store to shop from the broad selection of products. By mid-2011, the venture had opened six Best Price Modern Wholesale stores, and it planned to open another 20 stores in the subsequent

two years. As stated by Raj Jain, Bharti Walmart's chief executive, "In the next one or two years we do anticipate we will be in a market leadership position."[j] Clearly, Walmart will need to understand the political and market dynamics and exploit the lessons it has learned from entering other emerging markets in order to achieve success when the Indian market finally opens up.

Questions:

1. Why has Walmart viewed international expansion as a critical part of its strategy?

2. What did Walmart do to enable the company to achieve success in Canada and Latin America? Why did Walmart fail to achieve similar success in Europe?

3. What should Walmart do—or not do—to help ensure that the company achieves success in China and India?

[a] "ASDA Purchase Leads Way for Wal-Mart's International Expansion," *Wal-MartAnnual Report 2000,* p. 10.

[b] James Cox, "Great Wal-Mart of China Red-Letter Day as East Meets West in the Aisles," *USA Today,* September 11, 1996, p. B1.

[c] Tyler Marshall, "Selling Eel and Chicken Feet—Plus M&Ms and Sony TVs," *Los Angeles Times,* November 25, 2003, p. A15.

[d] Cox, "Great Wal-Mart of China Red-Letter Day."

[e] "Wal-Mart China Expansion to Accelerate," www.Walmartstores.com/newsstand/archive/prn_980605_chinaexpan.shtml (June 5, 1999).

[f] Ann Zimmerman and Emily Nelson, "With profits elusive, Wal-Mart to exit Germany," The Wall Street Journal, July 29, 2006, p. A1.

[g] Eric Bellman and Kris Hudson, "Wal-Mart Stakes India Claim," *The Wall Street Journal,* January 18, 2006, p. A9.

[h] "The Great Wal of India," The Economic Times, January 10, 2007, http://articles.economictimes.indiatimes.com/2007-01-10/news/27671456_1_wal-mart-indian-retail-chains-germany-s-metro (accessed July 15, 2011).

[i] Ibid.

[j] Rasul Bailay, "Bharti Walmart to Double Stores in India, Eyes Top Spot in Two Years," Livemint.com, May 5, 2011, www.livemint.com/2011/05/05230121/Bharti-Walmart-to-double-store.html (May 7, 2011).

Sources: Walmart 2010 Annual Report, http://walmartstores.com/sites/annualreport/2010/ (May 7, 2011); Peter Wonacott, "Wal-Mart Finds Market Footing in China," *The Wall Street Journal,* July 17, 2000, p. A31; "Big Chains Set for Post-WTO Scrap," *South China Morning Post,* November 3, 2000, p. 5; Glenn Hall, "Wal-Mart Germany Told to Raise Prices: Choking Small Retailers," *National Post,* September 9, 2000, p. D3; Mike Troy, "In South America, Ahold's Loss Is Wal-Mart's Gain," *DSN Retailing Today,* March 22, 2004, pp. 1–2; John Zimmerman and Emily Nelson, "With Profits Elusive, Wal-Mart to Exit Germany," *The Wall Street Journal,* July 29, 2006, p. A2; Ann Zimmerman and Emily Nelson, "With Profits Elusive, Wal-Mart to Exit Germany," *The Wall Street Journal,* July 29, 2006, p. A1; Matthew Boyle, "Wal-Mart's Painful Lessons," *Bloomberg Businessweek,* October 13, 2009, www.businessweek.com/managing/content/oct2009/ca20091013_227022.htm (May 7, 2011); and "Wal-Mart to Become Biggest Big-Box in China," http://money.cnn.com/2006/10/16/news/international/walmart_hypermarkets.reut/index.htm?postversion=2006101706 (October 17, 2006).

Organizational Design and Control

We are in the midst of a major transition from organization and management practices that began around the turn of the 20th century. Our cloudy crystal ball won't allow us to see which organization structure or model will dominate the 21st century. Since we're no longer in an age of mass production and standardization, there won't likely be just one type. Rather, we'll see our top organizations grow and shed a variety of structures and models to suit their changing circumstances.

—*Jim Clemmer, in "High Performance Organization Structures and Characteristics"*

Kraft Foods: Becoming a "Best of Global and Best of Local" Company by Reorganizing

When Kraft Foods announced a complex reorganization of its worldwide operations, the goal of this new organizational design was to transform the company into an integrated, global company. With more than $49 billion in sales and 127,000 employees worldwide at the end of 2010, Kraft is the largest branded-food and beverage company headquartered in North America and the second largest in the world, behind Nestlé. Kraft's mission is "to be widely recognized as the undisputed leader of the global food industry." The company's products—including such brands as Kraft cheese, Maxwell House coffee, Oreo cookies, Oscar Mayer meats, Cadbury chocolates, and Jello desserts—are sold in more than 150 nations.

Kraft's reorganization was triggered in part by slowing growth in several product categories, especially within developed country markets, which caused a decline in earnings in recent years. Many of Kraft's performance difficulties were attributed to problems with its prior organizational structure. To address this situation, under its new structure, Kraft created a matrix organization that included:

1. A new global marketing and category development group to accelerate growth and global expansion through developing global category strategies, new-product platforms, and marketing excellence.

2. Three geographic-based commercial units, for the regions of North America, Europe, and Developing Markets. The North American and European operations are managed by product category, while the Developing Markets unit is managed by geographic locale. These units are responsible for driving strong results, country by country, through local consumer and customer knowledge, local sales and marketing execution, and responsibility for profits and losses.

3. Key functions—including technology and quality, supply chains, finance, human resources, law, information systems, corporate and governmental affairs, and strategy and business development—are managed on a global basis in order to achieve greater economies of scale, leverage technologies and best practices internationally, and drive brands and ideas around the world faster.

4. The activities of the preceding three groups are coordinated with Kraft's six global product sectors—biscuits (snacks and cereals), confectionery, beverages, cheese, grocery (condiments and desserts), and convenient meals.

Kraft's CEO said, "The most important opportunities and pressing challenges that we face today and going forward demand that we become a more unified, global company. But in becoming more global, we must keep and strengthen the local expertise that has built our success. By moving quickly to create Kraft's new global 'One Company' structure, we can immediately begin to capture the 'best of global and best of local' and act with greater focus and speed than ever before." In terms of enhanced organizational effectiveness, Kraft's leadership anticipated that this outcome would be achieved through accelerated innovation, improved application of category/functional expertise, strong local execution, improved management development, and faster decision making. Enhanced efficiency would be facilitated by elimination of functional duplication and facility consolidation. The new organizational structure resembles that of other major consumer products companies, such as Gillette and Procter & Gamble.

A particular objective of the reorganization was to produce a more integrated and balanced global business by accelerating Kraft's growth outside its home market of the United States, where the market was maturing and profits were declining. Overall, Kraft's non-U.S. sales grew from less than a quarter of total company revenues in the early 1990s to nearly 61 percent in 2010. Kraft's executive vice president commented, "This new structure will help us accelerate our growth and move faster as a company in our decision-making process."

Another important objective of Kraft's reorganization was to enhance growth prospects within developing-country markets. Revenues from developing markets had increased from $1 billion in 1992 to $2 billion in 2000 and $5 billion in 2007, and jumping to nearly $14 billion in 2010. These markets grew from 12 percent of overall revenues at the time the company restructured to nearly 28 percent in less than 6 years. Part of this success was from expanding its core categories into large developing countries with the greatest growth potential, particularly Mexico, Brazil, Russia, and China.

Under the new structure, Kraft's strategy for developing-country markets was based on four main

components: (1) introduce additional snack, beverage, and cheese categories in developing markets where it already had a presence; (2) introduce additional brands across key price segments within the categories where it already had a presence; (3) enter developing markets where it did not yet have a presence; and (4) pursue tactical fill-in acquisitions, especially in snacks and beverages. Strategic and operational improvements from the new matrix structure were expected to enhance the implementation of these initiatives and Kraft's position in the global food and beverage industry.

To facilitate effective localization, Kraft mandated that an increasing proportion of decisions must be moved away from the company's Northfield, Illinois, headquarters and into the company's operating units. Full profit-and-loss accountability was given to the business units, and human and financial resources were placed closer to the marketplaces. Country managers were encouraged to create new products that appealed to local cultures, and Kraft allocated 30 percent more for marketing. One notable result involved the iconic Oreo cookie, which was reinvented as a wafer stick for the Chinese market. The new "biscuit" was an almost instant hit, capturing more than 23 percent of the $1.3 billion Chinese market for such products. Leveraging this success internationally, the wafers have subsequently been sold elsewhere in Asia, as well as in Canada and Australia.

Source: "Company Structure Encourages Best of Global, Best of Local," www.kraft.com/profile/company_structure.html (accessed June 20, 2006); Neil Buckley, "Kraft Works to Become a More Global Business," Financial Times, January 9, 2004, p. 20; "Kraft Foods Announces New Global Organizational Structure," January 8, 2004, www.lexdon.com/article/kraft_foods_announces_new_global/56574.html (accessed May 8, 2011); "Visuals from Presentation by Roger Deromedi, CEO, Kraft Foods, to Investment Community, January 27, 2004," http://media.corporate-ir.net/media_files/nys/kft/presentations/kft_o70127b2326.pdf (accessed July 24, 2004); "Kraft Foods Inc. Reports 2005 Results and Issues 2006 Outlook; Announces Expanded Restructuring Program as Part of Sustainable Growth Plan," Business Wire, January 30, 2006, p. 1; Julie Jargon, "Kraft Reformulates Oreo, Scores in China," The Wall Street Journal, May 1, 2008, pp. B1, B7; and Kraft Foods Inc., "Kraft Foods 10-K," www.kraftfoodscompany.com/Investor/sec-filings-annual-report/annual_reports.aspx (accessed May 8, 2011).

Organizations exist for the purpose of enabling a group of people to effectively coordinate their collective activities and accomplish objectives.[1] **Organizational structure** refers to the way that an organization formally arranges its various domestic and international units and activities and the relationships among these organizational components. A company's structure helps determine where formal power and authority will be located within the organization, and this structure is what is typically presented in a company's organization chart.

Creating and evolving the structure of an international organization over time are fundamental tasks of senior management. Few executives except those in the senior levels of the organization are capable of establishing or changing the overall structure of an international company, because people at an organization's lower levels lack the broad perspective necessary for making the various trade-offs that will influence the organization as a whole. Nevertheless, all of the company's managers have to perform their job responsibilities within the context created by this structure. Further, most managers need to be able to effectively structure the various activities that are within their area of responsibility and to do so in a manner that is consistent with the company's overall structure. As a result, developing an understanding of the different ways in which international companies can be structured and the relative strengths and weaknesses of each of the various structural alternatives is an essential skill for managers.

In this chapter, we discuss the different organizational forms an international company can take and key strategic issues that managers must address in choosing among these various organizational designs. Included in the discussion will be the identification of concerns that managers have regarding their ability to control the international activities of their companies.

What Is Organizational Design, and Why Is It Important for International Companies?

Organizational design is a process that deals with how an international business should be organized in order to ensure that its worldwide business activities are able to be integrated in an efficient and effective manner. As suggested in Figure 10.1, in designing an international organization, it is essential that the structures and systems being implemented are not merely consistent with each other but also consistent with the environmental context in which the organization is operating and the strategy the company is using for competing in this international environment. The size of the organization and the complexity of its business operations must also be considered in the design of a company.

The structure of an international company (IC) must be able to evolve over time, to allow the organization to respond to change and to efficiently and effectively reconfigure the way in which its competencies and resources are integrated within and across the company's various units. This is a major challenge for international companies, especially as their activities are increasingly dispersed across the globe as well as subject to rapid and ongoing environmental and strategic change. Failure to successfully deal with this challenge threatens the organization's performance and, indeed, its long-term survival.

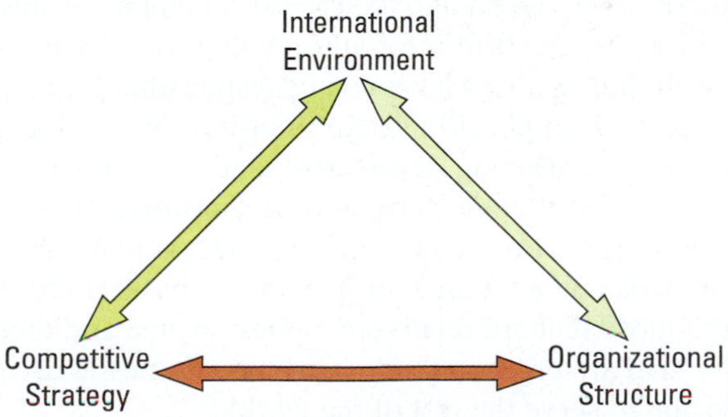

organizational structure
The way that an organization formally arranges its domestic and international units and activities, and the relationships among these various organizational components

LO10-1 Explain why the design of organizational structure is important to international companies.

organizational design
A process that deals with how an international business should be organized in order to ensure that its worldwide business activities are able to be integrated in an efficient and effective manner

FIGURE 10.1

The Relationship among International Environment, Competitive Strategy, and Organizational Structure

International Environment

Competitive Strategy

Organizational Structure

The international company's strategic planning process itself, because it encompasses an analysis of the firm's external environments as well as its strengths and weaknesses, often discloses a need to alter the organization. Changes in an international company's strategy may require changes in the organization, but the reverse is also true. For instance, a new CEO may join the firm, or the company may acquire a company in another nation or in another area of business activity. Strategic planning and organizing are so closely related that usually management treats the structure of the organization as an integral part of the strategic planning process.

ORGANIZATIONAL DESIGN CONCERNS

LO10-2 **Discuss** the organizational dimensions that must be considered when selecting organizational structures.

Two of the concerns that management faces in designing the organizational structure for an IC are (1) finding the most effective way to departmentalize to take advantage of the efficiencies gained from specialization of labor and (2) coordinating the activities of those departments to enable the firm to meet its overall objectives. As all managers know, these two concerns run counter to each other; that is, the gain from increased specialization of labor may at times be nullified by the increased cost of coordination. It is the search for an optimum balance between them that often leads to a reorganization of the international company's structure.

There are four primary dimensions that need to be considered when designing the structure of an international company:

1. *Product and technical expertise* regarding the different businesses that the company participates in.

2. *Geographic expertise* regarding the countries and regions in which the company operates.

3. *Customer expertise* regarding the similarity of client groups, industries, market segments, or population groups that transcend the boundaries of individual countries or regions.

4. *Functional expertise* regarding the various value chain activities that the company is involved with.

International companies vary with respect to the way these four dimensions are structured and integrated. No single structure is best for all companies and contexts. Rather, managers have to consider the nature of their company's international operating environment and strategy—both currently and how they are expected to change in the future—when deciding when and how to modify the company's organizational structure. In the following sections, we discuss the most common types of organizational designs for international companies. In reality, due to the complex nature of their operating environments and nuances of their historical origins and evolution, the structure of many ICs may deviate to some extent from these basic organizational designs. Nevertheless, understanding attributes associated with these basic designs can assist managers of international companies in selecting an organizational structure appropriate for their current and anticipated circumstances.

LO10-3 **Discuss** the various organizational forms available for structuring international companies.

EVOLUTION OF THE INTERNATIONAL COMPANY

international division

A division in the organization that is at the same level as the domestic division and is responsible for all non-home-country activities

As discussed in Chapters 2 and 13, companies often enter foreign markets first by exporting and then, as sales increase, by forming overseas sales companies and eventually setting up manufacturing facilities. As the firm's foreign involvement changes, its organization frequently changes as well. It might first have *no one* responsible for international business; the firm's marketing department might fill the export orders. Next, an export department might be created, possibly in the marketing department; and when the company begins to invest in various overseas locations, it could form an **international division** to take charge of all overseas involvement. Larger firms, such as Ford, IBM, and Walmart, commonly organize their international divisions on a regional or geographic basis (Figure 10.2). Today, we still see companies—both those that are relatively modest in size and those that are some of the largest in the world—that are organized into a primary domestic division, supplemented by an international division to serve the rest of the world.

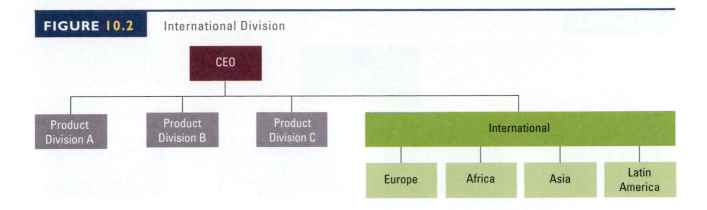

FIGURE 10.2 International Division

As their overseas operations increase in importance and scope, most managements feel the need to eliminate international divisions and establish worldwide organizations based on *product, region, function,* or *customer classes.* At secondary, tertiary, and still lower levels, these four dimensions—plus (1) process, (2) national subsidiary, and (3) international or domestic—provide the basis for subdivisions. As a result, as they grow over time, most international companies move away from the use of international divisions and instead implement one of the global structures that we present in the subsequent sections of this chapter. The initial choice of organizational structure after discarding the international division is usually one based on either global product or global geographic factors. These alternative paths for the design and evolution of the international company are presented in the international stages model of organizational structures, as shown in Figure 10.3.[2]

Managements that change to these types of organizations feel they will (1) be more capable of developing competitive strategies to confront the increasing global competition, (2) obtain lower production costs by promoting worldwide product standardization and manufacturing rationalization, and (3) enhance technology transfer and the allocation of company resources.

Global Corporate Form—Product Frequently, this structure represents a return to pre-export department times in that the domestic product division has been given responsibility for global line and staff operations. In the present-day global form, product divisions are responsible for the worldwide operations such as marketing and production of products

FIGURE 10.3

The International Structural Stages Model

Source: Based on John M. Stopford and Louis T. Wells, *Strategy and Structure of the Multinational Enterprise* (New York: Basic Books, 1970).

FIGURE 10.4   Global Corporate Form—Product

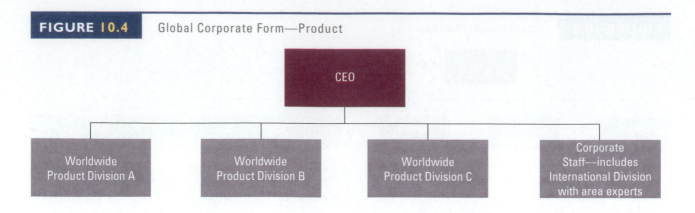

under their control. Each division generally has regional experts, so while this organizational form avoids the duplication of product experts common in a company with an international division, it creates a duplication of area experts. Occasionally, to avoid placing regional specialists in each product division, management will have a group of managerial specialists in an international division who advise the product divisions but have no authority over them (see Figure 10.4). For example, all of General Electric's businesses are managed through a global line-of-business structure, and investment opportunities are identified and assessed on a global basis by managers within each of these business areas.

Global Corporate Form—Geographic Regions   Firms in which geographic regions are the primary basis for division put the responsibility for all activities under area managers who report directly to the chief executive officer. This kind of organization simplifies the task of directing worldwide operations, because every country in the world is clearly under the control of someone who is in contact with headquarters (see Figure 10.5).

Of course, this organizational type is used for both multinational (multidomestic) and global companies. Global companies that use it consider the division in which the home country is located as just another division for purposes of resource allocation and a source of management personnel. Some U.S. global companies have created a North American division that includes Canada, Mexico, and Central American countries in addition to the United States, possibly in part to emphasize that the home country is given no preference.

The regionalized organization appears to be popular with companies that manufacture products with a rather low, or at least stable, technological content that require strong marketing ability. It is also favored by firms with diverse products, each having different product requirements, competitive environments, and political risks. Many producers of consumer products, such as prepared foods, pharmaceuticals, and household products, employ this type of organization. The disadvantage of an organization divided into geographic regions is that each region must have its own product and functional specialists, so although the duplication of area specialists found in product divisions is eliminated, duplication of product and functional specialists is necessary.

FIGURE 10.5   Global Corporate Form—Geographic Regions

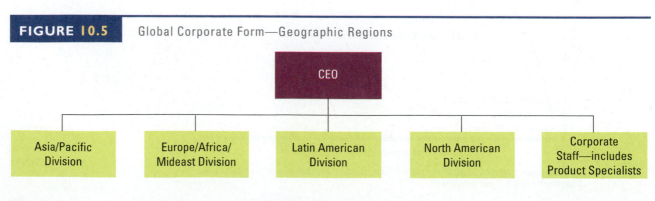

FIGURE 10.6 Global Corporate Form—Function

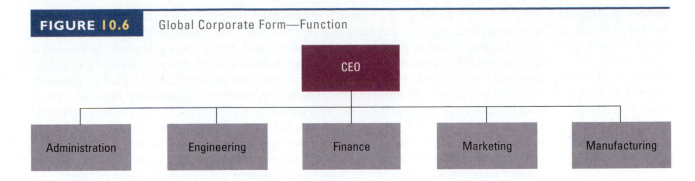

Production coordination across regions presents difficult problems, as does global product planning. To alleviate these problems, managements often place specialized product managers on the headquarters staff. Although these managers have no line authority, they do provide input to corporate decisions concerning products.

Global Corporate Form—Function

Few firms are organized by function at the top level. Those that are obviously believe worldwide functional expertise is more significant to the firm than is product or area knowledge. In this type of organization, those reporting to the CEO might be the senior executives responsible for each functional area (marketing, production, finance, and so on), as in Figure 10.6. The commonality among the users of the functional form is a narrow and highly integrated product mix, such as that of aircraft manufacturers or oil refining companies.

Hybrid Forms

In a **hybrid organization,** a mixture of the preceding organizational forms is used at the top level and may or may not be present at the lower levels as well. Figure 10.7 illustrates a simple hybrid form. Such combinations are often the result of a regionally organized company having introduced a new and different product line that management believes can best be handled by a worldwide product division. An acquired company with distinct products and a functioning marketing network may be incorporated as a product division even though the rest of the firm is organized on a regional basis. Later, after corporate management becomes familiar with the operation, it may be regionalized.

A mixed structure may also result from the firm's selling to a sizable, homogeneous class of customers. Special divisions for handling sales to the military or to original equipment manufacturers, for example, are often established at the same level as regional or product divisions.

hybrid organization
Structure organized by more than one dimension at the top level

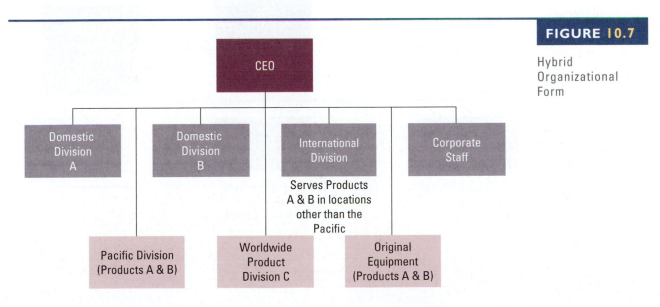

FIGURE 10.7

Hybrid Organizational Form

matrix organization
An organizational structure composed of one or more superimposed organizational structures in an attempt to mesh product, regional, functional, and other expertise

Matrix Organizations

The **matrix organization** has evolved from management's attempt to mesh product, regional, and functional expertise while still maintaining clear lines of authority. It is called a matrix because an organization based on one or possibly two dimensions is superimposed on an organization based on another dimension. In an organization of two dimensions, such as area and product, both the geographic area managers and the product managers will be at the same level, and their responsibilities will overlap. An individual manager—say, a marketing manager in Germany—will have a multiple reporting relationship, being responsible to the manager overseeing the geographic area that includes Germany and in some instances to an international or worldwide marketing manager at headquarters. Figure 10.8 illustrates an extremely simple matrix organization based on two organizational dimensions. Note that the country managers are responsible to both the area managers and the product-line managers.

Problems with the Matrix Although at one time it seemed that the matrix organizational form would enable firms to have the advantages of the product, regional, and functional forms, the disadvantages of the matrix form have kept most worldwide companies from adopting it. One problem with the matrix is that the two or three managers (if it is a three-dimensional matrix) must agree on a decision. This can lead to less-than-optimum compromises, delayed responses, and power politics in which more attention is paid to the process than to the problem. When the managers cannot agree, the problem goes higher in the organization and takes top management away from its duties. Dow Chemical Company, which has operations in more than 175 countries, changed its organizational structure from a geographic matrix to one of global business processes and 16 global business units that have individual global profit-and-loss responsibility.

matrix overlay
An organization in which top-level divisions are required to heed input from a staff composed of experts of another organizational dimension in an attempt to avoid the double-reporting difficulty of a matrix organization but still mesh two or more dimensions

Because of these difficulties associated with the matrix structure, many firms have maintained their original organizations based on product, function, region, or international divisions and have built into the structure accountability for the other organizational dimensions; this is called by some a **matrix overlay.**

Matrix Overlay The matrix overlay attempts to address the problems of the matrix structure by requiring accountability of all functions in the organization while avoiding the burdensome management stresses of a pure matrix structure. We have already mentioned how a firm organized by product may have regional specialists in a staff function with the requirement that they have input to product decisions. They may even be organized in an international division, as was mentioned previously. In the case of a regional organization, there would be product managers on its staff who provide input to regional decisions.

FIGURE 10.8

Regional–Product Matrix

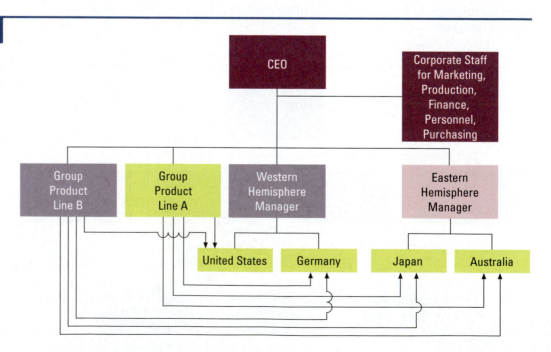

Strategic Business Units

Strategic business units (SBUs) are an organizational form in which product divisions have been defined as though they were distinct, independent businesses. An SBU is defined as a self-contained business entity with a clearly defined market, specific competitors, the ability to carry out its business mission, and a size appropriate for control by a single manager. Most SBUs are based on product lines, such as the 31 autonomous profit center business units that Caterpillar Inc. established.[3] If a product must be modified to suit different markets, a worldwide SBU may be divided into a few product/market SBUs serving various markets or groups of countries. Shell Chemical Company's SBUs, which it calls product business units (PBUs), are global.[4] BP's business units, which it calls strategic performance units (SPUs), are also global.[5]

CHANGES IN ORGANIZATIONAL FORMS

The rapidly changing business environment caused by increased global competition, customer preference for custom-made rather than mass-produced products, and faster technological change is pressuring companies to step up their search for organizational forms that will enable them to act more quickly, reduce costs, and improve the quality of product offerings. The ability to maintain alignment between the organization and its global and hypercompetitive environment has become a fundamental determinant of many organizations' ability to merely survive. As a result, change in organizational form has become an almost constant process. Not only are companies mixing older, established forms of organization; they are also changing to different forms, many of which are modified versions of long-established forms with new names.

The increasing acceptance by many companies of the need for frequent reorganization, called **reengineering** by many, is often accompanied by a significant reduction in the levels of middle management, restructuring of work processes to reduce the fragmenting of the process across functional departments, improvement in the speed and quality of strategy execution, empowerment of employees, and the use of computers for instant communication and swift transmittal of information. CEOs are striving to make their organizations lean, flat, fast to respond, and innovative.

CURRENT ORGANIZATIONAL TRENDS

Two organizational forms are now receiving the attention of many CEOs: the virtual corporation and the horizontal corporation.

Virtual Corporation

A **virtual corporation,** also called a *network corporation,* is an organization that coordinates economic activity to deliver value to customers using resources outside the traditional boundaries of the organization. In other words, it relies to a great extent on third parties to conduct its business. Outsourcing once was used for downsizing and cost reduction, but now companies are using it to obtain specialized expertise that they don't have but need in order to serve new markets or adopt new technology.

The evolution of the technology infrastructure has made possible changes in the work force and working methods, such as teleworking, home offices, and flexible working practices. All these factors have contributed to the increase in virtual corporations. Global networking on the Internet has made worldwide outsourcing possible for firms of all sizes. Dell Computer is a well-known example of a company that has used tight integration with its global network of suppliers in order to assemble and deliver semi-customized computers to its international customers within days of receiving an order, and without carrying large volumes of expensive inventory that is prone to losing value through technological obsolescence.

Although the name is new, the virtual corporation concept has existed for decades. It has been extremely common for a group of construction firms, each with a special area of expertise, to form a consortium to bid on a contract for constructing a road or a sports stadium, for example. After finishing the job, the consortium would disband. Other examples of network organizations are the various clothing and athletic shoe marketers such as DKNY, Nike, and Reebok. The latter firms are also called *modular corporations.*

The virtual corporation concept has several potential benefits. In particular, it permits greater flexibility than is associated with more typical corporate structures. Rather than building competence from the ground up and incurring high startup costs that could limit future production decisions, virtual corporations form a network of dynamic relationships that allow them to take advantage of the competencies of other organizations in order to respond rapidly to changing circumstances. However, this form of organization can have disadvantages, including the potential to reduce management's control over the corporation's activities (it is vulnerable to the opportunistic actions of partners, including cost increases, unintended "borrowing" of technical and other knowledge, and potential departure from the relationship at inappropriate times). From the standpoint of employees, the virtual corporation form of organization may replace the security of long-term employment and the promise of ever-increasing salaries with the insecurity of the market—a global market.

horizontal corporation
A form of organization characterized by lateral decision processes, horizontal networks, and a strong corporatewide business philosophy

Horizontal Corporation

Another organizational form, the **horizontal corporation,** has been adopted by some large technology-oriented global firms in highly competitive industries such as electronics and computers. Firms such as 3M, General Electric, and DuPont have chosen this organizational form to give themselves the flexibility to respond quickly to advances in technology and be product innovators. In many companies, *teams* are drawn from different departments to solve a problem or deliver a product.

This organization has been characterized as "antiorganization" because its designers are seeking to remove the constraints imposed by the conventional organizational structures. In a horizontal corporation, employees worldwide create, build, and market the company's products through a carefully cultivated system of interrelationships. In a horizontal corporation, marketers in Great Britain speak directly to production people in Brazil without having to go through the home office in Germany, for example.

Proponents of the horizontal organization claim lateral relationships incite innovation and new-product development. They also state that this approach to organizing helps to place more decision-making responsibility in the hands of middle managers and other skilled

Life in a Virtual Organization

Accenture Ltd. delivers a range of consulting, outsourcing, and technology services to clients around the world. Its 214,000 employees, located in some 120 countries, generated revenues of more than $23 billion in 2010. Although the company incorporated in Ireland in September 2009, according to the company's senior management, Accenture has neither an operational headquarters facility nor any formal branch facilities. Instead, the company's approach to organizing its global operations might be termed virtual.

Prior to 2000, Accenture had been the consulting arm of the now-defunct Arthur Andersen accounting company. During that time, the consulting operations had been managed for decades by the Swiss-based company, Andersen Worldwide. After consulting was split off from Andersen's accounting operations and subsequently became a separate organization under the name Accenture and incorporated in the tax haven of Bermuda, the partners could not agree on a location for the new company's headquarters. Because they typically spent a major portion of their time on the road, Accenture's executives decided to live where each of them wanted and forgo an organization built around a central headquarters. As a result, the chief financial officer lives in California's Silicon Valley, the chief technology officer lives in Germany, and many of the company's globally diverse workforce of consultants are traveling nearly nonstop to client sites worldwide.

Coordinating this geographically dispersed workforce is facilitated by technology. Employees log on to Accenture's intranet daily, either from home, from a hotel or airport, or from a temporary cubicle in one of the more than 120 locations that the company leases around the world. Every six weeks or so, the 23 members of the company's executive leadership team meet face-to-face for several days, with the location for the meetings rotating among different cities worldwide. Says the company's CFO, who lives in Boston, "We land somewhere, meet clients in the area, meet employees, then get together as a team to make decisions—and head out again." Accenture's Chief Leadership Officer commented, "Anyone who says managing this way is easy is lying."[a]

Question: What do you think might be the greatest strengths and weaknesses of working in a virtual organization like this?

[a]Accenture, "Company Overview," www.accenture.com/us-en/company/overview/Pages/index.aspx (accessed May 8, 2011); "Have Advice, Will Travel," *The Wall Street Journal*, June 5, 2006, pp. B1, B3; Yongsun Paik and David Y. Choi, "The Shortcomings of a Standardized Global Knowledge Management System: The Case Study of Accenture," *Academy of Management Executive* 19, no. 2 (2005), pp. 81–84; and Glenn Simpson, "The Economy: Consultants Accenture, Monday Take Steps That May Reduce Taxes," *The Wall Street Journal*, eastern ed., July 3, 2002, p. A2.

professionals, who do not have to clear each detail and event with higher-ups. The objective is to substitute cooperation and coordination, which are in the interest of everyone, for strict control and supervision. Pursued effectively, this approach can help to develop international communities of skilled workers that create and exploit valuable intangible assets.[6]

CORPORATE SURVIVAL IN THE 21ST CENTURY

Managers in many international companies can expect to make greater use of the *dynamic network structure* that breaks down the major functions of the firm into smaller companies coordinated by a small-size headquarters organization. Business functions such as marketing and accounting may be provided by separate organizations—some of them owned partially or fully by the international company, some of them not—that are connected by computers to a central office. To attain the optimum level of vertical integration, a firm must focus on its core business. Anything not essential to the business can often be done cheaper, faster, and better by outside suppliers.[7]

As companies engage in the global battles of the 21st century, we must remember that organizations, like people, have life cycles. In their youth, they are small and fast growing. However, as they age, they often become big, complex, and out of touch with their markets. The firms of tomorrow must learn how to be both large and entrepreneurial. As one CEO put it, "Small is not better; focused is better."

Control

Every successful company uses controls to put its plans into effect, evaluate their effectiveness, make desirable corrections, and evaluate and reward or correct executive performance. The challenges associated with achieving effective control are more complicated for an international company than for a one-country operation. In earlier chapters, we discussed several of the complicating causes. They include different languages, cultures, and attitudes; different taxes and accounting methods; different currencies, labor costs, and market sizes; different degrees of political stability and security for personnel and property; and many more. For these reasons, international companies need controls even more than do domestic ones.

SUBSIDIARIES

subsidiaries
Companies controlled by other companies through ownership of enough voting stock to elect board-of-directors majorities

The terms **subsidiaries** and **affiliates** sometimes are used interchangeably, and we first examine the control of those in which the parent has 100 percent ownership. This avoids for now the additional complications of joint ventures or subsidiaries in which the parent has less than 100 percent ownership. We deal with those later in the chapter.

WHERE TO MAKE DECISIONS IN WHOLLY OWNED SUBSIDIARIES?

affiliates
A term sometimes used interchangeably with subsidiaries, but more forms exist than just stock ownership

There are three possibilities. Theoretically, all decisions could be made either at the international company (IC) headquarters or at the subsidiary level. As common sense would indicate, they are not; instead, some decisions are made at headquarters, some are made at subsidiaries, and—the third possibility—some are made cooperatively. Many variables determine which decision is made where. Some of the more significant variables are (1) product and equipment, (2) the competence of subsidiary management and reliance on that management by the IC headquarters, (3) the size of the IC and how long it has been one, (4) the detriment of a subsidiary for the benefit of the enterprise, and (5) subsidiary frustration. We discuss each of these variables in the sections that follow.

LO10-4 Explain
why decisions are made where they are among parent and subsidiary units of an international company.

Product and Equipment   As to decision location, questions of standardization of product and equipment and second markets can be important for international companies. In Chapter 15, we will discuss how large global manufacturers of consumer products, such as Procter and Gamble (P&G) and Colgate, are developing standardized products from the outset for global or at least regional markets. In these situations, the affiliates have to follow company policy. Of course, representatives of the affiliates may have an opportunity to take part in the product design, contrary to the way new products were typically introduced before the globalization strategy became so popular. Then, as we discussed in Chapter 2 on the international product life cycle, new products often have been introduced first in the home market. After the production process has been stabilized, the specifications are sent to the affiliates (second markets) for local production, where adaptations can be made if the local managements deem them necessary for their markets.

In a firm without a global product policy, the preference of the operations management people in the home office has always been to standardize the product or at least the production process in as many overseas plants as possible, as we will explain in Chapter 15. If, however, any subsidiary can demonstrate that the profit potential is greater for a product tailored for its own market than what the company would realize from global standardization, the subsidiary ordinarily is allowed to proceed. Of course, the decision in such a case is cooperative in that the parent has the power to veto or override its subsidiary's decision.

Competence of Subsidiary Management and Headquarters' Reliance on It
Reliance on subsidiary management can depend on how well the executives know one another and how well they know company policies, on whether headquarters management feels that it understands host country conditions, on the distances between the home country and the host countries, and on how big and old the parent company is.

Moving Executives Around   Many ICs have a policy of transferring promising management personnel between parent headquarters and subsidiaries and among subsidiaries. Thus, the manager learns firsthand the policies of headquarters and the problems of putting those policies into effect at subsidiary levels.

A result of such transfers, which is difficult to measure but nevertheless important, is a network of intra-IC personal relationships. This tends to increase the confidence of executives in one another and to make communication among executives easier and less subject to error. Another development is that some ICs have moved their regional executives into headquarters to improve communications and reduce cost.

Understanding Host Country Conditions   One element in the degree of headquarters' reliance on subsidiary management is the familiarity of headquarters with conditions in the subsidiary's host country. The less familiar or the more different conditions in the host country are perceived to be, the more likely headquarters is to rely on subsidiary management.

How Far Away Is the Host Country?   Another element in the degree of headquarters' reliance on subsidiary management is the distance of the host country from home headquarters. Thus, an American parent is likely to place more reliance on the management of an Indonesian subsidiary than on the management of a Canadian subsidiary. This occurs for two reasons: American management typically perceives management conditions in Canada to be more easily understood than conditions in Indonesia, and Indonesia is much farther from the United States than Canada is—not merely geographically but also in terms of culture, politics, and other variables.

Size and Age of the IC
As a rule, a large company can afford to hire more specialists, experts, and experienced executives than can a smaller one. The longer a company has been an IC, the more likely it is to have a number of experienced executives who know company policies and have worked at headquarters and in the field. Successful experience builds confidence. In most ICs, the top positions are at headquarters, and the ablest and most persistent executives will typically get positions there eventually. Thus, over time, the headquarters of a successful company is run by experienced executives who are confident of their knowledge of the business in the home and host countries and in combinations thereof.

It follows that in larger, older organizations, more decisions are made at headquarters and fewer are delegated to subsidiaries. Smaller companies, in business for shorter periods of time, tend to be able to afford fewer internationally experienced executives and will not have had time to develop them internally. Smaller, newer companies often have no choice but to delegate decisions to subsidiary managements. However, with the increasing pace of change and intensity of competition in many markets of the world, as well as continued differences across many markets, even large and experienced companies are finding the need to delegate at least some decision-making authority to subsidiary managements in order to effectively sense pressures for adaptation, to serve as tools for developing and communicating innovation, and to promote effective execution of strategy.

Benefiting the Enterprise to the Detriment of a Subsidiary
An IC has opportunities to source raw materials and components, locate factories, allocate orders, and govern intrafirm pricing that are not available to a non-IC. Such activities may be beneficial to the enterprise yet may result in **subsidiary detriment.**

subsidiary detriment
Situation in which a small loss for a subsidiary results in a greater gain for the total IC

Moving Production Factors   For any number of reasons, an IC may decide to move factors of production from one country to another or to expand in one country in preference to another. In addition to the cost, availability, or skill levels of labor, other possible reasons include such factors as taxation, market, currency, and political stability issues.

The subsidiary from which factors are being taken would be unenthusiastic about giving up control over existing activities. Its management would be slow, at best, to cut the company's capacity or to downsize or eliminate local operations. Headquarters would typically have to make such decisions.

Which Subsidiary Gets the Order?   Similarly, if an order—say, from an Argentine customer—could be filled from a subsidiary in France or another in South Africa or a third in Brazil, parent headquarters might decide which subsidiary gets the business. Among the considerations in the decision would be transportation costs, production costs, comparative tariff rates, customers' currency restrictions, comparative order backlogs, governmental pressures, and taxes. Having such a decision made by IC headquarters avoids price competition among members of the same IC group.

Multicountry Production   Frequently, the size of the market in a single country is too small to permit economies of scale in manufacturing an entire industrial product or offering a full range of services for that one market. An example is Ford's production of a light vehicle for the Asian market. In that situation, Ford negotiated with several countries to the conclusion that one country would make one component of the vehicle for all the countries involved. Thus, one country makes the engine, a second country has the body-stamping plant, a third makes the transmission, and so forth. In this fashion, each operation achieves the efficiency and cost savings of economies of scale. Of course, this kind of multinational production demands a high degree of IC headquarters' control and coordination.

Which Subsidiary Books the Profit?   In certain circumstances, an IC may have a choice of two or more countries in which to declare profits. Such circumstances may arise where two or more units of the IC cooperate in supplying components or services under a contract with a customer unrelated to any part of the IC. Under these conditions, there may be opportunities to allocate higher prices to one unit or subsidiary and lower prices to another within the global price to the customer.

If the host country of one of the subsidiaries has lower taxes than the other host countries, it would be natural to try to maximize profits in the lower-tax country and minimize them in the higher-tax country. Other differences between host countries could dictate the allocation of profit to or from the subsidiaries located there. Such differences could include currency controls, labor relations, political climate, and social unrest. It is sensible to direct or allocate as much profit as reasonably possible to subsidiaries in countries with the fewest currency controls, the best labor relations and political climate, and the least social unrest, for example.

The intrafirm transaction may also give a company choices regarding profit location. Pricing between members of the same enterprise is referred to as **transfer pricing,** and while IC headquarters could permit undirected, arm's-length negotiations between itself and its subsidiaries, this might not yield the most advantageous results for the enterprise as a whole.

transfer pricing
Pricing that is established for transactions between members of the enterprise

Price and profit allocation decisions like these are usually best made at parent-company headquarters, which is supposed to maintain the overall view, looking out for the best interests of the enterprise. Naturally, subsidiary management does not gladly make decisions to accept lower profits, largely because its evaluation may suffer as a result of the apparent reduction in performance at the subsidiary level.

The following two tables illustrate how the total IC enterprise may profit even though one subsidiary makes less. Assume a cooperative contract by which two subsidiaries are selling products and services to an outside customer for a price of $100 million. The host country of IC Alpha levies company income taxes at the rate of 50 percent, whereas IC Beta's host country taxes its income at 20 percent. The customer is in a third country, has agreed to pay $100 million, and is indifferent to how Alpha and Beta share the money. The first table shows the enterprise's after-tax income if Alpha is paid $60 million and Beta is paid $40 million. Thus, after tax, the enterprise realizes $62 million.

	Receives ($ millions)	Tax ($ millions)	After Tax ($ millions)
Alpha	$60	$30	$30
Beta	40	8	32
			$62

The second table shows the after-tax income if Alpha is paid $40 million and Beta is paid $60 million. Thus, after taxes, the enterprise realizes $68 million.

	Receives ($ millions)	Tax ($ millions)	After Tax ($ millions)
Alpha	$40	$20	$20
Beta	60	12	48
			$68

These simple examples illustrate that the IC would be $6 million better off if it could shift $20 million of the payment from Alpha to Beta, while the customer is no worse off, because it pays $100 million in either case. Alpha, having received $20 million less in payment, is $10 million worse off after taxes, but Beta is $16 million better off—and the enterprise is $6 million ahead on the same contract. Given the number of countries and tax laws in the world, there are countless combinations for how such savings can be accomplished. Financial management awareness and control are the keys.

We do not mean to leave the impression that the host and home governments are unaware of or indifferent to transfer pricing and profit allocating by ICs operating within their borders. The companies must expect questioning by host and home governments and must be prepared to demonstrate that prices or allocations are reasonable. This may be done by showing that other companies charge comparable prices for the same or similar items or, if there are no similar items, by showing that costs plus profit have been used reasonably to arrive at the price. As to allocation of profits, the IC in our example would try to prove that the volume or importance of the work done by Beta or the responsibilities assumed by Beta—such as financing, after-sales service, or warranty obligations—justify the higher amount being paid to Beta. Of course, the questioning in this instance would come from the host government of Alpha if it got wind of the possibility of more taxable income for Beta and less for itself.[8]

Subsidiary Frustration   An extremely important consideration for parent-company management is that the management of its subsidiaries be motivated and loyal. If all the big decisions are made, or are perceived to be made, at the IC headquarters, the managers of subsidiaries can lose incentive and prestige or face with their employees and the community. They may grow hostile and disloyal.

Therefore, even though there may be reasons for headquarters to make decisions, it should delegate as many as is reasonably possible. Management of each subsidiary should

GlobalSoft: Profiting from International Transfer Pricing

GlobalSoft Inc. is a leading competitor in the international computer software industry. The company is headquartered in the United States and has subsidiaries in more than 100 nations of the world. More than 80 percent of Global-Soft's long-lived assets are located in the United States, and 60 percent of its revenues of $58 billion are generated from the U.S. operations. However, 60 percent of the company's $25 billion of income before taxes is generated in international markets, with much of that coming from nations with corporate tax rates that are much lower than the 35 percent tax rate that GlobalSoft is subject to in the United States.

One way that GlobalSoft has reduced the level of taxes that it pays is through the careful use of transfer pricing. For example, the company established a subsidiary in Ireland, where the corporate tax rate in 2011 was only 12.5 percent, one of the lowest levels in Europe. This subsidiary, called Emerald Isle Enterprises (EIE), serves as the regional headquarters for the licensing of GlobalSoft's software to European customers. Although most of GlobalSoft's software development occurs in the United States, the American organization then licenses this software at a relatively low rate to EIE. The outcome of this transfer pricing decision is that a lower level of revenues—and corresponding taxable income—is earned by GlobalSoft's American operations from EIE's activities. As a result, GlobalSoft pays a smaller amount of taxes in the United States than would be the case if it charged a higher license fee to EIE.

Although EIE licenses GlobalSoft's software from its parent company at a relatively low percentage rate, EIE charges a much higher fee to GlobalSoft's other European subsidiaries for this software. This approach to pricing allows EIE to have a high level of revenues and taxable income in Ireland, where the tax rate is low. The high license fee also reduces the level of taxable income in the other European subsidiaries, which are located in nations that charge higher tax rates than Ireland. Due to tax treaties, the after-tax profits of EIE are not subject to further taxation when they are transferred to the company's headquarters in the United States.

Through the creative use of transfer pricing techniques such as this, it is estimated that GlobalSoft has been able to reduce its worldwide tax bill by more than $500 million per year.

Questions:

1. If you were a shareholder in GlobalSoft, would you be supportive of the company's approach to transfer pricing? Why or why not?

2. If you represented the government of Ireland, would you be supportive of GlobalSoft's approach to transfer pricing? Why or why not?

3. If you represented the U.S. government, or the government of one of the other nations in Europe, would you be supportive of GlobalSoft's approach to transfer pricing? Why or why not?

---

be kept thoroughly informed and be consulted seriously about decisions, negotiations, and developments in its geographic area. The trend for many ICs of shifting power away from subsidiaries toward the parent has caused predictable frustration to subsidiary management, sometimes followed by resignations.

JOINT VENTURES AND SUBSIDIARIES LESS THAN 100 PERCENT OWNED

LO10-5 Discuss how an international company can maintain control of a joint venture or of a company in which the international company owns less than 50 percent of the voting stock.

A *joint venture,* as defined in Chapter 13, may be a corporate entity between an IC and local owners or a corporate entity between two or more companies that are foreign to the area where the joint venture is located, or it may involve one company working on a project of limited duration (e.g., constructing a dam) in cooperation with one or more other companies. The other companies may be subsidiaries or affiliates, but they may also be entirely independent entities.

All the reasons for making decisions at IC headquarters, at subsidiary headquarters, or cooperatively apply equally in joint venture situations. However, headquarters will almost never have as much freedom of action and flexibility in a joint venture as it has with subsidiaries that are 100 percent owned.

Loss of Freedom and Flexibility   The reasons for that loss of freedom and flexibility are easy to see. If shareholders outside the IC have control of the affiliate, they can block efforts of IC headquarters to move production factors away, fill an export order from another affiliate or subsidiary, and so forth. Even if outside shareholders are a minority and cannot directly control the affiliate, they can bring legal or political pressures on the IC to prevent it from diminishing the affiliate's profitability for the IC's benefit. Likewise, the local partner in a joint venture is highly unlikely to agree with measures that penalize the joint venture for the IC's benefit.

Control Can Be Had With less than 50 percent of the voting stock and even with no voting stock, an IC can have control. Some methods of maintaining control are:

- A management contract.
- Control of the finances.
- Control of the technology.
- Putting people from the IC in important executive positions.

As might be expected, ICs have encountered resistance to putting IC personnel in the important executive positions from their joint venture partners or from host governments. The natural desire of these partners and governments is that their own nationals have at least equality in the important positions and that they get training and experience in the technology and management.

REPORTING

For controls to be effective, all operating units of an IC must provide headquarters with timely, accurate, and complete reports. There are many uses for the information reported. Among the types of reporting required are (1) financial, (2) technological, (3) market opportunity, and (4) political and economic.

LO10-6 List the types of information an international company needs to have reported to it by its units around the world.

Financial A surplus of funds in one subsidiary should perhaps be retained there for investment or contingencies. On the other hand, such a surplus might be more useful at the parent company, in which case payment of a dividend is indicated. Or perhaps another subsidiary or affiliate needs capital, and the surplus could be lent or invested there. Obviously, parent headquarters must know the existence and size of a surplus to determine its best use.

Technological New technology should be reported. New technology is constantly being developed in different countries, and the subsidiary or affiliated company operating in such a country is likely to learn about it before IC headquarters hundreds or thousands of miles away does. If headquarters finds the new technology potentially valuable, it can gain competitive advantage by being the first to contact the developer for a license to use it.

Market Opportunities The affiliates in various countries may spot new or growing markets for some product of the enterprise. This could be profitable all around, as the IC sells more of the product while the affiliate earns sales commissions. Of course, if the new market is sufficiently large, the affiliate may begin to assemble or produce the product under license from the parent company or from another affiliate.

Other market-related information that should be reported to IC headquarters includes competitors' activities, price developments, and new products of potential interest to the IC group. Also of importance is information on the subsidiary's market share and whether it is growing or shrinking, together with explanations.

Political and Economic Not surprisingly, reports on political and economic conditions have multiplied mightily in number and importance over the past 20 or so years as revolutions—some bloody—have toppled and changed governments. Democracies have replaced dictatorships, one dictator has replaced another, countries have broken apart or reunited—changes have been occurring on almost every continent.

MANAGING IN A WORLD OUT OF CONTROL

The Internet may be the closest thing to a working anarchy the world has ever seen. Nobody owns it, nobody runs it, and most Internet users get along by dint of online etiquette, not rules and regulations. The Internet was built up without any central control because the U.S. Defense Department wanted to ensure that the Internet could survive a nuclear attack. The Internet has proved to be a paragon of hothouse expansion and constant evolution. Although it may be messier and less efficient than a similar system designed and run by an agency or company, this organically grown network is also more adaptable and less susceptible to a systemwide crash.

The consequence for management in a world out of control, such as the Internet, is a recipe developed at Massachusetts Institute of Technology for devising a system of distributed control: (1) do simple things first, (2) learn to do them flawlessly, (3) add new layers of activity over the results of the simple task, (4) don't change the simple things, (5) make the new layer work as flawlessly as the simple one, and (6) repeat ad infinitum. Many organizations would benefit by adopting organizing principles as deceptively simple as these.

Increasingly, the most successful companies, like the machines and programs so many of them now make, and the networks on which they all will rely will advance only by evolving and adapting in this organic, bottom-up way. Successful leaders will have to relinquish control. They will have to honor error because a breakthrough may at first be indistinguishable from a mistake. They must constantly seek disequilibrium.

Control: Yes and No

We have spoken of control within the IC family of parent, subsidiaries, affiliates, and joint ventures. This deals with where decisions are made on a variety of subjects under different circumstances. Timely and accurate reporting to the parent is necessary for success of the IC family. The trend in this area of control is toward centralized decision making, with more being done by the parent.

The other control of which we have spoken involves the design, production, and order-filling functions of companies. Here, the explosion of software, computer networks, and information technology, including the Internet, has tended to decentralize and de-job organizations. More and more, workers do evolving tasks with changing teams of other workers. Hierarchies dissolve and successful leaders relinquish control as workers are trained and encouraged to cope with evolving tasks and rewarded for coping well.

THE GLOBAL PATH AHEAD

Isaac Rush in Tianjin: So Much More Fun When You Don't Understand Everything!

Isaac Rush was an international business major at Cal Poly–San Luis Obispo whose interest in international work began with trips to Mexico to help build homes for people who were homeless. When he started seeing how other people lived their lives and how it worked for them, it sparked his interest. In his own words, "I was intrigued by different cultures and people—how they ate different foods, had different hobbies, and had completely different ways of doing things that sometimes made

sense to me and sometimes did not. I realized that there is so much more excitement and adventure when you don't understand everything; and that is why I chose to go international." He recently spent four months in China teaching English with AIESEC. Here's his report, which includes his advice:

Initially, I chose China because there were many teaching opportunities there and foreign teachers are in high demand. I went to China through the international business club, AIESEC, and they were able to provide internships connecting with another university in Tianjin, China. I knew that Mandarin Chinese is one of the hardest languages to learn and that living in China is really affordable. These two aspects were really appealing for me. Having just graduated from college, I was on a tight budget and looking for a new challenge that could really enhance my resumé.

(continued)

In order to prepare for my trip, I connected with students from China and gained some valuable advice: buy a map and make copies of your passport. I also got connected with a couple of Cal Poly students who were currently working abroad in China, and they helped me with many of the basics—for instance, what type of visa to apply for, the need for bringing basic medications, and to be picky about finding an apartment because cleanliness standards are much lower than in the United States. I also bought some books on Chinese culture and travel, as well as a simple phrase book, and I went on YouTube to practice pronunciation of basic phrases.

One of the most valuable things that I did when I was in China was e-mail and talk on Skype to family and friends, because then I didn't feel quite as removed from what was familiar. I also recommend getting involved in other activities to meet friends, because without a couple of good friends, I don't know how I would have survived. I also kept up with some typical routines that I did when I was in the United States like running, reading, and going to Starbucks for some coffee because instant coffee, which is dominant all over China, didn't cut it for me.

When I first began teaching, I was teaching a wide variety of students: primary school kids, high school students, college students, and even business professionals. I was traveling to several different companies in the city of Tianjin and changing up my lessons based on the audience. My main focus was oral English with all my students so that they could take an IELTS examination and pass. The IELTS would certify a student to study abroad, improve business opportunities, or simply provide evidence of being a better English speaker.

Some of my biggest challenges were ordering food in a restaurant because I didn't recognize any of the food, and navigating around the city, because I would have to memorize landmarks and then get around in the city in a taxi without being able to speak Chinese. The way I managed was finding restaurants with pictures to point to, buying an English map, and every time I had to get into a taxi, I would have an address written down on a note card in case the driver didn't understand my accent, which was 95 percent of the time.

One surprising discovery that I found out by experience is that you have to carry around toilet paper in public places in China because many places don't supply it. This I found out the hard way, but never left home without paper in my pocket again.

Some of my greatest enjoyments in China were going to my Chinese friends' homes and getting meals prepared by their parents. When I would arrive, they would offer me their best fruits, nuts, and snacks; then they would offer me cigarettes because most males in China smoke, and then they would bring out tons of food and would keep offering me more and more until I was absolutely full. The Chinese hospitality was amazing. I also really enjoyed the high value that Chinese place on family. Most Chinese have all of their relatives living in the same town and it has been that way for generations.

One thing that I would highly recommend is that when you're in China or any other foreign country, try as hard as possible to follow the same habits as the local people: eating, dress, and hobbies. This shows the local people that you actually care about their culture and want to see things from their perspective. It will open up more opportunities.

Some major learning points I can share with you are these: Do your best to learn the local language because this is the most difficult but necessary tool to learn about the foreign culture. Be disciplined because it takes determination and intensity. I also learned that I have to throw out all my standards of hygiene because trash is thrown out on the streets and smoking indoors is completely legal.

I am currently working in sales for a moving company and may open up a franchise in Orange County in the next year or two. Eventually, I will head back abroad to work once I have some industry experience. Perhaps we'll meet up!

Resources for Your Global Career

Enhancing coordination between manufacturing, marketing, and other related functions to manage the international corporation is becoming increasingly complex. A trend is to use decentralized and informal approaches for structural design and control of the multinational firm. Here are a range of resources to broaden your thinking about the structure of the global organization of the future to establish its best competitive position in global markets.

Organizational Design Considerations and Approaches:

http://jobfunctions.bnet.com/abstract.aspx?kw=organization+design&docid=68372&tag=bn-left

http://jobfunctions.bnet.com/abstract.aspx?kw=organization+design&tag=bn-left&docid=1863071&promo=100511

Matrix Structures and Their Management:

http://jobfunctions.bnet.com/abstract.aspx?kw=organization+design&tag=bn-left&docid=1908483&promo=100511

http://jobfunctions.bnet.com/abstract.aspx?kw=organization+design&tag=bn-left&docid=2337255&promo=100510

Organizational Design Forum:

www.organizationdesignforum.org/

The Networked International Firm:

http://smib.vuw.ac.nz:8081/www/ANZMAC1999/Site/B/BrownL.pdf

Establishing a Joint Venture in India:

http://docs.google.com/viewer?a=v&q=cache:DfSfYRKJXzEJ:www.usibc.com/sites/default/files/committees/files/jointventuresinindiaanoverview.pdf+establishing+joint+ventures+in+india+an+overview&hl=en&gl=us&piddocid=2337255bl&srcid=ADGEEShy7GwTQtgQI56mUf0ny33-el-HAMbRylacIkWrlg2sdq7FDqEcd7NAxiKbv5_1RJLV-9WzijGXnOaaSEYLVoQ6JYyb2oUXfHSX73Lmh0RzJdTuWxXwth9SiNmx-52WbeteqFolB&sig=AHIEtbRTyz1ujmECMVQ3di-Hw-6ZrLijhw

Ownership and Control of International Joint Ventures:

http://aib.msu.edu/awards/20_2_89_235.pdf

Summary

LO10-1 Explain why the design of organizational structure is important to international companies.

The structure of an international organization involves how its domestic and international units and activities are arranged and where formal power and authority will be located inside the company. It helps determine how efficiently and effectively the organization will be able to integrate and leverage its competencies and resources within and across various units of the enterprise, and thus contribute to successful implementation of the company's strategy.

LO10-2 Discuss the organizational dimensions that must be considered when selecting organizational structures.

The organizational structure selected for a company must be consistent with the organization's capabilities and resources, as well as with the environmental context in which the organization operates and with its strategy. In selecting an organizational structure, managers of an international company must consider the requirements for expertise in terms of product and technology, geography, customer, and function.

LO10-3 Discuss the various organizational forms available for structuring international companies.

Companies may (1) have an international division; (2) be organized by product, function, or region; or (3) have a mixture of them (hybrid form). To attain a balance between product and regional expertise, some companies have tried a matrix form of organization. Its disadvantages, however, have caused many companies to put a matrix overlay over a traditional product, regional, or functional form instead of using the matrix.

LO10-4 Explain why decisions are made where they are among parent and subsidiary units of an international company.

Several considerations govern where decisions are made in an IC family of organizations. They include the desirability of standardizing products as opposed to differentiating them for different markets, the competence of organization managements, the size and age of the IC, the benefit of one part of the family to the detriment of another, and building confidence or avoiding frustration of management.

LO10-5 Discuss how an international company can maintain control of a joint venture or of a company in which the international company owns less than 50 percent of the voting stock.

Control can be maintained over a joint venture or a company in which the IC owns less than 50 percent of the voting stock by several devices, including a management contract, control of the finances, control of the technology, and putting people from the IC in key executive positions.

LO10-6 List the types of information an international company needs to have reported to it by its units around the world.

Subsidiaries should report to the IC information about financial conditions, technological developments, market opportunities and developments, and economic and political conditions.

Key Words

organizational structure (p. 257)

organizational design (p. 257)

international division (p. 258)

hybrid organization (p. 261)

matrix organization (p. 262)

matrix overlay (p. 262)

strategic business unit (SBU) (p. 263)

reengineering (p. 263)

virtual corporation (p. 263)

horizontal corporation (p. 264)

subsidiaries (p. 266)

affiliates (p. 266)

subsidiary detriment (p. 268)

transfer pricing (p. 268)

Questions

1. Why is organizational structure an important issue for international companies?

2. What are the main strengths and weaknesses of the use of an international division as part of a company's organizational structure? Under what circumstances might such a structure be an appropriate choice for a company?

3. Compare and contrast geographic and product structures for international companies.

4. Your company's matrix organization isn't working; decisions are taking too long, and it seems to you that instead of best solutions, you're getting compromises. What can your company's CEO do to address this problem?

5. You are the CEO of Mancon Incorporated, and you have just acquired Pozoli, an Italian small-appliance maker (electric shavers, small household and personal care appliances). It has been in business for more than 40 years and has manufacturing plants in Italy, Mexico, Ireland, and Spain. Its output is sold in more than 100 markets worldwide, including the United States. Your company is now organized into two product groups—shaving and personal care—along with an international division at the top level. How are you going to include Pozoli in your organization? Explain your rationale.

6. It is obvious that in formulating new strategies, management may uncover a need to change its organization. Can you describe some situations in which the reverse may be true?

7. In determining whether decisions will be made by the parent company or by its subsidiaries, what are the considerations when equipment and products are standardized worldwide rather than tailored to individual national circumstances and markets?

8. Regarding issues of control in an international company:

   a. What are some decisions that could result in detriment for a subsidiary but greater benefit for the enterprise as a whole?

   b. In such circumstances, where will the decision be made—at IC headquarters or at the affected subsidiary?

9. What measures can be utilized to control subsidiaries that are less than 100 percent owned by the firm or joint venture partners in which the firm has no ownership?

10. Some companies use standardized organizational controls across their entire organization, in that the same control systems are used for each unit or operation worldwide. For example, companies such as Starbucks, Kentucky Fried Chicken, or McDonald's apply the same rigid quality controls throughout all aspects of their organizations, even as they expand internationally. Why would a company such as these impose rigorous corporate quality standards, regardless of the country in which it operates? What modifications in these quality standards, if any, should the company permit because of differences across nations or regions of the world? Why is the company allowing these modifications to occur?

---

 globalEDGE.msu.edu

Research Task

Use the globalEDGE site (http://globalEDGE.msu.edu/) to complete the following exercises:

1. You work at a U.S.-based food and beverage company that is currently planning to expand operations to other parts of the world. To design the structure of the international organization, management has requested additional information on the food and beverage sector abroad. Use the Industry Profiles in the globalEDGE website to prepare a risk assessment of the Food and Beverage industry that can help management gain a better understanding of the external environment in foreign markets.

2. *Fortune* magazine conducts an annual survey and publishes the rankings of the "World's Most Admired Companies." Locate the most recent publicly available ranking, follow the link to the best and worst companies, and focus on the nine factors highlighted by Fortune magazine. Based on these data, prepare an executive summary of the strategic and organizational success factors of a company of your choice.

Minicase: SemiConnected Inc.—Must It Reorganize?

SemiConnected, Inc. manufactures specialized electronic and electrical connectors used on such diverse products as computers, home appliances, telecommunications, and the air bag and antiskid systems of automobiles. The company has been in business since 1984. The accompanying table provides a summary of the important financial information for the last five years.

For some time, SemiConnected has been exporting to Asia, where its major markets are Australia, Singapore, Malaysia, Thailand, South Korea, China, and Taiwan. When its foreign sales were confined to exports, the company functioned well with an export department whose manager reported to the company's marketing manager. In 2010, however, another American firm tried to enter the Taiwan market, and there were rumors that a Taiwanese firm from a related industry was searching for a licensor in the United States to supply it with manufacturing technology. As a result, SemiConnected decided to set up its first foreign plant in Taiwan. When it did, it hired financial and marketing people with Asian experience and established an international division at headquarters to oversee the Taiwan operation. The president felt that the situation would be repeated in China, Singapore, and perhaps other nations. These were all good export markets at the time, but it was reasonable to suppose that some competitor would soon set up manufacturing facilities in one or more of them, which could dramatically affect the potential for exporting to these markets. Having a small international division with some Asian expertise responsible for monitoring these markets would help the firm avoid being surprised by a competitor's move.

After the Taiwan SemiConnected plant was in production, more firms in that nation were willing to do business with the company than had been the case when it had served the market through exports. In fact, the major portion of the 2011 sales increase was due to improved sales to Taiwan. However, the new customers also brought the company into a new, higher level of competition than it had known before. Other Taiwanese competitors were bringing out new

products at a considerably faster rate than SemiConnected. The president wondered if horizontal linkages across functions, such as the linkages automakers have used to reduce their design time, might help his firm. Also, on his trips to Taiwan, the marketing people told him things about the market and the competitors that were not being sent to the SemiConnected home office.

It was obvious to the president that overseas production and growth in overseas sales demanded a reorganization of the firm. Even though the company had only one plant overseas, in Taiwan, the president was confident that other plants would soon be needed. How should the company be organized to handle the new foreign production facilities? How can SemiConnected reduce the time needed to bring new designs to market?

	SemiConnected Five-Year Financial Highlight Summary ($ millions)				
	2011	2010	2009	2008	2007
Net sales	$353.0	$298.2	$271.9	$257.4	$231.1
Gross profit	134.1	116.3	110.3	106.7	94.9
Selling, general, and administrative expense	70.5	61.2	55.8	51.8	45.1
Income from operations	63.6	55.1	54.5	54.9	49.8
Income taxes	23.9	20.9	20.9	21.8	20.9
Effective tax rate (%)	37.6	37.9	38.3	39.7	42.0
Net income	39.7	34.2	33.6	33.1	28.9

Global Leadership Issues and Practices

Globalization and its demands have shifted the skill set necessary to lead in the twenty-first century. Headhunters are desperately trying to find executives with the right mix of skills, but they are rare and becoming difficult to find.

—*Mendenhall, Osland, Bird, Oddou & Maznevski, Global Leadership: Research, Practice, and Development*

The Challenge of Finding Global Leaders with the "Right Stuff"

Globalization is not only creating many new business opportunities, it is also creating opportunities for a new breed of leaders that have the "right stuff" for operating in an increasingly globalized world.

Rapid economic growth in the emerging markets, particularly the so-called BRIC nations (Brazil, Russia, India, and China), is creating large new markets for consumer and industrial goods. The revolution in communications and computer technology, including the Internet, social media, smartphones, and other developments, is enabling diverse and geographically dispersed groups of employees to collaborate in their work and to learn from and with each other. Developments in shipping and logistics are heightening pressure on companies to reconfigure their value chains in order to maintain competitiveness. Expanded geographic scope of operations is exposing companies to different regulatory environments, a more diverse set of suppliers and competitors, and exposure to a variety of unfamiliar risks.

International companies require a new type of leader in order to compete successfully in this complex and dynamic global environment. These global leaders need to not only be proficient in terms of their business acumen, but to also evidence an array of additional skills. They must be able to envision the nature and direction of change that is occurring within and across markets of the world and the implications of these changes for the company's strategy. They must show cultural understanding and adaptability, rather than being constrained by experiences only within their home country and culture. They must be able to understand, work with, and inspire individuals from a range of nations and cultures to create new technologies, businesses, and organizations. These skills and more are necessary in order for executives to lead their companies to success in the 21st century.

Where are such global leaders found? They can come from anywhere in the world. Indeed, we can see a Brazilian-born son of a French mother and a Lebanese father (Carlos Ghosn) as the leader of both Japan-based (Nissan) and Paris-based (Renault) automakers who are in a strategic alliance to compete in North America and the rest of the world. We can see a Turkish-American son (Muhtar Kent) who attended high school in Turkey and university in the United Kingdom, serving as the leader of U.S.-based Coca-Cola. Or we can see a woman born and educated in India (Indra Nooyi) move up to her role as CEO of a leading global consumer products company (PepsiCo). With the right preparation, global leaders with the "right stuff" can come from anywhere on the planet.

learning objectives

After reading this chapter, you should be able to:

LO11-1 **Discuss** the importance of creating a company "global mindset."

LO11-2 **Describe** what distinguishes the practice of global leadership from its domestic counterpart.

LO11-3 **Identify** the competencies required for effective global leadership.

LO11-4 **Discuss** approaches for selecting and developing effective global leaders.

LO11-5 **Explain** what skills a manager needs in order to effectively lead global teams.

LO11-6 **Identify** some of the challenges of leading global change.

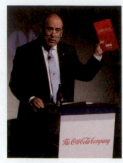

Can you be a global leader? If so, what will you need to do to prepare yourself for such a role? As we discuss in this chapter, the nature of the leadership challenge varies by company and context, so there is no universal approach to selecting and developing global leaders. However, obtaining a strong grasp of the business fundamentals that underlie international business is an important first step. Building from that foundation with a well-considered approach for developing cultural, linguistic, and other experiences and skills may also help you to develop the "right stuff" for understanding and managing the complex international challenges that global leaders confront, now and in the future.

This chapter focuses on key issues associated with leaders and leadership for international businesses in our increasingly complex and dynamic global world. Despite the opportunities that international business brings, most companies do not have the quantity and quality of leaders necessary to fully and successfully exploit these opportunities. As noted in the opening vignette, changes in the international environment are creating opportunities for leaders with a new set of skills and experiences, what we will refer to as *global leaders*. In this chapter, we will begin by discussing the concept of a global mindset and its importance for global companies. Then we will examine what global leadership is, how global leadership differs from leadership in domestic contexts, and why global leadership is important. We will identify some of the competencies that are required in order to be an effective global leader, as well as issues associated with selecting and developing candidates for global leadership positions. We will also discuss issues associated with leading global teams and managing global change initiatives.

The Global MindSet

LO11-1 **Discuss** the importance of creating a company "global mindset."

global mindset
Combines an openness to and an awareness of diversity across markets and cultures with a propensity and ability to synthesize across this diversity

Research indicates that many CEOs feel that developing a company **global mindset** is a "prerequisite for global industry dominance."[1] Global mindset is defined as "one that combines an openness to and awareness of diversity across cultures and markets with a propensity and ability to synthesize across this diversity." It has been argued that global mindset has two key components: (1) intellectual intelligence, which includes business acumen, and (2) global emotional intelligence, which includes self-awareness, cross-cultural understanding, cultural adjustment, and cross-cultural effectiveness.[2] These two components provide the foundation for the global behavior skills that comprise a person's global leadership style.

Percy Barnevik, who served as the leader for the merger of Swedish Asea with Swiss Brown Boveri to create the global engineering and manufacturing giant ABB, aptly observed, "Global managers have exceptionally open minds. They respect how different countries do things, and they have the imagination to appreciate why they do them that way. But they are also incisive; they push the limits of the culture. Global managers don't passively accept it when someone says, 'You can't do that in Italy or Spain because of the unions,' or 'You can't do that in Japan because of the Ministry of Finance.' They sort through the debris of cultural excuses and find opportunities to innovate."[3] Development of a company global mindset and of a cadre of managers with such a perspective is one of the key challenges that confront global leaders and helps to highlight what is different and important about the topic of global leadership.

What Is Global Leadership, and Why Is It Important?

LO11-2 **Describe** what distinguishes the practice of global leadership from its domestic counterpart.

Leadership is a complex and multidisciplinary concept. Even a cursory review of the academic or managerial literatures quickly reveals the existence of many different definitions of leadership.[4] Rather than review and debate this point, in this chapter we will use as our working definition the notion that **leadership** refers to the behaviors and processes involved with organizing a group of people in order to achieve a common purpose or goal.

Most experts agree that leadership is not the same thing as management, although there is overlap between the two concepts.[5] Warren Bennis differentiated between the two concepts, including the following distinctions:

- The leader innovates; the manager administrates.
- The leader develops; the manager maintains.
- The leader challenges the status quo; the manager accepts it.
- The leader has a long-range perspective; the manager has a short-term perspective.
- The leader asks "what?" and "why?"; the manager asks "how?" and "when?"
- The leader originates; the manager imitates.
- The leader inspires; the manager controls.[6]

leadership
The behaviors and processes involved with organizing a group of people in order to achieve a common purpose or goal

While the preceding distinctions highlight some of the differences between management and leadership, what is different about global leadership?

HOW GLOBAL LEADERSHIP DIFFERS FROM DOMESTIC LEADERSHIP

Most, or perhaps all, of the leadership competencies associated with leadership in domestic settings are also relevant to leadership within global contexts. However, global leaders confront different contexts than do leaders who operate domestically. Globalization introduces additional challenges for companies, including the development of managers who have the ability to understand and operate in the worldwide business environment and to provide a global perspective on leadership of their organizations.[7]

Scholars have identified four overlapping dimensions of complexity that are relevant to globalization and the challenge confronting global leaders: (1) *multiplicity* (the geometric growth in the volume and nature of issues that must be dealt with by global leaders), (2) *interdependence* (although dispersed geographically, the different units of the company are systematically linked to each other rather than being isolated and are increasingly dependent on external organizations), (3) *ambiguity* (the challenge of dealing with information that lacks clarity and incorporates both quantitative and qualitative dimensions, hindering the understanding of cause-and-effect relationships), and (4) *dynamism* (the international system itself is constantly changing).[8]

Globalization increases the complexity of both the external environment (including the geographic as well as cultural reach of the company) and the internal environment in which the firm's operates (e.g., a broader range of backgrounds and motivations of employees). As a result, globalization places increasing emphasis on recruiting and developing human resources with the capability for operating successfully in such a challenging environment.[9] For example, using leadership data from 17,000 managers in 62 countries, Project GLOBE found that different nations evidenced both similar and dissimilar perspectives regarding the traits of leaders.[10] The leadership traits that were found to be universally *acceptable* included decisive, informed, honest, dynamic, administratively skilled, coordinator, just, team builder, effective bargainer, dependable, win–win problem solver, plans ahead, intelligent, and excellence oriented. Leadership traits that were viewed universally as being *unacceptable* included ruthless, egocentric, asocial, nonexplicit, irritable, noncooperative, loner, and dictatorial. However, the acceptability of a number of leadership traits was found to be contingent on the cultural context in which the leader was operating, including enthusiastic, self-sacrificial, risk-taking, sincere, ambitious, sensitive, self-effacing, compassionate, unique, and willful. These findings help to highlight the context-specific aspect of global leadership and the traits of global leaders.

As mentioned before, most of the competencies associated with domestic leadership success are also required for leading within global contexts. However, the degree of difference in the level of demands on skills and their application is so great—and the nature of the possible outcomes that can be produced within a global context can be so profoundly greater—that global leadership can ultimately be regarded as being different in kind from domestic leadership.[11] As one team of researchers noted, global leadership:

> *differs from domestic leadership in degree in terms of issues related to connectedness, boundary spanning, complexity, ethical challenges, dealing with tensions and paradoxes, pattern recognition, and building learning environments, teams, and community and leading large-scale change efforts–across diverse cultures.*[12]

LO11-3 Identify the competencies required for effective global leadership.

What Competencies Are Required for Effective Global Leadership?

In order for an individual to perform successfully as a global leader, what competencies should he or she embody? In answering this question, it might first be of value to highlight the range of roles that a global leader may need to take. Henry Mintzberg and other researchers have identified a range of such roles, including:

- *Monitoring* (e.g., scanning environments, seeking information, monitoring different units of the company).
- *Spokesperson* (e.g., advocating and representing the company, communicating and disseminating information to and with different levels of stakeholders inside and outside the organization).
- *Liaison* (e.g., networking, coordinating, spanning boundaries within and across organizations).
- *Leader* (e.g., motivating and coaching individuals and teams, building and maintaining corporate culture).
- *Negotiator* (e.g., making deals, managing conflict).
- *Innovator* (e.g., seizing opportunities, generating new ideas, promoting a vision for the company).
- *Decision maker* (e.g., troubleshooting, making decisions).
- *Change agent* (e.g., taking action, developing and implementing change plans for the company).[13]

The broad range of duties of global leaders suggests that such individuals require a complex mix of competencies in order to be effective in their duties. Among the many studies that have examined these competencies, a survey conducted by the Corporate Leadership Council identified the following six skills that were considered the most important for global leaders:

- Adaptability across cultures.
- Capability to develop individuals from and across diverse cultures.
- Global strategic thinking.
- Ability to establish business in new markets.
- Capability for building global teams.
- Competency in interacting with local political interests.[14]

Research conducted by the Center for Creative Leadership found that, in order to be effective, global leaders required a similar pattern of traits, capabilities, and role-based skills, as did leaders operating in a strictly domestic setting. However, there was a more significant impact of emotional stability, ability to learn, and decision-making and negotiating roles for global leaders than was the case for domestic leaders.[15] Due to the impact of cultural differences on leadership attributes and performance, researchers from Project GLOBE asserted that a global mindset, cultural adaptability and flexibility, and tolerance for ambiguity were attributes that global leaders needed to have in order to be effective.[16] Terrence Brake created the Global Leadership Triad (see Figure 11.1), which incorporates three interrelated sets of competencies required for effective global leadership: (1) business acumen, (2) relationship management skills, and (3) personal effectiveness skills.[17] Dalton argued that global leaders needed to have four key competencies: (1) a high level of cognitive complexity, in order to collect

Business Acumen
- Depth of field
- Enterpreneurial spirit
- Professional expertise
- Stakeholder orientation
- Total organizational astuteness

Transformational
self

Relationship Management
- Change agentry
- Community building
- Conflict management and negotiation
- Cross-cultural communication
- Influencing

Personal Effectiveness
- Accountability
- Curiosity and learning
- Improvisation
- Maturity
- Thinking agility

Source: From Terence Brake, *The Global Leader: Critical Factors for Creating the World Class Organization,* 1997, p. 44. Copyright © 1997 The McGraw-Hill Companies. Reprinted with permission.

FIGURE 11.1

Blake's Global
Leadership Triad

and comprehend contradictory data from a variety of sources and to subsequently make effective decisions, (2) excellent interpersonal skills in order to enable them to understand how to behave within particular countries and situations, (3) capability for learning from experience, and (4) advanced capacity for moral reasoning in order to comprehend ethical dilemmas.[18]

In contrast to the preceding lists of leadership competencies, the five-level Pyramid Model of Global Leadership, presented in Figure 11.2, attempts to identify a progression of skills required for effective global leadership. At the bottom level is a baseline of global knowledge that is necessary in order for a global leader to perform at even a basic level of competence. Building on this knowledge is a second level of four threshold traits, including humility, integrity, inquisitiveness, and resilience. Level 3 includes attitudes and orientations

FIGURE 11.2

Pyramid Model of
Global Leadership

Level 5: System skills
Make ethical decisions
Influence stakeholders
Lead change   Span boundaries
Architecting   Build community

Level 4: Interpersonal skills
Mindful communication
Create and build trust
Multicultural teaming

Level 3: Attitude and orientations
Global mindset
Congnitive Complexity   Cosmopolitansim

Level 2: Threshold Traits
Intergrity   Humanity
Inquisitiveness   Resilience

Level 1: Global Knowledge

Source: Adapted from M. E. Mendenhall, J. S. Osland, A. Bird, G. R. Oddou, and M. L. Maznevski, *Global Leadership: Research, Practice, and Development* (New York: Routledge, 2008), Figure 3.3.

Are Women Appropriate for Global Leadership Positions?

The World Bank has stated that a core development objective is to achieve gender equality and full participation of women in business, particularly in developing nations. Despite this, as noted by Adler,[a] most of the research on leadership has focused on men, with only a minor portion dealing with the potential of women as leaders. Research has continued to show unevenness in terms of the level of participation of women in leadership roles, particularly as reflected in numbers of women leaders in business. Although women occupy more than 51 percent of the managerial and professional positions in U.S. organizations, there are few females in the top tier of corporate leadership.[b] Women CEOs such as Indra Nooyi at PepsiCo or Cynthia Carroll at Anglo American represent a very small minority of the leadership in publicly held corporations. Instead, most of the women who serve as CEOs have either started their own firms or have taken over the leadership of a family business. In a study involving 942 companies from the *Fortune* 1000, it was discovered that almost half of the companies had no women in their top executive ranks. Only 7 percent of the firms had more than two women executives and less than 3 percent had more than three women in top executive positions.[c] Only 14.4 percent of executive officer positions in *Fortune* 500 companies were filled by women in 2010, and only 15.7 percent of the positions on corporate boards.[d] Data such as these suggest that growth in the number of female CEOs in the United States may be constrained in the near future, given the limited quantity of women in the executive pipeline.

Research has shown that women and men differ in terms of their typical leadership styles. For example, women tend to view leadership as an opportunity to empower their subordinates and enhance their potential to excel; men tend to see their leadership position as a chance for exerting control over their subordinates.[e] Adler argues for an increased level of women in global leadership positions, due in part to research suggesting that traits and qualities typically associated with women are consistent with those linked to effective global leadership.[f] For example, she found that global leaders who were women:

- Came from diverse backgrounds, with no predictable pattern associated with their route to leadership positions.

- Were not selected for leadership positions only by women-friendly companies or countries.

- Symbolized hope, change, and unity through their selection as leaders, particularly in light of their position as outsiders who were going against the odds, thereby suggesting the potential for organizational or societal change.

- Were driven to achieve success based on vision, rather than desire for hierarchical status.

- Relied upon broad-based, popular support or support directly from the marketplace, instead of traditional, hierarchy-based structural or party support.

- Pursued paths to power that involved lateral transfers within their organizations, instead of the more traditional path up the hierarchy that was common among men.

- Leveraged the enhanced visibility that they received due to their status as women or as "the first woman." This special status meant that they received more attention from the media than did men, and they were able to use this visibility as a platform to enhance their position and performance.

Consistent with Adler's work, other research has found that women tend to have a leadership style that is more participative, interactional, and relational, with greater levels of emotional intelligence and empathy, than is the case for men.[g] These are attributes that have been suggested as being better suited for leadership performance within a global context. Women have also been found to attribute greater importance to the areas of social responsibility, inclusion and diversity, and global skills—and women were believed to be better prepared in these areas as well—than was the case for men.[h] Women have also been found to use leadership styles that are more participative or democratic and less directive or autocratic than the leadership styles used by men.[i]

Questions:

1. The research findings presented in this Global Debate suggest that perhaps women might be better suited for the challenges associated with global leadership positions than might be the case for men. Yet how could such a possibility be true, given the small number of women occupying executive leadership positions?

2. What options might be available for increasing the level of participation—and effectiveness—of women in global leadership positions?

[a]N. J. Adler, "Global Leadership: Women Leaders," *Management International Review* 37, no. 1 (1997), pp. 171–96; and N. J. Adler, "Global Leadership: Women Leaders," in M. Mendenhall, T. Kühlmann, and G. Stahl, Eds.) *Developing Global Business Leaders: Policies, Processes and Innovations* (Westport, CT: Quorum Books, 2001), pp. 73–97.

[b]U.S. Department of Labor, Women's Bureau, 2010, "Quick Facts on Women in the Labor Force in 2010," www.dol.gov/wb/factsheets/Qf-laborforce-10.htm (June 13, 2011).

[c]C. Helfat, D. Harris, and P. Wolfson, "The Pipeline to the Top: Women and Men in the Top Executive Ranks of U.S. Corporations," *Academy of Management Perspectives*, 20, no. 4, (2006), pp. 42–64.

(continued)

[d]Catalyst, 2010. "Statistical Overview of Women in the Workplace," March 2011, www.catalyst.org/publication/219/statistical-overview-of-women-in-the-workplace (June 13, 2011).

[e]J. Rosener, "Ways Women Lead," *Harvard Business Review* 68, no. 6 (1990), pp. 119–25.

[f]Adler (2001), pp. 90–96.

[g]For example, N. Fondas, "Feminization Unveiled: Management Qualities in Contemporary Writings," *Academy of Management Review* 2, no. 1 (1997), pp. 257–82; and M. A. Brackett, S. E. Rivers, S. Shiffman, N. Lerner, and P. Salovey, "Relating Emotional Abilities to Social Functioning: A Comparison of Self-Report and Performance Measures of Emotional Intelligence," *Journal of Personality and Social Psychology* 91 (2006), pp. 780–95.

[h]A. Lajtha and A. Carminati-Rabasse, *2008 Women's Research—One Step Ahead of 2011: A New Horizon for Working Women* (2008), https://microsite.accenture.com/mpw/experience/Pages/StepAhead2011.aspx (June 13, 2011).

[i]A. H. Eagly and B. T. Johnson, "Gender and Leadership Style: A Meta-Analysis. *Psychological Review* 109 (1990), pp. 573–98.

that affect the manner in which global leaders perceive and interpret their world, while the fourth level includes interpersonal skills that enable global leaders to effectively cross cultures. Level 5, at the apex of the pyramid, includes system skills that enable global leaders to effectively influence people and systems inside and outside the company.

The broad array of competencies identified in this section helps to highlight why there is no consensus on the set of competencies that a global leader must possess—simply, the jobs of global leaders tend to be quite diverse. Nevertheless, the preceding discussion identifies many of the attributes that have been identified as facilitating the effectiveness of those individuals who occupy global leadership positions.

Selecting and Developing Effective Global Leaders

LO11-4 Discuss approaches for selecting and developing effective global leaders.

ASSESSING GLOBAL LEADERSHIP COMPETENCIES

A key challenge confronting companies faced with the challenge of developing global leaders is assessing the competencies of candidates. As discussed earlier in this chapter, there are many different models of the skills and attributes required for effective global leadership, and the variation in components across these models complicates assessment.

To address this challenge of competence assessment, a number of different assessment instruments have been developed. These instruments include the Cross-Cultural Adaptability Inventory (a tool for self-assessment of cross-cultural adaptability),[19] the Intercultural Development Inventory (an instrument for identifying competencies associated with intercultural sensitivity),[20] the Global Competencies Inventory (an instrument to assess personality predispositions linked with effective intercultural behavior and the acquisition of global managerial skills),[21] and the Global Executive Leadership Inventory (a 360-degree feedback approach for identifying leadership competencies and awareness gaps associated with those competencies).[22] Each of these instruments has its own unique strengths and weaknesses, depending on the context in which it will be used.

MODELS FOR DEVELOPING GLOBAL LEADERS

An important issue facing international companies is developing an understanding of how to develop effective global leaders. Are candidates just "born global," with a special set of skills and attributes that makes them effective in global leadership contexts, or do these capabilities get developed over time as a result of some interplay among personal attributes, experience, and other factors? Most experts in the field tend toward the latter notion, that global leadership effectiveness is the result, at least in part, of a developmental process rather than innate capability.[23] As a result, various models of global leadership development have been proposed. Understanding these models may assist the international company in developing appropriate processes for enhancing the development of their own cadre of global leaders. This section discusses two models: the Global Leadership Expertise Development (GLED) model and the "right stuff" model.

The GLED Model A conceptual model designed for developing the expertise of global leaders, the GLED model (Figure 11.3) emphasizes the process by which expertise

FIGURE 11.3

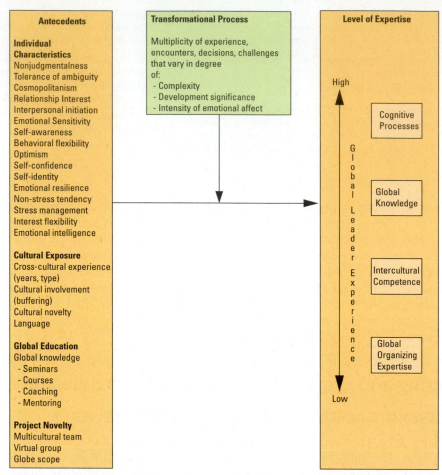

Source: From J. S. Osland and A. Bird, "Process Models of Global Leadership Development," in M. E. Mendenhall, J. S. Osland, A. Bird, G. R. Oddou, and M. L. Maznevski, *Global Leadership: Research, Practice and Development,* 2008, figure 5.2. Reproduced by permission of Taylor & Francis Books UK.

is developed.[24] This model includes antecedents for the development of global leaders and their expertise, divided among four categories: individual characteristics, cultural exposure, global education, and project novelty. The level of global leadership expertise is hypothesized as being determined collectively by four dependent variables: cognitive processes, global knowledge, intercultural competence, and global organizing expertise. The model asserts that the relationship between outcome measures and antecedents will be mediated by a transformational process. This transformational process is comprised of the set of experiences, interpersonal encounters, decisions, and challenges related to the global leader's expertise, and this process is asserted to be the primary cause of the different levels of global leadership expertise that are observed among leaders with global responsibilities.

The "Right Stuff" Model   This model (Figure 11.4) is focused on an outcome of developing global leaders that have the "right stuff" in terms of what they have learned and what they are able to do as leaders. Producing leaders with the right stuff is the result of interaction and partnership between the leader and the organization. The basic talent of the candidates being developed, combined with their developmental experiences and the context in which these experiences occur (and the developmental mechanisms that are employed—the policies and procedures used to ensure that the right people are channeled into the right experiences), will help to produce the right stuff in terms of the global leader's skills and capability. However, this model argues that the company's global business

FIGURE 11.4

The "Right Stuff" Model

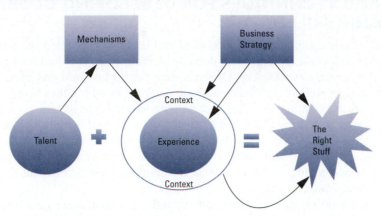

strategy is a major determinant of the relevant lessons that the global leader needs to learn and the skills that will be developed, and therefore what represents the right stuff for a global leader will vary across organizations. In this respect, the strategy and structure of the company determine the number of international jobs in the organization, the types and nationalities of the global leaders, and the skills that the company will require. For example, a company with a strategy that depends on extensive use of alliances with external organizations will require leaders with skills and experience of working with entities beyond the firm's formal boundaries. Correspondingly, an organization's decision to compete in a broad array of less economically developed nations will help determine the number and range of different cultural capabilities that the company's leaders will require.

As the preceding discussion shows, the development of global leaders is a complex process that demands flexibility in order to match the individual, organizational, and external contexts in which the leaders need to learn and to perform. A standardized approach applied to all leadership candidates and across all contexts is unlikely to be successful in developing effective global leaders.

TOOLS AND TECHNIQUES FOR DEVELOPING GLOBAL LEADERSHIP SKILLS

How can individuals aspiring to positions of global leadership develop the required set of skills and experiences? Development of global leadership skills is a nonlinear process comprised of a set of diverse experiences. Differences in the background and attributes of leadership candidates, as well as the companies and contexts in which they work, suggest that development efforts must be considered on an individualized basis and should consider a variety of different developmental tools and techniques. Global leaders will require strong training in business fundamentals, including international business. A robust comprehension of history, geography, and political science, among other topics, can be invaluable for enhancing understanding and performance within different international settings, as can training in language and culture.

Much of this learning may be achievable through traditional means, such as studying in universities, participating in intensive international business simulations, or attending executive short courses and seminars. However, gaining deeper, nuanced understanding of complex issues such as cross-cultural leadership can seldom be achieved solely through reading books and attending lectures. To develop the skills necessary to deal effectively with the complex, ambiguous, high-level challenges that global leaders face will require these individuals to consider an array of different techniques and experiences, some of which may be undertaken before, during, or shortly after their university studies. Examples include living with host families while studying abroad, in order to enhance language and cultural fluency; international internships, both paid and unpaid; personal and business travel to international locations; working with one's company to identify and participate in short-term or longer-term expatriate assignments within international markets; developing effective networks from contacts at university, work, and other contexts; pursuing opportunities to work within multicultural and virtual teams, including those of an international nature; or pursuing mentoring and coaching opportunities, both on the giving and the receiving end. Consciously considering one's developmental needs and pursuing an appropriate set of activities such as these can be invaluable in developing global leadership capability.

The goal of the leadership development process is to obtain the variety of transformational experiences that are needed in order to truly develop global leadership capability. Of course, not all international and cross-cultural experiences will have the same impact in terms of development of global leadership expertise, and an ongoing sequence of self-reflection and self-assessment will be necessary in order to identify remaining gaps and opportunities for further development. While monitoring career development of prospective global leaders is an important function for a corporation's executives as well as human resource personnel, they cannot force individuals to develop their potential. In that regard, it is important for aspiring leaders to recognize that they have an important role in monitoring and assessing their own development and undertake efforts to ensure that substantive progress is occurring.

Leading Global Teams

LO11-5 Explain what skills a manager needs in order to effectively lead global teams.

global team
A team characterized by a high level of diversity, geographic dispersion, and virtual rather than face-to-face interaction.

Global teams are an increasingly common form for international work. Such teams have members in multiple locations in more than one country. Further, they have several dimensions that add to their complexity. These additional dimensions include members from different national cultures whose locations are in different time zones, different available communication technologies, and different corporate and economic contexts in which their members are being embedded (see Table 11.1). Global teams are characterized by high levels of diversity, geographic dispersion, and virtual rather than face-to-face interaction. In this section, we begin with a discussion of team leading in general, examining the three activities that team leaders usually engage in. Then we explore the added challenges of leading global teams, including their performance management. Note that some scholars use the term *team* to suggest closer psychological bonding than is found in a group; here we are using the terms interchangeably.

| **TABLE 11.1** | Differences between Traditional and Global Teams |

Traditional Team—Single Context

Global Team—Multiple Contexts

Characteristics

1. One location for work
2. Common national culture in a shared geography
3. Common economic, political, and social conditions

4. Native language speakers, one work language
5. Professional expertise and communication skills

6. Task contained within organizational and national boundaries
7. Opportunities for frequent face-to-face and informal interactions
8. Work within single time zone

Characteristics

1. Multiple locations for work
2. Multiple national cultures in multiple geographies
3. Multiple dissimilar economic, political, and social conditions

4. Native and non-native speakers, several work languages
5. In addition to professional expertise and communication skills, cross-cultural competence and adaptability

6. Task spans organizational and national boundaries
7. Few opportunities for face-to-face and informal interactions, interaction structured and mediated by technology
8. Work across multiple time zones

Source: Adapted from J. Gluesing and C. Gibson, "Designing and Forming Global Teams" in *The Blackwell Handbook of Global Management* (Malden, MA: Blackwell Publishing, 2004), p. 203.

LEADING TEAMS IS A COMPLEX ACTIVITY

Leading teams in any context involve many activities. Scholars recognize three main activities that are common to most team leadership: establishing teams, coaching team members, and setting team norms.[25] We look at each of these activities and comment on their relevance to global team leadership, and then go on to explore how a global context for team leadership further affects the leadership activities.

The first leadership activity is to establish the team itself. In this process, the leader wants to encourage strong member identification with the team and its norms. Such identification has been shown to lead to better performance. When team members see one another as each member sees him- or herself, and when team members feel that their team is distinctive, even when the team is very diverse, high levels of motivation are likely to exist.[26] The basic task of creating an environment for these team norms to come into play is especially useful in global teams, characterized as they are by high levels of diversity.

The next group leader activity, coaching team members, is critically important in global teams, which usually have high levels of diversity. When faced with diversity, coworkers, if unfamiliar with the work of their group member, tend to expect that person to perform poorly. Chatman and Kennedy point out that such expectations tend to occur regardless of the person's actual skill level. Such expectations can be self-fulfilling.[27] The team leader can confront this bias by publicizing the strengths of team members. Motivational coaching is also important as the team begins their task, and strategic coaching may be valuable when strategic choices come into play, further along in the team's evolution.

Setting team norms is the third key activity for all team leaders. **Team norms** are defined as "legitimate, shared standards against which the appropriateness of behavior can be evaluated."[28] Team norms greatly influence the dynamics of the team, especially in two areas, cooperation and consideration. Cooperation is a critical issue with global teams, especially for those that are not co-located (where team members are not located in the same place). Often in work life, face-to-face interaction takes priority. To respond to requests for collaboration from a nearby coworker is much easier than to put off the coworker so that you can respond to the team member who may be geographically distant, so that synchronous connections are difficult. One way to support cooperation is to increase the level at which team members see one another as members of their in-group. Reward structures also can be set up to encourage group cooperation.

Norms of consideration are also important to teams, and especially so for global teams where the level of diversity is high. By consideration, we mean sensitivity to others. In some of the literature, this area of norms has been described as political correctness, but without the possibly negative associations. We mean something more akin to good manners. For example, when potentially offensive language is self-censored, diverse groups tend to build trust more quickly. The quicker the trust, the sooner the team can move to a constructive focus on the task at hand.

COMPLEXITY FOR TEAMS IN THE GLOBAL CONTEXT

In addition to these traditional team leader roles, the global team leader is acting within the context of globalization. As described earlier in this chapter, globalization involves a great shift towards increasing complexity. Three specific conditions identified in the international context that contribute to globalization's complexity are increased multiplicity, increased interdependence, and increased ambiguity.[29] We look at these forces a bit more closely in an effort to capture some of the complexity that global team leaders face.

Multiplicity arises from the increased number of players in the game. There are more competitors, more stakeholders, and more customers with globalization. There are many more relationships to manage and many more viewpoints to consider.

Interdependence arises from the very core of globalization and involves economic interdependence, interdependence along the value chain, and interdependence in alliances.

The increased ambiguity results from multiple ways we have to interpret data, of which we have an increasing amount. Yet, the more data we have, the less clear becomes the path for interpreting these data. Cause and effect relationships are not clear, there are multiple plausible interpretations of the same data, and the information itself may not be clear. We are left not knowing how to interpret the data we do have in a way that will guide decisions. This is the complex context in which global teams exist. Table 11.1 summarizes the differences between the simpler, single context team and the global team.

CULTURE AND GLOBAL TEAM LEADERSHIP

As you can see, global team leaders are challenged in several different ways. In addition to meeting the basic conditions of team performance, that have to do with the team's organization, social processes, and task processes, they face a far more complex context. A major part of this context is culture. Diverse team members bring different cultural expectations to the team environment. Culture controls how the team members even think of the team at deep levels. (Is the team a family? A tribe? A collection of friends? A sports team?) Addressing these differences in connection with the notion of culture can lead to superior performance. Researchers have pointed out, though, that the inclination in diverse teams is to suppress differences and focus on what team members have in common.[30]

As you may remember from Chapter 4, people have differing ways to think about how roles are defined and managed and what acceptable communication and conflict resolution norms are, depending on their cultural values. In cultures with high power distance, team members will expect, perhaps not fully aware of their expectation, a clear hierarchy and a single leader with decision-making power. These conditions describe the cultural assumptions about leadership in cultures such as Japan and Brazil. In Scandinavian cultures, a more fluid leadership model is expected, where leadership is shared and shifts depending on the task and the leader's ability. In individualistic cultures such as those in the United States or Britain, task roles are clearly defined and responsibility allocated, with individual rewards assumed. Contrast this to more collectivist cultures such as Malaysia and Thailand, where accountability is assumed at the group level and team-level reward assumed. Addressing these differences explicitly builds a foundation for understood and agreed upon roles in the team.

The assumptions about communication and how conflict is handled in the group also need to be directly addressed. Compare some Latin countries, where speaking up at any time is fine, even when someone else is talking, to some Asian countries, in which you respond only to questions and silence is a comfortable way to communicate. How does this cultural predisposition operate in the virtual world? How does the culture deal with disagreement? Is open disagreement appropriate? Or is harmony so valued that disagreement is withheld? It is important for the team to be able to resolve conflict constructively, but, as you can imagine, this may be a difficult process.

Understanding the various cultures of team members is important to the team's functioning. Maznevski suggests a process that can open up the cultural assumptions team members may have, involving three steps: map, bridge, and integrate.[31] *Mapping,* the first step, is to discuss the differences and similarities, that is, to map the relevant characteristics of team members. This is followed by a *bridging* effort. In bridging, team members communicate with each other about the differences and establish how the team members will work with one another. Bridging involves decentering—seeing the other person's point of view—and avoiding blame. Effective bridging also enables *integration,* which is the process of managing the various differences so that team members begin to understand the expectations and assumptions of their team members, as well as their backgrounds and skills.

VIRTUAL AND GEOGRAPHICALLY DISPERSED TEAMS

Many global teams are geographically dispersed and communicate through technology. Leading a team whose members are on different continents and in different time zones, and that connect through technology, creates unique leadership challenges. Virtual communication, even with video content, lacks the richness of face-to-face communication. Research suggests that initial face-to-face meetings for teams that plan to subsequently work virtually are a good way to build trust among team members. Such trust is critical for the functioning of the team. Most teams meet at their launch and during crises. Maznevski points out that virtual teams with high performance actually schedule regular face-to-face meetings to discuss progress and issues, and to further develop their relationships. Such regular meetings create a kind of regular heartbeat. "[T]eams that have a strong heartbeat can manage all other tasks virtually in between their face-to-face meetings, and . . . this is both less expensive and more effective than getting together 'whenever we need to.'"[32]

PERFORMANCE MANAGEMENT IN GLOBAL TEAMS

What do we understand about rewarding global team performance in these often culturally diverse, geographically dispersed, and virtual global teams? Researchers suggest that if we could point to one factor to account for many of the failures of global teams, that factor would be ineffective reward and recognition strategies.[33] The critical issues are:

- Are rewards based on individual performance, team performance, or a combination of the two?
- What factors come into play with team-based pay?
- What role can recognition play?

Individual-based rewards are most commonly used, despite the fact that individual contributions to global teams are difficult to discern, especially in a virtual environment. Team-based rewards are thought to suffer from social loafing. **Social loafing** is the tendency of some people to put forth less effort when they are members of a group. A combination of individual and group rewards is seen by many researchers as a good approach to resolving this issue. There are five areas that will benefit from consideration in establishing a balance of team and individual rewards:

1. What is the nature of the task? How interdependent is it? The greater the task interdependence, the higher the portion of team-based rewards should be.

2. How stable is the team membership? If the team boundaries are fluid or if membership changes are frequent, appropriate team rewards will be difficult to determine.

3. What are the national cultures of the team members? The individualism-collectivism dimension of the cultures needs to be considered. High levels of team rewards are appropriate for teams whose members are from collectivist cultures, and high levels of individual rewards are appropriate for teams whose members are from more individualist cultures. With high levels of cultural diversity, the team should be involved in the development of the reward system.

4. What are the labor laws that affect employee compensation? In many locations, salary levels are set by local or national laws or by labor unions, and their flexibility is constrained.

5. What are the available reward options? In addition to financial rewards, recognition is a valued reward. These rewards are most successful when they incorporate national cultural values of team members.[34]

Remember that performance appraisal for global teams will also be influenced heavily by national level culture and by the other team variables mentioned in our discussion of their rewards and recognition.

Global team leadership is an evolving skill that will be increasingly important going forward. Early research suggests that global teams require the leadership skills that basic teams need, and then the increased awareness and more subtle leadership skills that help the team build on its diversity and its geographic dispersion, all in a context that is increasingly complex.

Leading Global Change

LO11-6 Identify some of the challenges of leading global change.

Leading organizational change is always a difficult process, largely because it deals with changing individual behaviors. Leadership professor Jim Clawson believes that change is the central part of leadership. He writes that leadership has three elements: "(1) seeing what needs to be done; (2) understanding all the underlying forces at play in the situation; and (3) having the courage to initiate actions to make things better."[35] Key players in the change process have to alter their behavior. Their behavior rests on their assumptions, values, beliefs, perceptions, tasks and roles.[36] If the scope of the change that global managers hope to effect is global, then the process becomes exponentially difficult. The difficulty comes from the size of the organization, its geographical dispersion, and, most significantly, the varying expectations and values that surround personal assumptions about change in different national level cultures.

CHANGE MODELS

Research on global change is in its early stages, and it builds on the more general study of change. Here, we will look first at two models for change and its leadership, and then at the aspects of culture that may influence global change leadership. Each of the models is based on describing the *process* of change and its stages.

Probably the most well-known change model was developed by Kurt Lewin. It is a three-stage process that involves unfreezing, moving, and refreezing. The first stage, *unfreezing,* involves overcoming inertia and preparing people for change, including dealing with defense mechanisms against the proposed change. At this point, there is stress, tension, and recognition of the need for change. The second stage involves *moving* the proposed behaviors into practice, a period often characterized by confusion. *Refreezing* is the final stage, when the new behaviors are either accepted and institutionalized or rejected.

Expanding the level of description found in Lewin's model, John Kotter's approach to change suggests eight steps:

1. Increase urgency, so that people are inspired to move toward real and relevant objectives.

2. Develop the guiding team, so that those involved in leadership are the right people, with high emotional commitment and the right combination and levels of skills.

3. Develop a change vision and strategy.

4. Communicate the vision for buy-in.

5. Empower broad-based action by removing obstacles.

6. Generate short-term wins that are rewarded.

7. Don't let up; foster determination and persistence.

8. Make the change stick through leadership development and succession.[37]

These models might be misconstrued to imply that change is an orderly process and that the steps are nicely sequential. In practice, whether it is incremental or transformative, remember that change is not neat and orderly, largely because it rests on human behavior. Often it involves a lot of learning through trial-and-error approaches.

CHANGE AND CULTURE

It should not surprise us that aspects of culture are related to the process of change. These aspects of culture include cultural traits related to tolerance of ambiguity, power distance, attitude toward planning, communication styles, flexibility, and other cultural attributes that play out in the change process. Recent research suggests that the influence of national culture is stronger than the influence of organizational culture on change efforts.[38] In her work on the implementation of change, Osland looks closely at this issue, and our discussion is informed by her observations.[39] Cultures that are characterized by high tolerance of ambiguity—that is, cultures that have low uncertainty avoidance—are likely to be more change-friendly. The United States is a prime example of this. Cultures that have high uncertainly avoidance are inclined to avoid change. To lead change in such cultures as Japan, Germany, and France (relative to the United States, Ireland, Denmark, and Jamaica), the process has to be very well outlined and communicated with frequency.

THE GLOBAL PATH AHEAD

Chad Henry: Developing Global Leadership Skills and Experience, Beginning with an Internship to Croatia

I was born and raised in Sacramento, California, and went to Cal Poly–San Luis Obispo on a full scholarship to play college football. I initially intended to study architectural engineering, but switched into business administration with a concentration in finance.

After completing my degree and collegiate athletic career, I was searching for direction . I wanted to do something different with my life other than the traditional opportunities that were being offered. I didn't see myself as a traditional "finance" guy and was uncertain if these traditional careers paths would bring personal fulfillment. With the influence of

my parents and sports, I had already traveled extensively throughout the United States and thought to myself, "Why not take a step into a new frontier?" At the time, I didn't realize or think about the magnitude of such a decision. As a young man, to me it was an opportunity to work and live abroad.

I ended up applying for and accepting an AIESEC internship to Croatia, a place I knew almost nothing about. I tried to gather as much information as possible about Croatia before leaving. Due to a short time frame, approximately three weeks, I didn't place much thought into my travel. My main preparation focused on understanding exactly where I was going, ensuring that it was safe, and preparing information for my parents so they knew where I was going. The information I gathered was very general.

My internship was only for 12 months. However, I enjoyed the experience and ultimately became fluent with the language, took on a range of different jobs, and lived in Croatia for about 10 years. It was an exciting time in a country undergoing many changes. During this time, I lived in the cities of Split, Varazdin, and Zagreb. I also traveled to a number of countries, including

(continued)

Canada, the UK, Netherlands, Denmark, Finland, Germany, Austria, Spain, Italy, France, Belgium, Luxembourg, Switzerland, Poland, Czech Republic, Slovakia, Slovenia, Romania, Bulgaria, Hungary, Croatia, Serbia, Bosnia and Herzegovina, Montenegro, Russia, and the Ukraine, as well as the United States.

Among the jobs that I pursued during my decade abroad, I had positions in export development, strategic development and management consulting (on issues of foreign direct investment, business zone development, organic farming cooperatives, and business process management), investment development (creating a food processing facility), commercial real estate development (for Arena Zagreb, a multifunctional sports hall with 16,000 seats; Arena Centar, a multifunctional shopping and entertainment center; and Ciovo tourist development), and startup development. I also played professional baseball for a Croatian team and coached a team playing American football.

The keys to my successful adjustment while away from the United States included keeping a very open mind and maintaining my determination to succeed. This latter trait helped me deal with challenges as they presented themselves. The biggest challenges I confronted were learning to accept things as they are without making value judgments, remembering that things are more relative rather than absolute. While as individuals we are taught a certain way to do things or approach situations, this doesn't make it right or wrong. When you can learn to accept different viewpoints and see the value in them—even if not necessarily agreeing with them—then it allows you to enjoy and adapt to the culture in which you are immersed.

My greatest rewards from my time abroad included learning to successfully manage people who have intrinsically different values in regard to work; finding a way to work with people, and get the most out of them; and being accepted by peers and friends in another culture. The greatest learning points from my international experience included developing my ability to see and understand things from multiple perspectives and learning to adapt and react to adverse and sometimes hostile situations.

My recommendations regarding what is important to do or not to do to be successful when going abroad include the following:

- It is extremely important to understand the perspective of others while you are abroad. This is developed by cultural differences and values. Without understanding these different perspectives and values, it will be very difficult to resolve differences and disputes. This is also very important in the management of others in regard to both motivation of workers and gaining respect from colleagues.

- Learn the local language.

- Have a general understanding of the history of the country.

- Ask questions.

Resources for Your Global Career

Building a strong set of business and cultural skills, international experience, and global network of contacts is essential for promoting future success as a global leader. The following sites provide a wealth of different opportunities to assist you in nurturing this set of critical skills and experiences:

- Aperian Global offers a range of useful books, articles, and podcasts dealing with the development of skills for effective performance in cross-cultural and global leadership contexts, and they also have free subscriptions to their newsletter: www.aperianglobal.com/publications_newsletter.asp

- ITAP International, a consulting firm focused on building leadership capability across global and cultural boundaries, offers a variety of articles, recommended readings, YouTube videos, links, and cultural tips: http://itapintl.com/

- The Institute of International Education (IIE) is a nonprofit organization that offers opportunities for study and training for global leadership and development, including the Fulbright Program and Gilman Scholarships that are administered for the U.S. Department of State. Information and resources can be obtained by visiting www.iie.org/What-We-Do.aspx

- The Global Leadership Foundation provides assistance to public sector leaders and governments for improving the quality of governance and political leadership through the direct insights and experience of former national and international leaders: www.g-l-f.org/

- For insight on how to leverage your short-term business travel as a means of enhancing your global leadership potential, see http://onlinelibrary.wiley.com/doi/10.1002/1099-050X(200022/23)39:2/3%3C159::AID-HRM6%3E3.0.CO;2-J/abstract

- Using repatriation policies to enhance the development of global leaders is discussed at www.chrs.rutgers.edu/pub_documents/Article%2059%20Caligiuri%20(2).pdf

- For resources and links to international internships in different regions of the world, for both undergraduate or graduate students, see http://iccweb.ucdavis.edu/international/Internships.htm, http://www.aiesec.org/

- For internship or other job leads for developing international and leadership experience with General Electric, see www.ge.com/careers/students/index.html

- The Center for Creative Leadership provides a broad array of training programs, assessment tools, news, and blogs associated with the development of global leadership capability: www.ccl.org/leadership/index.aspx

People from cultures characterized by high power distance will feel most comfortable with hierarchy and will want top managers to make decisions and issue directives. Likewise, cultures in which respect for the past is strong are likely to resist change. The influence of these varying cultural issues suggests that an ability to communicate across cultural borders and to build trust is essential for global managers as they drive global change in their organizations.

One Consulting Company's Practical Take on Global Leadership

"It's the kiss of death to say, 'This is the way we do it back at headquarters.' If they see that you are there to do your job and they are just pawns, you are done and there will be no buy in."

Aperian Global, a consulting company whose goal is to open the world for its clients (*aperire* in Latin is to open), has researched the issues of how the global context changes what leadership is and what competencies are required for global leadership. Aperian interviewed a 51-member group of corporate leaders, all of whom had 18 months or more on international assignment to a wide variety of locations, where they were judged to be successful leaders. The interviewees came from 24 different countries and had assignments to 31 different countries.

On the first issue, the differences a global context adds to leadership, the responses included an ability to make quick shifts in strategy, business processes and personal styles in order to fit broader ranges of employee motivations and backgrounds. Here is what some of the respondents said:

The core leadership skills prevail, such as getting results through people . . . but you have to adapt your style to the people, the environment, the way things are done, the things that help you get it done.

Global leadership is very different, remarkably different. The business world has some global measures, but how to accomplish those things? We can all agree on growing 10%, but what are the means to get there? The process? The people skills? All these are different to reach the same result.

Aperian research identified five leadership activities that are important in global leadership, listed here.

Source: http://www.aperianglobal.com/newsletter_archive/publications_newsletter042.asp

- *Seeing differences* is self-awareness in a cultural context. Global leaders need to recognize that their leadership patterns are shaped by their culture, and that other ways to get things done exist.
- *Making connections* is more important in the global environment, because relationships are so important in many cultures, a prerequisite for getting things done. "Results through relationships" is a phrase used to describe this process.
- *Adjusting* is a kind of "frame-shifting" that requires cognitive flexibility to see and respond to differences.
- *Integration and change* describes a complex ability to adjust to some local practices while at the same time, selling other practices into the local environment. It involves a combination of adaptation and questioning the status quo.
- *Localization* is an ability to develop local talent.

In conclusion, global leadership is leadership plus much more, due to the exceedingly complex global environment. You can learn more about Aperian Global's view of global leadership at www.aperianglobal.com.

Summary

LO11-1 Discuss the importance of creating a company "global mindset."

Successful managers in international companies must demonstrate a combination of high knowledge differentiation and high knowledge integration.

LO11-2 Describe what distinguishes the practice of global leadership from its domestic counterpart.

Global leadership is leadership behavior that occurs in the more complex global context, where the challenge of leadership is exacerbated based on the dimensions of multiplicity, interdependence, ambiguity, and dynamism. The degree of difference between domestic and global leadership in the level of demands on skills and their applications is so great, and the nature of the possible outcomes that can

be produced within a global context can be so profoundly greater, that global leadership can ultimately be regarded as being different in kind from domestic leadership.

LO11-3 Identify the competencies required for effective global leadership.

The range of duties of global leaders suggests that such individuals require a complex mix of competencies in order to be effective in their duties. Different researchers have identified different sets of required competencies, including such dimensions as business acumen, adaptability across cultures, capability to develop individuals from and across diverse cultures, global strategic thinking, ability to establish business in new markets, capability for building global teams, competency in interacting with local political interests, emotional stability, ability to learn, decision-making and negotiating ability, global mindset, cultural adaptability and flexibility, and tolerance for ambiguity. Others have argued for the importance of (1) a high level of cognitive complexity in order to collect and comprehend contradictory data from a variety of sources and to subsequently make effective decisions, (2) excellent interpersonal skills in order to enable them to understand how to behave within particular countries and situations, (3) capability for learning from experience, and (4) advanced capacity for moral reasoning in order to comprehend ethical dilemmas. The Pyramid Model of Global Leadership refers to five levels of competencies, including global knowledge, threshold traits, attitudes and orientations, interpersonal skills, and system skills.

LO11-4 Discuss approaches for selecting and developing effective global leaders.

Various models of global leadership development have been proposed. Two models discussed in the text include the Global Leadership Expertise Development (GLED) model and the "Right Stuff" model. The GLED model involves antecedents and transformational processes that interact to produce global leadership expertise. The "right stuff" model suggests that the basic talent of the candidates being developed, combined with their developmental experiences and the context in which these experiences occur (and the developmental mechanisms that are employed—the policies and procedures used to ensure that the right people are channeled into the right experiences), will help produce the right stuff in terms of the global leader's skills and capability. However, this model argues that the company's global business strategy is a major determinant of the relevant lessons that the global leader needs to learn and the skills that will be developed, and, therefore, what represents the right stuff for a global leader will vary across organizations.

LO11-5 Explain what skills a manager needs in order to effectively lead global teams.

Global team leadership is an evolving skill that will be increasingly important going forward. Early research in this new area suggests that global team leadership requires all that basic team leadership needs and then the increased awareness and more subtle leadership skills that help the team build on its diversity and its geographic dispersion—all in a context that is increasingly complex. Among these skills is an understanding of the various cultures of team members. A tool to support this understanding throughout the team is the map-bridge-integrate model. In addition, an ability to create trust in virtual teams is an important skill for leaders of global teams.

LO11-6 Identify some of the challenges of leading global change.

Leading organizational change is always a difficult process, largely because it deals with changing individual behaviors. Global change involves, in addition to the many challenges of change, an ability to quickly grasp cultural differences in an environment that is often characterized by increased levels of multiplicity, interdependence, ambiguity, and flux.

Key Words

global mindset (p. 280)

leadership (p. 281)

global team (p. 288)

team norms (p. 290)

social loafing (p. 292)

Questions

1. What is a global mindset, and why is it important for international companies?

2. What is the difference between management and leadership?

3. How does global leadership differ from domestic leadership?

4. What are the different types of roles that a global leader may need to take?

5. How does Blake's Global Leadership Triad differ from the Pyramid Model of Global Leadership? How are the two models similar?

6. Compare and contrast the GLED model and the "right stuff" model of leadership development. What is similar between the two models? What is different?

7. What are some of the tools and techniques that an aspiring global leader might be able to use to develop his or her global leadership skills?

8. Describe global teams.

9. Many business managers will say, "Leadership is leadership the world over." What are they missing?

10. How might national level culture affect change?

Use the globalEDGE site (http://globalEDGE.msu.edu/) to complete the following exercises:

1. Your long-term goal is to be in a position of global leadership in a large, multinational corporation. As you take this course, you realize the importance of developing global leadership skills through international and cross-cultural experiences. As a result, you are now considering participating in an international internship program. Using the International Internship Directory provided by globalEDGE, identify internship opportunities in private corporations in Germany. Which three programs do you find most interesting?

2. During your university studies, you have been taking French lessons. Although you are now fluent in the language, you still do not feel comfortable speaking it. Your mentor, a global marketing director at a consumer products company, suggested that you live in France for a period of time to further enhance your French-speaking skills and, at the same time, to develop global leadership capability. Use *Exploring Abroad*—which contains information on working, teaching, studying, and traveling abroad—to prepare a short report on living in France.

Minicase: Justin Marshall—A Failed Global Leadership Opportunity?

Justin Marshall earned a bachelor's degree in business, with honors, from a prominent state university in the American Midwest. After graduation, he worked for two years in the finance department for a consumer products company and then two additional years in business development, consistently receiving excellent performance reviews from his superiors. He then returned to school to pursue a MBA degree at one of the top-ranked universities, ultimately graduating in the top 5 percent of his class. After being head-hunted by several corporations, Justin accepted a lucrative offer to work for a prominent computer software and services company, which we will call Compcorp. Demonstrating stellar performance, Justin quickly worked his way up the corporate hierarchy. By the age of 31, he was promoted to a position as divisional vice president for the United States, where he oversaw the transformation of his division from one with mediocre performance to one of the most profitable divisions in Compcorp's global operations.

Justin's performance as division VP caught the eye of the company's senior executives, and he was offered the opportunity to become VP of one of Compcorp's international operations, a division serving the Asia-Pacific region. Although growing in overall sales, this division had underperformed its major competitors in recent years, and Compcorp's executives told Justin that they wanted to see if he could replicate his earlier success and transform the Asia-Pacific unit's performance.

Justin leaped at this opportunity. He had always dreamed of living and working abroad, and he exuded confidence that he could quickly diagnose the unit's problems and turn things around. Within a month, he had transitioned out of his former position, packed up his family, and moved into an apartment near the Hong Kong headquarters of his division. Applying the skills and experiences he had honed in his earlier positions, Justin began an aggressive evaluation of his new division. He pored over the financial statements

and other documentation, met with dozens of key personnel throughout his division, and quickly initiated changes to help ratchet up performance. Rigorous reporting requirements and performance reviews were implemented, and Justin met with each of his country managers and other key personnel to agree on a set of ambitious cost-cutting and revenue growth targets. Individual unit performance was monitored closely and the results of each individual unit were shared across the unit's top managers. As Justin expected, performance showed a strong uptick during his second quarter as division VP. When he traveled back to headquarters for a quarterly review meeting with his superiors and the heads of other divisions, he proudly pointed out his unit's performance improvements and projected even stronger results for upcoming quarters. He basked in the positive feedback and attention he received from his bosses, as well as the substantial performance bonus he had earned. Justin felt that it was only a matter of time until he was promoted again, perhaps into a senior VP position back at headquarters.

During the months after he returned to Hong Kong, results for Justin's third quarter in office evidenced a slight decline, and he was also surprised to receive resignation letters from several key managers from his division. A few of these departing managers took comparable positions with Compcorp's competitors in the region, and rumors of morale problems began to filter back into the Hong Kong offices. Despite Justin's efforts to turn the situation around, the trend of personnel departures and performance declines continued into Justin's fourth quarter in office. A team from the American headquarters visited the region several times, meeting with Justin and a number of his executive team members and other subordinates, trying to discern what the problem was and how it should be resolved.

Justin realized that he needed to do something, and soon, to reverse the performance trend, or his position would be at risk.

Despite his efforts to initiate a number of rapid changes, performance did not improve. Shortly after his unit reported additional subpar performance for Justin's fifth quarter in office, he was invited back to company headquarters for a meeting with the company's president. At that meeting, Justin was informed that he was being reassigned to a VP position in one of Compcorp's less prestigious domestic units and that a replacement executive was being appointed to lead the Asia-Pacific region.

Although termed a lateral transfer, Justin knew that his reassignment was viewed in the company as a demotion and that his once high-flying career path had encountered serious turbulence. Despite his efforts to focus on his new position and reestablish his visibility in the company, and to regain the career trajectory he had once had, Justin felt that his actions were not paying off. Within a year of his transfer, he left the company to pursue opportunities with a different organization.

Questions:

1. What might explain Justin's failure to perform well in his new leadership role as the head of the Asia-Pacific division?

2. What might Compcorp have done to enhance prospects for Justin's successful performance? What might Justin himself have done to enhance the likelihood of success in his new assignment and to help avoid derailing an otherwise highly promising career in Compcorp?

Think locally, offer value, and be patient. That last one is key: You can make an elephant dance. But it takes time to learn the right tune.

—*Om Malik on Marketing to India, Business 2.0*

International Marketing Consultant In Focus: Faith Popcorn

Faith Popcorn, an international marketing consultant and president of the BrainReserve firm, seems more like a futurist, entertainer, or guru than a marketing consultant. Just her last name itself (she was born a Plotkin) suggests a playful cleverness and desire to be noticed and remembered. A former advertising agency creative director, she provides international businesses with predictions of future trends and then connects these trends to consumer behavior.

Some of her past predictions have been pretty accurate. She identified the consumer trends of cocooning, food coaches, and transcouture (using couture designs as a source of material, a bit like musical mixing and sampling)—all of which have come to pass. She also accurately predicted the growth of the entertainment industry in the recession. In her TrendBank, she includes the development of these trends over the next few years (adapting her descriptions):

- *99 lives:* living many different lives at the same time—the rush and role-multiplicity of the modern world, online, as a parent, as a student, as an organization member, and so on.

- *Anchoring:* reaching back to our spiritual roots; taking what was secure from the past to be ready for the future.

- *Atmosfear:* consumer fear and uncertainty stirred up by concerns about contaminated water, tainted food, and unclean air.

- *Being alive:* awareness that good health extends longevity and leads to a new way of life.

- *Cashing out:* working men and women question career satisfaction and goals and opt for a simpler life.

- *Eveolution:* the ways women think and behave are moving business from a hierarchical to a relational model.

- *EnGen:* the end of gender differences.

A *Los Angeles Times* reporter tracked Popcorn's predictions over a five-year period, and his conclusions were that she was bang-on in her predictions far and, hence, worth listening to.[a] Other trackers mark her predictions at a 95 percent accuracy rate. In fact, major corporations check out their marketing moves with her before they implement. Her site, www.faithpopcorn.com, is worth a visit because it lists her current trend predictions.

[a]Patrick Kevin Day, *Los Angeles Times,* September 30, 2008, http://latimes.com (accessed June 14, 2011).

learning objectives

After reading this chapter, you should be able to:

LO12-1 **Discuss** environmental analysis and two types of market screening.

LO12-2 **Explain** market indicators and market factors.

LO12-3 **Describe** some statistical techniques for estimating market demand and grouping similar markets.

LO12-4 **Discuss** the value to businesspeople of trade missions and trade fairs.

LO12-5 **Discuss** some of the problems market researchers encounter in foreign markets.

LO12-6 **Discuss** the different options for conducting survey-based research.

LO12-7 **Explain** the difference between country screening and segment screening.

As described in Section Two of this book, international environmental forces can complicate management efforts to assess the attractiveness of expanding into foreign markets. Companies have used a broad range of approaches to assess international markets, some of them rather unsystematic and prone to error. We think that many international managers might prefer to use a more systematic approach, and in the following pages, we describe in some detail a structured approach to the international market screening process.

The first step in the market screening process is determining the basic need potential. We describe this process in the next section. **Market screening** is a modified version of environmental scanning in which the firm identifies markets by using the environmental forces to eliminate the less desirable markets.

Environmental scanning, from which market screening is derived, is a procedure in which a firm scans the world for changes in the environmental forces that might affect it.[1] For some time, environmental scanning has been used by managers during the planning process to provide information about world threats and opportunities. Those who do environmental scanning professionally may belong to such organizations as the Society of Competitive Intelligence Professionals (www.scip.org). In addition, environmental scanning services are available from a number of private firms. Examples of such service providers include Smith Brandon International (www.smithbrandon.com) and Stratfor (www.stratfor.com).

Market Screening

Market screening is a method of market analysis and assessment that permits management to identify a small number of desirable markets by eliminating those judged to be less attractive. This is accomplished by subjecting the markets to a series of screenings based on the environmental forces examined in Section Two. Although these forces may be placed in any order, the arrangement suggested in Figure 12.1 is designed to progress from the least to the most difficult analysis based on the accessibility and subjectivity of the data. In this way, the smallest number of candidates is left for the final, most difficult screening.

Market screening assists two different kinds of firms. One is selling exclusively in the domestic market but believes it might increase sales by expanding into overseas markets. The other is already a multinational but wants to avoid missing potential new markets. In both situations, managers require an ordered, relatively fast method of analyzing and assessing the nearly 200 countries (and multiple market segments within countries) to pinpoint the most suitable prospects.

FIGURE 12.1

Selection of Foreign Markets

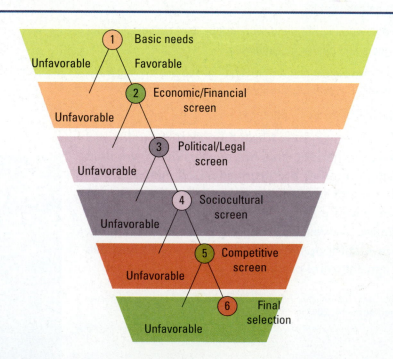

Two Types of Market Screening— Country and Segment

In this chapter, we will look at two types of market screening procedures. The first, **country screening,** uses countries as the relevant unit of analysis. The second, **segment screening,** is based on a subnational analysis of groups of consumers.

Country Screening

INITIAL SCREENING—BASIC NEEDS POTENTIAL

Basic Need Potential   An initial screening based on the basic need potential is a logical first step, because if the need is lacking, no reasonable expenditure of effort and money will enable the firm to successfully market its goods or services. For example, the basic need potential of certain goods is dependent on various physical forces, such as climate, topography, and natural resources. If the firm produces air conditioners, the analyst will look for countries with warm climates. Manufacturers of large farm tractors might not consider Switzerland a likely prospect because of its mountainous terrain. Manufacturers of large yachts might consider a landlocked country such as Paraguay to be an unattractive potential market, and only areas known to possess gold deposits are probable markets for gold-dredging equipment.

Generally, producers of specialized industrial materials or equipment experience little difficulty in assessing their basic need potential. A list of firms in an industry, often on a worldwide basis, is available either from the specific industry association for that industrial sector or from specialized trade journals. A builder of cement kilns, for example, can obtain the names and addresses of cement plants worldwide through the website of the Portland Cement Association. What about less specialized products that are widely consumed? For example, it is problematic to establish a basic need for chocolate and harder still to do so for MP3 players, consumer robots, or movies on Blu-ray discs. In these cases, we are moving from needs to wants.

country screening
Using countries as the basis for market selection

segment screening
Using market segments as the basis for market selection

Foreign Trade   Analysts who want to know where American competitors are exporting their products can go to the Web site of the International Trade Administration (ITA), www.ita.doc.gov. The U.S. Department of Commerce also has the report *U.S. Exports of Merchandise* on the National Trade Data Bank (NTDB), which is available online for a subscription fee. This report's information is especially useful because it includes both units and dollar values, permitting the analyst to calculate the average price of the unit exported. The Department of Commerce compiles and releases foreign trade statistics on a monthly and cumulative basis in its report *U.S. International Trade in Goods and Services,* commonly referred to as the FT900. It is published as a press release and can be found at www.census.gov/foreign-trade/Press-Release/current_press_release/index.html.

For help in their search for markets, analysts can obtain from the nearest Department of Commerce office numerous studies prepared by U.S. embassies. *Annual Worldwide Industry Reviews* and *International Market Research Reports* indicate major markets for many products.

The *Country Market Surveys* indicate products for which there is a good, established market in a given country. Other countries publish similar data. For example, the data office of the European Union (Eurostat) publishes an annual, *External Trade,* and JETRO (the Japanese External Trade Organization), publishes a wide assortment of trade and industry data, many of which are put on its Internet site.

Imports Do Not Completely Measure Market Potential

Even when a basic need is clearly indicated, experienced researchers will still investigate trade flows in order to have an idea of the magnitude of present sales. Of course, imports alone seldom measure the full market potential. Myriad reasons are responsible, among which are poor marketing, lack of foreign exchange, and high prices (potentially caused by transportation, duties and markups). Neither can imports give much indication of the potential demand for a really new product.

Moreover, import data indicate only that a market has been buying certain products from abroad and are no guarantee that these imports will continue. A competitor may decide to produce locally, which, in many markets, will cause imports to cease. Change in a country's political structure also may reduce or eliminate imports, as we saw in the case of Iran after the revolution there, when orders worth billions of dollars were suddenly canceled. Nevertheless, import data do provide the firm with an indication of how much product is currently being purchased and provide managers with a conservative estimate of the immediate market potential at the going price. If local production is being considered and calculations show that goods produced in the country could be sold at a lower price, the firm might reasonably expect to sell more than the quantity currently being imported.

SECOND SCREENING—FINANCIAL AND ECONOMIC FORCES

After the initial screening, the analyst will have a much smaller list of prospects. This list may be further reduced by a second screening based on the financial and economic forces. Trends in inflation, currency exchange rates, and interest rates are among the major financial points of concern. The analyst should consider other financial factors, such as credit availability, paying habits of customers, and rates of return on similar investments. It should be noted that this screening is not a complete financial analysis. That will come later if the market analysis and assessment disclose that a country has sufficient potential for capital investment.

Economic data may be employed in a number of ways, but two measures of market demand based on them are especially useful. These are *market indicators* and *market factors*. Other methods for estimating demand that depend on economic data are *trend analysis* and *cluster analysis*.

TABLE 12.1

TABLE 12.1 E-Commerce Potential: Rankings for Latin America

Countries	Market Size	Market Growth Rate	E-Commerce Readiness	Overall E-Commerce Potential
South America				
Argentina	4	17	3	6
Bolivia	17	5	15	15
Brazil	5	12	3	4
Chile	1	5	1	1
Colombia	11	7	9	9
Ecuador	14	1	9	6
Paraguay	12	16	15	17
Peru	12	3	15	11
Uruguay	7	20	9	12
Venezuela	2	19	7	9
Caribbean				
Dominican Republic	10	9	9	9
Haiti	20	18	20	19
Jamaica	3	14	2	3
Central America				
Costa Rica	6	2	3	2
El Salvador	15	13	9	12
Guatemala	17	11	9	12
Honduras	15	4	19	15
Mexico	6	15	3	6
Nicaragua	17	10	15	17
Panama	5	6	7	4

Source: Michael S. Minor and Alexandra Brandt, "A Possible Index of E-Commerce Potential for Latin America," working paper, January 8, 2002, updated June 2006 by Adesegun Oyedele and October 2008 by Michael S. Minor. Reprinted with permission of the authors.

Market Indicators

Market indicators are economic data that serve as yardsticks for measuring the relative market strengths of various geographic areas. As an example, we developed an index of e-commerce potential for Latin America so that the countries in the region could be compared. The results appear in Table 12.1. In this methodology, we assembled data on 20 Latin American countries and then ranked the countries against each other. We wanted to include indicators of the strength and growth rate of the overall economy, as well as factors related more specifically to e-commerce or to communications that would aid the growth of e-commerce. We developed three indices. Each indicator is given equal weight in each index.

Market size = Size of urban population + Electricity consumption

Market growth rate = Average growth rate in commercial energy use + Real growth rate in GDP

E-commerce readiness = Mobile phones per 1,000 + Number of PCs per 1,000 + Internet hosts per million people

The rankings on these three indexes were then used to form a composite ranking. We called this composite ranking the "e-commerce potential." As you can see in Table 12.1, by using our methodology, the countries with the most e-commerce potential appear to be Chile, Costa Rica, Jamaica, and Brazil, while Paraguay, Nicaragua, and Haiti appear to have the least potential.

LO12-2 Explain market indicators and market factors.

market indicators Economic data used to measure relative market strengths of countries or geographic areas

Market Factors

Market factors are similar to market indicators except that they tend to correlate highly with the market demand for a given product. If analysts of a foreign market have no factor for that market, they may be able to use one from the domestic market to provide an approximation for the foreign market. Moreover, analysts who work for a multinational firm may be able to obtain market factors developed by comparable subsidiaries. To be able to transfer these relationships to the country under study, the analysts must assume that the underlying conditions affecting demand are similar in the two markets.

We can illustrate this process, which is called **estimation by analogy,** by using the following example. If a supplier of laptops knows that one-fifth of all laptops are replaced every year in the United Kingdom, he or she might use the same relationship to estimate demand for replacement computers in a new overseas market. If there are 3 million existing laptops in the new market, the analyst might forecast that 3 million × 0.20, or 600,000, replacement laptops will be sold annually. The constant in the country under study may be somewhat different (it usually is), but with this approach, the estimates will represent a reasonable approximation and a base from which further analysis can be conducted. Many such factors exist, and generally research personnel, either at the home office or in foreign subsidiaries, are familiar with them.

Trend Analysis

When the historical growth rates of either the pertinent economic variables or the imports of a product are known, future growth can be forecast by means of **trend analysis.** A time series may be constructed in a manner similar to the way a regression model is made, or the arithmetic mean of past growth rates may be applied to historical data. Caution is advised when using the second method because if the average annual growth rate is applied mechanically, in just a few years the dependent variable may reach an incredible size. For example, a 5 percent growth rate, compounded annually, will result in a doubling of the original value in only 15 years. Because trend analysis is based on, the assumption that past conditions affecting the dependent variable will remain constant, analysts will generally modify the outcome to take into account any changes that can be foreseen or to create alternate scenarios for use in the company's analyses. Often, there are obvious constraints that will limit growth. One of these constraints is the near certainty that competitors will enter the market if large increases in demand continue for very long.

Cluster Analysis and Other Techniques
As multinationals extend their presence to more markets, managers are searching for ways to group countries and geographic regions by common characteristics. **Cluster analysis** divides objects (market areas, individuals, customers, and other variables) into groups so that the variables within each group are similar. For example, a team of college softball players sitting at a table in a restaurant might be a "cluster." Marketers, for example, use cluster analysis to identify a group of markets where a single promotional approach can be employed; attorneys can use it to group nations according to similarities in certain types of laws; and so forth. In other words, cluster analysis is used to classify a "mountain" of information into meaningful "piles."

LO12-3 Describe some statistical techniques for estimating market demand and grouping similar markets.

cluster analysis
Statistical technique that divides objects into groups so that the objects within each group are similar

Periodic Updating
If the estimates are altered appreciably in the periodic updatings that all long-term forecasts undergo, managers may change the extent of the firm's involvement to be in line with the new estimates. Fortunately, the alternative forms of participation in a market permit the firm to become progressively more involved, with corresponding increases in investment. As discussed in Chapter 13, most companies can enter a market in stages, perhaps in this sequence: exporting, establishment of a foreign sales company, local assembly, and, finally, local manufacturing.

Even when the decision is whether to produce overseas, management may plan to assemble a combination of imported and domestically produced parts initially and then progressively to manufacture more components locally as demand rises. Automobile manufacturers have begun a number of foreign operations employing this strategy.

THIRD SCREENING—POLITICAL AND LEGAL FORCES

The elements of the political and legal forces that can eliminate a market from further consideration (or make it more attractive) are numerous.

Entry Barriers
Import restrictions can be positive or negative, depending on whether managers are considering whether to serve the market by exporting (can the firm's products enter the country?) or by setting up a foreign plant (will competitive imports be kept out?). If an objective is 100 percent ownership, will the nation's laws permit it, or is some local participation required? Will the government accept a minority local ownership, or must a minimum of 51 percent of the subsidiary be in the hands of nationals? Are there laws that reserve certain industries for either the government or its citizens?[2] Is the host government demanding that the foreign owner turn over technology to its proposed affiliate that the foreign owner prefers to keep at the home-country plant? Perhaps the host government has local content restrictions that the prospective investor considers excessive. There may be a government-owned company that would compete with the proposed plant. Depending on the circumstances and how strongly management wishes to enter the market, any one of these conditions may be sufficient cause to eliminate a nation from further consideration.

Profit Remittance Barriers
When there are no objectionable requisites for entry, a nation may still be excluded if there are what management believes to be undue restrictions on the repatriation of earnings. Limits linked to the amount of foreign investment or other criteria may be set, or the nation may have a history of inability to provide foreign exchange for profit remittances.

Policy Stability
Another factor of importance to management in studying the possibilities of investing in a country is the stability of government policy. Is there continuity in policy when a new leader takes office, for example? What is the political climate? Is the government stable, or is there infighting among government leaders? How about the public? Is there visible unrest? Do the armed forces have a history of intervention when there are public disturbances? Business can adapt to the form of government and thrive as long as the conditions are stable. But instability creates uncertainty, and this complicates planning. An often-heard complaint is, "They've changed the rules again."

It is important to make a distinction between *political stability* and *policy stability*. Rulers may come and go, but if the policies that affect businesses do not change very much, these political changes really may not be important. In fact, if one measures political stability in terms of changes in leadership at the top, the United States is politically unstable compared with many countries!

Sources of analysis on political and policy stability are numerous. Some, such as Stratfor, have already been mentioned. In addition, Business Environment Risk Intelligence S.A. (www.beri.com) and Political Risk Services (www.prsgroup.com) publish rankings that compare countries on the issue of political risk.

FOURTH SCREENING—SOCIOCULTURAL FORCES

A screening of the remaining candidates on the basis of sociocultural factors is next and is often an arduous process. First, sociocultural factors are fairly subjective. Second, data are difficult to assemble, particularly from a distance. The analyst, unless he or she is a specialist in the country, must rely on the opinions of others. It is possible to hire consultants who typically are "old hands" with experience in the country or region. Others may have a particular methodology, such as Clotaire Rapaille, whose approach is mentioned in the Global Debate box elsewhere in this chapter, or Faith Popcorn, whose approach is mentioned in the chapter opening. Also, professional organizations and universities frequently hold seminars to explain the sociocultural aspects of doing business in a particular area or country.

Reading *Overseas Business Reports* (U.S. Department of Commerce), international business publications *(Business International, Financial Times, The Economist),* and specialized books will augment the analyst's sociocultural knowledge. The use of a checklist of the principal sociocultural components, many of which are described in Chapter 4, will serve as a reminder of the many factors the analyst must consider in this screening.

Clotaire Rapaille: Charlatan or Code Breaker Extraordinaire in International Market Research?

Clotaire Rapaille is a charlatan—or possibly an advisor your company simply cannot do without. Originally a psychologist treating autistic children in Europe, Rapaille now operates from a mansion in upstate New York, where top management seek his advice on "the code" that will allow them access to the Indian, French, or Norwegian psyche. And from there, this insight should help them understand the motivations that will draw these people to buy their products.

Rapaille's earlier insights came when comparing French and American attitudes toward cheese. For the French, he says, cheese is alive, and the French would not put cheese in the refrigerator any more than one would put one's cat in the fridge. Both are "alive." But for Americans, Rapaille's insight is that cheese is "dead," so Americans seal it in a plastic "casket" and put it in a refrigerator, which is really a "morgue." Americans are more concerned about safety than taste: the French reverse these preferences. So more French than American consumers die from eating cheese: but the Americans eat a relatively sterile and tasteless product, while the French enjoy a variety of cheeses that Americans cannot fathom.

Rapaille was also influential in the development of Chrysler's PT Cruiser, the retro car that has enjoyed great success. He has, in total, 50 of the *Fortune* 100 firms as clients. His claim is that teams under his direction have "broken the code" for "anti-Americanism," "China," "seduction," the "teen Internet," and more. A recent excursion to India led him to pronounce that the caste system was simply a "practical" way of signaling to all their places in society. "It's not a problem, it's a solution," he summarizes.

Rapaille displays a certain confidence bordering on arrogance, and he follows a research method that is unusual, to say the least. Rather than relying on focus groups or surveys, he "breaks the code" of certain countries in roughly three-hour sessions. In these sessions, paid

APJGP8 Alamy Images

respondents first discuss the topic of interest; then they are asked to tap into their emotional reactions; and finally Rapaille explores, as he puts it, their "reptilian brain." It is the last that he finds useful. "Never believe what people say," Rapaille says. "I want to understand why people do what they do." Ultimately, he has respondents on the floor in the fetal position, reliving childhood memories.

From this process, he says, he discovers cultural archetypes, which are long lasting, although opinions may change more readily. Former clients have scoffed at him, using "the cheese is dead" as a constant mantra, mocking his methods. For others, the idea that complex attitudes (such as the German code for Americans, which is "John Wayne") can be summarized in a word or phrase is, well, silly. Yet many of the same clients come back to him—P&G has come back 35 times.

As a manager, would you—or would you not—hire Clotaire Rapaille or his company to assist you in assessing and interpreting international market opportunities?

Sources: Danielle Sacks, "Crack This Code," *Fast Company*, April 2006, pp. 97–101; www.pbs.org/wgbh/pages/frontline/shows/persuaders/interviews/rapaille.html (accessed June 14, 2011); www.archetypediscoveries.com (accessed June 14, 2011); and "The Last Word: Clotaire Rapaille," *Newsweek*, international ed., www.msnbc.msn.com/id/4710897 (accessed June 14, 2011).

Although there are many difficulties, it is possible that recent immigrants or students from foreign countries may be used to shed light on potential sociocultural issues. A danger, of course, is that immigrants and students may not be "typical" representatives of their country, and there is also the prospect that they have been affected by their experience living abroad. Therefore, they are not necessarily reliable indicators of the reaction your product might receive from an audience "back home."

After the fourth screening, the analyst should have a list of countries for which an industry demand appears to exist. However, what management really wants to know is which of these markets seem to be the best prospects for the firm's products. A fifth screening based on the competitive forces will help provide this information.

FIFTH SCREENING—COMPETITIVE FORCES

In this screening, the analyst examines markets on the basis of such elements of the competitive forces as:

1. The number, size, and financial strength of the competitors.
2. Their market shares.
3. Their marketing strategies.
4. The apparent effectiveness of their promotional programs.
5. The quality levels of their product lines.
6. The source of their products—imported or locally produced.
7. Their pricing policies.
8. The levels of their after-sales service.
9. Their distribution channels.
10. Their coverage of the market. (Could market segmentation produce niches that are currently poorly served?)

Concerning item 10, it may be important to examine regional or ethnic subcultures in a particular foreign market. These subcultures may be natural or at least identifiable segments for which specific marketing programs may be successful. For example, there are sufficient Hispanic, Chinese, and other subcultures in the United States to merit the importation of Latin American and Chinese products into the United States.

Perhaps other countries have significant immigrant or subcultural populations whose needs you already understand and can serve. As an example, Japan has a small but growing population of immigrants from Latin America whose parents emigrated from Japan to Latin America in earlier times. These returnees tend to preserve their Latin heritage in Japan and might provide a market niche for firms whose strength is marketing to Latin Americans rather than to the Japanese.

Countries in which management believes strong competitors make a profitable operation difficult to attain are eliminated unless management (1) is following a strategy of being present wherever its global competitors are or (2) believes entering a competitor's home market will distract the competitor's attention from its home market, a reason for foreign investment that we discussed in Chapter 1.

FINAL SELECTION OF NEW MARKETS

While much can be accomplished through analysis, there is no substitute for personal visits to markets that appear to have the best potential. An executive of the firm or a team of company representatives should visit those countries that still appear to be good prospects. Before leaving, this person or team should review the data from the various screenings along with any new information that the researcher can supply.

On the basis of this review and experience in making similar domestic decisions, the executive or team should prepare a list of points on which information must be obtained on arrival. Management will want the facts uncovered by the desk study (the five screenings) to be corroborated. Management will also expect a firsthand report on the market, including information on competitive activity and an appraisal of the suitability of the firm's present marketing mix and the availability of support services (warehousing, media agencies, credit, and so forth).

LO12-4 Discuss the value to businesspeople of trade missions and trade fairs.

Field Trip   The field trip should not be hurried; as much or more time should be allotted to this part of the study as would be spent on a similar domestic field trip. The point is to try to develop a "feel" for what is going on, and this cannot be accomplished quickly. For example, while Japanese youths model themselves after American basketball stars by wearing Nike sneakers, it appears that they change into off-brand sneakers when they actually play basketball. As another example, it seems to be relatively more common for men to shop in grocery stores in Chile, as compared with elsewhere in Latin America. And there is not much tradition in East Asia of men taking on the "do-it-yourself" projects for which Home Depot and similar brands are famous. This type of insight is not likely to develop without actual visits to the market.

Government-Sponsored Trade Missions and Trade Fairs
When government trade specialists perceive an overseas market opportunity for an industry, they may organize a **trade mission.** The purpose is to send a group of executives from firms in the industry to a country or group of countries to learn firsthand about the market, meet important customers face-to-face, and make contacts with people interested in representing their products. Because of discounted airfares, hotels, and so forth, the cost to the firm may be less than it would pay if it arranged for its personnel to visit on their own. Moreover, the impact of a group visit is often greater than that of an individual company's visit. Before the mission's arrival, consulate or embassy officials will have publicized the visit and made contact with local companies they believe are interested. State governments, trade associations, chambers of commerce, and other export-oriented organizations also organize trade missions.

Probably every nation in the world holds a **trade fair** periodically. Usually, each nation has a specifically marked area (Chinese pavilion, Argentine pavilion, etc.) at the fairgrounds where its exhibitors have their own booths staffed by company sales representatives. Trade fairs are open to the public, but during certain hours (generally mornings), entrance is limited to businesspeople interested in doing business with the exhibitors.

While most fairs in developing countries are general, with displays of many kinds of products, those in Europe are usually specialized. A famous example is the annual CeBIT computer and telecommunications trade fair—the largest computer-related trade fair in the world—held annually in Hannover, Germany. Up to 400,000 people made the trip to this show in 2010 to see exhibits from 4,157 exhibitors from 68 countries.[3]

Besides making contact with prospective buyers and agents (direct sales are often concluded during these meetings), most exhibitors use these fairs to learn more about the market and gather competitive intelligence. They not only receive feedback from visitors to their exhibits but also have the opportunity to observe their competitors in action.

Sometimes Local Research Is Required
For many situations, the manager's field report will be the final input to the information on which the decision is based. Occasionally, however, the proposed human and financial resource commitments are so great that management will insist on gathering data in the potential market rather than depending solely on the desk and field reports.[4] This would undoubtedly be the position of a consumer products manufacturer that envisions entering a large competitive market of an industrialized country. It might also be the recommendation of the manager making the field trip if he or she discovered that market conditions were substantially different from those to which the firm was accustomed. Often, in face-to-face interviews, information is revealed that would never be written. In these situations, research in the local market not only will supply information on market definition and projection but also will assist in the formulation of an effective marketing mix.

trade mission
A group of businesspeople and/or government officials (state or federal) that visits a market in search of business opportunities

trade fair
A large exhibition, generally held at the same place and same time periodically, at which companies maintain booths to promote the sale of their products

Visitors explore the exhibits at the CeBIT Technology Fair in Hannover, Germany. Besides making sales contacts, most exhibitors use these fairs to learn more about the market and gather competitive intelligence. They not only receive feedback from visitors to their exhibits but also have the opportunity to observe their competitors in action.

Some Tips on International Marketing Surveys

How can companies begin to get that elusive "feel" for a country from survey data? As we mentioned, one way is to do it yourself via surveys and personal visits. Two other methods involve the use of an outside firm. Under one scenario, you can hire an outside firm to do customized research for your firm's needs. The second involves using surveys that are administered only partially, or not at all, with your specific firm in mind.

Customized Research Many firms that can do multicountry surveys on behalf of clients belong to ESOMAR (www.esomar.org), the European Society of Opinion and Marketing Research. Originally, the member-firms were European, but there are now 5,000 members from more than 100 countries.

Consumer products firms often utilize ethnographic research techniques, sometimes referred to as "corporate anthropology," to develop detailed understanding. A number of firms specialize in this type of research. These firms do extensive "on-the-ground" research, watching consumers actually use products, rather than relying on surveys or focus groups. An example of these specialist firms is Point Forward (www.pointforward.com). In one project, Point Forward helped Wrigley examine attitudes toward breath-freshening aspects of chewing gum, leading to a new Wrigley campaign in China. Another firm is Envirosell (www.envirosell.com), which specializes in research on shopping. A third firm, QualiData Research Inc., found that in Islamic households, men and women's clothing were usually washed separately.

General Surveys General surveys are not done with a specific firm in mind. There are three types of general survey. The first is the *omnibus survey*. Omnibus surveys are regularly scheduled surveys conducted by research agencies with questions from different clients (i.e., they are wholly or partially "syndicated"). Because several firms contribute questions, the cost is spread across several users, and the surveys are relatively fast. However,

---

LO12-5 Discuss some of the problems market researchers encounter in foreign markets.

social desirability bias
The custom of politeness toward everyone that can cause respondents to give answers calculated to please the interview rather than reflecting the respondent's true beliefs or feelings

Research in the Local Market

When a firm's research personnel have had no experience in the country, management should probably hire a local research group to do the work. Generally, home-country research techniques may be used, though they may need to be adapted to local conditions. It is imperative, therefore, that the person in charge of the project have experience either in that country or in one that is culturally similar and preferably in the same geographic area.

If secondary data are unavailable, the researchers must collect primary data, and here they face other complications caused by *cultural problems* and *technical difficulties*.

Cultural Problems. If the researchers are from one culture and are working in another, they may encounter some cultural problems. When they are not proficient in the local language or dialect, the research instrument or the respondents' answers must be translated. As we learned in Chapter 4's discussion of sociocultural forces, a number of languages may be spoken in a country, and even in countries where only one language is used, a word's meaning may change from one region to another.

Other cultural problems plague researchers as they try to collect data. Low levels of literacy may make the use of mail questionnaires virtually impossible. If a husband is interviewed in a market where the wife usually makes the buying decisions, the data obtained from him may be worthless. Nor is it always clear who should be interviewed. Respondents sometimes refuse to answer questions because of their general distrust of strangers. In other instances, the custom of politeness toward everyone will cause respondents to give answers calculated to please the interviewer; this is known as **social desirability bias.**

Often, people have practical reasons for not wanting to be interviewed. In some countries, income taxes are based on the apparent worth of individuals as measured by their tangible assets. In such countries, when asked if there is a stereo or TV in the household, the respondent may suspect the interviewer of being a tax assessor and refuse to answer.

these surveys can ask only a limited number of questions that are directly relevant to a particular client, and the sample may not be representative of a particular firm's potential target market.

One example of a firm involved in administering omnibus surveys is A.C. Nielsen (www.acnielsen.com). Although we may know Nielsen best from the "Nielsen ratings," its TV-watching media measurement service, the firm offers services in more than 100 countries. Nielsen does an omnibus survey in China, among other countries. Another familiar firm—the Gallup Organization (www.gallup.com)—is also involved in this type of research in a variety of countries.

In the second type of noncustomized general survey, market research firms do surveys of their own design and whose results they then market to a variety of firms. An example is the Asian Pacific Consumer Confidence Poll in 13 Asian Pacific markets, a Nielsen survey. Nielsen can even track TV-watching habits in China and India. Another firm that does industry-level surveys spanning a number of countries for general sale is Frost & Sullivan (www.frost.com).

Nonprofit Surveys The third type of survey is administered by a government or nongovernment agency, generally not for profit. The Eurobarometer surveys (http://ec.europa.eu/public_opinion/index_en.htm) are administered several times a year to thousands of respondents in European countries, under the auspices of the European Commission. Recent reports of Eurobarometer results with implications for consumer behavior include reports on attitudes toward vacations, food product safety, young people and drugs, and the family. Although these surveys are not specifically directed toward consumption issues, they are free and may be useful. A similar survey, called a *barómetro,* is conducted annually in 18 Latin American countries (www.latinobarometro.org).

The Internet Internet research is increasingly an option, and we are gradually moving toward a time when the technology of Internet surveys may offer any firm the opportunity to do its own surveys anywhere in the world. For example, in 2007 Publicis Groupe used the Internet to tap into French voters' views on French presidential elections. The use of the Internet allowed the firm to set up a blog as a substitute for a three-hour focus group session. The blog allowed participants to discuss their opinions over a two-week period. By the end of the survey period, the consensus had changed: Nicolas Sarkozy moved from "scary" as an unknown to someone articulating the need for change in France. Not only did the longer period result in a change of opinion, but 250 participants could be involved.

To overcome such a problem, experienced researchers often hire college students as interviewers because their manner of speech and their dress correctly identify them as what they are.

Technical Difficulties. As if the cultural problems were not enough, researchers may also encounter technical difficulties. First, up-to-date maps are often unavailable. The streets chosen for sampling may have three or four different names along their length, and the houses may not be numbered. In Japan, a grid system is used for addresses, and, it is said, only cab drivers can find street addresses. Telephone surveys can be a formidable undertaking.[5]

Mail surveys can be troublesome too, because mail deliveries within a city may take weeks or sometimes not made at all. For instance, the postal service in Italy has sometimes been so slow (two weeks for a letter to go from Rome to Milan) that some Italian firms have used private couriers to go to Switzerland to dispatch their foreign mail. The response to a mail survey is often low if the respondent must go to the post office to mail a letter. To increase returns, firms often offer such premiums as lottery tickets or product samples to persons who complete a mail questionnaire.

Research as Practiced   The existence of hindrances to marketing research does not mean it is not carried out in foreign markets. As you might surmise from the discussion of the availability of secondary data, marketing research is highly developed in many areas where markets are large and incorrect decisions are costly. Problems like the ones we have mentioned are prevalent in the developing nations, but they are well known to those who live there. It does not take long for the newcomer to become aware of them either, because longtime residents are quick to point them out.

Analysts tend to do less research and use simpler techniques in these nations because often the firm is in a seller's market, which means everything produced can be sold with a minimum of effort. Moreover, competition is frequently less intense in developing nations because (1) there are fewer competitors and (2) managements are struggling with problems other than marketing, which keep them from devoting more time to marketing issues. Even in Mexico, an important market for American firms, marketing research is less popular.[6] Although the situation

LO12-6 Discuss the different options for collecting survey-based research.

is changing, the most common technique continues to be a combination of trend analysis and the querying of knowledgeable persons such as salespeople, channel members, and customers. Researchers then adjust the findings on the basis of subjective considerations.

LO12-7 Explain the difference between country screening and segment screening.

Segment Screening

As was mentioned earlier, when a company intends to do business in several countries, managers can choose two broad market screening approaches: country or segment. In the first approach, Brazil may be viewed as a target market segment. Using the second approach, while Brazil is the physical location of a large group of consumers, the important variables for segmentation are commonalities in needs and wants among consumers *across nationalities*. These consumers may reside in different countries and speak different languages, but they have similar desires for a product or service. From this perspective, age, income, and psychographics (lifestyles) are the essential means of identifying market segments. The relevant marketing question is not where consumers reside but whether they share similar wants and needs. The targeted consumers may be global teens, middle-class executives, or young families with small children: each of these segments may share wants and needs across borders. An example comes from "phone surfers"—young Japanese who actively use their mobile phones to surf the Internet. The small phone screen and tiny keys may be a turnoff for older computer users in the West who have frequent and easy access to desktop or laptop PCs. But youngsters in the West have grown up with Nintendo DS devices, cell phone texting, and iPod nanos, and they readily adapt to the small screens and tiny buttons that are a part of using cell phones as an Internet device. On the other hand, baby boomers—whether in London, Los Angeles, or Lima, Peru—resist the thought of needing hearing aids. Swiss-based Phonak Group makes aids in 15 colors, fashions them like an ear phone, and calls them a "personal communication assistant" around the world. Also, because women around the world are buying similar clothing and cosmetics on the Internet, beauty regimens are becoming more universal.

Because we usually organize the world mentally in terms of countries, we naturally tend to want to analyze markets as country segments. It is much more difficult to think of ourselves as market segments that extend across borders. Also, as was mentioned in the discussion of sociocultural differences, these data can be difficult to secure. Nonetheless, it is important to do this because this approach is the logical outgrowth of the marketing concept. And the fact that certain types of data are difficult to gather does not mean that the data can be ignored. There is an old saying about research: "if you can count it, that ain't it." In our context, the easy-to-generate data are not necessarily the important data.

CRITERIA FOR IDENTIFYING AND ASSESSING SEGMENTS

Among the criteria managers should use when identifying and assessing segments, it is important that these segments be:

1. *Definable.* We should be able to identify and measure segments. The more we rely not on socioeconomic indicators but on lifestyle differences, the more difficult this becomes, but the more accurate the resulting analysis is likely to be.

2. *Large.* Segments should be large enough to be worth the effort needed to serve a segment. Of course, as we get closer to flexible manufacturing, the need to find large segments is beginning to recede. Further, the segments should have the potential for growth in the future.

3. *Accessible.* If we literally cannot reach our target segment for either promotional or distribution purposes, we will be unsuccessful.

Ronny Cheng-Ruggeberg: Risk It!

I was born in Austin, Texas, but raised in Berkeley, California. Growing up, I traveled and moved around quite a bit, living in Arizona and Connecticut, and I frequently visited Austin to spend time at my father's famous restaurant, Chinatown. In my junior year of high school, I had planned to major in mechanical engineering; I attended the National Student Leadership Conference at the University of Maryland—College Park to study just that. I spent three months bored out of my mind sitting through those lectures on engineering, and that's when I realized that I needed more excitement in my life than theorems and calculus could provide. This ultimately led to my decision to study international business and marketing at Cal Poly–San Luis Obispo and to eventually study abroad in Madrid, Spain.

While studying in Madrid, I traveled throughout Europe and have even made a return visit since then and visited many other cities and countries. I have also had the opportunity to do marketing work for a software company based out of Australia, and I am currently the channel marketing manager for a software company based out of Ireland. The best part of all of the international work and travel I have done has been the experiences. There's nothing more exciting than being able to climb up to the Acropolis in Athens, see a live bullfight in Madrid, or experience a soccer riot after a Real Madrid victory!

I have had quite a bit of international experience, and the best advice I can give is to keep an open mind, have a sense of humor, and learn from your mistakes. Don't go into another country with the mind-set that your culture is right and theirs is wrong, because you won't enjoy yourself and you'll experience nothing but conflict. Whether it's work or day-to-day life, everybody makes mistakes, and what matters is how you react and learn from them. The faster you are able to laugh at any mistakes you make and learn, the easier it is to adapt to a new culture and environment. Working and traveling internationally can be the most rewarding experience, but you have to risk it to get the biscuit. You have to forget about any hang-ups you may have, because the greatest stories and accomplishments don't happen from sitting on your butt because you are too scared to go out and seek adventure.

Resources for Your Global Career

Analyzing foreign markets and international projects is important for making decisions on expanding globally. These include tools to analyze market-entry projects including, but not limited to, demographics, economic structure, transportation infrastructure, and local and foreign competition. In any building process, the right tools are necessary to get the job completed. The end result is minimizing risk to increase profitability. Here are a number of solid analytical tools and skills that can be applied to analyzing global markets. If you understand how to use them and apply them appropriately, you will typically generate higher-quality analytical results and then be able to make better decisions. No tool is ever capable of giving you a clear "go/no go decision," but tools will help temper your judgment and allow you to make a more sound decision.

- The Project Management Process helps you manage complex tasks by identifying goals, setting benchmarks, and establishing timelines for assessing stages of project completion: www.businessballs.com/project.htm and www.method123.com/free-risk-management.php

- Market Development Planning is a project management application for bringing products to new or existing markets including the development and implementation of all related components of the marketing mix: www.businessballs.com/marketdevelopmentservice.htm

- Feasibility studies define the business problem or opportunity, identify and analyze alternative solutions, and recommend a solution to implement: www.readyplanning.com/business_plan_templates/feasibility_study_templates.htm

- SWOT analysis is a tool to analyze virtually any situation a business may encounter by looking at the strengths, weaknesses, opportunities, and threats presented by the situation: www.businessballs.com/swotanalysisfreetemplate.htm

- Porter's Five Forces Model analyzes a company's competitive position and competitive strength in the marketplace: www.businessballs.com/portersfiveforcesofcompetition.htm

- PEST and PESTELI Analysis provide tools to assess and understand a company's growth or decline in their industry: www.businessballs.com/pestanalysisfreetemplate.htm

- PROs & CONs Weighted Analysis is a simple tool to assist in making a "go/no go decision" based on weighted variables in the decision: www.businessballs.com/problemsolving.htm#pro%27s%20and%20con%20list%20decision-making%20template%20example

- Business Plan/Marketing Plan Writing provides information on how to write an effective business or marketing plan. You are unlikely to ever get a project approved or money allocated without a business or a marketing plan. Business and Marketing Plan Templates: www.businessballs.com/freebusinessplansandmarketingtemplates.htm

- Canada/Manitoba Business Service Centre shows you how to write an international business plan and export plan: www.canadabusiness.mb.ca/home_page/information_for_exporters/international_business_plan/

Using Secondary Data and Market Statistics.

High-quality secondary market data and economic statistics about global markets are becoming readily available with just a few keystrokes and will support your market understanding for better application of these tools. Make sure that you have enough analytical data to make a solid recommendation and then you own the recommendation. When you present your

(continued)

4. *Actionable.* If we cannot bring components of marketing programs (the 4 Ps of product, promotion, place, and price) to bear, we may not be successful. For example, in Mexico, the price of tortillas was formerly controlled by the government. Therefore, competition on the price variable was impossible. Foreigners could not penetrate the Mexican market for the standard tortilla by offering a lower price.

5. *Capturable.* Although we would love to discover market segments whose needs are completely unmet, in many cases these market segments are already being served. Nonetheless, we may still be able to compete. Where segments are completely "captured" by the competition, however, our task is much more difficult.[7]

TWO SCREENING METHODS, RECONSIDERED

In the final analysis, our view of the rest of the world is organized along national lines. However, it may be useful to attempt to leave that viewpoint behind when examining international markets.

With the increasing recognition of the existence of subcultures *within* nations and similarities between subcultures *across* nations, the international businessperson may wish to expand his or her horizon beyond the conventional view of the nation as the relevant "unit of analysis."

The next chapter takes up a series of related questions. Are our needs and desires becoming more and more alike, or are the differences in consumption preferences between us more relevant than the similarities?

Summary

LO12-1 Discuss environmental analysis and two types of market screening.

A complete market analysis and assessment as described in this chapter would be made by a firm that either is contemplating entering the foreign market for the first time or is already a multinational but wants to monitor world markets systematically to avoid overlooking marketing opportunities and threats. Many of the data requirements for a foreign decision are the same as those for a similar domestic decision, although it is likely that additional information about some of the international and foreign environmental forces will be needed. Essentially, the screening process consists of examining the various forces in succession and eliminating countries at each step. The sequence of screening based on (1) basic need potential, (2) financial and economic forces, (3) political and legal forces, (4) sociocultural forces, (5) competitive forces, and (6) personal visits is ordered so as to have a successively smaller number of prospects to consider at each of the succeedingly more difficult and expensive stages. Environmental analysis is a review of the external, environmental forces. Market screening is a method of market analysis and assessment that permits management to identify a small number of desirable markets by eliminating those judged to be less attractive. The two basic approaches are country screening and segment screening.

LO12-2 Explain market indicators and market factors.

Market indicators are economic data used to measure relative market strengths of countries or geographic areas, such as economic stability, economic growth rate, and population levels. Market factors are economic data that correlate highly with market demand for a product. The text example is the replacement rate for computers in the United Kingdom.

LO12-3 Describe some statistical techniques for estimating market demand and grouping similar markets.

Managers are always searching for ways to group countries by region or geographic clusters. Cluster analysis divides objects (market areas, individuals, customers, and other variables) into groups so that the variables within each group are similar. Trend analysis is another technique used to predict market demand.

LO12-4 Discuss the value to businesspeople of trade missions and trade fairs.

Trade missions and fairs allow potential buyers and sellers to explore market potential for their products is they are selling, and to explore import opportunities if they are seeking products.

LO12-5 Discuss some of the problems market researchers encounter in foreign markets.

There are both cultural and technical difficulties that await the market researcher in foreign markets. Language and dialect issues may be present. A social desirability bias may be present. Technical difficulties such as lack of up-to-date maps, unreliable mail service, or unreliable street names may be present, as well.

LO12-6 Discuss the different options for conducting survey-based research.

You can do your own survey research or use research done by a firm. Firm research is either customized to your needs or general. General research conducted by nonprofits may be a rich and inexpensive source if it can be adapted to your needs. The Internet holds great potential for customized survey research.

LO12-7 Explain the difference between country screening and segment screening.

In country screening, the country is viewed as a target market segment. The assumption is that the population is all the same. Using the second approach, while the country is the physical location of a large group of consumers, the important variables for segmentation are commonalities in needs and wants among consumers *across nationalities.* Segment screening looks at market segments across national borders. Segments should be definable, large, accessible, actionable, and capturable.

Key Words

market screening (p. 302)	**market indicators** (p. 305)	**cluster analysis** (p. 307)
environmental scanning (p. 302)	**market factors** (p. 306)	**trade mission** (p. 311)
country screening (p. 303)	**estimation by analogy** (p. 306)	**trade fair** (p. 311)
segment screening (p. 303)	**trend analysis** (p. 306)	**social desirability bias** (p. 312)

Questions

1. Select a country and a product that you believe your firm can market there. Make a list of the sources of information you will use for each screening.

2. What is the basis for the order of screenings presented in the text?

3. A firm's export manager finds, by examining the UN's *International Trade Statistics Yearbook,* that the company's competitors are exporting. Is there a way the manager can learn to which countries the U.S. competitors are exporting?

4. Do a country's imports completely measure the market potential for a product? Why or why not?

5. What are some barriers related to the political and legal forces that may eliminate a country from further consideration?

6. Why should a firm's management consider going on a trade mission or exhibiting in a trade fair?

7. What are the two principal kinds of complications that researchers face when they collect primary data in a foreign market? Give examples.

8. Consider the market segment screening method. Take a lifestyle segment—say, people who like do-it-yourself home decorating. How would the segment screening method suggest that you go about identifying potential foreign markets?

9. You are a consultant to the developers of the Spider-man computer game. You will tell the CEO where the likely overseas markets are. What do you do?

10. Assume that your academic unit (probably a college of business) wants to open a campus in a foreign country and that the dean has asked you to prepare a list of possible countries. How would you go about fulfilling the dean's requirement?

Use the globalEDGE site (http://globalEDGE.msu.edu/) to complete the following exercises:

1. The *Market Potential Index* (MPI) is an indexing study conducted by the Michigan State University Center for International Business Education and Research (MSU-CIBER) to compare emerging markets on a variety of dimensions. Provide a description of the indicators used for this index. Which of the indicators would have greater importance for a company that markets MP3 players? Considering the MPI rankings, which developing countries would you advise this company to enter first with such a product?

2. You are working at a firm that operates discount department stores across the United States and Canada. Top management has decided to expand to one of the following markets: France, Germany, Japan, Mexico or the United Kingdom. As part of the market analysis, you are asked to identify potential competitors in each market. Locate the National Retail Federation's *Stores* magazine's ranking of the *Top 250 Global Retailers* by annual sales, and provide a list of the top 10 companies for the latest year available. From this list, which companies (with a discount department store format) have operations in each of the markets you are assessing? Which countries are these companies from?

Minicase: The Sugar Daddy Chocolate Company

Jack Carlson started the Sugar Daddy Chocolate Company five years ago and is now selling about $1 million annually. Carlson would like to expand sales, but the U.S. market is very competitive. He has a friend with a small business who is now making 20 percent of his sales overseas. He wonders if any chocolates are exported. To find out, he calls a friend of his who is a professor of international business at the university and tells him that he wants to find out if chocolate is being exported. He asks the professor to research the following questions:

1. Is chocolate being exported?

2. Which are the six largest importing nations?

3. Which of these are growing markets?

4. Carlson's export competition would probably come from which countries?

Entry Modes

Our development strategy adapts to different markets addressing local needs and requirements. We currently use three business strategies: joint ventures, licenses, and company-owned stores.

—Starbucks Corporation

Market Entry in International Social Media

With the increasing business being done on the Internet, it might seem that anyone can easily become an Internet entrepreneur. In reality, it might be a little more complicated.[a]

It's true that there is a worldwide presence on the web. In the United States alone, some $1.5 billion worth of advertising will be done on social networking sites by 2012, and internationally it is becoming increasing common for companies to use social media as a key tool for conducting market research.[b] Social media sites such as Facebook, Myspace, LinkedIn, and hi5 have extensive foreign operations. For example, Facebook is the top social network in most of the nations it serves, such as the Philippines, Indonesia, Malaysia, Singapore, and Hong Kong, and its percentage penetration of web users ranges from 63 percent to 85 percent in each of those nations.[c]

As a result of the international expansion of social networking sites, the French luxury company Cartier began featuring separate pages for its "Love by Cartier" product line on Myspace's sites for the United Kingdom, China, France, Italy, Spain, and Japan. Two things are interesting here. First, because Myspace is best known as a youth site, the advertising of luxury brands seems out-of-place—you wouldn't think the audience would be there. Love by Cartier, after all, also has a campaign on the elite, invite-only social network A Small World, which has a jet-set user base that seems a much more appropriate target for a pricey jewelry brand. But Myspace representatives say their image as a teen hangout is a bit misleading, citing comScore statistics that estimate a quarter of its traffic comes from households with annual incomes greater than $100,000. Second, Cartier chose to enter Myspace's country-specific sites rather than stay with a single approach. Thus, for example, an Italian will see the site in Italian (written in Italian, not machine translated to Italian).

Yet, even with the international success of sites such as Facebook, in order to achieve deep penetration abroad, perhaps you also need to utilize localized or country-specific sites. This might give you a leg up when it comes to understanding the local environment, especially for younger citizens. In fact, although Facebook serves about 44 percent of the world's Internet users and is the leader in most of the nations it serves, it is not the top social network in a number of key developed and emerging markets, such as India, Brazil, South Korea, Russia, and Japan. Indeed, of the largest networking sites in the world, about half of them

13

Learning Objectives

After reading this chapter, you should be able to:

LO13-1 **Understand** the pros and cons of entering markets as a "market pioneer" versus being a "fast follower."

LO13-2 **Explain** the international market-entry methods.

LO13-3 **Discuss** why firms export and the options available for indirect and direct exporting.

LO13-4 **Explain** the potential benefits and disadvantages of joint ventures and how a company might exercise control over a joint venture, even as a minority shareholder.

are sites whose followers are primarily outside the United States. For example, Orkut has 100 million users, Badoo more than 86 million users, hi5 has an estimated 80 million users, and Odnoklassniki about 45 million users. Among these localized, country- or regional-specific sites are the following:

IN ASIA

In India, Orkut is popular, with nearly 50 percent penetration of the web-user market.[d] Bigadda.com and hi5 are also popular in India (and hi5 also has strong penetration in Mongolia, Thailand, Romania, Jamaica, Central Africa, Portugal, and Latin America). In China, three social networks are popular: Renren.com, Kaixin001.com, and 51.com. Facebook's site in China is blocked from that country's 420 million Internet users, although there are rumors that the company is exploring ways to gain approved entry to that market.[e] In South Korea, CyWorld.com is a major site, especially for young adults, and it reaches more than half of all web users in that country. CyWorld has a major music component, and many Korean socialites and celebrities post their tours and news of their work on it. Wretch.cc is a popular site in Taiwan, with nearly two-thirds' penetration of the web-user market, and Mixi.jp is popular in Japan. ZING Me is the leading social network site in Vietnam.

IN EUROPE

Hyves is the most popular social networking property in the Netherlands, penetrating about two-thirds of the market. The German site StudiVZalso records strong traffic, with 17 million visitors, and Grono.net is popular in Poland. Vkontakte dominates the Russian market with a penetration into about three-quarters of the market (more than seven times greater than Facebook's penetration rate in Russia), while Odnoklassniki has about 45 million users in Russia and former Soviet republics.[f]

IN LATIN AMERICA

Several sites are well-established, including Orkut, hi5, and Wamba. Orkut has more than 70 percent penetration of Brazil's social networking market. Another site that is important in Latin America is Sonico, based in Argentina. In addition, Peru is a hi5 stronghold, and Badoo is particularly strong in Venezuela.

Of course, the "just-around-the-corner" commercial battleground is mobile networking: 88 percent of Latin Americans own a mobile phone, versus the more than 60 percent worldwide average.[g] The largest single collection of cell phone users is in China. While American youth have the highest rate of mobile Internet usage, Chinese youth have a 50 percent higher rate of mobile data usage than is the case for the United States and more than double the rate for Europe.[h]

Given the importance of appealing to local tastes, are the obstacles to exporting created by a two-tiered social networking structure—where many citizens access major worldwide sites such as Facebook and Myspace, but also access a local or regional network—significant enough that only the largest companies should attempt to do this?

[a]Sources for this introductory vignette include: Nyay Bhushan, Berwin Song, and Mark Russell, "Rising in the East: A Guide to the Key Asian Social Networking Services," *Billboard,* May 24, 2008, p. 20, http://books.google.com/books?id=VxQEAAAAMBAJ&pg=PA20&lpg=PA20&dq=Rising+in+the+East:+A+Guide+to+the+Key+Asian+Social+Networking+Services&source=bl&ots=_iptto5_l8&sig=LJWb4YVqYvDSLytgCBzbZ30yLxU&hl=en&ei=x_wATrytD4f6swPj25S2DQ&sa=X&oi=book_result&ct=result&resnum=1&ved=0CBkQ6AEwAA#v=onepage&q=Rising%20in%20the%20East%3A%20A%20Guide%20to%20the%20Key%20Asian%20Social%20Networking%20Services&f=false (accessed June 21, 2011); "List of Social Networking Sites," *Wikipedia,* http://en.wikipedia.org/wiki/List_of_social_networking_websites (accessed June 21, 2011); "German Social Networking Community Reaches 14.8 Million," www.comscore.com/Press_Events/Press_Releases/2007/09/Social_Networking_Sites_in_Germany (accessed June 21, 2011); and Eric Eldon, "The Latin American Social Networking Wars," June 3, 2008, http://venturebeat.com/2008/06/03/the-latin-american-social-networking-wars-market-leader-hi5-has-been-growing-but-so-has-facebook-and-sonico/ (accessed June 21, 2011).

[b]Michael Stanat, "Social Media, the Future of Market Research?," www.greenbook.org/marketing-research.cfm/social-media-the-future-of-market-research (accessed June 21, 2011).

[c]**comScore, "Social Networking Habits** Vary Considerably Across Asia-Pacific Markets," www.comscore.com/Press_Events/Press_Releases/2010/4/Social_Networking_Across_Asia-Pacific_Markets (accessed June 21, 2011).

[d]Ibid.

[e]J.P. Mangalindan, "China: Facebook's Undiscovered Country," *CNNMoney,* January 17, 2011, http://tech.fortune.cnn.com/2011/01/17/how-facebook-can-conquer-china/ (accessed June 21, 2011).

[f]Jay Yarow and Kamelia Angelova, "Chart of the Day: The Countries Facebook Doesn't Dominate," September 23, 2010, www.businessinsider.com/chart-of-the-day-facebook-not-popular-in-countries-2010-9 (accessed June 21, 2011).

[g]Jose Fermoso, "U.N.World Report Picks Up Massive Growth in Mobile Phone Ownership," www.wired.com/gadgetlab/2009/03/report-60-of-wo/ (accessed June 21, 2011); and Euromonitor, International, "Latin America Enjoys Mobile Telephone Boom," May 28, 2010, http://blog.euromonitor.com/2010/05/regional-focus-latin-america-enjoys-mobile-telephone-boom.html (accessed June 21, 2011)

[h]"U.S. Youth Have Higher Smartphone Penetration Than Adults," www.marketingcharts.com/uncategorized/us-youth-have-higher-smartphone-penetration-than-adults-15665/nielsen-smartphone-penetration-jan-2011jpg/ (accessed June 21, 2011).

As you learned in Chapter 1, we can use a variety of names to identify large firms that operate on a multicountry scale: *global, multidomestic,* and *international* firm or company; *multinational enterprise (MNE)* or *multinational company (MNC); international company (IC); transnational company;* and even *multicultural multinational company.* Long before companies become any of these, however, they are usually smaller companies with only domestic experience. In this chapter we examine the very start—that is, the entry into international operations. We first examine issues associated with the decision whether to enter a market as a pioneer or as a fast follower. Then we discuss the different methods available for market entry, beginning with nonequity modes of market entry, followed by equity-based modes.

Entering Markets: Should You Be a Market Pioneer or a Fast Follower?

LO13-1 Understand the pros and cons of entering markets as a "market pioneer" versus being a "fast follower."

In the opening vignette, we gained some insight into which social networking sites are market leaders today. But we can't be sure that the same will be true by the time you are reading this book. Across industry after industry, market leaders rise, then plummet, sometimes disappearing completely. Compaq was once the undisputed leader in laptops and is not even a minor player now. Motorola dominated the first generation of cell phones, then its market share dropped precipitously as Nokia overtook it when second-generation cell phones appeared—subsequently, Nokia's market dominance has been threatened by companies such as Apple as a new generation of "smartphones" replaces second-generation technology. Not all pioneers capitalize on their potential advantages, yet some evidence does suggest that pioneers gain and maintain a competitive edge in new markets. For instance, researchers have found that surviving pioneers hold a significantly larger average market share when their industries reach maturity than do firms that were either fast followers or late entrants in the product category.

On the other hand, as Compaq illustrates, pioneers can certainly fail. One recent study that took failed pioneers into account and averaged their performances with those of the more successful survivors found that, overall, pioneers did not perform as well over the long haul as followers. Of course, what measures are used can be important here: volume and market share are not the only dimensions by which success can be measured. The truth is that there really is little evidence one way or the other concerning the effect of the *timing* of a firm's entry into a new market on its ultimate profitability in that market or the value it generates for shareholders.

In many cases, a firm entering into international markets becomes a follower by default, because a quicker competitor simply beats it by entering into the market first. But even when a company has the capability of being the first-mover, there are possible advantages to letting others go first and shoulder the initial risks while the follower observes the pioneers' shortcomings and mistakes.

A pioneering firm stands the best chance for long-term success in market-share leadership and profitability when (1) the pioneering firm is insulated from the entry of competitors (high-entry barriers), at least for a while, by strong patent protection, proprietary technology (such as a unique production process), or substantial investment requirements; or (2) the firm has sufficient size, resources, and competencies to take full advantage of its pioneering position and preserve it in the face of later competitive entries. Indeed, some recent evidence suggests that organizational competencies such as R&D and marketing skills not only affect a firm's success as a pioneer but also influence the company's decision about whether to be a pioneer in the first place. Firms that lack the competencies necessary to sustain a first-mover advantage may be more likely to wait for another company to take the lead and then enter the market later.

On the other hand, a follower will most likely succeed when there are few legal, technological, cultural, or financial barriers to inhibit entry (low-entry barriers) and when it has sufficient resources or competencies to overwhelm the pioneer's early advantage. The most successful fast followers tend to have the resources to enter the new market on a larger scale than the pioneer. Thus, they can quickly reduce their unit costs and offer lower prices than incumbent competitors.[1]

Thus, the evidence is not clear on whether the firm should be first—or nearly first—into a foreign market. Even after that decision, we have other decisions to make regarding which entry mode the firm should use in entering the market first (or not).

What Methods Are Available for Entering Foreign Markets?

LO13-2 **Explain** the international market-entry methods.

Once a company has decided to enter into a foreign market, it must decide which of the many different options for market entry would represent the optimal choice for the company's particular circumstances. We first examine nonequity modes of market entry, followed by equity-based modes.

NONEQUITY MODES OF ENTRY

If a company wishes to enter foreign markets through nonequity-based methods, a number of alternatives are available. In this section, we discuss exporting, turnkey projects, licensing, franchising, management contracts, and contract manufacturing as alternatives for nonequity modes of foreign market entry.

Exporting   Most firms begin their involvement in overseas business by exporting—that is, by selling some of their regular production overseas. This method requires little investment and is relatively free of risks. It is an excellent means of getting a feel for international business without committing a great amount of human or financial resources.

LO13-3 **Discuss** why firms export and the options available for indirect and direct exporting.

Benefits of Exporting   Many firms, both large and small, engage in exporting for reasons such as the following:

- To serve markets where the firm has no or limited production facilities. Many large multinationals, like DuPont or Procter & Gamble, supply some of their foreign markets by exporting because no firm, no matter how large, can afford to manufacture a complete product line in every country where its goods are sold. Markets without local factories are supplied through exports from the home country or from a foreign affiliate. In markets of sufficient size to justify the production of some but not all of the product mix, the affiliate will supplement local production with imports. A car plant in a developing nation may produce the least expensive cars and import luxury models. Also, the more vertically integrated plants may export semifinished products that are inputs for the less integrated subsidiaries.

- *To satisfy a host government's requirement that the local subsidiary have exports.* Governments of developing nations often require that the local affiliate export at least a portion of its output, and some require that it earn sufficient foreign exchange to cover the cost of its imports.

- *To remain price competitive in the home market.* Many firms import labor-intensive components produced in their foreign affiliates, or export components for assembly in countries where labor is less expensive and import the finished product.

- *To test foreign markets and foreign competition inexpensively.* This is a common strategy for firms that want to test a product's acceptance before investing in local production facilities. Exports may also enable firms to test market strategies and make adjustments with reduced risk in a smaller market. If the strategy or product fails, the firm can withdraw without having a costly and sometimes damaging failure to the entire firm. There is, however, a downside to this strategy: whatever the firm does in the foreign market may be seen by a competitor. This is especially true for large, global firms such as Unilever and Procter & Gamble. Former P&G CEO Edwin Artzt changed the company's strategy for introducing new products. Rather than postpone a global launch until the firm accumulated marketing experience in a country, P&G began to introduce products on a worldwide basis early in their development to avoid giving competitors time to react in other markets.

- *To meet actual or prospective customer requests for the firm to export.* This type of accidental exporting is fairly common. A foreign buyer often will search for something it cannot find locally by consulting the Internet or Thomas Net, a website listing North American producers for thousands of products.

- *To offset cyclical sales in the domestic market.*

- *To achieve additional sales,* which will allow the firm to use excess production capacity to lower per-unit fixed costs.

- *To extend a product's life cycle* by exporting to currently unserved markets where the product will be at the introduction stage of the life cycle.

- *To respond strategically to foreign competitors* that are in the firm's home market by entering their home market.

- *To achieve the success the firm's management has seen others achieve by exporting.*

- *To improve the efficiency of manufacturing equipment,* which usually works better at or near full capacity.

If management does decide to export, it can choose between *indirect* and *direct* exporting.

Indirect Exporting

Indirect exporting is simpler than direct exporting because it requires neither special expertise nor large cash outlays by the company producing the product. Instead, the work of exporting the product is done by other home country-based companies, which can (a) sell for the manufacturer, (b) buy for their overseas customers, (c) buy and sell for their own accounts, or (d) purchase on behalf of foreign middlemen or users. Although each type of exporter usually operates in the manner explained next, any given company may actually perform one or more of these functions.

indirect exporting
The exporting of goods and services through various types of home country-based exporters

A. Exporters That Sell for the Manufacturer

1. *Manufacturers' export agents* act as the international representatives for various noncompeting domestic manufacturers. They usually direct promotion, consummate sales, invoice, ship, and handle the financing. They commonly are paid a commission for carrying out these functions in the name of the manufacturer.

2. *Export management companies (EMCs)* act as the export department for several non-competing manufacturers. They also transact business in the name of the manufacturer and handle the routine details of shipping and promotion. When the EMC works on a commission basis, the manufacturer invoices the customer directly and carries any financing required by the foreign buyer. However, most EMCs work on a buy-and-sell arrangement under which they pay the manufacturer, resell the product abroad, and invoice the customer directly. Depending on the arrangement, the EMC may act in the name of the firm it represents or in its own name.

3. *International trading companies* are similar to EMCs in that they also act as agents for some companies and as merchant wholesalers for others. This, however, is only part of their activities. They frequently export as well as import, own their own transportation facilities, and provide financing.

B. Exporters That Buy for Their Overseas Customers

1. *Export commission agents* represent overseas purchasers, such as import firms and large industrial users. They are paid a commission by the purchaser for acting as resident buyers in the exporting nation.

C. Exporters That Buy and Sell for Their Own Accounts

1. *Export merchants* purchase products directly from the manufacturer and then sell, invoice, and ship them in their own names so that foreign customers have no direct dealings with the manufacturer, as they do in the case of an export agent. If export merchants have an exclusive right to sell the manufacturer's products in an overseas territory, they are generally called *export distributors*. Some EMCs may actually be export distributors for a number of their clients.

2. Sometimes called *piggyback exporters,* **cooperative exporters** are established international manufacturers that sell the products of other companies in foreign markets along with their own. Carriers (exporters) may purchase and resell in their own name, or they may work on a commission basis. Carriers, like EMCs, serve as the export departments for the firms they represent.

3. *Webb-Pomerene Associations* are organizations of competing firms that have joined together for the sole purpose of export trade. At this time, there are fewer than 25 such associations. The Motion Picture Association (MPA), which is the legacy of a Webb-Pomerene Association, is the primary organization combating movie piracy around the world.

cooperative exporters
Established international manufacturers that export other manufacturers' goods as well as their own

D. Exporters That Purchase for Foreign Users and Middlemen

1. *Large foreign users,* such as mining, petroleum, and international construction companies, buy for their own use overseas. The purchasing departments of all the worldwide companies are continually buying for their foreign affiliates, and both foreign governments and foreign firms maintain purchasing offices in industrialized countries.

2. *Export resident buyers* perform essentially the same functions as export commission agents. However, they are generally more closely associated with a foreign firm. They may be appointed as the official buying representatives and paid a retainer, or they may even be employees. This is in contrast to the export commission agent, who usually represents a number of overseas buyers and works on a transaction-by-transaction basis.

Drawbacks of Indirect Exporting   Indirect exporters pay a price for having another company handle their exports: (1) they pay a commission to the first three kinds of exporters, (2) foreign business can be lost if exporters decide to change their sources of supply, and (3) firms gain little experience from these transactions. This is why many companies that begin in this manner generally change to direct exporting.

direct exporting
The exporting of goods and services by the firm that produces them

Direct Exporting   To engage in **direct exporting,** the export business is handled by someone within the firm. The simplest arrangement is to give someone, often the sales manager, the responsibility for developing the export business. Domestic employees may handle the billing, credit, and shipping initially, and if the business expands, a separate export department may be set up. A firm that has been exporting to wholesale importers in an area and serving them with visits from either home office personnel or foreign-based sales representatives frequently finds that sales have grown to a point that will support a complete marketing organization.

Management may then decide to set up a **sales company** in the area. The sales company imports in its own name from the parent and invoices in local currency. It may employ the same channels of distribution, although the new organization may permit the use of a more profitable arrangement. This type of organization can grow quite large, often invoicing many millions of dollars annually. Before building a plant in Mexico, for many years Eastman Kodak imported and resold cameras and photographic supplies while doing a large business in local film developing. Many firms that began with local repair facilities later expanded to produce simple components. Gradually, they produced more of the product locally until, after a period of time, they were manufacturing all the components in the country.

The Internet has made direct exporting much easier. For the beginning exporter, the possibility of creating awareness that your product will be available abroad is dramatically increased. And although it is likely that a substantial international presence on the Internet will require a significant investment, the cost of trial is now very low.

sales company
A business established for the purpose of marketing goods and services, not producing them

Distribution Options for Direct Exporters
If the firm chooses to do its own exporting but not directly handle distribution in the market it is exporting to, then it has four basic types of overseas middlemen from which to choose: (1) manufacturers' agents, (2) distributors, (3) retailers, and (4) trading companies. These may be serviced by sales personnel who either travel to the market or are based in it. If the sales volume is sufficient, a foreign sales company may be established to take the place of the wholesale importer. The manufacturing affiliates of most worldwide companies also import from home country plants or from other subsidiaries those products that they themselves do not produce.

1. **Manufacturers' agents** are residents of the country or region in which they are conducting business for the firm. They represent various noncompeting foreign suppliers, and they take orders in those firms' names. Manufacturers' agents usually work on a commission basis, pay their own expenses, and do not assume any financial responsibility. They often stock the products of some of their suppliers, thus combining the functions of agent and wholesale distributor.

2. **Distributors,** or *wholesale importers,* are independent merchants that buy for their own account. They import and stock for resale. Distributors are usually specialists in a particular field, such as farm equipment or pharmaceuticals. They may be given exclusive representation and, in return, agree not to handle competing brands. Distributors may buy through manufacturers' agents when the exporter employs them, or they may send their orders directly to the exporting firm. Instead of hiring manufacturers' agents, exporters may employ their own salespeople to cover the territory and assist the distributors. For years, worldwide companies such as Caterpillar and Goodyear have utilized field representatives in export territories.

3. *Retailers,* especially of consumer products, are frequently direct importers. Contact on behalf of the exporter is maintained either by a manufacturers' agent or by the exporter's sales representative based in the territory or traveling from the home office.

4. **Trading companies** are relatively unknown in the United States but are extremely important importers in other parts of the world. In a number of African nations, trading companies not only are the principal importers of goods ranging from consumer products to capital equipment, but also export such raw materials as ore, palm oil, and coffee. In addition, they operate department stores, grocery stores, and agencies for automobiles and farm machinery. Another form of trading company is owned by the state. State trading companies handle exports and imports in North Korea and Cuba, and in noncommunist nations where an industry is a government monopoly, such as petroleum in Mexico, exporters or their agents must deal with these government-owned entities.

manufacturers' agents
Independent sales representatives of various noncompeting suppliers

distributors
Independent importers that buy for their own account for resale

trading companies
Firms that develop international trade and serve as intermediaries between foreign buyers and domestic sellers and vice versa`

Turnkey Projects

Turnkey project is an export of technology, management expertise, and, in some cases, capital equipment. The contractor agrees to design and erect a plant, supply the process technology, provide the necessary suppliers of raw materials and other production inputs, and then train the operating personnel. After a trial run, the facility is turned over to the purchaser.

The exporter of a turnkey project may be a contractor that specializes in designing and erecting plants in a particular industry, such as petroleum refining or steel production. It may also be a company in the industry that wishes to earn money from its expertise by delivering a plant ready to run rather than merely selling its technology. Another kind of supplier of a turnkey project is the producer of a factory.

Licensing

Frequently, worldwide companies are called on to furnish technical assistance to firms that have sufficient capital and management strength. By means of a **licensing** agreement, one firm (the licensor) will grant to another firm (the licensee) the right to use any kind of expertise, such as manufacturing processes (patented or unpatented), marketing procedures, and trademarks for one or more of the licensor's products.

The licensee generally pays a fixed sum when signing the licensing agreement and then pays a royalty of 2 to 5 percent of sales over the life of the contract (five to seven years with an option for renewal is one common way to structure such agreements). The exact amount of the royalty will depend on the amount of assistance given and the relative bargaining power of the two parties. In 2009, the total paid to American firms in foreign royalties and license fees amounted to $90 billion.[2]

In the past, licensing was not a primary source of income for international firms due to patent infringement, which can be considered a form of piracy. Licensing has changed in recent years, however, especially in the United States, because (1) the courts began upholding patent infringement claims more than they used to, (2) patent holders became more vigilant in suing violators, and (3) the federal government pressed foreign governments to enforce their patent laws.

As a result, more companies at home and abroad began to obtain licenses instead of making illegal copies. Texas Instruments (TI), for example, sued nine Japanese electronics

A woman sits beside her stall with Pierre Cardin shirts on a Hanoi street in June 2004. The shirts are made under French designer Pierre Cardin's firm license by a local garment factory. Each shirt sells for around 10 US dollars.

Piracy as a Means of Foreign Market Entry

Although we discuss elsewhere in this chapter the threats to companies from piracy of intellectual property such as brand names or patented technology, piracy can also contribute to the global spread of a product—sort of market entry by accident.[a]

Japanese *anime* has estimated global sales of $80 billion, 10 times what it was a decade ago. Former Japanese Prime Minister Junichiro Koizumi once called it the "savior of Japanese culture." Disney has purchased the American rights to a number of anime films. The Cartoon Network shows several anime series as part of its Adult Swim programming. TOKOPOP will publish 400 volumes of translated Japanese comics for U.S. consumption.

Two decades ago, there was no U.S. market for Japanese anime. The change occurred not through a concerted push from Japanese media companies but in response to American fans who pulled anime in.

Although Japanese anime was exported to the West in the early 1960s, some saw it as inappropriate for American children, and by the late 1960s it was available only in Japanese overseas communities. The advent of the videotape recorder allowed dubbing and sharing, and soon anime fans were contacting both Japanese citizens and American soldiers stationed in Japan for tapes. Fan clubs emerged as essentially lending libraries and dubbing

centers. In the late 1980s and 1990s, amateurs began dubbing these tapes into English: this "fansubbing" spread. In the early 1990s, large-scale anime conventions brought artists and distributors from Japan, who were astonished to see this thriving content they had never marketed. They returned to Japan ready to service this market commercially. The fan clubs continued their operations, but stopped fansubbing and distributing titles as they became commercially available.

This "piracy" is now supported by the commercial industry, which in fact sponsors events where fan-made *manga*,[b] a highly derivative version of the commercial product, is sold. The media companies use these events to publicize their own releases, spot new talent, and monitor shifts in audience tastes.

The idea that some piracy actually helps to diffuse new products is not limited to Japanese anime. It has also been tested for software.

Careful analysis actually found that software piracy is not necessarily harmful to a software firm seeking to launch a new product, because it establishes initial adopters (pirates) and speeds up software diffusion: these initial adopters then influence others to buy the product. Generally speaking, however, as the product diffuses in the market, the level of protection against piracy should be increased.

In a third industry, an international sample across 25 countries suggested that piracy of theatrical movies was actually slightly beneficial to the movie industry!

Questions:

1. How can piracy help a company to successfully, and profitably, enter foreign markets?

2. Consider the case of a small or medium-sized company that was producing software or applications for use on cell phones. If you were asked by this company to assist them in developing a strategy for using piracy as a means of entering foreign markets, what advice would you give them regarding how to successfully develop and implement such a strategy?

[a]Sources for this box include: Henry Jenkins, "When Piracy Becomes Promotion," *MIT Technology Review*, August 10, 2004, www.technologyreview.com/biomedicine/13722/ (June 21, 2011); Ernan Haruvy, Vijay Mahajan, and Ashutosh Prasad, "The Effect of Piracy on the Market Penetration of Subscription Software," *Journal of Business* 77, no. S2 (April 2004), pp. S81–S107; Ashutosh Prasad and Vijay Mahajan, "How Many Pirates Should a Software Firm Tolerate? An Analysis of Piracy Protection on the Diffusion of Software," *International Journal of Research in Marketing* 20, no. 4 (2003), pp. 337–53, www.sciencedirect.com/science/article/pii/S0167811603000491 (June 21, 2011); TorrentFreak, "Internet Piracy Boosts Anime Sales, Study Concludes," http://torrentfreak.com/internet-piracy-boosts-anime-sales-study-concludes-110203/ (June 21, 2011); and Sung Woo Ji, "Piracy Impact on the Theatrical Movie Industry," www.allacademic.com/meta/p172966_index.html (accessed July 4, 2008).

[b]*Anime* in Japan refers to an animated film, and *manga* is a printed cartoon.

manufacturers for using its patented processes without paying licensing fees. The defendants have paid TI more than $1 billion since 1986. Although the company does not publish its royalty receipts in its income statements, here's an idea of the magnitude of the earnings from royalties associated with TI's 6,000 patents: TI announced 10-year agreements with both Hyundai Electronics and Samsung Electronics projected to yield royalty payments of more than $1 billion.

Technology is not the only thing that is licensed to support a firm's market entry. In the fashion industry, a number of designers license the use of their names. Pierre Cardin, one of the largest such licensors, reported more than 400 licenses in more than 170 countries for thousands of different products, ranging from a broad range of clothing to such items as skis, frying pans, sardines, floor tiles, and silk cigarettes. These licenses have earned the company approximately $75 million annually. As Cardin himself commented, "If someone asked me to do toilet paper, I'd do it. Why not?"[3]

Are you giving Coca-Cola free advertising on your T-shirt? The company's manager for merchandise licensing expects the company to make millions from an agreement with the founder of Gloria Vanderbilt. He says the firm agreed to the arrangement because "clothes enhance our image. The money is not important."

Another industry, magazine publishing, is licensing overseas editions. For example, you can buy *Cosmopolitan* in more than 100 countries, and it is printed in 32 different languages.[4] *Playboy* is available in 23 different international editions, including in the Islamic nation of Indonesia.[5]

Despite the opportunity to obtain a sizable income from licensing, many firms, especially those that produce high-tech products, still will not grant licenses. They fear that a licensee will become a competitor upon expiration of the agreement or that the licensee will aggressively seek to market the products outside its home territory. At one time, licensors routinely inserted a clause in the licensing agreement that prohibited exports, but most governments will not accept such a prohibition.

franchising

A form of licensing in which one firm contracts with another to operate a certain type of business under an established name according to specific rules

Franchising

Firms have also gone overseas with a different kind of licensing— **franchising.** Franchising permits the franchisee to sell products or services under a highly publicized brand name and a well-proven set of procedures with a carefully developed and controlled marketing strategy. Of some 500 U.S. franchisers with approximately 50,000 outlets worldwide, fast-food operations (such as McDonald's, KFC, Subway, and Pizza Hut) are the most numerous. Other types of franchisers are hotels (Intercontinental), business services (Muzak, The UPS Store), fitness (Curves, Jazzercise), building maintenance (Service-Master, Nationwide Exterminating), and real estate (ReMax).

management contract

An arrangement by which one firm provides management in all or specific areas to another firm

Management Contract

The **management contract** is an arrangement under which a company provides managerial know-how in some or all functional areas to another party for a fee that typically ranges from 2 to 5 percent of sales. International companies make such contracts with (1) firms in which they have no ownership (e.g., Hilton Hotel provides management for nonowned overseas hotels that use the Hilton name, and Delta provides management assistance to foreign airlines), (2) joint venture partners, and (3) wholly owned subsidiaries. The last arrangement is made solely for the purpose of allowing the parent to siphon off some of the subsidiary's profits. This becomes extremely important when, as in many foreign exchange–poor nations, the parent firm is limited in the amount of profits it can repatriate. Moreover, because the fee is an expense, the subsidiary receives a tax benefit in the foreign subsidiary's country. This practice may also allow the parent firm to better manage its corporate-wide tax burden by reducing profits within higher-tax nations and moving them instead to countries with lower tax rates.

contract manufacturing

An arrangement in which one firm contracts with another to produce products to its specifications but assumes responsibility for marketing

Contract Manufacturing

International firms employ **contract manufacturing** in two ways. One way is as a means of entering a foreign market without investing in plant facilities. The firm contracts with a local manufacturer to produce products for it according to its specifications. The firm's sales organization markets the products under its own brand.

The second way is to subcontract assembly work or the production of parts to independent companies overseas. Although the international firm has no equity in the subcontractor, this practice does resemble foreign direct investment. When the international firm is the largest or only customer of the subcontractors, it has in effect created in another country a new company that generates employment and foreign exchange for the host nation. Frequently, the international firm will lend capital to the foreign contractor in the same way that a global or multinational firm will lend funds to its subsidiary. Because of these similarities, this practice is sometimes called *foreign direct investment without investment.*

EQUITY-BASED MODES OF ENTRY

When management does decide to make a foreign direct investment, it usually has several alternatives available, though not all of them may be feasible in a particular country:

1. Wholly owned subsidiary
2. Joint venture
3. Strategic alliances

Wholly Owned Subsidiary

A company that wishes to own a foreign subsidiary outright may (1) start from the ground up by building a new plant (greenfield investment) or (2) acquire a going concern. In the latter instance, a company might even purchase its distributor, thus obtaining a distribution network familiar with its products, although in such a case it will typically be necessary to build production facilities.

Historically, firms making a foreign direct investment have generally preferred wholly owned subsidiaries, but they have not had a marked preference for either of the two means of obtaining them. However, this has not been the case for foreign investors in the United States, who have demonstrated a general preference for acquiring going concerns for the instant access to the market they provide. Moreover, they also have one less competitor after the purchase. In 2008, 93 percent of the $261 billion that was invested in the United States was used to acquire existing companies, versus spent to create new businesses.

Sometimes it is not possible to have a wholly owned subsidiary in a foreign market. The host government may not permit it, the firm may lack either capital or expertise to

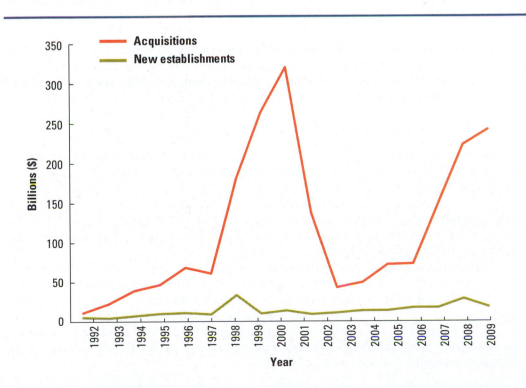

FIGURE 13.1

Investments into the United States for Acquisitions versus New Establishments, 1992–2009

undertake the investment alone, or there may be tax and other advantages that favor another form of investment, such as a joint venture.

Joint Venture   A **joint venture** may be (1) a corporate entity formed by an international company and local owners, (2) a corporate entity formed by two international companies for the purpose of doing business in a third market, (3) a corporate entity formed by a government agency (usually in the country of investment) and an international firm, or (4) a cooperative undertaking between two or more firms of a limited-duration project. Large construction jobs such as a dam or an airport are frequently handled by this last form.

Benefits of Joint Ventures

LO13-4 Explain the potential benefits and disadvantages of joint ventures and how a company might exercise control over a joint venture, even as a minority shareholder.

Reduced Risk and Competition or Increased Scale Economies   Sometimes, forming a joint venture can allow the partners to avoid making expensive and time-consuming investments of their own, while simultaneously helping to avoid dangerous competition with another company. Some firms, as a matter of policy, enter joint ventures to reduce investment risk. Their strategy is to enter into a joint venture with either native partners or another worldwide company. Still others have joined together to achieve economies of scale. Incidentally, any division of ownership in a joint venture is possible unless there are specific legal requirements.

Government Regulations for Local Participation   When the government of a host country requires that companies have some local participation, foreign firms must engage in joint ventures with local owners to do business in that country. In some situations, however, a foreign firm will seek local partners even when there is no local requirement to do so.

Strong Nationalism   Strong nationalistic sentiment may cause the foreign firm to try to lose its identity by joining with local investors. Care must be taken with this strategy, however. Although a large number of people in many developing countries dislike multinationals for "exploiting" them, they still believe, often with good reason, that the products of the foreign companies are superior to those of purely national firms. One solution to this ambivalence has been to form a joint venture in which the local partners are highly visible, give it an indigenous name, and then advertise that a foreign firm (actually the partner) is supplying the technology. Even wholly owned subsidiaries have followed this marketing strategy.

Expertise, Tax, and Other Benefits   Other factors that influence companies to enter joint ventures are the ability to acquire expertise that is lacking, the special tax benefits some governments extend to companies with local partners, and the need for additional capital and experienced personnel.

A Disadvantage of Joint Ventures: Loss of Control   Although a joint venture arrangement offers the advantage of a smaller commitment of financial and managerial resources and thus less risk, there are some disadvantages for the foreign firm. One, obviously, is that profits must be shared. Furthermore, if the law allows the foreign investor to have no more than 49 percent participation, it may not have equity-based control. If the stock markets in these countries are small or nonexistent, it is generally impossible to distribute the shares widely enough to permit the foreign firm with its 49 percent ownership position to be the largest stockholder.

Lack of full control over the joint venture is the reason many companies resist making such arrangements. They feel that they must have tight control of their foreign subsidiaries to obtain an efficient allocation of investments and production and to maintain a coordinated marketing plan worldwide. For example, local partners might wish to export to markets that the global company serves from its own plants, or they might want to make the complete product locally when the global company's strategy is to produce only certain components there and import the rest from other subsidiaries.

In the recent past, numerous governments of developing nations have passed laws requiring local majority ownership for the purpose of giving equity-based control of firms within their borders to their own citizens. Despite these laws, a substantial level of control may still be feasible, even with a minority ownership.

Control of Joint Ventures through Management Contracts   Management contracts, which were discussed earlier in this chapter under nonequity-based modes of entry, can enable the global partner to control many aspects of a joint venture even when holding only a minority position. If it supplies key personnel, such as the production and technical managers, the global company can be assured of the product quality with which its name may be associated. It may also be able to earn additional income by selling the joint venture inputs manufactured in the home plant. This is possible because the larger global company is more vertically integrated. A local paint factory, for example, might have to import certain semi-processed pigments and driers that the foreign partner produces in its home country for domestic operations. If these can be purchased elsewhere at a lower price, the local majority could insist on other sources of supply. This rarely happens, because the production and technical managers can argue that only inputs from their employer will produce a satisfactory product, especially if the production machinery being used has been purchased based on specifications from the foreign partner. The production and technical managers are the experts, and they generally have the final word.

Other Options for Exercising Control in Joint Ventures   Even as a minority shareholder, a partner company may be able to exercise some control over the joint ventures operations through such mechanisms as supermajority voting requirements (e.g., requiring a two-thirds or more vote in a venture with a 51 percent to 49 percent ownership split in order to approve strategic decisions), maintaining the right to appoint or approve key managerial positions, splitting control of the venture so that each partner may have primary influence over certain key activities (e.g., sourcing of raw materials or components, finance, production, technology), control over or participation in the design and implementation of performance appraisal and reward systems for top management and other personnel of the joint venture, and so forth.

Strategic Alliance

Faced with expanding global competition; the growing cost of research, product development, and marketing; and the need to move faster in carrying out their global strategies, many firms are forming **strategic alliances** with customers, suppliers, and competitors. In fact, in a 12-country study, consultants Ernst & Young found that 65 percent of non-U.S. and 75 percent of U.S. companies are engaged in some form of strategic alliance.[6] The aim of these companies is to achieve faster market entry and startup; gain access to new products, technologies, and markets; and share costs, resources, and risks. Alliances include various types of partnerships and may or may not include equity. Companies wanting to share technology may cross-license their technology, with each licensing its technology to the other. If their aim is to pool research and design resources, they may form an R&D partnership. For example, Nokia and Microsoft formed an alliance in 2011 to collaborate in the development of software for technologically advanced cell phones.

strategic alliance
A partnership between or among competitors, customers, or suppliers that may take one or more of various forms, both equity and nonequity

Alliances May Be Joint Ventures

Other companies carry the cooperation further by forming joint ventures in manufacturing and marketing.

Nissan of Japan was a struggling automaker in the 1990s, with $20 billion in debt and declining market share. Renault of France decided to form an alliance with Nissan rather than merge the companies. Renault sent Carlos Ghosn to become CEO and president of Nissan. Ghosn's team developed and implemented an aggressive turnaround plan, one that has provided benefits for both partners. They have leveraged their size and competencies to enter new markets more rapidly and with lower costs, because they do not need to build new plants. For example, Renault has used Nissan's assembly plants in Mexico, and Nissan uses Renault's Brazilian plant and distribution network. The alliance has increased sales, profitability, and market capitalization for both of the partners. In 2006, these two partners began discussing the possibility of an alliance with another ailing automaker, General Motors of the United States. However, these discussions ended without an alliance.

Joint Venture Challenges: Danone and Wahaha in China

Group Danone SA of France is a major player in the international food and beverage industry, with 90,000 employees spread across five continents. In contrast, the Chinese company Wahaha Group Co. Ltd. was established by Zong Qinhou in the late 1980s as a venture involving three people selling beverages to schoolchildren, later growing into the largest Chinese bottled-water company.

In 1996, Danone and Wahaha agreed to establish a joint venture (JV) in China, eventually expanding to 39 different JVs between them. Danone was the majority owner in the JVs, with a 51 percent share of the equity, and Zong was the chairman of the JVs' boards. Danone had limited involvement in the day-to-day operation of the JVs, delegating this task to Zong and his Chinese management team. In 2006, these ventures generated revenues of $2 billion and a strong position in the Chinese beverage market. From the outside, this partnership seemed to be a great success.

All was apparently not perfect between the partners, however. By 2005, Danone learned that Zong apparently had been setting up "mirror" businesses that produced and sold products that were nearly identical to those offered by the partners' JVs. These mirror companies, which would be a violation of the JV agreements, even used the Wahaha name to benefit from the JVs' advertisements and sales networks.

Danone negotiated quietly with Zong to resolve the newly discovered problem. In December 2006, an agreement was apparently achieved to combine the mirror companies with the JVs and to pay $566 million to Zong. Zong subsequently backed out of the deal, which he claimed to have only signed under "forced" conditions and for an amount far below the mirror companies' value.

After the agreement collapsed in 2007, the disputes between the partners first became public. Danone sought arbitration with Zong in Sweden. Danone also filed lawsuits in the United States and elsewhere for trademark infringement and violation of non-compete clauses. Danone accused Zong of masterminding the fraud with assistance from relatives and offshore entities.

Zong's response was to organize rallies and news conferences that denounced Danone's managers as "rascals" who had committed "evil deeds"; Zong even accused Danone of having engaged in poor treatment of the Chinese. Reflecting an escalation of tensions between the companies, Wahaha executives apparently prevented Danone officials from entering the JVs' buildings.

Zong also filed a request for arbitration in China, in Wahaha's headquarters' city of Hangzhou, arguing that the Wahaha trademark was owned by Wahaha and not the Danone-Wahaha JV. Zong acknowledged that he had signed an agreement with Danone to transfer use of Wahaha's trademark to the JV and to prevent Wahaha from expanding independently into the Chinese beverage market. However, Zong said he never submitted the agreement to the Chinese trademark office for approval, so the agreement never took effect. The Hangzhou Arbitration Commission upheld Zong's assertion that no agreement had been approved by the government and therefore Zong was not prevented from also using the Wahaha trademark or from entering the Chinese beverage market.

---

pooling alliance
An alliance driven by similarity and integration among partners

Pooling versus Trading Alliances A useful distinction can be made between pooling and trading alliances. **Pooling alliances** are driven by similarity and integration, while **trading alliances** are driven by the logic of contributing dissimilar resources. These two types are typically different in their goals (common versus compatible goals), optimal structures (many versus few partners), and managerial challenges (low versus high coordination needs).[7]

trading alliance
An alliance driven by the logic of partners contributing dissimilar resources

Alliances versus Mergers and Acquisitions Generally mergers and acquisitions are not considered alliances. However, both may be ways for firms to get their hands on new technology, by either acquiring or working with smaller, innovative firms. For example, the merger between Canadian brewer Molson and U.S. brewer Coors was analyzed by many as a union of two "struggling" mid-sized beer companies. The merged company was part of a joint venture with the U.S. operations of SABMiller plc, the maker of Miller beer. Sandoz, a Swiss pharmaceutical manufacturer, acquired Gerber for $3.7 billion in order to double the size of its food products division. Two years later, because of the increased global competition and the mounting cost of technology, Sandoz and Ciba Geigy, another Swiss drug company, merged to form Novartis, which became the second-largest pharmaceutical firm in the world. Novartis later sold Gerber to Nestlé.

Future of Alliances Many alliances fail or are taken over by one of the partners. The existence of two or more partners—which are often competitors as well as partners and

Several of Zong's companies also sued JV directors nominated by Danone, arguing that they violated non-compete clauses by serving not just on the Danone-Wahaha boards but also on boards of other companies in China that were competing with Wahaha.

Ultimately, the disagreement included at least a dozen lawsuits or arbitration cases filed in a variety of nations, including China, France, Sweden, the United States, Italy, British Virgin Islands, and Samoa. The situation became a major international dispute, including unsuccessful mediation efforts by the leaders of both France and China. Danone's public image and future competitiveness in China were put at risk. Strong feelings of nationalism caused many Chinese consumers and other observers to side with the local Chinese company, Wahaha. Zong was even viewed by some as a national hero for battling heroically against a giant, foreign bully, Danone. Heated debates appeared among Chinese bloggers to promote a boycott of Danone products. At the same time, the Chinese government was concerned about how the Danone-Wahaha dispute might affect the image of China as a desirable destination for international business investment as well as maintaining popular support within China.

In late 2009, Danone agreed to sell its 51 percent share of the JVs to Wahaha for cash and announced that all legal proceedings between the partners were concluded. Danone's CEO and chairman, Frank Riboud, commented, "The collaboration between Danone and Wahaha helped to build a strong and respected leader in the Chinese beverage industry. We are confident that Wahaha will continue to be highly successful under its future management guidance." Wahaha's chairman, Zong, said, "China is an open country. Chinese people are broadminded people. Chinese companies are willing to cooperate and grow with the world's leading peers on the basis of equality and reciprocal benefit."

Questions:

1. Why do you think the problems arose between Danone and Zong?

2. What might Danone have done to either avoid or reduce the problems that occurred over the life of the JVs?

Sources: Samual Shen and Jacqueline Wong, "Danone Ends Wahaha Dispute, to Sell China JV Stake," www.reuters.com/article/2009/09/30/us-danone-wahaha-idUSTRE58T12120090930 (June 21, 2011); "Danone v. Wahaha—Which of Us Is the Most China Rookie?," China Law Blog, www.chinalawblog.com/2007/04/danone_v_wahaha_which_of_us_is.html (June 21, 2011); "Danone Settles Dispute with Wahaha," China Daily, September 30, 2009, www.chinadaily.com.cn/china/2009-09/30/content_8758022.htm (June 21, 2011); David Barboza, "Danone Exits China Venture after Years of Legal Dispute," The New York Times, September 30, 2009, www.nytimes.com/2009/10/01/business/global/01danone.html (June 21, 2011); and Jingzhou Tao and Edward Hillier, "A Tale of Two Companies," China Business Review, May–June 2008, pp. 44–47.

typically have differences in strategies, operating practices, and organizational cultures—often causes alliances to be difficult to manage, particularly in rapidly changing international competitive environments.[8] Alliances can also allow a partner to acquire the firm's technological or other competencies, thereby raising important competitive concerns. The management consulting firm McKinsey & Co. surveyed 150 companies whose alliances with Japanese partners had been terminated. It found that three-quarters of the alliances had been taken over by Japanese partners.

Despite the challenges involved with forming and managing alliances successfully, there is no question that some alliances have accomplished what they set out to accomplish. For example, CFM International, the alliance between General Electric and France's Snecma (Société Nationale d'Étude et de Construction de Moteurs d'Aviation), has been producing jet engines for nearly four decades. It seems that alliances in their various forms will continue to be used as important strategic and tactical weapons, particularly given the financial, technological, political, and other challenges facing companies involved in increasingly competitive international marketplaces.

We began the chapter with a discussion of whether being first in the market meant profitability and discovered that the answer is, "It depends." Whether one is first, an early follower, or a late entrant, there are still chances for success, particularly if a company chooses an appropriate mode of entry and then manages the entry process in an effective manner.

THE GLOBAL PATH AHEAD

Mark Haupt: A Central California–based International Career

Mark Haupt graduated from Cal Poly with a business degree, concentrating in international business. He loved the area where he went to university and wanted to continue living there, so he put together a career that is both international and allows him to work near home. Here's his story:

I think my interest in international business started when I was little. My father had a job with IBM and he was constantly traveling domestically and internationally. I'm also a big soccer fan and soccer is such a global sport that you start learning more and more about different countries, cities, cultures, etc. . . . and that has always been fascinating to me. I grew up with a lot of different ethnicities and cultures around and it's the differences—and sometimes similarities—that make things interesting to me.

After graduation, I wanted to remain in the Central Coast region of California, near the ocean, but also have international business opportunities. Despite the rural nature of this area, I was able to find a position with a local sporting goods company. I am in charge of our specialty/sporting goods division and my title is "Specialty Sales Manager." I manage a network of sales representatives, domestic and international, as well as select independent accounts and key accounts.

In less than two years with the company, I have worked with customers in more than 30 different nations, including Australia, New Zealand, Canada, Mexico, Colombia, Brazil, Chile, Venezuela, Ireland, England, Germany, Italy, France, the Benelux Region (Belgium, Netherlands, Luxemburg), Scandinavia (Iceland, Sweden, Norway, Finland, Denmark), Romania, Latvia, Belarus, China, Japan, Singapore, Australia, New Zealand, South Africa, Egypt, and Russia. My business association with most of these customers is a distribution arrangement. Companies in these countries distribute my company's products as well as those of other firms.

To prepare for travel, I always like to research the country I am visiting. I start by finding out a little about that country's sport of choice. For me, that's always an easy conversation starter and something that almost everyone has an opinion on. Then I like to find out about popular venues, sights, etc. Finally, I find out what to do or not to do. I research online and talk to people who have already visited the country. I pack light because I never seem to need much besides a few business outfits and some casual clothes. English has been the accepted business language for all my travels, but I like to learn at least a few words of the native language. For me, that shows that I am interested in the country and people

seem to appreciate that. I don't have any routines for when I return from travel. I always seem to take way too long to unpack to the point where I run out of clothes. I am working on that.

To help myself adjust to being away, I always make sure I'm exhausted before I get on the plane. I sleep amazingly well on planes, probably because I have been flying ever since I was little. Usually, I wake up completely refreshed when I arrive.

To make my U.S. location convenient for my international counterparts, I have kept some odd hours. I rely on e-mail, but that usually creates a one-day delay and sometimes doesn't deliver the message effectively. If I use phone or video chat, I try to make the hours work for my customers, which isn't always easy. I have fielded calls as early as 5 A.M. and as late as midnight. That's all part of the job.

My biggest challenge to date has been working on a special order from one of my customers in Asia. Our factory is located in Taiwan, and I have encountered endless complications with molds, materials, packaging, etc. It's easy enough to say you can make a special product and give pricing. It is much more complicated once this actually comes to fruition. For big special orders, it's important that you get everything right. Errors that you might not think about can ruin a project and, potentially, a business relationship.

My greatest international-related enjoyment was going to New Zealand. I loved it over there. The scenery, people, and activities are all amazing. My greatest international business-related enjoyment was starting a relationship with what I first considered to be a mid-sized customer internationally and watching that customer blossom into one of our biggest customers. In sales, you don't always see your efforts pay off. Sometimes you work extra hours and put your heart and soul into something and get nothing out of it. It's extremely satisfying when you put in the extra effort, work extra hours, and it all pays off.

My greatest learning point from my international experience is that I have learned to assume nothing. I have become so incredibly detailed in everything I do because I can never assume that a customer or client understands something exactly the way I do, especially when English isn't their native language. It is much easier to go over something twice in the beginning rather than look back and try to correct a misunderstanding.

My advice for others who are interested in going abroad or working with others who are abroad is the following: if you have the chance, learn any language you can. This is an invaluable asset. Spend some time learning about the countries you are visiting or doing business with, and be extremely inquisitive. Do not act as if you already know everything. It's good to be knowledgeable and worldly, but people love talking about their country and culture and

(continued)

love it when you ask questions and are curious about their lifestyles. Be curious, but not ignorant. Make sure you don't ask anything that might bring up a sore subject.

Resources for Your Global Career

Making the "no go" decision is just as critical as making the "go" decision when considering if your organization should go international. The following articles and tools will assist you in objectively assessing the variables involved in this decision. The wrong decision will be costly to your organization in terms of money, staff time, and your organization's reputation. Take the time to do the analysis so the decision you make is the right decision. Here are some websites that can help you to make good decisions:

- KPMG's "Value and International Performance Research" on foreign market entry: www.kpmg.com.hk/en/virtual_library/Consumer_markets/Foreign_market_entry.pdf
- Should you go international? This article from the Washington *Business Journal* provides insight: http://washington.bizjournals.com/washington/stories/2005/06/06/smallb3.html
- Six major concerns about going into foreign markets: www.inc.com/magazine/20070401/features-how-to-get-started.html
- Strategies for identifying international markets: www.canadabusiness.ca/eng/88/194/

- Your portal for market-entry assistance: http://faculty.philau.edu/russowl/market.html
- How to select which foreign market to enter: http://marketingteacher.com/Lessons/lesson_international_marketing_entry_evaluation_process.htm
- Using FDI as a mode of entry: www.canadabusiness.ca/eng/105/175/ and http://jobfunctions.bnet.com/abstract.aspx?&docid=76544&promo=110000
- Modes of foreign market entry: http://jobfunctions.bnet.com/abstract.aspx?&docid=72028&promo=100511
- Research on corporate culture as a factor in foreign market-entry decisions: http://smib.vuw.ac.nz:8081/WWW/ANZMAC2001/anzmac/AUTHORS/pdfs/Evans1.pdf
- Exporting information from AUSTRADE, the Australian government's Office of Export Management and Assistance: www.austrade.gov.au/Getting-ready-for-export/default.aspx
- Case study: Campbell Soup Company's entry strategy into Russia: www.edamba.eu/userfiles/Permiakova.pdf
- Costs of developing foreign markets: www.smallbusiness-notes.com/aboutsb/rs241.html and archive.sba.gov/advo/research/rs241tot.pdf

---

Summary

LO13-1 Understand the pros and cons of entering markets as a "market pioneer" versus being a "fast follower."

A firm can succeed from any position, as the examples illustrate. In general, however, a follower is more likely to succeed if it has lots of resources. Smaller, less-well-financed followers are less likely to be successful. Pioneers appear to have the best chance for long-term success in market share profitability when they are insulated from entry by competitors due to strong patent protectin, proprietary technology, or substantial investment requirements, or if the pioneering firm has sufficient size, resources, and competencies to take full advantage of and preserve its pioneering position in the face of later competitive entry.

LO13-2 Explain the international market-entry methods.

Methods of entering foreign markets can be assessed as nonequity- or equity-based situations. Nonequity-based modes of entry include indirect or direct exporting, turnkey projects, licensing, franchising, management contracts, and contract manufacturing. Equity-based modes of market entry include wholly owned subsidiaries, joint ventures, and strategic alliances.

LO13-3 Discuss why firms export and the options available for indirect and direct exporting.

Firms can achieve many benefits from exporting, including serving markets where they have no or limited production facilities, responding to host government requirements for exports by local subsidiaries, remain price competitive in the home market,

inexpensively test foreign markets and competitors, meet foreign customer requests, offset cyclical sales in the domestic market, achieve additional sales and utilize excess production capacity, extend a product's life cycle, respond strategically to foreign competitors that are in the firm's home market by entering their home market, achieve success observed by other exporters, and improve the efficiency of manufacturing equipment. Indirect exporting can occur through exporters that sell for the manufacturer, exporters that buy for their overseas customers, exporters that buy and sell for their own accounts, and exporters that purchase for foreign users and middlemen. Direct exporting can occur through manufacturers' agents, distributors, retailers, and trading companies.

LO13-4 Explain the potential benefits and disadvantages of joint ventures and how a company might exercise control over a joint venture, even as a minority shareholder.

Joint ventures can allow the partner companies to benefit from reduced risk and competition or increased scale economies; ability to meet government regulations for local participation; respond to strong nationalism, and achieve expertise, tax, and other benefits. A major potential disadvantage of joint ventures is loss of control, but even as a minority shareholder a partner company may be able to exercise some control over the joint venture through management contracts, supermajority voting requirements, appointment of key managers, split control structures, and the design and implementation of performance appraisal and reward systems for the venture's personnel.

indirect exporting (p. 325)

cooperative exporters (p. 326)

direct exporting (p. 326)

sales company (p. 327)

manufacturers' agents (p. 327)

distributors (p. 327)

trading companies (p. 327)

turnkey project (p. 328)

licensing (p. 328)

franchising (p. 330)

management contract (p. 330)

contract manufacturing (p. 330)

joint venture (p. 332)

strategic alliances (p. 333)

pooling alliance (p. 334)

trading alliance (p. 334)

Questions

1. If a company wanted to be a pioneer for entering a market, what conditions might increase the likelihood of success? If the company wanted to instead be a fast follower, what would be different in terms of the conditions that would increase the likelihood of the company's successful entry?

2. What are the methods by which a firm can enter foreign markets?

3. Why might a company want to engage in exporting?

4. What is indirect exporting, and how does it differ from direct exporting? What are the main types of indirect exporting, and what are the primary strengths and weaknesses of each type?

5. What are the distribution options that a direct exporter can use, and what are the primary strengths and weaknesses of each type?

6. What entry mode do fashion designers such as Pierre Cardin, and some high-tech firms like Texas Instruments, share in common? Why might this be an attractive option for entering foreign markets?

7. Under what circumstances might piracy be beneficial to an exporter?

8. Why would a global firm or multinational require that a wholly owned foreign subsidiary sign a management contract when it already owns the subsidiary?

9. Under what conditions might a company prefer a joint venture to a wholly owned subsidiary when making a foreign investment?

10. How can a company control a joint venture if it only has a minority share of the equity?

11. What is the difference, if any, between a joint venture and a strategic alliance?

Research Task

 globalEDGE   globalEDGE.msu.edu

Use the globalEDGE site (http://globalEDGE.msu.edu/) to complete the following exercises:

1. *Entrepreneur* magazine annually publishes a ranking of America's top 200 *franchisers* seeking international franchisees. Provide a list of the top 10 companies that pursue franchising as a mode of international expansion. Study one of these companies in detail, and provide a description of its business model, its international expansion pattern, the qualifications it looks for in its franchisees, and the type of support and training it provides.

2. You are working for a computer manufacturer that is planning to set up an assembly unit in Uruguay to serve the region. Because this would involve importing parts from other countries and then exporting the finished products throughout Latin America, top management has requested information on the trading practices of Uruguay. In particular, these managers want to know (a) the average time to clear both imports and direct exports through Customs; (b) the percentage of losses from direct export due to theft, as well as, breakage; and (c) the percentage of firms identifying Customs and trade regulations as a major constraint. Using *Enterprise Surveys,* a site provided by the World Bank, that measures business perceptions of the investment climate, prepare a brief executive report summarizing your findings. How does Uruguay compare to other countries in Latin America on these measures?

Minicase: Method of Entry—The Foley Company

The Foley Company, a manufacturer of soybean harvesters, has for years sold a substantial number of machines in Brazil. However, a Brazilian firm has begun to manufacture them, and Foley's local distributor has told Jesse Osborne, Foley's president, that if Foley expects to maintain its share of the market, it will also have to manufacture locally. Osborne is in a quandary. The market is too good to lose, but Foley has had no experience with foreign manufacturing operations. Because Brazilian sales and repairs have been handled by the distributor, no one in Foley has had any firsthand experience in that country.

Osborne has made some rough calculations that indicate the firm can make money by manufacturing in Brazil, but the firm's lack of marketing expertise in the country troubles him. He calls in Joanne Poe, the export manager, and asks her to prepare a list of all the options open to Foley, with their advantages and disadvantages. Osborne also asks Poe to indicate her recommendation.

Questions:

1. Assume you are Joanne Poe. Prepare a list of all the options available to Foley, and give the advantages and disadvantages of each.

2. Which of the options would you recommend? Why?

3. Assuming that the president's calculations are correct and that a factory to produce locally the number of machines that Foley now exports to Brazil will offer a satisfactory return on investment, what special information about Brazil will you want to gather?

Export and Import Practices

The fact that trade protection hurts the economy of the country that imposes it is one of the oldest but still most startling insights economics has to offer. The idea dates back to the origin of economic science itself. Adam Smith's *The Wealth of Nations,* which gave birth to economics, already contained the argument for free trade: by specializing in production instead of producing everything, each nation would profit from free trade.

—*Jagdish Bagwati, professor, Columbia University,*
The Concise Encyclopedia of Economics

How a Box Transformed the World

Fifty years ago, on April 26, a war-surplus oil tanker, the *Ideal-X,* left port in Newark, New Jersey, with a steel frame welded to its deck. The frame held aluminum containers that were off-loaded five days later in Houston, onto trucks. That was the beginning of a revolution in shipping that has made our world smaller. Containerization drastically reduced shipping costs and allowed manufacturers to leave the waterfronts and move, literally, offshore, to take advantage of cheap labor to produce goods that previously could not be exported profitably.

Malcolm McLean, a North Carolina farm boy turned trucker, had hauled cotton bales to Hoboken, where he had to sit around a whole day for his shipment to be unloaded. He waited, and he watched the process. It was slow, hard labor and gave rise to pilferage, as well. His idea was to detach the truck bodies and ship them on boats made to hold them.

No one understood how the box would change everything having to do with export and import, ships and ports, goods traded, trade routes, and labor unions. Marc Levinson, author of *The Box: How the Shipping Container Made the World Smaller and the World Economy Bigger,* calls containerization a monument to the most powerful law in economics, the law of unintended consequences.

Source: Wally Bock, "A Man Who Changed the World," *Monday Memo,* June 11, 2001, www.mondaymemo.net/010611feature.htm (accessed June 16, 2011); Marc Levinson, *The Box: How the Shipping Container Made the World Smaller and the World Economy Bigger* (Princeton, NJ: Princeton University Press, 2006); Marc Levinson, "Unforeseen Consequence: How a Box Transformed the World," *Financial Times,* April 25, 2006, p. 17.

learning objectives

After reading this chapter, you should be able to:

LO14-1 **Identify** the sources of export counseling and support.

LO14-2 **Discuss** the meaning of the various terms of sale known as Incoterms.

LO14-3 **Identify** some sources of export financing.

LO14-4 **Describe** the activities of a foreign freight forwarder.

LO14-5 **Outline** the export documents required.

LO14-6 **Identify** import sources.

There are many reasons to export, as reviewed in the previous chapter. But why do companies *not* export? Two major reasons U.S. firms give for not exporting are a preoccupation with the vast American market and a reluctance to become involved in a new, unknown, and therefore risky operation. When managers of nonexporting firms are probed further on why they are not active in international markets, they generally mention the following three areas in which they lack knowledge: locating foreign markets, payment and financing procedures, and export procedures.

Considerable assistance is available from the federal and state departments of commerce, banks, the Small Business Administration, small business development centers, and private consultants, to mention just a few sources. Too few managers are taking advantage of this valuable assistance. In this chapter, we examine each of the areas that hinder managers in developing exporting capability: locating foreign markets, payment and financing procedures, and export procedures.

Locating Foreign Markets and Developing a Plan

The first step in locating foreign markets is to determine whether a market exists for the firm's products. The initial screening step described in Chapter 12 indicate a procedure to follow that will pose no problem for an experienced market analyst who is well acquainted with the available sources of information and assistance. However, newcomers to exporting, especially smaller firms, may still be at a loss as to how to begin their foreign market research. For them, a number of helpful export assistance programs are available. Once the potential exporter has established that there may be a market for the firm's products, it's time to draft the export marketing plan.

SOURCES OF EXPORT INFORMATION, COUNSELING, AND SUPPORT

LO14-1 Identify
the sources of export counseling and support.

Export.gov is the U.S. government's trade portal, established by the Department of Commerce. It brings together resources on exporting from a number of government agencies, including the U.S. International Trade Administration, U.S. Commercial Service, Department of Commerce, Export-Import Bank, Agency for International Development, Small Business Administration, Department of State, and Overseas Private Investment Corporation. Export.gov is packed with case studies of small businesses that have had recent export success and announcement of foreign trade missions and training programs that are open to small businesses.

For firms that already are exporting, the International Trade Administration (ITA) offers a wide range of export promotion activities that include export counseling, analysis of foreign markets, assessment of industry competitiveness, and development of market opportunities and sales representation through export promotion events. Four departments in ITA work together to provide these services:[1]

1. *Market Access and Compliance (MAC):* MAC specialists seek to open foreign markets to American products by developing strategies to overcome obstacles faced by U.S. businesses in foreign countries and regions. They also monitor foreign country compliance with trade agreements.

2. *Manufacturing and Services:* This department promotes the trade interests of American industries by helping to shape industry-specific trade policy. Its industry desk officers work by sector with industry representatives and associations to identify trade opportunities by product or service, industry sector, and market. They also develop export marketing plans and programs. Trade Development experts also conduct executive trade missions, trade fairs, and marketing seminars.

3. *U.S. and Foreign Commercial Service (USCS):* The USCS has commercial officers working in more than 100 U.S. domestic locations and around 80 countries who can provide background information on foreign companies and assist in finding foreign representatives, conducting market research, and identifying trade and investment opportunities for

American firms. The district offices also conduct export workshops and keep business-people informed about domestic and overseas trade events that offer potential for promoting American products.

4. *Import Administration:* This office enforces U.S. trade law and agreements to prevent unfairly traded imports and to safeguard the competitiveness of U.S. businesses.

The Office of International Trade of the Small Business Administration (SBA) offers assistance through SBA district offices to current and potential small business exporters through two programs that are provided in field offices around the country, Business Development and Financial Assistance. The Office of International Trade also works through the SCORE program, in which experienced executives offer free one-on-one counseling to small firms; Small Business Development Centers (SBDCs), located in many universities and colleges, which give export counseling, especially to inexperienced newcomers; Centers for International Business and Research (CIBERs), located in 30 U.S. universities, which also assist firms with exporting; and U.S. Export Assistance Centers, which are one-stop offices ready to help small and medium-size businesses with local export assistance.

The Department of Commerce Export Assistance Program (EAP) helps potential exporters narrow down their potential markets. It has offices in more than 100 U.S. cities and 80 foreign cities. After learning about the company and its products, the EAP international trade specialist might advise the potential exporter to consult the Foreign Trade Division of the U.S. Census Bureau, which tracks trade and economic data from federal agencies. The International Trade Administration of the Department of Commerce provides a comprehensive guide for new exporters and a source of specific product and regional information for experienced exporters searching for new markets.

Once the existence of a potential market is established, the firm must choose between exporting indirectly through U.S.-based exporters and exporting directly using its own staff. If it opts for indirect exporting as a way to test the market, the trade specialist can provide assistance. If the firm prefers to set up its own export operation, it must then obtain overseas distribution. The exporter may use the Export.gov portal to find agents, distributors, or joint venture partners.[2] Credit reporting agencies, such as Dun & Bradstreet, the Finance, Credit, and International Business Association (FCIB), and the exporter's bank will supply credit information.

If the firm wants to make a foreign trip, Commerce offers the Gold Key Matching Service through many U.S. embassies. This is tailored for managers of American companies who are coming to visit the country and includes orientation briefings, market research, introductions to potential partners, and assistance in developing a marketing strategy for the particular country. The U.S. Commercial Office makes the arrangements. The Foreign Agricultural Service of the U.S. Department of Agriculture offers similar services to potential exporters of agricultural products.

The Department of Commerce also organizes trade events known as "Show and Sells" that are helpful in both locating foreign representatives and making sales. There are four kinds:

1. *U.S. pavilions:* Commerce selects about 100 global trade fairs every year for which it recruits American companies to participate at a U.S. pavilion. Preference is given to fairs in markets suitable for firms that are ready to export. Exhibitors receive extensive support from Commerce in management and overseas promotional campaigns to attract business audiences.

2. *Trade missions:* These focus on an industry sector. Participants are given detailed marketing information, advanced publicity, logistical support, and prearranged appointments with potential buyers and government officials. Generally, a mission consists of 5 to 12 business executives.

3. *Product literature center:* Commerce trade development specialists represent U.S. companies at various international trade shows, where they distribute literature. They then tell the companies who the interested visitors were so that the companies can follow up.

4. *Reverse trade missions:* The U.S. Trade Development Agency may fund visits to the United States by representatives of foreign governments so that they can meet with American industry and government representatives. The foreign officials represent purchasing authorities interested in buying U.S. equipment for specific projects.

In addition to the federal government, other sources of assistance available to the exporter include state governments, all of which have export development programs and many of which have export financing programs. In the private sector, the World Trade Centers Association, a membership organization of more than 300 centers worldwide, provides networking opportunities and an online trading system. There are also industry-based trade groups that are a source of export guidance. In summary, there are many resources for the beginning exporter, and the U.S. government is a good place for U.S. businesses to start building their export knowledge.

MISTAKES MADE BY NEW EXPORTERS

Here is a list of the 12 most commonly made mistakes by new exporters.[3] Review them to help you build a sense of where the actual pitfalls are when firms launch export programs.

1. **Failure to obtain qualified export counseling and to develop a master international strategy and marketing plan before starting an export business.** To be successful, a firm must first figure out what its goals and objectives are and develop a plan for how they will be achieved. Unless the firm is fortunate enough to possess a staff with considerable export expertise, taking this crucial first step may require qualified outside guidance.

2. **Insufficient commitment by top management to overcome the initial difficulties and financial requirements of exporting.** Establishing a firm in foreign markets usually takes more time than doing so in domestic ones. Although the early delays and costs involved in exporting may seem difficult to justify compared to the situation in established domestic markets, the exporter should take a long-term view of this process and carefully monitor international marketing efforts through these early difficulties. If a good foundation is laid for export business, the benefits derived should eventually outweigh the investment.

3. **Insufficient care in selecting overseas sales representatives and distributors.** The selection of each foreign distributor is crucial. The complexity introduced by overseas communication and transportation requires that international distributors act with greater independence than do their domestic counterparts. Because a new exporter's history, trademarks, and reputation may be unknown in the foreign market, foreign customers may buy on the strength of a distributor's reputation. A firm should, therefore, conduct a personal evaluation of the personnel handling its account, the distributor's facilities, and the management methods employed.

4. **Chasing orders from around the world instead of establishing a basis for profitable operations and orderly growth.** If exporters expect distributors to promote their accounts actively, the distributors must be trained and assisted, and their performance must be monitored continually. This may require a company executive located in the distributor's geographic region. New exporters may want to concentrate their efforts in one or two geographic areas until they have sufficient business to support a company representative. Then, while this initial core area is expanded, the exporter can move into the next targeted geographic area.

5. **Neglecting export business when the home market booms.** Often companies turn to exporting when business falls off in their home market. When domestic business starts to boom again, they neglect their export trade. Such neglect can harm the profits and motivation of a company's overseas representatives, strangle its own export trade, and leave the firm without recourse when domestic business falls off again.

6. **Failure to treat international distributors and customers on an equal basis with their domestic counterparts.** Often, companies carry out institutional advertising campaigns, special discount offers, sales incentive programs, special credit term programs, warranty offers, and so forth, in the home market but fail to make similar assistance available to their international distributors and customers. This is a mistake that can destroy the vitality of overseas marketing efforts.

7. **Assuming that a given market technique and product will automatically be successful in all countries.** What works in one market may not work in others. Each market has to be treated separately until the company has sufficient knowledge about its export markets to generalize about them.

8. **Unwillingness to modify products to meet regulations or cultural preferences of other countries.** Local safety codes and import restrictions cannot be ignored, nor can cultural preferences. If necessary modifications are not made at the factory, the distributor must make them, often at greater cost and perhaps not as well

9. **Failure to provide service, sales, and warranty information in locally understood languages.** Although many people may speak English, assume that they will want to read instructions and product information in their own language. This holds for customers and distributors.

10. **Failure to consider the use of an export management company.** If a firm decides it cannot afford its own export department, it should consider the possibility of using an export management company (EMC).

11. **Failure to consider licensing or joint venture agreements.** Import restrictions in some countries, insufficient personnel or financial resources, or an overly limited product line can cause many companies to dismiss international marketing as unfeasible. Yet many products that compete on a national basis in a home market can be marketed successfully in many markets of the world through licensing or joint venture arrangements.

12. **Failure to provide readily available servicing for the product.** A product without the necessary service support can acquire a bad reputation in a short period, potentially preventing further sales.

EXPORT MARKETING PLAN

As soon as possible, the firm needs to draft its export marketing plan. An experienced firm will already have a plan in operation, but newcomers may need to wait until they have accumulated at least some information from foreign market research. Essentially, the export marketing plan is the same as the domestic marketing plan. It should be specific about the markets to be developed, the marketing strategy for serving them, and the tactics required to carry out the strategy. Sales forecasts and budgets, pricing policies, product characteristics, promotional plans, and details on arrangements with foreign representatives are required. In other words, the export marketing plan spells out what must be done and when, who should do it, and what the costs are. An outline for an export marketing plan appears in the appendix at the end of this chapter. In Chapter 15 we focus on the marketing mix, but two aspects of the mix require some explanation here: export pricing and sales agreements for foreign representatives.

INCOTERMS

One pricing area of concern for many firms beginning to export is the need to quote **terms of sale** that differ from those used in domestic markets. For foreign transactions, the exporter needs to be familiar with **Incoterms,** 11 three-letter trade terms that describe the responsibilities of the buyer and seller in international trade transactions.[4] They were created by the International Chamber of Commerce and have recently been revised into two categories, depending on mode of transportation, either general or water. Incoterms describe which party does which tasks, which party covers the costs, and which party bears the risk. Fox example, FOB means that the seller loads the goods on board the ship nominated by the buyer, clears them for export, and both cost and risk transfer at the ship's rail. Foreign customers will expect one of the following terms of sale, which are briefly described here. Note that these are new terms as of 2011. The responsibilities for various types of foreign sales are more fully described in Figure 14.1.

Two other areas of export differ from domestic sales: pricing and the sales agreement. On pricing, CIF and CFR terms of sale are more convenient for foreign buyers because to establish their cost, they merely have to add the import duties, landing charges, and freight

LO14-2 **Discuss** the meaning of the various terms of sale known as Incoterms.

terms of sale
Conditions of a sale that stipulate the point at which all costs and risks are borne by the buyer

Incoterms
Universal trade terminology developed by the International Chamber of Commerce

from the port of arrival to their warehouse. New exporters need to remember the miscellaneous costs—wharf storage and handling charges, freight forwarder's charges, and consular fees—incurred in making a CIF shipment. Note that the domestic marketing and general administrative costs included in the domestic selling price are frequently greater than the actual cost of making a CIF export sale.

FIGURE 14.1   Summary of Seller and Buyer Responsibilities by Incoterm Type of Sale

Incoterms	Load to truck	Export-duty payment	Transport to exporter's port	Unload from truck at port of origin	Landing charges at port of origin	Transport to importer's port	Landing charges at importer's port	Unload from truck from the importer's port	Transport to destination	Insurance	Entry-Customs clearence	Entry-Duties and taxes
EXW	No	No	No	No	No	No	No	No	No	No	No	No
FCA	Yes	Yes	Yes	No	No	No	No	No	No	No	No	No
FAS	Yes	Yes	Yes	Yes	No	No	No	No	No	No	No	No
FOB	Yes	Yes	Yes	Yes	Yes	No	No	No	No	No	No	No
CFR	Yes	Yes	Yes	Yes	Yes	Yes	Yes	No	No	No	No	No
CIF	Yes	Yes	Yes	Yes	Yes	Yes	No	No	No	Yes	No	No
CPT	Yes	Yes	Yes	Yes	Yes	Yes	Yes	Yes	Yes	No	No	No
CIP	Yes	Yes	Yes	Yes	Yes	Yes	Yes	Yes	Yes	Yes	No	No
DAP	Yes	Yes	Yes	Yes	Yes	Yes	No	No	No	No	No	No
DAF	Yes	Yes	Yes	Yes	Yes	Yes	No	No	No	No	No	No
DES	Yes	Yes	Yes	Yes	Yes	Yes	No	No	No	No	No	No
DAT	Yes	Yes	Yes	Yes	Yes	Yes	Yes	No	No	No	No	No
DEQ	Yes	Yes	Yes	Yes	Yes	Yes	Yes	No	No	No	No	No
DDU	Yes	Yes	Yes	Yes	Yes	Yes	Yes	Yes	Yes	Yes	No	No
DDP	Yes	Yes	Yes	Yes	Yes	Yes	Yes	Yes	Yes	No	Yes	Yes

Sources: Incoterms Wall Chart, 2010, www.winglobal.ca/incoterms_2010 (accessed 16 June, 2011); Wikipedia, http://en.wikipedia.org/wiki/Incoterms (accessed June 16, 2011).

The preferred pricing method is the use of the *factory door cost* (production cost without domestic marketing and general administrative costs), to which are added the direct cost of making the export sale, a percentage of the general administrative overhead, and a profit margin. This percentage can be derived from managers' estimates of the part of their total time spent on export matters. The minimum FOB, or Ex-Works, price is the sum of these costs plus the required profit margin. If research in a market has shown that either there is little competition or that competitive prices are higher, then of course the exporter is free to match the competition in that market (price skim) or set a low price to gain market share (penetration pricing). The course of action taken will depend on the firm's sales objectives, just as in the domestic market.

The other area of major difference in exporting is the sales agreement. It should specify as simply as possible the duties of the representative and the firm. Most of what is contained in the contract for a domestic representative can be used in export also, but special attention must be paid to two points: the designation of the responsibilities for patent and trademark registration and the designation of the country and state or province whose laws will govern any contractual dispute. To be absolutely safe, the firm should register all patents and trademarks. Policing them may be left to the local representative; however, the firm should have the help of an experienced international attorney when drawing up an agreement. Exporters from any country are likely to prefer to stipulate the laws of their home country. Many nations, especially those of Latin America, follow the Calvo Doctrine, which holds that cases should be tried under local and not foreign law.

Payment and Financing Procedures

Once new exporters build their understanding of export process, including pricing and the sales agreement, they need to address the issues related to getting paid for their sale, payment and financing procedures. We review the process of export payment and the terms used, approaches to export financing, and other government incentives that have been established to support exporters in the finance area.

EXPORT PAYMENT TERMS

Payment terms, as every marketer knows, are often a decisive factor in obtaining an order. As a sales official of an international grain exporter put it, "If you give credit to a guy who is broke, he'll pay any price for your product." This is somewhat exaggerated, but customers will often pay higher prices when terms are more lenient, especially in countries where capital is scarce and interest rates are high. Among the payment terms offered by exporters to foreign buyers are cash in advance, open account, consignment, letters of credit, and documentary drafts. We'll look at each of these payment methods in turn.

When the credit standing of the buyer is not known or is uncertain, *cash in advance* is desirable. However, very few buyers will accept these terms, because part of their working capital will be tied up until the merchandise has been received and sold. Furthermore, they have no guarantee that they will receive what they ordered. As a result, few customers will pay cash in advance unless the order is for a custom-made product.

When a sale is made on *open account,* the seller assumes all of the payment-related risk, and therefore such terms should be offered only to reliable customers. The exporter's capital is tied up until payment has been received. However, exporters that insist on less risky payment terms, such as a letter of credit, may find that they are losing business to competitors who do sell on open account. Well-known global firms such as Mercedes Benz do not accept the extra cost of obtaining letters of credit and give their business to suppliers that will offer them open-account terms. To establish the buyer's credit, exporters can get credit reports and credit information on foreign firms from several agencies such as Dun & Bradstreet, Owens Online, and Asian CIS.

Consignment means that goods are shipped to the buyer and payment is not made until they have been sold. All of the payment risk is assumed by the seller, so such terms should not be offered without making the same extensive investigation of the buyer and country as that recommended for open-account terms. Multinationals frequently sell goods to their subsidiaries on this basis.

letter of credit (L/C)
Document issued by the buyer's bank in which the bank promises to pay the seller a specified amount under specified conditions

Only cash in advance offers more protection to the seller than does an export **letter of credit (L/C).** In an L/C, the bank acts as an intermediary between the seller and buyer. The L/C document is issued by the buyer's bank, which promises to pay the seller a specified amount when the bank has received certain documents stipulated in the letter of credit by a specified time. Generally, the seller will request that the letter of credit be *confirmed* and *irrevocable.* In a **confirmed L/C,** a correspondent bank in the seller's country confirms that it will honor the issuing bank's letter of credit. With an **irrevocable L/C,** once the seller has accepted the credit, the customer cannot alter or cancel it without the seller's consent. Figure 14.2 is an example of a bank's confirmation of an irrevocable letter of credit. If the letter of credit is *not* confirmed, the correspondent bank (Merchants National Bank of Mobile) has no obligation to pay the seller (Smith & Co.) when it receives the documents listed in the letter of credit. Only the issuing bank (Banco Americano in Bogotá) is responsible. If sellers (Smith & Co.) wish to be able to collect from an American bank, they will insist that the credit be confirmed by such a bank. This confirmation is generally done by the correspondent bank, as it is in Figure 14.2. When the Merchants National Bank of Mobile confirms the credit, it undertakes an obligation to pay

---

FIGURE 14.2

Letter of Credit

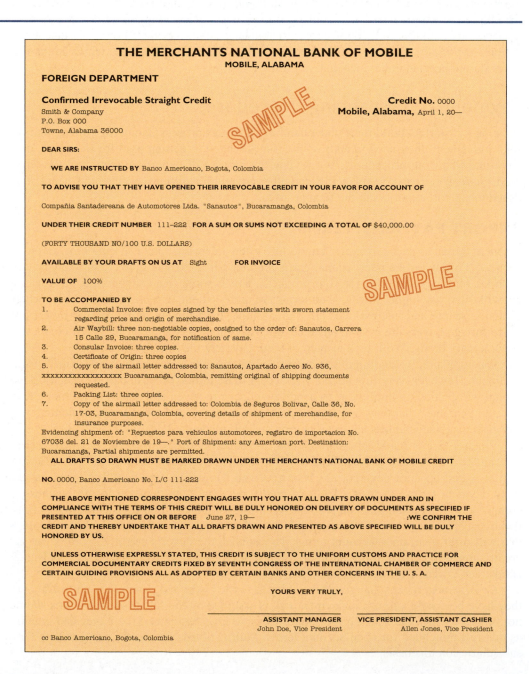

Section III   The Organizational Environment

Smith & Co. if all the documents listed in the letter are presented on or before the stipulated date. Note that nothing is mentioned about the goods themselves; the buyer has stipulated only that an **air waybill** issued by the carrier be presented as proof that shipment has been made. Even if bank officials know that the plane had crashed after the takeoff, they would still pay Smith & Co. Banks are concerned with documents, not merchandise.

Before opening a letter of credit, a buyer frequently requests a **pro forma invoice.** This is the exporter's formal quotation containing a description of the merchandise, price, delivery time, proposed method of shipment, ports of exit and entry, and terms of sale. It is more than a quotation, however. Generally, the bank will use it when opening a letter of credit, and in countries requiring import licenses or permits to purchase foreign exchange, government officials will insist on receiving copies.

Figure 14.3 illustrates the routes taken by the merchandise, letter of credit, and documents in a letter of credit transaction between a U.S. seller and a German buyer. When the German buyer accepts the terms of sale that provide for a confirmed and irrevocable letter of credit, she goes to her bank to arrange for opening the required letter. The buyer will furnish the bank with the information contained in the pro forma invoice, specify the documents that the exporter must present to obtain payment, and set the expiration date for the credit. The concept of the L/C is a simple one, the bank as intermediary between buyer and seller. In fact, a simple irrevocable L/C requires 11 steps to clear payment. Here are those steps:[5]

1. After the exporter and buyer agree on the terms of a sale, the buyer arranges for its bank to open a letter of credit that specifies the documents needed for payment. The buyer determines which documents will be required.

2. The buyer's bank issues, or opens, its irrevocable letter of credit includes all instructions to the seller relating to the shipment.

3. The buyer's bank sends its irrevocable letter of credit to a U.S. bank and requests confirmation. The exporter may request that a particular U.S. bank be the confirming bank, or the foreign bank may select a U.S. correspondent bank.

4. The U.S. bank prepares a letter of confirmation to forward to the exporter along with the irrevocable letter of credit.

confirmed L/C
A confirmation made by a correspondent bank in the seller's country by which it agrees to honor the issuing bank's letter of credit

irrevocable L/C
A stipulation that a letter of credit cannot be canceled

air waybill
A bill of lading issued by an air carrier

pro forma invoice
Exporter's formal quotation containing a description of the merchandise, price, delivery time, method of shipping, terms of sale, and points of exit and entry

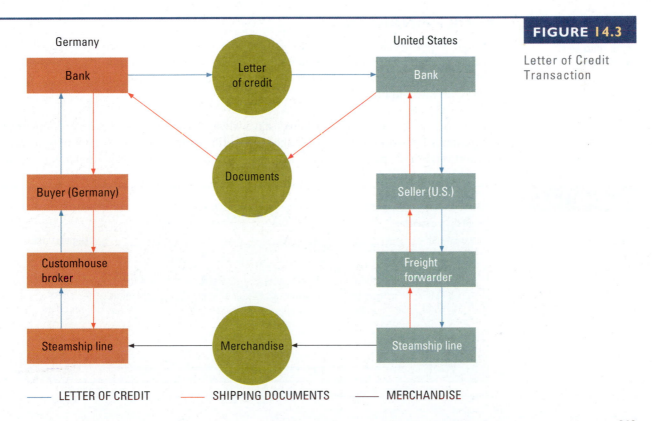

FIGURE 14.3

Letter of Credit Transaction

— LETTER OF CREDIT   — SHIPPING DOCUMENTS   — MERCHANDISE

5. The exporter reviews carefully all conditions in the letter of credit. The exporter's freight forwarder is contacted to make sure that the shipping date can be met. If the exporter cannot comply with one or more of the conditions, the customer is alerted at once.

6. The exporter arranges with the freight forwarder to deliver the goods to the appropriate port or airport.

7. When the goods are loaded, the freight forwarder completes the necessary documentation.

8. The exporter (or the freight forwarder) presents the documents, evidencing full compliance with the letter of credit terms, to the U.S. bank.

9. The bank reviews the documents. If they are in order, the documents are sent to the buyer's bank for review and then transmitted to the buyer.

10. The buyer (or the buyer's agent) uses the documents to claim the goods.

11. A draft, which accompanies the letter of credit, is paid by the buyer's bank at the time specified or, if a time draft, may be discounted to the exporter's bank at an earlier date.

If the exporter believes the political and commercial risks are not sufficient to require a letter of credit, the exporter may agree to payment on a *documentary draft basis,* which is less costly to the buyer. An **export draft** is an unconditional order drawn by the seller on the buyer instructing the buyer to pay the amount of the order on presentation *(sight draft)* or at an agreed future date *(time draft)*. Generally, the seller will ask its bank to send the draft and documents to a bank in the buyer's country, which will proceed with the collection as described in the letter-of-credit transaction.

Although documentary draft and letter-of-credit terms are similar, there is one important difference. A confirmed letter of credit guarantees payment to the seller if the seller conforms to its requirements. There is no guarantee with a documentary draft. An unscrupulous buyer can refuse to pay the draft when presented and then attempt to bargain with the seller for a lower price. The seller must then acquiesce, try to find another buyer, pay a large freight bill to bring back the goods, or abandon them. If the seller chooses the last alternative, customs will auction off the goods, and chances are that the original buyer will be able to acquire them at a bargain price. The seller would receive nothing. Figure 14.4 illustrates that the risks and costs vary inversely among the various export payment terms.

EXPORT FINANCING

Although exporters would prefer to sell on the almost riskless letter-of-credit terms, increased foreign competition and the universally tight money situation force them to offer credit. To do so, they must be familiar with the available sources and kinds of export financing, both private and public.

Private Source   Commercial banks have always been a source of export financing through loans for working capital and the discounting of time drafts. A bank may discount an export time draft, pay the seller and keep it until maturity or, if it is the bank on which

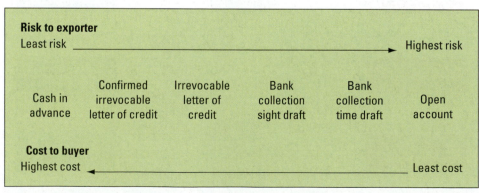

Source: *Business America* (U.S. Department of Commerce Publication), February 1995.

the draft is drawn, "accept" it. By accepting a time draft, a bank assumes the responsibility for making payment at maturity of the draft. The accepting bank may or may not purchase (at a discount) the draft. If it does not, the exporter can sell a **banker's acceptance** readily in the open market.

In recent years, two new types of financing have been developed, factoring and forfaiting. **Factoring** permits the exporter to be more competitive by selling on open account rather than by means of the more costly letter-of-credit method. This financing technique is the sale of export accounts receivable to a third party, which assumes the credit risk. Factoring is essentially discounting without recourse. A factor may be a factoring house or a special department in a commercial bank. Under the export factoring arrangement, the seller passes its order to the factor for approval of the credit risk. Once the order has been approved, the exporter has complete protection against bad debts and political risk. The customer pays the factor, which in effect acts as the exporter's credit and collection department. The period of settlement generally does not exceed 180 days.

Forfaiting is the purchase of obligations that arise from the sale of goods and services that fall due at some date beyond the 90 to 180 days that is customary for factoring. These receivables are usually in the form of trade drafts or promissory notes with maturities ranging from six months to five years. Because forfaited debt is sold without recourse, it is nearly always accompanied by bank security in the form of a guarantee, or *aval*. Whereas the guarantee is a separate document, the aval is a promise to pay that is written directly in the document. The forfaiter purchases the bill and discounts it for the entire credit period. Thus, the exporter, through forfaiting, has converted its credit-based sale into a cash transaction. Although banks have traditionally concentrated on short-term financing, they have become involved in medium- and even long-term financing because numerous government and government-assisted organizations are offering export credit guarantees and insurance against commercial and political risks.

Public Source

The **U.S. Export-Import Bank (Ex-Im Bank)** is the principal government agency responsible for aiding the financing of American exports, through a variety of loan, guarantee, and insurance programs. Ex-Im Bank's programs are available to any American export firm regardless of size. The bank provides two types of loans—direct loans to foreign buyers of American exports and intermediary loans to responsible parties, such as a foreign government lending agency that relends to foreign buyers of capital goods and related services. An example of the latter is a maintenance contract for a jet passenger plane. Both programs cover up to 85 percent of the value of the exported goods and services, with repayment terms of one year or more.

Ex-Im Bank's *Working Capital Guarantee* helps small businesses obtain working capital to cover their export sales. It guarantees working capital loans extended by banks to eligible exporters with exportable inventory or export receivables as collateral. The guarantee provides repayment protection for private sector loans to buyers of U.S. capital equipment and related services.

Ex-Im Bank also offers *export credit insurance*. An exporter may reduce financing risks by purchasing insurance to protect against the political and commercial risks of a foreign buyer's defaulting on payment. The coverage may be comprehensive or be limited to political risk only. Since its inception in 1934, Ex-Im Bank has supported more than $456 billion in American exports, mostly to developing markets.[6]

Other Public Incentives

Other government incentives for trade, although not strictly a part of export financing, are so closely related to it that we mention them here. These are the Overseas Private Investment Corporation and the foreign trade zone.[7]

The **Overseas Private Investment Corporation (OPIC)** is a government corporation formed to stimulate private investment in developing countries. It offers investors insurance against expropriation, currency inconvertibility, and damages from wars or revolutions. OPIC also offers specialized insurance for American service contractors and exporters operating in foreign countries. Exports of capital equipment and semiprocessed raw materials generally follow these investments.

---

banker's acceptance
A time draft with maturity of less than 270 days that has been accepted by the bank on which the draft was drawn, thus becoming the accepting bank's obligation; may be bought and sold at a discount in the financial markets like other commercial paper

factoring
Discounting without recourse an account receivable

forfaiting
Purchasing without recourse an account receivable whose credit terms are longer than the 90 to 180 days usual in factoring; unlike factoring, political and transfer risks are borne by the forfaiter

U.S. Export-Import Bank (Ex-Im Bank)
Principal government agency that aids American exporters by means of loans, guarantees, and insurance programs

Overseas Private Investment Corporation (OPIC)
Government corporation that offers American investors in developing countries insurance against expropriation, currency inconvertibility, and damages from wars and revolutions

Foreign trade zones (FTZs) are duty-free areas designed to facilitate trade by reducing the effect of customs restrictions. These areas may be free ports, transit zones, free perimeters, export processing zones, or free trade zones. In each instance, a specific and limited area is involved, into which imported goods may be brought without the payment of import duties. There are hundreds of these areas in more than 28 countries. Of the five types, the free trade zone is the most common.

The **free trade zone (FTZ)** is an enclosed area considered to be outside the customs territory of the country in which it is located. Goods of foreign origin may be brought into the zone for eventual transshipment, reexportation, or importation into the country. While the goods are in the zone, no import duties need be paid. Examples range from the Zhuhai Free Trade Zone, near Macao in China, to Chabahar in Iran. In the United States, free trade zones often are called foreign trade zones (and the FTZ acronym is used synonymously for both in the United States). They have been growing in popularity, and 250 of these zones, with more than 450 subzones, are now in operation.[8] Many are situated at seaports, but some are located at inland distribution points. Goods brought into the FTZ may be stored, inspected, repackaged, or combined with American components. Because of differences in the import tariff schedule, the finished product often incurs lower duty than would the disassembled parts. Bicycles have been assembled in the Kansas City FTZ for that reason. Importers of machinery and automobiles improve their cash flow by storing spare parts in an FTZ, because duty is not paid until they are withdrawn.

In addition to their advantages to importers, FTZs can also benefit exporters. By using FTZs, exporters may be eligible for accelerated export status in regard to excise tax rebates and **customs drawbacks.** These customs duty rebates are available for items such as tires, trucks, and tobacco products. The federal government collects the tax when the item is manufactured; when it is exported, the tax is rebated. The processing time for tax rebates can be initiated by putting the goods into FTZs because a product is considered exported as soon as it enters the FTZ. Although U.S. Customs has had the duty-drawback program in place for 200 years, many firms do not claim the money they're owed. As a result, each year up to $2 billion in customs duty refunds goes unclaimed.[9] FTZs offer another benefit to exporters: when manufacturing or assembly is done in FTZs using imported components, no duties need ever be paid when the finished product is exported.

Export Procedures

When those new to exporting are concerned about the complexity of export procedures, they are generally referring to documentation. Instead of dealing with the two documents used in domestic shipments, the freight bill and the bill of lading, export novices are suddenly confronted with five to six times as many documents, depending on the country. Table 14.1 summarizes documentation requirements for major locations and the United States.

"Exports move on a sea of documents" is a popular saying in the industry, and it seems an accurate description. Many firms give at least part of this work to a *foreign freight forwarder,* who acts as an agent for the exporter. Foreign freight forwarders prepare documents, book space with a carrier, and in general act as the firm's export traffic department. If asked, they will offer advice about markets, import and export regulations, the best mode of transport, and export packing. They also will supply cargo insurance. After shipment, they forward documents to the importer or to the paying bank, according to the exporter's requirements. We look now at the two basic elements of exporting, the paperwork and the actual transportation of goods. Then, in the next section, we look at import procedures, often the mirror image of export procedures.

EXPORT DOCUMENTS

Correct documentation is vital to the success of any export shipment. Interestingly enough, error rates reported for export and import documentation hover between 50 and 70 percent, largely because they are documents that come from different parties, yet their data need to be consistent.[10] Think of the impact of that statistic—goods waiting in a container, on a dock, or in a warehouse, tying up working capital. We'll review the two sets of documents required to ship and collect goods.

TABLE 14.1 Official Procedures for Exporting and Importing

Region or Economy	Documents for Export (number)	Time for Export (days)	Cost to Export (US$ per container)	Documents for Import (number)	Time for Import (days)	Cost to Import (US$ per Container)
East Asia and Pacific	6.2	22.7	889.8	6.9	24.1	934.7
Eastern Europe and Central Asia	6.4	26.7	1,651.7	7.6	28.1	1,845.4
Latin America and Caribbean	6.6	18.0	1,228.3	7.1	20.1	1,487.9
Middle East and North Africa	6.4	20.4	1,048.9	7.5	24.2	1,229.3
OECD	4.4	10.9	1,058.7	4.9	11.4	1,106.3
South Asia	8.5	32.3	1,511.6	9.0	32.5	1,744.5
United States	4.0	6.0	1,050	5	5	1,315

Source: World Bank, International Finance Corporation, www.doingbusiness.org/data/exploretopics/trading-across-borders (June 16, 2011).

Shipping Documents

Shipping documents are prepared by exporters or their freight forwarders so that the shipment can pass through U.S. Customs, be loaded on the carrier, and be sent to its destination. They include the domestic bill of lading, the export packing list, the shipper's export declaration, the export licenses, the export bill of lading, and the insurance certificate. The first two documents are nearly the same as those used in domestic traffic, so we'll focus here on the other four.

The **shipper's export declaration (SED)** is required by the Department of Commerce to control exports and supply export statistics. An SED contains:

1. Names and addresses of the shipper and consignee.
2. U.S. port of exit and foreign port of unloading.
3. Description and value of the goods.
4. Export license number and bill-of-lading number.
5. Name of the carrier transporting the merchandise.

Shippers or their agents (foreign freight forwarders) deliver the SED to the carrier, which turns it in to U.S. Customs with the carrier's manifest (list of the vessel's cargo) before the carrier leaves the United States. An **automated export system (AES)** with electronic filing was introduced in 2004. Because many errors can be flagged in the system, data entry on the forms has been greatly reduced and export processing has been sped up.

An *export license* from the U.S. federal government is required for all exported goods except those going to U.S. possessions or, with a few exceptions, to Canada. These licenses are either validated or general. A **validated export license** is required for strategic materials and all shipments to unfriendly countries. This is a special authorization for a specific shipment and is issued by the Department of Commerce Office of Export Administration. It is required for scarce materials, strategic goods, and technology. The Department of State issues the validated license for war materials. A **general export license** is used for all products that do not require the validated license.

An **export bill of lading (B/L)** serves three purposes: it functions as a contract for carriage between the shipper and the carrier, a receipt from the carrier for the goods shipped, and a certificate of ownership. B/Ls are either *straight* or *to order*. A straight bill of lading is nonnegotiable. Only the person stipulated in it may obtain the merchandise on arrival. An order bill of lading, however, is negotiable. It can be endorsed like a check or left blank. With an order B/L, the holder is the owner of the merchandise.

The *insurance certificate* is evidence that the shipment is insured against loss or damage while in transit. Unlike domestic carriers, oceangoing steamship companies assume no

shipper's export declaration (SED) U.S. Department of Commerce form used to control export shipments and record export statistics

automated export system (AES) U.S. Customs electronic filing system

validated export license A required document issued by the U.S. government authorizing the export of a strategic commodity or a shipment to an unfriendly country

general export license Any export license covering export commodities for which a validated license is not required; no formal application is required

export bill of lading (B/L)
Contract of carriage between shipper and carrier: straight bill of lading is non-negotiable; endorsed "to order" bill gives the holder claim on merchandise

responsibility for the merchandise they carry unless the loss is caused by their negligence. Marine insurance may be arranged by either the exporter or the importer, depending on the terms of sale. The laws of some countries may require that the importer buy such insurance, thus protecting the local insurance industry and saving foreign exchange. If the exporter has sold on sight draft terms, the firm carries the risk while the goods are in transit. In this case, the exporter should buy contingent interest insurance to protect it in the event that the shipment is lost or damaged and collection from the buyer is not successful. We believe that the exporter selling on CFR terms (the buyer purchases the insurance) should also buy contingent interest insurance to protect itself in case the buyer's insurance does not cover all risks.

There are three kinds of marine insurance policies: basic named perils, broad named perils, and all risks. *Basic named perils* include perils of the sea, fires, jettisons, explosions, and hurricanes. *Broad named perils* include theft, pilferage, nondelivery, breakage, and leakage in addition to the basic perils. *All risks* covers all physical loss or damage from any external cause and is more expensive than the other policies. War risks are covered under a separate contract. Premiums depend on a number of factors, such as the goods insured, the destination, the age of the ship, whether the goods are stowed on deck or under deck, the volume of business, how the goods are packed, and the number of claims the shipper has filed. Brokers will sometimes admit that in the long run, it is preferable not to file numerous small claims, even if justified, because the higher premiums charged for future shipments will be greater than the money recovered.

Collection Documents

The seller is required to provide the buyer with collection documents to receive payment. These documents vary among countries and customers, but some of the most common are invoices, both commercial and consular, certificates of origin, and inspection certificates.

Export invoices are similar to domestic invoices. The commercial invoice includes additional information, such as the origin of the goods, export packing marks, and a clause stating that the goods will not be transshipped to another country. Invoices for letter-of-credit sales name the bank and the credit numbers. Some importing countries require that the commercial invoice be in their language and be visaed or endorsed by their local consul. The *consular invoice* is a special form purchased from the consul, prepared in the language of the country, and then visaed by the consul. Along with the export invoice, many governments require a *certificate of origin,* which is usually issued by the local chamber of commerce and visaed by the consul.

CE (Conformité Européene) mark
EU mark that indicates that the merchandise conforms to European health, safety and environmental requirements

An *inspection certificate* is required frequently by buyers of grain, foodstuffs, and live animals. In the United States, inspection certificates are issued by the Department of Agriculture. Purchasers of machinery or products containing a specified combination of ingredients may insist that an American engineering firm or laboratory inspect the merchandise and certify that it is exactly as ordered. The EU requires the **CE (Conformité Européene) mark** is the European "trade passport": once a product has the mark, it can travel to any other EU member country without modification. This mark indicates that the merchandise conforms to European health, safety, and environmental requirements.[11] The certification process has been streamlined, and most merchandisers can self-certify that their merchandise conforms to EU regulations. Inspection by authorized testing houses is required of hazardous goods.

EXPORT SHIPMENTS

Most newcomers to exporting are so focused on making their sale and handling the documentation that they fail to be concerned about the actual physical movement of their goods. Innovations in material-handling techniques can help exporters reduce costs and perhaps reach markets they previously could not serve. Containerization, LASH, RO-RO, size, and air freight all offer increasingly cheaper, faster, and safer transportation solutions, shrinking our globe.

One means of drastically reducing both theft and handling costs is to use containers. *Containers* are large boxes—8 feet by 8 feet by 10, 20, or 40 feet—that the seller fills with the shipment in the firm's warehouse. Their origins are interesting, as explained in the

The Ethics of Exporting: Do Home Values Apply?

In early 2011, Australia banned the export of Australian cattle to Indonesia after reliable reports of cruelty in Indonesian slaughterhouses came to the attention of the Queensland government. At first glance, this action sounds like a responsible commitment to the humane treatment of animals.

Yet there is a dilemma or two here because there are beef ranchers in Queensland who depend totally on the live export market for their sales. And Indonesia is a huge market for them. One-third of the meat eaten in Indonesia is Australian beef.

In addition, as a result of the ban, there is less food for the 40 million Indonesians who live below the poverty line. "Ah, but they probably don't eat imported beef," you may be thinking. That's true, but when there's less food in the system, the poor will feel the effects first.

Other ethical issues related to exporting also touch on whether the home-country ethics should be upheld for the exports. Should the United Kingdom, which has outlawed the death penalty, export execution drugs to the United States? Should quality standards thought appropriate for the domestic market be maintained for the export markets in areas such as pharmaceuticals?

These issues about the ethics of exporting are the question here. To what degree are ethics domestic and to what degree are they universal? Another way to phrase the question is, Should exports have ethics embedded in them? What do you think?

Sources: *Ethics Newsline*, www.globalethics.org/newsline/2011/06/13/australia-cattle/, June 13, 2011 (accessed June 20, 2011); "British Company Exports Execution Drugs to U.S.," www.ethicsdaily.com/british-company-exports-execution-drugs-to-u-s-cms-17498 (accessed June 20, 2011).

---

chapter's opening story. Once packed, the containers are then sealed; they are opened when the goods arrive at their final destination. Containers are transported by truck or rail from the warehouse to shipside for loading. From the port of entry, railroads or trucks deliver them, often unopened even for customs inspection, to the buyer's warehouse. In most countries, customs officials go to the warehouse to examine the shipment. This integrated process reduces handling time and the risk of damage and theft because the buyer's own employees unload the containers.

If the importer or exporter has a warehouse on a river too shallow for ocean vessels, the firm can save time and expense by loading containers on barges. *LASH* (lighter aboard ship) vessels provide direct access to ocean freight service for exporters and importers located on shallow inland waterways. Sixty-foot-long barges ("lighters") are towed to inland locations, loaded, and towed back to deep water, where they are loaded aboard anchored LASH ships.

Another innovation in cargo handling is *RO-RO* (roll on–roll off) ships. Loaded trailers and any equipment on wheels can be driven onto these specially designed vessels. RO-RO service has brought the benefits of containerization to ports that have been unable to invest in the expensive lifting equipment required for containers.

Ship size continues to expand. Until recently, the standard largest size was "Panamax," which fit through the Panama Canal's locks with only feet to spare. "Post-Panamax" ("Suezmax," "capesize") ships are too big for the canal—nearly 44 feet too wide and more than 200 feet longer than the canal can accept. Some 160 of these ships will be put in operation over the next few years, many to carry Chinese exports. So, Panama must build a third set of even larger locks: work began in 2007 and may be completed by 2015.

Air freight has had a profound effect on international business because it permits shipments that once required 30 days to arrive in 1 day. Huge freight planes carry payloads of 200,000 pounds, most of which goes either in containers or on pallets. Airlines guarantee overnight delivery from New York to many European airports and claim that their planes can be loaded or unloaded in 45 minutes.

Newcomers to exporting might assume that ocean freight is a better choice than air freight because ocean freight is so much cheaper. Comparison of total costs of each mode may suggest otherwise. Total cost components that may be lower for air freight include insurance rates, because of much less chance of damage during shipment; packing costs, because the shipment does not need the heavier, more costly export packing, which is usually done by an outside firm; customs duties, when calculated on gross weights; replacement

TABLE 14.2 Sea-Air Total Cost Comparison, Shipment of Spare Parts

	Ocean Freight (with warehousing)	Air Freight (no warehousing)
Warehouse administrative costs	$1,020	—
Warehouse rent	1,680	—
Inventory costs		
Taxes and insurance	756	$ 396
Inventory financing	288	192
Inventory obsolescence	1,800	0
Seller's warehouse and handling costs	1,810	1,140
Transportation	420	2,400
Packaging and handling	300	120
Cargo insurance	72	36
Customs duties	132	127
Total	$8,278	$4,411

costs for damaged goods, again because of the reduced damage risk; and inventory costs, because the rapid delivery by air freight often eliminates the need for expensive warehouses. For example, Mercedes-Benz includes in the price of its luxury sports car Brabus SLR McLaren air freight from Bottrop, Germany, to anywhere in the world. Another cost saving is that machinery shipped by air does not require a heavy coat of grease to protect it from the elements, as does machinery sent by ship. Table 14.2 provides a sample comparison of the cost elements of ocean and air freight.

Even when the total shipping costs are higher for air freight, shipping by air may still be advantageous for several reasons:

1. *Total cost may decrease.* Getting the product to the buyer more quickly results in a more satisfied customer and faster payment, which speeds up the return on investment and improves cash flow. The firm's capital is released more quickly and can be invested in other profit-making ventures or used to repay borrowed capital, thus reducing interest payments. Production equipment may be assembled and sent by air so that it goes into production sooner, without the transit and setup delays associated with ocean shipments, a strong sales argument. These production and opportunity costs, although difficult to calculate, are part of the total cost.

2. *Either the firm or the product may be air-dependent.* Perishable food products being shipped to Europe, Japan, and the Middle East are in this category, as are live animals (newly hatched poultry and prize bulls) and fresh flowers. Without air freight, firms exporting such products would be out of business.

3. *The market may be perishable.* For goods with short life cycles, such as high-fashion products, delivery speed matters. When a fashion fad dies, its market goes with it.

4. *Competitive position may be strengthened.* The sales argument that spare parts and factory technical personnel are available within a few hours is a strong one for an exporting firm competing with overseas manufacturers.

LO14-6 Identify import sources.

Importing

In one sense, importers are the reverse of exporters: they sell domestically and buy in foreign markets. However, many of their concerns are similar. As in the case of exporters, there are small firms whose only business is to import, and there are global corporations for which importing components and raw materials valued at millions of dollars is just one of their functions. We will examine sources for imports, the role of customhouse brokers, and the payment of import duties here.

SOURCES FOR IMPORTS

Before importing, a firm may have difficulty determining whether the desired items exist and, if so, where to find them. How does the prospective importer identify import sources? There are a number of ways. First, similar imported products may already be in the market. By simple close examination, you can learn where they are made and often by whom. U.S. law requires that the country of origin be clearly marked on each product or on its container if product marking is not feasible (e.g., individual cigarettes). The consul or embassy of the country of origin can help with names of manufacturers. One of the principal duties of all foreign government representatives is to promote exports, and they do this through newsletters, trade shows, industry shows, and collaborative events with their home country chamber of commerce group and other organizations, such as, for Japan, the Japan External Trade Organization (JETRO), which has a number of offices outside Japan. The process is the same if the product is not being imported. You simply have less information with which to begin.

Other sources of information are electronic bulletin boards such as those of the World Trade Centers. Accidental importing also occurs with some frequency. When you visit a foreign country, look for products that may have a market at home. Finding one could put you into a new business, one that makes foreign travel tax-deductible.

Now we turn to some of the technical aspects of importing, customhouse brokers, and import duties.

CUSTOMHOUSE BROKERS

In every nation, there are **customhouse brokers,** whose functions parallel those of foreign freight forwarders but are on the import side of the transaction. As the agent for the importer, the customhouse broker brings the imported goods through customs, which requires that they know well the many import regulations and an extensive, complex tariff schedule. If a customs official places the import in a category requiring higher import duties than the importer had planned on, the importing firm may not be able to compete. To levy customs, evaluators everywhere generally use units shipped for products that carry specific duties and the invoice price for ad valorem duties. There are some exceptions. The practice of U.S. Customs is to use the transaction price, which appears on the commercial invoice accompanying the shipment, plus any other charges not included in the transaction price. These may be royalty or license fees, packing, or any assists. *Assist* is the U.S. Customs term applied to any item that the buyer provides free or at reduced cost for use in the production or sale of merchandise for export to the United States. Examples are molds and dies sent overseas to produce a specific product, a common practice of importers who want the goods produced using their design, and components and parts that the buyer provides for incorporation in the finished article.

Customhouse brokers also provide other services, such as arranging transportation for the goods after they have left customs if the exporter has not arranged for it. They also keep track of which imports are subject to import quotas and how much of the quota has been filled at the time of the import. No matter which port the goods arrive at, U.S. Customs knows immediately the quantity that has been imported. Merchandise subject to import quotas can be on the dock of an American port awaiting clearance through customs, but if the quota fills anywhere during the wait, those goods cannot be imported for the rest of the fiscal year. The would-be importer can put them in a **bonded warehouse** or a foreign trade zone, where merchandise can be stored without paying duty, and wait for the rest of the year; abandon them; or send them to another country. Importers of high-fashion clothing have lost millions of dollars when quotas became filled and they had a shipment that had not yet cleared. They could not sell the clothing until the following year, by which time it was out of fashion.

IMPORT DUTIES

Every importer should know how U.S. Customs calculates import duties and the importance of the product classification system, the **Harmonized Tariff Schedule of the United States (HTSA or HTSUS),** the American version of the global tariff code, the Harmonized

customhouse brokers
Independent businesses that handle import shipments for compensation

bonded warehouse
An area authorized by customs authorities for storage of goods on which payment of import duties is deferred until the goods are removed

Harmonized Tariff Schedule of the United States (HTSA or HTSUS)
American version of the Harmonized System used worldwide to classify imported products

Head of U.S. Export-Import Bank Calls Foul on China, India, and Brazil; Changes Game Rules

Ex-Im President Fed Hochberg recently pointed out that Brazil, India, and China provide export funding, particularly export credit, at levels that violate the export finance rules that bind the G7 and OECD countries. Together, Brazil, China, and India presently provide more export funding than do the combined nations of the G7 (the United States, Japan, France, Germany, Britain, Canada, and Italy).

This aid extended to foreign customers translates into more sales. Chinese telecoms manufacturer Huawei Technologies has experienced impressive market share growth that is based, Hochberg suggests, on a $30 billion credit line from the Chinese Development Bank that allowed it to offer its customers far better financing terms than could its developed nation competitors. "In less than 15 years, they have positioned themselves ahead of global leaders like Nokia and Siemens. In India, Huawei grew to $2.5 billion in sales from $50 million in one year," Hochberg said. "Folks, that kind of growth takes more than just good sales and marketing strategies."

Such Chinese "state-directed capital" threatens U.S. market share in renewable energy, aviation, biotechnology, and capital goods.

Currently, GE has been underbid by China on a lucrative 500-locomotive contract in Pakistan. China offered financing and credit terms that GE could not meet and stay within G7 and OECD rules. Hochberg's response to GE's complaint is to call for a change in the G7 rules so that when there is market distortion caused by state-directed capital, G7 members can respond with competitive support for developed nations' firms. Ex-Im Bank will help GE make this sale, Hochberg vows. Eventually, he thinks, the developing countries will have to renegotiate rules on export financing so that their unfair subsidies don't distort trade.[a] Under his leadership in 2010, his first full year on the job, Ex-Im Bank approved $24.5 billion in export financing, a 70 percent increase over the past two years. It sounds like he means business.

Questions:

1. There is an argument that developing countries ought to be able to maintain their subsidies, the ones to which Hochberg objects, because these countries need advantages to break into and become established in world markets. Do you agree?

2. Should a U.S. taxpayer-supported agency such as the Ex-Im Bank act internationally on behalf of American companies such as GE to support their export sales?

[a]"U.S. Must Confront China Export Advantages," *Reuters*, June 15, 2011, www.reuters.com/article/2011/06/15/us-usa-china-financing-idUSTRE75E6B820110615 (accessed June 17, 2011).

System. The Harmonized System is a classification system for the more than 200,000 commodities traded internationally, and it includes interpretive notes that help determine the classifications.

In HTSA each product has its own unique number. All member-countries use the same system, so it is possible to describe the product in any language by using the first six digits. The other four digits are for use just in the United States. The HTSA also shows the *reporting units,* which U.S. Customs uses in its paperwork. The last three columns have to do with the rate of duty. Rates of duty are broken down into three levels for each item—general, special, and a third-rate level for countries not considered friends of the United States. The HTSA is accessible on the Internet.[12]

New importers would do well to follow this advice: disclose fully to the U.S. Customs Service all foreign and financial arrangements before passing the goods through U.S. Customs. The penalties for fraud are high. Get the advice of a customhouse broker *before* making the transaction. Frequently, a simple change in the product description can result in a much lower import duty. For example, jeans carry higher duties if the label is outside the back pocket instead of under the belt. If the words on the label are stylized, the duties are higher as well. Any clothing that is ornamented has higher duty. One importer brings in plain sports shirts and then sews on an animal figure after the products are in the United States. One last word of advice: calculate carefully the landed price in advance. If you are unsure of the import category, ask U.S. Customs to determine the category in advance and to put it in writing, just like advanced rulings from the Internal Revenue Service. At the time of importation, customs inspectors must respect this determination.

Vadim Rozhkov: International All the Way!

I was born in Ekaterinburg, Russia. I enjoy active sports, surfing, rally, boxing, and hiking. My hobbies include history, travel, applied science, and listening to classical music. I have a BS degree in mechanical engineering from Ural State University in Russia; I then earned a BS in electrical engineering, MS in industrial technology, and MBA from California Polytechnic State University in San Luis Obispo.

My interest in international business came up a bit unexpectedly, a result of my interest in global heavy industries and their involvement in international trade and politics. Studying for my MBA gave me a better understanding of global trade, including knowledge about the economic aspects of manufacturing and production, price formation, and cross-border tariffs.

I am a sales manager, involved directly in business-to-business sales. Sales managers at my company are given different countries of responsibility, and my assigned countries include Italy, Germany, and Mexico.

My job is to identify and contact a circle of potential customers—namely, companies that purchase tooling for operating large-scale metallurgical mills. I use an information-based approach to identifying customers. First, I trace metals prices on the LME (London Metal Exchange), and I usually have a good idea of the average price for my product in my assigned countries. Then I contact and visit representatives from these companies' technical maintenance, engineering, and purchasing departments. After the initial meeting, where I am given drawings and specifications of the product they are interested in, I work with my company's accounting department to calculate manufacturing costs, and I determine logistics and insurance expenses (I am in constant contact with different shipping companies). It usually takes a few days to come up with a final quote for the product and a delivery option. Most of my customers request CIF Incoterms, which means my company as the seller pays the cost, insurance, and freight associated with shipping goods to the destination port. Then this quote is sent to my customer. If my customer accepts the price and delivery options, a purchasing/manufacturing contract is signed.

I visit a potential customer only when I am sure that I am well prepared for the trip, that the customer is expecting me, and that the topic of the visit is clearly laid out and ready for discussion. I usually have phone conversations in advance with the people I intend to meet during my visit. Not only do I know the financial aspect of a possible deal, I also come very well prepared technically. I study the products my customers use. I know how my products are installed and operated within complex, large-scale metallurgical mills. It is very important that my customers see that I have deep technical understanding of the products I am selling. I also study my competitors. I know the strong and weak points of their products, and I am knowledgeable about their business policies.

The biggest challenge of my job is coming to agreement with my international customers on common terms for the purchase. Cultural differences play a big role in dealing with people overseas and understanding the ways that people conduct their business in a particular country is crucially important. For example, as a result of my numerous business trips to Mexico, I have learned to respect the local pace of life. Sometimes rushing things will not necessarily make things happen more quickly!

The greatest enjoyment of my job, so far, was signing my first contract for supplying tooling to a company in Mexico. Actually, I was ecstatic, because it took me two years of work and relationship-building effort before this contract finally came through.

Doing business internationally teaches you a few great things. Patience is one of them. After all, you are a guest and a foreign business representative. Simply put, you are asking for a part of their business and you need them more than they need you.

In my opinion, to be successful in international business, you need common sense, cultural respect, and extensive knowledge of the subject or business area in which you are working. As for what *not* to do: never leave your customer aggravated, despite how ridiculous their suggestions or demands may seem. Even if you don't sign a deal today, make sure you will be able to come back tomorrow and have a friendly conversation with your potential customer.

Resources for Your Global Career

Consider a Job in Import/Export Management for Entry into International Business

With the growing volume of shipments between countries daily, there is demand for people to work in entry-level positions in import/export management. Managing the movement of products into and out of countries is a fundamental task in international trade, and job opportunities exist in every type of business dealing with foreign customers or suppliers and in size ranging from small businesses to *Fortune* 500 companies. To succeed in import/export management, you will need to know about the fundamentals of business; customer service; international business considerations; purchasing; marketing; import/export operations; and documentation for licenses, bills of lading, insurance, domestic and foreign country customs laws, and international trade regulations for the countries in which the importer/exporter is dealing. Language skills would be valuable. Entry-level salaries are in the range of $31,000 to $42,000, mid-level salaries are between $46,000 and $64,000, and top-level import/export manager salaries are between $69,000 and $96,000+ based on experience. Import/export management jobs can be found in or at the following:

- Import/export houses.
- International trading companies.
- Manufacturers of all sizes trading internationally.
- Wholesalers importing or exporting products.
- The corporate level for retail chains.

(continued)

- Purchasing departments for international companies.
- Customhouse brokers.
- Freight forwarders.
- Supply chain management organizations.
- Airlines and ocean shipping firms.

To advance your career and move into higher levels of import/export management, with greater responsibility, salary, and job mobility, you may want to earn the U.S. Customs Broker License:

www.cbp.gov/xp/cgov/trade/trade_programs/broker/brokers.xml
www.ncbfaa.org/About/content.cfm?ItemNumber=2302

Your Worldwide Resources on Import/Export Operations:

- In-depth information on import/export marketing: www.export911.com/
- Glossary of trade terms, shipping terms, ex-im terms, and trade laws: www.fibre2fashion.com/texterms/exim/exim_terms1.htm
- Your import/export library: www.the-acr.com/ie/library.htm
- Guide to starting your own import/export business: http://importexportcoach.com
- U.S. government import/export resources: http://export.gov
- International Trade Administration: http://trade.gov/index.asp
- U.S. Export Administration: www.access.gpo.gov/bis/
- U.S. Government Export Portal: www.export.gov/

- Bureau of Industry and Security: www.bis.doc.gov/exportlicensingqanda.htm
- Export Information Database: www.access.gpo.gov/bis/ear/ear_data.html
- Department of Commerce Export Controls: www.bis.doc.gov/licensing/exportingbasics.htm
- Resources for planning for import/export operations:
  - http://sbinfocanada.about.com/od/canadaexport/a/10exportsteps.htm
  - http://sbinfocanada.about.com/cs/marketing/a/export-markplan.htm
  - www.canadabusiness.ca/eng/105/
- Exporting information from Austrade, the Australian government's Office of Export Management and Assistance (see the checklist): www.austrade.gov.au/Getting-ready-for-export/default.asp
- Export compliance issues:
  - www.ytsbest.com/EXPORT-ADMINISTRATION-REGULATIONS-%28EAR%29-CLASSIFICATION-PROCESS-.html
  - www.exportcompliance.com/import-controls.html
  - www.exportcompliance.com/export-controls.html
  - www.exportcompliance.com/landed-cost-calculator.html
- Export articles, data and statistics: www.wisertrade.org/home/index.jsp?content=/news.jsp

Summary

LO14-1 Identify the sources of export counseling and support.

The Trade Information Center, Small Business Administration, Small Business Development Centers, Department of Agriculture, state offices for export assistance, and World Trade Centers Association are some sources of export counseling. The Department of Commerce, the federal department in charge of export assistance, offers many programs covering all aspects of exporting. Commerce also assists in locating foreign representatives and making sales through trade fairs, matchmaker programs, and catalog and video shows.

LO14-2 Discuss the meaning of the various terms of sale known as Incoterms.

There are 11 Incoterms used to describe the terms of sale in import/export transactions. Seven apply to general transportation, and four are reserved for water transportation. The general transportation terms are Ex-Works (named place), where

the seller makes goods available at factory or warehouse; FCA (named place), free carrier, where the seller hands over goods to carrier at a named place; CPT (named destination), where carriage is paid to destination, while risk passes when goods are handed to carrier; CIP (named place of destination), where carriage and insurance are paid to destination, while risk passes when goods are handed to carrier; DAT, where goods are delivered at terminal and seller pays for transport and insurance to terminal and has risk until goods loaded at terminal; DAP, where goods are delivered at place (name of destination) and the seller pays for carriage to the named place and assumes all risk until goods are unloaded; and DDP (destination place), where goods are delivers goods to destination and covers all duties, taxes, customs. The water transport terms include FAS (named loading port), where the goods are free alongside ship and the seller clears the goods for export and places them by the ship; FOB (named loading port), where the goods are free on board and the seller loads goods, with risk passing at rail; CFR (named destination port), where cost and freight is covered by seller and risk passes once goods are loaded; and, finally, CIF (named destination port), which is the same as CFR, but includes insurance. Risk still passes at ship's rail.

LO14-3 Identify some sources of export financing.

Some sources of export financing are commercial banks, factors, forfaiting, the Export-Import Bank (Ex-Im Bank), and the Small Business Administration.

LO14-4 Describe the activities of a foreign freight forwarder.

Foreign freight forwarders act as agents for exporters. They prepare documents, book space on carriers, and function as a firm's export traffic department.

LO14-5 Outline the export documents required.

Correct documentation is vital to the success of any export shipment. Shipping documents include export packing lists, export licenses, export bills of lading, shipper's export declaration, and insurance certificates. Collection documents include commercial invoices, consular invoices, certificates of origin, and inspection certificates.

LO14-6 Identify import sources.

Prospective importers can identify sources in a number of ways. They can examine the product label to see where the product is made and then contact the nearest embassy of that country to request the name of the manufacturer. Foreign chambers of commerce and trade organizations provide information on their countries' exporters. Electronic bulletin boards and data banks are also useful.

Key Words

terms of sale (p. 345)

Incoterms (p. 345)

letter of credit (L/C) (p. 346)

confirmed L/C (p. 347)

irrevocable L/C (p. 347)

air waybill (p. 347)

pro forma invoice (p. 347)

export, sight, and time drafts (p. 350)

banker's acceptance (p. 351)

factoring (p. 351)

forfaiting (p. 351)

U.S. Export-Import Bank (Ex-Im Bank) (p. 351)

Overseas Private Investment Corporation (OPIC) (p. 351)

foreign trade zone (FTZ) (p. 352)

free trade zone (FTZ) (p. 352)

customs drawbacks (p. 352)

shipper's export declaration (SED) (p. 353)

automated export system (AES) (p. 353)

validated export license (p. 353)

general export license (p. 353)

export bill of lading (B/L) (p. 354)

CE (Conformité Européene) mark (p. 354)

customhouse broker (p. 357)

bonded warehouse (p. 357)

Harmonized Tariff Schedule of the United States (HTSA or HTSUS) (p. 357)

Questions

1. In exporting, to what point does the seller pay transportation and delivery costs? Where does the responsibility for loss or damage pass to the buyer? Use Incoterms in your response.

2. Explain the various export payment terms that are available and the protection they offer the seller.

3. What is the procedure for a letter-of-credit transaction?

4. The manager of the international department of the Cape Cod Five Bank learns on the way to work that the ship on which a local exporter shipped some goods to Spain (Wellfleet oysters in salt-water tanks) has sunk in high seas. She has received all the documents required in the letter of credit and is ready to pay the exporter for the shipment. In view of the news about the ship, the manager now knows that the Spanish customer will never receive the goods. Should the manager pay the exporter, or should she withhold payment and notify the overseas customer?

5. What is a foreign trade zone? Check with a customhouse broker or a U.S. Customs official or do some online research to determine the advantages of a foreign trade zone over a bonded warehouse.

6. What are the purposes of an export bill of lading?

7. An importer brings plain sports shirts into the U.S. because the import duty is lower than it is for shirts with adornments. In New Jersey, the importer sews on a figure of a fox. Could the importer do this operation in a foreign trade zone?

8. How would you find sources for a product that you want to import?

9. What does a customhouse broker do?

10. What does a freight forwarder do?

Use the globalEDGE site (http://globalEDGE.msu.edu/) to complete the following exercises:

1. You own a small business and, for the first time, are considering exporting. As a new exporter, you want to consult several resources that offer guidance on how to export. Locate the "Trade Tutorials" category on globalEDGE, and identify three sources that you could use to learn more about *exporting*. Provide a description of the services available for new exporters through each of these sources.

2. Your company is planning to expand its operations to Spain. Because countries have different import requirements, top management has requested a report on Spain's procedures and regulations for imports. Utilize FedEx Country Profiles provided by the FedEx International Resource Center to find the information requested.

Minicase: State Manufacturing Export Sales Price

State Manufacturing Company, a producer of farm equipment, had just received an inquiry from a large distributor in Italy. The quantity on which the distributor wanted a price was sufficiently large that Jim Mason, the sales manager, felt he had to respond. He knew the inquiry was genuine, because he had called two of the companies that the distributor said he represented, and both had assured him that the Italian firm, Agricole Italiana, was a serious one. It paid its bills regularly with no problems. Both companies were selling to the firm on open account terms.

Mason's problem was that he had never quoted on a sale for export before. His first impulse was to take the regular Ex Works price and add the cost of the extra-heavy export packing plus the inland freight cost to the nearest U.S. port. This price should enable the company to make money if he quoted the price FAS port of exit.

However, the terms of sale were bothering him. The traffic manager had called a foreign freight forwarder to learn about the frequency of sailings to Italy, and during the conversation she had suggested to the traffic manager that she might be able to help Mason. When Mason called her, he learned that because of competition, many firms like State Manufacturing were quoting CIF foreign port as a convenience to the importer. She asked him what payment terms he would quote, and he replied that his credit manager had suggested an irrevocable, confirmed letter of credit to be sure of receiving payment for the sale. He admitted that the distributor, however, had asked for payment against a 90-day time draft.

The foreign freight forwarder urged Mason to consider quoting CIF port of entry in Italy with payment as requested by the distributor to be more competitive. She informed him that he could get insurance to protect the company against commercial risk. To help him calculate a CIF price, she offered to give him the various charges if he would tell her the weight and value of his shipment FOB factory. He replied that the total price was $21,500 and that the gross weight, including the container, was 3,629 kilos.

Two hours later, she called to give him the following charges:

1. Containerization	$ 200.00
2. Inland freight less handling	798.00
3. Forwarding and documentation	90.00
4. Ocean freight	2,633.00
5. Commercial risk insurance	105.00
6. Marine insurance (total of items 1–5 × 1.1 = $27,858.60 at 60¢/$100)*	167.15

*Total coverage of marine insurance is commonly calculated on the basis of the total price plus 10 percent.

During that time, Mason had been thinking about the competition. Could he lower the FOB price for an export sale? He looked at the cost figures. Sales expense amounted to 20 percent of the sales price. Couldn't this be deducted on a foreign order? Research and development amounted to 10 percent. Should this be charged? Advertising and promotional expense amounted to another 10 percent. What about that? Because this was an unsolicited inquiry, there was no selling expense for this sale except for his and the secretary's time. Mason felt that it wasn't worth calculating this time.

If you were Jim Mason, how would you calculate the CIF port of entry price?

Appendix: Sample Outline for the Export Business Plan

I. Purpose—Why has the plan been written?

II. Table of contents—Include a list of any appendixes.

III. Executive summary—This is short and concise (not longer than two pages) and covers the principal points of the report. It is prepared after the plan has been written.

IV. Introduction—Explains why the firm will export.

V. Situation analysis.

  A. Description of the firm and products to be exported.

  B. Company resources to be used for the export business.

  C. Competitive situation in the industry.

    1. Product comparisons.

    2. Market coverage.

    3. Market share.

  D. Export organization—personnel and structure.

VI. Export marketing plan.

  A. Long- and short-term goals.

    1. Total sales in units.

    2. Total sales in dollars.

    3. Sales by product lines.

    4. Market share.

    5. Profit and loss forecasts.

  B. Characteristics of ideal target markets.

    1. GNP/capita.

    2. GNP/capita growth rate.

    3. Size of target market.

  C. Identify, assess, and select target markets.

    1. Market contact programs.

      (a) U.S. Department of Commerce.

      (b) World Trade Centers.

      (c) Chamber of Commerce.

      (d) Company's bank.

      (e) State's export assistance program.

      (f) Small Business Administration.

      (g) Small Business Development Center in local university.

      (h) Export hotline directory.

    2. Market screening.

      (a) First screening—basic need potential.

      (b) Second screening—financial and economic forces.

        (1) GNP/capita growth rate.

        (2) Size of target market.

        (3) Growth rate of target market.

        (4) Exchange rate trends.

        (5) Trends in inflation and interest rates.

      (c) Third screening—political and legal forces.

        (1) Import restrictions.

        (2) Product standards.

        (3) Price controls.

        (4) Government and public attitude toward buying American products.

      (d) Fourth screening—sociocultural forces.

        (1) Attitudes and beliefs.

        (2) Education.

        (3) Material culture.

        (4) Languages.

      (e) Fifth screening—competitive forces.

        (1) Size, number, and financial strength of competitors.

        (2) Competitors' market shares.

        (3) Effectiveness of competitors' marketing mixes.

        (4) Levels of after-sales service.

        (5) Competitors' market coverage— Can market segmentation produce niches that are now poorly attended?

      (f) Field trips to best prospects.

        (1) Department of Commerce trade mission.

        (2) Trade missions organized by state or trade association.

  D. Export marketing strategies.

    1. Product lines to export.

    2. Export pricing methods.

3. Channels of distribution.
   (a) Direct exporting.
   (b) Indirect exporting.
4. Promotion methods.
5. After-sales and warranty policies.
6. Buyer financing methods.
7. Methods for ongoing competitor analysis.
8. Sales forecast.

VII. Export financial plan.
 A. Pro forma profit and loss statement.
 B. Pro forma cash flow analysis.
 C. Break-even analysis.

VIII. Export performance evaluation.
 A. Frequency.
  1. Markets.
  2. Product lines.
  3. Export personnel.
 B. Variables to be measured.
  1. Sales by units and dollar volume in each market.
  2. Sales growth rates in each market.
  3. Product line profitability.
  4. Market share.
  5. Competitors' efforts in each market.
  6. Actual results compared to budgeted results.

Marketing Internationally

A global company should always go about its business in a way that's responsive to the major differences from one country to another, in terms of, for example, how retailing or distribution or payment systems work. But the core product or service should remain unchanged, . . . since that is what is 'globalized.'

—*Theodore Levitt, author of the landmark* Harvard Business Review *piece on standardization, "The Globalization of Markets"*

But when it comes to questions of taste and, especially, aesthetic preference, consumers do not like averages. . . . The lure of a universal product is a false allure.

—*Kenichi Ohmae, corporate strategist and author*

Mongolia Joins Our Century

Mongolia, twice the size of Texas and stuck between Russia and China, seems a jumble of contradictions. These contradictions can be seen clearly in the capital of Ulan Bator, where half the population of the country lives, and where the hillsides are covered by the gers, a kind of yurt or portable dwelling, of 700,000 destitute former nomads.

In 1993, a statue of Lenin was removed from the capital's Sukhbattor Square. This statue has been replaced by . . . a Louis Vuitton store! Because of Mongolia's vast natural resources and China's voracious appetite for raw materials, Mongolia has grown a few thousand people who can afford luxury goods. And that, says Louis Vuitton CEO Yves Carcelle, is enough. "One to two thousand people is all you need. You can't judge by average income—average doesn't mean anything."

A few hundred miles south in Beijing, the numbers are much larger scale. British luxury fashion house Burberry is outfitting its stores with digital technology, including customer touchscreens the size of full-length mirrors. China will become the world's largest market for luxury goods by 2020, and the fashion houses are pouring in.

Sources: Laurie Burkitt, "Burberry Dresses Up China Stores with Digital Strategy," *The Wall Street Journal*, April 14, 2011, B9; and Maureen Orth, "The Luxury Frontier," *WSJ Magazine*, July/August 2011, pp. 60–67.

learning objectives

After reading this chapter, you should be able to:

LO15-1 **Explain** why there are differences between domestic and international marketing.

LO15-2 **Discuss** why international marketing managers may wish to standardize the marketing mix.

LO15-3 **Explain** why it is often impossible to standardize the marketing mix worldwide.

LO15-4 **Discuss** the importance of distinguishing among the total product, the physical product, and the brand name.

LO15-5 **Explain** why consumer products generally require greater modification for international sales than do industrial products or services.

LO15-6 **Discuss** the product strategies that can be formed from three product alternatives and three kinds of promotional messages.

LO15-7 **Discuss** some of the effects the Internet may have on international marketing.

LO15-8 **Explain** "glocal" advertising strategies.

LO15-9 **Discuss** the distribution strategies of international marketers.

367

Whether a policy or technique is first designed for global use and then adapted for local market differences or the idea comes from the home country and then is used overseas, marketers must know where to look for possible differences between marketing domestically and marketing internationally. Sometimes the differences are great; at other times, there may be few or even no differences. Marketers everywhere must know their markets; develop products or services to satisfy their customers' needs; price the products or services so that they are readily acceptable in the market; make them available to buyers; and inform potential customers, persuading them to buy.

Added Complexities of International Marketing

LO15-1 Explain why there are differences between domestic and international marketing.

Although the basic functions of domestic and international marketing are the same, the international markets served often differ widely because of the great variations in the uncontrollable environmental forces—sociocultural, resource and environmental, economic and socioeconomic, legal, and financial—that we examined in Section Two. Moreover, even the forces we think of as controllable vary across markets within wide limits. For example, distribution channels to which the marketer is accustomed may be unavailable. This is the case in Japan and in China. Certain aspects of the product may need to be different, for a number of reasons that range from taste and aesthetic preferences to voltage patterns and altitude issues. Then, too, the promotional mixes often must be dissimilar. Finally, distinct cost structures of specific markets may require that different prices be set.

The international marketing manager's task is complex. She or he frequently must plan and control a variety of marketing strategies, rather than a single unified and standardized one, and then coordinate and integrate those strategies into a single marketing program. Even marketing managers of global firms, who may want to use a single worldwide strategy, realize that doing so is impossible. They must know enough about the uncontrollable variables to be able to make quick and decisive implementation changes when necessary.

Both global and multinational marketing managers, much like their domestic counterparts, have the same general challenges. They must develop marketing strategies by assessing the firm's potential foreign markets and analyzing the many alternative marketing mixes. Their aim here is to select target markets that the firm can serve at a profit and then to formulate combinations of tactics for product, price, promotion, and distribution channels that will best serve those markets. We have examined the market assessment and selection process in the international domain; in this chapter, we shall study the formulation of the marketing mix for the international environment.

The Marketing Mix (What to Sell and How to Sell It)

marketing mix A set of strategy decisions made in the areas of product, promotion, pricing, and distribution in order to satisfy the needs and desires of customers in a target market

The **marketing mix** is a set of strategy decisions made in the areas of product, promotion, pricing, and distribution in order to satisfy the needs and desires of customers in a target market. The number of variable factors included in these four marketing areas is large, making possible hundreds of combinations. Often a company's domestic operation has already established a successful marketing mix, and the temptation to follow the same strategies and tactics overseas is strong. Yet, as we have seen, important differences between the domestic and foreign environments are likely to make a wholesale transfer of the mix—its standardization—impossible, however desirable such a transfer may be from a cost viewpoint. The question that the international marketing manager must resolve for each market is, "Can we standardize worldwide, should we make some changes, or should we formulate a completely different marketing mix?"

STANDARDIZE, ADAPT, OR FORMULATE ANEW?

LO15-2 Discuss why international marketing managers may wish to standardize the marketing mix.

Often, top management would prefer to standardize the marketing mix globally; that is, the strategic decision makers would prefer to use the same marketing mix in all of the firm's markets because standardization can produce significant cost savings. If the product sold in the domestic market can be exported, regardless of where the product is made, there can be longer production runs, which lower manufacturing costs. In addition to these economies of scale, the longer experience curve, or learning curve, can create economies as well: the more experience we have doing something, the better we get at that activity, usually. Both of these economies, scale and experience, apply to marketing. A standardized approach can result in significant savings.

When advertising campaigns, promotional materials (catalogs, point-of-purchase displays), and sales training programs can be standardized, the expensive creative work and artwork need be done only once. A standardized corporate visual identity (CVI) (firm name, slogan, and graphics) can help project a consistent image for a multinational with publics dispersed across geographic locales.[1] Standardized pricing strategies for firms that serve markets from several different subsidiaries prevent the embarrassment of having an important customer receive two different price quotations for the same product. In summary, in addition to the cost benefits from standardization of the marketing mix, control and coordination are easier, and time spent preparing the marketing plan is reduced significantly. For example, in 2009, Levi's standardized the fit of its 501 jeans worldwide, rather than have the fit vary by country, and launched its first global ad campaign.

In spite of the advantages of standardization, almost all firms find that this chapter's opening quote by Kenichi Ohmae is accurate for them: standardization is seldom as easy as it seems. Many firms find it necessary to modify the present marketing mix or develop a new one. The extent of the changes depends on the type of product, the environmental forces, and the degree of market penetration desired. Further, because the very concept of standardization is in a state of tension with the marketing principle—which centers on the needs of the buyer, not the seller—we probably should not be too disappointed that the economies that would come with complete standardization are seldom available to the seller, especially the seller in consumer goods.

Even Coca-Cola, the firm often portrayed as the exemplar of the standardized product, found that its increasingly standardized strategy had run its course. According to Coca-Cola's former chairman, Douglas Daft, "As the [20th] century was drawing to a close, the world had

LO15-3 **Explain** why it is often impossible to standardize the marketing mix worldwide.

Choosing not to market locally, Levi's 501 jeans are cut to fit the same way in every country.

Integrating Functions for New-Product Development

For a model of the pace of innovation, consider Moore's Law—the annual doubling of computer power or data storage capacity. Computing power and storage capacity increased exponentially from 1890 (with punch-card computing) to today, across countless technologies and human dramas.

As the pace of innovation continues to expand, the R&D function of the firm needs to expand in two directions. One is within the firm, by cooperating more closely both with production (which is where R&D meets the "rest of the firm" in terms of translating their ideas into products), and with marketing, (which is the firm's transition point with the outside environment, especially customers). The other direction of expansion, into new markets, is shown vertically in the accompanying figure. Expansion abroad can contribute to all three functions. Production, R&D and Marketing can each gain from expansion into new markets.

Gains from Expansion

Some suggest that while the information technology (IT) industry allowed for easy separation of design function in the United States and production in China (Apple is a good example), R&D, design, and production may be harder to separate in today's emerging technology sectors than they are in the IT industry. Most of the promising R&D and innovation in solar power involves cheaper and more efficient ways of manufacturing photovoltaics, a relatively mature technology. Companies such as China's Suntech Power Holdings Company have become major players in solar power by leveraging advanced manufacturing technologies, while others, such as the startup 1366 Technologies, are developing new ways of making solar cells that could dramatically redefine the costs of the technology. In both cases, the innovation is in the manufacturing.

There is a close connection between R&D and manufacturing in many of the emerging sectors because modularization just may not work as well for these technologies as it has for IT. R&D engineers may have to stay close to manufacturing to develop new strategies for making processes more efficient. The tighter integration of innovation and production may also present opportunities to bring design closer to end users, as advanced manufacturing technologies make it possible to produce higher-value goods at lower volume.

If firms need to keep production closely connected to their front-end innovative activities in order to bring new products and processes to the market, is that something that can be done in the United States? The advances we see emerging in areas like energy, life sciences, transportation, environment,

changed course, and we had not. The world was demanding greater flexibility, responsiveness and local sensitivity, while we were further consolidating decision making and standardizing our practices. . . . The next big evolutionary step of 'going global' now has to be 'going local.'"[2] The tuition for Coke's learning was its loss of international market share to its competition, both global and local.

PRODUCT STRATEGIES

LO15-4 Discuss the importance of distinguishing among the total product, the physical product, and the brand name.

The product is the central focus of the marketing mix. If it fails to satisfy the needs of consumers, no amount of promotion, price-cutting, or convenient distribution will persuade people to buy. Consumers will not repurchase a detergent, for example, if the clothes do not come out as clean as commercials say they will.

In formulating product strategies, international marketing managers must remember that the product is more than a physical object. The **total product,** which is what the customer buys, includes the physical product, brand name, accessories, after-sales service, warranty, instructions for use, company image, and package (see Figure 15.1). That the total product is what the customer purchases may present the company with product adaptation opportunities that are less expensive and easier than would be the case if every adaptation had to alter the product's physical characteristics. Different package sizes and promotional messages, for example, can create a new total product for a distinct market. The relative ease of creating a new total product without changing the manufacturing process explains why there is more physical product standardization internationally than one might expect. Remember that a product can be localized by adaptation of the package, brand name, accessories, after-sales service, warranty, instructions for use, and company image.

total product

What the customer buys, including the physical product, brand name, accessories, after-sales service, warranty, instructions for use, company image, and package

communication, construction, and security promise to transform modern economy and society. But it may well be that only those countries that can build powerful links between laboratory research and new manufacturing will be able to derive full benefit from their innovative capabilities. New manufacturing may not mean a larger manufacturing sector with large numbers of added jobs, but it certainly could mean radical change in the technologies and business models we have now.

Of course, one concern with expansion of R&D activities into other countries is the possibility for industrial espionage. The recent slate of hacking incidents (country versus country, company versus country, and company versus company) reminds us that this isn't a concept relegated to the past. But it also tells us that "staying at home" doesn't offer much security.

In fact, the Pentagon—and businesses—are fighting on a new front, created by two sources. Iran, unwilling to tolerate Western ideas, culture and influence in cyberspace, has begun building a "national" Internet to supplant the internationally controlled Internet we all use. And hackers—possibly from a variety of countries—have forced the Pentagon and private businesses to reconsider when an attack constitutes an "act of war." Iran intends that within two years, its government-controlled network will extend across the entire country, and expects that other Islamic countries will adopt its network. The country may also soon have its own operating system to replace Windows. At first "both Internets" will work in parallel: Myanmar, Cuba, and North Korea also already have dual Internet structures.

One reason for this development may be the success of hackers in disrupting Iran's nuclear program. Called "Stuxnet," the worm caused some of Iran's nuclear equipment to self-destruct. Although Iran blames the United States and Israel, the U.S. Pentagon has reacted to Stuxnet by reviewing the definition

of an "act of war." Sentiment seems to be that, if a hacker attack or worm causes damages similar to those of a physical attack, the worm is equivalent to an "act of war" and retaliation, including military action, is justified. Google announced that China attempted to compromise Gmail accounts of senior White House officials, Chinese activists, and others.

For businesses, danger looms as well. Some hack attacks—such as a prank that altered a Public Broadcasting System website to report that rapper Tupac Shakur, murdered 15 years ago, is alive in New Zealand—are less serious. But attacks on banks, defense contractor Lockheed, South Korean credit card provider Hyundai Card, and entertainment giant Sony Corporation promise to have wider repercussions. The hackers attempted to extract a ransom for a database of 1.7 million customers they stole from Hyundai Card; at Sony, hackers temporarily disabled its online PlayStation Network.

Questions:

1. Under what, if any, conditions should governments consider hacking "an act of war"?

2. If R&D and production need to be closely integrated, how might offshoring be affected?

Sources: Christopher Rhoads and Farnaz Fasshi, "Iran Vows to Unplug Internet," *The Wall Street Journal*, May 28–29, 2011, pp. Ai, A12; S Gorman and Julian E. Barnes, "Cyber Combat: Act of War," *The Wall Street Journal*, May 31, 2011, pp. A1, A2; Ben Worthen, Russell Adams, Nathan Hodge and Evan Ramstad, "Hackers Broaden Their Attacks," *The Wall Street Journal*, May 31, 2011, pp. B1, B2; Devlin Barrett and Siobhan Gorman, "Gmail Attack Targeted White House," *The Wall Street Journal*, June 3, 2011, pp. B1, B2; and Suzanne Berger, "Why Manufacturing Matters," www.technologyreview.com/business/37932/page2/ (accessed July 4, 2011).

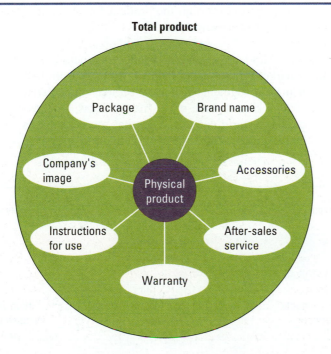

Total product

FIGURE 15.1

Components of the Total Product

Package

Brand name

Company's image

Accessories

Physical product

Instructions for use

After-sales service

Warranty

To illustrate the concept of total product, consider three consumer products: tonic water, chocolate, and instant coffee. Tonic water is a global product physically, but as a total product, it is multidomestic because people in different markets buy it for different reasons. The French drink tonic water straight, while the English mix it with alcohol. Chocolate is neither a global physical product nor a global total product; it is eaten as a snack in some areas, put in sandwiches in others, and eaten as a dessert elsewhere. Because of strong local preferences, it also varies greatly in taste, going from its pure, bitter taste to a quite sweet taste or a taste with some heat, depending on what is added to it. In the case of instant coffee, Nestlé produces it in different blends, across the world, all of which are sold under the same brand name: Nescafé. There is brand-name globalization and physical product localization. The worldwide slogan is "1 Now, 1 Nescafé."[3]

LO15-5 Explain why consumer products generally require greater modification for international sales than do industrial products or services.

Type of Product   The amount of change to be made in a product is affected by whether it is a consumer or industrial product or service and by the foreign environmental forces. Generally, consumer products require greater adaptation than do industrial products. If the consumer products are stylish or the result of a fad, they are especially likely to require changes. These product types form a continuum ranging from insensitive to the foreign environment to highly sensitive, as shown in Figure 15.2.

Industrial Products   As Figure 15.2 suggests, many industrial products can be sold unchanged worldwide. Memory chips, for example, are used wherever computers are manufactured, and there is no "cultural content" in nuts and bolts.

When product adaptations are necessary, they may be relatively simple ones, such as lengthening bicycle pedals and changing seat positions to compensate for consumer preferences among markets. However, somewhat more drastic modifications in the physical product may be necessary. In developing countries, there is a tendency to both overload equipment and overlook its maintenance. To overcome these market differences, manufacturers such as Caterpillar and Allis-Chalmers established training programs as a part of the total product purchase wherever their products are sold. The other alternative is to modify the equipment, perhaps using a simpler bearing system that requires little maintenance.

Adaptations are occasionally necessary to meet local legal requirements, such as those that govern noise, safety, or exhaust emissions. To avoid the need to change the product, some manufacturers design it to meet the most stringent laws even though it will be overdesigned for the rest of its markets. In some instances, governments have passed strict laws with the intent of protecting a local manufacturer from import competition. When this occurs, the company may prefer to design the product for the country with the next most stringent laws and stay out of the first market.

Consumer Products   Although consumer products generally require greater modification to meet local market requirements than do industrial products, some can be sold unchanged to certain market segments that have similar characteristics across countries. Consumer products of this kind include many luxury items, such as champagne and perfumes. Every country in the world contains a market segment that is more similar to the same segment in other countries with respect to economic status, buyer behavior, tastes,

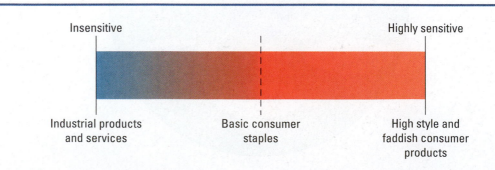

FIGURE 15-2

Continuity of Sensitivity to the Foreign Environment

Insensitive   Highly sensitive

Industrial products   Basic consumer   High style and
and services   staples   faddish consumer
                                                      products

and preferences than it is to the rest of the segments in the same country. This market segment includes the cosmopolitan consumers: foreign-educated and well-traveled citizens and expatriates. Many products and services foreign to local tastes and preferences have been successfully introduced in a number of countries by first being marketed to these similar groups. Gradually, members of other market segments have purchased these products and services until consumption has become widespread.

While "jet-setters" may share much in common across countries, marketers tend to find greater dissimilarities in social and cultural values as they go down the economic strata in each country. It follows from this that, in general, the deeper the desired immediate market penetration is, the greater must be the product modification. Remember that this observation does not suggest that for deeper market penetration, the physical product has to be changed. Perhaps a modification of one of the other elements of the total product is sufficient—a different size or color of the package, a change in the brand name, or a new positioning, if the product is consumed differently. Different emphasis in after-sales service may also be important.

An example illustrates the repositioning and repackaging possibilities. Mars faced a drop in Bahrain's imports of candy when it was ready to launch M&Ms. Fortunately, its marketing research discovered that Bahrainis consider the peanut to be a health food, so Mars repositioned its peanut M&Ms as a health food. The company also was able to turn the hot Gulf climate to its advantage by emphasizing the packaging through its traditional slogan, "M&Ms melt in your mouth, not in your hand." As you will see later in this chapter, Mars followed promotional strategy number 2 (same product—different message), although even part of the message (the slogan) remained the same.

Services   The marketing of services, like the marketing of industrial products, is generally less complex globally than is the marketing of consumer products. The consulting firm Accenture has 225,000 employees in 120 countries offering the same kinds of business expertise as the firm provides in the United States.[4]

However, laws and customs sometimes do mandate that providers alter their services. For example, Manpower cannot operate in some markets because in those countries, private employment agencies are against the law. Accounting laws vary substantially among nations, but the large accounting firms operate globally, making local adaptations where

necessary. The Sereno Spa on the west coast of India offers the same general sort of pampering as other expensive spas, but also uses its location to draw on local expertise in yoga and ayurvedic medicine.[5] VISA, MasterCard, and American Express are examples of successful companies in the global credit card industry. They had combined billings of $1.7 trillion in 1996; by 2010, VISA alone generated $2.1 trillion just in credit volume.[6]

Foreign Environmental Forces
In Section Two we examined the foreign environmental forces extensively, so here we limit our discussion to a few concrete examples of how some of these forces might affect product offerings.

Sociocultural Forces Dissimilar cultural patterns often require changes, either in the physical product or in aspects of the total product, in food and other consumer goods. The worldwide variation in consumer preferences for clothes washing is a challenge for appliance makers. The French want top-loading washing machines, and the British want front-loaders; the Germans insist on high-speed machines that remove most of the moisture in the spin-dry cycle, but the Italians prefer slower spin speeds because they let the sun do the drying. Hence, Whirlpool must produce a variety of models, although after buying Philips' appliance business in 1991 and acquiring Maytag in 2006, it has taken huge steps toward integrating a broad collection of independent national companies into regional manufacturing facilities and product platforms. For example, integration efforts in Whirlpool's European organization emphasize sharing across a few common platforms. When Whirlpool's European integration began in 1994, its CEO at the time argued that the national differences are exaggerated: "This business is the same all over the world. There is great opportunity to leverage that sameness."[7] After a painful restructuring in which Whirlpool closed a surplus Spanish plant, laid off 2,000 workers, centralized inventory control, and reduced its 36 European warehouses to 8, both European sales and operating margins improved. In fact, Whirlpool has created a "world washer," called Duet in the United States and Dreamspace in Europe, combining the U.S. preference for large-load capacity, the European preference for front-loading machines, and sensor technology that selects wash time and water consumption.[8]

While some international firms, such as Campbell's, have been extremely successful in employing the same brand name, label, and colors worldwide, other firms learn they must change names, labels, or colors because of cultural differences. Gold appears frequently on packages in Latin America because Latin Americans view it as a symbol of quality and prestige. Procter & Gamble found that a gold package has value in Europe, too, after it launched its silver-boxed Crest Tartar Control Formula in the United Kingdom, which was followed two months later by Colgate's equivalent in a gold box. P&G officials agreed that Colgate's choice of gold was better than their silver. They explained that silver was how the product was packaged in the United States.[9] The meaning that colors have for people in different cultures is also a marketing consideration. For example, in the Netherlands blue is considered warm and feminine, but the Swedes consider it masculine and cold. Figure 15.3 illustrates the color of several recent political revolutions.

FIGURE 15.3

The Revolution Will Be in Color

The Green Revolution in Iran follows a long tradition of "branding" uprisings, mainly by colors.		
Recent examples:		
Saffron Revolution	Myanmar	2007
Orange Revolution	Ukraine	2004
Blue Revolution	Kuwait	2005
Pink Revolution	Kyrgyzstan	2005
Purple Revolution	Iraq	2005

Sources: Jeremy Singer-Vine, "Garden Party or Uprising?" www.slate.com/id/2281845/ (accessed July 4, 2011); and "Colour Revolution," http://en.wikipedia.org/wiki/Colour_revolution (accessed July 4, 2011).

Even if the colors can remain the same, instructions on labels must be translated into the language of the market. Firms selling in areas where two or more languages are spoken, such as Canada, Switzerland, Belgium, and the United States, may need to use multilingual labels. Where instructions are not required, as with some consumer or industrial products whose use is well known, there is an advantage to printing the label in the language of the country best known for the product. A French label on a perfume helps strengthen the product's image in the United States.

A perfectly good brand name may have to be scrapped because of its unfavorable connotations in another language. An American product failed to survive in Sweden because its name translated to "enema." In Latin America, a product had to be taken off the market when the manufacturer found that the name meant "jackass oil." Of course, this problem occurs in both directions, as a Belgian brewery found when it tried to introduce its Delirium Tremens lager to the U.S. and Canadian markets. Authorities told the company the name was an incitement to drinking, and the beer was renamed "Mateen Triple" until the ban was subsequently lifted.[10] Sometimes a firm will not use a perfectly good name because the firm makes assumptions about the impact of the name on foreign locals and doesn't test these assumptions with locals. This is what happened with the Nova automobile. As the story goes, Chevrolet couldn't sell Novas in (the storyteller picks a Spanish-speaking country) because Nova means *no va* ("doesn't go") in Spanish. But the two words are pronounced very differently—*Nova* has the accent on the first syllable, whereas the accent for *no va* falls on the *va*. Therefore, to someone speaking Spanish, the words have very different meanings. Native Spanish-speaking people would be likely to connect *nova* with "star," which is probably what General Motors had in mind. You may be surprised to learn that Pemex, the government-owned petroleum monopoly in Mexico, once called its regular gasoline *Nova*.

An important difference in social forces to which American marketers are not accustomed is people's preference in other nations for making daily visits to small neighborhood specialty shops and large, open markets where they can socialize while shopping. More frequent buying involves smaller packages, which is important to a shopper who has no automobile in which to carry purchases. However, this custom is changing in Europe, where consumers are demanding the kinds of assortments that only a large store can offer. Shopping frequency is also slowing as European women, who traditionally have done the food shopping in most nations, are finding that they have less free time than previously. The solution has been the huge combination supermarket–discount house (*hypermarché* in France) with ample parking, located in the suburbs.

Pemex gasoline doesn't go.

There is a parallel here to the situation that began in the 1940s in the United States. The same conditions of rising incomes, a growing middle class, and a large number of working wives have combined to put a premium on the shopper's time, and just as occurred in the United States, mass merchandising and catalog and Internet shopping have moved in to fill this need.

Legal Forces. Legal forces can be a formidable constraint in the design of products because if the firm fails to adhere to a country's laws governing the product, it will be unable to do business in that country. Laws concerning pollution, consumer protection, and operator safety have been enacted in many parts of the world and limit the marketer's freedom to standardize the product mix internationally. For example, American machinery makers exporting to Sweden have found that Swedish operator safety requirements are stricter than those required by the Occupational Safety and Health Act (OSHA), so if they wish to market in Sweden, they must produce a special model. Of course, product standards set ostensibly to protect a nation's citizens can be effective in protecting indigenous industry from foreign competitors.

Laws prohibiting certain classes of imports are common in developing nations, as potential exporters learn when they research the world for markets. Products considered luxuries, as well as products already being manufactured, are among the first to be excluded from importation, but such laws also affect local production.

Food and pharmaceuticals are especially influenced by laws concerning product purity and labeling. Food products sold in Canada, whether imported or produced locally, are subject to strict rules that require both English and French on the labels as well as metric and inch/pound units. The law even dictates the space permitted between the number and the unit—"16 oz." is correct, but "16oz." is not. The Venezuelan government has decreed that the manufacturer or the importer must affix to the package the maximum retail price at which many products can be sold. Because of Saudi Arabians' concern about avoiding food that contains pork, the label of any product containing animal fat or meat that is sold in Saudi Arabia must identify the kind of animal used or state that no swine products were used.

Legal forces may also prevent a worldwide firm from employing its brand name in all its overseas markets. Managements accustomed to the American law, which establishes the right to a brand name by priority in use, are surprised to learn that in code law countries, a brand belongs to the person registering it first. Thus, the marketer may go into foreign markets expecting to use the company's long-established brand name only to find that someone else owns it. The name may have been registered by someone who is employing it legitimately for his or her own products, or it may have been pirated, that is, registered by someone who hopes to profit by selling the name back to the originating firm.

To avoid this predicament, the firm must register its brand names in every country in which it wants to use them or where it might use them in the future. And this must be done rapidly. The Paris Convention grants a firm that has registered a name in one country only six months' priority to register it elsewhere. To be certain that it has enough names for new products, Unilever, the English-Dutch manufacturer of personal care products, has more than 100,000 trademarks registered throughout the world, most of which are not in use but are kept in reserve. The U.S. Navy's Sea, Air and Land Teams, commonly referred to as SEALS, trademarked the name SEAL years ago, but after the success in finding Osama bin Laden in 2011, filed to enlarge their trademark to include Navy SEAL and SEAL Team.[11]

The use of domain names on the Internet shows that these problems have not decreased. A study found that American Express, for example, had registered the domain name "americanexpress" in 19 countries, while in 11 others the name was registered to someone other than American Express. In a more extreme example, CBS found that it had 4 registrations but others had 46. When *kanji* characters became an option for registering Japanese domain names, tiny Web Japan Co. got a head start by registering some 100 domain names, including those of major corporations.[12] This will become even more confusing when the number of domain names increases exponentially by late 2012, when companies may register their names under hundreds of country and company variants.

Economic Forces The disparity in income throughout the world is an obstacle to worldwide product standardization. Some products are priced too high for some consumers in developing nations, and so the firm must adjust to the consumers' ability to pay. Such adjustments may include simplification or repackaging. Procter & Gamble sells shampoo for individual use in India, in addition to the regular bottle quantity. In addition, many consumers throughout the world buy cell phone airtime by purchasing prepaid cards worth only a few dollars or even by renting cell phones by the call from intermediaries. As C. K. Prahalad pointed out in *The Fortune at the Bottom of the Pyramid,* the 5 billion people in poverty in developing nations have $14 trillion in purchasing power.[13]

In some cases, the foreign subsidiary cannot afford to produce as complete a product mix as does the parent. Automobile manufacturers may assemble the less expensive and higher-volume line locally and broaden the local product mix by importing the luxury cars. International firms practice this marketing technique whenever possible because a captive foreign sales organization is available to promote the sales of the home organization's exports and because the revenue derived helps pay the subsidiary's overhead. Yet GM has been successful with its Buick in China by introducing the Buick as a premium brand and then moving to mid-range and economy vehicles. GM had nearly 15 percent of the China market in 2011.[14]

Physical Forces   Physical forces, such as climate and terrain, also work against international product standardization. Manufacturers of clothes washers have found success in India by "hardening" their machines against heat, dirt, and power outages. The heat and high humidity in many parts of the tropics require that electrical equipment be built with extra-heavy insulation. Consumer goods that are affected by moisture must be specially packaged to resist its penetration. Thus, pills may be wrapped in foil or "blister packs."

High altitudes frequently require product alteration. Food manufacturers have found that they must change their cooking instructions for people who live at high altitudes because at such altitudes cooking takes longer. Water boils at a lower temperature. The thinner atmosphere requires that producers of cake mixes include less yeast as well.

Environmental forces may play a major part in foreign product strategies. Their influence is pervasive in the design of the entire marketing mix. A useful guide for the marketing mix preparation is a matrix in which the marketing mix variables are tabulated against the environmental forces. Such a guide is at the end of this chapter in Table 15.2.

PROMOTIONAL STRATEGIES

Promotion, one of the basic elements of the marketing mix, is communication that secures understanding between a firm and its publics to bring about a favorable buying action and achieve long-lasting confidence in the firm and the product or service it provides. Note that this definition employs the plural *publics,* because the seller's promotional efforts must be

promotion
Any form of communication between a firm and its publics

Cooking at high altitudes requires companies to post alternative instructions on food packaging.

LO15-6 **Discuss**
the product strategies
that can be formed
from three product
alternatives and three
kinds of promotional
messages.

directed to more than just the ultimate consumers, including retailers and other members of the distribution channel.

Promotion both influences and is influenced by the other marketing mix variables. Nine distinct promotion strategies are possible, by combining the three alternatives of (1) marketing the same physical product everywhere, (2) adapting the physical product for foreign markets, and (3) designing a different physical product with (*a*) the same, (*b*) adapted, or (*c*) different messages.[15] Here we examine the six strategies most commonly used:

1. *Same product–same message.* When marketers find that target markets vary little with respect to product use and consumer attitudes, they can offer the same product and use the same promotional appeals in all markets. Avon uses this strategy.

2. *Same product–different message.* The same product may satisfy a different need or be used differently elsewhere. This means the product may be left unchanged but a different message is required. Honda's early "You meet the nicest people on a Honda" campaign appealed to Americans who used their motorcycles as pleasure vehicles, but in Brazil Honda stressed the use of motorcycles as basic transportation. Honda has now captured about 90 percent of the Brazilian motorcycle market.

3. *Product adaptation–same message.* In cases where the product serves the same function but must be adapted to different conditions, the same message is employed with a changed product. In Japan, Lever Brothers puts Lux soap in fancy boxes because much of it is sold as gifts.

4. *Product adaptation–message adaptation.* In some cases, both the product and the promotional message must be modified for foreign markets. In Latin America, Tang is especially sweetened, premixed, and ready to drink in pouches, and in the Mideast comes in a pineapple flavor. Kraft localizes the vitamins in Tang to meet local deficiencies, for example adding iron in Brazil and the Philippines.

5. *Different product–same message.* In many markets, the potential customers cannot afford the product as manufactured for developed markets. To overcome this obstacle, companies frequently produce a very distinct product for these markets. Substituting a low-cost plastic squeeze bottle for an aerosol can and a manually operated washing machine for an automated one are two examples. The promotional message, however, can be very similar to what is used in the developed markets if the product performs the same functions.

advertising
Paid, nonpersonal presentation of ideas, goods, or services by an identified sponsor

6. *Different product for the same use–different message.* Frequently, the different product requires a different message as well. Welding torches rather than automatic welding machines would be sold on the basis of low acquisition cost rather than high output per hour. The governments of developing countries faced with high unemployment might be persuaded by a message emphasizing the job-creating possibilities of labor-intensive processes rather than the labor saving of highly automated machinery.

The tools for communicating these messages—the promotional mix—are advertising, personal selling, sales promotion, public relations, and publicity. Just as in the case of the product strategies, the composition of the promotional mix will depend on the type of product, the environmental forces, and the amount of market penetration desired.

Advertising   Among all the promotional mix elements, **advertising** may be the one with the greatest similarities worldwide. This is the case because much advertising is based on American practices. U.S. ad agencies have followed their corporate customers into the global realm through wholly owned subsidiaries, joint ventures, and working agreements with local agencies. The decision to go global, as Apple has with the iPod, or to go either local or regional, as an increasing number of iPad application developers have, is not an easy one. One commentator observes that the trend is toward localization, at least for a while.[16]

http://www.packagingdigest.com/article/518552-Affordable_convenient_packaging_helps_Tang_rocket_to_billion_dollar_status_in_developing_markets.php

Cultural dimensions play a major role in these decisions. Here is a summary of their influence, adapted from work by the scholar and researcher Lars Perner:[17]

- *Directness vs. indirectness.* U.S. advertising tends to be direct. What are the product benefits? Such bluntness may be considered too pushy for Japanese consumers, where directness is read as arrogance. How could the seller presume to know what the consumer would like?

- *Comparison.* Comparative advertising is banned in most countries and would probably be counterproductive in Asia, seen as an insulting instance of confrontation and bragging, even if it were allowed. In the United States, comparison advertising has proven effective (although its implementation is tricky).

- *Humor.* Although humor is a relatively universal phenomenon, what is considered funny differs greatly across cultures, so pretesting is essential. One example: the British are said to use irony in their jokes. Americans understand the jokes, but are much less likely to use irony in their own jokes.

- *Gender roles.* One study found that women in U.S. advertising tended to be shown in more traditional roles than in Europe or Australia. Some countries are more traditional than the United States. African television ads are also more likely to show women in traditional roles.

- *Explicitness.* Europeans tend to tolerate more explicit advertisements, often with sexual overtones, than do Americans.

- *Sophistication.* Europeans, particularly the French, demand considerably more sophistication than Americans, who may react more favorably to emotional appeals. Anecdotally, American ads seem more likely to use animals than does advertising in other cultures.

- *Popular versus traditional culture.* U.S. ads tend to employ contemporary, popular culture, often including current music, while those in more traditional cultures tend to refer more to older roots.

- *Information content versus fluff.* American ads often contain puffery, which was found to be ineffective in eastern European countries because it resembled communist propaganda. The eastern European consumer instead wants facts.

Global and Regional Brands Manufacturers are increasingly using global or regional brands for a number of reasons:

1. Cost is most often cited. By producing one TV commercial for use across a region, a firm can save up to 50 percent of the production cost.

2. There is a better chance of obtaining one regional source to do high-quality work than of finding sources in several countries that will work to the same high standard.

3. Some marketing managers believe their companies must have a single image throughout a region.

4. Companies are establishing regionalized organizations where many functions, such as marketing, are centralized.

5. Global and regional satellite and cable television are widely available.

Economies of scale are one reason some firms emphasize the regional or global standardization of advertising. Coca-Cola, for example, once estimated that it saved more than $8 million annually in the cost of thinking up new imagery by repeating the same theme everywhere.

The head of a consulting firm specializing in brands and corporate identity has a different idea. He says, "There are too many businesses out there doing the same thing. Global branding is a way of saying your company makes a difference, which moves you up the pecking order."[18] Look at the value placed on the world's most valuable brands (Table 15.1).

Global or National The debate continues among international marketers about using global, regional, or national brands. Companies that acquired successful regional or national brands when purchasing the original owner have been extremely cautious about converting them to their global brands. Nestlé is an example of a large global firm that uses both. Nestlé tries to achieve consumer familiarity and marketing efficiency by using two brands on a single product, a local brand that may be familiar and appeal only to a small group of

Rank 2010	2008	2006	Brand	Value ($M)
1	1	1	Coca-Cola, United States	$ 70,452
2	2	3	IBM, United States	64,727
3	3	2	Microsoft, United States	60,895
4	10	24	Google, United States	43,557
5	4	6	General Electric, United States	42,808
6	8	7	McDonald's, United States	33,578
7	7	5	Intel, United States	32,015
8	5	6	Nokia, Finland	29,495
9	9	8	Disney, United States	28,731
10	12	13	Hewlett-Packard, United States	26,867

*Google was 38th in 2005, and was not in the first 100 in 2004. Nokia lost 15 percent of its value in 2010 from the year before and Toyota lost 16 percent of its value during that same time period.

Source: www.interbrand.com/Libraries/Branding_Studies/Best_Global_Brands_2010_Poster.sflb.ashx (accessed June 22, 2011).

consumers and a corporate strategic brand such as Nestlé or Nescafé. In some markets, such as Asian ones, product quality across many categories is suggested by a shared brand. This developed from the *keiretsu* structure as evidenced by Mitsubishi, C. Itoh, and Mitsui.

Private Brands   Private brands have become serious competitors for manufacturers' brands and are responsible for a shift in power from manufacturers to retailers. A 2010 Nielsen survey found that, across 55 nations worldwide, 60 percent of consumers reported that they were purchasing more private-label products.[19] Private labels have flooded Japan's large supermarket chains and account for up to 25 percent of all supermarket sales in New Zealand and Australia. In Europe, private labels account for 46 percent, 43 percent, and 32 percent, respectively, of the Swiss, UK, and German markets. Private labels represent about 22 percent of American food store sales, and more than 18 percent in Canada. The trend toward private labels has also caught on in other nations and regions, although the practice lags the most in Asia and the Middle East. The Swedish food group Axfood AB notes that it profits twice from private-label manufacturing: first when it sells the product (at a lower price to its stores), and then when the profit margin is higher (when selling to the ultimate consumer).[20]

Availability of Media   Satellite TV broadcasters make possible numerous programming networks to provide service to millions of households in dozens of countries and in many languages. International print media include local, national, and regional editions. *The European,* a daily newspaper; the international edition of *The Herald Tribune;* the Asian and European editions of *The Wall Street Journal;* and the international editions of the *Manchester Guardian* and *The Financial Times* are some of the newspapers with wide circulation. Worldwide cell phone advertising more than doubled from 2010 to 2011. Advertisers can also go to other media to reach their markets. Cinema advertising is heavily used in many parts of the world (including Norway, Austria, the United Kingdom, and Brazil), as are billboards. In a number of developing countries, automobiles equipped with loudspeakers circulate through the cities announcing products, and street signs are furnished by advertisers whose messages hang on them. Homeowners can get a free coat of paint by permitting advertisers to put ads on their walls. Buses and trains carry advertisements. Probably one of the most ingenious campaigns ever was that of a tea company that gave away thousands of printed prayers with a tea advertisement on the other side to pilgrims bound for Mecca.

The point is that media of some kind are available in every market, and the local managers and advertising agencies are familiar with the advantages of each kind. Media selection is extremely difficult for international advertising managers who try to standardize their media mix from the home office. The variation in media availability is a strong reason for leaving this part of the advertising program to the local organization.

Internet Advertising   We mentioned the importance of the Internet as a market research tool in Chapter 12, and it is important as an advertising medium as well. Among the appealing factors of online advertising in the international sphere are the following:

LO15-7 **Discuss** some of the effects the Internet may have on international marketing.

1. The Internet provides an affluent, reachable audience. A high number of users in a wide variety of countries read English or other common languages well. Native-language sites are strongly preferred, though.

2. Unlike TV or newspaper ads, Internet communications are two-way. They are cheap. And they are possibly less regulated than other advertising forms. In Europe, where direct advertising of prescription drug products is banned, Internet sites are a way to provide potential consumers with product information. The disclaimer that the information is for U.S. audiences only may be ignored.

3. The possibility exists of involving customers in determining which messages and information they receive. For this reason, there is some possibility that company web offerings will be tailor-made by the user. This customization increases the application of the marketing concept.

4. Although the Internet doesn't reach all possible groups, for some groups it may be among the best media choices. For teenagers in particular, Internet advertising can be important because teenagers spend less time watching TV than any other demographic group, preferring to use social media or to play computer games.

Type of Product   Buyers of industrial goods and luxury products usually act on the same motives the world over; thus, these products lend themselves to a standardized approach. Such standardization enables manufacturers of capital goods, such as General Electric and Caterpillar, to prepare international campaigns that require very little modification in their various markets. Certain consumer goods markets are similar, too. Another set of characteristics also permits firms to use the same appeals and sales arguments worldwide: when the product is low priced, is consumed in the same way, and is bought for the same reasons. Examples of such products are gasoline, soft drinks, detergents, cosmetics, and airline services. Firms such as ExxonMobil, Coca-Cola, Apple, and Avon have used the international approach successfully. Generally, the changes they have made are a translation into the local language and the use of indigenous models.

Foreign Environmental Forces   Like variations in media availability, foreign environmental forces act as deterrents to the international standardization of advertising, and as you would expect, among the most influential of these forces are the *sociocultural* forces, which we examined in Chapter 4.

A basic cultural decision for the marketer is whether to position the product as foreign or local. Which way to go seems to depend on the country, the product type, and the target market. In Germany, for example, consumers are not at all impressed by a carmaker that announces it has American know-how. At the same time, such purely American products as bourbon, fast-food restaurants, and blue jeans have made tremendous inroads there and in the rest of Europe.

Similarly, in Japan and elsewhere in Asia, the national identity of some consumer products enhances their image. The rage among Chinese teenagers is anything from Korea. The influence of American-style fast-food restaurants on Japanese youth was emphasized in a survey taken by the Japanese Ministry of Agriculture, which found that more than 50 percent of the country's teenagers would rather eat Western foods than the traditional dishes. U.S.-based fast-food restaurants such as McDonald's (Japan's largest restaurant business), KFC (the third largest), Dairy Queen, and Mister Donut account for half the total restaurant business. While McDonald's is slimming down its menu in the West, in 2011 it introduced four new Big America 2 burgers in Japan. And KFC is zeroing in on an even larger Asian market—it had about 3,300 restaurants in China in 2011 and is expanding daily.[21] An indication of the significance of national identity is the Japanese *anime*-style cartoons that dominate the time slots in the after-school and Saturday morning American TV schedules.[22]

The experience of suppliers to the youth market indicates that this, too, is an international market segment, much like the market for luxury goods. A former director of MTV

Are these teens in Japan or the United States? Japan. But, like teens in the United States, they wear Levi's and carry American stateboards.

Europe observed that, "18-year-olds in Paris have more in common with 18-year-olds in New York than with their own parents. They buy the same products, go to the same movies, listen to the same music, sip the same colas. Global advertising merely works on that premise."[23] This similarity suggests that marketers can formulate global advertising campaigns for these consumers that will require little more than a translation into the local language, unless the product strategy goes with a foreign identity. That decision should be made with local input.

Because communication is impossible if the language is not understood, translations must be made into the language of the consumers. Unfortunately for the advertiser, almost every language varies from one country to another. The same word may be perfectly apt in one country while connoting something completely different in another. To avoid connotation errors in translation, the experienced advertising manager will use a back translation and often include plenty of illustrations with short copy.

Because a nation's laws generally reflect public opinion, the cultural forces tend to be closely allied to the legal forces, which exert a strong and pervasive influence on advertising. We have seen how laws affect media availability; they also restrict the kinds of products that can be advertised and the copy employed in the advertisements.

American firms accustomed to using comparative advertising at home may be surprised to find that legal restrictions on this technique exist in some markets. Since the early 1990s, PepsiCo has used comparative advertising to knock Coca-Cola, and wherever possible, Coke has used the courts to stop the ads. PepsiCo launched a series of TV commercials, the Pepsi Challenge campaign, in 1995 to test the comparative advertising laws of 30 countries. The ads presented the competitor's product in a way that is specifically prohibited in some countries as unfair advertising. The marketing head of PepsiCo said that the company "intended to push the envelope on comparison advertising in markets around the world."[24] Because of the grueling legal battle between PepsiCo and Coca-Cola over the Pepsi Challenge campaign, as well as other conflicts over comparative advertising, laws in various Latin American countries were found to be inadequate. To avoid the passage of more laws, members of the advertising industry have established self-regulatory bodies in a number of these nations to settle disputes out of court. In Europe, the EU Commission authorized comparative advertising subject to restrictions because some member countries permitted it while others did not. Germany's comparative advertising law is so strict that Goodyear couldn't use its multinational tire campaign stating that nylon tire cord is stronger than steel.

Advertisers in the Islamic countries face limitations, although these vary widely across the Middle East. A recent study shows that women appear about as often in Lebanese and Egyptian TV ads as in U.S. ads, although only half as often in Saudi ads. The women were just as likely to be dressed "immodestly" in Lebanese as in U.S. ads, although less often in Egyptian and never in Saudi ads.[25] In Japan, images of Western women in suggestive poses were acceptable, while similar images of Japanese women were not.

Globalization versus Localization   With so many obstacles to international standardization, what should be the approach of the international advertising manager? The opinion of some experts is that good brands and good product ideas can cross international borders, but each may have to be adjusted for the local market. Let's examine this situation more closely.

A global product and a global brand, such as Apple's iPad tablet, reach many markets unchanged or virtually unchanged. An ability to standardize both the product and the brand can lead to valuable cost savings.[26] Such products tend to be innovations. A global product with a local brand is often the result of mergers. Germany's Henkel—owner of Right Guard, Dial Soap, and other consumer products—has kept local packaging and standardized the physical product, its soap powder. Such a combination of localization of the product packaging and standardization of the contents makes manufacturing efficiencies possible. The final option, a local product with a local brand, is the most localized approach and is appropriate when, for perhaps cultural reasons, the product that sells well in one country will not transfer to another or does so for quite a different set of purposes. Dish soaps that are adjusted for the hardness of local water and sell under local names are an example. P&G's Fairy Liquid, a dishwashing soap that is a leading brand in the United Kingdom, similar to Joy in the U.S. market, is one example of localization of the product on both brand and content. Remember, too, that, as the director of multinational accounts at McCann-Erickson

---

 GLOBAL DEBATE

Lady Gaga Reaches India

When Lady Gaga wanted to replicate her superstardom in India, she had a problem. Unlike in the United States, in India the music industry is largely driven by the film industry, so hit songs are predominantly from hit movies. So she had her song, "Born This Way," remixed by Bollywood composers Salim and Salaiman to produce a hybrid song that would have more Indian appeal. A second song, "Judas," was remixed by Panjabi MC. In terms of these two songs, we can analyze her adaptation to the Indian market. First, the vocals and video were the same, the backing track was changed to use Indian instruments, and the "beat" was altered to be recognizably "Indian."

India has more than 700 million people under 30 years old, opening up a vast new potential market for the singer-songwriter. India is already a major entertainment market—Bollywood sells about 1 billion more tickets per year than does Hollywood.

Questions:

1. Although Lady Gaga did not re-record her singing in any of her songs, she did allow change in parts of the songs by changing the rhythm tracks. Is Lady Gaga's product in India unchanged, or not? What other examples can you think of where the line between a changed and unchanged product is difficult to draw?

2. Compared to modern film, contemporary foreign music doesn't seem to do very well abroad. Can you speculate about why that is?

Sources: Lee Hawkins, "Lady Gage Romances India," *The Wall Street Journal*, June 2, 2011, p. B9; www.bollywoodhungama.com/broadband/video/Parties-and-Events/IEBmhI77/3/Salim-Sulaiman-Launch-The-Lady-Gaga-Wall-Of-Fame.html (accessed June 19, 2011); and www.bbc.co.uk/news/business-13894702 (accessed June 25, 2011).

claims, social classes across different countries have shared sensibilities, "A male middle executive in Italy has more in common with a male middle executive in the U.K. than with a farmer in Italy. It is those shared sensibilities that make global branding possible."[27]

Such global branding approaches look for similarities across segments and countries to capitalize on them by providing promotional themes with worldwide appeal. A second approach believes that even though human nature is the same everywhere, it is also true that a Spaniard will remain a Spaniard and a Belgian a Belgian. Thus, it is preferable to develop separate appeals to take advantage of the differences among customers in different cultures and countries.

LO15-8 **Explain** "glocal" advertising strategies.

Neither Purely Global nor Purely Local   You probably have already gathered from this discussion that for most firms neither a purely global nor a purely local campaign is the best way to handle international advertising. In fact, companies at either end of the global–local spectrum, with purely global campaigns or only local campaigns, tend to be moving toward the middle, with a "glocal" approach. Advertisers have followed glocalization to reduce costs. It allows them to develop a common strategy for large regions. Coca-Cola says simply, "Think globally, but act locally."

Gillette's Panregional Approach   Gillette organizes its advertising in the following regional and cultural clusters: pan-Latin America, pan-Middle East, pan-Africa, and pan-Atlantic. The company believes it can identify the same needs and buying motives among consumers in regions or countries linked by culture, consumers' habits, and level of market development for their products. Gillette might use the same European-style advertising for Australia and South Africa, but in Asia, it would link developing economies such as the Philippines, Indonesia, Thailand, and Malaysia. Gillette introduced a modified version of its Mach 3 Turbo in India using a local marketing agency. The agency parked modified trucks with shaving booths, sound systems, and female marketers outside call centers and shopping malls. Trial led many of the consumers to switch immediately to the Gillette razor, giving up the traditional double-edged razor that is still common in India.[28] With its regional-where-possible approach to marketing, Gillette is moving toward a global marketing strategy in the markets where such an approach might be appropriate, while allowing for regional and national differences.

programmed-management approach
A middle-ground advertising strategy between globally standardized and entirely local programs

Programmed-Management Approach   The **programmed-management approach** is another middle-ground advertising strategy in which the home office and the foreign subsidiaries agree on marketing objectives, after which each subsidiary puts together a tentative advertising campaign. This is submitted to the home office for review and suggestions. The campaign is then market-tested locally, and the results are submitted to the home office, which reviews them and offers comments. The subsidiary then submits a complete campaign to the home office for review. When the home office is satisfied, the budget is approved and the subsidiary begins implementing the campaign. The result may be a highly standardized campaign for all markets or one that has been individualized to the extent necessary to cope with local market conditions. The programmed-management approach gives the home office a chance to standardize those parts of the campaign that can be standardized but still permits flexibility in responding to different marketing conditions.

Personal Selling   Along with advertising, personal selling constitutes a principal component of the promotional mix. The importance of this promotional tool compared with advertising depends to a great extent on the relative costs, the funds available, media availability, and the type of product sold.

Manufacturers of industrial products rely more on personal selling than on advertising to communicate with their overseas markets. However, producers of consumer products may also emphasize personal selling overseas, especially in the developing countries, because this may be more effective in the local environment.

Personal Selling and the Internet   Evidence suggests that the Internet, when used to build trust (through consumer orientation, competence, dependability, candor, and likability[29]), can be an effective tool in personal selling. It may be enhanced by face-to-face communication as well. There are evolving approaches to trust building in a virtual environment that seem to be working, such as the eBay community and other sales and social sites.

International Standardization By and large, the organization of an overseas sales force, sales presentation, and training methods are very similar to those employed in the home country, whenever possible. Avon was following the same plan of person-to-person selling in its major markets when, without notice, China outlawed door-to-door selling in 1998. The Chinese government claimed to be concerned about consumer safety and fraudulent pyramid schemes.[30] The success of Amway in China, whose personal selling may have come close to proselytizing, may also have been a concern. Avon had begun in China with a $40 million manufacturing base in Guangzhou, which started manufacturing in 1998. To comply with Chinese law, Avon China shifted to a retail model and in 2006 provided products through a network of 6,000 beauty boutiques and 1,000 beauty counters. In mid-2006, China approved Avon for person-to-person selling in China. It resumed the successful model, and by 2008 had some 600,000 sales promoters. Meanwhile, during the same period in Venezuela and Russia, Avon was extremely successful with the same personal selling approach it uses in the United States. It has also been successful in Mexico, but when it entered the Mexican market, local experts predicted that its plan would fail because the Mexican middle-class woman is not home during the day. She is socializing. The wall around the house would keep the Avon lady from reaching the front door, and when she rang the bell, the maid would not let her in. Other American firms had used this approach and had failed for these reasons. However, Avon made small but important changes. It mounted a massive advertising campaign to educate Mexicans as to what they could expect from the visits, which used the standardized U.S. advertising, adding some education about the selling approach. In addition, Avon recruited educated, middle-class women as representatives and trained them well. They were encouraged to visit their friends, too. In both China and Mexico, changing the essentially American plan as necessary for legal reasons and cultural differences supported Avon's successful entry.

Other firms also follow their home-country approach. Missionary salespeople from pharmaceutical manufacturers such as Pfizer and Upjohn introduce their products to physicians, just as they do in the United States. Salespeople calling on channel members perform the same tasks of informing middlemen, setting up point-of-purchase displays, and fighting for shelf space, as do their American counterparts.

Recruitment Recruiting salespeople in foreign countries is at times more difficult than recruiting them at home because sales managers may have to cope with the stigma attached to selling that exists in some areas. There is also the need to hire salespeople who are culturally acceptable to customers and channel members. This can be difficult and costly in an already small market that is further subdivided into several distinct cultures with different customs and languages.

Sales Promotion

Sales promotion provides the selling aids for the marketing function and includes activities such as the preparation of point-of-purchase displays, contests, premiums, trade show exhibits, money-off offers, and coupons.

sales promotion
Any of various selling aids, including displays, premiums, contests, and gifts

The international standardization of the sales promotion function is not difficult, because experience has shown that what is successful in the United States generally proves effective overseas, although often at a diminished rate. Couponing is a good example. A Nielsen report surveyed consumers on cost-saving measures that would move them to increased coupon use. In the United States, 46 percent of consumers stated that they would increase coupon use, while the global average was 19 percent.[31] One major difference on coupon use among markets is the method of distribution. In the United States, the freestanding insert is most frequently used, while in Europe coupons are distributed in stores, usually on the package itself. In some European countries, couponing is illegal. This is because price discrimination among consumers is illegal. In other countries, the selling price of specific goods is set within a narrow range.

When marketers are considering transferring sales promotion techniques to other markets, they must consider some cultural constraints.

Sociocultural and Economic Constraints Cultural and economic constraints influence sales promotions. For example, a premium used as a sales aid for the product must be meaningful to the purchaser. A kitchen gadget might be valued by an American but will not be particularly attractive to a Latin American of similar economic status with two maids. Putting a prize inside the package is no guarantee that it will be there when the purchaser takes the package home. While living in Mexico, one of this book's authors bought a product for the plastic toy it contained. When he opened the package at home, there was no toy. Examining the package closely, he found that a small slit had been made in the top. Where labor costs and store revenues are low, the income from the sale of these premiums is an extra profit for the retailer.

Contests, raffles, and games have been extremely successful in countries where people love to play the odds. If Latin Americans or the Irish will buy a lottery ticket week after week, hoping to win the grand prize playing against odds of 500,000 to 1, why shouldn't they participate in a contest that costs them nothing to enter? Point-of-purchase displays are well accepted by retailers, although many establishments are so small that there is simply no place to put all the displays that are offered to them. The marketing manager who prepares a well-planned program after studying the constraints of the local markets can expect excellent results from the time and money invested.

Public Relations

Public relations is the firm's communications and relationships with its various publics, including the governments where it operates, or as one writer has put it, "Public relations is the marketing of the firm." Although American ICs have had organized public relations programs for many years in the United States, they have paid much less attention to this important function elsewhere. Informing the local public of what they are doing has been overlooked by some U.S. corporations. For example, the Ford Foundation, a philanthropy begun by Edsel Ford and two Ford Motor Company executives, has an international graduate fellowships program (IFP) to provide $280 million in graduate fellowships for students from Africa, the Middle East, Asia, Latin America, and Russia between 2000 and 2012.[32]

Nationalism and anti-multinational feeling in many countries have made it imperative that companies with international operations improve their communications to their non-business publics with more effective public relations programs. International pharmaceutical manufacturers are viewed with suspicion by the public in developing nations because, although their products may alleviate suffering, they do so at a profit, made from the poor. To improve their images, major pharmaceuticals have begun programs related to disease globally. Their AIDS campaigns in Africa have received much public attention.

One of the most vexing problems for firms is how to deal with critics of their operations and motives. Some try to defuse criticism by holding regularly scheduled meetings at which topics of interest are debated. Others prefer to meet with critics privately, although they may find themselves caught in a never-ending relationship in which the critics continually escalate their demands.

A strategy that has been employed successfully by some firms is to address the issue without dealing directly with the critics. Instead, the firms work with international or governmental agencies. For example, in China a number of foreign firms that have achieved success recently—among them Toshiba, Philips, and Canon—have found themselves under fire by the Chinese media. Scott Kronick of Ogilvy Public Relations Worldwide recommended that if the coverage was too unbalanced, firms should complain to the Propaganda Department. Although the department is not actually part of the government, it is a committee of the Central Committee of the Communist Party of China, whose chairperson is an alternate member of the Politburo.[33]

Another alternative is to do nothing. If the criticism receives no publicity, it may die from lack of interest. Yet sometimes a libeled company chooses to defend its reputation in court. McDonald's decided it was the victim in London when Helen Steel and Dave Morris distributed leaflets accusing the company of starving the Third World, exploiting children in its advertising, and destroying the Central American rain forests. It was also cruel to animals, they alleged, because at times chickens were still conscious when their throats were cut. McDonald's sued Steel and Morris in 1994. It became the longest libel trial in history, ending two and a half years later. McDonald's was awarded $98,000 in damages in a case it had spent $16 million to pursue. Despite the award, which McDonald's has never collected, there is now a major anti-McDonald's website (www.McSpotlight.org) dedicated to protests against McDonald's, and October 16 has become established as Worldwide Anti-McDonald's Day.[34]

PRICING STRATEGIES

Pricing, the third element of the marketing mix, is an important and complex consideration in formulating the marketing strategy. Pricing decisions affect other corporate functions, directly determine the firm's gross revenue, and are a major determinant of profits. Most pricing research has been done on North Americans, and this raises serious problems for its generalizability.[35] Americans like sales, for example, while consumers in countries where goods are more scarce than they are in the United States may attribute sales to low quality rather than to a desire to gain market share. There is some evidence that perceived price–quality relationships are quite high in Britain and Japan. Thus, discount stores have had difficulty in both these markets. In developing countries, there is less trust of outsiders in the market. Cultural differences may influence the effort a buyer puts into evaluating deals in these markets, where buy decisions rest on relationships. That consumers in some economies are usually paid weekly rather than biweekly or monthly may influence the effectiveness of framing attempts as well. "A dollar a day" is a much bigger chunk from a weekly than a monthly paycheck.

Pricing, a Controllable Variable

Effective price setting consists of more than mechanically adding a standard markup to a cost. To obtain the maximum benefits from pricing, management must regard pricing in the same manner as it does other controllable variables. Pricing is one element of the marketing mix that can be varied to achieve the marketing objectives of the firm.

For instance, if the marketer wishes to position a product as a high-quality item, setting a relatively high price will reinforce promotion that emphasizes quality. However, combining a low price with a promotional emphasis on quality could result in a contradiction that would adversely affect credibility with the consumer. Pricing can also be a determinant in the choice of middlemen, because if the firm requires a wholesaler to take title to, stock, promote, and deliver the merchandise, it must give the wholesaler a much larger trade discount than would be demanded by a broker, whose services are much more limited.

These examples illustrate one of the reasons for the complexity of price setting: the interaction of pricing with the other elements of the marketing mix. In addition, two other sets of forces influence this variable: the interaction between marketing and the other functional areas of the firm and environmental forces.

Interaction between Marketing and the Other Functional Areas

To illustrate this point, consider the following:

1. The finance people want prices that are both profitable and conducive to steady cash flow.
2. Production supervisors want prices that create large sales volumes, which permit long production runs with their associated lower cost benefits.
3. The legal department worries about possible antitrust violations when different prices are set according to type of customer. It also worries about global trademark protection and intellectual property issues.
4. The tax people are concerned with the effects of prices on tax loads.
5. The domestic sales manager wants export prices to be high enough to avoid having to compete with company products that are purchased for export and then diverted to the domestic market (one aspect of parallel importing).

The marketer must address all these concerns and also consider the impact of the legal and other environmental forces that we examined in Section Two. Table 15.2 at the end of this chapter examines this aspect of pricing in greater detail.

foreign national pricing
Local pricing in another country

Standardizing Prices

Companies that pursue a policy of unified, global corporate pricing know that pricing is acted on by the same forces that inhibit the international standardization of the other marketing mix components. Pricing for the overseas markets is more complex because managements must be concerned with two kinds of pricing: **foreign national pricing,** which is domestic pricing in another country, and **international pricing** for exports.

international pricing
Setting prices of goods for export for both unrelated and related firms

Foreign National Pricing Some foreign governments fix prices on just about everything, while others are concerned only with pricing on essential goods. In nations with laws on unfair competition, the minimum sales price may be controlled rather than the maximum. The German law is so comprehensive that under certain conditions even premiums and cents-off coupons may be prohibited because they violate the minimum price requirements.

Prices can vary because of cost differentials on opposite sides of a border. One government may levy higher import duties on imported raw materials or may subsidize public utilities, while another may not. Differences in labor legislation cause labor costs to vary. Competition among local suppliers may be intense in one market, permitting the affiliate to buy inputs at better prices than those paid by an affiliate in another market.

Competition on the selling side may be diverse also. Frequently, an affiliate in one market will face heavy local competition and be limited in the price it can charge, while in a neighboring market a lack of competitors will allow another affiliate to charge a higher price. As regional economic groupings reduce trade barriers among members, such opportunities are becoming fewer because firms must meet regional as well as local competition.

International Pricing International pricing involves the setting of prices for goods produced in one country and sold in another. The pricing of exports to unrelated customers falls in this category and has been addressed in a prior chapter. A special kind of exporting, *intracorporate sales,* is common among large companies as they attempt to require that subsidiaries specialize in the manufacture of some products and import others. Their imports may consist of components that are assembled into the end product, such as computer chips made in one country that are mounted on boards built in another, or they may be finished products imported to complement the product mix of an affiliate. In either case, judgment is needed in setting a transfer price, the price charged for an intracompany sale, which is sometimes called intracorporate price.

It is possible for the firm as a whole to gain while both the buying and the selling subsidiaries "lose," that is, receive prices that are lower than would be obtained through an outside transaction. The tendency is for transfer prices to be set at headquarters so that the company may obtain a profit from *both* the seller and the buyer or locate its profit in lower-tax environments. The selling affiliate would like to charge other subsidiaries the same price it charges all customers, but when combined with transportation costs and import duties, such a price may make it impossible for the importing subsidiary to compete in its market. If headquarters dictates that a lower-than-market transfer price be charged, the seller will be unhappy because its profit-and-loss statement suffers. This can be problematic for managers whose promotion bonuses depend on the bottom line.

Increasingly, the Internet is redefining pricing options. It is a tremendous tool for comparing prices—already sites can scan hundreds of outlets for prices on certain goods—and so national boundaries may mean less and less. In a sense, world prices for consumers may be on the way to being achieved. The effect extends to business-to-business pricing as well.

DISTRIBUTION STRATEGIES

LO15-9 Discuss the distribution strategies of international marketers.

The development of distribution strategies is difficult in the home country and even more so internationally, where marketing managers must concern themselves with two functions rather than one: getting the products *to* foreign markets (exporting) and distributing the products *within* each foreign market.

Interdependence of Distribution Decisions Distribution decisions are often interdependent with the other marketing mix variables. For example, if the product requires considerable after-sales servicing, the firm will want to sell through dealers with the facilities, personnel, and capital to purchase spare parts and train service people. Channel decisions are critical because they are long-term decisions; once established, they are far less easy to change than those made for price, product, and promotion. Coca-Cola recently made a major decision to change its channel system in China; at great cost, it moved from using a traditional channel, where competing interests of the channel members were slowing up their connection to the market, to building relationships with its small retail sellers.[36]

Standardizing Distribution   Although management would prefer to standardize distribution patterns internationally, there are two fundamental constraints on doing so: the variation in the availability of channel members among the firm's markets and the environmental forces present in these different markets. International managers have found flexibility around an overall policy to be effective. The subsidiaries implement the distribution policy and design channel strategies to meet local conditions.

Availability of Channel Members   As a starting point in their channel design, local managers have the successful distribution system used in the domestic operation. Headquarters' support for a policy of employing the same channels worldwide will be especially strong when the entire marketing mix has been built around a particular channel type, such as direct sales force or franchised operators. McDonald's is an example of a firm that relies primarily on franchise operators at home and abroad.

Foreign Environmental Forces   Environmental differences among markets add to the difficulty in standardizing distribution channels. Basic geographic differences matter greatly in distribution, as explained in Chapter 5 Just think about Switzerland's challenges. Changes caused by the cultural forces generally occur over time, but those caused by the legal forces can be radical and quick. To illustrate, hypermarkets are changing distribution patterns everywhere, including Europe. The EU's Royer Law gives local urban commissions, often dominated by small merchants, the power to refuse construction permits for supermarkets and hypermarkets.

Japan's Large Scale Retailers Law, very similar to the Royer Law, had also slowed the opening of large retailers. However, the Japanese government scrapped the law completely in 1997. The Japanese have adopted Internet shopping, and one result is that retail stores now seem almost superfluous. When Sony launched its electronic pet *Aibo* (Japanese for "companion") in 1999, it sold out of stock in 20 minutes on SonyStyle.com; no units were shipped to stores. Sony later opened physical SonyStyle stores in addition to its existing Sony outlets.[37]

Another restriction of distribution has been tried in the EU. Manufacturers have attempted to prevent distributors from selling across national borders, but the EU Commission has prohibited them from doing so by invoking EU antitrust laws. Exclusive distributorships have been permitted, but every time the manufacturer has included a clause prohibiting the distributor from exporting to another EU country, the clause has been stricken from the contract. In effect, a firm that has two factories in the EU with different costs, and thus distinct prices, is practically powerless to prevent products from the lower-cost affiliate from competing with higher-cost products from the other affiliate.

Economic differences also make international standardization difficult, although marketers can adapt to economic changes. In Japan, many women no longer have time to shop and prepare the traditional Japanese foods. They fill their needs by purchasing more convenience foods advertised on TV with home delivery or by going to the more than 50 chains of convenience stores. The largest, 7-Eleven, has nearly 13,000 stores, many of which are run by former small shopkeepers.

Can retailing be globalized? Retailers such as France's Carrefour, with stores in France, Spain, Brazil, Argentina, and the United States, think it can. So do Safeway, Gucci, Cartier, Benetton, and Toys 'R' Us, which have made aggressive penetration in Canada, Europe, Hong Kong, and Singapore. Kaufhof, the German retailing giant, has 100 shoe stores located in Austria, France, Switzerland, and Germany and is also the leading mail-order shoe retailer in Europe. Walmart, now with operations in 15 countries, is learning that global retailing takes localization.

Disintermediation   The term *disintermediation* is a large word that refers to the unraveling of traditional distribution structures and is most often the result of being able to combine the Internet with fast delivery services such as FedEx and UPS. Increasingly, these tools are shaking up traditional distribution channels and making possible rapid service with or without a formal distribution structure. Our increasing ability to ship products quickly may mean that the lack of dedicated channels makes less difference over time. A good example is J. K. Rowling, who opened her own website to market her wildly popular "Harry Potter" series of novels.

Factors Limiting Standardization	Product	Price	Distribution	Personal Selling	Promotion
1. Physical forces	1. Climatic conditions—special packaging, extra insulation, mildew protection, extra cooling capacity, special lubricants, dust protection, special instructions 2. Difficult terrain—stronger parts, larger engines, stronger packing	1. Special product requirements add to costs 2. Difficult terrain—extra transportation costs, higher sales expense (car maintenance, longer travel time, more per diem expense)	1. Difficult terrain—less customer mobility, requiring more outlets, each with more stock 2. Varying climatic conditions—more stock needed when distinct products required for different climates	1. Buyers widely dispersed or concentrated—affects territory and sales force size 2. Difficult terrain—high travel expense, longer travel time, fewer daily sales calls 3. Separate cultures created by physical barriers—salespeople from each culture may be needed	1. Cultural pockets created by barriers—separate ads for languages, dialects, words, customs 2. Different climates—distinct advertising themes
2. Sociocultural forces	1. Consumer attitudes toward product 2. Colors of product and package—varying significance 3. Languages—labels, instructions 4. Religion—consumption patterns 5. Attitudes toward time—differences in acceptance of time-saving products 6. Attitudes toward change—acceptance of new products 7. Educational levels—ability to comprehend instructions, ability to use product 8. Tastes and customs—product use and consumption 9. Different buying habits—package size 10. Who is decision maker? 11. Rural-urban population mix	1. Cultural objections to product—lower prices to penetrate market 2. Lower educational level, lower income—lower prices for mass market 3. Attitudes toward bargaining—affects list prices 4. Customers' attitude toward price	1. More and perhaps specialized outlets to market to various subcultures 2. Buyers accustomed to bargaining—requires small retailers 3. Attitudes toward change—varying acceptance of new kinds of outlets 4. Different buying habits—different types of outlets	1. Separate cultures—separate salespeople 2. Varying attitudes toward work, time, achievement, and wealth among cultures—difficult to motivate and control sales force 3. Different buying behavior—different kinds of sales forces 4. Cultural stigma attached to selling?	1. Language, different or same but with words having different connotations—advertisements, labels, instructions 2. Literacy, low—simple labels, instructions, ads with plenty of graphics 3. Symbolism—responses differ 4. Colors—significances differ 5. Attitudes toward advertising 6. Buying influence—gender, committee, family 7. Cultural pockets—different promotions 8. Religion—taboos and restrictions vary 9. Attitudes toward foreign products and firms
3. Legal-political forces	1. Some products prohibited 2. Certain features required or prohibited 3. Label and packaging requirements	1. Varying retail price maintenance laws 2. Government-controlled prices or markups 3. Antitrust laws 4. Import duties 5. Tax laws	1. Some kinds of channel members outlawed 2. Government-controlled markups 3. Retail price maintenance 4. Turnover taxes	1. Laws governing discharge of salespeople 2. Laws requiring compensation on discharging salespeople	1. Use of languages 2. Legal limits to expenditures 3. Taxes on advertising 4. Prohibition of promotion for some products 5. Special legal requirements for some products (cigarettes, pharmaceuticals)

(continued)

Factors Limiting Standardization	Product	Price	Distribution	Personal Selling	Promotion
	4. Varying product standards 5. Varying patent, copyright, and trademark laws 6. Varying import duties 7. Varying import restrictions 8. Local production required of all or part of product 9. Requirements to use local inputs that are different from home-country inputs 10. Cultural stigma attached to brand name or artwork?	6. Transfer pricing controls	5. Only government-owned channels permitted for some products 6. Restrictions on channel members—number, lines handled, licenses for each line 7. Laws on canceling contracts of channel members	3. Laws requiring profit sharing, overtime, working conditions 4. Restrictions on channel members	6. Media availability 7. Trademark laws 8. Taxes that discriminate against some kinds of promotion 9. Controls on language or claims used in ads for some products
4. Economic forces	1. Purchasing power—package size, product sophistication, quality level 2. Wages—varying requirements for labor-saving products 3. Condition of infrastructure—heavier products, hand- instead of power-operated 4. Market size—varying width of product mix	1. Different prices 2. Price elasticity of demand	1. Availability of outlets 2. Size of inventory 3. Size of outlets 4. Dispersion of outlets 5. Extent of self-service 6. Types of outlets 7. Length of channels	1. Sales force expense 2. Availability of employees in labor market	1. Media availability 2. Funds available 3. Emphasis on saving time 4. Experience with products 5. TV, radio ownership 6. Print media readership 7. Quality of media 8. Excessive costs to reach certain market segments
5. Competitive forces	1. Rate of new product introduction 2. Rate of product improvement 3. Quality levels 4. Package size 5. Strength in market	1. Competitors' prices 2. Number of competitors 3. Importance of price in competitors' marketing mix	1. Competitors' control of channel members 2. Competitors' margins to channel members 3. Competitors' choice of channel members	1. Competitors' sales force—number and ability 2. Competitors' emphasis on personal selling in promotional mix 3. Competitors' rates and methods of compensation	1. Competitors' promotional expenditures 2. Competitors' promotional mix 3. Competitors' choice of media
6. Distributive forces	1. Product servicing requirements 2. Package size 3. Branding—dealers' brands	1. Margins required by channel members 2. Special payments required—stocking, promotional	1. Availability of channel members 2. Number of company distribution centers 3. Market coverage by channel members 4. Demands of channel members	1. Size of sales force 2. Kind and quality of sales force	1. Kinds of promotion 2. Amounts of promotion

Nicole Kissam

Nicole Kissam: Consider a Career in International Marketing

Nicole Kissam holds a BS in business administration with a concentration in international management from California Polytechnic State University, San Luis Obispo, California. Currently, Kissam is vice president, Western Financial Services Practice, for Matrix Consulting Group in Palo Alto, California, but prior to that she worked as an account manager for the Rust Advertising Agency located in Prague, Czech Republic. Rust Advertising is a small to mid-sized independently owned advertising agency with multinational clients such as Corinthia Hotels, Air Malta, and the United Arab Emirates, as well as prominent local clients such as Radegast, a Czech brewer. At Rust Advertising, Kissam was responsible for the company's English-speaking, Europe-based clientele, specifically Corinthia Hotels and Air Malta. She worked with the agency's clients to understand their needs for advertising campaigns and marketing materials; worked with creative staff to develop ideas and material prototypes; planned, managed, and implemented small campaigns in the Czech Republic; wrote advertising copy; and produced a monthly newsletter for the company's professional organization of independent international advertising agencies. Kissam's job required her to speak English with clients and Czech with company staff. Kissam lived and worked in Prague for three years and traveled to clients in the Czech Republic and Hungary. Kissam is multilingual and speaks Czech and Spanish.

I completed an internship through AIESEC International after I graduated from Cal Poly. This internship is what originally took me to a small town in the Czech Republic for a four-month assignment. The assignment was with an umbrella holding company that owned many types of

businesses. My role there as an intern was to research the marketing potential of a few of their products. I highly recommend using an international student organization such as AIESEC to do an internship right when you graduate from college. The contacts and experience I gained through my internship transitioned me into finding another job in Prague for a longer expat experience. Although I eventually chose to come back to America and not continue my international career in advertising, I had options to continue on and work for large multinational advertising companies. Working for the smaller agency was a great first work experience and could have easily been a stepping stone to a larger multinational corporate role.

Kissam suggests that these job-related skills are necessary for success in international business:

Adaptability, interpersonal skills, technical/specialized skills (depending on the field you are in), ability to learn other languages quickly, willingness to travel and "be on the road" away from home.

Regarding the personal skills necessary for success in international business, Kissam said,

Interesting for me was learning the protocols around different levels of friendships and how interaction is structured. For example, in adult life in America, we tend to call or make appointments to see each other, rather than just stop by. Very interesting to me was the way that Czech people, if they knew each other very well and were good friends, would always just stop over at each other's houses and apartments unannounced. When you did so, it was like a pleasant and welcoming reunion of friends. There would always be a pot of hot tea, shot of distilled spirits, and some bread and cheese available to nibble on and converse over for a half hour or so. It was common to show up and have meals together without notice as well.

Czech people also have a custom of always bringing something to share with them when they visit, such as chocolate, tea, bread, etc. I carry this custom over into my life in America with friends and sometimes close business associates.

Regarding how to succeed in international business, Kissam noted,

Business travel is not all it is cracked up to be. A lot of times traveling internationally is about hotel rooms, long flights, and long work hours. The payoff is an amazing experience that not many people can say they have had.

Success is really determined on your ability to perform quality work, of course, but also to be able to adapt to a foreign culture enough to get people to like you and give you what you want/need to do your job. Language skills

(continued)

are not necessarily essential at this point because most businesspeople speak English in the world. However, if you are talented in learning other languages, it will deepen your experience in a foreign country a thousandfold.

In commenting on her most memorable experience in international business, Kissam recounted the following:

Working in the Czech Republic showed me a lot I never knew about my own capacity and abilities. I learned the language in less than six months, was successful at planning and implementing advertising campaigns in a foreign country, and made wonderful friends that I still keep in touch with almost six years later. Working across cultures was also amazing. The approach to working and work life is different in every country and can sometimes take some getting used to.

(The) most memorable experience was really just the day-to-day experience of living and working in Prague. I walked from my apartment to my office every day, rode the metro to visit clients in various European cities, and enjoyed the beauty of Prague while getting my first work experience.

Resources for Your Global Career

In international business, the saying "Nothing happens until somebody sells something" holds critical meaning considering the significant investments of money, time, and human capital required to establish a base of sales in a foreign market. Marketing creates and drives sales in foreign as well as domestic markets. The principles of marketing apply to all markets globally, but the overriding international business concept of "think globally, act locally" requires marketing flexibility to be able to make strategic and tactical marketing decisions based on a keen understanding of local consumers and market conditions.

The Job Description for Your International Marketing Career

There will be special prospects in international marketing because international marketing employees are faced with a vast array of social, economic, and political conditions combined with added responsibilities due to decentralized decision making and the increased distance between foreign and central offices. International planning and managerial jobs are typically offered to those who have obtained some international marketing experience at the company's central offices. Beginning positions in international marketing at a company's central offices can include a vast array of different responsibilities, but for those with a master's degree, it normally includes research, planning, and coordination efforts.

Career Training and Qualifications Necessary for International Marketing

It is helpful to be fluent in related foreign languages and to have lived in one or more of the countries the company trades with.

Potential workers should have a solid and broad foundation in marketing, based particularly on sales management and market research.

The majority of firms hiring for international marketing positions will hire those with bachelor's degrees or MBAs.

Resources for International Marketing

- Careers leading to international marketing:
  www.careers-in-marketing.com/
- International market development:
  www.ftpress.com/articles/article.aspx?p=101588
- Vignette of an international market development manager:
  www.mba.com/why-b-school/meet-b-school-alums/marketing/megan-osorio.aspx
- The international 4 Ps:
  www.scribd.com/doc/36799681/4p-s-of-International-Marketing
- International marketing via the Internet:
  www.webworkswsisolutions.com/147/going-global-through-internet-marketing-cost-effective-ways-to-capitalize-on-the-dropping-dollar.html
- International product management:
  www.svproduct.com/global-product-management/
- International brand management:
  www.squidoo.com/01theone
- Global branding strategy:
  www.jrcanda.com/art_delphi.html
  www.jrcanda.com/art_globb.html
  www.jrcanda.com/art_brandmarriage.html
- International advertising resource center:
  www.bgsu.edu/departments/tcom/faculty/ha/intlad1.html
- Ads from around the world:
  www.theglobalmarketer.com/video/
  adsoftheworld.com/taxonomy/region/international
- International award-winning campaigns:
  www.theglobalmarketer.com/index.php
- International public relations association:
  www.ipra.org/
- International market research:
  http://text.tns-global.com/index.htm,
  www.marketresearchworld.net/
  www.fita.org/trade_info.html
- Articles on international marketing trends and issues:
  www.theglobalmarketer.com/marketingpulse/index.jsp
- International marketing and international business resource links:
  http://wtfaculty.wtamu.edu/~sanwar.bus/otherlinks.htm

Summary

LO15-1 Explain why there are differences between domestic and international marketing.

Sometimes there are great differences, and sometimes there are none. Although the basic functions of marketing are the same, the environmental forces can vary greatly. The marketing manager must decide whether the marketing program can be the same worldwide, if some changes must be made, or if a completely different marketing mix is required.

LO15-2 Discuss why international marketing managers may wish to standardize the marketing mix.

As a whole, firm executives are interested in the potential cost savings of using the same product and promotional mix. It is also easier to control the program and less time needs to be spent on the marketing plan.

LO15-3 Explain why it is often impossible to standardize the marketing mix worldwide.

Few countries, or the people within them, are the same. Usually some changes are necessary, and often these changes are substantial.

LO15-4 Discuss the importance of distinguishing among the total product, the physical product, and the brand name.

Each of the components of the total product can be altered as part of product adaptation. A brand name may be the same while the product is changed. On the other hand, sometimes the brand name is inappropriate and should be changed while the physical product may be fine without alteration.

LO15-5 Explain why consumer products generally require greater modification for international sales than do industrial products or services.

Industrial products (like, say, concrete) contain little or no "cultural input" and there are few personal preferences. On the other hand, consumer products reflect personal preferences. Notice that, for example, at the fashion end of the consumer market, there again may be few differences in country preferences. For example, a Louis Vuitton luxury purse may be the same all over the world.

LO15-6 Discuss the product strategies that can be formed from three product alternatives and three kinds of promotional messages.

Six commonly used promotional strategies can be formulated by combining the same, adapted, or newly designed product with the same, adapted, or different promotional message.

LO15-7 Discuss some of the effects the Internet may have on international marketing.

Among others, the Internet makes more pricing information available, increases the possibilities of distribution (for example the Burberry stores in China can broadcast runway events and clerks are equipped with iPads to make instant ordering of unstocked sizes), and can make the offering much more personal in terms of sizing and other variables.

LO15-8 Explain "glocal" advertising strategies.

The idea is to design an international program and then make local adjustments that local managers find necessary.

LO15-9 Discuss the distribution strategies of international marketers.

The fact is that the same channel members are not available everywhere and marketers must make adjustments for local conditions. For example, smaller stores are the norm in Japan as compared to the United States. Similarly, while 6 of the 10 fastest-growing emerging markets are in Africa, traditional distribution systems with elaborate warehousing systems are seldom available.

Key Words

marketing mix (p. 368)
total product (p. 370)
promotion (p. 377)
advertising (p. 378)

programmed-management
   approach (p. 384)
sales promotion (p. 385)
public relations (p. 386)

foreign national pricing (p. 387)
international pricing (p. 387)

1. Louis Vitton CEO Yves Carcelle says, "One to two thousand people is all you need. You can't judge by average income—average doesn't mean anything." Although he was speaking about the luxury goods market, do his comments about averages apply to other segments of the market as well? Why or why not?

2. What future do you see for global advertising?

3. What are two advantages of standardizing the marketing mix worldwide?

4. As people become more educated and living conditions improve, do their product preferences converge?

5. What is the basis of the reasoning for a panregional approach?

6. Arguably, food retailing in Japan and Europe is becoming more like that in the United States. What changes made this possible?

7. Assume you are a consultant to Nintendo, shortly before the introduction of the Wii U, the Nintendo home game console. What advice would you give Nintendo about making the device attractive to various foreign customers?

8. What cultural problems might you encounter in introducing the location sharing application Foursquare in foreign markets?

9. Farmville and Cityville are simple games played by millions of Facebook users, and the Chinese equivalent enjoys almost as much success. What do you think are the elements of the farming social network game Farmville that would appeal to consumers from many different cultures?

---

 globalEDGE.msu.edu

Research Task

Use the globalEDGE site (http://globalEDGE.msu.edu/) to complete the following exercises:

1. Locate and retrieve the most current ranking of *global brands*. Identify the criteria that are utilized in the ranking. Which country has considerable representation in the top 100 global brands list? Prepare a short report identifying the countries that possess top global brands and the potential reasons for success.

2. You are the marketing manager of a company that sells pet products, which have been of high demand in the United States. Given the huge success domestically, you want to explore opportunities abroad for your products. Utilize the Country Commercial Guides for U.S. Investors, and find a market research report on the pet products sector in Poland. Prepare an executive summary highlighting the opportunities and obstacles for your company in this country.

Minicase: Witty, Irreverent, a Little Over the Top?

Kraft, the 109-year old cheese company, released a new ad campaign in 2011 for its Athenos line of hummus, combining shock value, social media, and a little stereotyping. A young woman, Michelle, serves her friends Athenos hummus, and a Greek yiayia, or grandmother, comments that Michelle dresses like a prostitute. The hostess does a verbal double-take and the Greek grandmother repeats the word "prostitute" for good measure. Then the narrator points out that at least Yiayia endorses Athenos hummus. "Athenos may be the only thing approved by Yiayia," goes the tagline.

The ad is part of Kraft's efforts to shed its stodgy image and appeal to the denizens of Facebook and Twitter. In other recent efforts, Kraft has shown parents being arrested for eating their children's macaroni and cheese, handed out macaroni and cheese through Twitter, held a contest in which divorcing couples can win money if their split resulted from differences over Miracle Whip, and made the Yiayia popular enough to claim more than 150,000 Facebook hits.

Another ad features a couple declaring that they eat Athenos yogurt for breakfast, before Yiayia informs them they are going to hell for not being married. In another, the yiayia calls a stay-at-home husband a "wife."

Some Greeks have reported that they found the ads offensive, yet the ads may have persuaded a number of people to try hummus (although at least one commenter maintains that hummus isn't actually a Greek food at all).

Questions

1. View the ads. Did you find them offensive?

2. Do you think such ads will help Kraft shed its older, stodgy image?

3. Can you develop a similar campaign for another old-line brand or product that needs updating?

Sources: Ron Dicker, "Greek Outcry Over Kraft's Athenos Ads: Hummus and Hookers, Oh My!" www.walletpop.com/2011/02/28/greek-outcry-over-krafts-athenos-ads-hummus-and-hookers-oh-my/ (accessed July 1, 2011); Julie Jargon, "Kraft Spiffs Up Its Old Brands," *The Wall Street Journal*, June 30, 2011, p. B10; and "Kraft's Greek Grandmother Ads Draw Criticism," www.chicagotribune.com/business/ct-biz-yiayia-fashion-mar1,0,3786436.htmlpage (accessed July 1, 2011).

Global Operations and Supply Chain Management

Creating a national company is like rocket science . . . but creating an international company is like proton physics.

—*John Strand, Strand Consulting*

Zara: Transforming the International Fashion Industry through Innovative Supply Chain Management

After World War II, the leading designers of women's fashions typically looked to Paris and other European fashion centers for insight into what clothing to offer to the markets. Fashion houses like Chanel, Armani, and Gucci displayed their clothing lines twice a year in glamorous fashion shows, which provided the foundation for upscale boutiques to make their merchandise purchase decisions. These designs, which often cost thousands of dollars, were affordable only by the very rich. The designs were subsequently copied by mall retailers and sold to the masses at lower prices, helping to ensure that consumer trends moved in sync with the fashion industry. The limited parameters of what designs were being produced helped simplify planning and allowed clothing companies to survive even when they took six to nine months to bring a product from design to market.

That business model is disappearing rapidly. The international fashion industry is undergoing a major transformation toward "fast fashion"—involving up-to-the-minute fashion, low prices, and a clear market focus. Helping lead this revolution is a Spanish company called Zara. One of the world's most rapidly expanding retailers, with a chain of nearly 1,800 clothing stores located in leading cities across more than 80 countries, Zara's annual sales exceed €8 billion. The company is known for its fashionable and affordable clothing, offered in stores that project a modern, clean, and stylish image. Zara's competitive advantage, however, comes from its world-class supply chain management skills and its ability to reengineer the clothing supply chain.

The company's strategy of speed and flexibility has enabled Zara to shorten the fashion cycle almost to the point where it no longer exists. Store managers and roving observers use handheld devices to collect and send information regarding which designs are being well received by the buying public, which ones are not, and what will be the next hot trend. At headquarters, this information is used by its staff of more than 200 in-house designers to help stay on top of fashion trends. Zara's information systems also enable the company to better manage inventory, the primary cost of goods sold for clothing manufacturers and retailers. The textile manufacturers used by the company are mostly located close to Zara's headquarters, rather than lower-cost sources in the Far East that can lengthen the cycle time to market. For those cases in which it does buy fabric from more distant mills, Zara buys cloth only in four

learning objectives

After reading this chapter, you should be able to:

LO16-1   **Understand** the concept of supply chain management.

LO16-2   **Recognize** the relationship between design and supply chain management.

LO16-3   **Describe** the five global sourcing arrangements.

LO16-4   **Understand** the increasing role of electronic purchasing for global sourcing.

LO16-5   **Appreciate** the importance of the added costs of global sourcing.

LO16-6   **Explain** the potential of global standardization of production processes and procedures, and identify impediments to standardization efforts.

colors, enabling it to postpone dyeing and printing until the last possible moment.

Zara uses information technology and advanced supply chain management techniques to maintain tight control and integration of the various elements of the entire process, from textile mill to retail store. As a result, Zara has reduced the cycle time from initial garment design to appearance on hangers in the company's retail stores to as little as 14 days—versus a cycle time of 3 to 15 months for most of its rivals' products. Rapid turnaround times also mean the company can keep its best-selling designs well stocked, limit excess inventory of designs that do not resonate with the consumer, and add looks that were not initially in its collections. "If I tried to source my collections in Asia, I would not be able to get them quickly enough to our stores. By manufacturing close to home, I can scrap collections when they are not selling. And without this rapid response, I would not be able to extract a good relation between quality, price and fashion, which is what our customers have come to expect," said Jose Maria Castellano, the former CEO of Inditex and architect of Zara's fast-fashion business model.

As a result of these innovations, Zara can design merchandise inspired by and similar in style to what appears in fashion shows of the world's most prestigious fashion brands in Paris and Milan—and can have the merchandise on sale throughout the Zara chain long before the original designer's products have reached the market. A consequence, ironically, is that consumers may perceive the original product to be a copy, rather than Zara's offerings.

The company's business strategy also focuses on continual renewal of clothing lines. It ruthlessly removes its product lines, even ones that have been selling well, every two weeks or so. This approach enables Zara to have a near-continuous stream of new merchandise, always offer fresh styles, and help its customers to never feel out of fashion. Producing a range of 20,000 different items per year, Zara's culture of reacting very quickly to new fashion trends means that each time a customer walks into a Zara store, she can get the feel of entering a new place, one with fresh styles on display. Customers have thus come to know Zara as a chain offering a steady stream of new, "gotta-have-it" merchandise, and the limited availability of its merchandise promotes impulse purchases—a "grab it while you can" mentality among shoppers. To enhance its legitimacy in the fashion world and promote the style of its offerings, Zara uses top models in image ad campaigns that are placed in leading fashion magazines such as *Vogue.*

Even high-end shoppers who have traditionally been loyal to designer labels have begun to mix high fashion with the fast-fashion products pioneered by companies such as Zara. Cost, quality, and design have become lower priorities than an ability to deliver a constant stream of fashionable new merchandise. Attracted by the rapid introduction of new styles and the excitement of buying 10 inexpensive knockoff designs for less than the price of a single "authentic" jacket, even many wealthy customers have become loyal to Zara's fast-fashion approach. For example, a long pink boucle jacket similar to a current offering from the Chanel collection cost $129 at Zara, versus an original (albeit one with additional pearl buttons and a skirt) that was priced at $7,326. "Once it was embarrassing to be seen entering these stores. But now, not at all," proclaimed Franca Sozzani, the editor-in-chief of *Vogue Italia.*

Zara's revolutionary approach to the fashion industry means that it dictates industry standards on such dimensions as time to market, order fulfillment, costs, and customer satisfaction, as well as the ability to manage the linkages between these factors. The result is that high-end designers and fashion houses are being pressured to change their own operations and improve their ability to compete on speed. "What luxury brands can learn from these companies is their short time to market and constantly new merchandise. Even in the luxury business, customers want new merchandise all the time," explained Fabio Gnocchi, director of worldwide operations for the Italian fashion house Etro SpA. Building strong relationships with suppliers and improving capabilities in supply chain management seem to be requirements for other retailers hoping to respond to the fast-fashion model.

Propelled by the company's outstanding operational capabilities and execution in supply chain management, the Zara label has not only become the strongest Spanish consumer brand. It is also a label with impressive international pull within the fashion industry and a major factor in transforming the industry globally. Daniel Piette, fashion director for the upscale fashion house Louis Vuitton, described Zara as "possibly the most innovative and devastating retailer in the world." As Zara shows, effective supply chain management can indeed result in international competitive advantage.

Sources: Grupo Inditex, *2010 Annual Report,* www.inditex.com/ en/shareholders_and_investors/investor_relations/annual_reports (accessed June 21, 2011); Sarah Raper Larenaudie, "Inside the H&M Fashion Machine," *Time,* Spring 2004, pp. 48–50, www.time .com/time/2004/style/020904/article/inside_the_h_m_fashion_01a .html (June 21, 2011); "Branding Espana to the Rest of the World," *Brand Strategy,* March 2004, p. 12, http://goliath.ecnext.com/ coms2/gi_0199-161964/Branding-Espana-to-the-rest.html (June 21, 2011); Cecilie Rohwedder, "Style and Substance: Making Fashion Faster; As Knockoffs Beat Originals to Market, Designers Speed the Trip from Sketch to Store," *The Wall Street Journal,* February 24, 2004, p. B1; Teri Agins, "Pick-and-Mix Shoppers Force Fashion Industry to Abandon Old Models," *The Asian Wall Street Journal,* September 10–12, 2004, pp. A1, A10; and Stephen Tierney, "New Research Proves Link between Supply Line and Bottom Line," *Frontline Solutions,* October 2003, p. 31.

As firms continue to enter global markets, global competition increases. This forces management of both international and domestic companies to search for ways to lower costs while improving their products or services in order to remain competitive. Sometimes the desired results are obtained through improvements within existing operations. Other times, improved competitiveness is pursued by having the company open new—or transfer existing—operations abroad or find alternative outside sources for the labor, raw materials, or other inputs that it is currently sourcing from other organizations. A third option involves **outsourcing,** that is, hiring others to perform some of the noncore activities and decision making in a company's value chain, instead of continuing to do them in-house. Commonly, outsourcing firms provide key components of data processing, logistics, payroll, and accounting, although any activity in the value chain can be outsourced. It is common that management will pursue some combination of these different options in their efforts to enhance their company's international competitiveness. The efforts to improve the efficiency and effectiveness of a firm's international operations are often referred to as **supply chain management.** In this chapter, we discuss the topics of global supply chain management and critical issues in the management of global operations, including global sourcing, manufacturing systems, productivity and performance of international manufacturing operations, and issues associated with global standardization versus localization of international operations.

outsourcing
Hiring others to perform some of the noncore activities and decision making in a company's value chain, rather than having the company and its employees continue to perform those activities

Managing Global Supply Chains

Supply chain management has become an increasingly popular and strategically important topic in international business in recent years. *Supply chain* refers to the activities that are involved in producing a company's products and services and how these activities are linked together. The concept of supply chain management involves the applications of a total systems approach to managing the overall flow of materials, information, finances, and services within and among companies in the value chain—from raw materials and components suppliers through manufacturing facilities and warehouses and on to the ultimate customer.[1] Supply chains are an integral part of global quality and cost management initiatives, because a typical company's supply chain costs can represent more than 50 percent of assets and more than 80 percent of revenues.[2] Figure 16.1 illustrates a global supply chain for an American laptop computer company. This example broadly illustrates the activities and linkages involved in transforming initial designs into the finished goods and support services delivered to the consumer. These include product design, suppliers that provide the various inputs, assembly and testing activities, warehousing and distribution of finished goods, and the sales and technical support operations.

Because inventory is carried at each stage in the supply chain, and because inventory ties up money, it has been argued that the ultimate goal of effective supply chain management

supply chain management
The process of coordinating and integrating the flow of materials, information, finances, and services within and among companies in the value chain from suppliers to the ultimate consumer

LO16-1 Understand the concept of supply chain management.

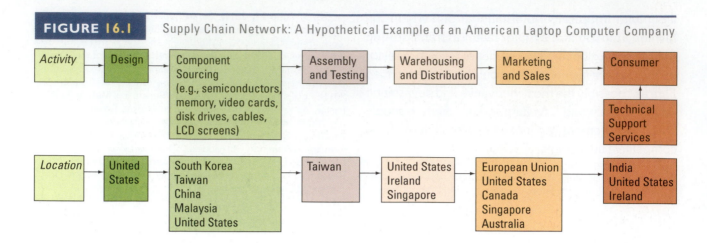

FIGURE 16.1 Supply Chain Network: A Hypothetical Example of an American Laptop Computer Company

systems is to reduce inventory, consistent with the prerequisites that the company's products be available when needed and at the desired level of quality and quantity. For that reason, it is critical that the operations at each stage in the supply chain are synchronized in order to minimize the size of these buffer inventories. Shorter, less predictable product life cycles, as well as the impact of unplanned economic, political, and social events, have placed further emphasis on the achievement of effective supply chain performance.[3] New technologies, including Web-enabled tools for supply chain planning, execution, and optimization, have enhanced the availability of data and integration with suppliers and customers, helping to enhance the international competitiveness of companies that have adopted and mastered these technologies.

As highlighted in the Balagny minicase at the end of this chapter and the Zara example at the beginning of the chapter, global supply chain management has been receiving increasing attention because many companies have achieved significant international competitive advantage as a result of the manner in which they have configured and managed their global supply chain activities. Some organizations, such as the computer and information technology company Dell, have reconfigured their international supply chains to substantially reduce or eliminate activities such as finished goods warehousing and retail stores, thus reducing costs and increasing effectiveness.[4] Other companies, such as the Hong Kong export trading company Li and Fung, have transformed their operations to enter into new, value-adding activities in an industry's value chain.[5] Effective supply chain management can also enhance a company's ability to manage regulatory, social, and other environmental pressures, both nationally and globally.

Design of Products and Services

LO16-2 Recognize the relationship between design and supply chain management.

An important factor in the structure and management of a company's global supply chain is the issue of design. The design of a company's products and services has a fundamental relationship with the type of inputs that the company will require, including labor, materials, information, and financing. As we discussed in Chapter 15, an important consideration in design is the extent to which the international company's products and services will be standardized across nations or regions or adapted to meet the different needs of various markets. The decision on standardization versus localization of designs is affected by a range of competitive, cultural, regulatory, and other factors and is an important strategic consideration for a company.

As an example, the multinational automaker Ford set up a pioneering assembly plant in Camacari, Brazil, that includes in-house suppliers, just-in-time parts delivery, and a "just-in-sequence" flexible assembly line that can produce a range of different models. However, Ford's performance in Latin America suffered due to attempts to sell "tropicalized" versions of autos designed for the United States and Europe that had only minor adaptations for the local market, such as reinforced suspensions to better handle rugged roads. In response,

Ford of Brazil developed a small team of local engineers dubbed the "Amazon group" to design a vehicle more specifically oriented toward consumer needs in Latin America. The final product—an affordable, light, sport-utility vehicle called the Ecosport that was well suited to the more rugged Latin American operating context—achieved such success with consumers that Ford captured 80 percent of the SUV market in Brazil. Export demand has also been brisk from nations such as Argentina, Chile, Venezuela, and Mexico. "Local design has been the key to success," said David Breedlove, Ford's product development director for South America. "We used to copy U.S. models and then we recognized the need to focus on the South American market."[6]

A traditional approach to product design has been termed the "over-the-wall" approach. This involves a sequential approach to design: an initial step in which the designers prepare the product's design, followed by sending the newly created design to the company's manufacturing engineers, who must then address the production-related problems that often result from their exclusion from the initial design activity.

An alternative approach to design is to promote cross-functional participation in the design stage, thereby helping to identify and avoid many of the potential sourcing, manufacturing, and other difficulties that can be associated with a particular design. Many companies also involve key customers in the design activities to ensure that designs are consistent with the customers' needs. Using this type of concurrent engineering approach allows the proposed designs to be subjected to earlier assessments on cost, quality, and manufacturability dimensions, thereby enhancing the efficiency and effectiveness of subsequent manufacturing and supply chain management activities. Indeed, design decisions must often be integrated with assessment of the various supply chain considerations, such as whether and where the company can obtain the inputs needed for the company's operations, whether the firm will source locally or from foreign locations, and whether the company has the capability to produce and deliver the product or service in a competitively viable manner.

A recent change in the approach to design is the penchant to solicit very broad input, increasingly from general customers, into the process. Examples of customer solicitation of input include Dell's IdeaStorm site and Starbucks' suggestion site. Within a week of Starbucks' opening of their MyStarbucksIdea.com site, more than 100,000 votes had been cast for one improvement idea or another. Other companies such as Nike are finding that such activities also help to engage the customer, possibly increasing loyalty.[7]

Sourcing Globally

REASONS FOR SOURCING GLOBALLY

Although the primary reason for sourcing globally is to obtain lower prices, there are other reasons. Perhaps certain products the company requires are not available locally and must be imported. Another possibility is that the firm's foreign competitors are using components of better quality or design than those available in the home country. To be competitive, the company may have to source these components or production machinery in foreign countries. The term **offshoring** is commonly used for a company's decision to relocate activities to foreign locations.

offshoring
Relocating some or all of a business's activities or processes to a foreign location

When deciding to source internationally, companies can either set up their own facilities or outsource the production to other companies. Outsourcing has become an increasingly common option for companies as they try to focus scarce resources on their core competencies and leverage the skills of other companies to reduce costs and capital investments, improve flexibility and speed of response, enhance quality, and provide other strategic benefits. The activities can be outsourced either to another company in the same country or to a company in another country (the latter would constitute "offshore outsourcing"). Any part of the value chain can be outsourced, including product design, raw material or component supply, manufacturing or assembly, logistics, distribution, marketing, sales, service, human resources, or other activities.

Outsourcing decisions, including the decision to use global sources of supply, are extensions of the make-or-buy decisions of earlier eras. The pros and cons of these decisions usually include comparisons of costs as well as managerial control of confidential product design specifications, delivered quantity, quality, design, and delivery time and method. Other considerations include the manufacturing expertise required to make the raw material or components as well as the added cost of not being able to take advantage of the scale or larger volumes a vendor may have. In global purchasing, these issues are exacerbated by such factors as distance, different languages of buyers and sellers, and different national laws and regulations. Over time, many organizations have developed the ability to manage these obstacles fully or in part, thus enabling global outsourcing to become a viable option for an increasing number of firms. When possible, it is better for companies to initially outsource simple activities and gradually outsource more complex activities as both the outsourcer and the service provider gain experience.

The lure of global sourcing is the existence of suppliers with improved competitiveness in terms of cost, quality, timeliness, and other relevant dimensions. For example, certain nations may provide access to lower-cost or better-quality minerals or other important raw materials or components compared to what might be available domestically (such as bauxite in Jamaica or dynamic random-access memory chips in South Korea). In addition, the existence of industrially less developed countries with inexpensive and abundant unskilled labor may provide an attractive source of supply for labor-intensive products with low skill requirements. This helps explain why many relatively standardized and labor-intensive operations (such as the assembly of athletic shoes or men's dress shirts) have moved away from the more industrialized countries, where labor is more expensive. The international product life-cycle theory, which was discussed in Chapter 2, helps explain this migration of operations from the developed to the developing areas of the world. These emerging economies have moved on the product and process continuum from high-labor-content products made with light, unsophisticated process equipment, to sophisticated processes and more complex, lower-labor-content machinery, or skill-intensive engineering and design services.

The ability to effectively and efficiently use global sources has been enhanced by the plummeting cost of communications, widespread use of standardized interfaces such as Web browsers, and the increasing pace at which companies are automating and digitizing data. As more of a company's operational activities are automated, it becomes easier and more economical to outsource these activities. Increasing numbers of companies have begun to compete for outsourcing business, and customers have become more accustomed to using these services.

GLOBAL SOURCING ARRANGEMENTS

LO16-3 Describe the five global sourcing arrangements.

Any of the following arrangements can provide a firm with foreign products:

1. *Wholly owned subsidiary.* May be established in a country with low-cost labor to supply components to the home country plant, or the subsidiary may produce a product that either is not made in the home country or is of higher quality.

2. *Overseas joint venture.* Established where labor costs are lower, or quality higher, than in the home country to supply components to the home country.

3. *In-bond plant contractor.* Home-country plant sends components to be machined and assembled or only assembled by an independent contractor in an in-bond plant, a plant located in a foreign country that manufactures for export only.

4. *Overseas independent contractor.* Common in the clothing industry, in which firms with no production facilities, such as DKNY, Nike, and Liz Claiborne, contract with foreign manufacturers to make clothing to their specifications with their labels.

5. *Independent overseas manufacturer.*

IMPORTANCE OF GLOBAL SOURCING

A strong relationship exists between global sourcing and ownership of the foreign sources. *Intrafirm trade,* which includes trade between a parent company and its foreign affiliates, accounts for 30 to 40 percent of exports of goods and 35 to 45 percent of imports in the case of the United States.[8]

In U.S. industry, the proportion of purchased materials in the overall cost of goods sold has been rising for several decades, from an average of 40 percent in 1945 to 50 percent in 1960 and 55 to 80 percent today.[9] There are several reasons for this phenomenon, including greater complexity of products and increasing pressure for firms to focus on their core business and outsource other activities in which they lack strong competitive ability.

In addition, competitive pressures and reduced concept-to-market cycle times in many product and service sectors have resulted in a rapid increase in the number of new products that are made available to the market. It has been estimated that at least 50 percent of products currently on the market were not available five years ago. This development has created additional pressure to locate suppliers worldwide that can provide inputs at competitive prices and quality and with quick responsiveness to market changes.

THE INCREASING USE OF ELECTRONIC PURCHASING FOR GLOBAL SOURCING

LO16-4 **Understand** the increasing role of electronic purchasing for global sourcing.

Simply entering "exporter" and the name of the product in a search engine will bring up the websites of dozens of exporters around the world that have online catalogs and information on how to order their products. There are also buyers, some of them from large companies, looking for products. In recent years, many firms have set up electronic procurement (e-procurement) exchanges, individually or in conjunction with other firms, to identify potential suppliers or customers and facilitate efficient and dynamic interactions among these prospective buyers and suppliers.

Ambitious B2B (business-to-business) e-procurement projects have been announced in healthcare and manufacturing (e.g., Covisint.com), chemicals (e.g., ChemConnect.com), insurance, petroleum, and hospital supplies. There is even a similar initiative in the advertising industry called NuIdea-Exchange, where marketers looking for advertising suggestions can connect with "creatives" who may have a good idea that has not found a home. In many companies, the purchasing function has been neglected for many years and is often viewed as a prime candidate for outsourcing to other firms. However, purchasing is increasingly being considered a strategic function, a trend encouraged by rapid developments in e-procurement.

While direct production–oriented goods have been the focus of management attention for many years, the purchasing of goods and services that are not part of finished goods—termed *indirect procurement*—is also critical. Including such items as maintenance, repair, operating supplies, office equipment, and other services and supplies, indirect procurement can account for as much as 70 percent of the total purchasing expenditures in a company. Although many organizations have continued to rely on traditional paper-based processes for indirect procurement despite their cost and inefficiency, new technologies are quickly encouraging change in this approach, even for small and mid-sized companies.

Options for Global Electronic Procurement
Among the most basic transactions that can occur over electronic purchasing exchanges are catalog purchases. Suppliers will provide a catalog of the products available, and buyers can access, review, and place orders for desired items at a listed price. The supplier can keep the catalog updated in real time, adjusting prices according to inventory levels and the need to move particular products. Electronic exchanges can also permit buyers and suppliers to interact through a standard bid/quote system in which buyers can post their purchasing needs online for all prospective suppliers to view, and the suppliers can then submit private quotes to the buyer. The buyer can then select among the submitted quotations on the basis of price, delivery times, or other factors. Industry-sponsored exchanges can also facilitate obtaining letters of credit, contracting for logistics and distribution, and monitoring daily prices and order flows, among other services.

Benefits of Global Electronic Procurement Systems
The benefits of electronic purchasing initiatives can be quite substantial, allowing companies to streamline operations, cut costs, and improve productivity in supply chain management and customer

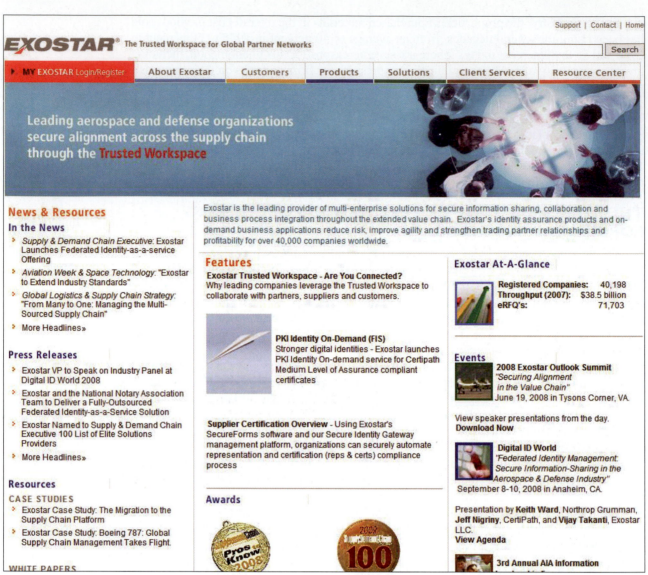

Web sites like Exostar help companies simplify and standardize procurement processes, streamline supply chains, reduce costs, improve productivity, and reach new markets.

Source: *Reprinted courtesy of Exostar.*

response. Research found that suppliers cut invoice and ordering errors by an average of 69 percent when using an e-marketplace, enhancing efficiency and reducing costs.[10] Websites like Exostar help companies simplify and standardize procurement processes, streamline supply chains, reduce costs, improve productivity, and reach new markets.

Smaller companies are also using the Internet to purchase raw materials as well as to sell their products to customers, often on a worldwide basis. Developments such as e-procurement exchanges have opened the door for many smaller suppliers, which now have to spend very little to get into the market, lowering barriers to entry to domestic and international market opportunities. As asserted by Amanda Mesler, managing director of KPMG Consulting in Houston, Texas, "The promise of an exchange is that it allows them [smaller companies] to leverage their size further and get into more markets, especially globally and internationally, than they ever have before."[11]

Overall, emerging industry-based B2B exchanges can help optimize the supply chain across an entire network of organizations, not merely within a single company. These exchanges can create value by aggregating the purchasing power of buyers, improving process efficiency, integrating supply chains, enhancing content dissemination, and improving overall market efficiency within and across nations.

PROBLEMS WITH GLOBAL SOURCING

LO16-5 **Appreciate** the importance of the added costs of global sourcing.

Although global sourcing is a standard procedure for half of the U.S. firms with sales greater than $10 million, it does have some disadvantages. In as much as lower price is the primary reason companies make foreign purchases, they may be surprised that what initially appeared to be a lower price is not really lower once all the costs connected to the purchase are considered.

For purchases of capital goods such as manufacturing equipment, many U.S. buying organizations now use "life-cycle costing" to analyze purchasing decisions through the life of the purchased item, including trade-in or future estimated salvage value. Even on components, firms are increasingly including full costing, including the use of activity-based costing systems, to ensure that all the costs associated with foreign sourcing (e.g., transportation, insurance, increased inventory levels to insulate against delays in delivery) are fully recognized when they make purchasing decisions.[12] It is essential that global sourcing decisions be closely linked to the organization's strategy and that explicit objectives for suppliers (such as delivery times and cost objectives) be defined and incorporated in contracts, ideally with incentives for meeting or exceeding them. Cross-company teams should also be developed in order to enhance the likelihood that best practices can be effectively shared between the organization and its suppliers, in order to avoid supply problems.

Added Costs   The buyer must understand the terms of sale because international freight, insurance, and packing can add as much as 10 to 12 percent to the quoted price, depending on the sales term used. The following is a list of the costs of importing, with an estimate of the percentage of the quoted price that each cost adds:

1. International freight, insurance, and packing (10–12 percent).
2. Import duties (0–50 percent).
3. Customhouse broker's fees (3–5 percent).
4. Transit or pipeline inventory (5–15 percent).
5. Cost of letter of credit (1 percent).
6. International travel and communication costs (2–8 percent).
7. Company import specialists (5 percent).
8. Reworking of products out of specification (0–15 percent).

One disadvantage an importer should not have to face is an increase in price because the home currency has lost value as a result of exchange rate fluctuation. For example, if an American importer requires that the exporter quote dollar prices, the importer has no exchange rate risk. However, if the firm has a large volume of imports and the dollar is unstable, management may want a quotation in foreign currency. In that case, the chief financial officer of the importing company probably will protect the company from exchange rate risk by using one of the hedging techniques discussed in Chapter 18. Hedging has been used for many years by companies that operate internationally, particularly if their raw materials include one or more of the commodities traded on established commodities markets. In most cases, such hedging has been done not for speculative reasons but as a means of protecting the company from the risk of rapid price fluctuations.

The emergence of e-procurement has also been accompanied by problems. E-procurement and electronic commerce as a whole cannot be isolated from the company's overall business system. Many early efforts at developing e-procurement systems have been made in isolation and have subsequently failed to deliver on their potential. Successful electronic commerce initiatives include connections to traditional systems for fulfilling procurement and other value chain activities, as well as considerations on how to manage the transition to new, electronic approaches. The traditional functions of purchasing—supplier determination, analysis, and selection—still have to be accomplished before the actual purchasing via e-procurement. In most instances, a company may be able to use the Internet for quicker data acquisition about possible suppliers and generally from a much broader information base than was previously available in a timely manner. Ensuring that a supplier is selected that

Cognizant Technology Solutions: Sourcing Low-Cost Talent Internationally to Achieve Global Competitive Advantage

India has become a global center for high-technology businesses in recent years, with an estimated 2.5 million information technology (IT) workers. The IT services sector has been supported by the Indian government for decades, a position enhanced by strong educational systems established by the British during colonial times. "The difference between India's universities and a school like Harvard is that an Indian university is harder to get into," said Mukesh Mehta, vice president of corporate systems for Metropolitan Life Insurance Company, which outsources IT services to an Indian supplier. Companies such as Microsoft, Oracle, and Sun have established research and development (R&D) facilities in Bangalore, Mumbai, and other Indian cities in an effort to utilize inexpensive and well-trained Indian engineers instead of expensive talent in the United States.

One company seeking to exploit this opportunity is Cognizant Technology Solutions of Teaneck, New Jersey. With an electrical engineering degree from Cambridge and an MBA from Harvard Business School, the company's chairman and CEO, Kumar Mahadeva, was well prepared to build a technology-based business. Observing the thriving software industry that was emerging in India in the early 1990s, Mahadeva recognized an opportunity. He realized that he could achieve a strong cost advantage over other U.S. companies by employing talented entry-level programmers in India for $6,000 to $9,000 per year, compared with an average salary in the United States of about $50,000. He founded Cognizant in 1994 as a division of Dun & Bradstreet Corporation, initially focusing on large-scale, full life-cycle software projects.

Providing software development and maintenance services, Cognizant competes on the basis of price, speed, and agility. The centerpiece of the company's operations is an innovative "offshore–onshore" business model. Under this model, about 30 percent of the

can meet all of the company's conditions for its raw material in terms of quality, delivery, price, and so forth, remains a challenge, particularly in a broadscale e-procurement network involving suppliers with which the company is not familiar. Suppliers located in emerging nations may also encounter difficulty in accessing and supporting sophisticated IT infrastructures, which can affect e-procurement performance.

Security also is often a significant concern for e-procurement. For B2B electronic commerce to achieve its full potential, access to the company's internal systems from outside is critical. Companies are wary of opening up the details of their business—including pricing, inventory, or design specifications—to competitors, to avoid risking the loss of brand equity and margins. In addition, exposing internal business systems to access via the Internet can expose the firm to a wide range of potential security issues, such as unauthorized entry ("hacking") and fraudulent orders. Although extensive research and development efforts have been undertaken in encryption technology and other technology and processes to ensure integrity, much progress still remains to be achieved before these systems can be considered fully secure. Different country standards are also of concern in attempting to implement international e-procurement systems. Governmental concerns with potential anticompetitive effects of collaboration among competitors may also cause problems for industrywide B2B exchanges.

Manufacturing Systems

Because international firms maintain manufacturing facilities in countries at various levels of development—facilities utilizing factors of production that vary considerably in cost and quality from one country to another—it is understandable that manufacturing

company's more than 111,000 computer science and engineering professionals work at customer sites in the United States or other Western nations, and the remainder work at one of its more than 50 development centers, primarily located in India. Cognizant's hourly billable rates were substantially below comparable rates from domestic American providers.

Once a contract has been signed, a global "virtual project team" is set up. Under its trademarked "Two-in-a-Box" client engagement model, a small portion of the team is located at the client's site, mainly Indian nationals who come for a couple of years to handle project management activities and manage client relationships on a daily basis. The remainder of the team is located in India or a select number of other locations, where software development, coding, maintenance, and other activities are completed on an around-the-clock, seven-days-a-week basis. This approach allows Cognizant's project managers to interact intensely with its clients during working hours in the West, intimately understanding the clients' strategies and needs, while prototype development, coding, and system upgrading activities are conducted overnight in a "chasing the sun" model of customer support.

To facilitate effective management of the offshore and on-site components of the multinational team, the company has set up a satellite- and fiber-optic-cable–based voice/data communications infrastructure, including e-mail and videoconferencing capabilities. To minimize misunderstandings and other problems as thoughts are translated from one culture to another, Cognizant's recruitment efforts target English-speaking students from computer science, engineering, and information technology programs at leading Indian universities. The company also provides extensive project management training programs. In addition, the company has a proprietary Project Management Tool that allows project managers to monitor the workflow of individual team members and track the status of components and various development activities.

Despite a fiercely competitive marketplace, Cognizant has achieved sustained success with its innovative business model. The company went public in 1998 on the Nasdaq, and by 2011 it had more than 500 clients from five continents and each major industry sector, including a number of prominent domestic and international companies. By 2011, 78 percent of Cognizant's revenue was from North America and 19 percent from Europe, with 42 percent of revenues coming from financial services and 25 percent from health care. Cognizant has received many awards and recognitions, including listings by *Fortune* as among the "Most Admired Companies" and by *Forbes* for being one of the "25 Fastest Growing Technology Companies in America." Cognizant has soared to revenues of $4.6 billion, and a rate of growth that is more rapid than the industry as a whole.

Questions:

1. What benefits might result from the use of a multi-nation client management team approach?

2. What challenges might result from such a set-up, and how could they be managed?

Sources: Interviews with executives at Cognizant Technology Solutions; "2011 Corporate Fact Sheet," www.cognizant.com/aboutus/company-highlights (June 23, 2011); Cognizant Technology Solutions, *2010 Annual Report*, http://investors.cognizant.com/ (accessed June 23, 2011); Alex Salkever, "Recognizing Cognizant as a High-Tech Bargain," *Bloomberg Businessweek*, www.businessweek.com/bwdaily/dnflash/mar2000/sw00328.htm (accessed June 23, 2011); and "Information Technology in India," http://en.wikipedia.org/wiki/Information_technology_in_India (June 23, 2011).

systems will also vary considerably, even within the same company. A single company may have a combination of plants that range from those with the most advanced production technology to those with far less advanced technology. The manufacturing systems in place within and across a company's international operations can have important implications for the way in which the company's global supply chain is set up and managed.

ADVANCED PRODUCTION TECHNIQUES CAN ENHANCE QUALITY AND LOWER COSTS

Growing international competition requires increasing efforts from companies to achieve efficiency and effectiveness in their international production activities. As a result, companies all over the world have pursued ways to improve their competitiveness, putting into place advanced production systems such as just-in-time supply chains or highly synchronized manufacturing systems. Others have installed computer-integrated manufacturing (CIM), utilizing computers and robots to further improve productivity and quality. Although these innovations can be a major challenge to implement successfully, their impact on international companies' competitiveness can be impressive.

LO16-6 Explain the potential of global standardization of production processes and procedures, and identify impediments to standardization efforts.

logistics
Managerial functions associated with the movement of materials such as raw materials, work in progress, or finished goods

Logistics

Logistics refers to managerial functions associated with the movement of materials such as raw materials, work in progress, or finished goods. The effectiveness of supply chain management efforts is strongly influenced by how a company manages the interface of logistics

Use of robots alongside humans within an auto assembly plant

with sourcing and manufacturing, as well as with other activities such as design, engineering, and marketing.[13] Given the strong emphasis on minimization of inventory and handling in supply chains, the way a product (or the components and materials that will go into a product) is designed can significantly influence the cost of delivering the product. For example, packaging and transportation requirements for a product can significantly influence logistics costs, and these factors should be addressed during design as well as in other steps in the value chain.

Many companies have chosen to outsource their logistics needs to outside specialists, particularly for managing international logistics activities. Companies such as Federal Express, DHL, and UPS have developed expertise in handling and tracking materials within and across nations, including sophisticated computer technology and systems for

tracking shipments. For example, FedEx's website www.fedex.com) allows a company to arrange pickups and then monitor the status of each item being transported, including information on the time the shipment was picked up; when and where it has been transferred within FedEx's network; and delivery location, time, and recipient. Many of these logistics companies have developed systems whereby their customers' in-house information systems are integrated with the logistics company's shipping and tracking systems. It is also common for logistics companies to offer a broad range of services beyond shipping, including warehousing, distribution management, and customs and brokerage services.

Standardization and the Management of Global Operations

Standards are documented agreements containing technical specifications or other precise criteria that will be used consistently as guidelines, rules, or definitions of the characteristics of a product, process, or service.

BENEFITS OF STANDARDIZATION OF GLOBAL OPERATIONS

Standards help ensure that materials, products, processes, and services are appropriate for their purpose. Credit cards and phone cards are produced to an accepted standard, including an optimal thickness of 0.76 mm, so that these cards can be used worldwide. The same symbols for automobile controls are displayed in cars throughout the world, no matter where the vehicles are produced.

In most countries, standards have been developed across product lines and for various functions. In the United States, for example, the standards developed by the American Society for Testing and Materials (ASTM) and other organizations are used in lieu of specific detailed requirements to ensure an expected level of use and quality. In Europe, the most used standard for quality is ISO 9000. This is a set of five universal standards for a quality assurance system that has been agreed to by the International Organization for Standardization (ISO), a federation of standards bodies from 162 countries.[14] The intention is that ISO 9000 standards will be applicable worldwide, avoiding technical barriers to trade attributable to the existence of nonharmonized standards between countries. If a product or service is purchased from a company that is registered to the appropriate ISO 9000 standard, the buyer will have important assurances that the quality of what was received will be what was expected. Indeed, registered companies have reported dramatic reductions in customer complaints as well as reduced operating costs and increased demand for their products and services. The United States has adopted the ISO 9000 series verbatim as the ANSI/AQC900 series.

The most comprehensive of the standards is now ISO 9001. It applies to industries involved in the design, development, manufacturing, installation, and servicing of products and services. The standards apply uniformly to companies, regardless of their size or industry. In general, companies that want to do business in Europe must have at least ISO 9000 registration, and many companies also require registration by their suppliers to provide further assurance of compliance.

Although it has been widely adopted as a standard for quality, not all quality "experts" agree that ISO 9000 is superior to other alternatives: "The focus of the standards is to establish quality management procedures, through detailed documentation, work instructions, and record keeping. These procedures . . . say nothing about the actual quality of the product—they deal entirely with standards to be followed." Phil Crosby, a noted quality expert and the author of several books on quality, states, "It is a delusion that sound management can be replaced by an information format. It is like putting a Bible in every hotel room with the thought that occupants will act according to its contents."[15]

An example of standardization is provided by Intel, the worldwide leader in supplying semiconductor memory products and related computer components, which introduced an approach called "Copy Exactly" for achieving standardization in its factories. "Copy Exactly solves the problem of getting production facilities up to speed quickly by duplicating everything from the development plant to the volume-manufacturing plant." Managers from high-volume facilities participate in the development plant as new process technology is created. "Everything at the development plant—the process flow, equipment set, suppliers, plumbing, manufacturing clean room, and training methodologies—is selected to meet high-volume needs, recorded, and then copied exactly to the high-volume plant. Time after time, factory yields start at higher levels, and even improve when multiple factories come online using Copy Exactly."[16]

An Intel employee checks wafers processing in a vertical diffusion furnace, one of the many tools through which wafers must pass as they go through the hundreds of steps that make up the manufacturing process. Intel, the worldwide leader in supplying semiconductor memory products and related computer components, uses a "Copy Exactly" strategy, which solves the problem of getting production facilities up to speed quickly by duplicating production facilities.

In addition to those just mentioned, there are other important, although perhaps less obvious, reasons for global standardization. The following sections discuss some of these reasons.

ORGANIZATION AND STAFFING

Some of the reasons for the global standardization of a firm's manufacturing systems are the effects on organization and staffing.

Simpler and Less Costly When Standardized
The standardization of production processes and procedures simplifies the manufacturing organization at headquarters because their replication enables the work to be accomplished with a smaller staff of support personnel. Fewer labor hours in plant design are involved because each new plant is essentially a scaled-up or scaled-down version of an existing one. The permanent group of experts that international companies maintain to give technical assistance to overseas plants can be smaller. Extra technicians accustomed to working with the same machinery can be borrowed from the domestic operation as needed.

Worldwide uniformity or standardization in manufacturing methods also increases headquarters' effectiveness in keeping the production specifications current. Every firm has hundreds of specifications, and those specifications are constantly being changed because of new raw materials or manufacturing procedures. If all plants, domestic and foreign, possess the same equipment, notice of a change can be given with one indiscriminate notification (e.g., an e-mail); there is no need for highly paid engineers to check each affiliate's list of equipment to see which ones are affected. Companies whose manufacturing processes are not unified have found that maintaining a current separate set of specifications for each of 15 or 20 affiliates is both more costly (larger staff) and more error-prone.

Logistics of Supply
As we discussed at the beginning of this chapter on the value of a supply chain management orientation, management has become increasingly aware that greater profits may be obtained by organizing all of its companies' production facilities into one logistical supply system that includes all the activities required to move raw materials, parts, and finished inventory from vendors, between enterprise facilities, and to customers. The standardization of processes and machinery provides a reasonable guarantee that parts manufactured in the firm's various plants will be interchangeable. This assurance of interchangeability enables management to divide the production of components among a number of subsidiaries in order to achieve greater economies of scale and take advantage of the lower production costs in some countries.

manufacturing rationalization

Division of production among a number of production units, thus enabling each to produce only a limited number of components for all of a firm's assembly plants

Rationalization
Manufacturing rationalization, as this production strategy is called, involves a change from a subsidiary's manufacturing only for its own national market to its producing a limited number of components for use by all subsidiaries. For example, SKF, a major bearing manufacturer with headquarters in Sweden, was able to reduce the number of types of ball bearings produced in five major overseas subsidiaries years ago from 50,000 to 20,000. Of the 20,000 remaining types, 7,000 have been rationalized among the five plants, and the other 13,000 are produced solely by one or another subsidiary for its local customers.[17]

For manufacturing rationalization to be possible, the product mix must first be rationalized; that is, the firm must elect to produce products that are identical worldwide or regionwide. Once this has been done, each subsidiary can be assigned to produce certain components for other foreign plants, thus attaining a higher volume with a lower production cost than would be possible if it manufactured the complete product for its national market only. Obviously, this strategy is not viable when consumers' tastes and preferences differ markedly among markets. For less differentiated products, however, manufacturing rationalization permits economies of scale in production and engineering that would otherwise be impossible.

Purchasing   When foreign subsidiaries are unable to purchase raw materials and machinery locally, they generally look for assistance from the purchasing department at headquarters. Because unified processes require the same materials everywhere, buyers can handle foreign requirements by simply increasing their regular orders to their usual suppliers and passing on the volume discounts to the subsidiaries. However, when special materials are required, purchasing agents must search out new vendors and place smaller orders, often at higher prices.

CONTROL

All the advantages of global standardization cited thus far also pertain to the other functions of management. Three aspects of control—quality, production, and maintenance—merit additional discussion.

Quality Control   When production equipment is similar, home office control of quality in foreign affiliates is less difficult because management can expect all plants to adhere to the same standard. The home office can compare the periodic reports that all affiliates submit and quickly spot deviations from the norm that require remedial action, such as a large number of product rejects. Separate standards for each plant because of equipment differences are unnecessary.

Production and Maintenance Control   A single standard also lessens the task of maintenance and production control. The same machinery should produce at the same rate of output and have the same frequency of maintenance no matter where it is located. In practice, deviations will occur because of the human and physical factors (dust, humidity, temperature), but at least similar machinery permits the home office to establish standards by which to determine the effectiveness of local managements. Furthermore, the maintenance experience of other production units in regard to the frequency of overhauls and the stock of required spare parts will help plants avoid costly, unforeseen stoppages from sudden breakdowns.

PLANNING

When a new plant can be built that is a duplicate of others already functioning, the planning and design will be both simpler and quicker because they are essentially a repetition of work already done:

1. Design engineers need only copy the drawings and lists of materials that they have in their files.
2. Vendors will be requested to furnish equipment that they have supplied previously.
3. The technical department can send the current manufacturing specifications without alteration.
4. Labor trainers experienced in the operation of the machinery can be sent to the new location without undergoing special training on new equipment.
5. Reasonably accurate forecasts of plant erection time and output can be based on experience with existing facilities.

In other words, the duplication of existing plants greatly reduces the engineering time required in planning and designing the new facilities and eliminates many of the startup difficulties inherent in any new operation. Just how important the savings from plant duplication are was emphasized in a study of the chemical and refining industries that indicated that the cost of technology transfer was lowered by 34 and 19 percent for the second and third startups, respectively.[18] If the case for global standardization of production is so strong, why do differences among plants in the same company persist?

Impediments to Standardization of Global Operations

Generally, it is easier for international corporations to standardize the concepts of total quality management and synchronous manufacturing in their overseas affiliates than it is to standardize the actual manufacturing facilities. Units of an international multiplant operation differ in size, machinery, and procedures because of the intervention of the foreign environmental forces, especially the economic, cultural, and political forces.

ENVIRONMENTAL FORCES

Let us examine the impact of the three kinds of forces just mentioned.

Economic Forces
The most important element of the economic forces that impede production standardization is the wide range of market sizes, discussed in Chapter 12.

To cope with the great variety of production requirements, the designer generally has the option of selecting either a *capital-intensive process* incorporating automated, high-semimanual-output machinery or a *labor-intensive process* employing more people and general-purpose equipment with lower productive capacity. The automated machinery is severely limited in flexibility (variety of products and range of sizes), but once set up, it will turn out in a few days what may be a year's supply for some markets.[19] For many processes, this problem may be resolved by installing one machine of the type used by the hundreds in the larger home plant. However, sometimes this option is not available; some processes use only one or two large machines, even in manufacturing facilities with large output, as we mentioned in the discussion of standardized manufacturing. Until recently, when the option was not available, plant designers had to choose between the high-output specialized machinery and the lower-output, general-purpose machines mentioned earlier. The major difference is that general-purpose machines require skills that are built into a special-purpose machine. The general-purpose machine usually produces a product of lower quality and higher per-unit costs than does the special-purpose machine.

A third alternative is available: computer-integrated manufacturing (CIM), which many international firms are using. However, its cost and high technological content generally limit its application to the industrialized nations and the more advanced developing nations. CIM systems enable a machine to make one part as easily as another in random order on an instruction from a bar code reader of the kind used in supermarkets. This reduces the economic batch quantity to one—the minimum number of a part that can be made economically by a factory—and it facilitates the potential for mass customization that we discussed earlier in this chapter. There is a limit, nevertheless, to the variety of shapes, sizes, and materials that can be accommodated.

Another economic factor that influences the designer's selection of processes is the *cost of production.* Automation tends to increase the productivity per worker because it requires less labor and results in higher output per machine. But if the desired output requires that the machines be operated only a fraction of the time, the high capital costs of automated equipment may result in excessive production costs even though labor costs are low. In situations where production costs favor semimanual equipment, the designer may be compelled to install high-capacity machines instead because of a lack of floor space. Generally, the space occupied by a few high-capacity machines is less than that required for the greater number of semimanual machines needed to produce the same output. However, because the correct type and quality of process materials are indispensable for specialized machinery, the engineers cannot recommend this equipment if such materials are unobtainable either from local sources or through importation. Occasionally, management will bypass this obstacle by means of **backward vertical integration;** that

backward vertical integration
Arrangement in which facilities are established to manufacture inputs used in the production of a firm's final products

is, manufacturing capacity to produce essential inputs will be included in the plant design even though it would be preferable from an economic standpoint to purchase those materials from outside vendors. For example, a textile factory might include a facility for producing nylon fibers.

The economic forces we have described are fundamental considerations in plant design, yet elements of the cultural and political forces may be sufficiently significant to override decisions based on purely economic reasoning.

Cultural Forces

When a factory is to be built in an industrialized nation that has a sizable market and high labor costs, capital-intensive processes will undoubtedly be employed. However, such processes may also be employed in developing countries, which commonly lack skilled workers despite their abundant supply of labor. This situation favors the use of specialized machines. Although a few highly skilled persons are needed for maintenance and setup, the job of *attending* these machines (starting, feeding stock) can be performed by unskilled workers after a short training period. In contrast, general-purpose machinery requires many more skilled operators.

These operators could be trained in technical schools, but the low prestige of such employment, a cultural characteristic, affects both the demand for and the supply of vocational education. Students do not demand it, and the traditional attitude of educational administrators in many developing nations causes resources to be directed to professional education instead of to the trades.

These economic and cultural variables, important as they are, are not the only considerations of management; the requirements of the host government must be met if the proposed plant is to become a reality.

Political Forces

When planning a new manufacturing facility in a developing country, management is frequently confronted by an intriguing paradox. Although the country desperately needs new job creation, which favors labor-intensive processes, government officials often insist on the most modern equipment. Local pride may be the cause, or it may be that these officials, wishing to see the new firm export, believe that only a factory with advanced technology can compete in world markets. They not only may be reluctant to take chances on "inferior" or untried alternatives, but also may feel that low-productivity technology will keep the country dependent on the industrialized countries. In some developing countries, this fear has been formalized by laws prohibiting the importation of used machinery.

Is Offshore Outsourcing Ending Its Run?

In 2003, nearly 900 workers at a cookware factory in Manitowoc, Wisconsin, switched off their machines. Their company was moving operations to Mexico. Now, however, many of the same workers are back, this time making pots and pans for Brazilian cookware maker Tramontina. Increasing growth in demand resulted in Tramontina acquiring land and building additional production facilities to allow a doubling of production output. In Japan, Sharp Corporation built a $9 billion factory complex that is the largest LCD and solar panel plant in the world. When plans for the plant were first announced, the trend in Japan was to build manufacturing offshore in places like China. But Sharp's chairman wanted to manufacture at home, and the company even included factories for many of its suppliers in its plans for the site. Sharp is bucking current trends in two directions. First, it is concentrating on manufacturing, rather than outsourcing production and concentrating on design and marketing. Second, it is building new production facilities in a high-cost country rather than in a low-cost area. So it is running against both the trend to outsource production and to "offshore" that production. In many economically developed countries, governments are offering a range of incentives to attract and retain jobs in manufacturing and other sectors of the economy.

This may represent a trend toward HCCS—high-cost country sourcing. The idea here is that being "at home," or in some cases "closer to home," may provide advantages, or at least make offshore production less attractive. First, as the cost of transportation increases, staying closer to home may become more economical. Second, while the labor costs of LCCS (low-cost country sourcing) will probably always be a reason to offshore, producing closer to home allows better control of quality and service. One furniture maker in Manitowoc says he can offer 150 different colors of furniture, a variety that is possible because he does not have to produce months in advance in order to bring product from offshore. As manufacturing moves from make-to-stock, repetitive production to more flexible approaches, other industries may find themselves in this situation.

In the first quarter of 2011, the total value of outsourcing contracts was $17.5 billion, a decline of 28 percent from the first quarter of 2010 and 25 percent below the last quarter of 2010. However, developments such as cloud computing, increased used of multiple-source supply systems, and risk management provide indications that extensive outsourcing and offshoring activity will continue. But only about 35 percent of outsourcing proposals directly met buyers' objectives, and outsourcing contracts generally appear to be decreasing in terms of average duration and contract value.

Questions:

1. What factors will determine whether or not more manufacturing and other activities will remain in—or come back to—high-cost countries such as the United States in coming years?

2. What are the implications of your analysis for economic prosperity—and job creation—in these countries?

Sources: Tramontina USA Inc., "Global Innovations . . . Made for the U.S.," www.tramontina-usa.com/global_innovations.pdf (June 23, 2011); David Jacoby and Bruna Figueiredo, "The Art of High-Cost Country Sourcing," *Supply Chain Management Review*, May/June 2008, pp. 32–38, http://trid.trb.org/view.aspx?id=867120 (June 23, 2011): Yukari Iwatani Kane, "Sharp Focuses on Manufacturing," *The Wall Street Journal*, July 9, 2008, p. B1, www.tectrends.com/tectrends/article/00170536.html (June 23, 2011); "Global Oursourcing Contract Volume Set to Climb in 2010," *PR Newswire*, March 18, 2010, www.prnewswire.com/news-releases/global-outsourcing-contract-volume-set-to-climb-in-2010-88404022.html (accessed June 12, 2010); "1Q11 Global TPI Index," www.tpi.net/newsevents/news/releases/110419-US.html (June 23, 2011); John Hill, "Manitowoc Plant Gets Second Chance to Make Cookware," *Corporate Report Wisconsin*, November 1, 2006, www.allbusiness.com/north-america/united-states-wisconsin/4104370-1.html (accessed June 23, 2011); Linda Wertheimer, "Are Outsourced Jobs Coming Back?" National Public Radio, February 2, 2009, www.npr.org/templates/story/story.php?storyId-100131296 (accessed June 23, 2011); Stephanie Overby, "Multi-billion-dollar Outsourcing Deals Turn Bad," *ITWorldCanada*, March 31, 2010, www.itworldcanada.com/news/multi-billion-dollar-outsourcing-deals-that-went-bad/140342 (accessed June 23, 2011); and Timothy Aeppel, "Export Boom Fuels Factory Town's Revival," *The Wall Street Journal*, July 18, 2008, pp. A1, A14, www.truthabouttrade.org/news/latest-news/12091-export-boom-fuels-factory-towns-revival (June 23, 2011).

For example, global automakers have announced investments of more than $10 billion in factories in China. However, most of the large automakers' plants are not designed to exploit China's large pool of low-cost labor. Rather, the plants are about as capital-intensive as American auto plants. Part of the reason for this is the Chinese government's desire to lure the latest technology, a goal it has promoted by a range of incentives. Acceding to these demands of the government can also be simpler for the automakers. As Mustafa Mharatem, the senior economist at General Motors, states, "Because of the way information travels these days, people in developing countries aren't any longer willing to buy cars that are one or two generations old. And if you're going to do the current-generation car, then keeping the process as similar as processes around the world makes sense."[20]

SOME DESIGN SOLUTIONS

More often than not, after consideration of the environmental variables, the resultant plant design will be a hybrid or one using intermediate technology.

Hybrid Design   Commonly, in designing plants for developing countries, engineers will use a hybrid of capital-intensive processes when they are considered essential to ensure product quality and labor-intensive processes to take advantage of the abundance of unskilled labor. For example, they may stipulate machine welding rather than hand welding but then use semimanual equipment for the painting, packaging, and materials handling.

Intermediate Technology   In recent years, the press of a growing population and the rise in capital costs have forced the governments of developing nations to search for something less than highly automated processes. They are becoming convinced that there should be something midway between the capital- and labor-intensive processes that will create more jobs, require less capital, but still produce the desired product quality. Governments are urging investors to consider an **intermediate technology,** which, unfortunately, is not readily available in the industrialized nations. This means that international companies cannot transfer the technology with which they are familiar but must develop new and different manufacturing methods. It is also possible that the savings in reduced capital costs of the intermediate technology may be nullified by higher startup costs and the greater expense of its transfer.

intermediate technology
Production methods between capital- and labor-intensive methods

Local Manufacturing System

BASIS FOR ORGANIZATION

Except for plants in large industrialized nations, the local manufacturing organization is commonly a scaled-down version of that found in the parent company. If the firm is organized by product companies or divisions (tires, industrial products, chemicals) in its home nation, the subsidiary will be divided into product departments. Manufacturing firms that use process organizations (departmentalized according to production processes) in the domestic operation will set up a similar structure in their foreign affiliates. In a paper-box factory, separate departments will cut the logs, produce the paper, and assemble the boxes. The only noticeable difference between the foreign and domestic operations is that in the foreign plant all these processes are more likely to be at one location because of the smaller size of each department.

HORIZONTAL AND VERTICAL INTEGRATION

The local manufacturing organization is rarely integrated either vertically or horizontally to the extent that the parent is. Some vertical integration is traditional, as in the case of the paper-box factory, and some will occur if it is necessary to ensure a supply of raw materials. In this situation, the subsidiary might be more vertically integrated than the parent, which depends on outside sources for many of its inputs. However, the additional investment is a deterrent to vertical integration, as are the extra profits gained by supplying inputs to these captive customers from the home plants. Some countries prohibit vertical integration for certain industries. In Mexico, for example, severe restrictions on private investment (Mexican or foreign) in the petroleum and petrochemical industry still exist and keep producers of products that use petrochemicals from achieving backward vertical integration. In contrast, some countries require a percentage of local content in finished products. When the subsidiary cannot meet the requirement by local sourcing, it may be forced to produce components that its parent does not.

Horizontal integration is much less prevalent in foreign subsidiaries, although restaurant chains, banks, food-processing plants, and other industries characterized by small production units will, of course, integrate horizontally in the manner of the domestic company. Overseas affiliates themselves become conglomerates when the parent acquires a multinational.

Jamie Cignetti at the Guataca School in San Pablo, Guatemala: A Life-Changing Experience

I am from Martinez, California, and I am completing a bachelor's degree in business administration, with a concentration in international business management, at Cal Poly in San Luis Obispo. I was drawn to international business because of my passion for culture and travel. My interest in service related to developing communities led me to explore Muhammad Yunis' microcredit and social business theories. After graduation, I plan to focus my career on facilitating sustainable economic development through social business, appropriate technology, and human empowerment. My studies and experiences in the field thus far have shown me the entrepreneurial sprit is universal—I believe that leveraging this creative drive, especially in developing communities, is a powerful tool to address our global community's mounting challenges.

Since September 2010, I have worked with Dr. Peter Schwartz, the village of San Pablo, and a team of fellow Cal Poly students to create an Appropriate Technology school in San Pablo *Tacaná*, a rural community of 800 people in the northwest highlands of Guatemala. An appropriate technology (or "intermediate technology," as coined by Schumacher's *Small Is Beautiful*) is often a small, inexpensive technology produced locally to serve the needs of the local people and provide local income with benign environmental impact. The school, called Guateca, consists of Cal Poly and San Pablo students

working collaboratively to design appropriate technologies and develop sustainable business models. In addition the students study relationships among energy, society, and the environment and take part in an active language exchange. Guateca aims to become a model for cross-cultural collaborative education, emphasizing sustainable SMEs (small and medium-sized enterprises) and fostering international community and local well-being.

My responsibilities with the program mostly include administrative support. To date, I have worked on our website development, marketing, recruitment, accounting and finance, event planning, data organization, communication with San Pablo, and most recently the development of a five-year business plan for the Cal Poly side of Guateca. While it has been exciting to help Guateca get started, my greatest enjoyment has come from the friends I've made at Cal Poly and in San Pablo. The program draws all kinds of people with such diverse backgrounds, experiences, and knowledge . . . I learn something new every day!

I traveled to San Pablo for the first time in December 2010 with 12 other Cal Poly students and Dr. Schwartz. For three months before our departure, we studied Guatemalan history and culture, as well as the history of San Pablo. At that time, we were fortunate enough to have Professor Luz Marina Delgado, a native Guatemalan who had personal ties with the community, to guide us through the many cultural differences. The instructors and students were careful to work from a place of mutual respect during our stay in San Pablo. We believe we had as much to learn from them as they have to learn from us. The importance of this attitude became so apparent that it profoundly shifted the long-term goals of the program. Rather than focus on technology and business development, we saw that a positive and empowering educational experience would be far more valuable than any widget we might create and sell.

I consider Guateca to be a life philosophy of sorts—the work we do is secondary to the relationships we are creating. Even in a heated or stressful situation, I challenge myself to step back and ask, "What kind of relationship are we developing with this approach?" It helps relieve internal tension and allows me to think about the next step with a clear head. This philosophy has been especially important for working in teams with the additional challenge of cultural differences and language barriers.

The physical distance that separates Cal Poly and San Pablo has only compounded these challenges. Most of our communication occurs via email; needless to say the messages are easily misinterpreted. To address this, we hired a Cal Poly Modern Language and Literature graduate to go to San Pablo, where she teaches English and acts as our main point of contact. She has vastly improved the clarity of our communications while keeping us in tune with feelings of the students and general community—a key aspect of communicating across cultures.

Working abroad can be confusing and frightening, especially as you start to look objectively at your culture and personal truths. Through my experiences with Guateca, I have learned to embrace the perspective this provides. In order to work successfully with others, whether at home or abroad, it is vital to be open-minded and to take time to assess a situation in context—I make a point to remind myself that the world view I hold is different from everyone else's. Every day I strive to be a student, teacher, and above all, a friend to those I meet.

(continued)

Resources for Your Global Career

Consider a Career in Global Logistics and Supply Chain Management

In international business, just-in-time manufacturing and lean manufacturing are increasingly important strategic concerns that can critically affect the bottom line of any organization operating globally. Third-party logistics suppliers are growing in importance because they are assuming responsibility for the logistics of supply chain management of many world-class corporations. There is increasing demand for professionals trained in purchasing, inventory control, warehouse management, and inbound/outbound distribution management worldwide. Managing global operations is an emerging field, and here are a number of career opportunities with salary range information for you to consider.

Entry level:

- Buyer/planner
- Inventory analyst
- Transportation coordinator
- Import/export clerk
- Quality assurance technician
- Salary ranges: mid $20,000s to mid $30,000s

Mid-level management:

- Purchasing manager
- Logistics manager
- Inventory control manager
- Director of quality assurance
- Manager of quality compliance
- International transportation manager
- Salary ranges: mid $40,000s to mid $50,000s

Senior-level management:

- Director of supply chain management
- Director of import/export management
- Vice president—logistics
- Vice president—production and inventory control
- Salary ranges: $70,000+

Resources on Global Logistics and Supply Chain Management:

- Logistics management: www.logisticsmgmt.com/
- Modern materials handling: www.mmh.com/
- Supply chain management review: www.scmr.com/
- Global logistics and supply chain strategies.
  - Articles, video interviews, data, and related information on global logistics management: www.supplychainbrain.com/content/index.php
- Building supply chains:
  - www.industryweek.com/articles/building_a_better_supply_chain_19610.aspx
  - www.forbes.com/2011/01/21/supply-chain-future-leadership-managing-mckinsey.html
  - www.s-ox.com/dsp_getFeaturesDetails.cfm?CID=2235
- Freight and logistics research and insights:
  - www.accenture.com/us-en/industry/freight-logistics/Pages/index.aspx?tab=2
  - www.handyshippingguide.com/shipping-news/freight-and-logistics-research-can-be-out-of-this-world_2537
  - www.d.umn.edu/~jvileta/industry/transportation.html
- Supply and demand chain executive, including multimedia, interactive global supply and demand chain map, research, news, and other materials: http://sdcexec.com/
- Supply chain digest: http://scdigest.com/
- Links to information about companies who transport goods internationally: www.business.com/directory/transportation_and_logistics/logistics/global_logistics/
- Sustainability within supply chains:
  - www.america.gov/st/env-english/2008/March/20080313154320wrybakcuh0.2632497.html
  - www.unglobalcompact.org/Issues/supply_chain/index.html
  - www.greenbiz.com/news/2011/05/02/simple-steps-tackle-complex-supply-chain-sustainability-issues
  - http://sic.conversationsnetwork.org/shows/detail4476.html

Summary

LO16-1 Understand the concept of supply chain management.

Supply chain management is the process of coordinating and integrating the flow of materials, information, finances, and services within and among companies in the value chain, from suppliers to the ultimate consumer. Supply chain management is integral to the achievement of cost and quality objectives in companies and to international competitiveness.

LO16-2 Recognize the relationship between design and supply chain management.

The design of a company's products and services has a fundamental relationship with the types of inputs the company will require, including labor, materials, information, and financing. Concurrent engineering approaches to design allow proposed designs to be subjected to earlier assessments on cost, quality, and manufacturability dimensions, enhancing the efficiency and effectiveness of subsequent supply chain management activities.

LO16-3 Describe the five global sourcing arrangements.

A firm may establish a wholly owned subsidiary in a low-labor-cost country to supply components to the home-country plant or to supply a product not produced in the home country. An overseas joint venture may be established in a country where labor costs are lower to supply components to the home country. The firm may send components to be machined and assembled by an independent contractor in an in-bond plant. The firm may contract with an independent contractor overseas to manufacture products to its specifications. The firm may buy from an independent overseas manufacturer.

LO16-4 Understand the increasing role of electronic purchasing for global sourcing.

The establishment of electronic purchasing systems on a company or industry basis can influence the number and type of suppliers available internationally to firms. Although there are a number of challenges to their use, electronic-purchasing systems can produce significant reductions in the costs of inputs, both direct and indirect products and services. These systems can also permit the optimization of supply chains across networks of organizations, not merely within a single company.

LO16-5 Appreciate the importance of the added costs of global sourcing.

International freight, insurance, and packing may add 10 to 12 percent to the quoted price, depending on the sales term used. Import duties, customhouse broker's fees, cost of letter of credit, cost of inventory in the pipeline, and international travel are some of the other added costs.

LO16-6 Explain the potential of global standardization of production processes and procedures, and identify impediments to standardization efforts.

Standards help ensure that materials, products, processes, and services are appropriate for their purpose, helping companies meet market and competitive demands. Standardization of activities helps simplify organization and control at headquarters because replication enables the work to be accomplished with a smaller staff of support personnel and internal best practices can more readily be applied across a company's international operations. However, differences in the foreign environmental forces, especially the economic, cultural, and political forces, cause units of an international multiplant operation to differ in size, machinery, and procedures, complicating efforts to achieve standardization of processes and procedures.

Key Words

outsourcing (p. 401)

supply chain management (p. 401)

offshoring (p. 403)

logistics (p. 409)

standards (p. 411)

manufacturing rationalization (p. 412)

backward vertical integration (p. 414)

intermediate technology (p. 417)

Questions

1. What recent developments have caused supply chain management to become increasingly important to international companies?

2. What are the main differences between sequential and concurrent approaches to the design of products and services?

3. Why would a company choose to source raw materials, components, or other products or services from a foreign supplier?

4. Why does the cost of raw materials represent about 55 to 80 percent of the cost of goods sold in U.S. industry, and why has this proportion been increasing over time?

5. Why is indirect procurement an important focus for management attention?

6. What are some of the primary problems or concerns associated with sourcing from a foreign supplier?

7. What is the benefit to a buyer company and to a vendor company of standards such as ISO 9000?

8. What are the advantages to a worldwide firm of global standardization of its production facilities?

9. Discuss the influence of the uncontrollable environmental forces in global standardization of a firm's production facilities.

10. Discuss some of the alternative design solutions available to a company that chooses not to completely standardize its production facilities.

Use the globalEDGE site (http://globalEDGE.msu.edu/) to complete the following exercises:

1. The World Bank's *Logistics Performance Index* (LPI) assesses the logistics environment of countries. Locate the most recent LPI ranking. How is the index constructed? Identify the top 10 and bottom 10 logistics performers. Prepare an executive summary highlighting the key findings from the LPI. How are these findings helpful for companies trying to build a competitive supply chain network?

2. Struggling to remain competitive in the medical devices industry, your firm has decided to begin sourcing components internationally. Though your firm's current operations are only in the United States and Germany, you must assess the relative costs for manufacturing medical devices in a variety of cities worldwide. Your manager, previously a consultant with KPMG, indicates that the *Competitive Alternatives* surveys published annually by KPMG may assist you. Develop a brief report addressing the following questions: (a) Which three cities in the survey have the lowest and highest manufacturing costs for your firm's specific industry? (b) Do you think that changing your firm's sourcing strategy will resolve the current problems? Why or why not?

Minicase: Balagny Clothing Company Outsources Domestic Production

Balagny Clothing Company Inc. is a major apparel manufacturer in the United States. It makes men's, women's, and children's casual wear such as denim jeans, cotton slacks, skirts, and sweaters. Balagny Clothing has taken the low-cost provider strategy and is constantly trying to find ways to cut costs and maintain their 4 percent profit margin while maintaining a competitive advantage over its major competitors. Because direct labor makes up approximately 65 percent of the total cost of an apparel item, Balagny Clothing closed all of its domestic manufacturing facilities and outsourced the production to contractors in China. In the United States, Balagny Clothing was paying an average hourly wage of $8.65 per hour. The Chinese labor rates average about $1.18 per hour, depending on the location of the factory. The company felt that relocating their production to China was a viable change for the long-term life of the company. Not only could it reduce labor costs by 86 percent, but it would no longer have to deal with labor unions; plant maintenance; and government regulatory offices such as the Occupational Safety and Health Administration (OSHA), the Fair Labor Standards Act (FLSA), and the Equal Employment Opportunity Commission (EEOC).

It took Balagny Clothing almost two years to complete the transition. After startup costs in China, domestic plant closings, and the associated costs, Balagny Clothing was ready to reap the benefits of its decisions. It slashed wholesale prices for the upcoming season to undercut the competition and planned for a 6 percent profit margin. Balagny Clothing had increased sales by more than 20 percent, garnering the majority of the business.

There were, however, a few discoveries that limited its cause to celebrate. It had relinquished almost all control over the manufacturing processes and product development after the initial designs were transmitted to their China contractors. Production was set up to be delivered in four batches per season (eight batches per year) with orders transmitted approximately four months in advance. These contracted production amounts were firm and, later that year when business slowed, Balagny Clothing could not lower the production rate nor refuse shipments. This resulted in large inventories of finished goods.

An additional and unexpected problem was caused by longer-than-expected transportation times from China to the Balagny Clothing distribution center. Balagny Clothing had originally planned for two-week in-transit inventory and customer delivery dates based on the import agents' estimated travel time across the Pacific, but the company had not foreseen an additional two- to three-week delay caused by the backlog at the port of Los Angeles. This pushed back shipment dates to Balagny Clothing's customers, resulting in a shorter selling period at retail and nullifying Balagny Clothing's expected refill orders, further enhancing already high finished goods inventory levels. The holding costs associated with these high inventory levels negated a large amount of the forecasted savings Balagny Clothing counted on for its profits.

In addition, customers were complaining that the fit and feel of the garments were different. The Chinese production facilities had altered the Balagny Clothing product to fit their production processes. The Chinese had their own raw material suppliers and their products were slightly different than Balagny Clothing's domestic suppliers.

Another problem that became evident was the producer's lack of flexibility. Because of the high inventories, model changes became more expensive because more inventory had to be marked down to clear the way for the new product. Balagny began to see a decline in sales and became concerned for the future of the company.

The CEO called the top management team together and charged each one of them to find ways to improve the situation.

William Duncan, vice president of operations, felt that he had an answer to the company's problems. After investigation, he proposed that they immediately buy or construct a wholly owned manufacturing subsidiary in Mexico in one of the border maquiladora parks. Finished goods could be transported from the maquiladora to the Balagny Clothing distribution center within 72 hours of completion. The plan would call for the maquiladora to produce the rapid turnover product needed for quick replenishment. The China contractors would be given the seasonal products that were not a part of the replenishment system and that could be produced and shipped in batches. The plan called for approximately 40 percent of the production to be moved to the Mexican maquiladoras while 60 percent would remain with China, yielding an average labor cost of $1.72 per hour. Duncan calculated that this change would decrease Balagny Clothing's on-hand and in-transit inventory dramatically, yielding a much higher profit.

Questions:

1. Identify specific concepts in the case found in this chapter, and discuss their relevance to the problems facing the company.

2. Considering all of the problems incurred in China and the immense effort and capital needed to start up the Mexico operation, would it have been a better idea for Balagny Clothing to keep its domestic operations? Why or why not?

Source: This case was contributed by Kevin Cruthirds of Nicholls State University.

Managing Human Resources in an International Context

Globalization . . . means globalizing every activity of the company. . . . Globalization especially means finding and attracting the unlimited pool of intellectual capital—the very best people—from all around the globe.

—*General Electric, "Key Growth Initiatives"*

Becoming an Expatriate, or Expat, as They Are Sometimes Called

You are happy and proud; you can hardly wait to get back to your office to phone your family with the news. Your boss has called you in and said, "We have a problem in Asia that we need you to solve." You are doing well with the company in the home, domestic market, but now the company has discovered markets away from home, and you have not seen anything away from home since you and your college friend backpacked in the Argentine mountains to Bariloche. You have read about dining at Singapore's Raffles Hotel with the ghost of Somerset Maugham, exploring Bangkok's temples, and enjoying the helicopter and Rolls-Royce service and harbor views of Hong Kong's Peninsula Hotel. A PricewaterhouseCoopers survey showed that 80 percent of 4,200 surveyed graduates from 44 countries said that they wanted to work internationally,[a] and now you have the chance to personally realize that dream.

You are about to become an **expatriate**. Your family will love it, and the foreign experience will be your passport to your company's top executive positions. Your career will be made. Right?

Maybe. You must be very careful. For too many employees who take foreign assignments, it is out of sight, out of mind, and you may find yourself well out of the loop. On the other hand, however, these assignments can be passports to the top if you take the right steps before you make the move.

If at all possible, arrange to have someone fairly high in the company hierarchy be your mentor, ideally a person who has also served in an expatriate role so that there can be a base of international experience that you can draw from. That home-country mentor should keep you advised of changes and developments in the company back at home and should keep your name in consideration and not forgotten while you are on your assignment abroad. You might also consider finding a mentor in the host country who can assist you in understanding the local culture, introduce you to valuable business contacts, and help you in interpreting situations that you encounter while in your position abroad.

Before you take the job, you should insist that your bosses tell you exactly what the company expects you to accomplish. Are you to get a plant up and running, install systems or practices that are currently in use in the home country, arrange customer financing, negotiate investment, or perhaps groom a host-country replacement? Will this be an extended on-site assignment, such as two to four years in length, or will it merely involve one or several short-term

learning objectives

After reading this chapter, you should be able to:

LO17-1 **Discuss** several of the major factors that may affect the quantity and quality of labor in a nation.

LO17-2 **Explain** the relationship between competitive strategies (international, multidomestic, global, and transnational) and international human resource management approaches (ethnocentric, polycentric, regiocentric, and global).

LO17-3 **Compare** home-country, host-country, and third-country nationals as international company executives.

LO17-4 **Explain** what an expatriate is, and identify some of the challenges and opportunities of an expat position.

LO17-5 **Discuss** the increasing importance of accommodating the trailing spouse of an expatriate executive.

LO17-6 **Identify** some of the complications of compensation packages for expatriate executives.

assignments that are primarily intended to work on a specific problem or transfer specific knowledge?

Of course, there is the chance that despite all your efforts and precautions, your company will forget or not value you. Realizing this possibility, you should make sure to profit from your foreign assignment by doing your job well; learning new markets; gaining proficiency in the language, which will permit you to better understand the culture; and networking. The networking can be done by being active in such things as local chambers of commerce, social clubs, and sports clubs.

All this will make you valuable to other companies and make them aware of you. In essence, you have received a million dollars' worth of training paid for by your company, and you and other companies can utilize it. After all, active expats are an important source of third-country national executives.

[a]*Up or Out: Next Moves for the Modern Expatriate* (London: The Economist Intelligence Unit, 2010), www.eiu.com/site_info.asp?info_name=uporout_expatriate&page=noads&rf=0 (May 30, 2011), p. 9.

---

expatriate
A person living outside his or her country of citizenship

The effectiveness of every organization depends to a great extent on the nature of its workforce and how well its human resources are utilized. Their effective use depends on management's policies and practices. Management of a company's human resources is a shared responsibility. The day-to-day supervision of people on the job is the duty of the operating managers, who must integrate human, financial, and physical resources into an efficient production system. However, the formulation of policies and procedures for (1) estimation of workforce needs, (2) recruitment and selection, (3) training and development, (4) motivation, (5) compensation, (6) discipline, and (7) employment termination is generally the responsibility of personnel managers working in cooperation with executives from marketing, production and operations, and finance, as well as the firm's lawyers.

Finding the right people to manage an organization can be difficult under any circumstances, but it is especially difficult to find good managers of overseas operations. Such positions require more and different skills than do purely domestic executive jobs. The right persons need to be bicultural, with knowledge of the business practices in the home country plus an understanding of business practices and customs in the host country. And to fully understand a culture, any culture, it is usually necessary to speak the language of its people. Only with a good grasp of the language, can one understand the subtleties and humor and know what is really going on in the host country. Although difficult to locate, such managers do exist, and they may be found in (1) the home country, (2) the host country, or (3) a third country. A key precursor for undertaking such a selection process is an examination of labor conditions and trends.

Worldwide Labor Conditions

LO17-1 Discuss several of the major factors that may affect the quantity and quality of labor in a nation.

labor market
The pool of available potential employees with the necessary skills within commuting distance from an employer

When a foreign company arrives in a **labor market,** it must take what it finds. Of course, the quantity and quality of labor vary across nations and regions of the world and also over time, so a prudent company will study the labor market when considering whether to invest in a country. Among the many information sources are *Foreign Labor Trends* and the *Handbook of Labor Statistics,* available from the U.S. Department of Labor in Washington, DC, and the *Yearbook of Labor Statistics,* published by the United Nations International Labor Office in Geneva, Switzerland. This section provides a brief review of several dimensions associated with labor conditions, including the overall size of the workforce, the aging of populations, urbanization of workforces, immigration, and labor unions.

OVERALL SIZE OF THE WORKFORCE

We begin by looking at the overall situation in the world in terms of some very macro demographic data. In 2011, the world had 6.9 billion inhabitants, 48 percent of whom were under the age of 25 and 31 percent under the age of 15.[1] Due to high birthrates and a decline in the rate of infant mortality, populations in the developing nations tend to be growing as well as becoming younger. Approximately 38 percent of the world's 15- to 24-year-olds, a key source of new workers during the next decade, live in just two developing countries: India and China.[2]

In contrast, populations in many developed countries are projected to decline in the coming years, due to factors such as low birthrates and low levels of immigration. For example, between 2006 and 2050, Japan's population is projected to decline from 127.5 million to 99.9 million, Russia's from 142.9 million to 110.8 million, and Germany's from 82.4 million to 73.6 million. Countries that have admitted large numbers of immigrants—such as the United States, the United Kingdom, Canada, and Australia—are projected to have continued population growth due to the younger age and higher birthrates of their immigrant populations. For example, between 2010 and 2050, the U.S. population is projected to grow from 310 million to 439 million, and Canada's from 33 million to 37.5 million.[3]

AGING OF POPULATIONS

In addition to examining population as a whole, we need to consider the effects on the workforce of an aging population, a trend affecting many nations worldwide. The rapid increase in the proportion of the world's population that is age 65 or older has received much attention in recent years. In 2010, 7.6 percent of the world's population was 65 or older, versus 6.6 percent only a decade earlier. The proportion of those 65 or older is projected to increase to 8.4 percent of the world's population in 2015 and 16.4 percent by 2050, with the distribution illustrated in Figure 17.1.[4]

As Figure 17.1 illustrates, the aging of populations is more pronounced for the developed countries, in which the percentage of the population 65 and above grew from 10 percent

FIGURE 17.1   Population Aged 65 and Above (2015)

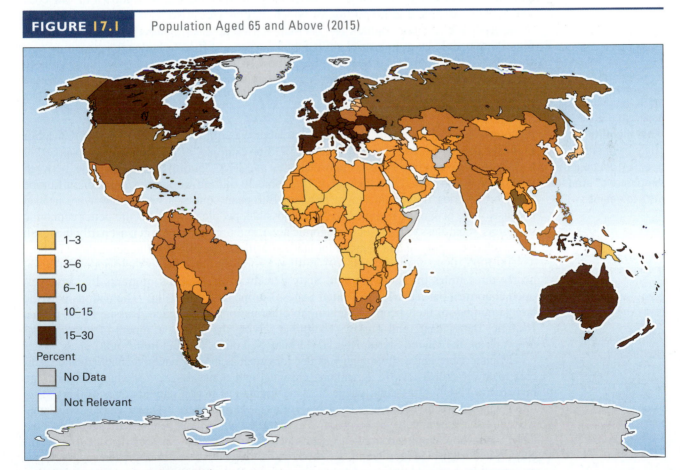

Source: http://globalis.gvu.unu.edu/ (May 29, 2011).

in 1996 to 12 percent in 2010 and is projected to rise to 25.4 percent by 2050. An aging population in most of the developed countries has implications for labor force size and skill; for policies regarding immigration; for economic growth; and for a range of political issues related to pension plans, health care, and other key social, economic, and political factors in those nations. For example, the European Commission predicts that Europe's share of world output could decline from its current 18 percent to 10 percent by 2050, and Japan's from 8 to 4 percent, unless major population-related policy changes are undertaken. In contrast, a more youthful United States could expand its world output share from 23 to 26 percent during the same time. Compared to developed countries, the developing countries will have only about one-half the proportion of people age 65 and older, at least through 2025. Take India, for example. A much larger proportion of Indians will be of traditional working age (20 to 64) than will be the case for most of the rest of the world, especially the developed countries. That may have important implications for international companies considering where to locate production as well as those seeking markets for products that target working-age adults.

URBANIZATION OF WORKFORCE

The population and labor force worldwide have been shifting dramatically from rural to urban during the past century. Less than 29 percent of the world's population lived in urban areas in 1950. By 2010, more than half of the world's population was urban, and this proportion is projected to increase to 60 percent by the year 2030. Although the level of urbanization is higher in developed countries, the rate of urbanization was four times faster in developing countries from 1975 to 2009 as these nations experienced rapid increases in population as well as increasing economic development.

As populations migrate from rural areas to urban areas, particularly within developing nations, they also move from agriculturally based employment to employment in industry and service sectors. Often, this influx of labor from rural areas creates a pool of low-cost, low-skilled workers, a large portion of which may be classified as part of the vulnerable workforce. While labor trainers for international companies in developing nations have found that people learn industrial skills rapidly, a more difficult challenge is teaching new workers who come from farms and villages how to adjust socially and psychologically to work life in industry or service sectors.

IMMIGRANT LABOR

labor mobility
The movement of people from country to country or area to area to get jobs

Although classical economists assumed that labor was immobile, we now know that **labor mobility** does exist, as shown in Figure 17.2. For example, at least 60 million people left Europe to work and live overseas between 1850 and 1970. During part of that time, between the end of World War II and the mid-1970s, some 30 million workers from southern Europe and North Africa flowed into eight northern European countries where they were needed because of the economic boom there. When possible, people move to secure better economic situations, regardless of their socioeconomic level, and immigration is at least partly the result of the relative supply of and demand for labor as well as regulations influencing those factors.

In 2005, there were at least 191 million people living outside their nation of birth, nearly three times the level in 1960. Sixty percent of the world's migrants live in developed countries, particularly the United States, Europe, and Australia.[5] The nations with the largest number of their people migrating to other nations are Mexico, Russia, India, China, Ukraine, Bangladesh, and Turkey. Nations receiving the largest numbers of international migrants are the United States, Russia, Germany, Ukraine, France, India and Canada.

Migrant labor ranges from highly skilled jobs such as in information technology and medicine to lower-skilled jobs in agriculture, cleaning, and domestic service. Many migrants are involved in "3-D" jobs—dirty, dangerous, and degrading—that a nation's own workers reject or for which there are not enough available workers. Many of these 3-D jobs employ vulnerable workers—that is, workers who do not have a contract, work without benefits, are paid "under the table," and whose employment often violates local laws. Often they are underaged, family members, or undocumented immigrants. Research on the wage effects of immigration suggest that it may result in depressed wages for a nation's workers. One study of workers in Canada between

FIGURE 17.2   Net Migration Rates, 2008

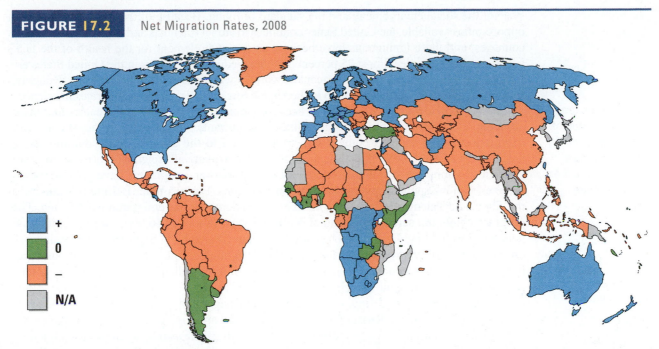

Source: *CIA Factbook* (accessed March 8, 2010); Wikipedia (accessed May 29, 2011).

1980 and 2000 reported that immigration contributed to a 7 percent decline in real wages for highly educated workers.[6] Wages were found to decline by 3 to 4 percent when the labor supply increased by 10 percent due to immigration. While immigration can be a net positive for inflation and international cost competitiveness of a nation's businesses, this effect of immigration on wage levels contributes to the opposition to immigration voiced by labor groups and others. The movement of large numbers of immigrants, both trained professionals and unskilled laborers, within and between nations has become an increasingly important issue for human resource managers.

Although the United States has only about 5 percent of the world's population, it has 20 percent of the world's migrants.[7] In 2008, 12.5 percent of the people residing in the United States were foreign-born, up from 5 percent in 1970, and more than half of the increase in the U.S. population between 2000 and 2009 came from immigration.[8] About 58 percent of the new jobs created since 1995 have been filled with foreign-born workers, including more than 85 percent of new positions for mechanics and construction workers and more than 60 percent of service positions. Overall, more than 23 percent of the U.S. population either is foreign-born or has one or both parents who were foreign-born. Immigrants come to the United States from all over the world, with the largest number of foreign-born coming from Latin America (53 percent), Asia (25 percent), and Europe (14 percent).

BRAIN DRAIN

Record numbers of immigrants are moving to many OECD countries in search of jobs. The OECD's annual *Trends in International Migration* notes that even recent economic downturns in some OECD countries have not affected the upward trend in international migration that began in the mid-1990s.[9] When skilled workers migrate from developing economies, a phenomenon known as **brain drain,** they generally do so for professional opportunities and economic reasons. Brain drain has become a serious problem for developing countries, because it involves the loss of such skilled professionals as scientists, IT specialists, engineers, teachers, and health care professionals. In some Central American and sub-Saharan African countries, more than half of the college-educated population emigrates, often to seek adequate infrastructures in the area in which they have trained. For example, 90 percent of doctors trained in Kenya's public hospitals subsequently emigrate, leaving many areas of the country without adequate medical care.[10]

Traditionally, a major destination for these skilled workers has been the United States, due to factors such as top-quality universities; dynamic companies; an open, merit-based economic

brain drain
The loss by a country of its most intelligent and best-educated people

system; the social environment; and the standard of living. Because of the salary and research opportunities available, the United States continues to attract scientists and engineers from other countries, and these immigrants have become an essential element for the health of the U.S. economy. For example, almost 25 percent of college-educated workers in the United States are foreign-born, as are more than 50 percent of workers with doctorates in engineering. Roughly, 53 percent of foreign students remain in the United States after receiving doctorates in science.

reverse brain drain
The return home of highly skilled immigrants who have made a contribution in their adopted country

Reverse brain drain has recently become a concern of American educators and businesspeople. The return home of highly skilled immigrants who have made significant contributions in their adopted country is a trend related to the growth of outsourcing and a willingness of the federal government to allow "controversial" scientists to move to other countries.[11] Some developing countries whose scientists and engineers have gone to industrialized nations sponsor reverse-brain-drain programs. For example, Beijing has launched the Thousand Talents Program in a bid to capture talent that has emigrated from China. The program offers top scientists grants of 1 million yuan (about $146,000), high salaries, and generous lab funding. Brain drain has also been exacerbated by U.S. government limitations on the number of work visas and long queues for naturalization.[12] The growth of outsourcing in developing economies such as India is also pulling Indian talent back home. American firms contribute aggressively to this aspect of reverse brain drain as they outsource knowledge work—engineering, software, product design, and development—to such countries as China, India, and Russia. In some controversial areas of science where the American government has limited research efforts, such as stem cell research, scientists—both native and non-native—move to environments where such cutting-edge research is supported.

labor unions
Organizations of workers

collective bargaining
The process in which a union represents the interests of workers bargaining in negotiations with management

LABOR UNIONS

Labor unions vary significantly from country to country. They tend to be more effective in developed countries, but even comparing Europe, the United States, and Japan, it is apparent that labor unions in various countries serve different purposes and influence employee matters differently. Labor legislation in the United States has mostly confined itself to the framework of **collective bargaining.** Collective bargaining is the process in which a union represents the interests of everyone in a bargaining unit (which may include both union members and nonmembers) in negotiations with management. In Europe, government's role is more active, with wages and working conditions frequently legislated. Many Latin American governments are also active in employer–employee relationships, frequently because the unions are weak and the union leaders inexperienced.

ethnocentric
As used here, related to hiring and promoting employees on the basis of the parent company's home-country frame of reference

In contrast to the adversarial relationship usually found between unions and management in Europe and the United States, Japanese unions tend to identify strongly with the interests of the company. For example, if Japanese unions are convinced a high wage increase would hurt the company's competitiveness, they tend to not ask for much of a pay raise. Japanese unions are also enterprise based rather than industrywide.

polycentric
As used here, related to hiring and promoting employees on the basis of the specific local context in which the subsidiary operates

The level of union membership varies substantially across countries, from single digits in some nations to more than 80 percent in others. For the past four decades, there has been a decline in the number of union members in most of the developed countries, especially among workers in industrial sectors. The reasons for this trend are several:

- Employers have made efforts to keep their businesses union-free, including putting employees on business boards and instituting profit-sharing plans. This co-optive approach has had its desired effect in many cases.

- More women and teenagers have joined the workforce, and because theirs are usually secondary incomes, they accept lower wages and have little loyalty toward organized labor.

regiocentric
As used here, related to hiring and promoting employees on the basis of the specific regional context in which the subsidiary operates

- The unions have been successful. Their results have led to wage increases, which have led to higher costs and lower competitiveness of their employers, which have led to layoffs, downsizing, and movement of jobs to lower-cost locations. So in this sense, unions have been the victims of their own success.

- As developed countries transition to a knowledge economy, their industrial jobs that have formed the core of union membership are declining.

Despite a general decline in union members in industrial sectors, many developed nations have seen an increase in union membership in recent years. This trend is particularly prominent in those nations where unions have successfully organized workers in the expanding service sectors of their post-industrial economies.

National unions have begun to perceive opportunities for companies to escape the organizing reach of unions through the relatively simple step of international outsourcing, transferring production to another country. Unions see such steps as dangerous. To combat those dangers, national unions have begun to (1) collect and disseminate information about companies, (2) consult with unions in other countries, (3) coordinate with those unions' policies and tactics in dealing with some companies, and (4) encourage international company codes of conduct. Such multinational labor activity is likely to increase, although unions are divided by ideological differences and are frequently strongly nationalistic. Vastly more effort and money have been spent on lobbying for protection of national industries than on cooperating with unions in other countries.

The International Human Resource Management Approach

Chapter 9 explained that two competing forces—the pressure to achieve global integration and reduce costs and the pressure to respond to local differentiation—determine which of four alternative competitive strategies (home replication, multidomestic, global, or transnational) a company should adopt. A company's competitive strategy should, in turn, drive the organization's approach to international human resource management (IHRM).

Heenan and Perlmutter developed a model that considers these four competitive strategies to determine whether the organization's approach to IHRM should be **ethnocentric, polycentric, regiocentric,** or **geocentric.**[13] Further, along with this decision, the employees used in the organization may be classified into one of three categories: (1) **home-country nationals** or **parent-country nationals (PCNs)**, (2) **host-country nationals (HCNs)**, or (3) **third-country nationals (TCNs).** These relationships are illustrated in Table 17.1.

Recruitment and Selection of Employees

The recruitment and selection of employees, frequently referred to as *staffing,* should be determined in a manner consistent with one of the four IHRM approaches the organization is pursuing, as discussed next.[14]

ETHNOCENTRIC STAFFING POLICY

Companies with a primarily international strategic orientation (characterized by low pressures for cost reduction and low pressures for local responsiveness) may adopt an ethnocentric staffing policy. In this approach, most decisions are made at headquarters, using the home country's frame of reference. International companies (ICs) utilize citizens of their own countries, or PCNs, in key foreign management and technical positions.

At first, PCNs usually are not knowledgeable about the host-country culture and language. Many such **expatriates** have adapted, learned the language, and become thoroughly accepted in the host country, although it is also common that such managers encounter difficulty both in overcoming the biases of their own cultural experience and in being able to understand and perform effectively within the new operating context.

Labor negotiators and other specialists may be sent to troubleshoot such problems as product warranty, international contracts, taxes, accounting, and reporting. Teams may be sent from the home country to assist with new plant startup, and they would probably stay until subsidiary personnel were trained to run and maintain the new facilities.

An advantage to using home-country citizens abroad is to expand their experience in preparation for becoming high-level managers at headquarters. Firms earning a large percentage of their profits from international sources require top executives who have a

geocentric

As used here, related to hiring and promoting employees on the basis of ability and experience without considering race or citizenship

home-country national

Same as parent-country national

LO17-2 Explain the relationship between competitive strategies (international, multidomestic, global, and transnational) and international human resource management approaches (ethnocentric, polycentric, regiocentric, and global).

parent-country national (PCN)

Employee who is a citizen of the nation in which the parent company is headquartered; also called *home-country national*

host-country national (HCN)

Employee who is a citizen of the nation in which the subsidiary is operating, which is different from the parent company's home nation

third-country national (TCN)

Employee who is a citizen of neither the parent company nation nor the host country

TABLE 17.1

TABLE 17.1 Strategic Approach, Organizational Concerns, and the International Human Resource Management Approach to Be Used

Aspects of the Enterprise	Orientation			
	Ethnocentric	**Polycentric**	**Regiocentric**	**Geocentric**
Primary strategic orientation/stage	Home replication	Multidomestic	Regional	Transnational
Perpetuation (recruiting, staffing, development)	People of home country developed for key positions everywhere in the world	People of local nationality developed for key positions in their own country	Regional people developed for key positions anywhere in the region	Best people everywhere in the world developed for key positions everywhere in the world
Complexity of the organization	Complex in home country, simple in subsidiaries	Varied and independent	Highly interdependent on a regional basis	"Global Web," complex, independent, worldwide alliances/network
Authority, decision making	High in headquarters	Relatively low in headquarters	High regional headquarters and/or high collaboration among subsidiaries	Collaboration of headquarters and subsidiaries around the world
Evaluation and control	Home standards applied to people and performance	Determined locally	Determined regionally	Globally integrated
Rewards	High in headquarters, low in subsidiaries	Wide variations, can be high or low rewards for subsidiary performance	Rewards for contribution to regional objectives	Rewards to international and local executives for reaching local and world-wide objectives based on global company goals
Communication, information flow	High volume of orders, commands, advice to subsidiaries	Little to and from headquarters, little among subsidiaries	Little to and from corporate headquarters, but may be high to and from regional headquarters and among countries	Horizontal, network relations
Geographic identification	Nationality of owner	Nationality of host country	Regional company	Truly global company, but identifying with national interests ("glocal")

Source: Adapted from David A. Heenan and Howard V. Perlmutter, *Multinational Organization Development* (Boston: Addison-Wesley, 1979).

worldwide perspective, both business and political. It is difficult to impossible to acquire that sort of perspective without living and working abroad for a substantial period of time.

If new technology for the subsidiary is involved, the parent company will probably station at least one of its technologically qualified experts at the subsidiary until its local personnel learn the technology. In this way, the home office can be confident that someone is immediately available to explain headquarters' policies and procedures, see that they are observed, and interpret what is happening locally for the IC's management. Positions that an IC must take or demands that it must make are sometimes not popular with a host government. It can seem unpatriotic for a host-country national to do such things, whereas the host government can understand, and sometimes accept, such positions or demands from a foreigner.

POLYCENTRIC STAFFING POLICY

LO17-3 **Compare** home-country, host-country, and third-country nationals as international company executives.

When the company's primary strategic orientation is multidomestic, with low pressures for cost reduction and high pressures for local responsiveness, a polycentric approach may be used. Polycentric staffing involves human resource policies that are created at the local level for the specific context of the local operations. Companies primarily hire HCNs for subsidiaries and PCNs for headquarters' positions; movement from the local subsidiaries to headquarters' positions is uncommon.

When HCNs are employed at the subsidiary level, there is no problem of their being unfamiliar with local customs, culture, and language. Furthermore, the first costs of employing them are generally lower (compared with the costs of employing home-country nationals and paying to move them and their families to the host country), although considerable training costs are sometimes necessary. If there is a strong feeling of nationalism in the host country, having nationals as managers can make the subsidiary seem less foreign. As Fujio Mitarai, chairman and CEO of Canon, said, "If you look at capital investment strategy, marketing, research and development, those types of activities are international. But if you talk about people, humans, it is quite local in nature."[15]

The government development plans and laws of some countries demand that employment in all sectors and at all levels reflect the racial composition of the society. In other words, more skilled and managerial slots must be given to the local people. If foreign-owned firms in Indonesia fail to hire enough *pribumi* (indigenous Indonesians), those firms are likely to encounter difficulties with reentry permits for foreign employees as well as with other government licenses and permits that they need. Bribery requests have been known to increase until more pribumi were hired and promoted.

A disadvantage of hiring local managers is that they are often unfamiliar with the home country of the IC and with its corporate culture, policies, and practices. As Liu Zhengrong, head of human resources for the German chemical group Lanxess, said of hiring local managers, "You lose something in terms of communication with the headquarters, but you get more hints about the local marketplace."[16] Differences in attitudes and values, as discussed in Chapter 4, can cause these locally hired managers to act in ways that surprise or displease headquarters. Also, local managers may create their own upward immobility if, because of strong cultural or family ties, they are reluctant to accept promotions that would require them to leave the country to work at parent headquarters or at another subsidiary.

Foreign-owned companies that hire and train local, host-country people frequently experience a common, and disruptive, IHRM problem. The best of these people may be pirated away by local firms or other IC subsidiaries, because local executive recruiters are constantly on the lookout to make raids and entice the most talented employees to leave the original IC and join another firm that is seeking to overcome its own shortage of skilled personnel.

Finally, there can be a conflict of loyalty between the host country and the employer. For example, the host-country national may give preference to a local supplier even though imported products may be less expensive or of better quality. Local managers may oppose headquarters' requests to set low transfer prices in order to lower taxes payable to the host government.

REGIOCENTRIC STAFFING POLICY

Companies with a regional strategic approach (with slightly higher pressures for cost reduction and slightly lower pressures for local responsiveness than the multidomestic strategy) can employ a regiocentric staffing approach. In this approach, regional employees are selected for key positions in the region, employing a variety of HCNs and TCNs.

The disadvantages often encountered when using employees from the home or host country can sometimes be avoided by sending third-country nationals to fill management posts. A Chilean going to Argentina may have little cultural or language difficulty, but IC headquarters should be careful not to rely too heavily on similarities in language as a guide to similarities in other aspects of cultures. Mexicans, for example, may have to make

Executives with the Right Stuff Are in Big Demand

Demand for executives with the "right stuff" is the case everywhere, but it is particularly true in developing economies. One can look at China and Latin America for examples of what is meant by this.

Kodak's Chinese operation brought in Western managers who were excellent with the technical aspects of their jobs. Nevertheless, they failed miserably because they did not understand the culture of the country.

In an attempt to solve the problem, Kodak and other foreign companies recruit Chinese-speaking staff from Asian and other countries. But there are still cultural considerations, says Kay Kutt, managing director of Cendant Intercultural Assignment Services, Asia-Pacific division. "It's almost worse than sending a Westerner, to send someone who has the Chinese language but not Chinese values," as she puts it. Local hires are less costly than expatriates, and they often have better understanding of the Chinese market and customers. Having a boss who is a local can

be motivating to ambitious junior employees, and can enhance communication and morale. As Walmart China executive Du Limin says about the response of her Chinese employees, "They take me as their big sister and they confide their family issues with me. That is impossible if you're an expatriate." Yet finding an adequate number of local talent, at an adequate quality level, in China can be difficult for international companies. "Companies want to localize but the majority of people who are local mainland Chinese don't have experience with global principles," said Joy Chen, a principal at the executive search firm Heidrick & Struggles. More than 65 percent of respondents reported in a *China Business Report* from the American Chamber of Commerce stated that they had experienced a negative impact on their operations in China due to difficulty finding and keeping skilled managerial and other personnel, and that the imbalance between demand and supply is not likely to change in the near future.

Hundreds of non–Latin American businesses trying to operate in that region have openings for bilingual executives. "Our objective is to find the best talent that we can for any position that is open . . . and

considerable adjustments if they are transferred to Argentina, and they would find a move to Spain even more difficult. This is because the Mexican culture, in general, differs considerably from that of both Argentina and Spain. Although Argentina and Chile are certainly not identical, they do have many similarities. A fair generalization is that after an executive has adapted once to a new culture and language, a second or succeeding adaptation is easier.

An employer should not count on cost savings in using third-country nationals. Although they may come from countries where salary scales are lower, in such countries as Brazil and most of the nations of northwestern Europe, salaries may be higher than American companies are paying at comparable position levels.

GEOCENTRIC STAFFING POLICY

Companies with a transnational strategic orientation, driven simultaneously by high pressures for cost reduction and high pressures for local responsiveness, follow a geocentric staffing policy. These organizations select the best person for each job without considering national origin and can therefore capitalize on the advantages of each staffing policy. With a geocentric staffing policy, HRM strategy tends to be consistent across all subsidiaries, borrowing best practices from wherever they may be found across the company's worldwide network of operations rather than showing preference only to the practices used at headquarters within a local context.

Training and Development

Training and development involve efforts to facilitate the acquisition of job-related knowledge, behavior, and skills. The training and development of managers and other key IC employees vary somewhat, depending on whether the candidate is from the home country, the host country, or a third country.

HOME- OR PARENT-COUNTRY NATIONAL

Relatively few recent college graduates are hired for the express purpose of being sent overseas. Usually they spend a number of years in the domestic (parent) company, and they may get into the company's international operations by design and persistence, by luck, or by

knowing a second language does create an advantage," said Mark Bailey, director of staffing at General Mills. But merely being fluent in the language does not mean that prospective employees have the skills required for a particular position. These companies are looking for people who can operate in a dual mode, combining U.S. efficiency and business culture with the Latin way of doing things, which is more personal and requires knowledge of Spanish or Portuguese.

An example of cultural contrast is given by Ignacio Kleinman of I-Network.com. An American might try to close a deal over the phone, but the Latin style is to take a plane ride to the customer's country, have lunch, and talk about soccer and the family. "Afterward, that Latin customer is going to feel closer to you," Kleinman says. "If there is no personal chemistry, there is likely to be no business."[a] It is important not to become insulated from the local culture. When arriving in a country, many expats choose to pursue a comfort zone familiar to them: they live in sections of a city favored by American visitors, travel everywhere in a chauffeured sedan with a driver who speaks English, and frequent stores, restaurants and bars that cater to Americans. Such managers are often termed "Teflon expatriates," because they are living abroad but nothing about the local culture sticks. As a result, they are not likely to develop the "right stuff" for working effectively with partners in the local culture.

Questions:

1. What does it take to have the "right stuff" for a foreign assignment?

2. How might a company go about assessing whether or not a candidate has the "right stuff"?

[a]Ida Relsted, "U.S. Firms Still Keen on China," *China Daily*, December 15–16, 2007, p. 10.

Sources: Julian Teixeira, "More Companies Recruit Bilingual Employees," May 13, 2008, www.hci.org/lib/more-companies-recruit-bilingual-employees (accessed May 29, 2011); Cui Rong, "More Firms in China Think Globally, Hire Locally," *The Wall Street Journal*, February 27, 2006, p. 29; "Leaders of the Right Stuff in Big Demand," *Financial Times*, June 7, 2000, p. 12; Jiang Yan, "Thirst for Talent," *China Business Weekly*, September 12–18, 2005, p. 4; Chris Kraul, "Latino Talent Pinch Hobbling U.S. Firms' Expansion Plans," *Los Angeles Times*, June 25, 2000, pp. C1, 5, http://articles.latimes.com/2000/jun/25/business/fi-44585 (May 29, 2011); and Amy Yee, "China's War for Talent Hots Up," *Financial Times*, February 16, 2006, p. 8, www.ft.com/intl/cms/s/0/b574c360-9e91-11da-b641-0000779e2340.html#axzz1Nmymfp00 (May 29, 2011).

a combination of those elements. They may first be assigned to the international division at the firm's headquarters, where they handle problems submitted by foreign affiliates and meet visiting overseas personnel.

If the company feels that it probably will send PCNs abroad, it will frequently encourage them to study the language and culture of the country to which they are going. Such employees will probably be sent on short trips abroad to handle special assignments and to be exposed to foreign surroundings. Newly hired PCNs with prior overseas experience may undergo similar but shorter training periods.

It is increasingly possible for American ICs to supplement their in-house training for overseas work with courses in American business schools. In recognition of the growing importance of international business, those schools are expanding the number and scope of international business courses they offer. In addition, a number of university-level business schools are now operating in other countries.

A major concern for employers involves families of executives transferred overseas. Even though the employee may adapt to and enjoy the foreign experience, the family may not, and an unhappy family may sour the employee on the job or even split up the marriage. In such cases, the company may have to ship the family and its possessions back home at great expense. Consequently, many companies try to assess whether the executive's family can adapt to the foreign ambience before assigning the executive abroad. This is part of the subject of expatriates that is dealt with later in this chapter.

HOST-COUNTRY NATIONAL

The same general criteria for selecting home-country employees apply to host-country nationals. Usually, however, the training and development activities undertaken for HCNs will differ from those used for home-country nationals in that host-country nationals are more likely to lack knowledge of advanced business techniques, particularly those that are specific to business applications and operations of the IC, and knowledge of the company as a whole.

HCNs Hired in the Home Country
Many multinationals try to solve the business technique problem by hiring host-country students upon their graduation from home-country business schools. After being hired, these new employees are usually sent

to IC headquarters to receive indoctrination in the firm's policies and procedures as well as on-the-job training in a specific function, such as finance, marketing, or production.

HCNs Hired in the Host Country   Because the number of host-country citizens graduating from home-country universities is limited, multinationals must also recruit locally for their management positions. To impart knowledge of business techniques, the company may do one or more things. It may set up in-house training programs in the host-country subsidiary, or it may utilize business courses in the host-country's universities. The IC may also send new employees to home-country business schools or to home-country training programs offered by the parent company. In addition, employees who show promise will be sent repeatedly to the parent-company headquarters, divisions, and other subsidiaries to observe the various enterprise operations and meet the other executives with whom they will be communicating during their careers. Such visits are also learning opportunities for the home office and the other subsidiaries.

THIRD-COUNTRY NATIONAL

Hiring personnel who are citizens of neither the home country nor the host country is often advantageous. TCNs may accept lower wages and benefits than will employees from the home country, and they may come from a culture similar to that of the host country. In addition, they may have worked for another unit of the IC and thus be familiar with the company's policies, procedures, and people. This can simplify the training and development requirements for such recruits.

The use of TCNs has become particularly prevalent in the developing countries because of shortages of literate, not to mention skilled, locals. It can be an advantage to get someone who already resides in the country and has the necessary work permits and knowledge of the local languages and customs.

Host-Country Attitudes   If the host government emphasizes employment of its own citizens, third-country nationals will not be welcomed any more than will home-country people. Actually, third-country nationals could face an additional obstacle in obtaining necessary work permits. For example, the host government can understand that the German parent company of a subsidiary would want some German executives to look after its interests in the host country. It may be harder to convince the government that a third-country native is any better for the parent than a local executive would be.

Generalizations about TCNs Are Difficult   We must be careful with generalizations about third-country personnel, partly because people achieve that status in different ways. They may be foreigners hired in the home country and sent to a host-country subsidiary either because they have had previous experience there or because that country's culture is similar to their own. Third-country nationals may have originally been home-country personnel who were sent abroad and became dissatisfied with the job but not with the host country. After leaving the firm that sent them abroad, they take positions with subsidiaries of multinationals from different home countries. Another way in which TCNs can be created is by promotion within an IC. For instance, if a Spanish executive of the Spanish subsidiary of an Italian multinational is promoted to be general manager of the Italian firm's Colombian subsidiary, the Spanish executive is then a third-country national.

As multinationals increasingly take the *geocentric* view toward promoting (according to ability and not nationality), we are certain to see greater use of TCNs. This development will be accelerated as more executives of all nationalities gain experience outside their native lands. Another, and growing, source for third-country nationals is the heterogeneous body of international agencies. As indicated in Chapter 3, these agencies deal with virtually every field of human endeavor, and all member-countries send their nationals as representatives to the headquarters and branch office cities all over the world. Many of those people become available to, or can be hired away by, international companies.

Expatriates

In Chapters 1 and 2, we discussed that international markets are becoming increasingly important to success for even small and medium-sized companies. To exploit these international opportunities, staffing of positions in international operations is an important strategic issue. Although many of the employees may be hired in the host country (sometimes called *inpatriates*), ICs have continued to send employees on foreign assignments. Some of the international positions, especially those that deal with addressing a specific technical problem or transferring specialized knowledge, will be staffed with home- or third-country employees who are on short-term assignments (called *flexpatriates*). Yet companies will continue to staff many key positions with expatriates, employees who are relocated to the host country from the home country or a third country, with the assignment lasting for an extended period of time (two to five years is a common length of time for an expatriate assignment).[17] In fact, about 80 percent of medium- and large-sized companies have employees working abroad, and 65 percent of surveyed companies said they were planning to increase the use of expats.[18] The average age of expats is getting somewhat younger, with 54 percent now being between 20 and 39 years, versus the historical average of 41 percent.[19] In addition, a higher proportion of expatriates are women, reaching 21 percent versus the historical average of 15 percent.

Why use expatriates rather than just hire local employees? Expatriates can bring technical or managerial skills that are scarce in the host country; they can help transfer or install companywide systems or cultures; they may provide a trusted connection for facilitating oversight or control over foreign operations, whether it is a new endeavor or an operation that is already in existence; or the international assignment may enable the expat to develop the skills and experiences that will allow a subsequent promotion into leadership positions of greater scope and responsibility within the IC. The most effective leaders in an increasingly complex and internationalizing world tend to be those who can understand and interact effectively with a variety of stakeholders, despite differences in culture or location. Expat assignments can demonstrate such skills, and these assignments have been reported to lead to faster promotions.[20] Ian Cloke, VP of Global Mobility and Reward Servives at the multinational consumer products company Unilever, reinforced the importance of international assignments by saying, "Out of our senior management cadre of a hundred people, only a few have never worked outside their home country."[21]

LO17-4 **Explain** what an expatriate is, and identity some of the challenges and opportunities of an expat position.

The costs of using expatriates are substantial, estimated at about $50 billion annually for U.S. companies, so the performance of expatriates is an important issue for ICs.[22] Yet various studies report that failure rates for expatriate assignments—including failing to achieve performance targets for an international assignment or prematurely returning from the assignment—range from 25 to 45 percent.[23] Approximately one-quarter of expats leave their firms during the course of their overseas assignment, and an additional 28 percent leave their companies within a year of their return from abroad, hindering the IC's ability to retain and leverage the skills and experience that the expatriate has gained from the international assignment.[24]

One important cause of expatriate performance problems is **culture shock,** which is the anxiety people often experience when they move from a culture that they are familiar with to one that is entirely different.[25] Because familiar signs and symbols are no longer present in the new culture, a person experiencing culture shock tends to feel lack of direction or inadequacy from not knowing what to do or how things are done in the new culture. Physical and emotional discomfort and feelings of disorientation and confusion are a common experience for people who go to other nations to work, live, or study. Many expatriates and members of their families are affected by culture shock, sometimes to a very great degree. As stated by Brian Friedman, founder of the Forum for Expatriate Management, "The initial period in a new posting involves considerable personal trauma. The main reason for expatriate failure is lack of adaptability, or the family unit's lack of adaptability."[26] Once a person has grown accustomed to a new culture, returning to one's home culture can produce the same experiences, referred to as *reverse culture shock.*

Researchers have identified three different dimensions associated with cross-cultural adjustment.[27] The first is associated with the work context, such as the extent of job clarity, inherent conflict in the person's role, and amount of discretion associated with completing the job tasks. Adjustment to the general environment, the second dimension, is associated with reacting to differences in housing, food, education, health, safety, and transportation. The third dimension, interaction with local nationals, involves adjusting to differences in behavioral norms, ways of dealing with conflict, communication patterns, and other relationship issues that can produce anger or frustration. An expatriate can experience some degree of culture shock associated with any or all of these three dimensions.

To enhance expatriate performance, ICs should consider the support that they provide to the employee during predeparture, while away on assignment, and upon repatriation.[28] Preassignment, the focus of support efforts should be on ensuring that the expatriate has the skills needed for successful performance in the foreign assignment, including language and cultural training, career counseling, and any needed technical or other skill development. Support during assignment includes the use of mentors (both home- and host-country), career counseling, and communication strategies to ensure that the expatriate remains connected to the IC's strategy, people, policies, and culture. Repatriation support, including management of the relocation to the home or other nation and reintegration into the company, is discussed later in this section. Organizational support has been shown to be a predictor of the success of expatriates' adjustment to their international postings.[29]

THE EXPATRIATE'S FAMILY

It has been suggested that as many as 9 out of 10 expatriates' failures are family related, and 81 percent of the employees who declined relocations in a recent study cited family concerns as the basis for their decision. In contrast to immigrants, who typically commit themselves to becoming part of their new country of residence, expats usually are only living temporarily in the new nation, so they often fail to adopt the host country's culture and seldom attempt to gain citizenship in that nation. The cultural adaptation pressures may be particularly great for the accompanying spouses, especially because they often

A family purchases train tickets in London. It has been suggested that as many as 9 out of 10 expatriates' failures are family-related.

are unable to work in the host country and may experience more challenges with regard to their personal identity. Spouses also typically need to interact more extensively with the local host community than do their expatriate partners, for such things as shopping, schools, and the management of domestic help, and related issues exacerbate adjustment pressures.[30] The stress an overseas move places on spouses and children will ultimately affect employees no matter how dedicated they may be to the company. Even worse, if the employee asks to go home early, the company is losing a "million-dollar corporate-training investment" in the executive. On the other hand, expatriates tend to have better satisfaction and performance when their spouses and other family members are able to adjust well to the new host country context.[31] Although a recent study reported that 77 percent of companies considered that cross-cultural training was highly valuable, only 21 percent of the companies required such training for their expats or their families.[32]

Trailing Spouses in Two-Career Families   While about 80 percent of expats are accompanied by a spouse or partner, the number of two-career families is growing. That is a major factor affecting expatriate adjustment and performance, and it can complicate matters when one spouse is offered a really good job abroad.[33] About 82 percent of expat spouses have university degrees, and nearly 90 percent were working prior to their partner's assignment.[34] Yet, in many countries, the employee's spouse does not have the legal right to work, as work permits for foreigners may be difficult or nearly impossible to acquire. As a result, as few as 8 percent were employed during the course of the assignment, which can increase financial pressures and strain relationships before, during, and after the expatriate assignment.[35] The trailing spouse must often make major adjustments in lifestyle, family balance of power, and self-image. They often experience stages of grief from derailment of their careers that is similar to the loss of a loved one—going through shock, denial, and anger—and sometimes fail to reach the reconciliation stage of adjustment.[36] Indeed, concern about the implications of an international assignment for the employee's partner and the partner's career prospects represented the second-highest reason for refusing an expatriate assignment, behind family concerns (such as children's education, family adjustment, resistance by the partner, difficult location for assignment, cultural adjustments, length of the assignment, and language).

LO17-5 Discuss the increasing importance of accommodating the trailing spouse of an expatriate executive.

In efforts to ease the problem, some companies are starting programs that give trailing spouses more help in adjusting. Such help may take the form of assisting with job hunting in the host country, writing résumés, providing language and cultural training, identifying career opportunities, or giving tips on local interview techniques. A reported 30 percent of companies provide education or training assistance to spouses, 36 percent sponsor work permits, and 69 percent provide language training to spouses. Many companies have made greater use of shorter international assignments, under the belief that this can be less disruptive to the expatriate family's lives while still permitting benefits from the international assignment of personnel. "People are going on assignments for 12, 9, even 6 months in much more dynamic arrangements than used to be the case," said Scott Sullivan, senior vice president at GMAC. "What it is to be an expatriate is changing."

Another option many companies apparently are pursuing is to hire people for expat assignments who are single and often younger as well, with more than 40 percent of such positions being filled by unmarried personnel.[37] It should be noted that hiring of single people for expatriate positions is not without its own set of potential concerns.

Expatriate Children May Suffer the Most   Children are an important but often overlooked consideration when planning for an international move, particularly because 45 percent of expats have children between the ages of 5 and 12.[38] Although an overseas stint may be seen as critical for career advancement of a parent, it can wreak havoc upon children's lives. Children are seldom involved in the initial decision-making process associated with a move abroad. This can result in the children experiencing many feelings (such as insecurity, frustration, and powerlessness) from being uprooted from friends and many of the sources of their own identity. A move does not merely involve changing schools; there are also new systems, new learning styles, new language, and so forth that the child must contend with. Sometimes these children are referred to as *third-culture kids* (or *TCKs*) because they often speak several different languages, hold passports from more than one country, and have difficulty explaining where they are from (where "home" is). As a consequence of these challenges, companies are increasing their focus on easing the disruptions faced by children.

PREPARATION FOR THE TRANSITION: LANGUAGE TRAINING

The English language has become the *lingua franca* of the world; in effect, it is everybody's second language. Nevertheless, foreign language skill has been shown to be a critical factor influencing effective adjustment of expatriates and their family members within the host country. When you are trying to sell to potential customers, it is much better to speak their language. As English speakers try to sell abroad, it is far more likely that their customers will speak English than that the English speakers will be able to speak the customers' language. Customers can then hide behind their language during negotiations. If your career involves international business—and few can avoid at least some exposure to it—it is likely to suffer if you speak English only.

EXPATRIATE SERVICES

Although most U.S. expatriates currently continue health coverage with their company's domestic plans, we can expect that to change in the near future as expatriate health care programs are being created to assist companies and expatriates with claims administration, language translations, currency conversions, and service standardization.[39] Similarly, banks are developing expatriate services, allowing expatriates to sign up for services online and providing 24-hour assistance to their customers, regardless of where in the world the expatriate is working.

In recognition of expatriate family issues, some companies have begun to prepare and assist these families. Assistance may take the form of realistic job previews for expatriates (and sometimes for their family members), training in the culture and language of the host country, assistance in finding suitable schools or medical specialists, or even arranging for long-distance care for elderly relatives or parents while the family is living abroad. House-hunting help may be given, and the new transplants should be taken on grocery and hardware shopping trips with locals and expats who have been in the host country for a while. Locals can teach you the social norms and where to shop and not to shop. Expats can teach you where to get things only expats want. Websites that focus on expatriate issues and can assist you in preparing for, adjusting to, or returning from an expatriate assignment include www.ExpatExpert.com and www.branchor.com.

REPATRIATION—THE SHOCK OF RETURNING HOME

As mentioned earlier, there is often reverse culture shock when an expatriate returns to the home company and country. The expatriate will have gained new skills and knowledge, and the company's attitudes and people will have changed. Expatriates who have become accustomed to high levels of autonomy while abroad often struggle with the more restrictive work context when they return home, as well as experiencing the common frustration of failing to be promoted or have their job expectations fulfilled after repatriation. If fully utilized, the repatriate can provide the company with rare, difficult to imitate, and competitively valuable knowledge and skills.

That is why planning for an expat's return should start well before the overseas assignment even begins. The person and the employer should discuss up front how the assignment will fit the employee's long-range career goals and how the company will handle the return. Challenges of repatriation should be discussed even before departure, and a mentor program should be considered between the expat and a mentor back home. During the assignment, expats should be encouraged to make regular visits back to the home country offices to help "stay in the loop" and feel part of the organizational network. When expats come back, companies have to understand that they are going to be different and should try to harness their new knowledge.[40] Efforts should be made to help the repatriates find appropriate

Are Women Appropriate for International Assignments?

Although women make up about 47 percent of the workforce in the United States, they represent a relatively small (albeit growing) fraction of the population of expatriates. Why this difference, especially with the pressing need for finding and developing competent global leaders? Adler examined three myths about women in international management:

Myth 1: Women do not want to be international managers.

Myth 2: Companies refuse to send women abroad.

Myth 3: Foreigners' prejudice against women renders them ineffective.

When Adler tested these myths empirically, neither the first nor the third was supported, but the second one was. Adler's research suggested that 70 percent of her sample of international companies were hesitant to select women for expatriate assignments. Why? Among the reasons expressed were that women in dual-career relationships would experience problems with international assignments, that gender-based prejudice would limit women's performance in many challenging countries or cultures, that women might feel lonely and isolated in an international assignment or be subjected to sexual harassment, or that the men making selection decisions regarding international assignments were themselves biased by traditional views and stereotypes regarding the appropriateness of assigning women to expatriate positions.

Is this hesitancy by companies regarding selecting women for international assignments justified? Research has shown that women are just as eager to go abroad as are men, sometimes more so. Additional research has shown that gender is unrelated to the performance ratings of expatriates, with the adjustment of expatriates to the host-country context, or with the intention of expatriates to leave their ICs. Recent studies have even suggested that the skills and identity typically associated with women (e.g., attentiveness to personal aspects of business and skill in building interpersonal relationships) may actually give women an edge over men for some expatriate assignments. In addition, rather than cultural attributes serving as a barrier to the effectiveness of women expats (e.g., a women-unfriendly environment in some host-country cultures), as has sometimes been argued in explaining why women could not or should not be assigned to international positions, these structural aspects may serve as an advantage for women in international roles.

Indeed, women may be able to divert attention from gender by demonstrating individualized sources of legitimacy and power, such as functional expertise and experience, and thereby enhance their effectiveness in international assignments. Similarly, although studies have reported that women assigned to countries where females have lower social status often have a more difficult time adjusting, they are nevertheless rated as being equally effective as men at their jobs. Some Japanese even refer to female expats as "the third gender" because they are accorded a different role and status than local women. A recent Australian study showed that childless single women were most likely to take expatriate roles because they did not encounter the same role conflicts and social pressures that married women or women with children might face. Women expatriates who are married are much less likely to take a partner overseas with them than is the case for male expatriates. Only 16 percent of women bring partners, versus 57 percent for male expatriates.

Questions:

1. Should ICs select more women for expatriate assignments?

2. Are there circumstances in which you believe that the use of women expatriates should be most strongly considered, or perhaps not considered at all?

Sources: Nancy J. Adler, "Women Do Not Want International Careers: And Other Myths about International Management," *Organizational Dynamics* 13, no. 2 (1984), pp. 66–80; Paula M. Caligiuri and Wayne Cascio, "Can We Send Her There? Maximizing the Success of Western Women on Global Assignments," *Journal of World Business* 33 (1998), pp. 394–417; Rosalie Tung, "Female Expatriates: The Model Global Manager?" *Organizational Dynamics*, August 2004, pp. 243–53; Phyllis Tharenou, "Disruptive Decisions to Leave Home: Gender and Family Differences in Expatriation Choices," *Organizational Behavior and Human Decision Processes*, March 2008, pp. 183–200; Ann Pomeroy, "Outdated Policies Hinder Female Expats," *HR Magazine*, December 2006, p. 16; and Jeremy Smerd, "More Women, Young Workers on the Move," *Workforce Management*, August 2007, pp. 9–10.

positions that use their newly developed skills and to help the expat and the family members re-acculturate, including access to counseling and other forms of support in order to promote adjustment success and build company loyalty. Nevertheless, only 49 percent of ICs have repatriation programs, and 68 percent of expatriates report that they do not have any guaranteed position in their IC after the end of their international assignment.[41] "We are seeing rapid globalization, and it's going to become a real problem to find people who are willing and qualified to go overseas if everyone hears about people who were not satisfied" after they are repatriated, said Lisa Johnson, the director of consulting services for Cendant Mobility.[42]

Compensation

Establishing a compensation plan that is equitable and consistent and yet does not overcompensate the overseas executive is a challenging, complex task, especially since a "one-size-fits-all" approach does not match up well with the reality of diverse company and country assignments. Rebecca Powers of Mercer Human Resource Consulting said, "More companies are now sending employees on expatriate assignments, so there is a greater need to keep pace with the cost of living changes. Employers need to be proactive in managing their expatriate programs to ensure they receive a proper return on their investment and employees are compensated fairly."[43] If ICs are not able to compensate in a manner that is perceived to be fair and attractive, it will become ever more difficult to attract the quantity and quality of potential expatriates needed to satisfy the company's international requirements. This can also fundamentally affect the extent to which a company's future leaders are shaped by such experiences and have developed the skills and experiences needed to lead effectively in an increasingly complex and internationalizing business environment.

The method traditionally favored by the majority of American ICs has been to pay a base salary equal to that paid to a domestic counterpart and then, in the belief that no one should be worse off for accepting foreign employment, to add a variety of allowances and bonuses. Table 17.2 provides an example of some of the compensation costs for sending an American manager on a two-year assignment to Russia. Many international assignments will entail significantly higher levels of additional costs, when compared with those in the home country, than suggested by this example.

Because of the high cost typically associated with expatriate assignments, some companies have attempted various schemes to help reduce these costs. In terms of salaries and other benefits, some companies have localized their workforce, replacing expatriates with qualified

---

TABLE 17.2 | Total Compensation Costs for Sending an Expatriate American Manager to Russia

The following compensation costs are illustrative of those an IC might encounter annually when sending an American manager and his or her family (spouse, two children) to Russia for a two-year assignment.

Compensation Component	Annual Cost (US$)
Base salary	$ 160,000
Incentive plan	16,000
Location differential (hardship premium)	7,000
Housing allowance	78,400
Cost-of-living allowance	8,500
Automobile allowance	36,500
Home leave	12,000
Educational assistance	24,000
Relocation/repatriation expenses	25,000
Total compensation before tax	**$367,400**
Tax assistance	54,200
Total compensation expense	**$421,600**
Other Expenses	
Preparation services (passports, visas, language training, etc.)	$ 3,800
Settling-in services	4,500
Emergency leave	6,700
Total annual cost for expatriate	**$436,600**

Source: Author estimates and "U.S. Firms Extend Global Reach," *Workforce Management,* December 2004, p. 142.

---

but lower-cost locals if such personnel are available. In other instances, an expatriate may begin with a higher salary and benefit package, but then have some but not all of this extra "expatriate package" phased out over time, creating a hybrid compensation scheme (e.g., key benefits such as children's schooling or housing subsidies may be maintained while other perks are eliminated). Another approach is to eliminate all expatriate compensation and benefits premiums, substituting a "local terms" package identical to what would be paid to an indigenous manager. This latter approach may be used from the point of initial recruitment or be applied after a certain trigger point is reached (such as time since initial appointment of the expat).[44]

SALARIES

The practice of paying home-country nationals the same salaries as their domestic counterparts permits worldwide consistency for this part of the compensation package. Because of the increasing use of third-country nationals, those personnel are generally treated in the same way.

Some firms take the equal-pay-for-equal-work concept one step further and pay the same base salaries to host-country nationals. In countries that legislate yearly bonuses and family allowances for their citizens, a local national may receive what appears to be a higher salary than is paid the expatriate, although companies usually make extra payments to prevent expatriates from falling behind in this regard. In the United Kingdom, it is a common practice to pay executives relatively lower salaries and to provide them with expensive perquisites, such as chauffeured automobiles, housing, and club memberships.

ALLOWANCES

Allowances are payments made to compensate expatriates for the extra costs they must incur to live as well abroad as they did in the home country. The most common allowances are for housing, cost of living, tax differentials, education, and moving.

allowances
Employee compensation payments added to base salaries because of higher expenses encountered when living abroad

Housing Allowances
Housing allowances are designed to permit executives to live in houses as good as those they had at home. A common rule of thumb is for the firm to pay all of the rent that is in excess of 15 percent of the executive's salary.

Cost-of-Living Allowances
Cost-of-living allowances are based on differences in the prices paid for food, utilities, transportation, entertainment, clothing, personal services, and medical expenses overseas compared with the prices paid for these items in the headquarters' city. Many ICs use the U.S. Department of State index, which is based on the cost of these items in Washington, DC, but have found it is not altogether satisfactory. For one thing, critics claim this index is not adjusted often enough to account for either the rapid inflation in some countries or the changes in relative currency values. Another objection is that the index does not include many cities in which the firm operates. As a result, many companies take their own surveys or use data from the United Nations, the World Bank, the International Monetary Fund, or private consulting firms. Figures and comparisons on costs of living, prices, and wages can also be found in private publications. Table 17.3 provides a ranking of the 10 cities with the highest cost of living, as of 2010, as well as a ranking of 10 cities with the highest quality of living.

Allowances for Tax Differentials
ICs pay tax differentials when the host-country taxes are higher than the taxes that the expatriates would pay on the same compensation and consumption at home. The objective is to ensure that expatriates will not have less after-tax take-home pay in the host country than they would at home. This can create a considerable extra financial burden on an American parent company because, among other things, the U.S. Internal Revenue Code treats tax allowances as additional taxable income. There are other tax disincentives for Americans to work abroad.

Education Allowances
Expatriates are naturally concerned that their children receive educations at least equal to those they would get in their home countries, and many want their children taught in their native language. Primary and secondary schools with teachers

TABLE 17.3	Cost-of-Living and Quality-of-Living Rankings of Top 10 Cities for 2010, from Highest to Lowest					
Cost-of-Living Rank	City	Country	Quality-of-Living Rank	City	Country
1	Luanda	Angola	1	Vienna	Austria
2	Tokyo	Japan	2	Zurich	Switzerland
3	N'Djamena	Chad	2	Geneva	Switzerland
4	Moscow	Russia	4	Vancouver	Canada
5	Geneva	Switzerland	5	Auckland	New Zealand
6	Osaka	Japan	6	Dusseldorf	Germany
7	Libreville	Gabon	7	Frankfurt	Germany
8	Hong Kong	Hong Kong	7	Munich	Germany
8	Zurich	Switzerland	9	Bern	Switzerland
10	Copenhagen	Denmark	10	Sydney	Australia

Note: Cost-of-living index includes cost of housing. Base City, New York City, USA = 100.

Sources: Mercer Human Resource Counsulting, *2010 Cost-of-Living Survey,* www.mercer.com/costofliving (accessed May 29, 2011); Mercer Human Resource Consulting, *2010 Quality of Living Survey,* www.mercer.com/qualityoflivingpr#City_Ranking_Tables (accessed May 29, 2011).

from most industrialized home countries are available in many cities around the world, but these are private schools and therefore charge tuition. ICs either pay the tuition or, if there are enough expatriate children, operate their own schools. For decades, petroleum companies in the Middle East and Venezuela have maintained schools for their employees' children. An Economist survey indicated that 39 percent of companies offered free private schooling to their expatriates' children.[45]

Moving and Orientation Allowances
Companies generally pay the total costs of transferring their employees overseas. These costs include transporting the family, moving household effects, and maintaining the family in a hotel on a full expense account until the household effects arrive. Some firms find it less expensive to send the household effects by air rather than by ship because the reduction in hotel expenses more than compensates for the higher cost of air freight. It has also been found that moving into a house sooner raises the employee's morale.

Companies may also pay for some orientation of the employees and their families. Companies frequently pay for language instruction, and some will provide the family with guidance on the intricacies of everyday living, such as shopping, hiring domestic help, and sending children to school.

BONUSES

bonuses
Expatriate employee compensation payments in addition to base salaries and allowances because of hardship, inconvenience, or danger

Bonuses (or *premiums*), unlike allowances, are paid by firms in recognition that expatriates and their families undergo some hardships and inconveniences and make sacrifices while living abroad. Bonuses include overseas premiums, contract termination payments, and home leave reimbursement.

Overseas Premiums
Overseas premiums are additional payments to expatriates and are generally established as a percentage of the base salary. They typically range from 10 to 25 percent. If the living conditions are extremely disagreeable, the company may pay larger premiums for hardship posts. The U.S. Department of State maintains a list of hardship differential pay premiums that is often used as a reference by ICs and expats. Table 17.4 shows the hardship differentials for 20 selected cities as of May 2011.

Contract Termination Payments
These payments are made as inducements for employees to stay on their jobs and work out the periods of their overseas contracts. The payments are made at the end of the contract periods only if the employees have worked out their

TABLE 17.4	Hardship Differential Pay Premiums for Selected Cities and Countries, 2011

City and Country	Differential Pay Premium (%)
Kabul, Afghanistan	35
Sarajevo, Bosnia-Herzegovina	20
São Paulo, Brazil	10
Phnom Penh, Cambodia	25
Guangzhou, China	25
Cairo, Egypt	15
Tbilisi, Georgia	25
Port-au-Prince, Haiti	30
Kolkata, India	25
Jakarta, Indonesia	25
Baghdad, Iraq	35
Kingston, Jamaica	15
Nairobi, Kenya	30
Mexico City, Mexico	15
Peshawar, Pakistan	35
Manila, Philippines	20
Riyadh, Saudi Arabia	20
Johannesburg, South Africa	10
Caracas, Venezuela	20
Harare, Zimbabwe	30

Source: U.S. Department of State, "Post (Hardship) Differential," May 22, 2011, http://aoprals.state.gov/Web920/hardship.asp (accessed May 29, 2011).

contracts. Such bonuses are used in the construction and petroleum industries and by other firms that have contracts requiring work abroad for a specific period of time or for a specific project. They may also be used if the foreign post is a hardship or not a particularly desirable one.

Home Leave[46]   ICs that post home-country—and sometimes third-country—nationals in foreign countries make it a practice to pay for periodic trips back to the home country by such employees and their families. The reasons for this are twofold. One, companies do not want employees and their families to lose touch with the home country and its culture. Two, companies want to have employees spend at least a few days at company headquarters to renew relationships with headquarters' personnel and catch up with new company policies and practices. A survey by *The Economist* revealed that 56 percent of companies gave regular, paid trips back home for their expatriate staff.[47]

Some firms grant three-month home leaves after an employee has been abroad about three years, but it is a more common practice to give two to four weeks' leave each year. All transportation costs are paid to and from the executive's hometown, and all expenses are paid during the executive's stay at company headquarters.

COMPENSATION PACKAGES CAN BE COMPLICATED

One might think from the discussion to this point that **compensation packages,** while costly—the extras frequently total 50 percent or more of the base salary—are fairly straightforward in their calculation. Nothing could be further from the truth.

What Percentage?   All allowances and a percentage of the base salary are usually paid in the host-country currency. What should this percentage be? In practice, it varies from 65 to 75 percent, with the remainder being banked wherever the employee wishes. One reason for such practices is to decrease the local portion of the salary, thereby lowering

compensation packages
For expatriate employees, packages that can incorporate many types of payments or reimbursements and must take into consideration exchange rates and inflation

host-country income taxes and giving the appearance to government authorities and local employees that there is less difference between the salaries of local and foreign employees than is actually the case. Another reason is that expatriate employees have various expenses that must be paid in home-country currency. Such expenses may include professional society memberships, purchases during home leave, payments on outstanding debts in the employee's home country (e.g., mortgage, school loans), and tuition and other costs for children in home-country universities.

What Exchange Rate?   Inasmuch as most of the expatriate's compensation is usually denominated in the host-country currency but established in terms of the home-country currency to achieve comparable compensation throughout the enterprise, a currency exchange rate must be chosen. In countries whose currencies are freely convertible into other currencies, this presents no serious problem, although the experienced expatriate will argue that an exchange rate covers only international transactions and may not represent a true purchasing power parity between the local and home-country currencies. For instance, such items as bread and milk are rarely traded internationally, and living costs and inflation rates may be much higher in the host country than in the home country. International companies attempt to compensate for such differences in the cost-of-living allowances.

More difficult problems must be solved in countries that have exchange controls and nonconvertible currencies. Without exception, those currencies are overvalued at the official rate, and if the firm uses that rate, its expatriate employees are certain to be shortchanged. Reference may be made to the free market rate for the host-country currency in free currency markets in, for example, the United States or Switzerland or to the black market rate in the host country, but these do not give the final answers. In the end, all companies must pay their expatriate employees enough to enable them to live as well as others who have similar positions in other firms, regardless of how the amount is calculated.

A common compensation component at many American companies is a stock plan that gives employees opportunities to acquire the company's stock on favorable terms. Such programs are designed to increase loyalty and productivity, but they sometimes run into problems outside the United States. Share ownership is unknown or restricted in numerous countries. DuPont, for example, discovered it could not give stock options in 25 of 53 nations, primarily because those countries' laws ban or limit ownership of foreign shares.

COMPENSATION OF THIRD-COUNTRY NATIONALS

Although some companies have different compensation plans for third-country nationals, there is a trend toward treating them the same as home-country expatriates. In either event, there are areas in which problems can arise. One of these areas is the calculation of income tax differentials when an American expatriate is compared with an expatriate from another country.[48] This results from the unique American government practice of taxing U.S. citizens even though they live and work abroad and treating tax differential payments made to those citizens as additional taxable income. No other major country taxes its nationals in those ways.

Another possible problem area is the home leave bonus. The two purposes of home leave are to prevent expatriates from losing touch with their native cultures and to have them visit IC headquarters. A third-country national must visit two countries instead of only one to achieve both purposes, and the additional costs can be substantial. Compare the cost of sending an Australian employee home from Mexico with that required to send an American from Mexico to Dallas.

Regardless of problems, the use of third-country nationals is growing in popularity. As businesses race to enlarge their ranks of qualified international managers, third-country nationals are in greater demand. They often win jobs because they speak several languages and know an industry or country well.

As the number of TCNs employed as executives by ICs continues to grow, the possible combinations of nationalities and host countries are virtually limitless, further complicating compensation efforts.

INTERNATIONAL STATUS

In all of this discussion, we have been describing compensation for expatriates who have been granted **international status.** Merely being from another country does not automatically qualify an employee for all the benefits we have mentioned. A subsidiary may hire home-country nationals or third-country nationals and pay them the same as it pays host-country employees. However, managements have found that although an American, for example, may agree initially to take a job and be paid on the local scale, sooner or later bad feeling and friction will develop as that person sees fellow Americans enjoying international status perquisites to which he or she is not entitled.

Sometimes firms promote host-country employees to international status even without transferring them abroad. This is a means of rewarding valuable people and preventing them from leaving the company for better jobs elsewhere.

Thus, international status means being paid some or all of the allowances and bonuses we have discussed, and there can be other sorts of payments as individual circumstances and people's imaginations combine to create them. Compensation packages for expatriates and other international executives are sufficiently important and complicated to have become a specialization in the personnel management field; at one firm, the title is "international employee benefits consultant." Help is also available from outside the IC. From time to time, the large consulting firms publish pamphlets advising about the transfer of executives to specific countries.

international status
Entitles the expatriate employee to all the allowances and bonuses applicable to the place of residence and employment

PERKS

Perks originated in the perquisites of the medieval lords of the manor, whose workers paid parts of their profits or produce to the lords to be allowed to continue working. Today, perks are symbols of rank in the corporate hierarchy and are used to compensate executives while minimizing taxes. Among the most common perks are:

- Cars, which may include chauffeurs, especially for executives higher up the organization ladder.
- Private pension plan.
- Retirement payment
- Life insurance.
- Health insurance.
- Emergency evacuation services (for medical or other reasons).
- Kidnapping, ransom, and extortion insurance.
- Company house or apartment.
- Directorship of a foreign subsidiary.
- Seminar holiday travel.
- Club memberships.
- Hidden slush fund (such funds may be illegal, but some corporations are said to have them).

WHAT'S IMPORTANT TO YOU?

When considering a relocation abroad, whether for a few months or many years, it is important for you to consider what elements of compensation and benefits are important for you. Common considerations include cost of living, safety of personnel, medical facilities, housing, and schools. They may also include availability of good restaurants, sports facilities, shopping facilities, and quality theatre or other entertainment venues. See Table 17.3 again, for a ranking of the top 10 cities in the world for quality of life; none of these cities is located in an emerging country. Also important to many employees may be the number of vacation days they are likely to receive annually. For example, the average number of vacation days in Japan is 25 per year, versus 35 in Germany, 37 in France, and 42 in Italy. In the United States, the average is 13 days, half of what Canadians enjoy.[49]

Laura Gunderson

I first caught the travel bug at age 6, as a result of growing up in Jakarta, Indonesia, as part of an expatriate family. Upon return to the U.S., I spent my life traveling, living, and studying all over the country, and then the world in places such as Australia, Mexico, New Zealand, and the United Kingdom. I had no idea that I could actually satisfy this craving for travel and international perspective while actually earning a living. I decided to attend Cal Poly–San Luis Obispo as a business administration major, but frankly at that point I really didn't even know what I wanted to do with my life.

It quickly became apparent that regardless of what level you were as a student taking business courses such as finance, accounting, economics, business law, or marketing, a common thread appeared amongst them all. This commonality was the incredible complications that arose when a business wanted to expand in any way internationally. This realization really struck me, and I wanted to understand how *do* all these aspects of business work together to create the best solutions . . . beyond just the United States. When it came time to select a concentration, I distinctly remember thinking, "How could I *not* do international business?"

I embarked on my newfound educational course, taking all classes related to how to resolve the issues posed by doing business internationally. International human resource management (IHRM), in particular, captured my interest. Although I didn't know how, I knew I wanted to work with a company to leverage their greatest assets, their people, to achieve business success. I could combine my passion for people with my passion for business success (dating back to my childhood summer

sidewalk lemonade café business venture). As I was graduating at one of the most difficult economic times the country had seen in decades, making this dream a reality seemed near to impossible. However, after much hard work and preparation, I have now worked in IHRM for a little over a year coordinating expatriate, repatriate and host-to-host assignees on three different continents for a Fortune 100 company. My experience has been working with assignees, business leaders and HR colleagues across all functions and located around the country and globe. Throughout my experience, I faced numerous challenges specific to IHRM supporting business success, including but not limited to:

- *Relocation:* How do we coordinate an employee's immigration and tax considerations? How do we prepare them for the cultural differences they will experience?

- *Talent management:* How do we best leverage the experiences and knowledge of individuals who have gone on assignment? How do we avoid the dreaded "out of sight, out of mind" experience felt by many assignees upon repatriation?

- *Recruitment:* What criteria are we selecting candidates based on?

- *Employee development:* Are we a culture that supports assignments as a career steppingstone? How do we ensure that assignees are still receiving an equivalent access to HR programs and support as domestic employees?

- *Compensation:* How can we properly incentivize employees to live and work in less desirable areas, especially if they have a family?

- *Labor relations:* Does a union-represented environment affect an employee's ability or desire to go on an assignment?

- *Information systems:* How are we managing employee data in countries where our typical infrastructure or software systems may not exist?

Considering the economic climate, cost considerations were a huge component of every single decision: what is the best option to balance what is best for the company strategically and what is best for the assignee personally, while keeping the bottom line in mind. In addition, many of these challenges were completely unique, and our team had to stretch to use all resources available to take action, usually on a short timeframe. I learned the best way to resolve these situations was to ask as many questions as possible and to continuously learn from my own and others' experience. As an entry-level professional, no one will expect you to be an expert—otherwise they would have hired one—and you don't get to be an expert without starting somewhere. A large majority of the lessons learned during my college courses were directly applicable from my first day on the job, so believe it or not, it was incredibly helpful to keep my course notes and textbooks available.

An inspiring mentor of mine explained to me that luck was nothing more than being prepared for an opportunity when it arises, which allows you to make the most of any situation. I have

(continued)

found this to be absolutely true in every situation, which is why as an HR professional and as someone who recently went through the long and exhausting job search process, my strongest advice is simply to be prepared. This doesn't mean you have to have a dozen internships abroad or speak five languages, because I definitely didn't, though it certainly wouldn't hurt. I suggest that you apply and interview for as many positions as possible in order to gain comfort and experience speaking with recruiters. Send your resumé to everyone, including teachers, mentors, alumni, family, and friends for editing and review; it may even open unexpected doors and networks. If you are currently employed and an IHRM position is not readily available, volunteer or suggest HR projects related to your international business and learn as much as possible about your firm's international programs. Continue to build your networks and communicate your interests to as many people as possible; there is always an opportunity out there. It is imperative to advertise yourself and your interests while doing as much as possible to prepare for when that great IHRM job does present itself.

Although challenging and sometimes stressful, working in IHRM has always been incredibly rewarding. I feel I am truly helping people and program success by finding the best solutions for both the company and the individual employee. By stretching me in so many ways, both personally and professionally, working in IHRM has given me a great international business foundation because I truly understand how HR directly supports international business ventures. Everyone can gain from this experience and take their careers as far as possible—the sky is the limit, and I hope to see you there!

Resources for Your Global Career

Resources on Global Labor Trends and Labor Issues

- **Foreign labor trends** from the U.S. Department of Labor with links to labor data for 20 countries and the European Union: www.dol.gov/ilab/media/reports/flt/main.htm

  The Bureau of labor Statistics' **Foreign Labor Statistics (FLS)** gives international comparisons of hourly compensation, productivity, unit labor costs, labor force employment and unemployment rates, and consumer prices internationally: www.bls.gov/fls/

  The Human Capital Institute offers webcasts and white papers on emerging labor trends and topics related to the global workforce: www.humancapitalinstitute.org/hci/tracks_future_labor_trends.guid

The Human Capital Institute offers webcasts and white papers on managing global talent: www.hci.org/webcasts/schedule

The Herman Group defines itself as "Strategic Business Futurists" who address future workforce and workplace trends. Thought-provoking ideas are offered on their website: www.hermangroup.com/index.html

The **Herman Trend Alert** is a free weekly e-mail newsletter on issues of international HRM: www.hermangroup.com/trend_alert_main.html

Become a World-Class Certified Human Resources Specialist

SHRM (Society for Human Resources Management) is recognized as *the* professional association for HR managers worldwide. Become SHRM certified and you will be in a highly qualified group of HR specialists. SHRM offers three categories of certification:

1. Professional in Human Resources (PHR) with 50,000+ members certified at this level.
2. Senior Professional in Human Resources (SPHR) with 38,000+ certified members.
3. Global Professional in Human Resources (GPHR) with 800+ certified members.

The GPHR is the world-class standard of HR certification and the top level of global HR certification attainable. For more information on SHRM, visit: www.shrm.org/Pages/default.aspx.

Your Worldwide Resources for International Human Resource Management

IPMA-HR for managers working in the public sector: www.ipma-hr.org/

HRM Guide on international human resources: www.hrmguide.net/buscon1.html

AHR guide articles on international human resources: www.hrmguide.net/

AHRMIO (Association for Human Resources Management in International Organizations): www.ahrmio.org/

Comprehensive guides and links to international HR management information and articles: www.hr-guide.com/

Also of importance in decisions on where to locate a business operation are considerations such as cost of living, business environment, and office rents. Despite labor market problems and less attractive market opportunities, the quality of the business environment in western European and North American countries remains higher than that in most emerging markets because those countries possess sophisticated institutions, such as advanced financial sectors, reliable legal systems, and political stability, that companies value. See again Table 17.3 for cost-of-living comparisons for a number of the world's cities. The survey compares the prices of goods and services typically consumed by the families of executives being sent abroad. You will note that several of the cities ranked in the top 10 are located in emerging countries.

Summary

LO17-1 Discuss several of the major factors that may affect the quantity and quality of labor in a nation.

Forces that affect the quantity and quality of labor in a nation include such characteristics of the population as overall size, age, urbanization, immigrant labor availability, and unionization.

LO17-2 Explain the relationship between competitive strategies (international, multidomestic, global, and transnational) and international human resource management approaches (ethnocentric, polycentric, regiocentric, and global).

Recognize that competitive strategy should be a primary determinant of the IHRM policies that an IC will use. Alternative competitive strategies of home replication, multidomestic, global, or transnational are linked to the organization's use of ethnocentric, polycentric, regiocentric, or geocentric approaches to international human resource management.

LO17-3 Compare the use of home-country, host-country, and third-country nationals as international company executives.

Sources of IC executives may be the home country, host countries, or third countries, and their differing culture, language, ability, and experience can strengthen IC management. Home or parent country nationals may know the IC's home country culture, language, and approach to doing business, but they usually are not knowledgeable about the host-country culture and language, which can limit their effectiveness. Host-country nationals generally have familiarity with local, host nation customs, culture and language and may be less expensive than using expatriates from the home country, although considerable training costs may be necessary to familiarize them with the IC's corporate culture, policies, and practices. Host-country nationals may be pirated away by local companies or subsidiaries of other Ics once they are trained, and they may also experience a conflict of loyalty between the host country and the employer. Third-country nationals may be able to overcome cultural or language difficulties, as well as reduce the problem of limited availability of suitably qualified host-country managers.

LO17-4 Explain what an expatriate is, and identify some of the challenges and opportunities of an expat position.

Expat positions allow employees to work in foreign locations, providing a foundation for learning and growth, both personally and professionally, and a basis for movement upward in an IC's hierarchy. Expats can also find themselves "out of sight, out of mind," with unclear performance objectives and bases for performance evaluation. The families of many expat find the adjustment to a foreign posting difficult to manage successfully.

LO17-5 Discuss the increasing importance of accommodating the trailing spouse of an expatriate executive.

The growing prevalence of two-career families is complicating problems of accommodating the spouse of an executive who is being transferred to another country. The leading cause of expatriate failure is family-related issues, especially the ability of accompanying spouses to adjust to the cultural adaptation pressures of the foreign posting. In many countries, the expatriate's spouse does not have the legal right to work, which can increase financial pressures and strain relationships before, during, and after the expatriate assignment.

LO17-6 Identify some of the complications of compensation packages for expatriate executives.

Expatriate manager compensation packages can be extremely complicated. Among other sources of complications are fluctuating currency exchange rates and differing inflation rates. Basic elements of those packages are salaries, allowances, and bonuses.

Key Words

expatriate (p. 426)

labor market (p. 426)

labor mobility (p. 428)

brain drain (p. 429)

reverse brain drain (p. 430)

labor unions (p. 430)

collective bargaining (p. 430)

ethnocentric (p. 430)

polycentric (p. 430)

regiocentric (p. 430)

geocentric (p. 431)

home-country national (p. 431)

parent-country national (PCN) (p. 431)

host-country national (HCN) (p. 431)

third-country national (TCN) (p. 431)

culture shock (p. 438)

allowances (p. 443)

bonuses (p. 444)

compensation packages (p. 445)

international status (p. 447)

1. Why is the average age of the population increasing in some nations, particularly the developed countries? What are some of the implications of this trend, especially for international companies?

2. Classical economists assumed the labor factor of production to be immobile. Is this assumption correct in the modern world? Explain.

3. What is brain drain, and why does it occur? What actions might countries take in order to reduce or even reverse brain drain?

4. Why should the international human resource management approaches used by an international company be closely linked to the competitive strategy the company is using?

5. Compare and contrast ethnocentric, polycentric, regiocentric, and geocentric staffing policies.

6. In staffing a multinational organization for service outside the IC home country, what are some advantages and disadvantages of hiring home-country personnel?

7. Why has there been an increasing use of third-country nationals in the foreign operations of ICs?

8. Why are problems involving the trailing spouses of expatriate executives so common? What are some companies doing to solve those problems?

9. Why are expatriate employees frequently paid more than their colleagues at equivalent job levels in the home office?

10. Why are compensation packages for expatriates more complicated than those for domestic employees?

11. What are some of the quality-of-life issues executives should consider before taking their families into an expatriate experience?

12. Suppose you are the CEO of an American multinational. On your staff and in the U.S. operating divisions of your company are several bright, able, dedicated female executives. They are also ambitious, and in your company, international experience is a must before an executive can hope to get into top management. An opening comes up for the position of executive vice president in the company's Mexican subsidiary. One of the women on your staff applies for the position, and she is well qualified for the job, better than anyone else in the company. Would you give her the position? What are the arguments pro and con?

13. Using the company example in question 12, suppose another position becomes available, this one as treasurer of the Japanese subsidiary. The chief financial officer of the company's California division applies for this job. She has performed to everyone's satisfaction, and she seems thoroughly qualified to become the treasurer in Japan. In addition, she speaks and writes Japanese. She is the daughter of a Japanese mother and an American father, and they encouraged her to become fluent in both English and Japanese. Would you give her the job? Why or why not?

---

 globalEDGE.msu.edu

Research Task

Use the globalEDGE site (http://globalEDGE.msu.edu/) to complete the following exercises:

1. *HSBC Expat Zone,* which provides insight into expatriate life, publishes an Expat Experience report every year. Locate and download the most recent report. What does this report focus on? Specifically, what factors are considered when ranking the countries with the best life experience? Briefly summarize the key findings of this report, and identify the top five countries that offer the best overall experience to expatriates. Are these findings surprising?

2. The text discusses the importance of establishing a good compensation plan for foreign employment. Using the *Quarterly Reports for Living Costs Abroad,* published by the U.S. Department of State, provide a report comparing the cities of Rio de Janeiro and Mexico City.

Minicase: Brittany Miller: Should She Accept an International Assignment?

Brittany Miller, a 37-year-old manager with Techtonics International, had just returned to her office early on a Thursday afternoon. During a lunchtime meeting in the company's executive lunchroom, her boss had just offered her a chance to move to Shanghai, China, where she would be in charge of establishing the company's new office for the East Asia region. As she sat at her desk looking out over the Los Angeles skyline, she was filled with a mix of excitement and trepidation. Should she accept the position she was offered? Or should she pass on this opportunity and wait for something else in the future? What factors should she consider in making this important decision?

Miller had joined Techtonics shortly after completing her bachelor's degree in business, starting as an assistant sales manager. Since then, she had been promoted several times and was now the vice president in charge of North American operations for one of Techtonics's main business areas, overseeing a workforce of more than 2,100 people and sales in excess of $500 million. Identified as one of the "rising stars" in Techtonics, and mentored by one of the senior vice presidents of the company, she seemed to have no limits to her career path.

Miller had always dreamed of living and working abroad. As a student, she studied abroad for a semester in Spain and spent a month afterward traveling around Europe with several friends. After graduation, she worked on a six-month internship with AIESEC, working for a small exporting company based in Poland. Since joining Techtonics, her international experience had primarily consisted of business trips to Canada or Mexico, attending several conferences and visiting a few selected client companies in Europe and Asia, and going on two extended vacations: one to Thailand and another to the Caribbean. When her boss mentioned the possibility of going to China, she could barely contain her enthusiasm!

However, Miller also began to think about her family and how an international assignment might affect them. Her husband, Jerry, was an accountant in the Los Angeles office of a large accounting firm. Although he had a successful career, she thought that he might be open to a change. She also had two children: Jerry Jr., who was 8, and Susan, who was 5. How would they respond to moving to a new country? Would now be a good time for such a move, or would it be better to wait for a few years?

And what if she was to accept the offer to go to China? What issues would she need to discuss with the company regarding the implications of a move to China? Her boss said that he would like to have Miller's decision within about a week and that she would need to move to Shanghai within four to six months if she accepted the job.

As she watched the traffic begin to jam up on the freeway outside her office building, Miller thought about reaching for her cell phone and calling her good friend for advice on how to deal with the job opportunity that she had been offered.

Questions:

1. If you were a good friend of Brittany Miller, what recommendation would you give regarding whether she should accept the international assignment that has been offered to her?

2. What issues she should focus on in making such a decision?

International Accounting and Financial Management

Quick decisions are unsafe decisions.

—*Sophocles, 496–406 B.C.*

Arrange whatever pieces come your way.

—*Virginia Woolf*

Sovereign Wealth Funds: Globalization at Work

Sovereign wealth funds are investment funds that are controlled by governments. The funds themselves may be from national reserves, pension funds, and other monies controlled by the government. Recently, the growth of sovereign wealth funds in China and the oil-rich states has created pools of dollars so large, in the range of $4 trillion, that they can influence the market and readily acquire assets in the developed world. The Sovereign Wealth Funds Institute, an organization that tracks these funds, lists the United Arab Emirates as having the largest fund or group of funds, at $738.9 billion. China follows at $732.5 billion, then Saudi Arabia weighs in at $436.3 billion.[a]

Governments invest to get a return on their assets for their citizens and to diversify their national risk. For example, if the country's main earnings are in the oil sector, investments in nonrelated industries will protect it from a down oil market (if we can imagine such a thing).

"What's the problem?" you might ask. Why not use Arab, Chinese, and Brazilian wealth to leverage growth in the developed world? There are a couple of interesting issues connected to sovereign wealth funds. First of all, it is an odd twist on the prevalent trend toward privatization. Except for dire situations such as the recent financial crisis in which governments bailed out some private companies, the developed nations tend to preach that business should be controlled by private risk takers. Keep the government out. Yet sovereign wealth funds are government owned, so their investments actually represent a foreign government's ownership.

In addition to the counter-trend aspect of sovereign wealth funds, there's the issue that they are not purely commercial in their interests and might choose objectives other than to maximize return to the shareholder. For example, the Chinese Investment Corporation, one of the major Chinese sovereign wealth funds, might choose to influence procurement decisions, favoring China's companies over less costly suppliers, on the basis of self-interest. Or Chinese government economic policy could favor job creation over profitability. Or a foreign government might invest in a firm that's important to national defense. Once government ownership is established, the business decisions may be influenced by political objectives or other objectives not in the best interest of the firm's economic results. Besides, these are

18

learning objectives

After reading this chapter, you should be able to:

LO18-1 **Identify** the major international accounting issues that international firms face when operating in foreign currencies.

LO18-2 **Describe** the relationship between accounting and culture.

LO18-3 **Describe** the international accounting standards' convergence process and its importance to international firms.

LO18-4 **Outline** the arguments for and against 3BL.

LO18-5 **Explain** the capital structure choices open to international firms and their significance.

LO18-6 **Describe** why ICs move funds.

LO18-7 **Explain** the utility of an international finance center.

LO18-8 **Describe** multilateral netting and its benefits.

LO18-9 **Categorize** foreign exchange risks faced by the international firm into transaction exposure, translation exposure, and economic exposure.

LO18-10 **Describe** ways to hedge transaction exposure.

private funds and have limited transparency, so what the fund is doing is difficult to assess.

Many of these concerns can be answered by government legislation that limits foreign investment directly, requires disclosure or requires approval of foreign investments. By and large, these processes have been legislated. There are many examples of government-owned businesses, both domestic and foreign. In the United States, public pension funds constitute more than 40 percent of all institutional investment. More than a whopping 80 percent of all the oil pumped in the world is pumped by government-owned firms. CITGO is owned by the Venezuelan government.[b] (Don't you wonder what the Red Sox Nation thinks of that?[c])

There's still another noteworthy point to be made about sovereign wealth funds. They represent a global shift—a trend toward a transfer of ownership away from the United States, Europe, and Japan and toward developing nations.

Sovereign wealth funds represent globalization at work. In addition, for the developed world, they provide benefits because they leverage continued growth and provide an ability to cushion financial crises. Remember, developing country assets are growing around twice as fast as those in the developed nations.[d] A McKinsey study predicts that by 2020, more than half of the world's saving and investment will take place in developing markets![e]

[a]Sovereign Wealth Funds, www.swfinstitute.org (accessed April 16, 2011).

[b]James Surowiecki, "The Financial Page: Sovereign Wealth World," *The New Yorker,* November 26, 2007, p. 70; and Alan Murray, "The Outlook: Ascent of Sovereign Wealth Funds Illustrates New World Order," *The Wall Street Journal,* January 28, 2008.

[c]See www.redsoxconnection.com/citgo.html for explanation.

[d]Diana Farrell and Susan Lund, "Power Brokers," McKinsey Global Institute, October 2007, referenced by Murray, "The Outlook," www.mckinsey.com/mgi/mginews/powerbrokers.asp (accessed April 16, 2010).

[e]"Farewell to Cheap Capital? Implications of Long-Term Shifts in Global Investment and Saving," McKinsey, October 2010 (accessed April 16, 2011).

In Chapter 8, we reviewed some of the major financial forces international managers face in their daily operations. These forces include fluctuating currency values, currency exchange controls, taxation, and inflation and interest rates. Managers are not helpless before these forces, and now we look at methods these managers have developed to deal with them, some of which are imaginative and elegant, and, of course, all of them are legal. *A word here about the general area.* Some find these topics uninteresting or perhaps too complex. One of our goals in this chapter is to help you see that these issues are at the core of how companies work, they often make the difference between moderate and outstanding results, and they can be exciting and interesting. True, there's no doubt; international finance is complex. Our approach is to help you gain access to the major issues, assuming that you do not have an advanced background in finance.

We'll begin with accounting because it is a fundamental tool of financial management and because accounting practices and standards change across national borders. First, we look at the differences in how countries record stored value (the essence of accounting). Fortunately, there is a strong movement toward a convergence of accounting standards, which will make the process much easier for the international company. In our discussion, we'll use the U.S.-based international company (IC) for the sake of simplicity, remembering that ICs can be any nationality. Note, too, that increasingly major ICs are headquartered in emerging-market economies such as China, India and Brazil.

That's the first half of our job in this chapter, to address issues of international accounting. The second half is to review the major issues in IC financial management. If you are concerned that this material is too complex, rest assured that we are not condensing an international finance course into a chapter. We begin with how the IC's capital is structured and then move on to cash management, including techniques such as multilateral netting and approaches to currency fluctuations. Finally, we discuss some aspects of taxation. Our goal is to describe these areas in an understandable way so that you can appreciate their contributions to the IC's success.

International Accounting

The purpose of accounting in all countries is to provide managers with financial data for use in their decision making and to provide external constituencies (investors, governments, lenders, suppliers, and others) the quantitative information they seek to inform their decisions. Accounting also provides the data governments need to levy taxes. If you think back to Chapter 4's coverage of cultural values that vary across nations, the idea that the basic concept of what useful accounting data is varies from country to country shouldn't surprise you. For example, in Germany, the primary users of financial information have been creditors, so accounting focuses on the balance sheet and the company's assets. By contrast, in the United States, investors are major users of financial information, and they look to the income statement as a sign of the company's future and are less interested in the balance sheet than are the Germans.[1]

An international company such as the Indian Tata Group, the Chinese household appliance company Haier Group, or the American consumer goods company Procter & Gamble has to address transactions in foreign currencies, with an obvious impact on the practice of accounting. And, as mentioned in our contrast of the Germans and Americans, different needs in different countries have led to large variations in financial statements across the globe. There is one additional source of variation, and this goes more directly to cultural differences: assumptions that underlie the country's legal, political, and economic systems, as well as the country's history, influence the commonly shared understanding of the purpose of accounting. That is to say, culture plays a significant role in the practice of accounting. In this section, we examine both transactions in foreign currencies and the role of culture in accounting, and then we go on to look at possible convergence among the main accounting approaches.

ACCOUNTING AND FOREIGN CURRENCY

LO18-1 Identify the major international accounting issues that international firms face when operating in foreign currencies.

There are only two points at which operating in a foreign currency raises issues from an accounting perspective: when transactions are made in foreign currencies and when branches and subsidiaries operate in foreign currencies and their results need to be made a part of the parent company's financial reports. We look first at transactions and then at translation and consolidation, the two processes involved in merging subsidiary financial results with those of the parent company.

When the U.S.-based company has foreign currency–based transactions such as sales, purchases, and loans (made and taken), they need to be recorded as revenues, expenses, assets, or liabilities. Here's an example.

Suppose the U.S.-based company buys Swiss watches in Geneva for 25,000 Swiss francs (CHFs) on June 1. Because the company's books are in U.S. dollars, the transaction is entered in dollars at the exchange rate on June 1. Let's say it's $0.963149/CHF. That is, 1 CHF buys $0.963149. The purchase entry would be $24,078.73. Accounts payable would also be $24,078.73 and the exchange rate notation "CHF 25,000 @ $0.963149" would be made.

Now, if the payment is immediate or stipulated in U.S. dollars (US$), that would be the end of it. But suppose there is a time lag, the payment is made on August 1 and in the meantime, the exchange rate has changed. If the transaction is in CHF, the underlying dollar value of the purchase would change. Let's say the Swiss franc weakens against the dollar, moving to $0.94300/CHF on August 1, when the payable is due. Now the U.S. company has to pay $23,575, or less than their original purchase entry. The $503.73 difference constitutes a foreign exchange gain. In this case, the journal entries would remain the same, and the gain (or loss) would be recorded in the income statement. This process is described by U.S. Financial Accounting Standards Board Statement 52 (FASB 52), which requires that companies record foreign currency–based transactions at the spot rate at the time of the transaction. Any gains or losses from changes in exchange rates for items carried as payables or receivables are posted in the income statement. The International Accounting Standards Board (IASB), the international accounting standards organization that we'll soon discuss when we look at the convergence of accounting standards, has the same rule.

consolidation The process of translating subsidiary results and aggregating them into one financial report

current rate method An approach in foreign currency translation in which assets and liabilities are valued at current spot rates

temporal method An approach in foreign currency translation in which monetary accounts are valued at the spot rate and accounts carried at historical cost are translated at their historic exchange rates

functional currency The primary currency of a business

Now to our second concern about foreign currencies in accounting operations. When a U.S. IC's foreign subsidiary reports results, these results need to be translated into the parent company's operating currency, in our discussion, dollars, and made to conform to U.S. generally accepted accounting principles (GAAP). Then these various results from foreign subsidiaries are aggregated into one financial report. This process is called **consolidation.**

So the question arises, what exchange rate should be used, today's or the one in effect on the day of the transaction? As you can see, there are two basic approaches to translation, and these are called the current rate method and the temporal method. They both have as their objectives to accurately reflect business results. By the **current rate method,** assets and liabilities are translated at the rate in effect the day the balance sheet is produced. By the **temporal method,** monetary items such as cash, receivables, and payables are translated at the current exchange rate. Fixed assets and long-term liabilities are translated at the rates in effect the date they were acquired or incurred.

So when is each of these translation methods used? The choice hinges on which currency the operation uses, its **functional currency**. The functional currency is the primary currency of the operation, the currency in which cash flows, pricing, expenses, and financing are denominated. Usually the functional currency is the local one, but every once in a while, an IC will operate in its parent currency in a foreign location. You can find all the details for the translation process in FASB 52 and IASB 21. Figure 18.1 summarizes implications of using the local or parent company currency as the functional currency.

ACCOUNTING AND CULTURE

LO18-2 **Describe** the relationship between accounting and culture.

We know that accounting follows different patterns in different parts of the world. Sidney Gray's research measures how two accounting functions, what information companies provide and how companies value assets, are influenced by culture. Accounting terms for these functions are disclosure practices and accounting measurement. His study, summarized in Figure 18.2, classifies countries on two dimensions, secrecy–transparency and optimism–conservatism.[2]

The dimension of secrecy–transparency measures the degree to which companies disclose information to the public. Germany, Japan, and Switzerland tend to value secrecy or privacy over transparency. In the United Kingdom and the United States, there is more disclosure and less privacy. The dimension of optimism–conservatism measures the degree to which a company is cautious in its valuing of assets and measuring of income. Accounting reports in countries with more conservative asset-valuing approaches tend to understate assets and income, while those in countries whose asset-valuing approach is more optimistic

FIGURE 18.1

Functional Currency and Translation Methods

When Functional Currency Is:	Local Currency	Parent Company Currency
Translation method is:	Current method	Temporal method
Assets are translated at:	Spot rate on date balance sheet prepared	Spot rate for monetary assets Historic cost for fixed assets
Income statement is translated at:	Average exchange rate for reporting period	Cost of goods sold and depreciation at historic rates Average exchange rate for reporting period Other items at average rate for period
Owner's equity is translated at:	Rates in effect when stock issued	Rates in effect when stock issued
Retained earnings are translated at:	Rates in effect when earnings posted	Rates in effect when earnings posted

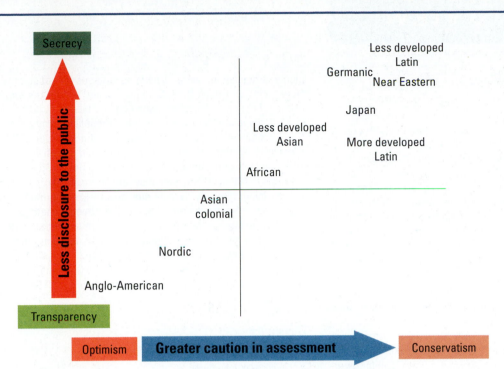

FIGURE 18.2

Cultural Differences in Measurement and Disclosure for Accounting Systems

Source: Adapted from Lee Radebaugh and Sidney J. Gray, *Accounting and Multinational Enterprises*, 5th ed. (New York: John Wiley & Sons, 2002).

tend toward overstatement. In France, Germany, and Japan, public companies' capital structure tends to depend more on debt rather than equity, with banks being a major source of the debt. Banks are concerned with liquidity. A conservative statement of profits may reduce tax exposure and dividend payouts, contributing to cash reserves that can be tapped for debt service. On the optimism measure, U.S. and, in a more restrained way, U.K. companies want to show impressive earnings that will attract investors and raise the share value sooner rather than later.

CONVERGENCE OF ACCOUNTING STANDARDS

LO18-3 Describe the international accounting standards' convergence process and its importance to international firms.

There are now two main accounting standards at play in the global arena. The private organization that establishes accounting standards in the United States is the Financial Accounting Standards Board. The FASB's standards are the U.S. generally accepted accounting principles. The international body is the International Accounting Standards Board, whose standards are the International Financial Reporting Standards (IFRS). In 2002, FASB and IASB agreed in principle to harmonize standards and converge. Convergence would create a standard for a global market and allow ICs to list stock in foreign markets, so they could tap into their potential as a source of shareholders. There is general political agreement to move toward the principles-based IASB standards (IFRS) from the rules-based FASB standards, but as we approached and then saw the initial 2011 deadline reset, some U.S. companies voiced their dissatisfaction with IFRS standards, especially in the cost area. The recession has also slowed down progress toward convergence. Significant progress has been made on this commitment by a negotiating group, with a target date of June 2011, a date later extended to 2015, but the negotiations are complex. With two very different basic sets of assumptions and so many important and heavily detailed aspects of specific standards to be reconciled, the progress so far toward convergence is impressive.

On the path of convergence, the EU Parliament and the Council of Europe decided to require IASB standards for financial reporting as of 2005. Australia and New Zealand have joined the EU in this step forward. The transition seems to have gone smoothly. Presently there are more than 90 countries that require public companies to list using IFRS and another 30 that permit it. Many other countries, including those in the EU, have adopted IFRS with

WORLD VIEW

The Ongoing Effects of SOX as a Symptom, Not a Cause

When the U.S. Congress passed the Sarbanes-Oxley Act (SOX) in the wake of the corporate scandals of 2001, Harvey Pitt, former chairman of the Securities and Exchange Commission (SEC) (2001–2003), lashed out at Congress for its required export of a hastily written and poorly conceptualized law. Its "one size-fits-all" approach to regulation stifles innovation, creativity, risk taking, and competitiveness. All foreign companies listing in the United States had to conform to SOX listing requirements, which are seen to be overly complex, until 2007, when the SEC changed its regulation. Worse, Pitt says, "Congress's exportation of SOX's standards has created huge difficulties for multinational companies and produced scorn for U.S. standards." He suggests that the scorn is justified, that there are better standards out there.[a]

What Pitt characterizes as "American geocentrism" has resulted in the loss of foreign listings on U.S. exchanges and the movement of IPOs to non-U.S. sites. In fact, London overtook New York as the world's top financial center in 2007.[b] A 2011 report on the top financial centers by the Qatar Financial Centre Authority lists London as the foremost city in the world economy, followed by New York, Hong Kong, Singapore and Shanghai.[c] Many financial reporters note that financial business has fallen off in New York due to "heavy-handed regulations." John Ross, director of economic and business policy for London's former mayor, Ken Livingstone, said that "the predictability and

clarity of regulations were obvious advantages for London over New York. . . . I don't think Sarbanes-Oxley is even the worst aspect of it, nor do the companies I have talked to. It is the litigious and apparently arbitrary culture of regulation and policy." Ross mentioned the political opposition to the takeover of P&O Ports by Dubai Ports World, owned by the United Arab Emirates, as an example of the uncertainty found in the United States.

Faced with evidence that they are increasingly irrelevant in the global economy, largely due to SOX-like approaches to regulation and enforcement, U.S. stock exchanges made a gallant effort to change their position. They went out to the market, trying to buy into foreign exchanges. Instead, following the old "buy on weakness; sell on strength" approach, Belgian Euronext merged with the NYSE in 2007. In 2011, the German Deutsche Börse made a $9.53 billion all stock purchase of the NYSE that is awaiting approval.

Questions:

1. Explain the goals of SOX legislation.

2. Why is SOX a symptom?

[a]Harvey Pitt, "Sarbanes-Oxley Is an Unhealthy Export," *Financial Times*, June 21, 2006, p. 15.

[b]Alan Beattie, "London Named Top Financial Centre," *Financial Times*, June 12, 2007, p. 3.

[c]Qatar Financial Centre Authority, Financial Centre Futures, "The Global Financial Index 9," www.zyen.com/GFCI/GFCI%209.pdf (accessed April 21, 2011).

minor modifications, called *carve-outs,* on the path to full IFRS acceptance. As of 2007, the U.S. Securities and Exchange Commission (SEC) decided that foreign companies listing their shares in the United States no longer needed to restate their financial statements to comply with FASB standards. As of April, 2011, the SEC had yet to decide whether to require or allow a switch to IFRS for U.S. public companies Incidentally, in 2002, when the U.S. Congress passed the Sarbanes-Oxley Act (SOX), in response to the corporate scandals in which accounting practices were at the center (Tyco, Enron, and WorldCom among them), it also noted in the legislation its desire for convergence in accounting standards. SOX named the SEC as the responsible party for recognizing the IASB.

One of the largest differences between GAAP and the IFRS has to do with their general approach. Thinking back to new institutional theory (Chapter 3) will help us here. GAAP relies on rules and regulations; we can think of it as a formal institution, with compliance based on expedience. The IFRS has greater reliance on principles, a normative institution, with compliance based on social obligation. Shared principles suggest the need for reasoned judgment because they allow for interpretations, unlike the application of rules, so accountants with GAAP approaches will have to get used to a new way of thinking. At this point, the United States is the only major nation that follows GAAP.

With convergence, financial markets around the world will become more integrated because the statements will be directly comparable. Investors and other interested parties will be able to see company performance across borders, companies will no longer have to restate their financials, and the complex process of consolidation will be much less so. These features of standardization mean substantial cost reductions for companies and better information for everyone.

TRIPLE-BOTTOM-LINE ACCOUNTING

L018-4 **Outline** the arguments for and against 3BL.

As mentioned in Chapter 5 in our sustainability discussion, increasingly, companies have made efforts to report on their environmental, social, and financial results. This reporting framework has been termed triple bottom line (3BL), a term credited to John Elkington in his 1997 book, *Cannibals with Forks: The Triple Bottom Line of 21st Century Business.*[3] The book's argument is that capitalism can become civilized; capitalists can be taught to eat with forks, due to consumer pressure and other social forces. Corporate capitalism can become sustainable capitalism. Elkington describes seven drivers of this transformation: markets, values, transparency, life-cycle technology, partnerships, time, and corporate governance. This approach supports sustainability and corporate social responsibility (CSR). As we have seen in our earlier discussion, *sustainability* is a systems concept that has three major aspects: the environmental or ecological, the social, and the economic. Currently, we measure at the economic level and, where required by government or social pressure, we measure at the environmental level (as with emission controls and hazardous waste) and at the social level (as with the Equal Employment Opportunity Commission's enforcement of the federal civil rights laws). Yet even in the environmental and social areas, we tend to know more about the problems—what is reported in the media—than about the company-level thinking on these important issues. Companies should measure and make public the environmental and social effects of their decisions. These are, in summary, the major argument for 3BL.

The major argument against 3BL is neither a substantive disagreement with the desirability of ecologically responsible business practices that support sustainability nor a disagreement with the idea of business being socially responsible; rather, it is the claim that measurement will not get us closer to the desired state. Wayne Norman and Chris MacDonald argue that social performance and environmental impact cannot be objectively measured in ways that are comparable to our economic measurements of a firm's activities.[4] They point out that the rhetoric may be appealing, but no widely implementable framework exists for measuring a company's performance in environmental and social areas, although there are high levels of consulting in these areas. In fact, they suggest that a focus on the measurement of these activities may well detract from efforts to figure out ways to combine sustainability and social responsibility with positive economic results, which is a more difficult challenge. There is a parallel with codes of ethics: what matters is what a company actually does, not whether a code of ethics is hanging on the wall of every office. The poster is rhetoric. Posting it is not ethical action. Decisions in the field that have to do with implementation are what matter, as well as how the organization's members understand the company's values and what those values say about their duties to stakeholders.[5]

Perhaps such reporting requires a reframing of how we think about organizational outcomes, a process that is incremental and subtle. Notable efforts to develop a framework that supports substantive reporting on the environmental, social, and financial aspects of business have been made by the Global Reporting Initiative (GRI), an international network of stakeholders from thousands of organizations, including private sector businesses, nongovernmental organizations, and government organizations, both local and international. There are more than 20,000 stakeholders from more than 80 countries. GRI is independent and collaborates with the United Nations Environmental Program (UNEP). Details can be accessed at www.globalreporting.org.

International Financial Management

We now look at how the firm manages funds across borders. This process of transferring value internationally is interesting and complex because it involves many variables, among them, exchange rates among currencies, varying restrictions on the movement of funds, differing tax systems, and differing economic environments. You might think of this challenge as an exceedingly complex game that involves managing risk, opportunity and complexity.

We begin our financial management review with a focus on the capital structure of the firm. Then we move on to cash flow management across borders, looking at both the financial flows themselves and the techniques used to move them. Foreign exchange (FX) risk management follows. We also look at taxation issues. This review's goal is to introduce you to the type of challenges international financial managers face and how they resolve them.

Capital Structure of the Firm

LO18-5 Explain the capital structure choices open to international firms and their significance.

We have seen that firms are becoming increasingly international in their markets and their sourcing in order to exploit attractive opportunities. Such an opportunity is also available for the capital structure of the firm, and, increasingly, chief financial officers (CFOs) have been tapping international financial markets, both public and private. Because financial markets are not globally integrated, though they are increasingly interconnected, varying opportunities arise among them with varying costs. If a CFO can raise capital in a foreign market at a lower cost than in the home market, such an opportunity may be attractive as a way to increase shareholder value.

The firm raises capital internally through its retained earnings and then, externally, through either equity (the issuing of shares) or debt (leveraging). Many firms choose the equity approach, to issue stocks in foreign markets, in part to tap into a broader investor pool, which can raise the stock price and reduce the cost of capital. Selling stock in foreign markets may have a significant marketing advantage, too, raising the profile of the brand name abroad. Foreign companies that have issued shares in the United States include Unilever, Fuji Film, Canadian Pacific, KLM, Sony, Toyota, and Cemex. Sometimes, foreign shares are directly traded in the American stock markets, but many times, they are traded in the form of **American depository receipts (ADRs).** These receipts represent shares that are held by a custodian, usually an American bank, in the stock's home market. They are denominated in dollars and traded on the U.S. exchange, eliminating the need to have a broker in the country of issue and the need for currency exchange.

American depository receipts (ADRs)
Foreign shares held by a custodian, usually a U.S. bank, in the issuer's home market and traded in dollars on the U.S. exchange

The sale of increasingly more shares of a company in foreign stock markets may raise concerns about foreigners having control of domestic assets, especially when the sectors involved are perceived as essential to national security. In these cases, governments restrict foreign ownership of equity. These restrictions are more prevalent in developing countries. For example, in China, India, Mexico, and Indonesia, foreign ownership in specific sectors is limited. Some sectors in developed nations are also protected from foreign ownership, often through an approval process. Such an example in the United States is found with airlines, which must be directed and operationally controlled by a U.S. citizen.[6] In addition, foreign acquisitions are approved by the U.S. Treasury's Committee on Foreign Investment in the United States, with final decision made by the president. In 2008, CFIUS investigated just under 2,000 proposed acquisitions. In 2005, this committee refused approval of China National Offshore Oil Corporation's acquisition of the California oil company UNOCAL, which later merged with Chevron.

Debt markets are the other source of capital for the firm, and increasingly the tendency is to tap local markets first. That may mean that a foreign subsidiary of the Japanese firm Toyota would look first to its market in the United States for funds to use in their U.S. operations. Multinational corporations, in addition to obtaining funds at the corporate level, can explore borrowing in their domestic and international debt markets, increasing the opportunities to reduce the cost of capital. They also have access to **offshore financial centers,** locations that specialize in financing by nonresidents, where the taxation levels are low and the banking regulations are slim. Switzerland, the Cayman Islands, Hong Kong, and the Bahamas are examples of offshore financial centers.

offshore financial center
Location that specializes in financing nonresidents, with low taxes and few banking regulations

Debt financing is thought to be less expensive than is equity financing, because the interest paid on the debt is usually tax deductible, while dividends paid out to investors are not. Yet the choice of debt or equity financing is also influenced by local practice. Companies in the United States, the United Kingdom, and Canada tend to rely on equity more heavily than do companies in many other countries. In both Japan and Germany, banks traditionally play a more central role than do the stock markets in the financing picture. In Japan, we find the interlocking relationships of the *keiretsu,* where related companies in a larger family—such as Mitsubishi, Sumitomo, or C. Itoh—are connected with interlocking ownership of stocks and bonds, with the company bank at their center. Essentially, this structure eliminates the stakeholder conflicts between bondholders and stockholders, an appropriate characteristic for a national culture where harmony is an important cultural value.

How the local government treats taxes may also influence how the IC structures its capital. If the local tax rate is high, and interest paid on debt is tax deductible, debt may be a way to partially protect profits from taxes. National policies also influence this decision. For example, exchange controls may limit dividend payments to foreign equity holders, and national policies designed to encourage local reinvestment may control the remission of dividends. In summary, local practices, taxation and other country-level policies may influence the firm's capital structure. Figure 18.3 illustrates capital structure percentages for selected countries.

Decisions a financial manager would make in the process of raising capital are as follows:

1. In what currency should the capital be raised, considering an estimate of its long-term strength or weakness?

2. How should the capital raised be structured between equity and debt?[7]

3. What are the sources of capital available? Should money be borrowed from a commercial bank by an ordinary loan; a bank as part of a swap; another company as part of a swap; another part of the MNC; or a public offering in one of the world's capital markets, for example, in the New York or eurobond market?

4. If the decision is made to use one of the world's capital markets, management must then decide in which of those markets it can achieve its objectives at the lowest cost.

5. Are there other sources of money available? For example, a joint venture partner, private capital, or a host government may be some sources. A host government may be a source of funds or tax abatement if the move is expected to bring the IC's technology, management knowledge, or the jobs that will be created.

6. How much money does the company need and for how long? For instance, if the company is moving into a new market or product, there will probably be a period during product introduction or plant construction when the new venture will need more capital than it can generate.

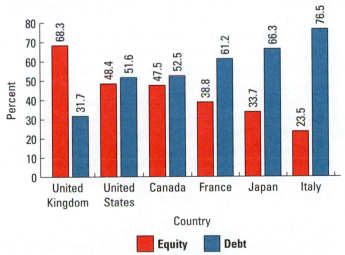

Source: Data extracted from S. Besley and E. Brigham, *Essentials of Managerial Finance* (Oklahoma City, OK: Southwestern Publishing, 2008, Table 12.7.

FIGURE 18.3

Capital Structure Percentages for Selected Countries

Cash Flow Management

The management of cash flows is an important part of international financial management that builds on the activities of domestic financial management. For example, both purely domestic and international firms would want to source funds in low-cost markets and place excess funds where they would get the best return. The global cash management picture is more complex than that of a domestic firm due to the number of different markets involved, each with its own economic characteristics, currency, and regulations. Operating in 25 local currencies is not uncommon for the international firm. The overall goal of cash flow management is to reduce risks and position the firm so it can benefit from opportunities. Some of the sources of these risks and opportunities are foreign exchange movements, interest rates, inflation, government regulation, and taxes. We first look at the major reasons for which an international company moves funds and then at its international finance center's activities.

WHY FUNDS ARE MOVED AND USEFUL TECHNIQUES

Firms move funds for many reasons, among them dividends, royalties, and fees from the subsidiary to the parent company; loans from the parent to the subsidiary or among subsidiaries; and transfer pricing of sales between subsidiaries and the parent company. Dividends result from the parent company's equity interest in the subsidiary, while royalties and fees are payments made for the use of company assets such as trade names, technology, consulting, and management systems. These payments are important to the business in and of themselves and are additionally are useful in cash flow management in several ways. They may serve as vehicles for moving profits from subsidiaries in high-tax environments to lower-tax environments. They may be a way to move profits out of countries where repatriation of profits is blocked or limited. They may also be a way to reduce FX risk by moving currency from environments that have a high risk of devaluation to lower risk ones. Note, too, that these payments are business expenses, so they may be used to impact tax liability.

Loans also may be useful in cash flow management. Parent companies may loan funds directly to the subsidiary, yet these direct loans face some risk because the host government is able to restrict the subsidiary's remittances, including the loan payments, back to the parent. A **fronting loan** is an approach that achieves the same objective for the firm, with much less risk. In a fronting loan, the parent company deposits money in an international bank, which then lends to the subsidiary, *fronting* for the parent company. The host government is not inclined to restrict subsidiary loan payments, especially to a major international bank. There is a small cost to the parent company, while the bank has no risk because it is holding a fully collateralized loan. If the deposit is made from a tax haven, there will be tax advantages as well. Such loans may also be a way to get around blocked funds. Such funds may be blocked because the host government is making an effort to protect its balance of payments position.

One additional method of transferring funds within the firm that may serve as a cash management technique is transfer pricing. The **transfer price** is the bookkeeping cost of goods transferred (sold) from one unit of a business to another in another country.

LO18-6 Describe why ICs move funds.

fronting loan
A loan made through an intermediary, usually a bank, from parent company to subsidiary

transfer price
The bookkeeping cost of goods transferred from one unit of a business to another in another country

Such transfers are common with globally dispersed firms, making up 60 percent of world trade. Because the sale that creates the transfer is internal, its cost can be seen as somewhat flexible. In this flexibility lies the potential to move funds from high-tax, weak-currency environments in ways that are beneficial to the firm. Transfer pricing may also be used to circumvent host-country currency transfer controls and tariffs. Because it may often represent lost tax revenues for host governments, transfer pricing is carefully reviewed by host-government authorities. Transfer pricing can be seen to raise ethical issues, too, because the maneuvers, although they may be legal, are often not in the spirit of the host-country tax and monetary laws. The OECD and the U.S. Internal Revenue Service have issued guidelines on transfer pricing. Some firms now voluntarily agree in advance with the host country on their approach to internal pricing. Such agreements, in addition to offering ethical guidelines to decision makers, reduce the firm's legal and tax audit risks.

INTERNATIONAL FINANCE CENTER

LO18-7 Explain the utility of an international finance center.

The increasing complexity of global financing, combined with increasing global competition, has encouraged firms to pay more attention to financial management. In many firms, the finance operation has become centralized and established as a profit center, a bit like a company bank. Developments that lead to the establishment of finance centers are (1) floating exchange rates, whose fluctuations are sometimes volatile; (2) growth in the number of capital and foreign exchange markets, where the firm can shop for lower interest costs and better currency rates; (3) different and changing inflation rates from country to country; (4) advances in electronic cash management systems; (5) realization by financial managers that through innovative management of temporarily idle cash balances of the subsidiaries, they can increase yields and, thereby, profit; and (6) the explosive growth of derivatives to protect against commodity, currency, interest rate, and other risks. These centralized finance centers can balance and **hedge** currency exposures, tap capital markets, manage inflation rate risk, manage cash management technological innovation, manage derivatives use, handle internal and external invoicing, help a weak-currency subsidiary, and strengthen subsidiary evaluation and reporting systems. Hedging is the process of taking a position in one market in order to offset exposure to price changes in an opposite position. Hedging is widely used to cover risk. We now move to cash flow management and look at multilateral netting and leading and lagging as two approaches the firm's finance center may use to manage cash flows.

hedge
To take a position in one market in order to offset exposure to price changes in an opposite position

MULTILATERAL NETTING

LO18-8 Describe multilateral netting and its benefits.

There are many possible types of cash flows between subsidiaries and the parent company and among subsidiaries. The parent company makes loans to the subsidiary and may increase investment in the form of equity capital. In the other direction, cash from sales, dividends, royalties, and fees move from the subsidiary to the parent. Flows also exist among subsidiaries. One common strategy finance centers use to manage and optimize these flows is **multilateral netting.** This is a centralized approach in which subsidiaries transfer their net cash flows within the company to a cash center that disperses cash to net receivers. A single transaction to or from each member settles the net result of all cash flows. The structure is essentially the wheel-and-spoke model.

multilateral netting
Strategy in which subsidiaries transfer net intracompany cash flows through a centralized clearing center

Why do companies consider multilateral netting? First of all, the transfer of funds has a cost attached to it, the *transaction cost,* and at the same time, the funds while in transit present an opportunity cost: they are not working for the company. In addition, FX costs are incurred. By reducing the transfer transactions, there is less inactive time for funds, the actual transfer costs are reduced, and there are fewer FX transactions, as well. As an example, consider multilateral netting among the European and Middle Eastern subsidiaries of a firm. Each subsidiary with a net payable position would transfer its funds to a central

FIGURE 18.4

Advantages of
Multilateral Netting

US$-000			
Subsidiary	**Receivables**	**Payables**	**Net**
Chinese	350	450	(100)
German	250	300	(50)
Indian	150	300	(150)
Mexican	450	150	300

MNC, Inc. intra-subsidiary cash positions

**(a) MNC Inc., intrasubsidiary cash flows
(US$-000)**

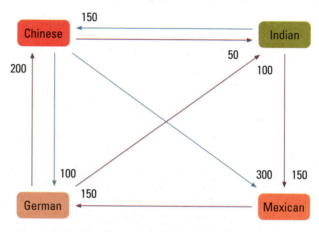

**(b) MNC Inc., intrasubsidiary cash flows
with netting (US$- 000)**

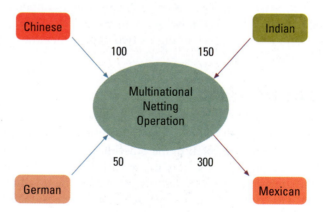

account once a month, where the central account manager would then transfer funds to the net receivers. Compare the two approaches in Figure 18.4. Without netting, reconciling the positions would require eight transactions and $1.2 million in transit. With netting, there are four transactions, and $600,000 in transit. Plus, the foreign exchange transaction costs are reduced.

LEADING AND LAGGING

Currency exchange rates that float, as do today's, create a risk for the multinational firm. To minimize such a risk, one useful technique is **leading and lagging,** which involves the timing of payments. This is actually a simple technique that you may practice already: collect payments as early as possible (lead) and pay out as late as possible (lag). In the international arena, leading and lagging also can be used to limit FX risk. A *lead* approach is to collect receivables early when the foreign currency is expected to weaken and fund payables early when the foreign currency is expected to strengthen. A *lag* approach is to collect receivables late when the currency is expected to strengthen and fund payables late when the currency is expected to weaken. If we now think about combining the multilateral netting approach, leading and lagging can be coordinated among IC subsidiaries to reposition funds and help to compensate for blocked funds or funds about to be blocked.

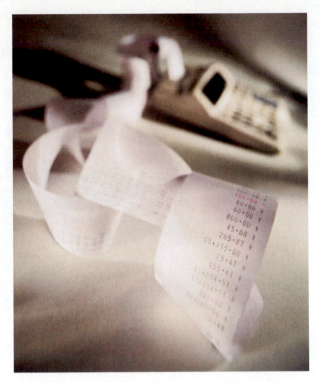

Foreign Exchange Risk Management

When operating across different currencies, MNC managers regularly encounter currency exchange rate movements. These unanticipated shifts present risks to the international business because they represent unplanned-for changes in the value of assets and liabilities. These significant risks are usually categorized into three types: transaction exposure, translation exposure, and economic exposure. These exposures describe positions that are either uncovered or covered, that is, hedged.

TRANSACTION EXPOSURE

Transaction exposure occurs when the firm has transactions denominated in a foreign currency. The exposure is due to currency exchange rate fluctuations between the time the commitment is made and the time it is payable. For example, an order for German diesel truck engines is placed by a Massachusetts company, for payment in 180 days in euros, €150,000 (US$189,000 at the then-prevailing exchange rate of $1.26 per euro). This agreement to buy in a foreign currency creates a transaction exposure for the buyer in Massachusetts. If the euro strengthens against the dollar to $1.38 when the company converts its dollars to euros, the engines' price in dollar terms would increase by $18,000 to US$207,000. In this case, there would be a cash flow effect for the importer but no effect for the exporter. Had the exporter quoted the engines' price in U.S. dollars, the situation would have been reversed.

There are many ways to cover the risk a transaction exposure creates. An initial observation is that the company could avoid transaction exposure altogether by refusing to enter into foreign currency contracts. That's true, yet the desire to conduct business across currency borders suggests a willingness to accept this risk. Besides, one party will always have to, and doing so might be a part of the contract negotiation strategy. There are other approaches to dealing with eliminating the risk of a transaction exposure, or hedging, at the firm's operations level. Remember our discussion of leading and lagging? Let's look at an example.

The U.S. company Nucor is exporting to Spain a €20 million boutique steel order, made from recycled steel, payable in euros. Nucor has accepted the foreign exchange risk as a part

leading and lagging
Timing payments early (lead) or late (lag), depending on anticipated currency movements, so that they have the most favorable impact for company

LO18-9 Categorize foreign exchange risks faced by the international firm into transaction exposure, translation exposure, and economic exposure.

LO18-10 Describe ways to hedge transaction exposure.

transaction exposure
Change in the value of a financial position created by foreign currency changes between the establishment and the settlement of a contract

Microloan Bankers: Charity or For-Profit Business Model?

This is Sophia Maimu, a melon stand owner and microloan client of ACCION Tanzanian partner, Akiba Commercial Bank.

You might think it would be utter folly to lend money to the poor in a developing country. What about a loan to a new small business or entrepreneur such as a vegetable peddler, tailor, or candle maker? Worldwide, development organizations are finding that some of the world's poorest entrepreneurs repay their debts at rates approaching 100 percent. To encourage grassroots private business in Latin America, Asia, and Africa, microlending organizations are expanding programs that already lend thousands of small entrepreneurs amounts ranging from $50 to several hundred dollars. Tiny businesses in developing countries commonly repay these microloans faithfully because of community pressure and the security of a favorable credit rating. Microloans give them small spurts of working capital when they need it, allow them to establish credit, and let them borrow again in hard times. The money helps them start or expand their businesses—selling vegetables, sewing, repairing shoes, making furniture, and the like—and boosts the local economy.

The microcredit concept was developed by Professor Muhammad Yunus, a U.S.-trained Bangladeshi PhD economist, through the Grameen Bank in Bangladesh (which he established to administer his program), and ACCION, a U.S. microcredit organization. Dr. Yunus was awarded the Nobel Peace Prize in 2006 for his work fighting poverty.

The microloan repayment performance shines when compared with that of some sovereign nations. It also looks very good compared with a default rate of 13.8 percent among U.S. recipients of federally guaranteed student loans. ACCION reports a repayment rate over the life of its program of 97 percent. A Mexican program, Compatramos, reports a 1 percent default rate.

Critics point out, though, that one microloan is not going to pull a budding entrepreneur out of poverty, let alone a whole country. When Tufts University received an endowment to set up a microloan program, specialists were ready to warn Tufts of the ethical aspects of microloans: its program needs to be much more than banking. A series of loans is probably necessary, combined with training and support.

Recently, several not-for-profit microloan operations have changed. Because of their success, they have become banks, and in one case, Mexico's Banco Compartamos sold 30 percent of its shares to the public, with the IPO share price moving up 34 percent. Their 2007 IPO also brought a lot of difficult issues forward. Compartamos began as a charity grant program, then became a bank, and then a publicly listed bank. The move to private ownership that seeks a return on investment changes the microloan business model substantially, from *charity* to *business*. The charity model uses donated funds and funds from international financial institutions such as the World Bank and the European Bank for Reconstruction and Development, and they have low interest rates. Some of the microcredit organizations even make profits, but they are cooperatives, such as Grameen Bank, so their profit moves back into their stakeholder community. Compartamos, in contrast, now charges its credit customers in the range of 100 percent (on an annualized basis) to cover loan interest, fees, and taxes. That is three times the cost of borrowing from other microcredit lenders. To make matters a little more complicated, many of the shareholders who profited greatly from the Compartamos IPO are themselves microlenders, such as ACCION. Tufts University splits the revenues from its microloans 50–50 with the loan program and the university itself. In 2008, the university reported a $6.60 million payout from its share of the microlending operations.[a]

Is it right to profit from loans to the poor? Dr. Yunis thinks definitely not, and "refuses to mention the words *Compartamos* and *microfinance* in the same breath."[b] At the same time, here's an explanation from the two friends who founded Compartamos in 1990. They suggest that, much like food crisis and famine, the issue isn't the existence of the needed good; both food and money exist. The issue is one of distribution: the food and money frequently are not where they are needed most desperately. The argument is that a profit potential brings private capital in touch with the people who need it, the world's poor, quickly and efficiently. It is a way to align the world's wealth with the world's poor. Big investment firms and banks have begun to participate in profitable microlending. Firms such as CITI Group, Morgan Stanley, TIAA-CREF, and Deutsche Bank are active in the sector now. With returns like Compartamos has, at 53 percent, investors are interested. Here's how the loans work: they are small, usually to women, guaranteed by peers, paid off on time, and often followed immediately by another loan.[c]

(continued)

of its marketing strategy. It may also even have factored a currency shift expectation into its euro pricing. Here are the foreign exchange and interest data. They are hypothetical:

EU interest rate:	4.00
U.S. interest rate:	5.00
Spot rate	$1.534
Forward rate	$1.527 (one year forward)

Nucor faces transaction exposure in its receivable. The markets have figured out clever ways to reduce the risks, and we look briefly at six of these maneuvers, leading and lagging, exposure netting, forward market hedge, currency option hedge, money market hedge, and a swap contract. These maneuvers may sound complex, but they are simply ways Nucor has to cover its risk because it made a sale in a foreign currency.

First, Nucor could lead its receivable, because the market indicates that the dollar may well strengthen against the euro. (Moving from a spot rate of $1.534 to a forward rate of $1.527 means that the market expects the euro to buy fewer dollars a year out. So the dollar is strengthening against the euro.) The Spanish customer may well want to lag the payment, though, if there is no incentive for early payment.

In another way to hedge on transaction exposure through company actions, Nucor could follow a centralized practice similar to multilateral netting: *exposure netting*. The firm will run a centralized clearing account that matches and nets out foreign exchange exposures across currencies or across currency families. Working with currency families recognizes that some currencies tend to move in lockstep with one another. Many ICs follow this approach.

There are also ways to hedge foreign currency exposure by engaging in contracts known simply as *hedges*. A **forward market hedge** involves a quite simple transaction: the company sells forward its foreign currency receivables for its home currency, matching the time forward to the due date of the receivables. When the Spanish company pays, Nucor will deliver the amount to its bank, the partner in the forward market hedge contract. Nucor will not have been exposed to currency risk in the Spanish sale. Because the forward market hedge is a way to cover the complete exposure in a given transaction, it is the most widely used approach. Yet, because the forward market hedge assumes all of the foreign exchange risk, it eliminates the chance of gaining from a currency move in the company's favor.

An approach to hedging an exposure but not losing the opportunity to gain from a currency appreciation is a *foreign currency option*. With a **currency option hedge,** you purchase an option to buy or sell a specific amount of currency at a specific time, but the option can be exercised or not. These hedges are *calls*—or contracts with an option to buy—for foreign currency payables and *puts*—or contracts to sell—for foreign currency receivables. Because these are options, if the market works against you, you can exercise the contract. If the market works for you, you don't need to exercise the option.

forward market hedge

Foreign currency contract sold or bought forward in order to protect against foreign currency movement

currency option hedge

An option to buy or sell a specific amount of foreign currency at a specific time in order to protect against foreign currency risk

money market hedge
A method to hedge foreign currency exposure by borrowing and lending in the domestic and foreign money markets

The money markets also afford an opportunity to hedge a foreign transaction. In a **money market hedge,** Nucor would borrow euros in the European money market in the amount of the receivables from the Spanish sale. The basic idea here is to match the balance sheet asset with a liability in the same currency. Here's how the money market hedge works: Nucor borrows the equivalent of $20 million in euros, or €13,035,300, for a period that matches the receivable's due date. Nucor then converts the euros to dollars at the spot rate and then invests them. The euros that are received from the Spanish company will be used to close out the euro loan. Then the invested dollars plus their interest provide Nucor the dollar amount for the Spanish sale.

swap contract
A spot sale/purchase of an asset against a future purchase/sale of an equal amount in order to hedge a financial position

Swap contracts are also used to hedge foreign currency exposure. A swap is an agreement to exchange currencies at specified rates and on a specified date or sequence of dates. Swaps are quite flexible and may be undertaken for long periods, much longer than in the forward market. So if Nucor had a series of sales in the EU over the next 10 years, all denominated in euros, it could enter into a series of swaps so that the exchange rate or series of exchange rates would be known in advance.

TRANSLATION EXPOSURE

translation exposure
Potential change in the value of a company's financial position due to exposure created during the consolidation process

Translation exposure occurs when subsidiary financial statements are consolidated at the corporate level for the companywide financial reports. Because the foreign subsidiaries operate in non-dollar currencies, there is a need to translate subsidiary financial reports to the parent company's currency during the corporate consolidation process. Exchange rate movements can have substantial impact on the value of these financial statements, which may affect per-share earnings and stock price. Take a U.S. company that has subsidiaries in Brazil, Japan, Spain, and the United Kingdom. Each subsidiary will prepare financial reports in its own currency, so amounts in four currencies will need to be translated. Any changes in the exchange rates will affect the dollar values or these results. Such changes, either gains or losses, are not reflected in cash flow; they are paper or unrealized changes.

The key question related to translation exposure is what currency exchange rate to use for the translation. The two basic approaches to translation, the current rate method and the temporal method, and their exchange rate use rules are reviewed earlier in this chapter in our discussion of international accounting. Approaches to translation exposure differ by country.

Many organizations do not hedge translation exposure because hedging a translation exposure can actually increase transaction exposure. For example, if the translation exposure is hedged through a matching foreign exchange liability, such as a debt, then that debt is an exposure at the transaction level. Transaction exposure is fundamental to a corporation's value.

ECONOMIC EXPOSURE

economic exposure
The potential for the value of future cash flows to be affected by unanticipated exchange rate movements

Economic exposure occurs at the operations level and results from exchange rate changes on projected cash flows. Unlike transaction exposure, which addresses the individual transaction, economic exposure is firm-wide and long term. For example, when the dollar strengthens, as it did in the 1990s, U.S. export prices increased in terms of other currencies. U.S. exported goods became less price-competitive in foreign markets, so sales plummeted. Yet when the dollar weakens, U.S. export prices become more attractive in foreign markets. These changes are examples of the possible effects of economic exposure. Economic exposure can affect both the dollar value of the company's foreign assets and liabilities and the company's cash flow, because it has an impact on foreign sales. Asset exposure includes the firm's fixed assets as well as their financial assets. The exposure of cash flow to currency fluctuation is known as *operating exposure.* Operating exposure is difficult to measure because it involves both the cash flows and the larger commercial context, the competitive conditions connected to obtaining inputs and selling. The management of economic exposure draws on the hedging and swap contracts we have discussed as ways to manage transaction exposure, on flexibility in sourcing, and on a portfolio approach to foreign market involvement.

Taxation

In Chapter 8, we discussed taxation as a financial force and outlined three major types of taxation that governments around the world use—income tax, value-added tax, and withholding tax. **Income tax** is a direct tax levied on earnings. **Value-added tax (VAT)** is an indirect tax, in that the tax authority collects it from the person or firm that adds value during the production and marketing process, not from the owner of the item taxed. The ultimate user of the product pays the full amount of tax that is rebated to the others in the value chain. Thus, the government is collecting the tax on the value added in the process. The **withholding tax** is also an indirect tax, in that it is paid not by the person whose labor generates the income but by the business that makes the payment for the labor. Usually, the withholding tax is levied on passive income such as royalties, dividends, and interest.

As for what territories a government's tax covers, we find two approaches to this jurisdiction issue, either worldwide or territorial. A worldwide approach taxes residents of the country on their worldwide income. The United States follows a policy of worldwide taxation, and it can be argued convincingly that, despite tax treaties, such taxation puts U.S. firms operating foreign subsidiaries at a disadvantage compared with their foreign domestic competitors.[8] A territorial taxation policy taxes income earned within the nation's borders. There are tax credits, based on treaties that reduce or eliminate double taxation for U.S. residents and companies, as long as the foreign tax liability is less than the U.S. equivalent would be.

How the foreign operations of a company are organized is key to its U.S. tax liability on foreign earnings. If the operation is a **branch,** that is, an extension of the parent company, not a separate legal entity incorporated in the foreign country, its losses may be deducted by the parent company from its U.S. taxable income. If the foreign entity is a **subsidiary,** that is, a separate legal entity incorporated in the foreign country, its ownership by the IC may be minority, that is, between 10 and 50 percent. Such minority company income, both active and passive, is taxed only when it is remitted to the parent company. If the foreign subsidiary is actually controlled by the parent company, with more than 50 percent ownership, it is known as a *controlled foreign corporation (CFC),* and its active income is taxed in the United States when that income is remitted to the parent company, but its passive income (royalties, licensing fees, dividends, service fees) is taxed as it occurs. When deciding where to locate and how to structure a foreign operation, IC managers review the tax rates of possible locations and also consider what legal form their operations should take. Often, startups have several years of losses, so establishment of a branch rather than a subsidiary might generate valuable losses, from a tax point of view, for the parent company. Transfer pricing, which we discussed earlier, offers international businesses a way to reduce tax liability. Some ICs are remarkable in their ability to manage their tax exposure. A recent *New York Times* article reported that GE paid no U.S. taxes in 2010 on U.S. profits of $5.1 billion and actually claimed a tax benefit of $3.2 billion.[9]

In Chapter 18, we have examined two basic areas that are fundamental to the financial management of an international business, international accounting and the process of financial management. Our review of accounting looked at accounting issues related to foreign currency, culture, convergence of accounting standards, and 3BL accounting efforts. In financial management, we reviewed the capital structure of the international firm, cash flow management, foreign exchange risk, and taxation. Financial management is becoming increasingly central to capturing efficiencies in the international firm. The green eyeshades are passé—it's an exciting area in which to develop a career.

income tax
Direct tax levied on earnings

value-added tax (VAT)
Indirect tax collected from the parties as they add value to the product

withholding tax
Indirect tax paid by the payor, usually on passive income

branch
Legal extension of the parent company

subsidiary
Separate legal entity owned by the parent company

Bryan Goldfinger: Microfinance in Latin America with Kiva

I was born and raised in San Diego, California, surfing, playing soccer, and generally living a pretty stereotypical California life. My first two years at Cal Poly, San Luis Obispo, I was a business administration major with an undeclared concentration. I spent my third year of university studying abroad in Puntarenas, Costa Rica, where I lived with a Spanish-speaking host family and completed primarily Spanish classes. During this year, I became infatuated with travel and the Latin people and culture and gained fluency in Spanish and a desire to in some way help those less fortunate. Upon my return, I declared a concentration in international business management and later that same year, also declared a concentration in accounting. I graduated in June 2007 with a minor in Spanish and a contract to begin auditing with KPMG in January 2008. The months between graduation and entering the "real world," I spent taking an overland trip from Nicaragua to Argentina. This travel experience proved to be more valuable than I could have imagined.

I began my time at KPMG with high hopes of completing the CPA examinations, spending a minimum of two years auditing and hopefully being able to complete an international rotation at one of its overseas offices. My time at KPMG was extremely valuable, although not quite what I had expected. I had the opportunity to work with clients in the roofing and construction, real estate, telecommunications, insurance, and agriculture industries. However, at the end of my first year, I began feeling as though the work I was doing did not satisfy my goals of helping others, and the lifestyle of public accounting was not consistent with one I desired to live. Just after completing my first year, I left KPMG.

During this time, a friend asked me what my ideal dream job would entail. The dream job that I conjured up would involve international business travel, allow me to utilize my Spanish skills, involve more time in the field and less in an office, and be more socially fulfilling than my previous work. Two days later,

he sent me an e-mail about a friend who was currently working in Paraguay with a company called Kiva, and he included a link to the website (www.kiva.org). Kiva's mission is to connect people through lending to help alleviate poverty. Individuals like you or me provide funds in increments of $25, via the organization's website, to entrepreneurs in developing countries and the United States. Kiva then sends the funds to their partner microfinance institutions (MFIs), which provide loans to the selected entrepreneurs.

The work of a Kiva Fellow varies greatly, depending on his or her experience, skill set, and which partner institution he or she is assigned to work with. Kiva Fellows are volunteers who work closely with the partner institutions to help them implement Kiva policies, meet and interview borrowers, and complete verifications of the information the MFIs provide to Kiva. Essentially, the Kiva Fellows are Kiva's eyes and ears in the field and connect all four stakeholders involved with Kiva: the borrowers, the lenders, the MFIs and Kiva headquarters.

I completed two placements as a Kiva Fellow, the first as a roaming Fellow in Peru, and the second in Managua, Nicaragua. The primary objective of my placement in Peru was borrower verification. I would select a small sample of loans from several MFIs, visit the borrowers, and verify that the information Kiva had on the website was consistent with what was actually taking place in the field. During these visits, I would also write a short journal entry on the progress of the borrowers. This journal entry would then be uploaded to the Kiva website and sent out to everyone who had lent money to that particular borrower. In Nicaragua, I worked primarily with one MFI to complete a review of its social performance. Social performance monitoring is a new and growing subject in microfinance. There are a variety of tools and companies whose sole purpose is social performance monitoring. The goal is to review and identify strengths and weaknesses of an MFI's social performance. More specifically, what is the mission statement of the MFI and is the mission being applied in the field? Kiva has recently begun administering social performance questionnaires to many of its partner MFIs and utilizing Kiva Fellows to assist MFIs in filling out and reviewing the questionnaires.

Due to the vastly different locations and duties Kiva Fellows are assigned, each Fellow tends to have wildly different experiences, challenges and rewards. In my opinion, the most rewarding part of being a Kiva Fellow was visiting and interviewing borrowers and having the opportunity to witness, firsthand, the effects of microfinance. To trek out into the field with a loan officer to a place you would likely never go otherwise, meet people you would likely never meet otherwise, ask them in-depth questions about their business and life, and at the end ask, "what are your hopes and dreams?" is quite a unique and rewarding experience.

Aside from the small frustrations of working in and learning the work culture of a new country and MFI, I was lucky to have very few, if any, difficulties in relation to my work as a Kiva Fellow. Reflecting on both of my placements, as a Kiva Fellow, the biggest challenge I experienced, particularly

(continued)

during my placement in Peru and the first half of my placement in Nicaragua, was loneliness and lack of a social network. Although an incredibly rewarding and equally valuable experience, work travel is not the same as tourist travel or a study abroad experience. One does not necessarily have the built-in support group that is often present in a study abroad program or the free time and lodging situations that "tourist" travel provides—which are helpful in facilitating social interactions. That said, by the end of each placement, I found myself wishing I did not have to leave so soon. In my experience, the most important thing to do when in such a situation is to not resort to crawling into a ball and secluding yourself. The Internet and comforts of home can easily become a crutch to lean on, which ultimately serve no purpose in alleviating the situation. Go out by yourself, put your pride on the line, meet random people, and be willing to experience situations you normally would never dream of.

As far as Kiva is concerned, one of the most important aspects of an applicant is his or her experience living, working, studying, and traveling abroad. Obviously, work experience and study background weigh in heavily, but with no experience abroad, Kiva will likely not even consider your application. The reasoning behind this is that there are a multitude of applicants who are qualified to do the work of a Kiva Fellow. The reality is that Kiva trains the Fellows on what they need to know once in the field. They realize that cultural sensitivity, adaptability, and general decision making when abroad are knowledge abilities primarily gained through experience and travel, and they cannot be taught in a classroom at Kiva Headquarters.

My advice to anyone who wishes to pursue international work opportunities is to get as much international experience as possible before entering the "workforce." Whether it is through study abroad, international internships, small jobs abroad like working at a restaurant, bar, or hostel, or just flat out travel, one gains knowledge and experience that cannot be taught in any classroom.

Resources for Your Global Career

Careers in International Accounting

- http://career-advice.monster.com/job-search/company-industry-research/global-accounting-careers/article.aspx
- www.ehow.com/how_7451915_plan-international-career.html
- www.internationalaccountingjobs.com/a/jobs/find-jobs

Sustainability and Triple-Bottom-Line Accounting

- www.green2sustainable.com/media/docs/TripleBottomLine.pdf
- http://globaledge.msu.edu/resourcedesk/gbr/gbr4-6.pdf
- www.businessethics.ca/3bl/triple-bottom-line.pdf

Careers in International Finance

- www.expatfinancejobs.com/
- http://bx.businessweek.com/international-finance/jobs/
- www.guidetoonlineschools.com/careers/international-business

Jobs and Careers in Foreign Exchange Currency Analysis and Trade

- www.princetonreview.com/Careers.aspx?cid=70
- www.jobmonkey.com/forex/traders-analysts.html
- www.job-search-engine.com/keyword/currency-exchange/

International Microlending Issues, Resources, and Job Opportunities

- www.microfinancefocus.com/
- www.kiva.org/
- www.accion.org/

Summary

LO18-1 Identify the major international accounting issues that international firms face when operating in foreign currencies.

International accounting has to deal with many major issues. The chapter discusses issues related to foreign currency, such as which values to be used to translate currencies during consolidation, the current rate or the temporal rate; the influence of national culture on assumptions we make in the process of accounting; issues related to differing accounting standards; and issues related to accounting for social and environmental impacts of business decisions, in additional to the economic impacts.

LO18-2 Describe the relationship between accounting and culture.

Accounting is a product of assumptions about human behavior and the need to control. These assumptions are influenced by culture.

LO18-3 Describe the international accounting standards' convergence process and its importance to international firms.

The body that establishes accounting standards in the United States is a private organization, the Financial Accounting

Standards Board (FASB), whose standards are the generally accepted accounting principles (GAAP). The more international body is the International Accounting Standards Board (IASB), whose standards are the International Financial Reporting Standards (IFRS). Convergence requires harmonization of many standards and procedures, and it is a time-consuming process. With so many important and heavily detailed aspects of specific standards to be reconciled, the progress toward convergence is impressive. The EU Parliament and the Council of Europe requires IASB standards for financial reporting, along with Australia and New Zealand. There are more than 75 countries that require public companies to list using IFRS and another 50 countries, including those in the EU, that have adopted IFRS with minor modifications. In 2007, the U.S. Securities and Exchange Commission (SEC) decided that foreign companies listing their shares in the United States no longer needed to restate their financial statements to comply with FASB standards. In the United States, the SEC is the responsible party for recognizing the IASB. One of the largest differences between GAAP and the IFRS is their general approach. GAAP relies on rules and regulations; the IFRS has greater reliance on principles.

LO18-4 Outline the arguments for and against 3BL.

Currently, we measure at the economic level and, where required by government or social pressure, we measure at the environmental level (as with emission controls and hazardous waste) and at the social level (as with the Equal Employment Opportunity Commission's enforcement of the federal civil rights laws). Yet in the environmental and social areas, we tend to know more about the problems—what is reported in the media—than about the company-level thinking on these important issues. Companies should measure and make public the environmental and social effects of their decisions. These are, in summary, the major argument for 3BL. The major argument against 3BL is neither a substantive disagreement with the desirability of ecologically responsible business practices that support sustainability nor a disagreement with the idea of business being socially responsible; rather, it is the claim that measurement will not get us closer to the desired state.

LO18-5 Explain the capital structure choices open to international firms and their significance.

The firm raises capital through its retained earnings, and then, externally, through equity, the issuing of shares, or debt (leveraging). Firms may choose to issue stocks in foreign markets, in part to tap into a broader investor pool, which can raise the stock price and reduce the cost of capital. Such local issues may also have a significant marketing advantage. Debt markets are the other source of capital for the firm, and increasingly the tendency is to tap local markets first. Offshore financial centers, where taxation is low and banking regulations are slim, are also a source of debt financing. Debt financing is thought to be less expensive than equity financing, but local practices and taxation are some of the factors that are considered in making decisions about the capital structure of the firm.

LO18-6 Describe why ICs move funds.

Firms move funds for many reasons, among them dividends, royalties, and fees from the subsidiary to the parent company;

loans from the parent to the subsidiary or among subsidiaries; and transfer pricing of sales between subsidiaries and the parent company.

LO18-7 Explain the utility of an international finance center.

Centralized finance centers offer ICs a way to address the increasingly complex financial environment. They can balance and hedge currency exposures, tap capital markets, manage inflation rate risk, manage cash management technological innovation, manage derivatives use, handle internal and external invoicing, help a weak-currency subsidiary, and strengthen subsidiary evaluation and reporting systems. Developments that increase complexity and often lead to the establishment of finance centers are (1) floating exchange rates, whose fluctuations are sometimes volatile; (2) growth in the number of capital and foreign exchange markets, where the firm can shop for lower interest costs and better currency rates; (3) different and changing inflation rates from country to country; (4) advances in electronic cash management systems; (5) realization by financial managers that through innovative management of temporarily idle cash balances of the subsidiaries, they can increase yields and, thereby, profit; and (6) the explosive growth of derivatives to protect against commodity, currency, interest rate, and other risks.

LO18-8 Describe multilateral netting and its benefits.

Multilateral netting is a centralized approach in which subsidiaries transfer their net cash flows within the company to a cash center that disperses cash to net receivers. A single transaction to or from each member settles the net result of all cash flows. The structure is essentially the wheel-and-spoke model. The advantages are that it reduces transaction costs and, at the same time, avoids the opportunity cost that would be incurred by the funds in transit.

LO18-9 Categorize foreign exchange risks faced by the international firm into transaction exposure, translation exposure, and economic exposure.

Transaction exposure occurs when the firm has transactions denominated in a foreign currency. The exposure is due to currency exchange rate fluctuations between the time the commitment is made and when it is payable. Translation exposure occurs when subsidiary financial statements are consolidated at the corporate level for the companywide financial reports. Because the foreign subsidiaries operate in non-dollar currencies, there is a need to translate subsidiary financial reports to the parent company's currency during the corporate consolidation process. Economic exposure is at the operations level and results from exchange rate changes on projected cash flows. Unlike transaction exposure, which addresses the individual transaction, economic exposure is firmwide and long term.

LO18-10 Describe ways to hedge transaction exposure.

There are many ways to cover the risk a transaction exposure creates. (The company could avoid transaction exposure altogether by refusing to enter into foreign currency contracts.) The company could hedge through leading and lagging, through exposure netting, or through a currency option, a forward market hedge, a money market hedge, or a swap. The key goal is to cover the exposure to foreign currency.

consolidation (p. 458)

current rate method (p. 458)

temporal method (p. 458)

functional currency (p. 458)

American depositary receipt (ADR) (p. 462)

offshore financial center (p. 462)

fronting loan (p. 464)

transfer price (p. 464)

hedge (p. 465)

multilateral netting (p. 465)

leading and lagging (p. 467)

transaction exposure (p. 467)

forward market hedge (p. 469)

currency option hedge (p. 469)

money market hedge (p. 470)

swap contract (p. 470)

translation exposure (p. 470)

economic exposure (p. 470)

income tax (p. 471)

value-added tax (VAT) (p. 471)

withholding tax (p. 471)

branch (p. 471)

subsidiary (p. 471)

Questions

1. The cultural analysis of accounting Gray presents suggests that transparency is the result of a cultural characteristic of some countries and secrecy of others. Could the same attributes be explained by the hypothesis that transparent cultures are less trusting and need the transparency to satisfy their cultural distrust? What do you think?

2. How might Sarbanes-Oxley influence the progress of the convergence of international accounting standards?

3. How might triple-bottom-line accounting improve the social and environmental behavior of companies?

4. What is your assessment of the movement pushing for 3BL? Explain your thinking.

5. You are establishing your first overseas subsidiary. As you consider how to capitalize your business, what are your concerns about using the local and home-country debt and equity markets?

6. A local exporter has signed a sales contract that specifies payment of $3 million in Saudi riyals in six months. Discuss the hedge options you would advise the exporter to consider.

7. One of the characteristics of centralized structures is that they are slow and reduce innovation. Why would an MNC set up a centralized cash management operation?

8. What aspect of how foreign operations of a company are organized is key to its U.S. tax liability?

9. What are the differences between transaction and translation exposure?

10. Describe how mircolending has developed as a result of its success.

Research Task

 globalEDGE.msu.edu

Use the globalEDGE site (http://globalEDGE.msu.edu/) to complete the following exercises:

1. Deloitte Touche Tohmatsu hosts an *International Accounting Standards* (IAS) webpage that provides information and guidelines regarding accounting guidelines approved by IASC. Locate the website, go to the section on standards, and prepare a short description of the international accounting standards for recording intangible assets.

2. The top management of your company has requested information on the tax policies of Denmark. Using the Denmark business guide on *Deloitte International Tax and Business Guides*—a resource that provides information on the investment climate, operating conditions, and tax system of the major trading countries—prepare a short report summarizing your findings on Denmark's business taxation.

Minicase: Dealing with Transaction Risk in a Renminbi Contract

You are the finance manager of an American multinational that has sold US$6 million of your high-tech product to a Chinese importer. Because of stiff competition for the contract against European and other American companies, you agreed that the negotiators could sign a renminbi-based contract, although this is not standard practice for the firm. This concession may have won you the deal, actually.

The sales contract calls for the Chinese importer to make three equal payments at 6, 12, and 18 months from the date of delivery, which is in 60 days. Your plan is to translate the renminbi to dollars on their receipt; your company has no operations in China and no need for the currency. You realize, though, that this arrangement involves transaction exposure. How could you cover this risk?

CHAPTER 1

1. For example, see Cornelis A. de Kluyver and John A Pearce II, *Strategy: A View from the Top,* 2nd ed. (Upper Saddle River, NJ: Pearson Prentice Hall, 2006), p. 38; *InvestorDictionary.com,* "Multinational Corporation" www.investordictionary.com/definition/multinational-corporation (May 28, 2011); and "Multinational Corporation," http://en.wikipedia.org/wiki/Multinational_corporation (May 28, 2011).

2. UNCTAD, "Transnational Corporations Statistics," www.unctad.org/templates/Page.asp?intItemID=3159&lang=1 (May 28, 2011).

3. Anil K. Gupta, Vijay Govindarajan, and Haiyan Wang, *The Quest for Global Dominance,* 2nd ed. (San Francisco: Jossey-Bass, 2008); Yves Doz, Jose Santos, and Peter Williamson, *From Global to Metanational* (Boston: Harvard Business School Press, 2001); Anne-Wil Harzing, "An Empirical Analysis and Extension of the Bartlett and Goshal Typology of Multinational Corporations," *Journal of International Business Studies,* First Quarter 2000, pp. 101–19; and C. A. Bartlett and S. Goshal, *Managing across Borders: The Transnational Solution* (Boston: Harvard Business School Press, 1989).

4. "The Black Death," www.insecta-inspecta.com/fleas/bdeath/bdeath.html (May 2, 2010); and Robbie Robertson, "Globalization Is Not Made in the West," www.globalpolicy.org/globaliz/define/2005/0413notmadeinthewest.htm (May 28, 2011).

5. "A Quick Guide to the World History of Globalization," www.sas.upenn.edu/~dludden/global1.htm (May 28, 2011); "Dutch East India Company," http://en.wikipedia.org/wiki/Dutch_East_India_Company#History (May 28, 2011); BBC News, "Globalization: What on Earth Is It About?" http://news.bbc.co.uk/1/hi/special_report/1999/02/99/e-cyclopedia/711906.stm (May 28, 2011); and "The Growth of Global Industry," *The Wheel Extended,* no. 4 (1989), p. 11.

6. "Multinationals Come into Their Own," *Financial Times,* December 6, 1999, p. 16, http://proquest.umi.com/pqdweb?index=3&did=46873498&SrchMode=2&sid=5&Fmt=3&VInst=PROD&VType=PQD&RQT=309&VName=PQD&TS=1306621686&clientId=17870 (May 28, 2011).

7. Bayer, "History," www.bayer.com/bayer-group/history/page701.htm (May 28, 2011).

8. Alfred D. Chandler Jr. and Bruce Mazlish, eds., *Leviathans: Multinational Corporations and the New Global History* (New York: Cambridge University Press, 2005), pp. 66, 88–89.

9. UNCTAD, "Largest Transnational Corporations Adversely Affected by Financial and Economic Crisis, Report Says," September 19, 2009, www.unctad.org/templates/webflyer.asp?docid=11926&intItemID=5266&lang=1 (May 28, 2011).

10. *Fortune,* "2010 Global 500," http://money.cnn.com/magazines/fortune/global500/2010/full_list/ (May 28, 2011); The World Bank, "GNI, Atlas Method (current US$)," http://data.worldbank.org/indicator/NY.GNP.ATLS.CD (May 28, 2011).

11. Calculation based on information found in *Walmart 2010 Annual Report,* http://investors.walmartstores.com/phoenix.zhtml?c=112761&p=irol-reportsannual (May 28, 2011), where value added is based on net operating profit before tax.

12. *World Investment Report 2001,* United Nations Conference on Trade and Development, Geneva, October 2001; and *World Investment Report 2010,* United Nations Conference on Trade and Development, Geneva, www.unctad.org/Templates/webflyer.asp?docid=13423&intItemID=5539&lang=1&mode=downloads (May 28, 2011).

13. World Trade Organization, "Trade Growth to Ease in 2011 but Despite 2010 Record Surge, Crisis Hangover Persists," April 7, 2011, www.wto.org/english/news_e/pres11_e/pr628_e.htm (accessed May 28, 2011).

14. World Trade Organization, "Trade in Commercial Services," http://stat.wto.org/StatisticalProgram/WSDBStatProgramSeries.aspx?Language=E (May 28, 2011); and World Trade Organization, "Trade Growth to Ease in 2011."

15. Fred W. Riggs, "Globalization Is a Fuzzy Term But It May Convey Special Meanings," The Theme of the IPSA World Congress 2000, July 1999, www2.hawaii.edu/~fredr/ipsaglo.htm (May 28, 2011); and "Globalization," http://en.wikipedia.org/wiki/Globalization (May 28, 2011).

16. Theodore Levitt, "The Globalization of Markets," *Harvard Business Review 61,* no. 3 (May–June 1983), pp. 92–93.

17. "Running a Global Company Well Poses Major Operational Challenges," http://knowledge.wharton.upenn.edu (May 28, 2011), p. 2.

18. United Nations Development Programme (UNDP), "Economy and Inequality," *Human Development Report 2009* (New York: United Nations Development Programme, 2009), pp. 195–98.

CHAPTER 2

1. World Trade Organization, "Trade Growth to Ease in 2011 But Despite 2010 Record Surge, Crisis Hangover Persists," April 7, 2011, www.wto.org/english/news_e/pres11_e/pr628_e.htm (accessed May 10, 2011).

2. Ibid.

3. United Nations Industrial Development Organization, *International Yearbook of Industrial Statistics 2011,* (Northampton, MA: Edward Elgar Publishing, 2011).

4. "International Merchandise Trade—World Exports by Provenance and Destination," *Monthly Bulletin of Statistics,* July 2009, Table 40, http://unstats.un.org/unsd/mbs/table_list.aspx (April 29, 2011); *Monthly Bulletin of Statistics,* July 2001, pp. 266–71, July 2000, pp. 258–61, June 1997, pp. 255–62, June 1993, pp. 266–71 (New York: United Nations); and *Statistical Yearbook* (New York: United Nations, 1969), pp. 376–83.

5. World Trade Organization, *International Trade Statistics 2010,* (Geneva, Switzerland: World Trade Organization, 2010), p. 5.

6. U.S. Census Bureau, "Trade in Goods with Canada," www.census.gov/foreign-trade/balance/c1220.html (May 10, 2011).

7. U.S. Census Bureau, "Trade in Goods with Mexico," www.census.gov/foreign-trade/balance/c2010.html#1991 (May 10, 2011).

8. Government administrators involved in project evaluation are increasingly applying socioeconomic rather than purely financial criteria. For example, social rates of discount and opportunity costs are considered rather than the pure costs of borrowing money. Although marketing managers do not have to be development economists any more than they need to be specialists in marketing research, they should have knowledge of the basic concepts.

9. Peter Navarro, *Report of "The China Price Project"* (Irvine, CA: Merage School of Business, University of California, January 2007), www.peternavarro.com/chinaprice.html (May 10, 2011).

10. David Ricardo "The Principles of Political Economy and Taxation," in *International Trade Theory: Hume to Ohlin,* ed. William R. Allen (New York: Random House, 1965, 62–67.

11. Ibid., pp. 174–77.

12. R. Vernon "International Investment and International Trade in the Product Cycle" *Quarterly Journal of Economics*, pp. 190–207.

13. Many new products come not from the manufacturer's laboratories, but from its suppliers of machinery and raw materials.

14. Bela Belassa, *A Stages Approach To Comparitive Advantage* (Washington DC: World Bank 1997), pp. 26–27.

15. Kimberly C. Gleason, Jeff Madura, and Joan Wiggenhorn, "Operating Characteristics, Risk, and Performance of Born-Global Firms," *International Journal of Managerial Finance* 2, no. 2 (2006), pp. 96–120; and N. Hashai and T. Almor, "Gradually Internationalizing 'Born Global' Firms: An Oxymoron?" *International Business Review* 13 (2004), pp. 465–83.

16. Richard B. Chase, F. Robert Jacobs, and Nicholas J. Aquilano, *Operations Management for Competitive Advantage,* 11th ed. (Burr Ridge, IL: McGraw-Hill Irwin, 2005).

17. Alfred Marshall, *Principles of Economics,* 8th ed. (London: Macmillan, 1920).

18. Michael E. Porter, *The Competitive Advantage of Nations* (New York: Free Press, 1990).

19. For example, see Christophe Lecuyer, *Making Silicon Valley: Innovation and the Growth of High Tech, 1930–1970* (Cambridge, MA: MIT Press, 2005).

20. U.S. Department of Commerce, Bureau of Economic Analysis, "International Investment Position of the United States at Yearend, 1976–2009," www.bea.gov/international/ (May 10, 2011).

21. Ibid.

22. Central Intelligence Agency, "Stock of Direct Foreign Investment—Abroad," *The World Factbook,* www.cia.gov/library/publications/the-world-factbook/fields/2199.html?countryName=World&countryCode=xx&regionCode=oc (May 10, 2011); and United Nations Conference on Trade and Development, *World Investment Report,* "Annex Table 4: FDI Outward Stock, By Region and Economy, 1990–2009," www.unctad.org/ztemplates/Page .asp?intItemID=5545&lang=1 (May 10, 2011).

23. Murray Weidenbaum and Samuel Hughes, *Bamboo Network: How Expatriate Chinese Entrepreneurs are Creating a New Economic Superpower in Asia* (New York: Free Press, 1996); and Joe Quinlan, "China's Capital Finds New Targets across South-East Asia," *Financial Times,* November 14, 2007, www.ft.com/cms/s/0/8a38bba8-9254-11dc-8981-0000779fd2ac.html#axzz1KyYAMtwi (May 10, 2011).

24. "Sovereign Wealth Funds 2011 Rankings," www.photius.com/rankings/sovereign_wealth_fund_country_ranks_2011.html (May 10, 2011).

25. United Nations Conference on Trade and Development, *World Investment Report,* "Annex Table 2: FDI Outflows, By Region and Economy, 1990–2009," www.unctad.org/templates/Page.asp?intItemID=5545&lang=1 (May 10, 2011).

26. United Nations Conference on Trade and Development, *World Investment Report,* "Annex Table 1: FDI Inflows, By Region and Economy, 1990–2009," www.unctad.org/templates/Page.asp?intItemID=5545&lang=1 (May 10, 2011).

27. Charles Kindleberger, *American Business Abroad* (New Haven, CT: Yale University Press, 1969), pp. 43–44.

28. Stephen Hymer, *The International Operations of International Firms: A Study in Direct Investment* (Cambridge, MA: MIT Press, 1976).

29. E. M. Graham, "Transatlantic Investments by Multinational Firms: A Rivalistic Phenomenon," *Journal of Post-Keynesian Economics,* Fall 1978, pp. 82–99.

30. John H. Dunning, *International Production and the Multinational Enterprise* (London: George Allen & Unwin, 1981), pp. 109–10; P. Buckley and M. Casson, *The Future of Multinational Enterprise* (New York: Macmillan, 1976); D. Teece, *The Multinational Corporation and the Resource Cost of International Technology Transfers* (Cambridge, MA: Ballinger, 1986); and A. M. Rugman, *Inside the Multinationals: The Economics of International Markets* (New York: Columbia University Press, 1986).

CHAPTER 3

1. Martin Wolfe, "Why Washington and Beijing Need Strong Global Institutions," *Financial Times,* April 19, 2006, p. 13.

2. W. Richard Scott, *Institutions and Organizations,* 3rd ed. (Thousand Oaks, CA: Sage, 2008) p. 48.

3. Talcott Parsons, "Prolegomena to a Theory of Social Institutions," *American Sociological Review* 55 (1934/1990) pp. 319–39, as referenced by Scott (2008), p 14.

4. Douglass North, *Institutions, Institutional Change and Economic Performance* (Cambridge UK: Cambridge University Press, 1990), p. 4, as quoted in Scott (2008). Also see Gerry Everding, "Douglass North Prizes Economic History," *Washington University Record,* October 21, 1993, p. 3. Douglass North received the Nobel Prize, along with Robert Fogel, for work using economic theory to explain institutional change. Douglas C. North, *Understanding the Process of Economic Change* (Princeton, NJ: Princeton University Press, 2005).

5. Scott, *Institutions and Organizations.*

6. Ibid.

7. Geert Hofstede, *Cultures and Organizations: Software of the Mind* (San Francisco: Jossey Bass, 1991).

8. M. W. Peng, "How Entrepreneurs Create Wealth in Transition Economies," *Academy of Management Executive* 15 (2001), pp. 95–108, as cited in M. W. Peng, *Global Business* (Mason, OH: South-Western Cengage, 2009), p. 33.

9. Scott, *Institutions and Organizations,* p. 100, referencing John Boli and George M. Thomas, "World Culture in the World Polity: A Century of International Nongovernmental Organization," *American Sociological Review* 62, 1997, pp. 171–90.

10. UNCTAD, http://unctadstat.unctad.org/UnctadStatMetadata/Documentation/UNCTADstatContent.html (March 8, 2011). This is a new, continuously updated site. CIA. The World Factbook, https://www.cia.gov/library/publications/the-world-factbook/geos/xx.html (March 8, 2011).

11. See http://www.un.org/partners/business/index.asp (accessed March 8, 2011).

12. United Nations, *On the Front Line,* p. 13, http://www.unaids.org/en/media/unaids/contentassets/documents/document/2011/20110519_OnTheFrontLine.pdf. (accessed May 10, 2011).

13. See www.icj-cij.org/docket/index.php?p1=3&p2=1 (accessed March 9, 2011).

14. See www.endpoverty2015.org/en/goals (accessed March 10, 2011).

15. See www.imf.org (accessed March 9, 2011).

16. See www.imf.org/external/np/exr/facts/quotas.htm (accessed March 9, 2011).

17. See www.imf.org/external/np/sec/memdir/members.htm#3 for charts of new voting and quota allocations (accessed March 10, 2011).

18. Alan Beattie, "Retread Required," *Financial Times,* December 1, 2009, p. 7.

19. See www.imf.org/external/pubs/ft/survey/so/2011/NEW021911A.htm (accessed March 10, 2011).

20. See http://web.worldbank.org/WBSITE/EXTERNAL/EXTABOUTUS/EXTANNREP/EXTANNREP2010/0,,contentMDK:22626653~menuPK:7148629~pagePK:64168445~piPK:64168309~theSitePK:7074179,00.html (accessed 10 March, 2011).

21. See http://web.worldbank.org/WBSITE/EXTERNAL/EXTABOUTUS/IDA/0,,contentMDK:21206704~menuPK:83991~pagePK:51236175~piPK:437394~theSitePK:73154,00.html (accessed March 10, 2011).

22. *The World Bank Annual Report 2010: The Year in Review,* p. 1. See http://web.worldbank.org/WBSITE/EXTERNAL/EXTABOUTUS/

EXTANNREP/EXTANNREP2010/0,,contentMD
K:22626653~menuPK:7148629~pagePK:641684
45~piPK:64168309~theSitePK:7074179,00.html
(accessed March 10, 2011).

23. See http://icsid.worldbank.org/ICSID/Front
Servlet?requestType=GenCaseDtlsRH&action
Val=ListPending (accessed March 10, 2011).

24. IMF, "Articles of Agreement," www.imf.
org/external/pubs/ft/aa/aa01.htm (accessed
March 11, 2011).

25. "Brazil Rejects U.S. Demands in Doha
Round," *Forexyard,* www.forexyard.com/en/
news/Brazil-rejects-demands-in-Doha-round-
2011-02-18T141859Z-UPDATE-2-US (accessed
March 11, 2011).

26. See Yale Center for the Study of Globalization, www.ycsg.yale.edu/, for resources on
issues related to globalization and equity.

27. www.wto.org/english/tratop_e/region_e/
region_e.htm (accessed March 11, 2011).

28. See www.OECD.org (accessed March 12,
2011).

29. See www.ers.usda.gov/AmberWaves/
September07/Findings/NAFTA.htm (accessed
March 12, 2011).

30. OECD, "China-DAC (Development
Assistance Committee) Study Group,"
www.oecd.org/document/63/0,3746,en_
2649_34621_44173540_1_1_1,00.html
(accessed March 12, 2011).

31. See the EU website for information on
accession: http://europa.eu (accessed March 12,
2011).

32. See http://europa.eu/pol/comm/index_
en.htm (accessed March 12, 2011).

33. "Eurozone Should Get Seat in G20, IMF:
EU's Rehn," *Eurobusiness,* January 11, 2010,
www.eubusiness.com/news-eu/economy-
budget-g20.27l (accessed January 23, 2010).

34. See cia.gov (accessed March 14, 2011).

CHAPTER 4

1. I. Brady and B. Isaac, *A Reader in Cultural
Change,* vol. 1 (Cambridge. MA: Schenkman
Publishing, 1975), introduction, p. x.

2. Hi Mariampolski, *Ethnography for Marketers: A Guide to Consumer Immersion* (Thousand Oaks, CA: Sage Publications), p. 123.

3. "What Is Culture?" Center for Advanced
Research on Language Acquisition, University
of Minnesota, www.carla.umn.edu/culture/
definitions.html (accessed March 17, 2011).

4. Vern Terpstra and Kenneth David, *The
Cultural Environment of International Business*
(Cincinnati, OH: South-Western, 1985), p. 7.

5. E. T. Hall, *Beyond Culture* (Garden City, NY:
Doubleday, 1977), p. 54.

6. "How to Win Friends and Influence Clients,"
The European, January 21–27, 1994, p. 11.

7. C. Berrgren, *Alternatives to Lean Production: Work Organization in the Swedish Auto
Industry* (Ithaca, NY: Cornell, 1992).

8. C. Kluckhohn and K. Strodtbeck, *Variations
in Value Orientations* (Westport, CT: Green-
wood, 1961).

9. E. T. Hall, *The Silent Language* (New York:
Doubleday, 1959); *The Hidden Dimension* (New
York: Doubleday, 1966; *Beyond Culture* (New
York: Doubleday, 1976).

10. Robert J. House et al., *Culture, Leadership
and Organizations: The Globe Study of 62 Societies* (Thousand Oaks, CA: Sage, 2004).

11. Geert Hofstede, *Culture and Organizations: Software of the Mind* (London: McGraw-
Hill, 1991).

12. Fons Trompenaars, *Riding the Waves of
Culture* (Burr Ridge, IL: Irwin, 1993).

13. S. Schwartz, "A Proposal for Measuring
Value Orientations across Nations," http://
en.wikipedia.org/wiki/Shalom_H._Schwartz,
n.d. (accessed March 17, 2011).

14. E. T. Hall and Mildred Hall, *Hidden Differences: Doing Business with the Japanese* (Garden City, NY: Anchor Press/Doubleday, 1987).

15. Carol Kaufman-Scarborough and Jay D.
Lindquist, "Time Management and Polychronic-
ity: Comparisons, Contrasts, and Insights for
the Workplace," *Journal of Managerial Psychology,* 14, no. 3–4 (1999), pp. 288–312, http://
crab.rutgers.edu/~ckaufman/polychronic.html
(accessed March 18, 2011).

16. Hofstede's work has received considerable critical commentary, which centers on
methodological survey issues: that his analysis
is done on one level (organization) and then
extrapolated to another (national); his data are
dated; and his five dimensions are oversimpli-
fied and perhaps not robust enough to describe
a culture. While these are important issues,
managers have found his work helpful. We look
forward to continued refinement in this area.

17. Geert Hofstede, "Cultural Dimensions in
Management and Planning," *Asia Pacific Journal of Management,* January 1984, pp. 81, 84.

18. The source of the descriptions of the
dimensions is Hofstede's Web site, which
is well worth a visit because it has the raw
scores for the countries against the five dimensions: www.geerthofstede.com (accessed
March 18, 2011).

19. Stella Ting-Toomey and others use Confu-
cian dynamism to describe this dimension:
Communicating across Cultures (New York:
Guilford Press, 1999).

20. Fons Trompenaars and Charles Hampden-
Turner, *Riding the Waves of Culture* (New
York: McGraw-Hill, 1997); John Bing, "The Use
and Misuse of Questionnaires in Intercultural
Training," ITAP International, www.itapintl.
com/facultyandresources/articlelibrarymain/
the-use-and-misuse-ofquestionnaires-in-
intercultural-training.html (accessed March 18,

2011); David Thomas, *Essentials of International
Management: A Cross-Cultural Perspective*
(Thousand Oaks, CA: Sage, 2002); Vas Tara
et al., "Half a Century of Measuring Culture:
Review of Approaches, Challenges, and Limitations Based on the Analysis of 121 Instruments
for Quantifying Culture," *Journal of International Management* 15 (2009), pp. 357–73.

21. Joyce S. Osland and Allan Bird, "Beyond
Sophisticated Stereotyping: Cultural Sense-
Making in Context," *Academy of Management
Executive 14,* no. 1 (2000), p. 65.

22. Shakespeare, *Hamlet,* Act 2, Scene 2.

23. Anita Snow, "Ad Featuring 'Che' Guevara
Sparks Furor," *The Monitor,* August 10, 2000,
p. 8a.

24. K.M. Fisher, J. McNett, and P. Scherer,
"Religion in the Workplace." In *Understanding
and Managing Diversity,* 6th ed., C. Harvey and
J. Allard, Eds. (Upper Saddle River, NJ: Prentice Hall, 2011).

25. The descriptions of the five major religions
is written by Kathleen M. Fisher and from the
ar-ticle cited in note 24.

26. E. T. Hall, *The Hidden Dimension* (Garden
City, NY: Doubleday, 1969), pp. 134–35.

27. M. Mauss, *The Gift: Forms and Functions
of Exchange in Archaic Societies* (London:
Routledge, 1990; originally published in 1922).

28. Internet resources may be helpful, such as
Neil Payne, "International Gift Giving Etiquette,"
www.buzzle.com/editorials/10-23-2004-60743.
asp (accessed March 19, 2011).

29. Herskovits, *Man and His Works,* (New
York: A. A. Knopf, 1967), p. 303.

CHAPTER 5

1. Rhoads Murphey, *The Scope of Geography,* 2nd ed. (Skokie, IL: Rand McNally, 1973),
pp. 65–67.

2. M. E. Porter, *The Competitive Advantage of
Nations* (New York: Free Press, 1990).

3. Federal Research Division, Library of Congress, "Afghanistan," *Country Studies/Area
Handbook Series,* http://countrystudies.us/
afghanistan/32.htm (accessed March 23, 2011).

4. "Facts about Afghanistan," *World Facts,*
http://worldfacts.us/Afghanistan
.htm (accessed March 23, 2011).

5. "Spain's Regions," *The Economist,* November 16, 1996, pp. 55–56.

6. United Nations Population Information Network, 2010 data. www.un.org/popin/data.html
(accessed March 23, 2011).

7. Fiona Harvey, "Analysis: A Costly Thirst,"
Financial Times, April 4, 2008, p. 7. See www
.ft.com/cms/s/0/71ea7cce-01e1-11dd-a323-
000077b07658.html?nclick_check=1 (accessed
March 23, 2011).

8. WaterAid is a nonprofit organization based in London, United Kingdom, whose mission is to help poor communities establish sustainable water supplies and latrines. It is referenced in Fiona Harvey's *Financial Times* piece, "Analysis: A Costly Thirst."

9. Murphey, *The Scope of Geography*, pp. 188–89.

10. Jared Diamond, *Guns, Germs, and Steel: The Fates of Human Societies* (New York: W. W. Norton, 1997).

11. Andrew M. Karmack, *The Tropics and Economic Development* (Washington, DC: World Bank, 1976), p. 5.

12. Kenneth Deffeyes, *Hubbert's Peak: The Impending World Oil Shortage* (Princeton, NJ: Princeton University Press, 2001), p. 146; Peter Jackson, "What Are the Real Decline Rates for Global Oil Production?" Cambridge Energy Research Associates, 2007.

13. International Energy Agency, *Oil Market Report*, January, 2011.

14. Cambridge Energy Research Associates, "The Future of the Global Oil Supply: Understanding the Building Blocks," November 4, 2009, www.cera.com/aspx/cda/client/report/report.aspx?KID=5&CID=10720 (accessed March 24, 2011).

15. Association for the Study of Peak Oil and Gas, www.peakoil.net (accessed March 24, 2011).

16. Energy Information Administration, "Annual Energy Outlook 2010," www.eia.doe.gov/ (accessed March 24, 2011).

17. Sasol, "Sasol Oil-from-Coal Process," www.sasol.com/sasol_internet/downloads/SASOL_global_force_March07_1172224987155.pdf (accessed March 26, 2011).

18. Carol Kopp, "The US Air Force Synthetic Fuels Program," Technical Report APA-TR-2008-0102, www.ausairpower.net/APA-USAF-SynFuels.html (accessed March 26, 2011).

19. Carola Hoyos, "Running on Empty? Fears oOver Oil Supply Move into the Mainstream," *Financial Times*, May 20, 2008, p. 9.

20. Sylvia Pfeifer, "Industry Thrown into Turmoil," Oil & Gas Special Report, *Financial Times*, March 21, 2011, p. 1.

21. International Atomic Energy Agency, www.iaea.org/programmes/a2/ (accessed March 26, 2011).

22. www.world-nuclear.org/info/inf63.html (accessed March 26, 2011).

23. www.nei.org/keyissues/newnuclearplants (accessed March 26, 2011).

24. www.world-nuclear.org/info/inf16.html (accessed March 26, 2011).

25. www.eia.doe.gov/oiaf/ieo/coal.html (accessed March 26, 2011).

26. http://tonto.eia.doe.gov/energyexplained/index.cfm?page=coal_reserves (accessed March 26, 2011).

27. www.iea.org/techno/etp/etp10/English.pdf (accessed March 26, 2011).

28. *Renewables 2010 Global Status Report*, REN21_GSR_2010.pdf, www.ren21.net/REN21Activities/Publications/GlobalStatusReport/GSR2010/tabid/5824/Default.aspx (accessed July 3, 2011).

29. "China Soon May Need to Import Rare Earths, Mining Official Says," *Bloomberg.com*, March 15, 2011. (accessed March 28, 2011).

30. Phillip Sutton, "Sustainability, What Does It Mean?" *Green Innovations* homepage, August 28, 2000, www.green-innovations.asn.au/sustblty.htm (accessed March 31, 2011)

31. The Environmental Leader, July 30, 2010 www.environmentalleader.com/2010/07/30/executives-link-sustainability-with-business-strategy/?graph=full&id=1 (accessed April 4, 2011).

32. Paul Hawken, *The Ecology of Commerce* (New York: HarperCollins, 1994), p. 139.

33. Economics Network, UK Higher Education Academy, "Development Survey on Definitions: Sustainable," www.economicsnetwork.ac.uk/projects/esd/def_survey.pdf (accessed March 29, 2011).

34. "Oil Firms in Nigeria Cut Output," *BBC News*, www.vanityfair.com/politics/features/2007/02/nigeria_photoessay200702 (accessed March 6, 20100); Dino Mahtani, "Nigerian Oil Industry Helpless as Militants Declare War on Obasanjo," *Financial Times*, February 21, 2006. For Michael Kamber's photographs of the Nigerian issue, see www.vanityfair.com/politics/features/2007/02/nigeria_slide0702 (accessed March 29, 2011); Amnesty International, March 2010, www.amnesty.org/en/library/info/AFR44/017/2006 (accessed July 3, 2011); John Vidal, Nigeria's Agony Dwarfs the Gulf Oil Spill," *Gardianco.uk*, May 30, 2010, (accessed March 29, 2011).

35. Francesco Guerrera and Richard Waters, "IBM Chief Wants End to Colonial Companies," *Financial Times*, June 12, 2006, p. 1; Samuel Palmisano, "Multinationals Have Been Superseded," *Financial Times*, June 12, 2006, p. 15.

36. R. Edward Freeman, *Strategic Management: A Stakeholder Approach* (Boston: Pitman, 1984).

37. R. Edward Freeman, Andrew C. Wicks, and Bidhan Pamar, "'Stakeholder Theory' and the Corporate Objective Revisited," *Organizational Science* 15, no. 3 (May–June 2004), pp. 364–69.

38. Quoted in *Religious Education*, Vol. 73 (1978), p. 292, December 10, 1968.

39. Partner in the Smith and Hawken business and author of *Natural Capitalism: Creating the Next Industrial Revolution*, (Boston: Little Brown and Co., 1999).

40. Interface, www.interfaceglobal.com/Sustainability/Our-Journey/Interface-Model.aspx (accessed April 2, 2011).

41. Interface at www.interfaceglobal.com/Sustainability/Our-Journey/7-Fronts-of-Sustainability.aspx (accessed April 3, 2011).

42. "Environmentalism: What We Do," Patagonia.com, www.patagonia.com/web/us/patagonia.go?assetid=2329 (accessed April 3, 2011)

43. Y. Chouinard, *Patagonia: The Next Hundred Years*, http://uwsustainability.com/ (accessed April 3, 2011).

44. www.bluegreenalliance.org (accessed April 3, 2011).

CHAPTER 6

1. Gerhard Pohl, Robert Anderson, Stijn Claessens, and Simeon Djankov, "Privatisation and Restructuring in Central and Eastern Europe," *World Bank Technical Paper No. 386* (Washington, DC: World Bank, June 1997); and Kevin Done, "Europe's Privatisation Fast Track," *Financial Times*, July 4, 1997, p. 10.

2. John Lancaster, "U.S. Arms Sales in Gulf Risk Being Eroded by China and Others," *International Herald Tribune*, July 17, 1997, p. 6.

3. Maplecroft, "Somalia Overtakes Iraq, Afghanistan, Pakistan and Columbia to Become World's Terror Capital—Global Study," http://maplecroft.com/about/news/terrorism.html (June 23, 2011).

4. Nick Miroff, "As Kidnappings for Ransom Surge in Mexico, Victims' Families and Employers Turn to Private U.S. Firms Instead of Law Enforcement," *Washington Post*, February 26, 2011, www.washingtonpost.com/wp-dyn/content/article/2011/02/26/AR2011022603384.html (June 23, 2011); and Peter Apps, "Factbox: Global Kidnap Hotspots and Ransom Costs," *Reuters*, February 17, 2011, www.reuters.com/article/2011/02/17/us-crime-kidnap-hotspotsidUSTRE71G42D20110217?pageNumber=2 (June 23, 2011).

5. "The Price of Paying Ransoms," *The Economist*, September 2, 2000, p. 17, *www.economist.com/node/353978* (June 23, 2011).

6. "Kidnap and Ransom: Negotiating Lives for Cash," *Reuters*, February 17, 2011, www.reuters.com/article/2011/02/17/us-crime-kidnap-ransom-idUSTRE71G3U520110217 (June 23, 2011); and Joann S. Lublin, "Keeping the CEO Safe Can Be Costly," *The Wall Street Journal*, June 9, 2008, p. B.1, http://online.wsj.com/article/SB121296823263355759.html (June 23, 2011).

7. See Chapter 2 for more on the growth of FDI.

8. "Footwear Industry Tells Congress 'Shoe Gap' Threatens U.S. Defense," *The Wall Street Journal*, August 24, 1984, p. 21; and Thomas A.

Pugel, *International Economics,* 13th ed. (New York: McGraw-Hill Irwin, 2007), pp. 197–98.

9. Lance Davis and Stanley Engerman, "History Lessons: Sanctions: Neither War nor Peace," *Journal of Economic Perspectives* 17, no. 2 (Spring 2003), p. 187, www.aeaweb.org/articles.php?doi=10.1257/089533003765888502 (June 23, 2011).

10. Gary C. Hufbauer, "Economic Sanctions: America's Folly," in *Economic Casualties: How U.S. Foreign Policy Undermines Trade, Growth and Liberty,* S. Singleton and D. T. Griswold, Eds. (Washington DC: Cato Institute, 1999), pp. 90–99; and Hossein Askari, John Forrer, Jiawen Yang, and Tarek Hachem, "Measuring Vulnerability to U.S. Foreign Economic Sanctions," *Business Economics* 40, no. 2 (April 2005), pp. 41–55, www.palgrave-journals.com/be/journal/v40/n2/abs/be200513a.html (June 23, 2011).

11. "How to Lower Price of Ethanol; Kill the Tariff, Help Consumers," *Rocky Mountain News,* May 14, 2006, p. 5E, www.highbeam.com/doc/1G1-145753434.html (June 23, 2011); and Scott Learn, "Rice University Analysis Questions Ethanol Subsidies," www.oregonlive.com/environment/index.ssf/2010/01/rice_university_analysis_quest.html (accessed June 23, 2011).

12. "Brie and Hormones," *The Economist,* January 7, 1989, pp. 21–22; "Europe's Burden," *The Economist,* May 22, 1999, p. 84; Office of the Foreign Trade Representative, *2006 National Trade Estimate Report on Foreign Trade Barriers,* March 2006, www.ustraderep.gov/Document_Library/Reports_Publications/2006/2006_NTE_Report/Section_Index.html (accessed June 23, 2011); and Juliane von Reppert-Bismarck, "U.S. Lifts Sanctions in EU Beef Hormone Row," *Reuters,* www.reuters.com/article/2011/05/27/us-sanctions-beef-hormone-idUSTRE74Q63L20110527 (June 23, 2011).

13. Robert Anderson, "Slovakia's 'Soviet' Skills Set to Create Car World-Beater," *Financial Times,* April 20, 2006, p. 4, www.ft.com/cms/s/0/0902aeda-d0a-11da-80fb-0000779e2340.html#axzz1Q9YKfuhA (June 23, 2011); John Gapper, "It Is Time for the Big Three to Shut Up," *Financial Times,* October 20, 2005, p. 19; "The New Rules of Trade," *National Review,* April 18, 1994, pp. 40–44, *www.therathouse.com/Rafe_s_Roundup_1994-96.pdf (June 23, 2011);* and Marc Champion and Adam Z. Horvath, "EU Expansion Fuels Debate on Taxes," *The Wall Street Journal,* May 3, 2004, p. A18.

14. Catherine Moreddu, *Distribution of Support and Income in Agriculture,* OECD Food, Agriculture and Fisheries Working Papers, No. 46, OECD Publishing, 2011, http://dx.doi.org/10.1787/5kgch21wkmbx-en (June 23, 2011).

15. European Commission, "United States Barriers to Trade and Investment: Report for 2007" (Brussels: European Commission, April 2008), trade.ec.europa.eu/doclib/docs/2008/april/tradoc_138559.pdf.pdf (June 23, 2011).

16. Office of the United States Trade Representative, *2010 National Trade Estimate Report on Foreign Trade Barriers, www.ustr.gov/about-us/press-office/reports-and-publications/2010 (June 23, 2011).*

17. "International Trade of Genetically Modified Foods," http://en.wikipedia.org/wiki/International_trade_of_genetically_modified_foods (June 23, 2011).

18. The OECD published *Costs and Benefits of Protection,* which evaluates a wide range of studies on import restrictions of manufactured goods in OECD countries. Patrick A. Messerlin, *Measuring the Costs of Protection in Europe: European Commercial Policy in the 2000s* (Washington, DC: International Institute for Economics, 2001), http://bookstore.piie.com/book-store//102.html (June 23, 2011), examined costs in 22 highly protected industries in the EU. The 2002 annual report of the Federal Reserve Bank of Dallas, www.dallasfed.org/fed/annual/2002/ar02f.html (accessed July 9, 2006), provides a listing of the jobs saved and total costs of protecting these jobs for 20 selected industries.

CHAPTER 7

1. "Shanghai Sees Law as Key to Being Commercial Hub," *Financial Times,* July 1, 2002, p. vi.

2. WIPO Arbitration and Mediation Center, "Administrative Panel Decision: Research in Motion Limited v. Georges Elias," www.wipo.int/amc/en/domains/decisions/html/2009/d2009-0218.html (accessed June 25, 2011).

3. A. H. Herman, "Growth in International Trade Law," *Financial Times,* March 30, 1989, p. 10.

4. Avery Johnson, "Pfizer Buys More Time for Lipitor," *The Wall Street Journal,* June 19, 2008, p. B1, http://online.wsj.com/documents/print/WSJ_-B001-20080619.pdf (June 25, 2011): "Avorastatin," http://en.wikipedia.org/wiki/Lipitor (accessed June 25, 2011).

5. Office of the United States Trade Representative, "U.S., Participants Finalize Anti-Counterfeiting Trade Agreement Text," Novmber 2010, www.ustr.gov/about-us/press-office/press-releases/2010/november/us-participants-finalize-anti-counterfeiting-trad (accessed June 25, 2011).

6. Chester Yung, "Hong Kong's Antitrust Law Proposal Is Rapped for Lacking Punch," *The Wall Street Journal,* June 19, 2008, p. A10, www.global-report.com/hongkong/a302538-hong-kong-s-antitrust-law-proposal-is-rapped-for-lacking-punch (June 25, 2011).

7. Pierre Verkhhovsky and Clifford Chance, "Advising Japanese Clients on EU Competition Law," *International Journal of Competition Policy and Regulation,* www.globalcompetitionreview.com/apar/jap_eu.cfm (accessed July 30, 2004); and Lee Youkyung, "Japan's Antitrust Watchdog Fines Samsung SDI, Ex-LG Affiliate for Price-Rigging," March 30, 2010, www.highbeam.com/doc/1G1-222922727.html (accessed June 25, 2011).

8. "Japan's Fair Trade Commission, Pussycat," *The Economist,* October 23, 1993, pp. 85–86; "Japanese Competition Law," http://en.wikipedia.org/wiki/Japanese_competition_law (June 25, 2011); and James D. Fry, "Struggling to Teethe: Japan's Antitrust Enforcement Regime," *Law and Policy in International Business,* Summer 2001, http://business.highbeam.com/61320/article-1G1-83249553/struggling-teethe-japan-antitrust-enforcement-regime (June 25, 2011).

9. Molly S. Boast and Hannah M. Pennington, "Extraterritorial Applications of U.S. Antitrust Laws: An Overview," www.abanet.org/antitrust/at-committees/at-ic/pdf/spring/05/boast.pdf (accessed June 25, 2011); John M. Connor and Darren Bush, "How to Block Cartel and Price Fixing: Using Extraterritorial Application of the Antitrust Laws as a Deterrence Mechanism," *Penn State Law Review* 112, no. 3 (April 2008), pp. 813–57, www.pennstatelawreview.org/articles/112%20Penn%20St.%20L.%20Rev.%20813.pdf (June 25, 2011); and Leon B. Greenfield and David Olsky, "From Bananas to Vitamins: The Evolving Doctrine of the Extraterritorial Application of US Antitrust Law," *The Licensing Journal,* March 2006, pp. 7–12, www.wilmerhale.com/files/Publication/29ff537f-7ac7-4cd9-a3b8-de6c2814314b/Presentation/PublicationAttachment/d05eb7a7-df27-4479-ac00-ef5eb197a3ce/Greenfield_Olsky.pdf (June 25, 2011).

10. George Trefgarne, "Brussels Clears Way for $220bn Merger," *The Telegraph,* www.telegraph.co.uk/finance/4468341/Brussels-clears-way-for-220bn-merger.html (June 25, 2011); and Stephen Castle, "EU Fine Sends Message to Microsoft and Others," www.nytimes.com/2008/02/27/technology/27iht-msft.4.10498942.html (accessed June 25, 2011).

11. "Caught in a Web of Jurisdiction," *Financial Times,* May 15, 2002, p. 13.

12. "Alan Beattie, "From a Trickle to a Flood—How Lawsuits Are Coming to Dictate the Terms of Trade," *Financial Times,* March 20, 2007, p. 11, www.ft.com/cms/s/0/a4fdfdf0-d688-11db-99b7-000b5df10621.html (June 25, 2011).

13. Harvey Kaplan and Jon Strongman, "United States: Developments in U.S. Product Liability Law and the Issues Relevant to Foreign Manufacturers," January 5, 2010, www.mondaq.com/unitedstates/article.asp?articleid=89684 (accessed June 25, 2011).

14. Barbara Crutchfield George and Linda McCallister, "The Effect of Cultural Attitudes on Product Liability Laws," Southwestern

Association of Administrative Disciplines, March 4, 1993; and Craig P. Wagnild, "Civil Law Discovery in Japan: A Comparison of Japanese and US Methods of Evidence Collection in Civil Litigation," *Asia-Pacific Law and Policy Journal* 3, no. 1 (Winter 2002), www.hawaii.edu/aplpj/articles/APLPJ_03.1_wagnild.pdf (accessed June 25, 2011).

15. T. Markus Funk, "Another Landmark Year: 2010 FCPA Year-in-Review and Enforcement Trends for 2011," *Bloomberg Law Reports,* January 3, 2010, www.perkinscoie.com/files/upload/11_01_03_FunkArticle.pdf (June 25, 2011).

16. "United Nations Convention Against Corruption," http://en.wikipedia.org/wiki/United_Nations_Convention_against_Corruption (June 25, 2011).

17. Clayton Utz, "UK Bribery Act Starts on 1 July 2011—Are You Ready?" April 4, 2011, www.claytonutz.com/publications/news/201104/04/uk_bribery_act_starts_on_1_july_2011-are_you_ready.page (June 25, 2011).

CHAPTER 8

1. Cheol S. Eun and Bruce G. Resnick, *International Financial Management,* 4th ed. (Burr Ridge, IL: McGraw-Hill Irwin, 2007), p. 25.

2. Charles N. Henning, William Pigott, and Robert Haney Scott, *International Financial Management* (New York: McGraw-Hill, 1978), p. 149.

3. Albert C. Whitaker, *Foreign Exchange,* 2nd ed. (New York: Appleton-Century-Crofts, 1933), p. 157; Richard Cooper, "The Gold Standard: Historical Facts and Future Prospects,: *Brookings Papers on Economic Activity* 1982, no. 1 (1982). The increases were gradual until the 1970s, when the price of gold spiked, largely as a result of the 1973 oil crisis.

4. Jacques Rueff, *La réforme du système monétaire international* (Paris: Plon, 1973).

5. Paul Krugman, "The Gold Bug Variations," November 1996, www.pkarchive.org/ (accessed April 8, 2011).

6. *Federal Reserve Bulletin,* September 1969 and January 1974.

7. *Federal Reserve Bulletin,* December 1971 and January 1974.

8. www.bis.org/publ/qtrpdf/r_qt1012e.htm (accessed April 9, 2011).

9. Michael B. Devereux and Shouyong Shi, "Vehicle Currency," No. 10, Globalization and Monetary Policy Institute Working Paper from Federal Reserve Bank of Dallas, updated March 2011, Vehicle Currency, http://ideas.repec.org/p/fip/feddgw/10.html (accessed April 10, 2011).

10. "U.S. Probes Whether Big Banks Stifle Rival in Currency Trading," *The Wall Street Journal,* May 15, 2002, p. A1.

11. Susie Gharib, "Slowing Global Growth May Energize the Dollar," February 28, 2008, PBS, *Nightly Business Report,* www.pbs.org/nbr/site/onair/transcripts/080208a (accessed April 11, 2011).

12. Eun and Resnick, (2007) *International Financial Management,* pp. 147–48. The technical explanations here are clearly described and well illustrated.

13. Ibid., p. 149.

14. Ibid., p. 151.

15. Cheol Eun and Sanjiv Sabherwal, "Forecasting Exchange Rates: Do the Banks Know Better?" *Global Finance Journal,* 2002, pp. 195–215; Lillie Lam, Lawrence Fung, and Ip-wing Yu, "Comparing Forecast performance of Exchange Rate Models," Hong Kong Monetary Department, 2008.

16. David Kocieniewski, "GE's Strategies Let It Avoid Taxes Altogether," *New York Times,* March 24, 2011, p. 1, www.nytimes.com/2011/03/25/business/economy/25tax.html (accessed April 12, 2011).

17. "The Case for Open Trade," World Trade Organization, www.wto.org/english/thewto_e/whatis_e/tif_e/fact3_e.htm (accessed April 12, 2011).

18. H. Kohler and J. Wolfensohn, "We Can Trade Up to a Better Financial World, " *Financial Times,* December 12, 2003.

CHAPTER 9

1. For a discussion of strategy, see Michael E. Porter, "What Is Strategy?" *Harvard Business Review,* November–December 1996, pp. 61–78.

2. Jay B. Barney, "Looking Inside for Competitive Advantage," *Academy of Management Executive* 9 (1995), pp. 49–61; M. A. Peteraf, "The Cornerstones of Competitive Advantage: A Resource-Based View," *Strategic Management Journal* 14 (3) (1993), pp. 179–91; B. Wernerfelt, "A Resource Based View of the Firm," *Strategic Management Journal* 5, no. 2 (1984), pp. 171–80; and Jay Barney, *Gaining and Sustaining Competitive Advantage,* 2nd ed. (Upper Saddle River, NJ: Prentice Hall, 2002).

3. "An Executive Takes on the Top Business Trends: A McKinsey Global Survey," *The McKinsey Quarterly,* April 2006, www.mckinseyquarterly.com/article_print.aspx?L2=21&L3=114&ar=1754 (accessed May 1, 2011).

4. Darrell Rigby and Barbara Bilodeau, "Management Tools and Trends 2009," Bain & Company, www.bain.com/management_tools/home.asp (accessed May 1, 2011), p. 14.

5. "How Companies Act on Global Trends: A McKinsey Global Survey," *The McKinsey Quarterly,* March 2008, pp. 1–9.

6. Reggie Van Lee, Lisa Fabish, and Nancy McGaw, "The Value of Corporate Values," *Strategy+ Business,* www.strategy-business.com/article/05206?gko=7869b-1876-9176155&tid=230&pg=all (accessed May 22, 2010).

7. Samsung, "Values and Philosophy," www.samsung.com/hk_en/aboutsamsung/samsunggroup/valuesphilosophy/SAMSUNGGroup_Values Philosophy.html# (accessed May 1, 2011).

8. Amazon.com, "Does Amazon.com Have a Mission or Vision Statement?" http://phx.corporate-ir.net/phoenix.zhtml?c=97664&p=irol-faq#14296 (accessed May 1, 2011).

9. Sumitomo Corporation, "SC Values," www.sumitomocorp.co.jp/english/company/principles/index.html (accessed May 22, 2010).

10. "Intel's Mission Statement, Values, and Objectives," www.intel.com/intel/company/corp1.htm (accessed May 1, 2011).

11. Jeroen van der Veer, "Shell Energy Scenarios to 2050," www.shell.com/home/content/aboutshell/our_strategy/shell_global_scenarios/shell_energy_scenarios_2050/ (accessed May 1, 2011).

12. Peter Schwartz, *The Art of the Long View—Planning for the Future in an Uncertain World* (New York: Doubleday, 1996).

13. Cornelius A. de Kluyver and John A Pearce II, *Strategy: A View from the Top,* 2nd ed. (Upper Saddle River, NJ: Pearson Prentice Hall, 2006), p. 9.

14. Gary Hamel, "Strategy as Revolution," *Harvard Business Review,* July–August 1996, p. 70.

15. Eric D. Beinhocker and Sarah Kaplan, "Tired of Strategic Planning?" *The McKinsey Quarterly,* 2002 (special edition on risk and resilience), www.mckinseyquarterly.com/article_print.aspx?L2=21&L3=37&ar=1191 (accessed May 1, 2011).

16. Andrew Campbell and Marcus Alexander, "What's Wrong with Strategy?" *Harvard Business Review,* November–December 1997, p. 46.

17. Frederick W. Gluck, "A Fresh Look at Strategic Management," *Journal of Business Strategy,* Fall 1985, p. 6.

CHAPTER 10

1. Nitin Nohria, *Note on Organization Structure* (Boston: Harvard Business School, 1991).

2. John M. Stopford and Louis T. Wells, *Strategy and Structure of the Multinational Enterprise* (New York: Basic Books, 1972).

3. Caterpillar Inc., *2007 Annual Report,* www.cat.com/cda/files/887773/7/AR_2007_final.pdf (accessed May 8, 2011).

4. Shell Chemical Company, "About Shell Chemicals," www.shell.com/home/content/chemicals/aboutshell/ (accessed May 8, 2011).

5. BP p.l.c., "About BP," www.bp.com/sectionbodycopy.do?categoryId=2&contentId=7065607 (accessed May 8, 2011).

6. Lowell L. Bryan and Claudia Joyce, "The 21st-Century Organization," *The McKinsey Quarterly*, no. 3 (2005), www.mckinseyquarterly.com/article_print.aspx?L2=18&L3=30&ar=1628 (accessed May 8, 2011).

7. Remo Häcki and Julian Lighton, "The Future of the Networked Company," *The McKinsey Quarterly*, no. 3 (2001), pp. 26–39, www.mckinseyquarterly.com/The_future_of_the_networked_company_1091 (accessed May 8, 2011).

8. Glenn R. Simpson, "Wearing of the Green: Irish Subsidiary Lets Microsoft Slash Taxes in U.S. and Europe," *The Wall Street Journal*, November 7, 2005, p. A1, www.hondoazul.com/MSIrish.pdf (accessed May 8, 2011).

CHAPTER 11

1. C. A. Bartlett and S. Ghoshal, *Managing Across Borders: The Transnational Solution*, (Boston: Harvard Business School Press, 1989); Vijay Govindarajan and Anil Gupta, *The Quest for Global Dominance: Transforming Global Presence into Global Competitive Advantage* (San Francisco: Jossey-Bass, 2001), p. 106; and M. F. R. Kets de Vries and E. Florent-Treacy, "Global Leadership from A to Z: Creating High Commitment Organizations," *Organizational Dynamics* 30 (2002), pp. 295–309.

2. S. Rhinesmith, "Basic Components of a Global Mindset," in M. Goldsmith, V. Govindarajan, and A. Vicere, Eds., *The Many Facets of Leadership* (Upper Saddle River, NJ: Financial Times Prentice Hall, 2003).

3. Govindarajan and Gupta, *The Quest for Global Dominance*, p. 111.

4. For example, the following approaches used to examine leadership—(1) traits, (2) behaviors, (3) power-influence, (4) situational, and (5) integrative)—were identified and reviewed in G. Yukl, *Leadership in Organizations*, 6th ed. (Upper Saddle River, NJ: Pearson Prentice Hall, 2006).

5. Ibid., pp. 6–7.

6. Warren Bennis, *Learning to Lead: A Workbook on Becoming a Leader* (New York: Perseus Books, 1997), p. 9.

7. N. Adler and S. Bartholomew, "Managing Globally Competent People," *Academy of Management Executive* 6, no. 23 (1992), pp. 52–64; and M. Mendenhall, R. Jensen, J. S. Black, and H. Gregersen, "Seeing the Elephant: HRM Challenges in the Age of Globalization," *Organizational Dynamics* 32, no. 3 (2003) pp. 261–74.

8. H. W. Lane, M. L. Maznevski, and M. E. Mendenhall, "Hercules Meets Buddha," in H. W. Lane, M. Maznevski, M. E. Mendenhall, and J. McNett, Eds., *The Handbook of Global Management: A Guide to Managing Complexity* (Oxford: Blackwell, 2004), pp. 3–25.

9. For example, J. Osland, A. Bird, M. E. Mendenhall, and A. Osland, "Developing Global Leadership Capabilities and Global Mindset: A Review," in G. K. Stahl and I. Bjorkman, Eds., *Handbook of Research in International Human Resource Management* (Cheltenham, UK: Edward Elgar, 2006), pp. 197–222; and AsperianGlobal, *What Is Global Leadership?*, www.asperianglobal.com/newsletter_archive/publications_newsletter042.asp (June 12, 2011).

10. D. N. Den Hartog, R. J. House, P. J. Hanges, S. A. Ruiz-Quintanilla, P. W. Dorfman, and Associates, "Culture Specific and Cross-Culturally Generalizable Implicit Leadership Theories: Are Attributes of Charismatic/Transformational Leadership Universally Endorsed?" *Leadership Quarterly* 10, no. 2 (1999) pp. 219–56.

11. M. E. Mendenhall, J. S. Osland, A. Bird, G. R. Oddou, and M. L. Maznevski, *Global Leadership: Research, Practice, and Development* (New York: Routledge, 2008), p. 17.

12. J. S. Osland and A. Bird, "Global Leaders as Experts," in W. Mobley and E. Weldon, Eds., *Advances in Global Leadership*, vol. 4 (Stamford, CT: JAI Press, 2006), pp. 123–42.

13. H. Mintzberg, *The Nature of Managerial Work* (New York: Harper and Row, 1973); J. P. Kotter, "What Leaders Really Do," *Harvard Business Review* 68, no. 3 (1990), p. 103; J. S. Osland, "The Multidisciplinary Roots of Global Leadership," in M. E. Mendenhall, J. S. Osland, A. Bird, G. R. Oddou, and M. L. Maznevski, *Global Leadership: Research, Practice, and Development* (New York: Routledge, 2008), Ch. 2.

14. Corporate Leadership Council, *The New Global Assignment: Developing and Retaining Future Leaders* (Washington, DC: Author, 2000).

15. J. B. Leslie, M. Dalton, C. Ernst, and J. Deal, *Managerial Effectiveness in a Global Context. A Center for Creative Leadership Report* (Greensboro, NC: CCL Press, 2002), p. 63.

16. M. Javidan, P. Dorfman, M. Sully de Luque, and R. House, "In the Eye of the Beholder: Cross Cultural Lessons in Leadership from Project GLOBE," *Academy of Management Perspectives*, February 2006, pp. 67–90.

17. T. Brake, *The Global Leader: Critical Factors for Creating the World Class Organization*, (Chicago: Irwin Professional Publishing 1997).

18. M. A. Dalton, "Developing Leaders for Global Roles," in C. D. McCauley, R. S. Moxley, and E. Van Velsor, Eds., *The Center for Creative Leadership Handbook of Leadership Development* (San Francisco: Jossey-Bass, 1998), pp. 379–402.

19. C. Kelley and J. Meyers, *The Cross-Cultural Adaptability Inventory* (Minneapolis, MN: National Computer Systems, 1995).

20. M. R. Hammer, M. J. Bennett, and R. Wiseman, "Measuring Intercultural Sensitivity: The Intercultural Development Inventory," *International Journal of Intercultural Relations* 27, no. 4 (2003), pp. 421–43.

21. Kozai Group Inc. *The Global Competencies Inventory* (St. Louis, MO: Author, 2002).

22. M. F. R. Kets de Vries, P. Vrignaud, and E. Florent-Treacy, "Global Executive Leadership Inventory: Development and Psychometric Properties of a 360-Degree Feedback Instrument," *International Journal of Human Resource Management* 15, no. 3 (2004), pp. 475–92.

23. M. W. McCall Jr. and G. P. Hollenbeck, *Developing Global Executives: The Lessons of International Experience,* (Boston: Harvard Business School Press, 2002).

24. J. Osland, A. Bird, M. E. Mendenhall, and A. Osland, "Developing Global Leadership Capabilities and Global Mindset: A Review," in G. K. Stahl and I. Björkman, Eds., *Handbook of Research in International Human Resource Management* (Cheltenham, UK: Edward Elgar, 2006), pp. 197–222; and J. S. Osland and A. Bird, "Process Models of Global Leadership Development," in M. E. Mendenhall, J. S. Osland, A. Bird, G. R. Oddou, and M. L. Maznevski, *Global Leadership: Research, Practice, and Development* (New York: Routledge, 2008), Ch. 5.

25. J. Chatman and J. Kennedy, "Psychological Perspectives on Leadership," in N. Nohria and R. Khurana, Eds., *Handbook of Leadership Theory and Practice* (Boston: Harvard Business Press, 2010), pp. 159–83.

26. M. Swann, L. Milton, and J. Polzner, "Should We Create a Niche or Fall In Line? Identity Negotiation and Small group Effectiveness," *Journal of Personality and Social Psychology* 79, no. 2 (2000), pp. 238–50.

27. Chatman and Kennedy, "Psychological Perspectives on Leadership," p. 166.

28. A. Birenbaum and E. Sagarin, *Norms and Human Behavior* (New York: Praeger, 1976) as referenced in Chatman and Kennedy, "Psychological Perspectives on Leadership."

29. Lane, Maznevski, and Mendenhall, "Globalization: Hercules Meets Buddha," pp. 3–25. This portion of the discussion draws heavily on introduction to the handbook.

30. M. L. Maznevski, "Leading Global Teams," in M. Mendenhall et al., *Global Leadership: Research, Practice and Development* (London: Routledge, 2008), pp. 94–113. The discussion on global teams is strongly influenced by Maznevski's work.

31. H. Lane, et al. *International Management Behavior: Leading with a Global Mindset* (Chichester, UK: Wiley, 2009), p. 79.

32. M. Maznevski, "Leading Global Teams," p. 108.

33. B. L. Kirkman and D. N. Den Hartog, "Performance Management in Global Teams," in H. W. Lane, M. Maznevski, M. E. Mendenhall, and J. McNett, Eds., *The Handbook of Global Management: A Guide to Managing Complexity* (Oxford: Blackwell, 2004), pp. 250–67.

34. These suggestions are drawn from the work of Kirkman and Den Hartog, "Performance Management in Global Teams."

35. J. Osland, "Leading Global Change," in M. Mendenhall et al., *Global Leadership: Research, Practice and Development* (London: Routledge, 2008) p. 131; J. G. Clawson, *Level Three Leadership: Getting Below the Surface* (Upper Saddle River, NJ: Prentice Hall, 2006), p. 6. Joyce Osland's work on international change management has greatly influenced this discussion of change leadership.

36. M. Maznevski, "Global Leadership Issues and Practices," in H. Lane et al., *International Management Behavior: Leading with a Global Mindset* (Chichester, UK: Wiley, 2009), p. 250.

37. www.kotterinternational.com (accessed June 11, 2011).

38. T. Savolainen, "Challenges of Intercultural Management: Change Implementation in the Context of National Culture," *Proc. 12th International Conference on ISO 9000 & TQM*, 2007, Samuel Ho, Ed., http://uef.academia.edu/TainaSavolainen/Papers/398527/Challenges_of_Intercultural_Management_Change_Implementation_In_the_Context_of_National_Culture (accessed June 12, 2011).

39. J. Osland, "Building Community through Change," in H. W. Lane, M. Maznevski, M. E. Mendenhall, and J. McNett, Eds., *The Blackwell Handbook of Global Management: A Guide to Managing Complexity*, pp. 143–51.

CHAPTER 12

1. A good introduction to scanning the environment is "Environmental Scanning," http://en.wikipedia.org/wiki/Environmental_scanning (accessed June 14, 2011).

2. Virtually all governments have barriers to foreign direct investment and at the same time offer a variety of incentives to potential foreign investors. For example, Mexico currently restricts foreign investment in the petroleum industry. See, for example, UNCTAD's series of *World Investment Reports,* which is published in an annual edition: www.unctad.org/Templates/Page.asp?intItemID=1485&lang=1 (accessed June 9, 2010).

3. "CeBIT 2010 Has Been Very Impressive," www.cebit.de/end_of_show_report_2010 (accessed June 15, 2011).

4. Secondary data and sometimes primary data will be gathered on a field trip, but the visitor rarely has the time or ability to conduct a complete field study.

5. Yuezhi Zhao "The 'People's Phone' on Hold," *Foreign Policy,* July–August 2002, pp. 83–85.

6. For a sophisticated example in Mexico, see www.pearson-research.com/english/informacion-america-latina-mexico.phtml (accessed June 15, 2011).

7. Carol Hymowitz, "Marketers Focus More on Global 'Tribes' than on Nationalities," *The Wall Street Journal,* December 10, 2007, p. B1. The segment screening approach was inspired by Masaaki Kotabe and Kristiaan Helsen, *Global Marketing Management* (New York: Wiley, 2008).

CHAPTER 13

1. This discussion owes a great deal to Orville C. Walker Jr., John Mullins, and Harper W. Boyd Jr., *Marketing Strategy: A Decision-Focused Approach* (Burr Ridge, IL: Irwin/McGraw-Hill, 2011).

2. The World Bank, "Royalty and License Fees, Receipts (BoP, current US$)," http://data.worldbank.org/indicator/BX.GSR.ROYL.CD/countries (accessed June 21, 2011).

3. Thayne Forbes, "Set the Right Royalty Rate," *Intellectual Asset Management*, www.intangiblebusiness.com/Brand-Services/Marketing-services/News/Set-the-right-royalty-rate~317.html (accessed June 21, 2011); and Christina Passariello, "Pierre Cardin Ready to Sell His Overstretched Label," *The Wall Street Journal*, May 2, 2011, http://online.wsj.com/article/SB10001424052748704547604576263541408680576.html (June 21, 2011).

4. "Cosmopolitan," www.hearst.com/magazines/cosmopolitan.php (accessed June 21, 2011).

5. "International Editions," www.playboy.com/magazine/international-editions (accessed June 21, 2011).

6. Frank Tian Xie and Wesley J. Johnston, "Strategic Alliances: Incorporating the Impact of E-Business Technological Innovations," *Journal of Business and Industrial Marketing* 19, no. 3 (2004), pp. 208–22, www.emeraldinsight.com/journals.htm?articleid=856907&show=html (accessed June 21, 2011).

7. Edward J. Zajac, "Creating an Academic Framework for Strategic Alliances," www.kellogg.northwestern.edu/kwo/sum02/indepth/theory.htm (accessed June 21, 2011).

8. For discussion of challenges in managing international joint ventures and alliances, see Colette A. Frayne and J. Michael Geringer, "Challenges Facing General Managers of International Joint Ventures," in *Readings and Cases in International Human Resource Management*, 2nd ed., ed. M. Mendenhall and G. Oddou (Cincinnati, OH: South-Western, 1995), pp. 85–97; J. Michael Geringer and C. Patrick Woodcock, "Agency Costs and the Structure and Performance of International Joint Ventures," *Group Decision and Negotiation* 4, no. 5 (1995), pp. 453–67; J. Michael Geringer and Louis Hebert, "Control and Performance of International Joint Ventures," *Journal of International Business Studies,* 20, no. 2 (1989), pp. 235–54; and Colette A. Frayne and J. Michael Geringer, "Joint Venture General Managers: Key Issues in Research and Training," in *Research in Personnel and Human Resources Management,* ed. K. M. Rowland, B. Shaw, and P. Kirkbride (Greenwich, CT: JAI Press, 1993), supplement 3, pp. 301–21.

CHAPTER 14

1. International Trade Administration, http://trade.gov (accessed June 18, 2011).

2. The SBA has a handy book-length guide to the export process, "Breaking into the Trade Game: A Small Business Guide to Exporting," available at www.sba.gov/idc/groups/public/documents/sba_program_office/bitg3rd_full.pdf (July 17, 2008).

3. Adapted from *Small Business Success,* Vol. 1, Pacific Bell Directory, in cooperation with the U.S. Small Business Administration, 2006.

4. "Rules at the Core of World Trade," www.iccwbo.org/incoterms/id3045/index.html (July 16, 2008).

5. "A Basic Guide to Exporting," www.unzco.com/basicguide/c12.html (accessed June 16, 2011).

6. Export Import Bank, "Mission," www.exim.gov/about/mission.cfm (June 16, 2011).

7. A third support for exporters, the Foreign Sales Corporation (FSC), offered tax breaks for U.S.-owned foreign subsidiaries meeting specific criteria. This amounted to an export subsidy, claimed the EU. The claim was upheld by the WTO. Congress enacted legislation to end the FSC in May 2006.

8. Foreign-Trade Zone Corporation, "Foreign-Trade Zone Resource Center," www.foreign-trade-zone.com (June 16, 2011).

9. See http://alliancechb.com (July 15, 2008).

10. www.tradebeam.com/solutions/finance/export_letters_of_credit (accessed June 17,2011).

11. CE Directory, "What Does CE Mark Stand For," www.cedirectory.com/ce-mark.php (June 17, 2011).

12. The HTSA is available at www.usitc.gov/tata/hts/index.htm (July 18, 2008).

CHAPTER 15

1. T. C. Melewar and John Saunders, "International Corporate Visual Identity: Standardization or Localization?" *Journal of International Business Studies,* Third Quarter 1999, pp. 583–98; and Adesegun Oyedele, Osama J. Butt, and Michael S. Minor, "The Extent of Global Visual Identity as Expressed in Web Sites: An Empirical Assessment," working paper, 2011.

2. Douglas Daft, "Back to Classic Coke," *Financial Times,* March 27, 2000, p. 16.

3. "Nescafe Worldwide," www.nescafe.com/nescafe (accessed June 22, 2011).

4. "Accenture," *Wikipedia,* http://en.wikipedia.org/wiki/Accenture (accessed June 20, 2011).

5. "Sereno Spa, Goa," http://goa.park.hyatt.com/hyatt/pure/spas/ (accessed July 4, 2011); "Gorgeous Spas: Sereno Spa at Park Hyatt Goa, www.bing.com/travel/content/search?q=Gorgeous+Spas%3a+Sereno+Spa+at+Park+Hyatt+Goa&FORM=TRSSPG (accessed July 4, 2011).

6. Visa, "Visa Confirms Global FIFA Relationship," June 28, 2007, http://corporate.visa.com/media-center/press-releases/press336.jsp (accessed July 4, 2011); and Visa, *Annual Report 2010*, http://investor.visa.com/phoenix.zhtml?c=215693&p=proxy (accessed July 4, 2011).

7. "Call It Worldpool," *BusinessWeek,* November 29, 1994, pp. 98–99.

8. Peter Marsh, "The World's Wash Day," *Financial Times,* April 29, 2002, p. 6; "High Efficiency Front-Load Washers," www.whirlpool.com/Laundry-1/Laundry_Laundry_Washers-3/102110047+4294966820/ (accessed July 4, 2011); and "Whirlpool Corporation Announces Changes at Several Manufacturing Facilities in North America," October 3, 2006, http://investors.whirlpoolcorp.com/releasedetail.cfm?ReleaseID=532036 (accessed July 4, 2011).

9. "A Global Comeback," *Advertising Age,* August 20, 1987, p. 146.

10. Hilary Clarke, "Belgium's Strong Drinks," *International Management,* June 1992, p. 65, www.faqs.org/abstracts/Business-international/Buyers-market-Belgiums-strong-drinks.html (accessed July 4, 2011); and "Delirium Nocturnum," http://en.wikipedia.org/wiki/Delirium_Nocturnum (accessed July 4, 2011).

11. Jana Winter, "Navy Fights Mickey Mouse for SEALs Trademark," May 25, 2011, www.foxnews.com/politics/2011/05/25/navy-seals-fights-mickey-mouse-trademark/ (accessed July 4, 2011).

12. http://currents.net/newstoday/00/03/07/news4.html (accessed December 1, 2000); http://globalarchive.ft.com/globalarchive/article.html?id_001205001403 (accessed December 5, 2000); and Sam Holmes and Christopher Rhoads, "Web Addresses Enter New Era," http://online.wsj.com/article/SB10001424052702303936704576396963900727284.html, (accessed June 28, 2011).

13. C. K. Prahalad, *The Fortune at the Bottom of the Pyramid: Eradicating Poverty through Profits* (Upper Saddle River, NJ: Wharton School Publishing, 2005).

14. www.bloomberg.com/news/2011-04-02/gm-china-s-march-sales-growth-slows-for-second-month-on-end-of-incentives.html (accessed June 20, 2011).

15. Warren J. Keegan, "Multinational Product Planning Strategic Alternatives," *Journal of Marketing,* January 1969, pp. 56–62, combines these strategies to formulate five product and promotional strategies.

16. Geoffrey Fowler, "Intel's Game: Play It Local but Make It Global," *The Wall Street Journal,* September 30, 2005.

17. Lars Perner, "International Marketing," www.consumerpsychologist.com/international_marketing.html (accessed July 2, 2011).

18. "Shimmering Symbols of the Modern Age," *Financial Times,* October 17, 1997, p. 12.

19. "The Global Staying Power of Private Label," August 25, 2010, http://blog.nielsen.com/nielsenwire/consumer/the-global-staying-power-of-private-label/ (accessed July 4, 2011).

20. "About Axfood: Strategic Matters," www.axfood.se/en/About-Axfood/Private-labels (accessed July 26, 2011).

21. Yum Press Release, 2011, www.yum.com/company/china.asp (accessed July 4, 2011); and Peter Siris, "U.S. Consumer Brand Exports like McDonald's, KFC, Starbucks Are Big Hits in China," *The Daily News,* June 21, 2011, http://articles.nydailynews.com/2011-06-21/news/29704418_1_building-brands-volcom-major-brand (accessed July 4, 2011); and http://online.wsj.com/article/SB10001424052748703791904576075450692538030.html (accessed June 25, 2011).

22. Douglas McCray, "Japan's Gross National Cool," *Foreign Policy,* May–June 2002, pp. 44–54.

23. Referenced in Marieke de Mooij, Consumer Behavior and Culture: Consequences for Global Marketing and Advertising Los Angeles, (CA: Sage Publishing, 2011) p. 9.

24. "PepsiCo's New Campaign to Knock Rival Coca-Cola," *Financial Times,* January 19, 1995, p. 12.

25. Morris Kalliny, Grace Dagher, Michael S. Minor, and Gilberto de los Santos, "Television Advertising in the Arab World: A Status Report," *Journal of Advertising Research,* June 2008, pp. 215–223.

26. Gerrit Wiesmann, "Brands That Stop at the Border," *Financial Times,* October 6, 2006, p. 10, www.ft.com/cms/s/0/71f1d064-54d6-11db-901f-0000779e2340.html (accessed July 4, 2011).

27. Rachel Kaplan, "Ad Agencies Take On the World," *International Management,* 49, no. 3 (April 1994), pp. 50–52.

28. Eric Pfanner, "On Advertising: A Race to Connect in India," *International Herald Tribune,* November 27, 2005, www.nytimes.com/2005/11/27/business/worldbusiness/27iht-ad28.html (accessed July 1, 2011).

29. Stephen X. Doyle and George Thomas Roth, "Selling and Sales Management in Action: The Use of Insight and Coaching to Improve Relationship Selling," *Journal of Personal Selling & Sales Management,* Winter 1992, p. 62.

30. Melissa Campanelli, "Avon's Calling in China," *DM News,* March 10, 2006, www.dmnews.com/cms/dm-news/international/36010.html (accessed June 15, 2011).

31. "Our Social Lives and Personal Image the First to Suffer When the Going Gets Tough," ACNielsen, April 18, 2006, http://my.nielsen.com/news/20060418.shtml (accessed July 4, 2011).

32. "Ford Foundation International Fellowships Program," www.fordfound.org (accessed June 28, 2011).

33. "Agencies Responsible for Censorship in China," U.S. Congressional Executive Commission on China, www.cecc.gov/pages/virtualAcad/exp/expcensors.php (accessed July 4, 2011).

34. "McDonald's Wins Its Libel Case against Two Activists in the UK," *The Wall Street Journal,* June 20, 1997, p. B2; and www.mcspotlight.org/case/index.html (accessed June 23, 2011).

35. Lars Perner, "International Marketing," http://pptbusiness.net/international-marketing-lars-perner-instructor.html (accessed June 29, 2011).

36. "Coke Ends Year on the Better Side of Earnings," *Financial Times,* December 31, 2005, www.ft.com/cms/s/0/7d8bb15c-7894-11da-a356-0000779e2340.html (accessed July 4, 2011).

37. Alexandra Nusbaum and Naoko Nakamae, "Store Wars in Cyberspace," *Financial Times,* February 8, 2000, p. 18; and www.sonystyle.com (accessed June 22, 2011).

CHAPTER 16

1. Donald J. Bowersox, David J. Closs, and M. Bixby Cooper, *Supply Chain Logistics Management,* 2nd ed. (Burr Ridge, IL: McGraw-Hill Irwin, 2007), pp. 2–18.

2. Robert D'Avanzo, "The Reward of Supply-Chain Excellence," *Optimize,* December 2003, p. 68.

3. David Demers and Priya Sathyanarayanan, "Charting the Supply Chain DNA," *Supply Chain Management Review,* November–December 2003, pp. 48–58.

4. Joan Magretta, "The Power of Virtual Integration: An Interview with Dell Computer's Michael Dell," *Harvard Business Review,* March–April 1998, pp. 73–84.

5. Joan Magretta, "Fast, Global, and Entrepreneurial: Supply Chain Management, Hong Kong Style—An Interview with Victor Fung," *Harvard Business Review,* September–October 1998, pp. 3–14.

6. Geraldo Samor, "Ford Discovers Future Ideas in Brazilian Unit," *Pittsburgh Post-Gazette,* www.post-gazette.com/pg/06191/704782-185.stm (accessed June 21, 2011); and Raymond Colitt, "Brazil Engineers Turnaround for Ford," *Financial Times,* September 28, 2004, p. 20.

7. Elizabeth M. Gillespie, "Online Starbucks Suggestion Box Is a Hit," April 10, 2008, www.mailtribune.com/apps/pbcs.dll/article?AID=/20080410/BIZ/804100332 (accessed June 21, 2011).

8. William J. Zeile, "U.S. Affiliates of Foreign Companies: Operations in 2000," *Survey of Current Business,* August 2002, p. 161.

9. L. J. Krajewski and L. P. Ritzman, *Operations Management,* 5th ed. (Boston: Addison-Wesley, 1999), p. 456; J. Heizer and B. Render, *Principles*

of Operations Management, 4th ed. (Upper Saddle River, NJ: Prentice Hall, 2001), p. 436, table 11.2; and Bowersox, Closs, and Bixby Cooper, *Supply Chain Logistics Management,* p. 81.

10. Sam Fortescue, "Companies Warm to Doing Deals on e-Marketplaces," *Supply Management,* June 10, 2004, p. 10.

11. David Hannon, "Owens Corning Plans to Go 80% Paperless by End-2004," *Purchasing,* January 15, 2004, pp. 16–17.

12. Ronald C. Ritter and Robert A. Sternfels, "When Offshore Manufacturing Doesn't Make Sense," *The McKinsey Quarterly,* no. 4 (2004), www.mckinseyquarterly.com/article_print. aspx?L2=1&L3=106&ar=1510 (accessed June 21, 2011).

13. Richard B. Chase, F. Robert Jacobs, and Nicholas J. Aquilano, *Operations Management for Competitive Advantage,* 11th ed. (Burr Ridge, IL: McGraw-Hill Irwin, 2006), pp. 413–14.

14. International Organization for Standardization, "About ISO," www.iso.org/iso/about.htm (June 21, 2011).

15. J. Heizer and B. Render, *Principles of Operations Management,* 4th ed. (Upper Saddle River, NJ: Prentice Hall, 2001), p. 173.

16. Intel, "Copy Exactly, Factory Strategy," www.intel.com/pressroom/kits/manufacturing/copy_exactly_bkgrnd.htm (accessed June 21, 2011); and Intel, "Copy Exactly!," www.intel.com/design/quality/mq_ce.htm (June 21, 2011).

17. Conversation with SKF executive.

18. D. J. Teece, "Technology Transfer by Multinational Firms," reprinted in M. Casson, ed., *The International Library of Critical Writings in Economics I* (London, UK: Edward Elgar, 1990), pp. 185–204.

19. A highly automated machine may make only one or two sizes or types of a product, whereas a general-purpose machine may be capable of producing not only all sizes of a product but other products as well. Its output, however, may be as little as 1 percent of that of a specialized machine.

20. David Wessel, "China Rewrites Rules for Building Wealth," *The Wall Street Journal,* January 29, 2004, p. A2.

CHAPTER 17

1. U.S. Census Bureau, International Data Base, www.census.gov/ipc/www/idb/region.php (accessed May 29, 2011).

2. Ibid.

3. U.S. Census Bureau, International Programs, "Midyear Population, by Age and Sex," http://www.census.gov/population/international/data/idb/informationGateway.php (accessed July 15, 2011).

4. Ibid.

5. *Costs and Benefits of International Migration* (New York: Council on Foreign Relations, September 2005).

6. Eric Beauchesne, "Immigration Cuts Wages; StatsCan Study Finds 7% Slide at Top of Pay Scale," *National Post,* May 26, 2007, p. FP7.

7. *Costs and Benefits of International Migration.*

8. Aaron Terrazas and Jeanne Batalova, *Migration Information Source* (Washington, DC: Migration Policy Institute, 2009); www.migrationpolicy.org (accessed March 10, 2010).

9. OECD, "Migration and the Brain Drain Phenomenon," www.oecd.org/document/16/0,3343,en_2649_33935_39269032_1_1_1_1,00.html (accessed May 29, 2011).

10. "Africa Economy: EU Foreign Ministers Bid to Stop Africa's Brain-Drain," *EIU ViewsWire,* New York, March 30, 2006.

11. Alan M. Webber, "Reverse Brain Drain Threatens U.S. Economy," *USA Today,* February 23, 2004, www.usatoday.com/news/opinion/editorials/2004-02-23-economy-edit_x.htm (accessed May 29, 2011).

12. Vivek Wadhwa, "The Reverse Brain Drain," *BusinessWeek Online,* August 23, 2007, www.businessweek.com/smallbiz/content/aug2007/sb20070821_920025.htm (accessed May 29, 2011).

13. David A. Heenan and Howard V. Perlmutter, *Multinational Organization Development* (Boston: Addison-Wesley, 1979).

14. Consistency between mind-set and IHRM practices was reported in Linda K. Stroh and Paula M. Caligiuri, "Strategic Human Resources: A New Source for Competitive Advantage in the Global Arena," *International Journal of Human Resource Management* 9, no. 1 (1998), pp. 1–17.

15. David Pilling and Francesco Guerrera, "We Are a Mixture: Western Style in Management but with an Eastern Touch," *Financial Times,* September 26, 2003, p. 13.

16. Geoff Dyer, "A Spun-out Tale of Two Corporate Cultures," *Financial Times,* May 22, 2006, www.ft.com/cms/s/1/5db1846e-e9b0-11da-a33b-0000779e2340.html#axzz1Nmymfp00 (May 29, 2011).

17. *Up or Out: Next Moves for the Modern Expatriate* (London: The Economist Intelligence Unit, 2010), www.eiu.com/site_info.asp?info_name=uporout_expatriate&page=noads&rf=0 (May 30, 2011).

18. GMAC Global Relocation Services, *Global Relocation Trends 2007 Survey Report,* www.gmacglobalrelocation.com/2007survey (accessed July 10, 2008); and Mary G. Tye and Peter Y. Chen, "Selection of Expatriates: Decision-Making Models Used by HR Professionals," *Human Resource Planning* 28, no. 4 (2005), pp. 15–20.

19. "Expatriate Workforce Demographics," *HR Magazine* 51, no. 5 (May 2006), p. 16, http://findarticles.com/p/articles/mi_m3495/is_5_51/ai_n26865604/ (May 29, 2011).

20. GMAC Global Relocation Services, *Global Relocation Trends 2007 Survey Report.*

21. *Up or Out: Next Moves for the Modern Expatriate,* p. 7.

22. John C. Beck, "Globalization: Don't Go There . . .," www.accenture.com/Global/Research_and_Insights/ (accessed June 8, 2010).

23. Juan I. Sanchez, Paul E. Spector, and Cary L. Cooper, "Adapting to a Boundaryless World: A Developmental Expatriate Model," *Academy of Management Executive* 14, no. 2 (May 2000), pp. 96–106.

24. GMAC Global Relocation Services, *Global Relocation Trends 2007 Survey Report.*

25. Lalervo Oberg, "Culture Shock and the Problem of Adjustment to New Cultural Environments," www.worldwide.edu/travel_planner/culture_shock.html (accessed May 29, 2011).

26. *Up or Out: Next Moves for the Modern Expatriate,* p. 12.

27. Margaret A. Shaffer, David A. Harrison, and K. Matthew Gilley, "Dimensions, Determinants, and Differences in the Expatriate Adjustment Process," *Journal of International Business Studies* 30, no. 3 (1999), pp. 557–81.

28. Deirdre McCaughey and Nealia S. Bruning, "Enhancing Opportunities for Expatriate Job Satisfaction: HR Strategies for Foreign Assignment Success," *Human Resource Planning* 28, no. 4 (2005), pp. 21–29; and Jie Shen, "International Training and Management Development: Theory and Reality," *Journal of Management Development* 24, no. 7 (2005), pp. 656–666.

29. Shaffer, Harrison, and Gilley, "Dimensions, Determinants, and Differences in the Expatriate Adjustment Process."

30. Margaret A. Shaffer and David A. Harrison, "Forgotten Partners of International Assignments: Development and Test of a Model of Spouse Adjustment," *Journal of Applied Psychology* 86, no. 2 (2001), pp. 238–254.

31. Riki Takeuchi, Seokhwa Yun, and Paul E. Tesluk, "An Examination of Crossover and Spillover Effects of Spousal and Expatriate Cross-Cultural Adjustment on Expatriate Outcomes," *Journal of Applied Psychology* 87, no. 4 (August 2002), p. 655.

32. GMAC Global Relocation Services, *Global Relocation Trends 2007 Survey Report.*

33. GMAC Global Relocation Services, *Global Relocation Trends 2003/2004 Survey Report,* www.nftc.org/default/hr/GRTS_2003-4.pdf (accessed September 19, 2008); and GMAC Global Relocation Services, *Global Relocation Trends 2007 Survey Report.*

34. *Up or Out: Next Moves for the Modern Expatriate,* p. 14.

35. Michael Harvey, "Dual-Career Expatriates: Expectations, Adjustment and Satisfaction with International Relocation," *Journal of International Business Studies* 28, no. 3 (1997), pp. 627–58; and Perri Capell, "What 'Trailing Spouses' Can Do," *The Wall Street Journal,* May 2, 2006, p. B6.

36. Alison Langley, "Always Beginning Again: The Opportunity to Make a Home Abroad Can Sound Exciting but the Spouses of Overseas Workers Face Particular Challenges," *Financial Times,* November 4, 2006, p. 1.

37. Jeremy Smerd, "More Women, Young Workers on the Move," *Workforce Management,* August 2007, pp. 9–10, www.workforce.com/section/news/article/more-women-young-workers-move.php (May 29, 2011).

38. Expatica, "Helping Families Meet the Challenge of Moving Abroad," www.expatica.com/hr/story/helping-families-meet-the-challenge-of-moving-abroad-10453.html (accessed May 29, 2011); and Expatica, "How Children View Moving Abroad," www.expatica.com/hr/story/how-children-view-moving-abroad-10567.html (accessed May 29, 2011).

39. Joanne Wojcik and Sarah Veysey, "Expatriate Health Coverage Often Hard to Coordinate," *Crain Communications,* 2004, p. 10, www.highbeam.com/doc/1G1-112695014.html (May 29, 2011).

40. Annette Haddad and Scott Doggett, "Road Home Hard after Working Overseas," *Los Angeles Times,* March 13, 2000, p. C2, http://articles.latimes.com/2000/mar/13/business/fi-8316 (May 29, 2011); and Leslie Gross Klaff, "The Right Way to Bring Expats Home," *Workforce,* July 2002, pp. 40–44, http://findarticles.com/p/articles/mi_m0FXS/is_7_81/ai_89269493/ (May 29, 2011).

41. GMAC Global Relocation Services, *Global Relocation Trends 2003/2004 Survey Report;* and Kathryn Tyler, "Retaining Repatriates," *HR Magazine* 51, no. 3 (March 2006), pp. 97–102, www.shrmindia.org/article/hr-magazine-retaining-repatriates (May 29, 2011).

42. Tyler, "Retaining Repatriates."

43. "Worldwide Cost of Living Survey 2006—City Rankings," www.mercerhr.com/press release/details.jhtml/dynamic/idContent/1142150 (accessed July 23, 2006).

44. Tess Lyons, "Betting Big on 'Internationalising' Local Employees," *China Staff,* May 2005, pp. 12–14, http://findarticles.com/p/articles/mi_qa5478/is_200505/ai_n21373013/ (May 29, 2011); and *Up or Out: Next Moves for the Modern Expatriate,* p. 9.

45. *Up or Out: Next Moves for the Modern Expatriate,* p. 11.

46. Some writers regard paid home leave as an allowance, but our experience convinces us that it is a bonus, because ICs consistently give more frequent or longer home leaves to employees working in less desirable assignments.

47. *Up or Out: Next Moves for the Modern Expatriate,* p. 11.

48. Tom Herman, "Americans Working Overseas May See Big Jump in Tax Bill," *The Wall Street Journal,* May 20, 2006, p. B4, http://online.wsj.com/article/SB114808112290258454.html (May 29, 2011).

49. World Tourism Organization, "Average Number of Vacation Days around the World per Year," www.infoplease.com/ipa/A0922052.html (accessed May 29, 2011).

CHAPTER 18

1. John Daniels, Lee Radebaugh, and Daniel Sullivan, *International Business: Environments and Operations,* 11th ed. (Upper Saddle River, NJ: Pearson, 2007), p. 639.

2. Sidney J. Gray, "Towards a Theory of Cultural Influence on the Development of Accounting Systems Internationally," *Abacus* 24, no. 1 (1998), pp. 1–15.

3. John Elkington, *Cannibals with Forks: The Triple Bottom Line of 21st Century Business* (Gabriola Island, BC, Canada: New Society Publishers, 1997).

4. Wayne Norman and Chris MacDonald, "Getting to the Bottom of 'Triple Bottom Line,'" *Business Ethics Quarterly,* April 2004, www.businessethics.ca/3bl/triple_bottom_line_abstract.html (accessed July 17, 2011).

5. A good example of this is BP. For years they ran an advertising campaign based on their sensitivity to the environment. In fact, their observed behavior through crises in the first decade of the 21st century in Texas, Alaska, and the Gulf of Mexico shows different priorities: 1993–1995, Hazardous substance dumping in Alaska; 2006–2007, Prudhoe Bay Alaska pipeline corrosion; 2010, Texas City chemical leak (two weeks before oil spill); 2010 Gulf of Mexico Oil Spill (http://en.wikipedia.org/wiki/BP).

6. James Oberstar, House Transportation and Infrastructure Committee testimony before the U.S. Senate Committee on Commerce, Science and Transportation, May 9, 2006; U.S. Department of Treasury, Committee on Foreign Investment in the United States, www.treasury.gov/resource-center/international/Pages/Committee-on-Foreign-Investment-in-US.aspx (accessed April 19, 2011).

7. When equity securities (stock shares) are issued, part of the ownership is being sold. No money is being borrowed that must be repaid, as is the case when debt securities (bonds) are issued.

8. Daniel Mitchell, "Job Creation and the Taxation of Foreign Earned Income," *Executive Memorandum 911,* The Heritage Foundation, 2004.

9. David Kocieniewski, "G.E.'s Strategies Let It Avoid Taxes Altogether," *The New York Times,* March 24, 2011 (accessed April 20, 2011).

Glossary

A

absolute advantage Theory that a nation has absolute advantage when it can produce a larger amount of a good or service for the same amount of inputs as can another country or when it can produce the same amount of a good or service using fewer inputs than could another country

achievement vs. ascription What a person does vs. who a person is

ad valorem duty An import duty levied as a percentage of the invoice value of imported goods

advertising Paid, nonpersonal presentation of ideas, goods, or services by an identified sponsor

aesthetics A culture's sense of beauty and good taste

affiliates A term sometimes used interchangeably with subsidiaries, but more forms exist than just stock ownership

air waybill A bill of lading issued by an air carrier

allowances Employee compensation payments added to base salaries because of higher expenses encountered when living abroad

American depository receipts (ADRs) Foreign shares held by a custodian, usually a U.S. bank, in the issuer's home market and traded in dollars on the U.S. exchange

Andean Community (CAN) South American five-nation trading bloc

antitrust laws Laws to prevent price fixing, market sharing, and business monopolies

appropriate technology The technology (advanced, intermediate, or primitive) that most closely fits the society using it

arbitrage The process of buying and selling instantaneously to make profit with no risk

arbitration A process, agreed to by parties to a dispute in lieu of going to court, by which a neutral person or body makes a binding decision

ask price Lowest priced sell order that is currently in the market

Association of Southeast Asian Nations (ASEAN) Ten-member body formed to promote peace and cooperation in the Southeast Asian region

associations Social units based on age, gender, or common interest, not on kinship

automated export system (AES) U.S. Customs electronic filing system

B

backward vertical integration Arrangement in which facilities are established to manufacture inputs used in the production of a firm's final products

balance of payments (BOP) Record of a country's transactions with the rest of the world

banker's acceptance A time draft with maturity of less than 270 days that has been accepted by the bank on which the draft was drawn, thus becoming the accepting bank's obligation; may be bought and sold at a discount in the financial markets like other commercial paper

Bank for International Settlements (BIS) Institution for central bankers; operates as their bank

bank swap Swap made between banks to acquire temporary foreign currencies

barter A direct exchange of goods or services for goods or services without the use of money

benchmarking A technique for measuring a firm's performance against the performance of others that may be in the same or a completely different industry

bid price Highest priced buy order that is currently in the market

biomass A category of fuels whose energy source is photosynthesis, through which plants transform the sun's energy into chemical energy; sources include corn, sugarcane, wheat

blocked funds Funds whose conversion from a host currency or repatriation is not allowed by a host government

bonded warehouse An area authorized by customs authorities for storage of goods on which payment of import duties is deferred until the goods are removed

bonuses Expatriate employee compensation payments in addition to base salaries and allowances because of hardship, inconvenience, or danger

boomerang effect Situation in which technology sold to companies in another nation is used to produce goods to compete with those of the seller of the technology.

bottleneck Operation in a manufacturing system whose output sets the limit for the entire system's output

bottom-up planning Planning process that begins at the lowest level in the organization and continues upward

brain drain The loss by a country of its most intelligent and best-educated people

branch Legal extension of the parent company

Bretton Woods (System) The New Hampshire town where treasury and central bank representatives met near the end of World War II; established the IMF, the World Bank, and the gold exchange standard

bribes Gifts or payments to induce the receiver to do something illegal for the giver

budget An itemized projection of revenues and expenses for a future time period

C

caste system An aspect of Hinduism by which the entire society is divided into four groups (plus the outcasts) and each is assigned a certain class of work

CE (Conformité Européene) mark EU mark that indicates that the merchandise conforms to European health, safety, and environmental requirements

Central American Free Trade Agreement (CAFTA) FTA among the United States and several Central American nations

central reserve asset Asset, usually currency, held by a government's central bank

child labor The labor of children below 16 years of age who are forced to work in production and usually are given little or no formal education

clearing account arrangement A process to settle a trading account within a specified time

climate Meteorological conditions, including temperature, precipitation, and wind, that prevail in a region

cluster analysis Statistical technique that divides objects into groups so that the objects within each group are similar

collective bargaining The process in which a union represents the interests of a bargaining unit (which sometimes includes both union members and nonmembers) in negotiations with management

Collective Security Treaty Organization (CSTO) Security alliance of six members of the Commonwealth of Independent States (former Union of Soviet Socialist Republics)

common market Customs union that includes mobility of services, people, and capital within the union

communitarianism Belief that the group is the beneficiary of actions

comparative advantage Theory that a nation having absolute disadvantages in the production of two goods with respect to another nation has a comparative or relative advantage in the production of the good in which its absolute disadvantage is less

compensation Countertrade in which the developing country makes payment in products produced by use of developed country equipment

compensation packages For expatriate employees, packages that can incorporate many types of payments or reimbursements and must take into consideration exchange rates and inflation

competencies Skills or abilities required in order to adequately complete a task

competition laws The EU equivalent of antitrust laws

competition policy The European Union equivalent of antitrust laws

competitive advantage The ability of a company to have higher rates of profits than its competitors

competitive strategies Action plans to enable organizations to reach their objectives

competitor analysis Process in which principal competitors are identified and their objectives, strengths, weaknesses, and product lines are assessed

competitor intelligence system (CIS) Procedure for gathering, analyzing, and disseminating information about a firm's competitors

complete economic integration Integration on both economic and political levels

compound duty A combination of specific and ad valorem duties

concentrating solar thermal power (CSP) Uses mirrors or lenses to collect sunlight heats water running in tubes behind the collectors

confirmed L/C A confirmation made by a correspondent bank in the seller's country by which it agrees to honor the issuing bank's letter of credit

confiscation Government seizure of the property within its borders owned by foreigners without payment to them

Confucian dynamism Another term for long-term orientation

Confucian work ethic Drive toward hard work and thrift; similar to Protestant work ethic

consolidation The process of translating subsidiary results and aggregating them into one financial report

context The relevant environment

contingency plans Plans for the best- or worst-case scenarios or for critical events that could have a severe impact on the firm

contract manufacturing An arrangement in which one firm contracts with another to produce products to its specifications but assumes responsibility for marketing

controllable forces Internal forces that management administers to adapt to changes in the uncontrollable forces

cooperative exporters Established international manufacturers that export other manufacturers' goods as well as their own

copyright Exclusive legal rights of authors, composers, creators of software, playwrights, artists, and publishers to publish and dispose of their works

Council of the European Union Group that is the EU's primary policy-setting institution

counterpurchase Countertrade in which the goods supplied do not rely on the goods imported

countertrade The trade of goods or services for other goods or services

countervailing duties Additional import taxes levied on imports that have benefited from export subsidies

country risk assessment (CRA) An evaluation, conducted by a bank or business having an asset in or payable from a foreign country or considering a loan or an investment there, that assesses the country's economic situation and policies and its politics to determine how much risk exists of losing the asset or not being paid

country screening Using countries as the basis for market selection

cross investment Foreign direct investment by oligopolistic firms in each other's home countries as a defense measure

culture Sum total of beliefs, rules, techniques, institutions, and artifacts that characterize human populations

culture shock The anxiety people often experience when they move from a culture that they are familiar with to one that is entirely different

currency devaluation The lowering of a currency's price in terms of other currencies

currency option hedge An option to buy or sell a specific amount of foreign currency at a specific time in order to protect against foreign currency risk

currency swap An exchange of debt service of a loan or bond in one currency for the debt service of a loan or bond in another currency

current rate method An approach in foreign currency translation in which current assets and liabilities are valued at current spot rates and noncurrent assets and liabilities are translated at their historic exchange rates

customhouse brokers Independent businesses that handle import shipments for compensation

customs drawbacks Rebates on customs duties

customs union Collaboration that adds common external tariffs to an FTA

D

demonstration effect Result of having seen others with desirable goods

derivative A contract whose value is tied to the performance of a financial instrument or commodity

direct exporting The exporting of goods and services by the firm that produces them

direct investment Investments located in one country that are effectively controlled by residents of another country

discretionary income The amount of income left after paying taxes and making essential purchases

distributors Independent importers that buy for their own account for resale

Doha Development Agenda WTO extended conference on trade; also called *Doha Round*

domestic environment All the uncontrollable forces originating in the home country that surround and influence the firm's life and development

dumping Selling a product abroad for less than the cost of production, the price in the home market, or the price to third countries

dynamic capability Theory that for a firm to successfully invest overseas, it must have not only ownership of unique knowledge or resources but the ability to dynamically create and exploit these capabilities over time

E

eclectic theory of international development Theory that for a firm to invest overseas, it must have three kinds of advantages: ownership-specific, internalization, and location-specific

Economic and Social Council (ECOSOC) UN body concerned with economic and social issues such as trade, development, education, and human rights

economic exposure The potential for the value of future cash flows to be affected by unanticipated exchange rate movements

economic globalization The tendency toward an international integration of goods, technology, information, labor and capital, or the process of making this integration happen

Economies of scale Situation where the average cost of producing each unit of output decreases as a plant gets larger and output increases

efficient market approach Assumption that current market prices fully reflect all available relevant information

environment All the forces surrounding and influencing the life and development of the firm

environmental scanning A procedure in which a firm scans the world for changes in the environmental forces that might affect it

environmental sustainability Economic state in which the demands placed upon the environment by people and commerce can be met without reducing the capacity of the environment to provide for future generations

estimation by analogy Process of using a market factor that is successful in one market to estimate demand in a similar market

ethnocentric As used here, related to hiring and promoting employees on the basis of the parent company's home country frame of reference

ethnocentricity Belief in the superiority of one's own ethnic group (see the *self-reference criterion* in Chapter 1)

European Central Bank (ECB) Institution that sets and implements EU monetary policy

European Commission Institution that runs the EU's day-to-day operations

European Court of Justice (ECJ) Court that rules on issues related to EU policies

European Free Trade Agreement (EFTA) Four-nation non-EU FTA in Europe

European Monetary Union (EMU) Group that established use of euro (€) in the 12-country eurozone

European Parliament EU legislative body whose members are popularly elected from member-nations

European Union (EU) A body of 25 European countries dedicated to economic and political integration

exchange rate The price of one currency stated in terms of another currency

Ex-Im Bank Principal government agency that aids American exporters by means of loans, guarantees, and insurance programs

expatriate A person living outside his or her country of citizenship

experience curve Reduction of unit costs of production as accumulated volume increases, due to improved efficiency resulting from increased cumulative experience and learning

explicit knowledge Knowledge that is easy to communicate to others via words, pictures, formulae, or other means

export bill of lading (B/L) Contract of carriage between shipper and carrier: straight bill of lading is nonnegotiable; endorsed "to order" bill gives the holder claim on merchandise

export draft An unconditional order drawn by the seller that instructs the buyer to pay the draft's amount on presentation (sight draft) or at an agreed future date (time draft) and that must be paid before the buyer receives shipping documents

exporting The transportation of any domestic good or service to a destination outside a country or region; the opposite of importing, which is the transportation of any good or service into a country or region, from a foreign origination point

export processing zone A government-designated zone in which workers are permitted to import parts and materials without paying import duties, as long as these imported items are then exported once they have been processed or assembled

export trading company (ETC) A firm established principally to export domestic goods and services and to help unrelated companies export their products

expropriation Government seizure of the property within its borders owned by foreigners, followed by prompt, adequate, and effective compensation paid to the former owners

extended family Family that includes blood relatives and relatives by marriage

extortion Demand for payment to keep the receiver from causing harm to the payer

extraterritorial application of laws A country's attempt to apply its laws to foreigners or nonresidents and to acts and activities that take place outside its borders

Ex-Works INCOTERM equivalent of FOB

F

factor conditions Attributes that a country inherits, such as climate and natural resources, and those a country can mold, such as the labor force and infrastructure

factor endowment Heckscher-Ohlin theory that countries export products requiring large amounts of their abundant production factors and import products requiring large amounts of their scarce production factors

factoring Discounting without recourse an account receivable

fiscal policy Policy that addresses the collecting and spending of money by the government

Fisher effect The relationship between real and nominal interest rates; the real interest rate will be the nominal interest rate minus the expected rate of inflation

fixed currency exchange rates Rates that governments agree on and undertake to maintain

floating currency exchange rates Rates that are allowed to float against other currencies and are determined by market forces

FOB (free on board) Pricing policy in which risks pass from seller to buyer at the factory door; U.S. equivalent of Ex-Works

Foreign Corrupt Practices Act (FCPA) U.S. law against making payments to foreign government officials for special treatment

foreign direct investment (FDI) Direct investments in equipment, structures, and organizations in a foreign country at a level that is sufficient to obtain significant management control; does not include mere foreign investment in stock markets

foreign environment All the uncontrollable forces originating outside the home country that surround and influence the firm

foreign national pricing Local pricing in another country

foreign sourcing The overseas procurement of raw materials, components, and products

foreign tax credits Allowances by which U.S. taxpayers who reside and pay income taxes in another country can credit those taxes against U.S. income tax

foreign trade zone (FTZ) Duty-free area designed to facilitate trade by reducing the effect of customs restrictions

forfaiting Purchasing without recourse an account receivable whose credit terms are longer than the 90 to 180 days usual in factoring; unlike factoring, political and transfer risks are borne by the forfaiter

formal institutions Institutions that influence behavior through laws and regulations

forward currency market Trading market for currency contracts deliverable 30, 60, 90, or 180 days in the future

forward market hedge Foreign currency contract sold or bought forward in order to protect against foreign currency movement

forward rate The exchange rate between two currencies for delivery in the future, usually 30, 60, 90, or 180 days

franchising A form of licensing in which one firm contracts with another to operate a certain type of business under an established name according to specific rules

free trade area (FTA Area in which tariffs among members have been eliminated, but members keep their external tariffs

free trade zone An area designated by the government as outside its customs territory

fronting loan A loan made through an intermediary, usually a bank, from parent company to subsidiary

functional currency The primary currency of a business

fundamental approach Exchange rate prediction based on econometric models that attempt to capture the variables and their correct relationships

G

General Agreement on Tariffs and Trade (GATT) International agreement that functioned to encourage trade liberalization from 1947 to 1995

General Assembly Deliberative body of the UN made up of all member-nations, each with one vote regardless of size, wealth, or power

general export license Any export license covering export commodities for which a validated license is not required; no formal application is required

geocentric As used here, related to hiring and promoting employees on the basis of ability and experience without considering race or citizenship

geothermal power Power derived from heat stored in the earth

global company (GC) An organization that attempts to standardize and integrate operations worldwide in all functional areas

global mindset A mindset that combines an openness to and an awareness of diversity across markets and cultures with a propensity and ability to synthesize across this diversity

Global team A team characterized by a high level of diversity, geographic dispersion, and virtual rather than face-to-face interaction

gold standard The use of gold at an established number of units per currency

gross national income (GNI) The total value of all income generated by a nation's residents from international and domestic activity

Group of Eight (G8) Group of government leaders from industrialized nations that meets regularly to discuss issues of concern

guest workers People who go to a foreign country legally to perform certain types of jobs

H

Harmonized Tariff Schedule of the United States (HTSA) American version of the Harmonized System used worldwide to classify imported products

heavy oil Oil that does not flow easily

hedging A process to reduce or eliminate financial risk

home-country national Same as parent-country national

horizontal corporation A form of organization characterized by lateral decision processes, horizontal networks, and a strong corporatewide business philosophy

host-country national (HCN) Employee who is a citizen of the nation in which the subsidiary is operating, which is different from the parent company's home nation

human-needs approach View that defines economic development as a reduction of poverty and unemployment as well as an increase in income

hybrid organization Structure organized by more than one dimension at the top level

hydropower Power derived from the force of moving water

I

import substitution The local production of goods to replace imports

in-bond plants (maquiladoras) Production facilities in Mexico that temporarily import raw materials, components, or parts duty-free to be manufactured, processed, or assembled with less expensive local labor, after which the finished or semifinished product is exported

income distribution A measure of how a nation's income is apportioned among its people, commonly reported as the percentage of income received by population quintiles

income tax Direct tax levied on earnings

INCOTERMS Universal trade terminology developed by the International Chamber of Commerce

indirect exporting The exporting of goods and services through various types of home-based exporters

industrial cooperation An exporter's commitment to a longer-term relationship than that in a simple export sale, in which some of the production occurs in the receiving country

industrial espionage Act of spying on a competitor to learn secrets about its strategy and operations

informal institutions Institutions that influence behavior through customs and ideologies

inland waterways Waterways that provide access to interior regions

instability Characteristic of a government that cannot maintain itself in power or that makes sudden, unpredictable, or radical policy changes

intellectual property Patents, trademarks, trade names, copyrights, and trade secrets, all of which result from the exercise of someone's intellect

interest rate swap An exchange of interest rate flows in order to manage interest rate exposure

intermediate technology Production methods between capital- and labor-intensive methods

internalization theory An extension of the market imperfection theory: the concept that to obtain a higher return on its investment, a firm will transfer its superior knowledge to a foreign subsidiary rather than sell it in the open market

international company (IC) Either a global or a multidomestic company

International Court of Justice (ICJ) UN body that renders legal decisions involving disputes between national governments

international division A division in the organization that is at the same level as the domestic division and is responsible for all non-home country activities

international environment Interaction between domestic and foreign environmental forces or between sets of foreign environmental forces

international Fisher effect Concept that the interest rate differentials for any two currencies will reflect the expected change in their exchange rates

International Monetary Fund (IMF) Institution that coordinates multilateral monetary rules and their enforcement

international pricing Setting prices of goods for export for both unrelated and related firms

international product life cycle (IPLC) A theory explaining why a product that begins as a nation's export eventually becomes its import

international status Entitles the expatriate employee to all the allowances and bonuses applicable to the place of residence and employment

international strategy The way firms make choices about acquiring and using scarce resources in order to achieve their international objectives

intervention currency A currency used by a country to intervene in the foreign currency exchange markets, often to buy (strengthen) its own currency

irrevocable L/C A stipulation that a letter of credit cannot be canceled

iterative planning Repetition of the bottom-up or top-down planning process until all differences are reconciled

J

Jamaica Agreement The 1976 IMF agreement that allows flexible exchange rates among members

joint venture A cooperative effort among two or more organizations that share a common interest in a business enterprise or undertaking

just-in-time (JIT) A balanced system in which there is little or no delay time and idle in-process and finished goods inventory

K

knowledge management The practices that organizations and their managers use for the identification, creation, acquisition, development, dispersion, and exploitation of competitively valuable knowledge

Kyoto Protocol United Nations Framework Convention on Climate Change, which calls for nations to reduce global warming by reducing their emissions of the gasses that contribute to it

L

labor market The pool of available potential employees with the necessary skills within commuting distance from an employer

labor mobility The movement of people from country to country or area to area to get jobs

labor quality The skills, education, and attitudes of available employees

labor quantity The number of available employees with the skills required to meet an employer's business needs

labor unions Organizations of workers

language trap A situation in which a person doing international business can speak only his or her home language

law of one price Concept that in an efficient market, like products will have like prices

leadership The behaviors and processes involved with organizing a group of people in order to achieve a common purpose or goal

leading and lagging Timing payments early (lead) or late (lag), depending on anticipated currency movements, so that they have the most favorable impact for company

letter of credit (L/C) Document issued by the buyer's bank in which the bank promises to pay the seller a specified amount under specified conditions

licensing A contractual arrangement in which one firm grants access to its patents, trade secrets, or technology to another for a fee

lingua franca A foreign language used to communicate among a nation's diverse cultures that have diverse languages

M

management contract An arrangement by which one firm provides management in all or specific areas to another firm

manufacturers' agents Independent sales representatives of various noncompeting suppliers

manufacturing rationalization Division of production among a number of production units, thus enabling each to produce only a limited number of components for all of a firm's assembly plants

market factors Economic data that correlate highly with market demand for a product

market indicators Economic data used to measure relative market strengths of countries or geographic areas

market screening A version of environmental scanning in which the firm identifies desirable markets by using the environmental forces to eliminate the less desirable markets

mass customization The use of flexible, usually computer-aided, manufacturing systems to produce and deliver customized products and services for different customers worldwide

material culture All human-made objects; concerned with *how* people make things (technology) and *who* makes *what* and *why* (economics)

matrix organization An organizational structure composed of one or more superimposed organizational structures in an attempt to mesh product, regional, functional, and other expertise

matrix overlay An organization in which top-level divisions are required to heed input from a staff composed of experts of another organizational dimension in an attempt to avoid the double-reporting difficulty of a matrix organization but still mesh two or more dimensions

mercantilism An economic philosophy based on the belief that (1) a nation's wealth depends on accumulated treasure, usually gold, and (2) to increase wealth, government policies should promote exports and discourage imports

Mercosur (Mercosul) Economic free trade area in South America modeled on the EU

minorities A relatively smaller number of people identified by race, religion, or national origin who live among a larger majority

mission statement A broad statement that defines the organization's purpose and scope

monetary policy Government policy that controls the amount of money in circulation and its growth rate

money market hedge A method to hedge foreign currency exposure by borrowing and lending in the domestic and foreign money markets

monochronic Having to do with linear time, sequential activities

monopolistic advantage theory Theory that foreign direct investment is made by firms in oligopolistic industries possessing technical and other advantages over indigenous firms

most-favored nation (MFN) clause Agreement that GATT member-nations would treat all members equally in trade matters

multidomestic company (MDC) An organization with multicountry affiliates, each of which formulates its own business strategy based on perceived market differences

multilateral netting Strategy in which subsidiaries transfer net intracompany cash flows through a centralized clearing center

N

national competitiveness A nation's relative ability to design, produce, distribute, or service products within an international trading context while earning increasing returns on its resources

natural resources Anything supplied by nature on which people depend

neutral vs. affective Withholding emotion vs. expressing emotion

new institutional theory Understanding of institutions that sees them as social constructs, a collection of norms that structure the relations of individuals to one another

newly industrialized economies (NIEs) The fast-growing upper-middle-income and high-income economies of South Korea, Taiwan, Hong Kong, and Singapore

newly industrializing countries (NICs) The four Asian tigers and the middle-income economies such as Brazil, Mexico, Malaysia, Chile, and Thailand

nonrenewable energy sources The principal nonrenewable energy sources are the fossil fuels—petroleum, coal, and natural gas—and nuclear power

nonrevenue tax purposes Purposes such as redistributing income, discouraging consumption of products such as tobacco and alcohol, and encouraging purchase of domestic rather than imported products

nontariff barriers (NTBs) All forms of discrimination against imports other than import duties

North American Free Trade Agreement (NAFTA) Agreement creating a free trade area among Canada, Mexico, and the United States

North American Treaty Organization (NATO) Security alliance of 26 North American and European nations

O

ocean energy Power derivved from the ocean, either as a result of the sun's heat on the ocean or the mechanical energy of the tides and waves

offset Trade arrangement that requires that a portion of the inputs be supplied by the receiving country

offshore financial center Location that specializes in financing nonresidents, with low taxes and few banking regulations

offshoring Relocating some or all of a business's activities or processes to a foreign location

orderly marketing arrangements Formal agreements between exporting and importing countries that stipulate the import or export quotas each nation will have for a good

Organisation for Economic Cooperation and Development (OECD) Group of developed countries dedicated to promoting economic expansion in its member-nations

Organization of Petroleum Exporting Countries (OPEC) Cartel of 11 petroleum-exporting countries

organizational design A process that deals with how an international business should be organized in order to ensure that its worldwide business activities are able to be integrated in an efficient and effective manner

organizational structure The way that an organization formally arranges its domestic and international units and activities, and the relationships among these various organizational components

outsourcing Hiring others to perform some of the noncore activities and decision making in a company's value chain, rather than having the company and its employees continue to perform those activities

overlapping demand Theory that trade in manufactured goods will be greater between nations with similar levels of per capita income and that the goods traded will be those for which consumers in both countries demand the same good

Overseas Private Investment Corporation (OPIC) Government corporation that offers American investors in developing countries insurance against expropriation, currency inconvertibility, and damages from wars and revolutions

P

parallel loans Matched loans across currencies that are made to cover risk

parent-country national (PCNs) Employee who is a citizen of the nation in which the parent company is headquartered; also called home country national

par value Stated value

particularist Condition in which context determines what concepts apply

passive processing The finishing or refining in Eastern European countries of semifinished goods from the West, which are then returned to the West after finishing; similar to Mexican maquiladora operations

patent A government grant giving the inventor of a product or process the exclusive right to manufacture, exploit, use, and sell that invention or process

policies Broad guidelines intended to assist lower level personnel in handling recurring issues or problems

polycentric As used here, related to hiring and promoting employees on the basis of the specific local context in which the subsidiary operates

polychronic Having to do with simultaneous activities; multi-tasking

pooling alliance An alliance driven by similarity and integration among partners

population density A measure of the number of inhabitants per area unit (inhabitants per square kilometer or square mile)

population distribution A measure of how the inhabitants are distributed over a nation's area

portfolio investment The purchase of stocks and bonds to obtain a return on the funds invested

preferential trading arrangement An agreement by a small group of nations to establish free trade among themselves while maintaining trade restrictions with all other nations

preventive (planned) maintenance Maintenance done according to plan, not when machines break down

private international law Laws governing transactions of individuals and companies that cross international borders

privatization The transfer of public sector assets to the private sector, the transfer of management of state activities through contracts and leases, and the contracting out of activities previously conducted by the state

procedures Specified ways of performing a particular task or activity

product differentiation The development of products that have unique differences, with the intent of positively influencing demand

product liability Standard that holds a company and its officers and directors liable and possibly subject to fines or imprisonment when their product causes death, injury, or damage

pro forma invoice Exporter's formal quotation containing a description of the merchandise, price, delivery time, method of shipping, terms of sale, and points of exit and entry

programmed-management approach A middle-ground advertising strategy between globally standardized and entirely local programs

promotion Any form of communication between a firm and its publics

promotional mix A blend of the promotional methods a firm uses to sell its products

public international law Legal relations between governments

public relations Various methods of communicating with the firm's publics to secure a favorable impression

purchasing power parity (PPP) The number of units of a currency required to buy the same amounts of goods and services in the domestic market that one dollar would buy in the United States; the theory that predicts that currency exchange rates between two countries should equal the ratio of the price levels of their commodity baskets

Q

questionable or dubious payments Bribes paid to government officials by companies seeking purchase contracts from those governments

quotas Numerical limits placed on specific classes of imports

R

random walk hypothesis Assumption that the unpredictability of factors suggests that the best predictor of tomorrow's prices is today's prices

rare earths A group of 17 elements used in technological applications

reciprocal currency/direct quote In FX, using the dollar as the base currency, a currency that is quoted as dollars per unit of currency instead of in units of currency per dollar; also known as *direct quote*

reengineering Redesigning organizational structure, hierarchy, business systems and processes in order to improve organizational efficiency

regiocentric As used here, related to hiring and promoting employees on the basis of the specific regional context in which the subsidiary operates

reserve currency Currency held by national governments to use in case of financial need; *see also* central reserve currency

resource endowment Theory that countries export products requiring large amounts of their abundant production factors and import products requiring large amounts of their scarce production factors

reverse brain drain The return home of highly skilled immigrants who have made a contribution in their adopted country

Rhine waterway A system of rivers and canals that is the main transportation artery of Europe

rural-to-urban shift The movement of a nation's population from rural areas to cities

S

sales company A business established for the purpose of marketing goods and services, not producing them

sales forecast A prediction of future sales performance

sales promotion Any of various selling aids, including displays, premiums, contests, and gifts

scenarios Multiple, plausible stories about the future

Secretariat The staff of the UN, headed by the secretary-general

Security Council Main policy-setting body of the UN, composed of 15 members including 5 permanent members

segment screening Using market segments as the basis for market selection

self-reference criterion Unconscious reference to one's own cultural values when judging behaviors of others in a new and different environment

shale A fissile rock (capable of being split) composed of laminated layers of claylike, fine-grained sediment

shipper's export declaration (SED) U.S. Department of Commerce form used to control export shipments and record export statistics

Six Sigma Business management process for reducing defects and eliminating variation

social desirability bias The custom of politeness toward everyone that can cause respondents to give answers calculated to please the interview rather than reflecting the respondent's true beliefs or feelings

social loafing Tendency of some people to put forth less effort when they are members of a group

sociocultural Description of the social world through which we observe the effects of culture

sogo shosha The largest of the Japanese general trading companies

solar photovoltaic power (PV) Type of power based on the voltage created when certain materials are exposed to light

special drawing right (SDR) An international reserve asset established by the IMF; the unit of account for the IMF and other international organizations

specific duty A fixed sum levied on a physical unit of an imported good

specific vs. diffuse Life divided into public and private vs. life undifferentiated

spot and forward market swaps Use of the spot and forward markets to hedge foreign currency exposure

spot rate The exchange rate between two currencies for delivery within two business days

stability Characteristic of a government that maintains itself in power and whose fiscal, monetary, and political policies are predictable and not subject to sudden, radical changes

stakeholder theory An understanding of how business operates that takes into account all identifiable interest holders

standards Documented agreements containing technical specifications or other precise criteria that will be used consistently as guidelines, rules, or definitions of the characteristics of a product, process, or service

strategic alliances Partnerships between competitors, customers, or suppliers that may take one or more of various forms

strategic business unit (SBU) Business entity with a clearly defined market, specific competitors, the ability to carry out its business mission, and a size appropriate for control by a single manager

strategic planning the process by which an organization determines where it is going in the future, how it will get there, and how it will assess whether and to what extent it has achieved its goals

strict liability Standard that holds the designer/manufacturer liable for damages caused by a product without the need for a plaintiff to prove negligence in the product's design or manufacture

subsidiaries Companies controlled by other companies through ownership of enough voting stock to elect board-of-directors majorities

subsidiary Separate legal entity owned by the parent company

subsidiary detriment Situation in which a small loss for a subsidiary results in a greater gain for the total IC

subsidies Financial contributions, provided directly or indirectly by a government, which confer a benefit; include grants, preferential tax treatment, and government assumption of normal business expenses

supply chain management The process of coordinating and integrating the flow of materials, information, finances, and services within and among companies in the value chain from suppliers to the ultimate consumer

swap contract A spot sale/purchase of an asset against a future purchase/sale of an equal amount in order to hedge a financial position

synchronous manufacturing An entire manufacturing system with unbalanced operations that emphasizes total system performance

T

tacit knowledge Knowledge that an individual has but that is difficult to express clearly in words, pictures, or formulae, and therefore difficult to transmit to others

tariffs Taxes on imported goods for the purpose of raising their price to reduce competition for local producers or stimulate local production

tax treaties Treaties between countries that bind the governments to share information about taxpayers and cooperate in tax law enforcement; often called tax conventions

Taylor's scientific management system System based on scientific measurements that prescribes a division of work whereby planning is done by managers and plan execution is left to supervisors and workers

Team norms Legitimate, shared standards against which the appropriateness of behavior can be evaluated

technical analysis An approach that analyzes data for trends and then projects these trends forward

technological dualism The side-by-side presence of technologically advanced and technologically primitive production systems

temporal method An approach in foreign currency translation in which monetary accounts are valued at the spot rate and accounts carried at historical cost are translated at their historic exchange rates

terms of sale Conditions of a sale that stipulate the point at which all costs and risks are borne by the buyer

terrorism Unlawful acts of violence committed for a wide variety of reasons, including for ransom, to overthrow a government, to gain release of imprisoned colleagues, to exact revenge for real or imagined wrongs, and to punish nonbelievers of the terrorists' religion

third-country national (TCN) Employee who is a citizen of neither the parent company nation nor the host country

top-down planning Planning process that begins at the highest level in the organization and continues downward

topography The surface features of a region

torts Injuries inflicted on other people, either intentionally or negligently

total product What the customer buys, including the physical product, brand name, accessories, after-sales service, warranty, instructions for use, company image, and package

total quality management (TQM) System in which the entire organization is managed so that it excels on all dimensions of product and services that are important to the customer

trade fair A large exhibition, generally held at the same place and same time periodically, at which companies maintain booths to promote the sale of their products

trade mission A group of businesspeople and/or government officials (state or federal) that visits a market in search of business opportunities

trade name A name used by merchants or manufacturers to designate and differentiate their products

trade-related intellectual property rights (TRIPS) The acronym TRIPS refers to the WTO agreement that protects copyrights, trademarks, trade secrets, and other intellectual property matters

trade secret Any information that a business wishes to hold confidential

trademark A shape, a color, design, catchy phrase, abbreviation, or sound used by merchants or manufacturers to designate and differentiate their products

trading alliance An alliance driven by the logic of partners contributing dissimilar resources

trading companies Firms that develop international trade and serve as intermediaries between foreign buyers and domestic sellers and vice versa

transaction exposure Change in the value of a financial position created by foreign currency changes between the establishment and the settlement of a contract

transfer price Intracorporate price, or the price of a good or service sold by one affiliate to another, the home office to an affiliate, or vice versa

translation exposure Potential change in the value of a company's financial position due to exposure created during the consolidation process

treaties Agreements between countries, which may be bilateral (between two countries) or multilateral (involving more than two countries); also called conventions, covenants, compacts, or protocols

trend analysis Statistical technique by which successive observations of a variable at regular time intervals are analyzed to establish regular patterns that are used for establishing future values

Triffin paradox The concept that a national currency that is also a reserve currency will eventually run a deficit, which eventually inspires a lack of confidence in the reserve currency and leads to a financial crisis

triple-bottom-line (3BL) accounting An approach to accounting that measures the firm's social and environmental performance in addition to its economic performance

U

uncontrollable forces External forces over which management has no direct control, although it can exert an influence

underground economy The part of a nation's income that, because of unreporting or underreporting, is not measured by official statistics

United Nations (UN) International organization of 191 member-nations dedicated to the promotion of peace and global stability; has many functions related to business

unit labor costs Total direct labor costs divided by units produced

universalist Condition in which concepts apply to all

unspoken language Nonverbal communication, such as gestures and body language

Uruguay Round The last extended conference of GATT negotiations

V

validated export license A required document issued by the U.S. government authorizing the export of a strategic commodity or a shipment to an unfriendly country

value-added tax (VAT) Indirect tax collected from the parties as they add value to the product

value chain analysis An assessment conducted on the chain of interlinked activities of an organization or set of interconnected organizations, intended to determine where and to what extent value is added to the final product or service

values statement A clear and concise description of the fundamental values, beliefs, and priorities of the organization's members

variable levy An import duty set at the difference between world market prices and local government-supported prices

vehicle currency A currency used as a vehicle for international trade or investment

vertically integrated Descriptive term for a firm that produces inputs for its subsequent manufacturing processes

virtual corporation An organization that coordinates economic activity to deliver value to customers using resources outside the traditional boundaries of the organization

vision statement A description of the company's desired future position if it can acquire the necessary competencies and successfully implement its strategy

voluntary export restraints (VERs) Export quotas imposed by the exporting nation

W

wind power Power derived from the wind, as with a windmill

withholding tax Indirect tax paid by the payor, usually on passive income

World Bank Institution that focuses on funding of development projects

World Trade Organization (WTO) A multinational body of 149 members that deals with rules of trade between nations

Photo Credits

Πσγοσμιο Business Los negocios internacionales Παγοσμιο
Gli Affari Internazionali
Negócios Internacionais Internationales Geschäft 國際商務

Page Number	Credit
4	© Michael S. Yamashita/Corbis.
7	© AFP/Getty Images.
8	© Mark Elias/Bloomberg via Getty Images.
17	© Daniel Sheehan/Liaison Agency/Newsmakers/Getty Images.
24	Photo courtesy of Ryan Hultzman.
30	© Royalty-Free/Getty Images.
43	© DAJ/Getty Images/DAL.
52	© Andrzej Gorzkowski/Alamy/DAL.
55	© PhotoLink/Getty Images/DAL.
56	Photo courtesy of Kerry Thwing.
62	© AP Photo/Osamu Honda.
70	© AP Photo/Mikhail Metzel.
75	© AP Photo/Khalfan Said.
82	Photo courtesy of Katie Emick.
85	© Ingram Publishing/SuperStock/DAL.
92	© Punchstock/Digital Vision/DAL.
106	© Hilary Duffy/Corbis.
107	© Medio Images/Corbis/DAL.
113	Photo courtesy of Mallory Wedeking.
118	© Royalty-Free/Corbis/DAL.
123	© Royalty-Free/Corbis/DAL.
124	© Royalty-Free/Corbis/DAL.
129	© 1997 IMS Communications Ltd/Capstone Design. All rights reserved./DAL.
135	© Getty Images/DAL.
146 top	© Getty Images/Steve Allen/DAL.
146 bottom	© Reuters/Corbis.
150	Interface, Inc.
151 top	© Peter Hvizdak/The Image Works.
151 bottom	Photo courtesy of Jeremy Capdevielle.
156	© AP Photo/Visar Kryeziu.
160	© 2008 Linden Research, Inc.
168	© Getty Images/DAL.
169	© AP Photo/Kent Gilbert.
174	Photo courtesy of Fernando Villanueva.
180	© AP Photo/George Osodi.
186	© Wolfgang Kaehler/Corbis.
188	© 2008 Linden Research, Inc.
192	© Scott Ferrell/Congressional Quarterly/Getty Images.
198	Photo courtesy of Rory Burdick.
202	© Ryan McVay/Getty Images/DAL.
205	© Photographer's Choice/Getty Images/DAL
216	© Mike Clarke/AFP/Getty Images.
219	Photo courtesy of Andrew Crane.
228	© Royalty-Free/Corbis/DAL.
237	© Bobby Yip/Reuters/Landov.
240	© Comstock Images/Jupiterimages/DAL.
242	© AP Photo/Eric Gay.

248	Photo courtesy of Eduardo Rangel.
254	© Tim Boyle/Getty Images.
264	© India Today Group/Getty Images.
266	© M. Scott Brauer/Onasia.com
272	Photo courtesy of Isaac Rush.
278	© Roberto Schmidt/AFP/Getty Images.
280 left	© AP Photo/Kaji Sasahara.
280 center	© AP Photo/John Amis.
280 right	© AP Photo/Pepsico Inc.
287	© AP Photo/Mohammed Zaatari.
293	Photo courtesy of Chad Henry.
300	© Weng lei - Imaginechina via AP Images.
301	© Marcus Brindicci/Reuters/Corbis.
303	© Cali/Iconotec.com/DAL.
306	© Fabrice Dimier/Bloomberg via Getty Images.
308	© Getty Images.
309	© Mark Bassett/Alamy.
311	© Sean Gallup/Getty Images.
312	© Liu mingxiang - Imaginechina via AP Images.
315	Photo courtesy of Ronny Cheng-Ruggeberg.
320	© James Hardy/PaloAlto/DAL.
322	© Roberts Publishing Services. All rights reserved.
328	© Hoang Dinh Nam/AFP/Getty Images.
329	© Brendan Smialowski/AFP/Getty Images.
335	© Zhan yanlin - Imaginechina via AP Images.
336	Photo courtesy of Mark Haupt.
340	© Hafen Hamburg/VISUM/The Image Works.
358	© Andrew Harrer/Bloomberg via Getty Images.
359	Photo courtesy of Vadim Rozhkov.
366	© Erica Simone Leeds 2007/DAL.
369	© Red fx/Alamy/DAL.
373	© The McGraw-Hill Companies, Inc./Erica Simone Leeds, photographer/DAL.
375	Photo courtesy of Victoria Ball.
377	© Blend Images/Getty Images/DAL.
378	© Kraft Foods Inc. (Brazil).
382	© Catherine Karnow/Woodfin Camp.
383	© AP Photo/Evan Agostini.
392	Photo courtesy of Nicole Kisum.
396	© Aliki Sapountiz image library/Alamy.
398	Photo courtesy of Inditex.
406	Courtesy of Exostar LLC. Used by permission.
408	© G. Krishnaswamy/The India Today Group/Getty Images.
410 top	© 1998 Eyewire, Inc./DAL.
410 bottom	© The McGraw-Hill Companies, Inc./Jill Braaten, photographer/DAL.
412	Photo courtesy of Intel Corporation.
415	© AFP/Douglas E. Curran/Getty Images.
418	Photo courtesy of Jamie Cignetti.
424	© Stockbyte/Getty Images/DAL.
437	© Digital Vision/Getty Images/DAL.
438	© Yellow Dog Productions/Getty Images/DAL.
448	Photo courtesy of Laura Gunderson.
454	© Bohemian Nomad Picturemakers/Corbis.
464	© Robert Llewellyn/Getty Images.
467	© Stockbyte/Punchstock Images/DAL.
468	© John Rae for ACCION International.
472	Photo courtesy of Bryan Goldfinger.

Company/Name Index

Capital account, 222
Capital account surplus, 222
Capital-intensive processes, 414, 415–416
Capital mobility, 19
Capital structure
    decisions on raising capital
        debt financing, 462–463
        equity approach, 462
        national comparisons, 463
        opportunities in international
            markets, 462
        and taxation, 463
Capturable segment, 316
Carnegie Endowment for International
    Peace, 19
Cartels, legal in European Union, 190
Carve-outs, 460
Cash flow management
    international financial centers, 465
    leading and lagging techniques, 467
    loans, 464
    multilateral netting, 465
    reasons for moving funds, 464–465
    transfer prices, 464–465
Cash in advance, 347
Catalan, 123–125
Catalog purchases, 405
"Catalogue of Instruments for Measuring
    Culture," 96
Catalonia, 122–125
Centers for International Business
    and Research, 343
Central American Free Trade
    Agreement, 78
Central American Integration System, 76
Central banks
    Bank for International Settlements, 210
    of G-7 nations, 208–209
    intervention in exchange rates, 210
Central Intelligence Agency *World
    Factbook,* 76, 85
CEOs
    and international orientation, 6
    merits of foreign experience, 5
    women as, 284
Certificate of origin, 354
CFR (cost and freight-foreign port), 185,
    345–346
Chahabar, Iran, 352
Change agent, 282
Change models
    eight steps for, 293
    moving, 292
    refreezing, 292
    unfreezing, 292
Channel decisions, 388
Channel member availability, 389
Cheap foreign labor, protecting jobs
    from, 166
Chemical terrorism, 162

Chernobyl disaster, 137
Chief financial officer, 462
Child labor, 177–178
    decrease in, 18
Children, of expatriates, 439–440
Chile, privatization in, 158–159
China
    arms sales to Arab states, 159
    Asian foreign direct investment
        directed to, 51
    automaker investments in, 416
    ban on door-to-door selling, 385
    convertibility of currency, 216
    decline in poverty, 18
    early trade with, 13
    exports of rare earths, 144
    FDI in Africa, 78
    as fortress of mercantilism, 38
    Google's problems in, 236–237
    Group Danone in, 334–335
    guanxi concept, 65–66
    inland waterways, 130–132
    language map, 126
    languages and dialects, 125
    Nokia in, 12
    oil reserves and share of
        production, 136
    overseas investments, 162
    production of solar voltaic
        supply, 141
    social and economic statistics, 293
    software piracy, 74
    sovereign wealth fund, 455
    statistics on, 78
    Thousand Talents Program, 430
    Three Gorges Dam, 131–132, 144
    topographical map, 126
    trade with Africa, 75
    versus U.S. on global stage, 66
    value of imports and exports, 34
    violations of export rules, 357
    Walmart in, 251–252
    and World Trade Organization, 74
    Zuhai Free Trade Zone, 352
China Business Report, 434
Chinese family businesses, 49
Chocolate production, 177–178
Choice-of-forum clause, in
    contracts, 184
Choice-of-law clause, in contracts, 184
Christianity, 107
CIF (cost, insurance, freight-foreign port),
    185, 345–346
Cinema advertising, 380
CIP, 346
Civil liberties, 18
Civil penalties, antitrust cases, 191
Clean Air Act, 148
Clean energy sources, 155
Clean Water Act, 148

Climate
    definition, 132
    North-South divide, 132–133
Climate Change Convention, 67
Cluster analysis, 307
Coal
    conversion to oil, 137
    distribution in top six countries, 139
    and greenhouse gases, 139–140
    and Kyoto Protocol, 139–140
    major deposits, 139
    projected increase in use, 139
    reserves in U.S., 139
Cognitive informal institution, 65
Cold War, 121–122
Collection documents; *see* Export
    documentation
Collective bargaining, 429
Collectivist cultures, and global
    teams, 291
Collectivistic cultures, 100
Colombia, effect of Andes
    Mountains, 125
Colors, changes in, 374–375
Columbia-Snake River system, 132
COMECON, collapse of, 122
Committee on Foreign Investment in the
    U.S. (Treasury Dept.), 462
Common market, 76
Common Market for Eastern and Southern
    Africa, 78
Common Market of the South, 76, 78
Communication
    in global teams, 291
    improved, 21
    revolution in, 279
Communications technology, 15–17
Communications Workers of
    America, 155
Communist Party of China, 386
Communitarianism, 103
Compacts, 183
Companies; *see also* International
    companies
    born globals, 46
    influence of institutions, 67
    reasons for nationalization, 158
    in societal context, 149
    terrorist attacks on, 161
Comparative advantage
    compared to overlapping demand, 44
    definition, 40
    example, 39–40
    gains from specialization, 40
    gains from trade, 40
    and offshoring of jobs, 41–42
    and Ricardo, 39
    specialization, 40
    terms of trade, 40
Comparison advertising, 379

Foreign currency option, 469
Foreign direct investment, 32
  annual inflows, 54
  annual outflows, 50–51
  of Asia into China, 51
  associated with mergers and
      acquisitions, 51
  bamboo network, 49
  book value of, 49
  by China in Africa, 78
  decline of U.S. proportion
      1980–2010, 49
  definition, 14
  impact on export performance, 53
  increase 1980–2010, 16
  increased by developing countries, 49
  increase in European Union, 49
  information sources on, 57
  level and direction of, 52–53
  major role of oligopolistic
      industries, 56
  and Multilateral Investment Guarantee
      Agency, 72–73
  national and regional
      comparisons, 50
  outstanding stock of, 49–50
  outward volume
      from developed countries, 50–51
      for developing countries, 50
  reasons for growth 2006–2009, 31
  sovereign wealth funds in, 50
  theories of international investment
      dynamic capability, 55
      eclectic theory of international
          production, 55–56
      internalization theory, 55
      monopolistic advantage theory, 54
  trade leading to, 54
  world stock in 2010, 14
Foreign direct investment without
    investment, 331
Foreign environment
  analysis of, 232–233
  different values, 11
  forces difficult to assess, 11
  interrelated forces, 11–12
Foreign environmental forces
  and advertising, 381–382
  and distribution strategies, 389
  in international marketing
      economic forces, 376–377
      legal forces, 375–376
      physical forces, 377
      sociocultural forces, 374–375
Foreign exchange, lack of, 22–23
Foreign exchange market
  ask price, 212
  average annual turnover, 212
  bid-ask spread, 212
  bid price, 212
  exchange rate quotations, 211–212

forward currency market, 211
  forward rate, 211
  over-the-counter market, 212
  spot rate, 211
Foreign exchange quotations, 211
Foreign exchange risk management
  case, 476
  economic exposure, 470–471
  hedging, 465
  reduced by moving funds, 464
  transaction exposure, 467–470
  translation exposure, 470
Foreign experience, value of, 6
Foreign investment
  direct, 48, 49–54
  distinction between components,
      48–49
  liberalization of attitudes toward, 14
  portfolio investment, 48, 49
  reduced barriers to, 15
  uneven results, 18–19
Foreign Labor Trends, 426
Foreign markets; *see also* Modes of entry
  barriers to entry, 307
  entry to protect markets, profits,
      and sales
      to acquire raw materials, 23
      to acquire technology/
          know-how, 23
      attack competitor in home
          market, 22
      creating new markets, 20–21
      downstream markets, 23
      faster-growing markets, 21
      finding new markets, 20
      following customers overseas, 22
      geographic diversification, 23
      greater profits, 21
      greater revenue, 21–22
      higher overseas profits, 22
      improved communication, 21
      lack of foreign exchange, 22–23
      local production by
          competitors, 23
      lower cost of goods sold, 22
      lower-cost production, 22
      management's desire to
          expand, 23
      protectionism, 23
  export market plan, 345
  Incoterms, 345–347
  locating, 342–344
  mistakes made by new exporters,
      344–345
  stock issues, 462
Foreign market selection
  country screening, 303–314
      basic needs potential, 303–304
      economic and financial forces,
          304–307
      political and legal forces, 307–308

  sociocultural forces, 308–309
  steps in final selection, 310–313
      field trips, 310–311
      local research, 311–313
          cultural problems, 312–313
          technical difficulties, 313
      trade missions or fairs, 311
Foreign national pricing, 387
Foreign-owned companies, 7–9
Foreign ownership of American
    securities, 49
Foreign production, and international
    product life cycle, 44–45
Foreign securities, American ownership
    of, 49
Foreign trade, data sources, 304
Foreign Trade Division of Census
    Bureau, 343
Foreign trade zones, 352
Foreign venture capitalists, 49
Forfaiting, 345
Formal institutions
  definition and functions, 65
  influence on firms and managers, 67
  social agreement in, 66
Formulate anew, for international
    marketing, 368–370
Fortune at the Bottom of the Pyramid
    (Prahalad), 376
Fortune 500 companies, 22, 41
Fortune Global 500, 31
Forum for Expatriate Management, 438
Forward currency market, 211
Forward market hedge, 469
Forward rate, 211
Fossil fuel crisis, 138
France
  capital structure, 463
  hypermarché, 375
  number of vacation days, 447
  reliance on nuclear energy,
      138–139
  value of imports and exports, 34
Franchising
  definition, 330
  as mode of entry, 330
Free-association societies, 112
Free trade
  enhancing socioeconomic
      development, 18
  more and better jobs from, 18
  uneven results, 18–19
  and World Trade Organization, 73
Free trade areas, 76
Free trade zones, 352
Fronting loans, 464
Fukushima incident, Japan, 137, 138, 139
Functional currency
  definition, 458
  translation method, 458
Functional expertise, 258

International managers
  awareness of population densities, 128
  competitive challenges facing,
    230–231
International marketing
  added complexities, 368
  information sources, 491
  marketing mix
    distribution strategies, 388–389
    environmental constraints on
      standardization, 390–391
    pricing strategies, 387–388
    product strategies, 370–377
    promotional strategies, 377–386
    standardize, adapt, or formulate
      anew, 368–370
  in Mongolia, 367
International marketing managers, 368
*International Market Research
  Reports,* 304
International Medical Products Anti-
  Counterfeiting Taskforce, 181–182
International Monetary Fund, 63, 81
  collaborative relationships, 71
  and cost-of-living allowance
    survey, 443
  criticisms of, 72
  establishment of, 70, 206
  and exchange rates, 71
  functions, 70–71
  and global financial crisis, 71–72
  growth predictions for Africa, 75
  number of members, 71
  quota formula, 71
  rebalancing global currency, 72
  reserve accounts, 207
  role in international monetary
    system, 204
  Special Drawing Rights, 71
International Monetary Fund Articles of
  Agreement, 71, 206
International monetary system
  Bank for International Settlements, 210
  Bretton Woods system, 206–207
  components, 204
  current currency arrangements,
    208–209
  floating exchange rates, 207
  and funding of terrorism, 203–204
  gold standard, 204–206
  information sources, 219–220
International Organization for
  Standardization, 189, 411
International orientation, 6
International pricing
  definition, 387
  description, 388
International product life cycle
  definition, 44
  and direction of trade, 44–46
  foreign competition in export markets, 45

foreign production begins, 45
import competition in U.S., 45–46
and outsourcing, 404
repeated in less developed countries, 46
stages, 44
and subsidiaries, 266
and U.S. exports, 44–45
International Programme on the
  Elimination of Child Labor, 178
International Rivers Network, 132
International Seabed Authority, U.S.
  avoidance of, 148
International social media, 322–323
International stages model of
  organizational structure, 259
International standardization
  of distribution, 389
  environmental constraints, 389–390
  of personal selling, 385
  of sales promotion, 385
International status
  and compensation, 447
  definition, 447
International strategy; *see also* Global
  strategic planning *entries*
  bottom-up planning, 244–245
  competitive challenges, 230–231
  definition, 231
  goals
    competitive advantage, 231
    development of competencies, 231
  Google Inc., 236–237
  information sources, 249
  iterative planning, 245–246
  new directions in planning, 246–247
  and organizational levels, 244
  plan features and implementation
    budgets, 243
    performance measures, 243–244
    policies, 243
    procedures, 243
  scenario planning, 229–230
  strategic management process, 246
  summary of planning process, 247
  time horizon, 244
  top-down planning, 244
  in uncertain times, 229–230
International Telecommunications
  Union, 68
International trade; *see also* Direction of
  trade; Trade restrictions
  age of mercantilism, 13
  balance of payments accounts,
    221–222
  British and Dutch trading companies, 13
  and Buy America Act, 173
  developing countries and share of
    value, 34
  direct government participation in,
    172–173
  economic growth from liberalization, 18

effect of Ottoman Empire, 13
effect of Smoot-Hawley Tariff Act of
  1930, 171
effects of economies of scale, 46
effects of experience curve, 46
effects on public health, 13
evenness of growth, 33–34
exporting, 15
  with gold standard, 204–205
impact on economies
  less costly then foreign direct
    investment, 54
  relation to foreign direct
    investment, 54
  social development, 52–53
importing, 15
increasing regionalization, 35
information sources on, 57
leading exporters and importers, 34
major trading partners
  reasons for focusing on, 35
  of United States, 36–37
most-favored-nation principle, 73
rapid expansion of exports since
  1980, 34
regionalization of, 35
value in goods and services 2010, 33
value of analysis for finding
  opportunities, 37
value of merchandise trade, 15, 16
value of services trade, 15, 16
volume of, 32–33
World Trade Organization
  principles, 73
zero-sum view, 38
International Trade Administration,
  31–32
International trade association, 26
International trade theories
  absolute advantage, 38–39
  and Adam Smith, 37
  comparative advantage, 39–42
  factors affecting direction of trade,
    42–48
  mercantilism, 37–38
  summary of, 48
International trading companies, 326
Internet, 16–17
  and personal selling, 384
  to purchase raw materials, 406
  redefining pricing strategies, 388
  as working anarchy, 272
Internet advertising, 380
Internet domain names, 376
Internship opportunities, 26–27
Intervention currency, 211
Intracorporate sales, 388
Intrafirm trade, 404–405
Intraindustry trade, 44
Inventory, in supply chain management,
  401–402

Investments, in U.S. for acquisitions vs. new establishments, 331
Investors
    cross-border Chinese, 49
    patent trolls, 187
Iran
    Green Revolution, 374
    nuclear program, 371
    oil reserves and share of production, 136
Iraq, oil reserves and share of production, 136
Irish Republican Army, 160
Irrevocable letter of credit, 348–349
Islam, 107
Islamic countries, advertising in, 383
ISO 9000 standard, 411
ISO 9001 standard, 411
Israel, public relations problem, 157
Italy
    capital structure, 463
    value of imports and exports, 34
Iterative planning, 245–246

J

Jamaica Agreement, 207
Japan
    antitrust policy, 190
    capital structure, 463
    earthquake/tsunami of 2031, 122, 209, 230
    foreign direct investment by, 49
    keiretsu, 463
    labor unions, 429
    Large Scale Retailing Law, 389
    Ministry of Agriculture, 382–383
    Ministry of International Trade and Industry, 190
    number of vacation days, 447
    product liability law, 194–195
    projected decline in output, 428
    projected population decline, 427
    supplier relationships with U.S., 65
    Tokyo subway attack of 1995, 162
    versus U.S. antitrust policy, 190
    value of imports and exports, 34
    voluntary export restraints, 172
    zaibatsu, 190
Japanese *anime,* 329, 381
Japanese Antimonopoly Law, 190
Japanese Red Army, 160
Japan External Trade Organization, 304, 357
Job opportunities
    in finance, 220
    international resources for, 25–26
Jobs
    cost of saving, 173
    created by free trade, 18
    held by immigrants, 428–429
    lost to offshoring, 41

migrating to foreign countries, 19
other than business, 26
Joint ventures
    benefits of
        expertise, tax, and other benefits, 332
        government regulation for local participation, 332
        reduced risk, 332
        scale economies, 332
        strong nationalism, 332
    control in, 270–271
    definition, 332
    Group Danone in China, 334–335
    strategic alliances as, 333
Journal of the United Nations, 68
Judaism, 108
Jurisdiction
    for cross-border litigation, 184
    determining country of, 201
    taxing authority, 471

K

Kazakhstan, oil reserves and share of production, 136
Keiretsu, 463
Kidnap, ransom, and extortion insurance, 161
Kidnapping for ransom
    annual number of situations, 160
    countermeasures my industry, 161–162
    in Mexico, 160
    paying as counterproductive, 160–161
    by Somalian pirates, 160
Kinship societies, 112
Know-how, entry into foreign markets to acquire, 22
Knowledge management, 234–235
Kosovo, 157
KPMG, *Competitive Alternatives,* 421
Kuwait
    invasion by Iraq, 159
    oil reserves and share of production, 136
Kyoto Protocol, 67, 139–140, 148

L

Labels
    changes in, 374–375
    language translation, 375
Labor
    as external force, 10
    negative effect of globalization, 19
Labor conditions, worldwide, 426–431
Labor-intensive processes, 414, 415–416
Labor market
    and aging of populations, 427–428
    and brain drain, 429–430

definition, 426
immigrant labor, 428–429
information sources, 426, 449
labor mobility, 428
overall size of workforce, 426–427
and unions, 430–431
urbanization of, 428
Labor mobility, 428
Labor standards
    in developing countries, 19
    negative effect of globalization, 19
Labor unions
    collective bargaining, 430
    definition, 430
    increase in developed countries, 431
    in Japan, 430
    membership variations, 430
    multinational activity, 430
    opposition to outsourcing, 430
    protectionist lobbying, 430
    variations worldwide, 430
Lag approach, 467
Language
    and advertising, 382
    conversational distance, 111
    cross-cultural communication, 108–111
    nonverbal communication, 108–111
    and spatial relationships, 111
    world map, 110
Languages
    of China, 125
    map of China, 126
    of Spain
        Catalan, 123–125
        Euskara, 123–125
    of Switzerland, 125
Language training for expatriates, 440
Large foreign users, 326
Large Scale Retailing Law, Japan, 389
Large segment, 314
LASH (lighter aboard ship), 356
Latin America
    e-commerce potential, 305
    Foreign direct investment in, 51
    inflation problems, 217
Laws
    extraterritorial application, 183–184
    international, 183
    worldwide standardization
        antitrust, 188
        commercial arbitration, 188
        international sales agreements, 188–189
        organizations for, 189
        taxation, 188
Lawyers, patent trolls, 187
Lead approach, 467
Leader role, 282
Leaders, new breed for globalization, 279

Nature, cultural attitudes, 104
Negotiator, 282
Netherlands, value of imports and exports, 34
Network computing, 16–17
Neutrality of Austria in Cold War, 121–122
Neutral vs. affective, 103
New institutional theory, 64
New market creation, 20–21
New markets, 20
New product development, 370–371
Newspaper advertising, 380
New York Times, 471
Nigeria, oil reserves and share of production, 136
No Enchanted Palace (Mazower), 63
Nominal interest rate, 213
Nonequity modes of entry
    contract manufacturing, 330–331
    exporting
        direct, 326–327
        indirect, 325–326
    franchising, 330
    licensing, 328–330
    management contracts, 330
    piracy, 329
    turnkey projects, 328
Nonexporting firms, 342
Nonfuel minerals, 144
    major U.S. sources, 145
Nonquantitative nontariff barriers
    customs and administrative procedures, 173
    direct government participation in trade, 172–173
    standards, 173
Nonrenewable energy sources
    coal, 139–140
    definition, 133
    future fossil fuel crisis, 138
    International Energy Agency Report 2010, 140
    natural gas, 141
    nuclear power, 137–139
    petroleum, 133–137
    world use by fuel types, 140
Nontariff barriers
    definition, 171
    nonquantitative, 172–173
    orderly marketing agreements, 172
    quantitative, 171–172
Nonverbal communication, 108–111
Normative informal institution, 65
Norms of consideration, 290
North American Free Trade Agreement, 12, 15, 35, 36, 76, 122
    definition and functions, 77–78
    effect on World Trade Organization, 75
    and environmental standards, 19
    Labor Secretariat, 19
    statistics on, 78

North-South divide, 132–133
Nuclear power
    Chernobyl disaster, 137
    in France, 138–139
    Fukushima incident, Japan, 137, 138, 139
    growth in developing countries, 138
    projected decline in use, 137–138
Nuisance tariffs, 171

O

Objectives
    corporate, 235–238
    of Kraft Foods, 256
Occupational Safety and Health Act, 375–376
Ocean energy, 144
Office of Export Administration, 353
Office of Harmonization in the Internal Market (EU), 187
Office of International Trade (SBA), 343
Official prices and tariffs, 171
Official reserves account, 222
Offshore financial centers, 462
Offshoring
    and comparative advantage, 40
    definition, 40, 403
    pros and cons of, 42
Oil-bearing shale, 134–137
Oil sands, 134–135
Oligopolistic industries, 54
    major role in foreign direct investment, 56
    monopolistic advantage, 54
OLI model, 56
Omnibus surveys, 312–313
Open account, 347
Operating exposure, 470–471
Operational plans, 243
Optimism-conservatism measure in accounting, 458–459
Order bill of lading, 353
Order getting, by subsidiaries, 268
Orderly marketing arrangements, 172
Organizational design
    ability to evolve over time, 257
    current trends
        dynamic network structure, 265
        horizontal corporation, 264–265
        virtual corporation, 263–264
    definition, 257
    evolution of international company, 258–263
    hybrid organizations, 261
    information sources, 273
    matrix organizations, 262
    matrix overlay, 262
    primary dimensions
        customer expertise, 258
        functional expertise, 258
        geographic expertise, 258
        product and technical expertise, 258

    product business units, 263
    strategic business units, 263
Organizational knowledge base, 234
Organizational structure; *see also* Organizational design
    definition, 257
    evolution of international companies, 258–263
    global corporate forms, 259–261
    international stages model, 259
    local manufacturing systems, 417
    reengineering, 263
    relation to competitive strategy, 257
    relation to international environment, 257
    reorganization, 275–276
    reorganization at Kraft Foods, 255–256
    task of senior managers to evolve, 257
Organization for Economic Cooperation and Development, 64, 196
    agricultural support subsidies, 172
    Business and Industry Advisory Committee, 76
    cost of petroleum, 137
    country surveys, 76
    definition, 75
    guidelines on transfer prices, 465
    number of members, 75, 76
    origin, 75
    Trends in International Migration, 429
Organization of Petroleum Exporting Countries, 12, 23
Organizations involved in country risk assessment, 163–164
Orientation allowances, 444
Ottoman Empire, 13
Output
    expanded in United States, 428
    projected decline in Europe and Japan, 428
Outsourcing, 401
    case, 421–422
    decline in value of contracts, 416
    of logistics, 410
    potential for Brazil, 59–60
    result of reverse brain drain, 430
    trend away from, 416
Outsourcing decisions, 403–404
Outsourcing firms, tasks performed by, 401
Overlapping demand theory, and direction of trade, 44
Overseas Business Reports, 308
Overseas premiums, 444
Overseas Private Investment Corporation, 342
    functions, 351
Over-the-counter market, 212
Over-the-wall approach to design, 403